African-American History

CHRONOLOGY OF

African~ American History

Significant Events and People from 1619 to the Present

Alton Hornsby, Jr.

Fuller E. Callaway Professor of History
and Chairman
Morehouse College
Atlanta, Georgia

 Gale Research Inc.   Detroit • London

Library of Congress Catalog Card Number 91-17303
ISBN 0-8103-7093-X

Gale Research, Inc.
835 Penobscot Building
Detroit, MI 48226-4094

Printed in the United States of America

Published simultaneously in the United Kingdom
by Gale Research International Limited
(An affiliated company of Gale Research Inc.)

To the memory of

ALTON PARKER HORNSBY, SR.

and

LILLIE M. NEWTON HORNSBY,

my parents

Contents

Preface ix

Acknowledgments xi

Introduction xiii

Chapter 1   Involuntary Servitude, 1619-1860   1

Chapter 2   War and Freedom, 1861-1876 33

Chapter 3   The Nadir, 1877-1900 49

Chapter 4   The Age of Booker T. Washington, 1901-1917 59

Chapter 5   Between War and Depression, 1918-1932 71

Chapter 6   A New Deal—A New Life? 1933-1940 81

Chapter 7   War Again, 1941-1945 89

Chapter 8   The Attack against Segregation, 1946-1954 93

Chapter 9   "The Second Reconstruction," 1954-1964 101

Chapter 10   "The Second Reconstruction" Wanes, 1964-1972 121

Chapter 11   "The Second Reconstruction" Betrayed, 1973-1990 207

Appendix 439

Selected Bibliography 489

Index 507

Preface

The *Chronology of African-American History* is designed to provide a convenient repository of important facts relating to the cultural experiences of African-Americans in the United States. Those occurrences which have significantly affected the lives of black Americans, materially as well as emotionally, have been selected. In making selections, we have been conscious of gender, region, class, patterns and trends, cultural innovations, and race relations, especially. *Chronology* contains biographical information on representative African-Americans, depictions of significant events, legislation, court decisions, programs, manifestos, and data on social, economic, political and educational milestones. It can, thus, prove valuable to students at all levels as well as the general reader. The book is subdivided into the eleven most significant eras affecting African-Americans in the United States. There is also a Selected Bibliography and an Appendix containing excerpts from court decisions, laws, speeches, and proclamations, as well as tables with demographic data.

Several persons have assisted with the publication of this book, and I wish here to express my gratitude. Professor Abraham L. Davis and the late Professor Edward A. Jones of Morehouse College, the late Professor C.A. Bacote of Atlanta University, and Professor-Emeritus Robert Moran of Southern University in Baton Rouge offered helpful suggestions. My student assistants, Betty Reedy, Raymond Gordon, Leslie Pickens, Walter Green, Jeffrey A. Green, Jr., Barry Lee and my student scholars in the Morehouse Scholars Program, Maurice R. Mander, Frederick Knight, Frederick McCuiston, Shawn A. Sabater, and Fanon Wilkins performed numerous detailed chores. Angela Culmer, Cleta Winslow, Mozell Powell, Arnold Sails, Jr., and Iris Singleton typed various drafts of the manuscript. I wish to thank the editorial staff at Gale Research Inc., particularly Christine Nasso, Director of New Product Development (General Reference), and my editor, Robyn Young (Literary Criticism Series), who helped guide the manuscript to a better-finished product.

I also wish to thank President Leroy Keith, Jr., Vice President for Academic Affairs, Weldon Jackson, and my colleagues in the Morehouse College Department of History for encouragement and support. A portion of the research for the work was made possible by a grant from the Faculty Research Committee of Morehouse College.

I must also express especial appreciation to my family, Anne, Alton III, and Angela Mandee, not only for denying them the use of our dining room table for several months, but also for assisting with typing, organizing, filing, and other chores.

Alton Hornsby, Jr.
Atlanta, Ga.
January 31, 1991

Acknowledgments

The editors wish to thank the copyright holders of the excerpted material included in this edition, and the permissions managers of the book, magazine, and newspaper publishing companies for assisting us in securing reprint rights. The following is a list of the copyright holders who have granted us permission to reprint material in this edition of *Chronology of African-American History*. Every effort has been made to trace copyright, but if omissions have been made, please contact us.

COPYRIGHTED EXCERPTS IN *CHRONOLOGY OF AFRICAN-AMERICAN HISTORY* WERE REPRINTED FROM THE FOLLOWING SOURCES:

The Atlanta Constitution, January 6, 1975; May 30, 1978; September 11, 1978; December 15, 1982; July 13, 1988. All reprinted by permission of the publisher.

The Atlanta Journal-Constitution, 1989. Reprinted by permission of the publishers.

The Final Call, v. 10, April 8, 1991. Reprinted by permission of the publisher.

Muhammad Speaks, January 22, 1971. Reprinted by permission of *The Final Call.*

The New York Times, September 13, 1987. Copyright © 1987 by The New York Times Company. Reprinted by permission of the publisher.

United Press International, 1975. Copyright 1975. Reprinted with the permission of United Press International, Inc.

The Wall Street Journal, April 7, 1983 for "Martin Luther King, Jr.: A Dream Deferred" by Hodding Carter III. © 1983 Dow Jones & Company, Inc. All rights reserved. Reprinted with permission of *The Wall Street Journal* and the author.

• • • • •

Johnson, James Weldon and J. Rosamond Johnson. From a song entitled "*Lift Every Voice and Sing.*" Marks Music Corp., 1926. Copyright 1926, renewed 1953 by Edward B. Marks Music Corporation. Used by permission of Edward B. Marks Music Company.

King, Martin L., Jr. From his oration "*I Have a Dream,*" delivered on August 28, 1963. Copyright © by Martin Luther King, Jr. Reprinted by permission of Joan Daves Agency.

Rice, Thomas "Daddy." From "Jump Jim Crow" in *The Negro in American History.* Mortimer J. Adler, Charles Van Doren, George Ducas, eds. Encyclopedia Britannica Educational Corp., 1969. Reprinted by permission of the publisher.

PHOTOGRAPHS AND ILLUSTRATIONS APPEARING IN *CHRONOLOGY OF AFRICAN-AMERICAN HISTORY* WERE RECEIVED FROM THE FOLLOWING SOURCES:

Prints and Photographs Division, Library of Congress: **pp. 2, 6, 24, 26, 30, 52;** Fort Shaw, Montana: **p. 37;** U.S. Signal Corps: **p. 39;** U.S. War Department, National Archive: **p. 68;** Consulate General of Jamaica: **p. 72;** Photograph by Cecil Layne: **p. 83;** UPI/Bettmann Newsphotos: **pp. 86, 94, 114, 125, 130, 256;** U.S. Army: **pp. 87, 398;** U.S. Navy: **p. 90;** AP/Wide World Photos: **pp. 104, 105, 107, 109, 123, 129, 132, 346, 365, 372, 411, 413, 435;** NBC: **pp. 115, 116;** Photograph by Ed Druck: **p. 118;** The White House: **p. 119;** Brooklyn Museum: **p. 122;** U.S. Marine Corps: **p. 146;** Photograph by Carl Nesfield: **p. 160;** Schomberg Center for Research in Black Culture, The New York Public Library, Astor, Lenox and Tilden Foundations: **p. 284;** NASA: **p. 341.**

Introduction

Out of Africa (300-1619)

The ancestors of most black Americans came from the area of the continent of Africa known as the Western Sudan. This area extended from the Atlantic Ocean in the west to Lake Chad in the east, and from the Sahara desert in the north to the Gulf of Guinea in the south.

From about 300 A.D. to the late 1500s, three powerful empires dominated the Western Sudan in succession. The empires were Ghana, Mali and Songhai. Each originated as a small, generally peaceful kingdom but subsequently expanded and gained dominance over the entire region. The economies of the Sudan empires were based on farming and mining gold. Although the topography of the Sahara provided an often frustrating barrier, there was continuous trade between the Western Sudanese and the then-known world through the Muslims of North Africa.

The cultivation of crops was most prominent in the savanna, the rain forests of the Guinea Coast south of the savanna, and in the Sahara north of the savanna. West African agriculture was conducted under a system which combined private enterprise and communitarianism. Farm land was owned collectively by the descendants of the first occupant. Individual descendants of the elder were given parcels of land to cultivate, but once cultivation ended, the land reverted back to the collective community. The administrator of the land, the Master of the Ground, determined the usages of the soil.

While agriculture and gold mining were the principal occupations of blacks living in the Western Sudan, others supported themselves by undertaking numerous crafts, including basketry, pottery, and woodwork.

The first of the great Sudanic empires to gain control of the Western Sudan was Ghana. The Ghanians were mostly black Soninke people who spoke a language in the Manda branch of the Sudanic language group. While Ghana's economy was centered on agricultural pursuits in the various villages, its people also engaged in a lucrative trade from their principal commercial center at Koumbi (Kumbi). The Ghanaians served as middlemen in the trade between North and West Africa, obtaining gold from the mines in Wangara, a forest region south of Ghana, which they exchanged for salt mined by the Berbers and later the Arabs in the northern Sahara. While gold was plentiful in the Sudan, salt was a scarce commodity. Consequently, salt became extremely valuable and was often bartered for gold. The Ghanaians also traded ivory and slaves for textiles and beads which were brought in from North Africa. The government of Ghana levied taxes on all caravans, merchants, and commercial transactions. Once the kingdom expanded, it increased its wealth further by exacting tribute from other peoples whom it had conquered and brought under its control. Because of its vast wealth, many of the residents of Ghanaian cities constucted homes of wood and stone.

Once the Arabs occupied North Africa in the seventh and eighth centuries, Islamic missionaries moved into the Western Sudan and quickly became an important cultural force in the region. At about the same time, the Ghanaians began to raise large armies to subjugate many of their neighbors. Since they were the first West Africans to learn how to smelt iron ore, the Ghanaians were able to make arrows, swords, and other weapons which they used to easily conquer less technologically advanced peoples. One of the more noted kings of Ghana, Tenkhamenen, reportedly had 200,000 warriors in his army in 1067.

Following a drought, compounded by religious divisions, the Ghanaian empire began to decline in the twelfth century. The weakening of Ghana opened the way for many of its former subject kingdoms to increase their strength and influence in the area. Two of the principal candidates to replace Ghana as the superior power in West Africa were Koniaga, inhabited by the Soso people, and Mali, occupied by the Malians. Led by Sundiata Keita, Mali defeated Koniaga in the battle of Karina in 1235 and five years later, subdued the once dominant Ghanaians.

The Malians were also a Sudanic-speaking people who lived principally as farmers and traders. They constructed a prosperous capital city at Niani on the Niger River. The chief administrator of the nation was the emperor. He ruled, however, through a decentralized system of regional and local officials, which included *ferbas,* or governors of provinces, and *mochrifts,* or mayors of important cities. One of the most fabled Malian emperors was Mansa Musa, who ruled the empire from 1309 to 1332.

Much of Musa's notoriety stemmed from descriptions of his famous pilgrimage to Mecca in 1324. A contemporary picture drawn by the Arab traveler, Ibn Batuta, in his *Travels in Asia and Africa, 1325-1354,* depicts the emperor being sent on his journey to the sound of drums, trumpets, and bugles. In addition,

John Hope Franklin commented in his *From Slavery to Freedom* that Musa's entourage "was composed of 60,000 persons." Franklin reported: "Books, baggagemen, and royal secretaries there were in abundance. To finance the pilgrimage, the king carried eighty camels to bear more than 24,000 pounds of gold." The exact amount of the gold carried on the journey totaled more than $5 million.

Once Mansa Musa arrived in the Middle East, he spent so much money, according to Edgar Allan Toppin in his book *A Biographical History of Blacks in America Since 1528,* that he "depressed the price of gold in the great commercial center of Cairo." After running low on funds, however, Musa had to borrow money from local gold merchants. Following the grand pilgrimage of 1324, the Malian kingdom and its emperor were placed on many of the maps of the medieval world, and Musa was given the title "Rex Melle (Mali), King of the Gold Mines."

In addition to Mali's great wealth, Ibn Batuta also observed that the kingdom was virtually free of crime—an astonishing feat for any nation, then as now. But the Malians were not strangers to violence, for they had achieved their control of the Western Sudan through the subjugation of their neighbors. Eventually, the Malians had to defend their hegemony against the growing power of other rivals.

After 1332, Mali was ruled by an increasingly inept group of monarchs. Spending continued to be lavish, and local officials often threatened secession from the central government. The people of Songhai were more unified and were led by stronger rulers. Songhai, then, emerged as Mali's strongest rival for supremacy in the Western Sudan.

The Sunni dynasty of Songhai, which was established in 1335, contested Mali for control of the Western Sudan for more than a century. The empire emerged victorious during the reign of King Sunni Ali Ber in 1473. The Sunni dynasty remained in power through Ali Ber and his son until it was overthrown by Askia Muhammad Touré, one of Ali Ber's generals, in 1492. Askia Muhammad expanded Songhai's boundaries to the salt mines of the Sahara, the Hansa states of the Lake Chad region, and the Mossi of the Volta region.

Askia Muhammad established a government which included an efficient central administration as well as appointed local officials. He also made a great pilgrimage to Mecca between 1495 and 1497. Unlike Mansa Musa, however, Askia had a much smaller entourage and spent his money more wisely. Instead of depleting his funds on lavish goods, Askia engaged the services of several Arabic scholars and physicians. The scholars were employed to teach in the empire's two major universities at Timbuktu and Jenne. Because of these and other accomplishments, Edgar Allan Toppin called Askia Muhammad "the greatest of the emperors of West Africa."

Even before Christopher Columbus sailed for the New World, Songhai had become the largest and richest country in Africa. Much of its wealth and the products of that affluence could be seen in the city of Timbuktu, which became a principal center of learning and trade in the Muslim world. An Arab traveler, Al-Hasan Ibn Muhammad, observed in 1526 that all of the houses in Timbuktu were built of "chalke, and covered thatch." There was also "a stately temple" and a "princely palace" built "by a most excellent workman of Granada." All of the inhabitants, especially the "strangers" residing there, "seemed exceeding[ly] rich."

Timbuktu was best known for its multitude of educational institutions. Boys and men studied history, medicine, astronomy, mathematics, and literature. The scholars who taught in the schools and universities were well maintained at the king's expense.

While Askia Muhammad ruled Songhai effectively and efficiently for more than forty years, the empire began to weaken after his sons deposed the aging emperor in 1528. As Askia neared death, warfare over his succession disrupted the kingdom. Both Askia Ishak I and Askia Dared made valiant but unsuccessful efforts between 1539 and 1582 to restore the efficient, centralized rule which had existed under the great Askia Muhammad. Thus, when a smaller Moroccoan army equipped with cannons and gunpowder invaded the empire in 1590, they were able, in the words of Benjamin Da Silva, et al. in their book, *The Afro-American in United States History*, to "cut Songhai to pieces. The days of the great black kingdoms of West Africa were over."

But these great Western Sudanic kingdoms, which served as an ancestral home for African-Americans, had demonstrated sophisticated economic activities, a capacity for government which was highly developed, and a complex social structure.

Political life in these African nations consisted of local rule at the tribal and village level, but also a combination of hereditary monarchy and aspects of representative government, particularly at the national or central levels. In some instances, councilors elected their leaders. More typically, however, West African kingdoms were governed by three hereditary families: royal, electing, and enthroning. The monarch was generally selected from the hereditary royal family, but the hereditary electing family made the selection from among those considered the quintessential members of the royal family. Hence, it was not always a matter of primogeniture, where the deceased king's eldest son ascended to the throne. In many situations, the hereditary enthroning family exercised the right to confirm the choice in installing the new ruler. The character of the monarchs and their influence on their subjects ranged from tyrannical to benevolent, from great nation builders to inept and corrupt charlatans. A common characteristic was that, particularly after the eighth century, almost all of them were Muslim.

While Islamic influence became pervasive in West African life and directly affected governance, economic, social, and intellectual activities among the Sudanese, animistic worship, which advocated the propitiation of the spirit of the ancestors, also persisted. Animism was often practiced through chants, sacred songs, and ceremonial dancing. The oldest living relative or descendant of a common ancestor served as the local priest for this form of religion.

The priest of the more ancient, indigenous religions was also known as the Master of the Ground in the extended family, the most common form of social organization. The extended family was composed of several generations of people who were descended from a common ancestor. They all lived in a common village or similar residential area. Individuals who were not obviously related to the group could often become a part of the family in return for performing services for the actual members of the family. Because of its size, both the usual as well as any extraordinary needs of any member of the family, either legitimate or adopted, could normally be supported within the extended family itself. Most disputes could be settled by the Master of the Ground.

Aside from family, work, and worship, there were African cultural expressions in song, instrumental music, dance, art, and literature. Singing took the form of chants, festive tunes, and lullabies as well as sacred songs. Traditional musical instruments included the flute, guitar, harp, and violin. Dancing was used for ritualistic and recreational purposes as well as religious ones. Because of the multitude of languages within a single empire, writing was limited; most of the surviving literature is, understandably, written in Arabic. However, a rich oral tradition—which included such literary forms as fables, legends, and myths—flourished. By the fourteenth century, the Griot, a professional storyteller, appeared. This elder usually collected and recited tales for a living. In art, utilitarian, ceremonial, and religious themes were prevalent. Cookware, eating utensils, latches, and pulleys were often decorated. Carvers produced masks, dolls, and statuettes. Generally, Edgar Allan Toppin contends, African art was "non-representational, distorting natural shapes, such as the human figure, with marvelous plasticity to achieve a truer artistic reality."

Yet, despite the existence of complex political and social systems and highly developed intellectual and cultural activities, the West Africans were not above participating in the ancient practice of owning other human beings.

Slavery developed along with civilization in ancient Europe, Asia, and Africa. Normally, an individual became the slave of another through birth (the child of a slave often was consigned to slavery himself), through capture (such as a prisoner of war), through kidnapping (particularly as a result of pirate attacks on ships), through sale by a relative or another person, and as a result of capture and sale by slave traders.

African slaves were generally treated as lesser members of the extended family, but were, for the most part, treated humanely and could share in some of the privileges afforded other members of the family. But they could also be sold as chattel by their owners. The largest category of sales was probably the result of monarchs disposing of surplus prisoners who had become slaves.

In ancient times West Africans sold their slaves to Arab traders from northern Africa. By the early 1500s, however, after they had established colonies in Latin America and in the West Indies, Portugal and Spain became increasingly involved in the African slave trade. Portugal placed African slaves on the sugar plantations which its colonists developed in Brazil. Spain used Africans on its sugar plantations in the West Indies. After 1600, England, France, and the Netherlands also began to import African slaves into their colonies in North America.

Many of the African slaves obtained by Europeans were sold or traded by other Africans for cloth, rum, and other items, especially weapons. Guns were a precious commodity in the interminable warfare between neighboring African peoples. Other black slaves were caputred by traders on the continent, pirated from ships, or kidnapped elsewhere, including Europe.

The nefarious European slave trade took several triangular routes. One of the routes guided ships from Europe transporting manufactured products to the west coast of Africa, where traders exchanged the goods for slaves. Then, on the infamous "Middle Passage," the blacks were carried across the Atlantic Ocean to the West Indies and sold for huge profits. The slave traders then purchased coffee, sugar, and tobacco in the West Indies to be sold in Europe. Over another route, ships from New England colonies took rum and other products to Africa, where they were exchanged for slaves. These blacks were also transported to the West Indies to be sold. Some of the profits were used to purchase molasses and sugar, which they took back to New England and sold to rum producers.

Most of the slave voyages across the Atlantic took several months. Since the slave trade was conducted for profit, the captains of slave ships tried to deliver as many blacks as possible. Some captains used a system called "loose packing" to deliver their cargo. This meant that fewer slaves than the ships could carry would be transported in the hope that sickness and death among them could be reduced. Other captains, seeking larger profits and believing that many blacks would die on the voyage nonetheless, carried as many slaves as their ships could hold. The blacks were generally chained together below deck all day and night except for brief periods of exercise. These crowded and filthy conditions resulted in stench, diseases, and death. This system was called "tight packing." Approximately twelve percent of all slaves died during the crossings of the Atlantic. Thus, the story of the "Middle Passage" is a tale of horrors.

The Euro-American slave trade continued from the 1500s to the 1800s. Although the exact number of Africans who were enslaved during these four centuries is unknown, the most reliable estimates range from ten million to twenty million blacks. Between 400,000 and 1,200,000 of this total arrived in North America.

Slavery in the New World began in the Caribbean and on the Latin American mainland. The Spanish, shortly after the establishment of Santo Domingo (the first permanent European settlement in the New World) in 1496 employed slaves on their sugar plantations. The first Africans were seen there as early as 1501. After the Spaniards virtually exterminated the Carib Indians, natives of the Caribbean islands, larger numbers of blacks were imported. Fearing that blacks would eventually outnumber Europeans in the region, Spanish authorities soon placed restrictions on their importation. In 1517, Bishop Bartholomew Las Casas and others persuaded King Charles I of Spain to rescind the restrictions in order for Africans to augment the dwindling supply of Indian labor. Subsequently, in 1518 large numbers of blacks were imported directly from Africa. Those newly-arrived slaves were known as *bozal* Negroes, which distinguished them from the group of Africans who were initially transported to Europe and Christianized before being sent to the Caribbean.

The Spanish, Portuguese, and eventually the English developed great plantations in the West Indies where cocoa, coffee, tobacco, and sugar were produced. Slaves grew and processed all of these crops, but most were employed in the furious labor of producing sugar. The Europeans also maintained several colonies on the South American mainland, in such places as Brazil and the territory that now comprises Columbia. Here, in addition to agricultural labor, the slaves worked in mines.

As the black population increased, there was always fear among the settlers that the slaves would rebel against their captivity. Thus, harsh slave codes which mandated severe punishments for insurgency were enacted. These codes served to deter large scale violence, but did not prevent another common form of rebellion—escape. Large numbers of black runaways, known as Maroons, formed camps called *quilombos* (cabins). One of the largest *quilombos* was at Palmares, in the northeastern section of Brazil. Between 1630 and 1697, the Maroons established a succession of three republics at Palmares, which contained a government, enacted laws, and elected a king. Their economy was based upon agriculture and trade, although much of their food and supplies was attained by raiding nearby plantations. Finally, in 1697, an army of settlers broke through the Maroon fortifications and destroyed the community. Several of the republic's leaders committed suicide rather than be returned to slavery.

The patterns of black enslavement which developed in Latin America, including the Christianization of Africans, provided ready examples and precedents for the establishment of an even larger "slavocracy" in the English colonies to the north. There, beginning in the first half of the seventeenth century, millions of Africans would begin the long cultural process of becoming African-Americans.

Involuntary Servitude (1619-1860)

The beginning of the history of African-Americans in the United States is that period of involuntary servitude from 1619 to 1860, when the large majority of blacks were chattels. Although blacks are known to have accompanied the early explorers to the New World, the first permanent settlers were the twenty blacks deposited at Jamestown, Virginia in 1619. These blacks, who had been captured in Africa and sold to the highest bidders (as many lower-class whites had been similarly captured or kidnapped and sold in Europe) were not slaves, but indentured servants.

African-Americans were probably indentured servants in the American colonies until 1640, and perhaps as late as 1650. After serving their period of indenture, (normally seven years), some of these blacks became property holders and politically active citizens. Throughout the seventeenth century, however, the numbers of blacks—servants, slaves, or free—were still relatively small. There were about 300 blacks in the colonies by 1650. The first rapid increase in their number occurred during the close of the seventeenth century. By the time of the American Revolution, almost half of the population in several Southern states was black. Virginia and Maryland, for example, had a total population of approximately 480,000 at the time of the Revolutionary War, about 206,000 of these people were black. South Carolina's black population was larger than the white one. However, slavery was not confined to the South. The first black slaves arrived in New England probably in 1638. By 1700, there were about 1,000 blacks out of a population of 90,000 in the New England colonies, and at the time of the American Revolution there were 16,000 slaves in the region. Massachusetts and Rhode Island became great slave-trading colonies, while Connecticut was the leading New England slave colony. On the eve of the American Revolution, there were about half a million black slaves in the American colonies.

In the South, the slaves were principally employed in producing the staple crops which were the basis of the Southern economy. By 1700 they had proved to be the most reliable form of cheap labor for the Southern planters. The typical slave, however, did not work on a large plantation. He would be found more likely on a small farm, with one or two other blacks, where he worked alongside the master and his family. The majority of blacks were field slaves who worked under one of two systems—the Gang Plan or the Task System. Under the Gang Plan, large groups of blacks, especially on the larger plantations, worked long hours in the fields. In the Task System, individual blacks were given various specific chores to perform. Most urban slaves worked under the Task System in such occupations as messengers, domestic servants, and craftsmen. A smaller group of favored slaves (selected principally because of their light skin color, loyalty, or old age) worked in and around the master's house as domestic servants.

The climate and soil in New England prevented huge profits from agriculture, but skilled and unskilled labor was in much demand on small farms and in homes, ships, factories, and shipyards, as well as on fishing and trading ships. Since Indians and indentured servants proved to be insufficient laborers, black slaves were a welcome supplement. In the Middle Colonies and later states, black slaves were employed in similar occupations and in larger numbers.

Since English law did not define the status of a slave, the colonies were left to adopt their own regulations. Essentially, all the colonies and states aimed first to protect the property rights of the master, and, secondly, to protect white society from what was considered an alien and savage race. The codes grew out of laws regulating indentured servitude, but the slave had practically no rights, while the servant had many.

The first statutory recognition of slavery came from Massachusetts in 1641. Rhode Island passed a law regulating slavery in 1652. Virginia's regulations, which were to set the standards for the South, were passed in 1661. The status of the mother would determine whether a child was slave or free. Children born to slave mothers would become slaves. Most interracial unions and unions of slaves and free persons were of black women and white men, so the products of such unions would be classified as slaves. This practice ran counter to the English tradition which determined the status of a child according to that of his father.

Generally speaking, the slave codes prohibited the assembling or the wandering of blacks without permission from masters. Slaves could not, for instance, own weapons, testify against white persons, and received harsher punishment for some crimes, lesser for others. An attack, for example, on a white person usually meant severe punishment, while petty theft often went unpunished. A master or any white man could not kill a slave with impunity, but was likely to receive less punishment than for killing a free man. Cases involving relations between slave and master could be tried in special courts without juries. Justices of the Peace and a selected group of planters heard such cases and passed judgment. The strictness of enforcement of slave codes varied from region to region, from colony to colony, from state to state, and even from one plantation to another. The Massachusetts code was less restrictive than the Mississippi one, for example, where blacks could be emancipated or manumitted only with legal approval. Urban slaves were less restricted than rural ones. Slaves on small farms enjoyed more freedom than those on huge plantations.

Physical cruelties were inflicted upon some slaves, primarily for insubordination, refusal to work, slave plots or revolts, and for running away. The cruelest punishment was likely to be seen on large plantations and was received at the hands of foremen or slave drivers. Modern historians tend to indict American Negro slavery not so much for physical cruelty and the psychological effects of the slave system, but because of the harshness of the slave codes, wherein the blacks had little legal protection. In the view of many, the slave system almost completely distorted the Negro's personality.

Early historians disagreed vehemently on the question of the slaves' acceptance or rejection of his status and on many related matters, such as whether or not religion stifled resistance or served as a vehicle for leadership and protest. One school, commonly associated with the Southern-born historian Ulrich B. Phillips, portrayed a docile, contented African, naturally pliable, and logically a slave. Another school, taking its name from the New England historian Stanley Elkins, assessed the psychological consequences of slavery and concluded that the blacks' personalities were so distorted by the harshness of the system that they assumed a docile "Sambo," character. Still another school, which includes such liberal historians as Kenneth Stampp and the Marxist scholar Herbert Aptheker, saw the slave as rebellious and troublesome to his master. Contemporary historians widely agree that the slave community was a complex environment. Many, perhaps most slaves accomodated themselves to their immediate surroundings, with the realization that open rebellion was futile and suicidal. Others were openly rebellious. Many others sought any means available, other than violent insurrection, to show their displeasure with their bondage. This "day to day resistance" was carefully documented as early as 1943 by historians Alice and Raymond Bauer.

Slaves did, in fact, protest their enslavement from the very beginning. Aside from daily acts of rebellion, which took such forms as escape, destruction of property, feigned illness, and disloyalty, there were a number of plots and at least one major mutiny and one major revolt. Black slaves joined with white servants in a conspiracy in Gloucester County, Virginia in 1663; fifty-five whites were killed in the slave rebellion led by Nat Turner in Southhampton County, Virginia in 1831; and slaves mutineered on the *Amistad* off the coast of Long Island in 1839. In the final analysis, Negro slave plots, mutinies, and revolts resulted in the freeing of only a few blacks, although vicious reprisals often followed such acts. Many more slaves secured freedom by escape and by manumission or emancipation.

The origins of the free black population in America came after the Revolutionary War. In appreciation of the service of approximately 5,000 blacks in the War for Independence, and as a result of the libertarian and egalitarian spirit which the Declaration of Independence and the war inspired, many masters, especially Northerners, manumitted their slaves. Soon individual states in the North decreed the gradual abolition of the institution, beginning with Vermont's action in 1777. In 1776, the population of the United States was about two and one-half million, with more than 500,000 black slaves and approximately 40,000 free blacks. More than one-half of these free blacks lived in the South. The Revolutionary leaders, including George Washington and Thomas Jefferson, anticipated a continuation of this trend toward manumission and emancipation until eventually slavery would disappear from the land. This expectation was to be drowned, almost literally, by the whirling noise of Eli Whitney's cotton gin. The invention of this native of Massachusetts made cotton production increasingly profitable and caused rapid and substantial increases in the slave population. On the eve of the Civil War, there were four million black slaves in the South.

Free blacks in the rural South worked primarily as farm workers or as independent farmers. In the urban areas, North and South, free blacks were employed in factories, such as tobacco plants and textile mills, and also worked in ship yards and in railroad construction. There were some independent merchants and many personal servants and artisans. The principal professional occupation was preaching, hence the first black leader of national stature was Bishop Richard Allen of Philadelphia, one of the founders of the African Methodist Episcopal (A.M.E.) Church.

Prior to the American Revolution, free blacks were so small in number that they did not pose a threat to whites in most of the states. Then, during the Revolutionary era, thousands of slaves were freed from Delaware to the north. This rapid increase in the free black population resulted in more severe restrictions. By 1790, free blacks faced regulations similar to those governing slaves. In the early history of New England, blacks could not serve in the militias as combatants (the black military hero, Peter Salem, had to beg his master's permission to serve during the American Revolution), although they could be called upon to work on the roads and other menial tasks. Free blacks could not walk on the streets at night without a pass or visit a town other than the one in which they lived without passes. They could not entertain black or Indian slaves without permission. In the South, they ran the risk of being enslaved themselves if caught without proof of their status. In early Rhode Island history, free blacks were not allowed to keep horses, sheep, or any other domestic animals. In Boston, they could not own hogs. The possession of weapons was severely restricted. In one New England state, blacks could not possess walking sticks or canes unless demonstrably required for the actual support of the person. There was constant conflict in places like New York as free blacks and whites competed for jobs.

By 1840, the free black population in the United States was almost completely disfranchised. More than ninety percent of the American free black population lived in states which totally, or in part, restricted their right to vote. On the eve of the Civil War, blacks voted with relative freedom and safety only in Massachusetts, Vermont, New Hampshire, and Maine.

Restrictions on the political and civil rights of free blacks were motivated by racial prejudice and, additionally, in the South by beliefs that the group had a disquieting influence on the institution of slavery. Free blacks were implicated in a number of the slave plots and uprisings and their very existence pointed to a different life, although not a very radical one, for black men in America. In the final analysis, a free black in pre-Civil War America was little better off than a slave. The inferior status of this group has led historians to classify them appropriately as quasi-free Negroes.

Despite the inferior civil, social, and political status of quasi-free blacks, many managed to achieve considerable distinction in American society. Although discriminated against in employment and in other economic endeavors, a number of free blacks acquired substantial wealth. Even in the pre-Civil War era, there were prosperous free black communities in Philadelphia, Baltimore, Charleston, New Orleans, and elsewhere. Such black individuals as John Jones and Paul Cuffe acquired considerable fortunes. In the military, the arts and sciences, and in religion there were free blacks who distinguished themselves and won recognition even from White America. The free black communities, especially in the North, were vociferous opponents of slavery and discrimination, and the abolition movement of the 1830s and the convention movement of the 1840s and 1850s were interrelated vehicles used by blacks to protest their status in America, whether slave or quasi-free.

War and Freedom (1861-1876)

Momentous changes in the lives of black Americans occurred in the years between 1861 and 1876. These were the years of the American Civil War, Emancipation, and Reconstruction. Four million Negroes were freed as a result of a war in which many of them participated. Then, for the first time, large numbers of blacks had an opportunity to direct their own social and economic destinies; and some, during the Reconstruction era, were able to assert political leadership. Despite the war and the resulting freedom, however, these were still very difficult years for the black masses as they struggled to survive in a hostile environment, and even the gains made during Black Reconstruction failed to provide lasting security.

After the Confederate attack on Fort Sumter, South Carolina on April 12, 1861 and President Abraham Lincoln's call for 75,000 volunteers to "defend the Union," many Northern blacks rushed to answer the President's appeal. The blacks erroneously interpreted the unfolding conflict as a war against slavery. They soon discovered that Lincoln's war aims did not include interference with slavery where it already existed and that they were not to be permitted combat roles. Abraham Lincoln judged that a war against slavery would drive additional Southern and Border states into the Confederacy and that such a program, along with the employment of black troops, would anger most Northern whites. Blacks and their white abolitionist supporters, in and out of Congress, clearly expressed their opposition to a war whose aims did not include the abolition of slavery, as well as the refusal to employ blacks as troops.

The first year of the Civil War was for the most part a frustrating one for Abraham Lincoln and the Union. In addition to inept military commanders, he had to contend with apathy and even disloyalty in the North; the possibility of an alliance between the Confederacy and cotton-seeking European nations; abolitionist and Negro agitation; runaway slaves crossing into Union lines; unauthorized slave emancipation by military leaders; and the employment of blacks in fatigue duties by the Confederacy. There was also the continuous matter of preventing the secession of additional slave states. By the summer of 1862, President Lincoln concluded that the emancipation of certain slaves and the eventual employment of black troops had become military necessities. There were risks involved in such an act: the Border states might join the Confederacy; many Northern whites might become alienated; and morale in the Union Army might be lowered. On the other hand, England and the rest of Europe would not likely oppose a war against slavery; abolitionist sentiment in the North would enthusiastically support the effort; and thousands of blacks would be lost to the Confederacy while thousands more could be drawn to the Union.

The Emancipation Proclamation specifically excluded all slave states and areas loyal to the Union, hence preserving the Border States for the North and having little immediate effect in most of the South, which the Confederate Army controlled. At the same time, the Proclamation and the employment of Negro troops convinced blacks and abolitionists that the "Day of Jubilee" was at hand. Bells rang from the spires of Northern black churches and blacks rejoiced when the emancipation edict took effect on January 1, 1863.

The moral crusade known as abolitionism had sprung up during the 1830s. This new, militant movement resulted from the efforts of such New England and Midwestern reformers as William Lloyd Garrison, James Finney, Lewis

Tappan, and Theodore Dwight Weld. The talents of former slaves like Frederick Douglass, Henry Highland Garnett, and Harriet Tubman, as well as members of the free black communities in the North, were joined with the efforts of the white reformers. These people were successors to the Quaker protestors of earlier centuries, the moderate abolitionists of the eighteenth and early nineteenth centuries, and the colonizationists of the early 1800s, who would rid the land of the Negro problem by shipping blacks back to Africa or to other foreign lands. In 1863, the abolitionists' long and painful efforts finally received political sanction at the highest level when emancipation became a war objective, even though prompted not by moral suasion or moral right, but by military necessity.

Almost 200,000 blacks fought for the Union during the Civil War. Although they faced discrimination of one type or another throughout the conflict, many rendered distinguished service and won commendations from the Commander-in-Chief himself. A few rose to the ranks of officers. About 40,000 blacks died in the fight for freedom—most of these deaths were disease-related, reflecting the poor medical attention received by black soldiers as well as the disproportionate number of blacks on the front line and other hazardous duties. The Confederacy debated the use of black troops until 1864, but when the decision to employ them was grudgingly made, the war was nearing its end. Blacks never saw combat duty for the Confederacy.

The generous terms of surrender which General Ulysses S. Grant offered the Confederates on April 9, 1865 were symptomatic of much of Northern white opinion at the close of the Civil War. It certainly reflected the attitude of President Lincoln toward the seceded states which should, in his view, be returned to the Union as expeditiously as possible in a spirit of leniency and reconciliation. Lincoln's mild Reconstruction program was aborted by an assassin's bullet on April 14, 1865, but his successor, Andrew Johnson, a Southerner, continued the lenient policies toward the white South. Following Lincoln's example, Johnson (who did not believe in Negro equality) supported ratification of the Thirteenth Amendment abolishing slavery, but did not push Negro enfranchisement or the protection of civil rights. He tolerated anti-Negro violence in Louisiana, Tennessee, and Mississippi, as well as the Black Codes which the Southern white or "Johnson" governments enacted in 1865 and 1866. These codes, reminiscent of the ante-bellum slave codes, proscribed the Negro to an inferior status once again in Southern society.

Republican leaders in Congress correctly viewed the Johnson program as an invitation to restore white Democratic supremacy in the South. Some of these leaders, motivated by a desire to institute Republican party supremacy in the region, and others motivated by a sincere interest in protecting Negro civil rights, combined to form a solid front of opposition to the President's programs. The "Radical Republicans" favored a harsh program of Southern Reconstruction, one which would delay the reentrance of the Southern states until Republican strength could be garnered; until the blacks could be enfranchised with the premise that they would form a bloc of Southern Republican votes; and one which would guarantee civil rights for Negroes. In addition, the Republicans believed that Southern white Democratic agriculturists should not be allowed to regain economic and political ascendancy in the nation.

In 1866 and 1867 the Republican leadership, using the party's majorities in Congress, took the Reconstruction of the South from President Johnson's control and instituted their own program. Their plans included an extension of the Freedmen's Bureau (originally proposed by Lincoln) to help freed blacks and poor whites eat, attain clothing and shelter, secure job protection, receive medical attention and some education. Negroes were to be made citizens of the United States and granted all rights and privileges enjoyed by other American citizens. This was accomplished through the Civil Rights Act of 1866 and the Fourteenth Amendment (ratified in 1868). The blacks' right to vote was to be insured through the Fifteenth Amendment (ratified in 1870).

The Radical Republican Reconstruction program, which was guided through the House by the Pennsylvania egalitarian Thaddeus Stevens and through the Senate by Charles Sumner, a Massachusetts humanitarian, paved the way for the first large scale participation by blacks in the State conventions in the South. These conventions were called in 1867 and 1868 to establish new fundamental laws to replace the pro-Democratic, anti-Negro documents instituted by the Johnson governments. In South Carolina, more blacks than whites attended these conventions, and in Louisiana the races attended in equal numbers. Elsewhere, Northern whites ("carpetbaggers"), some of them economic and political opportunists, and Southern whites ("scalawags"), political and economic allies of the Northern Republicans, dominated the conventions. The latter group had exercised the greatest influence in the new Southern governments, except in South Carolina, where blacks had a majority in the Legislature throughout the early years of Radical or Black Reconstruction.

Although blacks never really controlled any part of the Southern governments (with the exception of South Carolina) during the whole Reconstruction era (1865-1877), they voted in large numbers and elected members of their own race and sympathetic whites to offices ranging from city councilman to United States Senator. There were, for example, four black lieutenant governors, twenty U.S. congressmen, two U.S. senators, three secretaries of state, a state supreme court justice, two state treasurers, and numerous other minor black officials. P.B.S. Pinchback served briefly as acting governor of Louisiana.

Black voters and elected officials tended to pursue an attitude of charity and reconciliation toward their former slave masters and their descendants. They refrained from passing or supporting vindictive legislation and insisted that Southern whites reap equal benefits from the reformist acts which they passed. The Black Reconstruction governments, despite examples of waste and corruption, made great strides in the physical reconstruction of the South: in providing free public schools; in eliminating anachronistic penal institutions; and in guaranteeing civil rights. In these matters, black and white alike could look for a better life.

The Nadir (1877-1900)

The growing Republican strength in the Northwest, economic ties between Northern and Southern capitalists, anti-Negro intimidation and violence by the Ku Klux Klan and other hate groups, and the economic helplessness of black Americans eventually caused the waning of Northern Republican enthusiasm for Black Reconstruction. The nadir came with the disputed election of 1876. In return for Republican pledges of federal aid for internal improvements in the South and the withdrawal of the remaining federal troops supporting Radical Reconstruction, Southern Democratic leaders allowed Congress to proceed in certifying Rutherford B. Hayes as President of the United States instead of the Democratic contender, Samuel Tilden. Following his inauguration, Hayes removed the last federal troops from the South, and the remaining Radical or Black Reconstruction governments in Florida, Louisiana, and South Carolina toppled.

Historian Rayford Logan of Howard University and others have called the period between 1877 and 1900 the nadir in Negro life and history. Following the disputed election of 1876 and the so-called Compromise of 1877 which settled it, the Republican party abandoned the Negro and left him in the hands of Southern "redeemers," those native whites who reasserted white supremacy. From Hayes through William McKinley, the national government exhibited a "hands off" policy toward the "Southern problem." With little or no relief to be expected from state and local authorities, blacks faced an environment reminiscent of slavery. Legalized segregation, discrimination, and political disfranchisement became the order of the day. The United States Supreme Court in 1883 and 1896 conclusively stamped legality on racial separation. In the Civil Rights cases of 1883, the Court struck down the Civil Rights Act of 1875, which, among other things, had guaranteed blacks equal access to public accommodations. In 1896, in the historic *Plessy v. Ferguson* decision, the Court sanctioned the principle of separate-but-equal facilities for blacks and whites. In practice, however, the facilities were separate and unequal. Beginning with a Mississippi law in 1890, one Southern state after another adopted ingenious devices for denying the ballot to blacks. These ranged from literacy tests to the infamous white primary, in which blacks were excluded from the most important state and local elections. Ku Klux Klan-type violence, of which the most notorious form was lynching, continued to augment the legal oppression. Out of this nadir, however, were to come two outstanding voices who would leave large imprints upon African-American history—Booker T. Washington and W.E.B. DuBois.

The Age of Booker T. Washington (1901-1917)

Booker T. Washington was the only black American invited to speak at the 1895 Cotton States International Exposition in Atlanta. Most prominent Southern whites were aware of the significant work he was performing at Tuskegee Institute in Alabama, where as principal since 1881, Washington was producing trained black agriculturists, artisans, and teachers. He also encouraged cleanliness, respect for hard labor, and fostered racial harmony. In his address at the Exposition, latter dubbed "the Atlanta Compromise," Washington admonished blacks for agitating for political power and social equality, and called on whites to assist them in education, principally agricultural-industrial training, and economic advancement.

The formula for racial peace and progress which Washington outlined at the Exposition met wide approval from Southern and Northern whites. The *Atlanta Constitution* called it the greatest speech ever delivered in the South, and President Grover Cleveland sent Washington a congratulatory telegram. While many blacks supported Washington's ideas, others, particularly publisher William Monroe Trotter and scholar W.E.B. DuBois, disagreed with Washington's remarks and launched attacks against him. Although Trotter was his first and most vociferous antagonist, the best known opposition to Washington was W.E.B. DuBois.

The publication of DuBois' *The Souls of Black Folk* in 1903 crystallized the opposition to the "accommodationist" philosophy of Booker T. Washington. A group of black "radicals" led by DuBois and Trotter met at Niagara Falls, Canada, in June of 1905 and adopted resolutions calling for aggressive action to end racial discrimination in the United States. The lynchings, riots, intimidation, and disfranchisement of the previous decade had taught them that temporizing would not guarantee security to black Americans. The Niagara group held other meetings in the United States, recruiting black intellectuals in nearly every major city. The protest group has become known to history as the Niagara Movement.

Following the anti-Negro riots in Brownsville, Texas, Atlanta, Georgia, and Springfield, Illinois between 1906 and 1908, the Niagara Movement, with the exception of Trotter (who was suspicious of white people), merged in 1910 with a group of white progressives and founded the National Association for the Advancement of Colored People (NAACP). The NAACP became the most militant civil rights organization in the United States, as it sought to obtain racial equality for all Americans.

Despite the activities of the Niagara "radicals" and the NAACP, the policies and practices of Booker T. Washington and his "Tuskegee Machine" remained in vogue, and continued to garner substantial financial subsidies from wealthy white Americans as well as political endorsements from the White House to state and local authorities. The Niagara "radicals" were hard put in their efforts against Washington. Indeed, the period in African-American history following the "Atlanta Compromise" to the death of "the wizard of Tuskegee" in 1915 was the Age of Booker T. Washington.

Between War and Depression (1918-1932)

After the death of Booker T. Washington, several members of the NAACP and other individuals gained the ascendancy in black leadership, for there could really be no one successor to the Tuskegee "king pin." White America, however, was resistant in accepting these militant demands, and racial oppression continued to be commonplace. Legal and extra-legal discrimination in employment, housing, education, and political disfranchisement were combined with police brutality and atrocious lynchings. Tuskegee Institute kept a running count of lynchings in the United States and published annual reports—as many as eighty-three were recorded in one year—and it was 1952 before none was recorded. When the United States intervened in World War I, some seemed to believe that the participation of blacks in the conflict would prick the conscience of white Americans and lead to concessions for blacks. Such precedents, in fact, existed in the War for Independence and in the Civil War. The contemporary story, however, turned out be one of harassment of black soldiers, even while in uniform at home and abroad, and the war itself was followed by one of the worst series of racial clashes in American history. During the summer of 1919, at least twenty-five cities witnessed racial disturbances in what the poet and civil rights leader James Weldon Johnson called "the Red Summer."

The "Red Summer," a product of the post-war depression and the growing black migration to large urban areas, produced a wave of disillusionment in Black America. This disenchantment had positive as well as negative effects. In the early 1920s, for example, scores of black intellectuals, centered in Harlem, began producing literary and artistic works depicting Negro life in the ghettoes and often crying for relief from oppression. The Harlem Renaissance, as the new movement was called, came of age in 1922 with the publication of Claude McKay's volume of poetry, *Harlem Shadows*. His poem "If We Must Die" was a militant protest against white attacks in the North and lynchers in the South and urged blacks to resist physical assaults against them. Other notable literary works from this period include Jean Toomer's *Cane*, Jessie Fauset's *There Is Confusion*, Countee Cullen's *Color*, Walter White's *Flight*, and Langston Hughes' *The Weary Blues*. The era was synthesized in Alain Locke's anthology, *The New Negro*.

In this same period, such singers as Marian Anderson, Roland Hayes, and Paul Robeson carried performances of Negro spirituals to new heights while black musicians and composers, including Louis Armstrong, Fletcher Henderson, Duke Ellington, Scott Joplin, King Oliver, and Bessie Smith brought jazz and blues from Southern "honky tonks" to the major cities of the North.

Black nationalism was revived in the movement of Marcus Garvey. The West Indian immigrant taught race pride and urged large-scale emigration of blacks to Africa. Garvey's would-be African empire collapsed behind the cell doors of the Atlanta Federal Penitentiary, where he was incarcerated after being convicted of mail fraud.

The Great Depression which hit the country in 1929 stung the Negro. Most blacks were already on the lowest rung of the economic ladder, now they were in serious danger of touching ground. The Depression, of course, stifled much of the growing militancy among the race while doing little to relieve discontent. Blacks contended that even in the midst of common woes, they were still singled out and made the victims of discrimination. Their plight in the area of employment, for instance, was depicted by the slogan "the last hired and the first fired." When Franklin D. Roosevelt took office as President in 1933, American blacks were certainly ready for a New Deal.

A New Deal—A New Life? (1933-1940)

Such New Deal measures as the Civilian Conservation Corps (CCC), the National Youth Administration (NYA), and the Works Progress Administration (WPA) lifted blacks as well as whites out of the depths of the Depression, but some blacks felt that they did not receive their fair share of the benefits. Since many of the recovery and reform programs were administered by the state and local governments, this meant all-white control, especially in the

South. Discriminatory handling of the measures for relief, in many instances, would not be difficult to imagine. In any case, the New Deal Administration was a segregated one. Nonetheless, President Roosevelt established his so-called "Black Cabinet," Negro advisers on African-American affairs. These individuals included Mary McCleod Bethune, an educator, Ralph Bunche, a political scientist, William Hastie, an attorney, and Robert Weaver, an economist. In the end, the New Deal, despite its imperfections, was viewed by blacks as well as whites as an era of progress—certainly a marked advance over the Depression years.

War Again (1941-1945)

The outbreak of the Second World War in Europe, like its predecessor, encouraged a new wave of black emigration to the North. As the nation entered a state of defense-readiness, blacks sought to obtain a share of the increasing number of jobs in defense industries. Again, they met a good deal of frustration resulting from discrimination. Finally, after blacks threatened to stage a massive protest march in Washington, D. C., President Franklin D. Roosevelt issued an executive order forbidding discrimination in defense related industries. Once the United States entered the world war, hundreds of thousands of black Americans served with distinction. This service, along with the growing black populations in the urban centers, a rise in the literacy rate among blacks, and increasing economic opportunities appeared to foster a new determination to end racial discrimination in American life. The NAACP, bolstered by the records of black servicemen, an increased membership, a new corp of brilliant young lawyers, and steady financial support from white philanthropists, led the way toward freedom.

The Attack against Segregation (1945-1954)

The existence of segregation and discrimination in the most democratic nation in the world constituted an American dilemma, according to the Swedish social scientist Gunnar Myrdal, who in 1944 had concluded a year-long study of the race problem entitled *An American Dilemma*. The NAACP had long been aware of the dilemma and was determined to resolve it by eliminating segregation and discrimination from American society. The NAACP leaders, like most Americans, revered the constitutional structure of the United States and thus sought to implement its program through legal channels. Prior to World War II, the organization's legal minds were chipping away at the foundations of segregation and discrimination by winning important decisions before the United States Supreme Court. After the war, there was a virtual avalanche. From 1945 to 1954, the NAACP attacked legalized segregation and discrimination in almost every domain and its foundations slowly crumbled. Ingenious devices for denying blacks the right to vote, discrimination in housing, bias in transportation, and segregation in recreation and educational facilities fell victim to NAACP-sponsored law suits. The Supreme Court decisions on school segregation, which are highlighted by the Brown case in 1954, were so far-reaching and portended so much for the future that they inaugurated a whole new era in African-American history, the era of civil rights.

"The Second Reconstruction" (1954-1964)

The schoolhouse had long been considered an integral part of the democratic process. It was, in fact, a bulwark of American society. Indeed, its ability to socialize individuals made it an almost sacred institution. The destruction of segregation and discrimination in the schools could then bring the day closer when America would boast of an integrated society. The school decisions inspired a literal stampede for equality. Court decisions quickly knocked down the remaining vestiges of legalized segregation. Congress, in the face of skillful lobbying by black organizations and increasing black voter registrants in the North, began passing laws designed to insure Negro voting rights against extra-legal trickery in the South. President Harry S. Truman issued an executive order banning segregation in the armed forces; several years later, President Dwight Eisenhower signed a bill which prohibited discrimination in housing assistance by the FHA and the Veterans' Administration. Civil rights committees were established to investigate and report injustices. Boycotts, such as the famous one in Montgomery, Alabama in 1955-56, broke down Jim Crowism on local buses. With segregation and discrimination by law a dead letter, black groups turned to overt and covert bias in the private sector. Centering their attention on the humiliating separate lunch counters and restaurants, the sit-in technique (aided by the boycott) was revived and used frequently to wipe out discrimination in restaurants and other public accommodations from hotels to cemeteries. The Civil Rights Act of 1964 acknowledged the correctness of sit-ins by, among other things, outlawing discrimination in public accommodations. The American dilemma seemed to be over, all citizens would be free in "the land of the free." The dream which Martin Luther King, Jr. had so eloquently described at the March on Washington in August, 1963 seemed near fulfillment.

In assessing the gains in civil rights and human freedoms which blacks had made in a single decade, 1954-1964, it was easy for some to see them as a continuation of the progress aborted by the end of Reconstruction in the 1870s and 1880s. The achievements and the prospects seemed so significant that many felt that the era could properly be called "The Second Reconstruction."

"The Second Reconstruction" Wanes (1964-1973)

President Lyndon B. Johnson's signature on the Civil Rights Act of 1964 had barely become law when a serious racial disturbance erupted in Harlem. That same summer several other Northern ghettoes were the scenes of violence. Then in August, 1965, the black ghetto of Watts in Los Angeles exploded, leaving many dead and injured, and property losses in the millions of dollars. For the next two summers, peaking with the equally destructive Detroit riot of 1967, scores of major racial outbursts, often times sparked by clashes between blacks and white police officers, occurred. The nation sought an answer to these eruptions, particularly at a time when the millenium appeared at hand. The Presidential Commission on Civil Disorders (Kerner Commission) offered its findings in March, 1968. In spite of all the court decisions, the sit-ins, marches and boycotts, the average black American was disillusioned with his status in American society, for he still found himself ill-housed, ill-clothed, poorly paid, (if at all), segregated, and discriminated against (through covert and extra-legal means) in all walks of American life. Ingrained white racism, the Commission reasoned, blocked the legitimate aspirations of black people. The slaying of Martin Luther King, Jr., the nation's leading apostle of non-violent resistance to racism and bias, in April of 1968 increased the disillusionment and, in fact, led to some outright despair. New cries of black nationalism, black separatism, and violent resistance were heard in African-America.

In three and one-half centuries of life in America, the African race has seen momentous changes in the legal and social structures of the country which relate directly to its own status. The legal foundations of segregation and discrimination which kept it in a straitjacket were toppled in the last decade. The attainment of these goals involved a long, painful, often times frustrating and disillusioning struggle. Yet, as the Kerner Commission Report so dramatically depicted, the long fight for dignity and justice was by no means completed, for the real victory would have to involve the repression of white racism. White Americans would have to confront its ingrained and often unconscious bias on the subject of race, and work consciously to erase its effects from the land.

"The Second Reconstruction" Betrayed (1973-1990)

The landslide proportions of Richard Nixon's re-election as President in 1972 cast a dark cloud over Black America. During his first term, the President had consistently reaffirmed his commitment to racial equality and justice, but at the end of his term many of the most prominent leaders in Black America found Nixon's record on civil rights seriously wanting. Some even claimed that there had been an erosion of the gains made under the two previous Democratic administrations. They cited, for example, the President's failure to appoint blacks to top level positions in the federal government (i.e., under Nixon, the cabinet returned to an all-white status); his nominations of G. Harold Carswell and Clement Haynsworth, both "conservative" Southerners, for seats on the United States Supreme Court; his vehement opposition to busing to achieve school desegregation; and his indifference towards desegregated housing and support of black institutions of higher education. The United States Commission on Civil Rights joined its voice with that of the black leaders, charging that the Nixon administration was derelict in its enforcement of existing civil rights laws.

President Nixon used several occasions, including press conferences and meetings with blacks inside and outside of government, to express concern with the disillusionment and disenchantment with his administration within Black America. Yet he refused to alter his course. Nixon was prone to cite the phenomenal progress of black Americans in the past decade in the areas of civil rights, economic opportunity, and political development. He seemed to suggest that the remaining problems of blacks were less a matter of race and more of initiative, self-reliance, and economic development, and discussed the need for "black capitalism" and black entrepreneurship. As Nixon approached the election campaign of 1972, he predicted substantial black support for his candidacy and did, in fact, win endorsement from several prominent blacks in his bid for re-election. However, the leaders of most of the major black civil rights organizations in the country urged Nixon's defeat, and on election day he amassed only about thirty percent of the total black vote.

The President began his second administration amid the aura of the greatest election victory in American history, while the growing cancer of Watergate still only slowly creeping into his political life. The "Watergate" scandal, whose discovery was attributed to a black security guard, Frank Wills, would soon bring down the presidency of Richard Nixon. Meanwhile, the President continued his policies of "benign neglect" toward Black America.

The indifference of a national administration toward the peculiar problems of black Americans, combined with a growing economic recession, created a certain amount of confusion among blacks. Ironically, this was also a time of substantial political progress at the local level, particularly in the South. The problem, however, in large measure, was that the local political prowess which blacks were gaining could not be transformed or translated into influence at the national level, and could not halt the growing spiral of black unemployment and underemployment. The indifference manifested by the national administration had its impact in other facets of black American life. The drive for "affirmative action" in recruiting blacks to higher paying jobs seemed to lose some of its furor, as did the preferential recruiting of black students to previously all-white or majority-white schools and colleges. The economic decline was a part of the explanation; the cry by some whites of "reverse discrimination" was another, but the complacent tone set in Washington was also of great significance. What should blacks, still the most ill-fed, ill-housed, poorly trained segment of the American population, do now? Would the disillusionment of the past become outright despair? Would there be new Wattses, Detroits, and Atlantas? Would the black masses again take to the streets to vent their frustrations at still not being able to share fully in the American Dream? There were, as always, voices in the black community urging such a course of action, but they were, as in the past, on the fringe of the black mainstream without a substantial following.

During the Nixon nadir, the black mainstream would continue to look to the leadership of the black middle class, as exemplified in the major civil rights organizations—the NAACP, the Southern Christian Leadership Council (SCLC), Operation PUSH (People United to Save Humanity), the Urban League—for the right path to the Promised Land. That leadership, faced with the political and economic realities of the 1970s and the growing displays of overt racism in the North, could only sprout the old shibboleths of the Civil Rights era and espouse similar strategies. In fact, black American leaders were now faced with problems, policies, and practices which defied simple solutions; such previous tactics as marches, court edicts, or even a brick thrown through a plate-glass window seemed to be less than effective. Black America needed influence at the highest levels of political and economic decision-making, and that it did not have.

While the Nixon administration undoubtedly exaggerated the extent of black progress in America in the 1960s, it was nevertheless true that all indexes relating to income, education, housing, and the like revealed numerical and often percentage gains for black Americans during the 1960s. In many respects, Black America was still a colonized nation, but its colonial status was closer to that of America in the 1760s than to Rhodesia in the 1970s. These facts, together with the apparent futility of violent outbursts, seemed to suggest to Black America, the masses as well as the elite, that after a decade of disillusionment, a return to the mainstream would best promote physical and psychological well-being. The mood of Black America suggested a harvesting of gains to prevent further erosions; to place education above demonstration; to seek whatever securities that were inherent in the middle-class society in America; and to acknowledge the fact that America was still a nation of two societies—one black, one white—separate and unequal.

The "Watergate" scandal of the early 1970s, in which President Richard Nixon was recorded on tape as allegedly condoning criminal conspiracy, did what black voters had been unable to do in 1972—remove him from office. Nixon's successor, Vice President Gerald R. Ford, a "more moderate" Republican, came into the White House under the major constraint of not having been elected to the Oval Office. The next presidential campaign was less than two years away.

Given the constraints under which he assumed office, Ford, who eventually pardoned former President Nixon, acted in the manner of a caretaker. He continued many of his predecessor's policies while trying "to heal the nation" in the aftermath of Watergate. President Ford made no new major civil rights initiatives and generally opposed "forced busing" to achieve school desegregation. One of his cabinet members, Agriculture Secretary Earl Butz, was forced to resign after uttering a racial slur against blacks.

Ford's propensity for simplicity, particularly in foreign affairs, a continued downturn in the economy, and the "stain" which Watergate left on the Republican party, particularly its "conservative wing," left the President particularly vulnerable as the 1976 elections approached. Jimmy Carter, a relatively unknown peanut farmer and the former governor of Georgia, emerged from the close race victorious.

Carter had sprung on the nation during the Democratic primaries as a populist who would strengthen the economy so that both farmers and laborers could reap a better harvest. As a former Southern governor, he was suspect among blacks, particularly in the North. Although the Southerner from the small town of Plains had captured the Georgia governor's office as a segregationist, he declared in his inaugural address that the time for racial bigotry in his state was over. Carter won the allegiance of many of Georgia's black leaders, particularly in the capital city of Atlanta. Since Atlanta was the headquarters of the Civil Rights Movement, the Atlanta black leadership cadre, which included the father and widow of slain civil rights leader Martin Luther King, Jr. as well as such civil rights veterans as John Lewis and Andrew Young, was highly respected throughout the nation. The Atlanta group was thus able to win over other influential blacks in other parts of the nation to join them in their support of Carter's candidacy. Even when Carter stumbled in a speech in Gary, Indiana, in which he discussed "the ethnic purity" of neighborhoods, the Atlanta leadership group stuck with him and helped save him from disaster in Black America. The strong showing which Carter made among blacks in the

South, particularly, gave him, according to several journalists and political analysts, his margin of victory over President Ford.

Many blacks apparently believed that they had put Jimmy Carter in the White House and placed great expectations on him when he took the oath of office in January, 1977. There were predictions of several black Cabinet officers, increased financial support of black institutions, and greater sensitivity toward other special aspirations and needs of Black America. But even after Carter, in an unprecedented and unexpected move, named the black Georgia congressman Andrew Young U. S. Ambassador to the United Nations and appointed Patricia Roberts Harris, a former Howard University law professor, Secretary of Housing and Urban Affairs, some blacks began to grumble that the President had made too few high level black appointments. There were even some complaints that Mrs. Harris, a fair-complexioned, middle class African-American, was "not black enough " in her racial consciousness. Harris, a former civil liberties lawyer, bristled at the suggestion.

As President Carter developed his financial policies in the midst of a continuing economic downturn in the nation, Vernon Jordan, the head of the National Urban League, began a chorus of protests that the President was not doing enough to help the most depressed segment of the nation, Black America. In the beginning, Jordan's comments drew few adherents, but shortly thereafter only Carter's staunchest supporters among America's black leadership establishment were withholding criticisms. Carter himself vacillated between bristling and appeasing his black critics. On one occasion, he noted that he was under no compulsion to have a "quota" of blacks in his cabinet; on another, he expressed disappointment that he had not been able to recruit more highly qualified, high-level black appointees. On some occasions, Carter extolled the progress that his administration had made in civil rights and in other major issues of concern to blacks; on other occasions, he admitted that much remained to be done.

Yet it was the soaring inflation which brought higher gasoline prices and diminished supplies, and the Iran hostage crisis of 1979 which crippled the Carter presidency. Carter's inability to restore a full, healthy economy and to secure the release of American citizens from Iran brought accusations of a "malaise" at the White House. Finally, when Ronald Reagan, the former Hollywood star and governor of California, who ran an unsuccessful campaign for the Republican presidential nomination in 1976, told voters in the 1980 elections that he would restore the economy and make Americans proud of their nation again, the American electorate turned Jimmy Carter out of the White House. Although black voters still provided Carter with the heaviest support of any segment of the American population, there was less enthusiasm for him in the 1980 election. Many blacks apparently agreed that the President was not forceful enough in solving the problems of the economy or in dealing with terrorists. Others seemed to believe that he had still done too little to advance the major concerns of Black America: fuller employment, better education, and enhancement of civil rights.

In the end, Jimmy Carter, by any fair assessment, was the strongest supporter of Black America's "Agenda" than any American president since Lyndon Baines Johnson. While only two blacks served in his Cabinet, others were generously sprinkled throughout other high levels of government. They included Clifford Alexander, Secretary of the Army; Mary Frances Berry, Assistant Secretary of Education; and Drew Days, Assistant Attorney General. Carter appointed more black federal judges than all of his predecessors combined. He consulted with such black leaders as Jesse L. Jackson, Martin Luther King, Sr., and Benjamin Mays to a degree much larger than Johnson, and took more initiatives to support black colleges than any of his predecessors. But President Carter's gestures toward Black America were not only hampered by a slow economy, but also by a growing white backlash against affirmative action and other preferential and compensatory programs for African-Americans as well as continued opposition to school desegregation. In a similar fashion, if not outright overtly, Ronald Reagan had also appealed to such sentiments in his 1980 campaign, while at the same time declaring himself a proponent of "equal opportunity."

Exponents of one version of a cyclical theory of history relate the nature and character of events of certain periods to the policies and practices of the presidential party or administration in power. Often, such an analysis takes into account the personality of the President himself. For example, both Lyndon Johnson and Jimmy Carter were Southerners of somewhat humble origins who later achieved considerable wealth. Even after rising to social and political prominence, however, they tended to eschew lavishness and elitism. Both were raised among substantial black populations in the segregated South. Both overcame their backgrounds to become proponents of racial equality and racial justice. Reagan, on the other hand, emerged from modest means to fame and fortune as a Hollywood star. During his acting career and later as governor of California, Reagan associated primarily with his peers, whose lifestyles reflected glamor and power. Although he later referred to his appointments of blacks to high positions in the California state government, Reagan rarely, if ever, identified with the black masses or their particular circumstances, aspirations, and needs.

While one can make too much of the relationships between the cycles of party and administration policies and practices, and the differing characters of chief executives, it was, nevertheless, true that the "Second Reconstruction" blossomed under Democratic administrations, whose leaders, although men of substantial wealth, exhibited a special sensitivity to all of Black America. The new era of progress and hope first waned under Republican presidents, one of whom allowed arrogance to place him outside of the law. The "Second Reconstruction" gained new life under a Southern Democrat who once made a living producing peanuts with poor blacks. This interlude was ended when the Republican governor of California occupied the White House.

Ronald Reagan appointed only one black person, Samuel R. Pierce, a "conservative" lawyer, to his Cabinet. When Pierce left the White House, he was being investigated by Congress for possible corruption in office. Another Reagan black appointee was William Allen, another "conservative" who left his post as head of the U.S. Civil Rights Commission in disgrace under clouds of mismanagement and buffoonery. President Reagan rarely consulted with members of the black leadership establishment largely because he felt that they were partisan (almost all of them were either Democrats or Independents) and because they continuously complained that he was insensitive to their "Black Agenda." While Reagan did not sway in his opposition to such "Black Agenda" items as affirmative action and mandatory busing to achieve desegregation, he boasted of strengthening the economy and its subsequent benefits to all Americans, including black ones. President Reagan also took offense at any suggestion that he was a racist. However, as he prepared to leave the White House in 1989 after serving two terms, Reagan suggested on network television that some of the black leadership establishment deliberately continued to fan the fires of racism for self-gain, while distorting the declining significance of race in American life as well as his own record in behalf of civil rights and equal opportunity.

While Reagan did sign a bill extending the provisions of the historic Civil Rights Act of 1965 and the legislation creating the Martin Luther King, Jr. federal holiday (both with some initial reluctance), he advocated tax exemptions for segregated private schools and opposed two civil rights bills designed to strengthen the provisions of the Civil Rights Act of 1964. These protections were struck down by a Supreme Court dominated by Reagan appointees. The "Reagan Court" emerged after the President appointed three justices and elevated another to Chief Justice, jurists who were widely suspected of being "conservative idelogues." One of his nominees, Robert Bork, was rejected by the United States Senate. Reagan appointed only two blacks to federal judgeships.

Indeed, it was Reagan's appointments to the judiciary, particularly the United States Supreme Court, which highlighted the "betrayal of the Second Reconstruction." After all, the new era of human and civil rights for blacks, women, other ethnic minorities, and dissidents had begun with the high Court's decision in *Brown v. Board of Education of Topeka, Kansas* in 1954. Then, after blacks took control of their own destinies beginning with the Montgomery Bus Boycott of 1955, the Supreme Court remained steadfast in guarding and protecting their liberties under constitutional guarantees. When Reagan appointees joined the "conservative" minority on the high Court, however, affirmative action and other preferential and compensatory programs to readdress past discrimination, as well as mandatory busing to achieve school desegregation, were rebuffed time and time again. The concept of "reverse discrimination" gained new prominence as the Court frequently agreed with the complaints of white males, particularly, that they were the victims of bias because of their race or sex.

While the policies of the Reagan administration and the rulings of the Supreme Court may have accurately reflected the current mood of White America, i.e., that the "Second Reconstruction" had achieved its objectives in granting full constitutional rights to black Americans, many blacks continued to blame President Reagan for "rolling back the [civil rights] clock." Some even suggested that despite what opinion polls might say about race conscious policies, the President had a constitutional and moral duty to promote such ideas and programs until the "Second Reconstruction" was, in fact, completed. They often enlisted in their assessments the history of the first Reconstruction which ended when another Republican president, Rutherford B. Hayes, made a "corrupt bargain" with racism in 1876.

During what some black and white leaders, scholars, and other individuals came to call "the Reagan Nadir," a number of proponents of the "Black Agenda" turned their focus away from traditional politics into independent parties, apolitical postures, or new structures of political activity. Others chose to remain within the traditional structure. Some placed their hopes on the shoulders of the Reverend Jesse Louis Jackson, a veteran African-American minister and civil rights leader. The former SCLC leader, through his organizations Operation PUSH and the Rainbow Coalition, emerged in the 1980s as the most popular national black leader since the late Martin Luther King, Jr. In 1984, Jackson sought the Democratic nomination for President and was promptly hailed as the first major black figure to seek that office. But Jackson's candidacy seriously divided the black leadership establishment. Several contended that his candidacy would further polarize the races in the United States, while others believed that it would undermine the solidarity which the Democratic presidential nominee would need in the general election to defeat Ronald Reagan. Furthermore, the black leadership establishment insisted that Jackson had absolutely no chance of capturing his party's nomination, let alone the White House.

Jackson persisted, however, insisting that he could win both the nomination and the presidency by galvanizing black Americans, bringing additional minorities (a rainbow coalition) into his ranks, and winning the support of whites "of goodwill." Although his campaign did inspire a significant increase in new black voters, particularly in the South, Jackson stumbled with other minorities and whites when he became associated with the Nation of Islam leader Louis Farrakhan, and after making allegedly anti-Semitic remarks himself.

Louis Farrakhan had long been accused of harboring anti-Semitic views. He allegedly called Judaism "a gutter religion" and Adolph Hitler, the Nazi dictator, "wickedly great." At the time these comments were made, Farrakhan

was a strong supporter of Jesse Jackson. There were loud outcries from Jews, gentiles, and even some African-Americans, particularly when Jackson procrastinated in disassociating himself from Farrakhan. However, Jackson himself created his most crucial political mistake when he was quoted as having privately referred to Jews by the epithet "hymie." After initial denials and vacillations, the presidential candidate apologized, but severe, perhaps irreparable damage had been done to his quest to broaden his Rainbow Coalition beyond black people.

The black opposition to the Jackson candidacy took on more strident tones after the "hymie" remark. There were more assertions that the Jackson campaign represented divisiveness and futility. At the Democratic National Convention in San Francisco, Andrew Young, the mayor of Atlanta, Georgia, and a colleague of Jackson's in the Civil Rights Movement, publicly severed ties with the African-American candidate and seconded the nomination of the leading contender, former Vice President Walter Mondale. Young was roundly jeered by Jackson delegates and supporters and open warfare between pro and anti-Jackson blacks seemed a real possibility in the Golden Gate city. With deep divisions among blacks and barely five percent of support from whites, the Jackson campaign of 1984 was doomed.

No matter what the outcomes were in 1984, the candidacy of Jesse Jackson for the Democratic nomination inspired thousands of blacks to enter or reenter the traditional political process and to pin their hopes on a candidate who espoused, for the most part, a "Black Agenda." Jackson's showing among whites, while not very impressive, was the best ever attained by a black presidential candidate. Furthermore, the barrier against a major African-American candidate for a major party's nomination was shattered.

By 1988, even amidst continuing racial divisions, blacks were mayors in almost all of the nation's larger cities. Other American cities were on the verge of electing blacks to high office and even smaller municipalities, some with minority black populations, had elected black mayors. Black representation in state legislatures, school boards, and state courts were increasing, especially in the South. There was a black lieutenant-governor in Virginia. These trends were encouraging to Jesse Jackson and his hard-core supporters. Despite the results of 1984, they decided that the preacher-politician should make a new effort for the White House in 1988.

The lessons to be learned from the Jackson campaign of 1984 included the imperative to solidify African-Americans, particularly the black leadership establishment, to avoid the appearance of being an exclusive "Black Agenda" candidate, and to avoid such embarrassing episodes as the Farrakhan affair and the "hymie" remark so as not to alienate white voters. In the 1988 campaign Jackson succeeded remarkably well in unifying blacks; almost all of the nation's prominent black Democrats rallied around his candidacy or remained neutral. He kept arm's length from Farrakhan and made overtures to Jewish leaders (Jackson had begun these gestures during his address at the 1984 Democratic Convention). Jackson carried his populist theme to urban black ghettos as well as rural hamlets, and courted the white working class laborer as well as the Midwestern and Southern farmer. He said he wanted to give hope to the hopeless and make America a better place for all people. Black voters gave him ringing endorsements and Jackson increased his white support at least threefold, but far short of enough to win the Democratic nomination for President of the United States.

Nevertheless, Jackson's primary successes, which resulted in him finishing second with more than 1,200 delegates at the 1988 Democratic Convention, had some immediate and long-range results. It helped to reduce the alienation felt among the black masses and gave them new hope that their agenda could become reality through the traditional political process. Jackson helped to shape his party's platform and secured new high-ranking positions for African-Americans in the Democratic party; one of his campaign managers, Ron Brown, was subsequently elected Chairman of the Democratic National Committee. Most importantly, Jackson helped reduce white antipathy to the election of blacks to high offices. Within months of the end of Jackson's campaign, L. Douglas Wilder was elected governor of Virginia and David Dinkins mayor of New York City with substantial white support. However, many believed that Jackson had driven the Democratic party "too far to the left," which contributed to its defeat in the 1988 presidential election. Also, despite his populist appeals, many still viewed Jackson as the candidate of the "Black Agenda." Indeed, several commentators suggested that while Jackson's efforts may have helped to pave the way for Wilder in Virginia and Dinkins in New York City, these triumphs were only secured by an abandonment of a "Black Agenda" in favor of one which suited "mainstream" White America. Such an agenda deemphasized "race conscious" policies and practices.

To be sure, even in the euphoria among most blacks over the Jackson candidacies, others, including academicians Thomas Sowell and Robert Woodson, contended that such an adherence to a "Black Agenda" would impair efforts to promote equal opportunity for African-Americans. They deplored "race conscious" policies and practices, including affirmative action programs, which they implied lowered black self-esteem and increased racial animosity. Instead, they argued, the black leadership establishment should encourage initiative and enterprise among blacks and focus their attention on the serious internal problems of African-American communities: the disproportionate number of unwed mothers and school drop-outs, drug abuse, crime and violence, poverty, and other social ills. While many in the black leadership establishment had acknowledged such problems, they all too often, the black "conservatives" asserted, placed blame upon white racism and were too dependent on relief from the federal government. The black "conservatives" would have middle income blacks promote their agenda to the black masses which could lead to solutions. Smaller numbers of blacks during the "betrayal of the Second Reconstruction" shunned the traditional political processes altogether and sought refuge in African national parties, the Nation of Islam and other such groups, or withdrew entirely from structured political involvement. They had apparently abandoned all hope of achieving a "Black Agenda," however defined, in any variation of the American political process. Many of these people were leaders or promoters of a new wave of Afro-centricity, which gained momentum, particularly among intellectuals and students.

The new Afro-centricity, which was by no means confined to non-traditional partisans or apolitical blacks, was in reality a continuation of the Black Consciousness Movement of the 1960s and 1970s, whose political anthem was "Black Power" and whose cultural themes were "Black Is Beautiful" and "I'm Black and I'm Proud." The earlier movement led to many changes in the students, faculties, and curricula of the nation's institutions of higher education. Hand-in-glove with affirmative action programs, the movement changed the physical and intellectual complexion of many educational facilities and even made an impact in libraries, museums, the media, and other institutions. The Black Consciousness Movement was the mother of the Black Studies or Afro-American Studies programs, inspired the epic television production "Roots" in 1977, and was instrumental in establishing African and African-American history as important areas of scholarly research and study. In literature, its progenitors and leading practitioners included such poets as Gwendolyn Brooks and Dudley Randall; novelists Margaret Walker Alexander, Ernest Gaines, and James Baldwin; dramatists Imanu Amiri Baraka (LeRoi Jones) and Ron Milner; and literary critics Houston A. Baker, Jerry Ward, and Larry Neal. In art, its promoters included David Driskill, Jacob Lawrence, and Elizabeth Prophet. In music, Bernice Johnson Reagon and Quincy Jones were among the leading exponents of the Movement, while Ossie Davis and Ruby Dee were the leaders on the Broadway stage. Among historians, Vincent Harding, Lawrence Reddick, and Lenore Bennett emerged as vocal and prolific adherents. Former SNCC leader Stokely Carmichael and Black Panther founders Huey P. Newton and Bobby Seale were among its political pioneers. Culturally and politically, the older movement was far from monolithic. Although some partisans might argue vigorously for their concept of Afro-centricity, the tenets and practices actually ranged from infusion into

xliv

Euro-centered scholarship and institutions to distinct and separate emphases and institutions.

The earlier Afro-centric or Black Consciousness Movement began to wane during the Nixon presidency. There appeared to be increased apathy, disillusionment, and some return to the mainstream. Enrollment in Black Studies courses decreased as did the demand for them, and new questions were even raised about the academic legitimacy of the discipline. Then, during the "Reagan Nadir," there appeared what some called "a resurgence of racism" in the United States. Black men were assaulted and killed by whites in New York City when they "intruded" into all-white neighborhoods. Blacks in Miami, Florida rioted at least three times during the 1980s after alleged racially-motivated killings of black men by white and Hispanic police officers. Non-violent demonstrators were assaulted in Forsyth County, Georgia in 1986 by Ku Klux Klansmen and other white supremacists on the eve of the first Martin Luther King, Jr. national holiday. Black students were subjected to verbal and physical abuse on hundreds of high school and college campuses throughout the nation.

This "resurgence" of racism led to new demands that colleges and universities increase the diversity of their student bodies and faculties and that there be a greater infusion of ethnic studies, particularly African and African-American curricula. But some African-American youths decided to turn inward, electing instead to attend or to transfer to all-black or majority black colleges in order to "escape" the throes of academic racism while immersing themselves in their own culture. Meanwhile, on the nation's black campuses, there were, in addition to demands that such institutions should become "blacker," i. e., a greater infusion of Black Studies and black administrative control, there was a new insistence that these historical institutions be reformed internally, in terms of physical facilities, efficiency, and effectiveness.

As in the Black Consciousness Movement, exponents of the new Afro-centricity espoused a levelling of African-American society. They challenged the black social and economic elite to move away from any attempt at assimilating into the white world and to identify with their black "brothers and sisters," regardless of class. Indeed, like the black "conservatives," the Afro-centrists contended that the black elite had an obligation to help pull the black underclass out of its quagmire of poverty, illiteracy, drug abuse, crime, and despair.

The new Afro-centrists tended to be boldly nationalistic in their orientation. They identified closely with the continent of Africa. Many came to reject the racial designation Negro, as their predecessors had done, and even the term black itself, preferring instead to be known as African-American. Some took African names and wore African dress, as in the 1960s movement. New slogans, often proudly worn on tee shirts and other clothing, proclaimed "Black Is Back" and "It's a Black Thing; You Wouldn't Understand" (an apparent taunt to whites). While Martin Luther King, Jr. remained a revered martyr, other civil rights heroes and heroines slipped in esteem among the new Afro-centrists. The black "radicals" of earlier periods: W.E.B. DuBois, Paul Robeson, Angela Davis, and Malcolm X, were elevated to new heights of respect and admiration. The suggestion was that aggressive, nationalist strategies, not non-violent assimilationist or integrationist attitudes, were the key to achieving the "Black Agenda."

The intellectual foundation for the new Afro-centricity was laid by black scholars, including Molefi Kete-Asante of Temple University, Maulena Karenga of the University of California, and Ronald Bailey of the University of Mississippi. These scholars were also leaders in the National Council of Black Studies, which had emerged during the earlier movement as a major coordinator, along with the older Association for the Study of Afro-American Life and History and the Association of Social and Behavioral Scientists, of the changing scholarship. Kete-Asante and others wrote that black culture, even human civilization itself (because of its African origins) must be studied and understood with Africa—its history, folkways, philosophy, geography, diaspora, etc.—at the center.

The Afro-centrist scholars, however, faced strong challenges not only from white intellectuals, but from some black ones as well. Historians, including Nell Painter of Princeton University and Armstead Robinson of the University of Virginia, argued that African-American experiences could not be fully understood from a narrow, internally-centered focus. They contended that such matters as class and gender must be strongly considered and, indeed, that these factors may well emerge as more central to the understanding of issues than race. In fact, the research and publication of the peculiar roles of black women in American and African-American societies became one of the major fields of scholarship in the 1980s.

Other cultural manifestations in African-American life during "the betrayal" included new motion pictures and new musical forms delineating the Black Experience. A young black filmmaker, Spike Lee, emerged in the 1980s with new media presentations of black people. Lee began his career with a racy comedy, *She's Gotta Have It,* and later established himself in the film industry with *School Daze,* a film about fraternity antics and color consciousness on a black college campus. *Do the Right Thing,* Lee's third film, was probably the best of his productions. With its theme of violent racial confrontation set in the Bedford-Stuyvesant section of Brooklyn, New York, it was certainly Lee's most controversial effort to date. Some critics even suggested that the film risked provoking the "race war" that it had so graphically depicted. Nonetheless,

Lee's work in *Do the Right Thing* garnered an Academy Award nomination for Best Original Screenplay in 1990.

While gospel, jazz, blues, and soul music remained staples of the African-American musical diet in the 1980s, "rap," a new form, appeared. Although rap music could be used for nearly any purpose—from comedy to sex to politics—it was often employed to express a description of, and offer an opinion on, life in the black ghetto. Some of the messages, which were presented as musical essays in verse, addressed such problems as drug abuse, violence against women, inferior education, and gang-related crime. Leading rappers of the period included 2 Live Crew, Run DMC, M.C. Hammer, and Public Enemy.

It should be clear that the new Afro-centrists did not represent a majority view in Black America during "the betrayal." African-American aesthetics continued to run the gamut from assimilationist to nationalist. Still, there were variations among all people, so that an "assimilationist" and a "nationalist" could both condemn the racist South African system of apartheid and celebrate the release of African National Congress leader Nelson Mandela in February of 1990. Both camps could also find common ground in supporting the retention of black colleges and other race institutions. A more definitive line between them came on the issue of full participation in the American political process and on social relations with white people. Many of the more zealous Afro-centrists, however, tended to reject both ideals.

Many of those African-Americans who still believed that the "Black Agenda" could be achieved through traditional political avenues had their spirits dampened in the election of another Republican president, George Bush, in 1988. They had voted overwhelmingly for the Democratic candidate, Massachusetts governor Michael Dukakis. But despite minimal black support, once in office, Bush promised, without criticizing his predecessor Ronald Reagan, "a kinder and gentler nation." He pledged his commitment to equal opportunity and justice and invited black establishment leaders to the White House for consultation. Such early gestures raised some hope that "the betrayal" might be reversed and that the "Second Reconstruction" could be resurrected once again.

Chapter 1
Involuntary Servitude, 1619-1860

1619

August 20. A Dutch ship with twenty Negroes aboard arrived at Jamestown, Virginia. The twenty had been captured in Africa and sold to the highest bidders, as many impoverished whites were similarly kidnapped in Europe. These blacks were not the first of their race to arrive in North America, however; blacks traveled with Spanish, Portuguese, and French explorers in the Americas throughout the sixteenth century. Pedro Alonso Nino, a member of Christopher Columbus's crew, was perhaps a Negro. On Columbus's last voyage to the New World, which set out in July, 1502, Diego el Negro, a black man, was a member of the crew on the *Capitana*. Certainly as many as thirty blacks, including Nuflo de Olano, were with Vasco Núñez de Balboa when the explorer discovered the Pacific Ocean.

The most noted black explorer was Estevanico (Esteban), a Moroccan. He was a member of the ill-fated Narvaez expedition that left Spain in 1527 to explore the western coast of the Gulf of Mexico. The Narvaez ships were blown off its original course and landed far to the east at what is now known as Tampa Bay, Florida in 1528. Moving westward, the expedition party shipwrecked on Galveston Island off the Texan coast. Only four survivors, Cabeza de Vaca, Alonzo del Castillo, Andres Dorantes, and his slave Estevanico were able to continue the trek. Because of his good rapport with the Indians, Estevanico became a valuable member of the party. The explorers reached Mexico City around 1536 and excited Spanish officials there with stories the Indians had told them of the seven golden cities of Cibola located in the Northwest. Francisco Coronado was subsequently assigned to conquer Cibola, and in 1539 sent an advance party led by Friar Marcos but guided by Estevanico. Friar Marcos sent Estevanico ahead and the black scout soon discovered Arizona

1

and New Mexico. The Zuni Indians of Cibola then killed Estevanico and the rest of the party retreated.

The twenty blacks left at Jamestown in 1619 were, nonetheless, the first permanent involuntary settlers of their race, hence the history of Afro-Americans in what is now the United States begins with their arrival.

1638

Negro slaves were brought into New England. Prior to this date blacks had been sold in Boston, but it is not definitely known when the first Negro slaves were brought into the region. Authorities who claim that Negro slaves were first brought to New England in 1638 base their contention on an entry in John Winthrop's *Journal*. Winthrop recorded on December 12, 1638 the arrival of the ship *Desire* to Boston. The cargo of the vessel, according to Winthrop, included salt, cotton, tobacco, and Negroes. The statement of Governor Winthrop is the first recorded account of Negro slavery in New England.

First black indentured servants arrive in Jamestown, Virginia.

1641

Massachusetts recognized slavery as a legal institution, the first of the North American colonies to do so. Section ninety-one of the *Body of Liberties* of 1641 read: "There shall never be any bond slaverie, villinage or Captivities amongst us, unless it be lawful Captives taken in just warres, and such strangers as willingly sell themselves or are sold to us. And these shall have all the liberties and Christian usages which the law of God established in Israell. . . . This exempts none from servitude who shall be Judged thereto by Authoritie."

1661

————. Slavery was recognized by statute in Virginia; the status of the mother would determine whether a black child would be slave or free. The slave codes of Virginia, and those which followed them, were motivated by the growth of the black population and the fears of slave uprisings. They were designed to protect the property in slaves and to protect white society from an "alien and savage race." Generally, slaves were not allowed to leave the plantation, to wander, or to assemble without permission from the master. They could not own weapons and could not testify against white people in court. Slaves found guilty of murder or rape were to be executed. For petty offenses, slaves were whipped, maimed, or branded. The slave codes grew out of the laws regulating indentured servitude, but the slaves, unlike the indentured servants, had practically no rights at all. (See Appendix for excerpts taken from the Virginia Slave Laws, 1660-1669.)

1663

September 13. The first major conspiracy of people in servitude was documented in Colonial America. A plot of white servants and black slaves was betrayed by a servant in Gloucester County, Virginia.

1664

September 20. Maryland took the lead in passing laws against the marriage of English women to black men. The preamble of the statute justified the prohibition of intermarriage because "divers freeborn English women, forgetful of their free condition, and to the disgrace of our nation, do intermarry with Negro slaves," causing, among other things, questions to arise over the status of such blacks. The law was passed to remove this problem and to deter "such freeborn women from such shameful matches."

1688

February 18. Quakers at Germantown, Pennsylvania adopted the first formal anti-slavery resolution in American history. The Society of Friends declared that slavery was in opposition to Christianity and the rights of man. The Quakers continued their anti-slavery protests throughout the seventeenth century.

1704

————. One of the first schools in the colonies to enroll slaves was opened by Elias Nau, a Frenchman, in New York City.

1712

April 7. A Negro slave revolt occurred in New York City. Nine whites were slain and twenty-one blacks were executed as participants. Six other alleged participants committed suicide. The insurrection was spearheaded by twenty-seven armed slaves who met in an orchard near the center of the city. A fire was set to an outhouse of a white man, and as other whites attempted to extinguish the blaze, they were shot by the blacks. The state militia was called out to pursue and capture the black rebels, and New Yorkers responded to the uprising by strengthening their slave code. The number of slave crimes punishable by death was increased to include willful burning of property. Conspiracy to murder was also made a capital offense.

1739

September 9. The first serious slave uprising took place in South Carolina. Twenty-five to thirty whites were slain, and more than thirty blacks were killed for alleged participation. The uprising, led by a black man named Cato, began about twenty miles west of Charleston at Stono. The slaves killed two warehouse guards, secured arms and ammunition, and fled south, hoping to reach Florida. They marched to the beating of two drums and killed all whites who attempted to interfere. Armed whites pursued the rebels, capturing all but a dozen.

1761

December 15. Jupiter Hammon, born a slave in 1720, published *Salvation by Christ with Penitential Cries*, the first known poetical work by an American Negro. Hammon's masters had given him a rudimentary education, including religious instruction, and helped to publish his verse. Scholars do not accord much literary merit to Hammon's work, but he is an important figure because of his place in the chronology of black American literature. Hammon is also known for his *Address to the Negroes of the State of New York* (1787), in which he called upon blacks to be faithful and obedient to their masters. Hammon believed that the race should endure its bondage humbly and patiently until it earned its freedom by honest and good conduct.

1764

————. Brown University was founded at Providence, Rhode Island. The university was named for the wealthy New England shippers, the Brown Brothers, who made substantial profits from the African slave trade.

1770

March 5. Crispus Attucks of Framingham, Massachusetts, an escaped slave, died along with four other Americans in the so-called Boston Massacre. He was in the forefront of the group that taunted British soldiers during the altercation and is commonly said to have been the first to fall from their fire. Massachusetts has honored Attucks with a statue in Boston.

1773

————. George Leile and Andrew Bryan organized the first Negro Baptist Church in the American colonies at Savannah, Georgia. Leile and Bryan were both former slaves with modest education. When they first began preaching (at very young ages) there were no black denominations. Leile and Bryan preached without compensation. Leile supported himself as a laborer-for-hire after being freed by his pious master. Opposition to Negro worship eventually forced Leile to flee to Jamaica. Bryan's master defended him against other whites who were alarmed over the growth of the black church, and although Bryan bought his wife's freedom, he did not purchase his own until after his master's death, because of the sense of gratitude Bryan had for his master's support of him.

————. Phillis Wheatley, an African-born poet, published *Poems on Various Subjects, Religious and Moral,* becoming the second American woman to publish a book. Wheatley was born in Senegal circa 1753 and was sold as a slave in 1761 to a Boston tailor, John Wheatley, whose wife tutored young Phillis, enabling her to become literate. Wheatley began writing verse in her early teens. Manumitted in 1773, she travelled to London and was received by the Lord Mayor and other influential Londoners. On February 28, 1776, Wheatley had

5

Crispus Attucks

an audience with General George Washington at his Cambridge, Massachusetts headquarters, in order that he might express his appreciation for her poem
in his honor.

————. Jean Baptiste Point DuSable, the first permanent settler of Chicago,
purchased the property of Jean Baptiste Millet at "Old Peoria Fort." DuSable
was born in St. Marc, Haiti, in 1745, the son of a successful Frenchman who
had emigrated to Haiti from Marseilles, France, and a black slave. DuSable
was educated in France and later worked in his father's business in New
Orleans in 1765. When the Spanish occupied Louisiana that same year,
DuSable and an associate, Jacques Clemorgan of Martinique, left for the
French-settled areas of the upper Mississippi River. They stopped at St. Louis
and carried on a successful fur trade with the Indians there for two years. Later,
DuSable and Clemorgan moved farther north into Indian territory and lived
with the Peoria and Potawatomie tribes. At the same time, DuSable participated in fur trapping expeditions which carried him to the present sites of Chicago,
Detroit, and Ontario, Canada. In 1772, DuSable decided to build a fur trading
post on the Chicago river near Lake Michigan. A successful trading center grew
around the post and the Chicago settlement developed. After Illinois came
under the jurisdiction of the United States, DuSable sold his property and
returned to Missouri, where he died in 1818.

1775

April 14. The first abolitionist society in the United States was organized in Philadelphia. The group, which had many active Quaker participants, was known as the Pennsylvania Society for the Abolition of Slavery. The Society first directed its efforts toward obtaining an abolition law in Pennsylvania and protecting free blacks from being kidnapped and sold into slavery. After a successful campaign for adequate protective legislation, the Society helped to enforce the new laws through committees of correspondence and by employing lawyers to secure the conviction of offenders. The Society suspended its operations during the Revolutionary War, although individual members continued active work. The group was reorganized in 1787 as the Pennsylvania Society for Promoting the Abolition of Slavery, the Relief of Free Negroes Unlawfully held in Bondage, and for Improving the Condition of the African Race.

April 19. The War for Independence began at Lexington and Concord, Massachusetts. Blacks were among the Minutemen who opposed the British.

June 17. Two blacks, Peter Salem and Salem Poor, were commended for their participation on the side of the Patriots at the Battle of Bunker Hill. Salem had been a slave in Framington, Massachusetts but was manumitted in order that he might serve in the Revolutionary Army. The Committee on Safety of the Continental Congress had decreed in May, 1775 that only free blacks could serve in the American army. During the Battle of Bunker Hill, Salem killed the British commander, Major John Pitcairn. Although the Americans did not achieve victory at Bunker Hill, the death of Pitcarn raised the rebels's morale at the time. The Massachusetts General Court later commended Salem for the act. Salem Poor also won commendation from the Massachusetts Court and from his officers. He was described by his officers as an excellent soldier. On July 9, 1775, however, General George Washington announced that there would be no further enlistments of blacks. The Continental Congress sanctioned Washington's decree in October.

October 23. The Continental Congress prohibited black enlistment in the American army.

November 7. Lord Dunmore, British Royal Governor of Virginia, issued a proclamation promising freedom to slaves who joined the British forces in the Revolutionary War. Southerners, especially Virginians, were alarmed and angered. Virginia responded by attempting to convince blacks that the British motives were purely selfish, and promised them good treatment if they remained loyal to the Patriot cause. On December 13, 1775, a Virginia Convention promised to pardon all slaves who returned to their masters within ten days. It is not clear how many slaves served with the British, but the war did have an unsettling effect on the institution of slavery. At least 100,000 blacks ran away from their masters during the conflict. The Dunmore Proclamation helped to bolster Southern support for the Patriots as the British threatened slavery, at least in this respect.

December 31. General George Washington, revising an earlier decision, ordered recruiting officers to accept free Negroes in the American army. More than 5,000 Negroes, mostly Northern blacks, fought against the British. Georgia and South Carolina steadfastly opposed the enlistment of black soldiers. In 1770, the Continental Congress agreed to pay owners of slaves in Georgia and South Carolina $1,000 for each slave allowed to serve in the American army, but at the end of the war the blacks were to be freed and given fifty dollars. The two Southern states rejected the offer.

1776

July 4. The Declaration of Independence was approved in Philadelphia. A section which alleged that King George III had forced the slave trade and slavery on the colonies was eliminated at the insistence of representatives from Georgia and South Carolina. Thomas Jefferson had charged King George with waging "cruel war against human nature itself, violating its most sacred rights of life and liberty in the persons of a distant people who never offended him, captivating and carrying them into slavery in another hemisphere, or to incur miserable death in their transportation thither." In the monarch's determination "to keep open a market where men should be bought and sold," Jefferson said he had suppressed "every legislative attempt to prohibit or to restrain this excerable commerce." Historians agree that this was one example of the American exaggerations in the list of grievances against King George III.

1777

July 2. Vermont took the lead in abolishing slavery. By 1804, all the states north of Delaware had taken action leading to the gradual abolition of slavery. (Some slaves were seen in New Jersey as late as 1860, however.) Pennsylvania passed a law for gradual abolition in 1780. New Hampshire's law was passed in 1783. In 1784 Connecticut and Rhode Island took similar action. Manumission acts were passed in New York in 1785 and in New Jersey in 1786, though effective legislation stipulating gradual abolition was not achieved in the two states until 1799 and 1804, respectively. In 1783, the courts of Massachusetts upheld the contention of blacks that slavery in that state violated a section of the state constitution of 1780 which asserted that "all men are born free and equal." One immediate result of the Northern manumissions was the establishment of schools for free blacks by the early abolition and philanthropic societies. The African Free School in New York City, for example, was opened on November 1, 1787.

1787

April 12. Richard Allen and Absalom Jones organized the Free African Society, a Negro self-help group, in Philadelphia. Allen was perhaps the most conspicuous Negro leader in the country before the rise of Frederick Douglass. His stature rested upon his leadership in the establishment of such organizations as the Free African Society and the African Methodist Episcopal (A.M.E.) Church. Jones was a close associate of Allen for many years, but the two parted when Jones, who was attracted by Anglicanism, became rector of the first Protestant Episcopal congregation for blacks. Jones was born a slave in Sussex, Delaware. His master took him to Philadelphia to work as a handyman in a store, where he was taught to write by one of the clerks. He later attended night school and completed his education. Saving money that visitors to his master's house had given him, together with his earnings, Jones purchased both his own freedom and that of his wife. He became a member of the St. George's Methodist Church in Philadelphia. While attending services there one Sunday in 1786. Jones, along with Richard Allen and other worshippers, was pulled from his knees and ordered to move to the reserved worship area for blacks in the church's balcony. Out of this incident grew the Free African Society. The Free African Society was basically a quasi-religious organization. Its program included a fund for mutual aid, burial assistance, relief for widows and orphans, strengthening of marriage ties and personal morality, cooperation with abolition societies, and correspondence with free Negroes in other areas. It was probably the first stable, independent black social organization in the United States. Among the various other joint efforts of Allen and Jones were the organization of relief measures for the black population in Philadelphia during the yellow-fever epidemic in 1793, and the raising of a company of black militia during the War of 1812.

July 13. The Continental Congress prohibited slavery in the Northwest Territory under the famous Ordinance of 1787. Specifically, there could be neither slavery nor involuntary servitude in the region northwest of the Ohio River except as punishment for a crime.

September 12. Prince Hall, a veteran of the War for Independence, received a charter for a Masonic Lodge for blacks. Hall was born in Barbados, British West Indies, in 1735, the son of an Englishman and a free black woman. He was apprenticed as a leather worker but abandoned that training to emigrate to Boston. During the Revolutionary War, Hall and twelve other free blacks were inducted into a Masonic Lodge by a group of British soldiers stationed in

Boston. When the British evacuated the area, Hall organized a Masonic Lodge for blacks. This group was chartered in England in 1787 as African Lodge No. 459. Hall, the first master of the organization, set up additional African lodges in Pennsylvania and Rhode Island during 1797. Following his death in 1807, the African Grand Lodge became the Prince Hall Grand Lodge. Hall, a self-educated clergyman, also championed the establishment of schools for black children in Boston, urged Massachusetts to legislatively oppose slavery, and proposed measures to protect free Negroes from kidnapping and enslavement. The Prince Hall Masonic Lodge, Hall's principal legacy, has become a major social institution in Black America.

September. The Constitution of the United States was adopted. The "Three-fifths Compromise," which allowed the South to count three-fifths of the slave population in determining representation in the House of Representatives was incorporated. The Constitution also prohibited any legislation which might close the slave trade before 1808, but allowed a tax of ten dollars per head on each slave imported before that date and demanded that fugitive slaves be returned to their owners.

1791

January. Free blacks in Charleston, South Carolina presented a petition to the State Legislature protesting laws restricting their freedoms. The blacks pointed specifically to an Act of 1740 which deprived slaves and free blacks of the right to testify under oath in court and of the right to trial by jury. The blacks reminded the legislators that they were taxpaying citizens of South Carolina and were considered free citizens of the state, and thus hoped to be treated as such. At the same time, the blacks acknowledged that they did not "presume to hope that they shall be put on an equal footing with the free white citizens of the state in general." The petitioners were seeking the repeal of the objectionable clauses of the Act of 1740.

———. Newport Gardner, one of the first black music teachers in America, opened a music school in Newport, Massachusetts. Gardner, born in 1746, was a slave of Caleb Gardner, one of Newport's leading merchants. The slave taught himself to read and to sing, and later wrote music. One of his compositions, "Crooked Shanks," was included in the collection *A Number of Original Airs, Duettos and Tiros,* published in 1803. Among Gardner's music students was his former mistress, Mrs. Sarah Ann Gardner. Newport Gardner was also active in religious affairs. He was a founder of the Newport Colored Union Church and Society and became a missionary in Africa in 1826, the estimated year of his death.

November 9. Benjamin Banneker, a notable astronomer, inventor, mathematician, and gazetteer, was born in Ellicott, Maryland. Banneker, the grandson of a white woman, secured a modest education from a school for free blacks near Joppa, Maryland, but received assistance in his study of science from George Ellicott, a Maryland Quaker, planter, and philanthropist. While still a youth, Banneker made a wooden clock which is said to have remained accurate throughout his lifetime. Between 1791 and 1802, Banneker published a yearly *Almanac,* which was widely read, and was also the first black man to publish astronomical materials in the United States. His other publications included a treatise on bees. Banneker is also credited with computing the cycle of the seventeen-year locust.

In 1791, Banneker was appointed upon the recommendation of Thomas Jefferson to serve as a member of a commission to survey plans for Washington, D.C. In August of the same year, Banneker wrote a famous letter to Jefferson appealing for a more liberal attitude toward blacks, using his own work as evidence of Negro intellectual equality. Banneker said in part:

"I apprehend you will embrace every opportunity to eradicate that train of absurd and false ideas and opinions which so generally prevail with respect to us [blacks]; and that your sentiments are concurrent with mine which are: that one universal Father hath given being to us all; that He not only made us all of one flesh, but that He had also without partiality afforded us all with these same faculties and that, however diversified in situation or color, we are all the same family and stand in the same relation to Him."

Jefferson accepted, then later rejected, the notion of black mental equality and even entertained doubts about Banneker's intellectual capabilities.

1793

February 12. Congress passed the first Fugitive Slave Act, making it a crime to harbor an escaped slave or to interfere with his or her arrest.

March 14. Eli Whitney of Massachusetts, a white inventor, obtained a patent for his cotton gin. The invention strengthened the institution of slavery, especially in the South.

1794

June 10. Richard Allen of Philadelphia founded the Bethel African Methodist

Episcopal Church, the first A.M.E. church in the United States. (See also entry dated April 12, 1787, for further information about Allen.)

1797

January 30. Blacks in North Carolina presented a petition to Congress protesting a state law that required slaves, although freed by their Quaker masters, to be returned to the state and to the status of slavery. This first recorded anti-slavery petition by Negroes was rejected by the Congress.

August 30. A slave uprising planned by Gabriel Prosser and Jack Bowler near Richmond, Virginia was suspended because of bad weather and betrayal. Prosser was born in Virginia in 1776. In 1800, the young insurrectionist planned to seize an arsenal at Richmond, attack whites in the area, and free the slaves. It was hoped that the revolt would spread throughout the state. Perhaps as many as 1,000 slaves were prepared to participate in what would have been one of the largest slave revolts in United States history. Prosser had won such a large following by telling fellow blacks that he was their chosen leader, quoting Scripture to bolster his claim. The rebels had made or obtained swords, bayonets, and bullets in preparation for the uprising when a storm hit the area. Two slaves belonging to Mosby Sheppard, betrayed Prosser's plot. Governor James Monroe declared martial law in Richmond and called up 600 members of the state militia. Prosser fled but was captured in Norfolk on September 25. He was later convicted and, with fifteen others, sentenced to hang on October 7. Another thirty-five blacks were later executed. Although interviewed by Governor Monroe himself, Prosser refused to implicate others. The demeanor of the captured rebels led John Randolph of Virginia to declare that "the accused have exhibited a spirit, which if it becomes general, must deluge the southern country in blood. They manifested a sense of their rights, and a contempt of danger."

1804

January 5. The Ohio legislature took the lead in passing "Black Laws" designed to restrict the rights and freedom of movement of free Negroes in the North. The laws indicated the steady deterioration of the legal and social status of free Negroes since the Revolutionary War. Although Northern blacks had endured severe restrictions in the Colonial period—in some areas of New England they faced curfews at night, could not visit a town other than the one in which they resided without permission, and could not own certain types of property—these were somewhat relieved by the atmosphere of freedom which prevailed in the North after 1776. By 1835, however, several Northern states had prohibited free Negro immigration and severely restricted or completely disfranchised Negro voters. By 1860, according to Professor John Hope Franklin, it was actually difficult to distinguish, in terms of legal status, between slaves and free Negroes.

1808

January 1. A federal law prohibiting the importation of African slaves into the United States went into effect. The law was passed in March, 1807 and stipulated that persons convicted of violating it were to be fined anywhere form $800 (for knowingly buying illegally imported blacks) to $20,000 (for equipping a slave vessel), or imprisoned. Illegally imported blacks were to come under the jurisdiction of the state legislatures, which would decide their disposition. The coastwide trade of slaves was prohibited also if it was carried on in vessels of less than forty tons. This new law was poorly enforced. The responsibility for the enforcement was given first to the Treasury Department, then to the Secretary of the Navy, and sometimes to the Secretary of State. Neither department put any vigor in its efforts in view of the shifting responsibility. Some Southern states passed laws against the illegal importation of blacks, while other states took no action at all. Some of the newly-imported blacks were sold in these states with the proceeds going into the state treasury. Northern commercial interests as well as Southern planters ignored the law with impunity.

1811

January 8-10. United States troops suppressed slave uprisings in two Louisiana parishes near New Orleans.

1812

May 6. Martin R. Delany, pioneer black physician, colonizationist, and Union Army officer, was born in Virginia. Delany was educated in the African Free School of New York City, the Canaan Academy in New Hampshire, the Oneida Institute in upper New York state, and at the Harvard University Medical School, where he took his medical degree in 1852. Delany attempted to practice medicine in Pittsburgh, but prejudice and poor profits drove him into other areas. He became a member of the British Association for the Promotion of Social Science, published two books, *The Condition, Elevation, Emigration and*

Destiny of the Colored People of the United States (1852) and *Principle of Ethnology* (1879). In 1843, Delany had published an unsuccessful newspaper, The *Mystery*, and had joined Frederick Douglass in the publication of The *North Star* in 1847. He was also a leader of the national convention movement of black Americans. Following the passage of the Compromise of 1850, with its new Fugitive Slave Act, Delany became convinced that the United States was too inhospitable for people of African descent and turned his attention to colonization. He helped organize an expedition to Nigeria in 1858, negotiated treaties with eight African chiefs who granted lands for prospective American black settlers, and began plans for the expanded production and exportation of cotton in the region. During the Civil War, Delany was a medical officer with the rank of major in the 104th Union Regiment in South Carolina. He settled in Charleston after the war, working with the Freedmen's Bureau, and later served as a justice of the peace there. He was defeated in a bid for lieutenant governor of South Carolina in 1874. Delany died in 1885.

1816

April 9. The African Methodist Episcopal (A.M.E.) Church, the first all-black religious denomination in the United States, was formally organized in Philadelphia. Richard Allen was named the first bishop of the Church. Allen was born a slave in Philadelphia and was sold as a youth to a white man in Delaware. He became a preacher shortly thereafter and received permission to hold services in his master's home. Allen preached to both blacks and whites and was allowed, at the same time, to hire himself out. He bought his freedom by hauling salt, wood, and other products, and by laboring in a brickyard. After leading the A.M.E. Church for fifteen years, Allen died in 1831. He was succeeded by Morris Brown, an exile from South Carolina who had resided in Philadelphia since 1823.

December 28. The American Colonization Society, formed to ease American race problems by transporting free blacks to Africa, was organized in Washington, D. C. John C. Calhoun of South Carolina and Henry Clay of Kentucky were among its sponsors.

1817

January. Philadelphia Negroes, meeting at the Bethel A.M.E. Church, formally protested against the American Colonization Society's efforts to deport blacks from the United States to Africa.

————. Paul Cuffe, a black New England shipbuilder and African colonizer, died. Cuffe was born in New Bedford, Massachusetts in 1758 as a free man. In

1797, he purchased a farm and built a school for the children in his hometown. An activist in the cause of civil rights, Cuffe and his brother John unsuccessfully sued the state of Massachusetts for the right to vote. Disillusioned over the future of free Negroes in America, Cuffe transported a group of thirty-eight blacks to Sierra Leone, a British colony on the West Coast of Africa, in 1811. Failing health and uncertainty about the colonization scheme caused him to withdraw from the venture shortly before his death. At his death, Cuffe left an estate valued at more than $20,000, making him one of the wealthiest blacks in early American history.

1818

April 18. A force of Indians and Negroes were defeated in the Battle of Suwanne, Florida, ending the First Seminole War by United States troops under General Andrew Jackson. Jackson characterized the hostilities as a "savage and negro war."

1820

March 3. The famous Missouri Compromise was approved by Congress. Slavery was prohibited north and west of the 36-30 parallel line within the Louisiana territory. Missouri itself entered the Union as a slave state, Maine entered as a free state.

1821

———. The black Republic of Liberia was founded under the auspices of the American Colonization Society. American Negroes were encouraged to emigrate to the West African country as a means of alleviating the race problem. In the end, only about 20,000 did so. The capital city, Monrovia, was named for President James Monroe.

1822

May 30. A slave conspiracy led by Denmark Vesey in Charleston, South Carolina, was betrayed. Vesey, a former slave, had been free since 1800 and had worked as a carpenter in Charleston. He plotted his slave uprising for several years, during which he carefully chose his associates, collected weapons, and sought assistance from Santo Domingo. Vesey's revolt, in which as many as 5,000 blacks were prepared to participate, was first set for the second Sunday in July, 1822, but the authorities, having been alerted, thwarted their efforts. Thereafter, South Carolina and other states tightened their control of slaves and free Negroes as a result of the plot. Morris Brown, the preeminent A. M. E. leader in South Carolina, was one of those free blacks who became suspect. Brown fled to the North and eventually succeeded Richard Allen as Bishop of the A.M.E. Church.

1824

November. American politics were becoming democratized as the elimination of the caucus system for choosing presidential candidates was accompanied by the removal of property qualifications for voting. The way was being paved for virtual universal male suffrage in the United States. At the same time, the Northern and Western states adopted measures denying blacks the right to vote.

1827

March 16. Two blacks, John Russwurm (the first American Negro college graduate) and Samuel Cornish began publication of *Freedom's Journal*, the nation's pioneer Negro newspaper, in New York City. The paper was not very successful, and two years later Cornish began a second publication, *Rights of All*, a militant but also short-lived paper. In 1836, Cornish published the unsuccessful *Weekly Advocate*, and the following year co-edited the *Colored American*. Most of the Negro newspapers founded before the Civil War were principally abolitionist propaganda sheets, with Frederick Douglass's *North Star* being the most successful.

1829

March 4. Blacks attended the inaugural reception for President Andrew Jackson at the White House. A South Carolina woman observed one black female "eating jelly from a gold spoon," and disapproved.

September 28. David Walker's militant anti-slavery pamphlet calling on blacks to revolt was discovered in several areas of the country. Walker's *Appeal*, published in Boston, stirred slaveholders in several Southern states. Walker was a free black who had wandered across the South before settling in Boston as the proprietor of a secondhand clothing store. He had become widely acquainted with anti-slavery and revolutionary literature. The *Appeal*, which was probably smuggled into the South by black sailors, was a carefully written trumpet call for mass slave uprisings, with violent reprisals against slaveowners. Although perhaps only a few literate blacks could read it, Southern states took

Mastheads from Abolitionist Newspapers.

extreme precautions. The mails were scrutinized, ships arriving in Southern ports were searched, and black seamen were restricted. The circulation of the work became a crime and a bounty was placed on Walker's life. Walker died under mysterious circumstances in 1830.

1830

April 6. James Augustine Healy, the first black Catholic bishop in America, was born on a plantation near Macon, Georgia. Healy was the son of an Irish immigrant and a mulatto slave. His father sent him and his brothers to the North for their education, but after being rejected by several academies, the Healys entered a Quaker school on Long Island. Later, they transferred to the College of the Holy Cross at Worcester, Massachusetts, where Healey James was the most outstanding pupil. In 1852, he entered the Sulpician Seminary in Paris, and on June 10, 1854 he was ordained a priest in Notre Dame Cathedral, Paris. Healy's first assignment as a priest was in a white parish in Boston. He became secretary to the Bishop of Boston, and when his superior died he became pastor of the New St. James Church. Healy's stature in the New England Catholic hierarchy continued to rise; in 1874, he was appointed bishop of Maine, and was consecrated in the Cathedral at Portland on June 2, 1875. Healy proved to be energetic and devoted to duty. He ministered to an all-white following, but only occasionally was subjected to racial abuse. Shortly before his death on August 5, 1890, Healy was promoted to the rank of Assistant at the Papal Throne.

September 20-24. The initial National Negro Convention met at Bethel A.M.E. Church in Philadelphia. Delegates from Delaware, Maryland, New York, Pennsylvania, and Virginia attended. The convention, under the leadership of Richard Allen (other prominent black leaders present included James Forten, the wealthy abolitionist and shipmaker, and the journalist Samuel Cornish), adopted resolutions calling for improvements in the social status of American blacks. The delegates considered projects to establish a black college and to encourage Negroes to emigrate to Canada. Neither of these proposals was adopted. Opposition even arose to the idea of a Negro convention at all. Yet these ad-hoc conventions continued to meet and occasionally were attended by white abolitionists and reformers. In the ten years before the Civil War, there was a rash of such conventions held in Cleveland, Rochester, and New York City as well as in Philadelphia. One of the most important meetings was held in Rochester in 1853, during which a National Council of Colored People was formed. This group issued a memorable statement denouncing racial oppression in America while at the same time citing instances of black progress. These conventions were in the American tradition of assembling for redress of grievances and increased solidarity among the blacks.

1831

January 1. William Lloyd Garrison published the first issue of the militant anti-slavery newspaper, the *Liberator*, with financial aid and moral support from prominent blacks, including James Forten of Philadelphia.

August 21-22. The most momentous slave revolt in United States history occurred in Southhampton County, Virginia. It was led by the black minister Nat Turner, who had on a previous occasion run away but decided to return to his master. Approximately sixty whites were slain in the revolt. Turner was captured on October 30 and hanged on November 11. Thirty other blacks who were implicated with Turner were also executed. The revolt caused near pandemonium in the South. Slave codes were vigorously enforced, slave patrols were increased, and suspicious blacks were either incarcerated or killed. No other major slave revolt or conspiracy followed the Turner insurrection until John Brown's raid on the United States Arsenal at Harpers Ferry, Virginia, in 1859.

Members of Pennsylvania Anti-Slavery Society. Abolitionist leader William Lloyd Garrison in front row, first from right.

1835

June 1-5 The fifth National Negro Convention met in Philadelphia and urged blacks to abandon the use of the terms "African" and "colored" when referring to Negro institutions, organizations, and to themselves.

1836

————. The infamous "gag rule" was adopted in the United States House of Representatives. Under the act, anti-slavery petitions were simply laid on the table without any further action. This denial of the right of petition angered former President John Quincy Adams, then a congressman from Massachusetts. Adams fought vigorously against the rule, helping to rouse public opinion in the North. Anti-slavery petitions began to pour into Washington, more than 200,000 of them in a single session. In 1844 the gag rule was rescinded. Its opponents saw it as an effort to deny white men their right of freedom of petition in an attempt to keep black men slaves.

1838

March 14. Blacks held a mass meeting in Philadelphia to protest the action of the Pennsylvania Reform Convention of 1837 which denied them the right to vote. The Convention, acting on the basis of a State Supreme Court decision (*Fogg v. Hobbs*, 1837) that blacks were not freemen and restricted the suffrage to white males. At the Philadelphia mass meeting the blacks, claiming to represent 40,000 of their number threatened with disfranchisement, said the denial of suffrage would make political rights dependent upon the "skin in which a man is born," and divide "what our fathers bled to unite, to wit, TAXATION AND REPRESENTATION." The blacks argued that they were indeed citizens, having been recognized as such by article four of the Articles of Confederation which stated: "The free inhabitants of each of these states, paupers, vagabonds, and fugitives from justice excepted, shall be entitled to all privileges and immunities of free *citizens* in the several states." The Constitution of the United States, according to the black petition, made no changes as to their rights of citizenship. The petitioners asked the state court to reverse its decision in *Fogg v. Hobbs* and/or the people of Pennsylvania to reject the new Constitution. The court's action stood, however, and the new constitution's disfranchising clauses won popular approval.

————. Frank Johnson, one of America's first black bandleaders, gave a command performance before Queen Victoria at Buckingham Palace. He was presented with a silver bugle. Johnson was born in 1792, and by 1820 had established himself as a versatile musician, playing with white bands in Philadelphia. When he organized his own band, principally a woodwind ensemble, it won national acclaim for its excellent performances at parades and dances. Frank Johnson's Colored Band, as it was called, even performed on plantations as far south as Virginia. Johnson became noted for his ability to "distort a song into a reel, jig, or country dance." He also composed music, including the "Recognition March on the Independence of Hayti" in 1825. Johnson died in 1844.

1839

July. The most famous slave mutiny in United States history took place on the Spanish ship *Amistad*. A group of Africans, led by Cinque, brought the captured vessel into Montauk, Long Island, where they were arrested. Former President John Quincy Adams defended the rebels before the Supreme Court, which granted their freedom.

1843

August 22. A national convention of black men was held in Buffalo, New York. The black abolitionist Henry Highland Garnet called for a slave revolt and a general strike to improve the lot of blacks in the United States. Many of the delegates, including Frederick Douglass, denounced the speech. Garnet, a minister, had served as pastor to whites and blacks in Troy, New York.

1844

June 24. A mass meeting of blacks in Boston adopted a resolution declaring that segregated public schools in that city violated the State Constitution. They urged the city's School Committee to abolish separate schools and to extend to black citizens the right to send their children "to the schools established in the respective district" in which they resided. Their request was denied and the schools in Massachusetts remained segregated until 1855.

1846

August. Norbert Rillieux obtained his first patent for the revolutionary multiple-effect vacuum evaporation process, which refines sugar whiter and grainier. The technique became the basic manufacturing process in the sugar as well as other industries. Rillieux, born in New Orleans in 1806, was the son of a white engineer and a free mulatto woman. His father was the inventor of a steam-operated cotton-baling press. Rillieux was educated in Paris and in 1830 he became an instructor of applied mechanics at the L'Ecole Centrale. It is believed that he developed the theory for his later invention about this time. Rillieux had built and installed a triple-effect evaporator on a Louisiana plantation in 1834. He reached a permanent solution in 1845 and obtained a patent the following year. Frustrated by racial discrimination in Louisiana, he returned to Paris in 1861 and died in France in 1894.

1847

June 30. Dred Scott, a slave, filed suit in the St. Louis Circuit Court claiming that his temporary residence in a free territory should have made him a free man. Scott was a semi-literate man whose travels throughout the country—specifically into the free portions of the Louisiana territory where slavery had been excluded by the Missouri Compromise of 1820, and into free Illinois—formed the basis for the case. (See also entry dated March 6, 1857.)

December 3. The black abolitionist Frederick Douglass began publication of his own newspaper, the *North Star*. Douglass, a former slave, became the principal black anti-slavery speaker and writer. Born in Tuckahoe, Maryland in 1817, Douglass was separated in infancy from his mother, and had harsh masters as a child. While still very young, Douglass became a house servant in Baltimore, where white playmates taught him to read. His first attempt at escape was thwarted, but in 1838, while working as a ship calker, he managed a successful break from slavery. Further education by anti-slavery groups in the North made Douglass a very lucid speaker and writer. The publication of the *North Star* was one of the factors which led to Douglass's break with William Lloyd Garrison, the noted white abolitionist and publisher of the *Liberator*. Garrison saw no need for two major rival anti-slavery publications, but Douglass and other blacks had become convinced that they must play a more leading role in the abolitionist movement, including the printing of a newspaper. In later years Douglass was appointed to several political and diplomatic posts, including unofficial advisor to Presidents Lincoln and Johnson, marshal of the District of Columbia, recorder of deeds of the District of Columbia, and minister to Haiti. He also served as president of the Freedmen's Bank in 1874.

1848

February. The Treaty of Guadalupe Hidalgo was concluded between the United States and Mexico, ending the two years of combat between the

Frederick Douglass

countries. Under the terms of the treaty, the present states of New Mexico and California were ceded to the United States. Many pro-slavery Southerners had supported the war, anticipating that new lands would be opened to slavery. Many anti-slavery Northerners had opposed the war, fearing that it was the result of a pro-slavery conspiracy designed to open new territory to slavery. Shortly after the war began in 1846, Democratic Representative David Wilmot of Pennsylvania introduced an amendment to a pending bill in Congress. This "Wilmot Proviso" sought to prohibit slavery in any territory acquired as a result of the Mexican War. The proviso passed in the House of Representatives, but was defeated in the Senate. The Mexican Cession and the status of slavery there precipitated bitter debate between North and South in the years from 1848 to 1850. One proposed solution was offered by President Zachary Taylor, who suggested that California and New Mexico bypass the territorial stage of government and apply directly for statehood, thus nullifying the question of slavery in the Mexican Cession territories. This proposal was unacceptable to the South, for both New Mexico and California would enter the Union as free states, thus upsetting the precarious sectional balance in the United States Senate which now stood at fifteen states each. The grounds were laid for the famous Compromise of 1850. (See also entry dated September 18, 1850.)

1849

July. Harriet Tubman escaped from slavery in Maryland. Tubman, the best-known black female abolitionist, returned to Maryland and Virginia at least twenty times, and is credited with freeing more than three hundred slaves. The daring abolitionist was born in Dorchester County, Maryland in 1823. While working as a field hand as a young girl, she suffered a severe head injury by a weight that an enraged overseer had thrown at another slave. The damage from that blow caused Tubman to suffer from "sleeping seizures" for the rest of her life. In 1844, she married a free black, John Tubman, but remained a slave. In 1849, her master died and rumors emerged that his slaves were to be sold into the Deep South. Tubman, along with two of her brothers, escaped. Fearing capture and punishment or death, the brothers returned to the plantation, but Tubman, using the North Star for directions, marched on until she reached Philadelphia. In 1850, Tubman returned to Maryland for a sister and a brother, and in the following year she led a party of eleven blacks from the South into Canada, leaving her husband, who had married another woman, behind. In 1857, Tubman made one of her last trips into Maryland, rescuing her parents and three additional brothers and sisters. The family then settled in Auburn, New York. The family home, purchased from anti-slavery Senator William H. Seward, was later turned into a home for elderly and indigent blacks. After serving in the Civil War as a nurse and a spy, Tubman devoted all of her energy and earnings to this home during the twilight of her life. Tubman, often called "the Moses of her People," died in Auburn in 1913.

————. Benjamin Roberts, a black parent in Boston, sued the city for denying his daughter admission to a white public school. The Massachusetts Supreme Court rejected the suit, establishing the "separate but equal" doctrine instead.

————. Elder Peter Lowery became pastor of a black church in Nashville, Tennessee, making him probably the first black pastor of a church in the South. Lowery, who was born a slave, had managed to purchase his freedom and that of other members of his family, including his mother, brothers, and sisters, over a period of more than forty years. In his endeavor, he was substantially aided by his wife, Ruth, a free woman of color.

1850

September 18. Congress enacted the famous Compromise of 1850. Senator Henry Clay of Kentucky and other "moderate" statesmen from both sections drew up this omnibus solution to the problem of slavery in the Mexican Cession as well as other outstanding differences between North and South. The provisions of the Compromise relating to slavery included the outlawing of the

Harriet Tubman (first from left) with several slaves she helped guide to freedom.

slave trade in Washington, D.C. but the retention of slavery itself, the passage of a new, tougher fugitive slave law to replace the poorly enforced act of 1793, and the admission of California as a free state. (See also entry dated February, 1848.)

1851

————. Elizabeth Taylor Greenfield, the "Black Swan," made her debut at a concert sponsored by the Buffalo Musical Association. Greenfield, a soprano, was born a slave in Natchez, Mississippi in 1809. As an infant, she was taken to Philadelphia and adopted by a Quaker woman named Greenfield who arranged for her to study music and to sing at private parties. After her debut in Buffalo, Greenfield toured the Northern states between 1851 and 1853. She toured England in 1854 and gave a command performance before Queen Victoria in Buckingham Palace. A contemporary critic described her voice as one of "amazing power," "flexibility," and "ease of execution." America's leading historian of black music, Eileen Southern, says that "Greenfield was the best known black concert artist of her time."

1852

March 20. *Uncle Tom's Cabin*, a novel by a Northern white woman, Harriet Beecher Stowe, was published in Boston. The book, which exaggerated the cruelties of slavery, evoked sympathy for the blacks in the North and greatly angered the South.

1853

July 6-8. The National Council of Colored People was founded in Rochester, New York. An outgrowth of the ante-bellum Negro Convention Movement, the new organization was formed as a permanent body to advance the cause of blacks. A notable feature of the Rochester convention was a proposal to erect a national industrial school for the race. The institution was to be financed by the issuance of $50,000 worth of stock in shares of ten dollars each, through the sale of scholarships "at judicious rates," and by the raising of a $100,000 endowment. The school was to be co-educational and was to be governed by a board of trustees, residents of the state wherein the institution was located. The sponsors of the measure, which was never implemented, hoped that the education of black youths would "give them means of success adapted to their struggling condition; and ere long, following the enterprise of the age . . . see them filling everywhere positions of responsibility and trust, and gliding on the triple tide of wealth, intelligence, and virtue, reach eventually to a sure resting place of distinction and happiness."

———. William Wells Brown, a former slave, abolitionist, historian, and physician, published *Clotel,* the first novel written by a Negro American, in London. The work, an account of the life of a black woman whose father was an American president, draws on the legend that Thomas Jefferson had fathered many children by his slave mistresses. Brown was born to a slave and a white slave-owner in Lexington, Kentucky in 1816. He was educated in St. Louis, Missouri, where he served as an apprentice to the martyred abolitionist editor, Elijah P. Lovejoy. Brown also published *Three Years in Europe: or, Places I Have Seen and People I Have Met* (1852), in which he gave his impressions of such notables as Richard Cobden, Victor Hugo, and Alexis de Tocqueville. Brown was also a regular contributor to William Lloyd Garrison's the *Liberator,* the London *Daily News,* and the *National Anti-Slavery Standard.* His reputation as an historian rests largely upon such works as *The Black Man* (1863) and *The Negro in the American Rebellions* (1867). Brown's principal anti-slavery work was as a "conductor" on the Underground Railroad and as an anti-slavery lecturer. He died in 1884.

CLOTEL;

OR,

THE PRESIDENT'S DAUGHTER:

A Narrative of Slave Life

IN

THE UNITED STATES.

BY

WILLIAM WELLS BROWN,

A FUGITIVE SLAVE, AUTHOR OF "THREE YEARS IN EUROPE."

With a Sketch of the Author's Life.

"We hold these truths to be self-evident: that all men are created equal; that they are endowed by their Creator with certain inalienable rights, and that among these are LIFE, LIBERTY, and the PURSUIT OF HAPPINESS." — *Declaration of American Independence.*

Title page of William Wells Brown's novel, Clotel.

1854

January 1. Lincoln University, the nation's first Negro college, was chartered as Ashmum Institute at Oxford, Chester County, Pennsylvania.

May 30. The Kansas-Nebraska Act was approved by Congress and President Franklin Pierce. In addition to providing formal organization for the two territories of Kansas and Nebraska, the act repealed the Missouri Compromise of 1820, thus removing anti-slavery restrictions north and west of the 36-30 parallel line in the Louisiana territory. According to the bill's author, Senator Stephen A. Douglas of Illinois, Congress, in the Compromise of 1850, had abandoned all efforts to protect or to prohibit slavery in the territories. Therefore, it was only consistent, Douglas reasoned, that the new principle be applied in the Louisiana territory as elsewhere. Southerners viewed Kansas as ripe for slavery. Northern anti-slavery men opposed the prospects of a slave Kansas and the repeal of the Compromise of 1820. The contest for control of Kansas between the pro- and anti-slavery forces led to several years of bitter, often bloody, strife in the territory and in Congress. In fact, Kansas came to be known as "Bleeding Kansas." The most significant acts of violence were (1) the sacking of the anti-slavery town of Lawrence, Kansas in May 1856 and the subsequent retaliation by John Brown. Brown and his followers slaughtered five pro-slavery men at Pottawatomie Creek; (2) the beating of anti-slavery Senator Charles Sumner of Massachusetts by Congressman Preston S. Brooks of South Carolina on the floor of the United States Senate, also in the spring of 1856. Sumner had denounced the South and some of its representatives for the "crime against Kansas," the rape of a virgin territory by slaveholders. His remarks against Senator Andrew P. Butler of South Carolina led to the attack by Brooks, Butler's nephew. The acrimony and political confusion in Kansas prevented the territory from being admitted into the Union by Congress until just before the Civil War. On January 29, 1861, Kansas joined the Union as a free state, representing the will of the majority of the bona fide residents there.

June 3. Anthony Burns, a fugitive slave, was arrested in Boston. His master refused an offer of $1,200 made by Boston citizens for his freedom. Burns was escorted through the streets of Boston by United States troops to be returned to the South. The incident was indicative of a growing anti-slavery sentiment in the North, especially following the passage of the Kansas-Nebraska Act.

1855

————. John Mercer Langston was elected clerk of Brownhelm Township in Lorain County, Ohio, making him the first black to win an elective political office in the United States. Langston was born to a white man and a black slave on a Virginia plantation in 1829. After his father's death, Langston was sent to

Ohio, where he was reared by one of his father's friends. By 1854, Langston was engaged in an active law practice in Chillicothe, Ohio, and in 1855, as the only black attorney in Brownhelm, he was elected clerk. Langston won a seat on the Brownhelm City Council the following year, a post he held until 1860. In 1865, he was named president of the National Equal Rights League and in 1867 he became a member of the Board of Education in Oberlin, Ohio. After his return to the South during Reconstruction, Langston served as inspector general to the Freedman's Bureau Schools (1868-1869); teacher, law school dean, and acting vice-president of Howard University (1869-1876); minister to Haiti (1877-1885); president of the Virginia Normal and Collegiate Institute (1885-1888); and congressman from Virginia (1889-1891). Langston, who died in 1897, was one of the last blacks elected to the United States Congress in the nineteenth century, and was the great-uncle of the Harlem Renaissance poet Langston Hughes.

1857

March 6. The Supreme Court rendered its decision in the case of *Dred Scott v. Sandford*, declaring that Negroes were not citizens of the United States, and denying to Congress the power to prohibit slavery in any federal territory. Scott was eventually freed by new owners. Meanwhile, he remained as a slave, albeit a famous one, in St. Louis where he worked as a porter. The Dred Scott decision, a clear-cut victory for the South, alarmed abolitionists men in the North and fueled the fires leading to the Civil War. (See also entry dated June 30, 1847.)

June. The California legislature defeated by a narrow margin of thirty-two to thirty an attempt to prevent the immigration of blacks into the state. The opposition to the measure was lead by Representative G. A. Hall. Despite the defeat of the immigration measure, California blacks continued to protest instances of racial discrimination against them. An excerpt from a protest of two black businessmen in 1857 follows:

"During a residence of seven years in California, we, with hundreds of other colored men, have cheerfully paid city, state and county taxes on real estate and merchandise, as well as licenses to carry on business, and every other species of tax that has been levied from time to time for the support of the government, save only the 'poll tax' that we have persistently refused. On the day before yesterday, the Tax Collector called on us, and seized and lugged off twenty or thirty dollars' worth of goods, in payment, as he said, of this tax. . . . Now, while we cannot understand how a 'white' man can refuse to pay each and every tax for the support of government, under which he enjoys every privilege—from the right to rob a negro up to that of being Governor of the State—

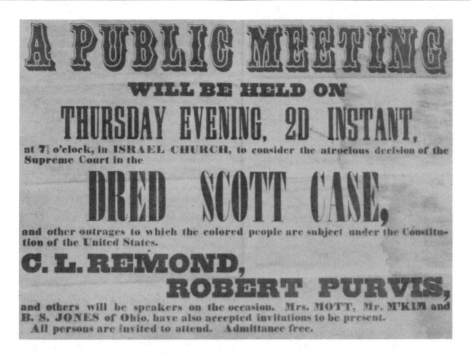

Handbill advertising the Dred Scott case, circa 1856-57.

we can perceive and feel the flagrant injustices of compelling 'colored men' to pay a special tax for the enjoyment of a special privilege, and then break their heads if they attempt to exercise it. We believe that every voter should pay poll-tax, or every male resident who has the privilege of becoming a voter; but regard it as low and despicable, the very quintessence of meanness, to compel colored men to pay it, situated as they are politically. However, if there is no redress, the great State of California may come around annually, and rob us of twenty or thirty dollars' worth of goods, as we will never willingly pay three dollars as poll tax as long as we remain disfranchised, oath-denied, outlawed colored Americans."

1859

March 7. The Acting Commissioner of General Lands for the United States, J. S. Wilson, stated that blacks were not citizens of the United States "as contemplated by the preemption law of September, 1841" and, therefore, were "not legally entitled to preempt public lands."

October 16. John Brown, a white abolitionist from Kansas, attacked the

United States Arsenal at Harpers Ferry, Virginia. Brown, who had unsuccess-fully sought the aid of leading abolitionists, including Frederick Douglass, was accompanied by a dozen white men and five blacks. The raid, which was to be a prelude to a general slave uprising, was foiled by local, state, and federal forces. Two blacks were killed for their part in the affair. Brown was executed on December 2.

————. The *Clothilde*, the last slave ship to stop at an American port, landed at Mobile Bay, Alabama.

————. The United States Supreme Court, in *Ableman v. Booth*, overruled an act by a Wisconsin state court declaring the Fugitive Slave Act of 1850 unconstitutional. The Fugitive Slave Act and its methods of enforcement were increasingly opposed by Northern residents. Many Northern cities and states passed Personal Liberty Laws, denying the use of Northern jails for the housing of fugitive slaves and prohibiting local law enforcement officers from assisting in their capture, in an attempt to offset the Fugitive Slave Act. The Wisconsin case arose when a journalist was arrested for rousing a mob to free a captured runaway. The state court ordered him released on a writ of *habeas corpus* and declared the federal statute unconstitutional.

Escaped slaves rest in front of Underground Railroad "station."

1860

January 1. A law went into effect in Arkansas which prohibited the employment of free blacks on boats and ships navigating the rivers of that state.

November 6. Abraham Lincoln, viewed by Southerners as an abolitionist, was elected President of the United States on a platform opposed to the further expansion of slavery into the territories.

December 17. South Carolina seceded from the Union, partly because of Lincoln's election as President.

————. The Pony Express began operations in the West. Eastern mails went by railroad to St. Joseph, Missouri, then were picked up by professional riders who, working in relays, delivered letters as far west as San Francisco. Two of the earliest black Pony Express riders were George Monroe and William Robinson.

Chapter 2
War and Freedom, 1861-1876

1861

April 12. The Confederates attacked Fort Sumter in South Carolina. President Lincoln called for 75,000 volunteers to defend the Union; the Civil War begins. Many blacks viewed the conflict as a war for freedom. Some rushed to join the Union forces, but were refused because of their race.

August 6. Congress passed the Confiscation Act providing that any property used by the owner's consent and with his knowledge in aiding or abetting insurrection against the United States could be captured wherever found. When the property consisted of slaves, they were to be forever free. President Lincoln refused to order vigorous enforcement of the law.

August 23. James Stone, a very light complexioned fugitive slave, enlisted in the First Fight Artillery of Ohio. Stone, whose wife was a white woman, was taken for white himself. Having fought for the Union in Kentucky, where he had been a slave, Stone died from a service-related illness in 1862. After his death, some blacks revealed his true racial identity. Thus, Stone was actually the first black man to fight for the Union during the Civil War—almost two full years before blacks were authorized to join Union forces.

September 25. The Secretary of the Navy authorized the enlistment of blacks in this branch of the armed forces.

————. General John C. Fremont proclaimed military emancipation in Missouri. President Lincoln countermanded the order.

1862

March 6. President Lincoln proposed to Congress a plan for gradual, compensated emancipation of slaves. Lincoln urged the congressional delegations from Delaware, Kentucky, Maryland, Missouri, and West Virginia to support his proposal. They opposed it, as did Northern abolitionists who felt slaveholders should not be paid for property which they could not rightfully own. Congress, however, passed a joint resolution on April 10, 1862, endorsing the concept of gradual, compensated emancipation.

April 16. The United States Senate passed a bill abolishing slavery in the District of Columbia. Slaveowners were to be compensated at the rate of $300 per slave. One hundred thousand dollars was also allocated for the voluntary emigration of these freedmen to Haiti or Liberia.

May 9. General David Hunter issued a proclamation emancipating slaves in Georgia, Florida, and South Carolina as "contrabands of war." President Lincoln overruled Hunter's order.

May 13. Robert Smalls, a black pilot, sailed the Confederate steamer the *Planter* out of Charleston, South Carolina, and turned the ship over to the United States. Smalls, a former slave, had received some education through the indulgence of his master. He was a member of a crew in the Confederate Navy when he performed his Civil War heroics. Smalls's war deeds aided his rise in South Carolina politics and business endeavors during Reconstruction. He later served five terms in the U. S. House of Representatives.

June 19. President Lincoln signed a bill abolishing slavery in the federal territories.

July 17. Congress authorized President Lincoln to accept Negroes for service in the Union Army. The blacks were to receive less pay than white soldiers. A white soldier, for example, was paid $13 a month and $3.50 for clothing, while blacks of the same rank were to receive $7 and $3 respectively. Eventually, more than 186,000 blacks served in the Union Army; approximately 38,000 lost their lives. Many of the deaths were non-combat related, due principally to overwork and poor medical care.

August 14. President Lincoln called in a group of blacks for the first discussion by an American president with Negroes on public policy. He urged Negroes to emigrate to Africa or to Latin America. Many blacks denounced the President's suggestion.

September 22. President Lincoln issued a preliminary Emancipation Proclamation, giving rebellious states and territories until January 1, 1863 to abandon their hostilities or lose their slaves.

1863

January 1. President Lincoln signed the Emancipation Proclamation. Based upon military necessity, it declared slaves free in all states and territories then in rebellion against the United States.(See Appendix for the text of the Emancipation Proclamation.)

May 1. The Confederate Congress passed a resolution calling Negro troops and their officers criminals, thus permitting captured black soldiers and their officers to be murdered or enslaved.

May 27. Two Louisiana Negro regiments made six unsuccessful charges on the Confederate fortifications at Port Hudson, Louisiana.

July 9. Eight Negro regiments played a vital role in the siege of Port Hudson which, with the capture of Vicksburg, Mississippi, allowed the Union to control the Mississippi River.

July 13-16. Four days of rioting ensued in New York City in protest of the Union's Draft Law. The disturbance left more than one thousand people, mostly blacks, dead or wounded, and resulted in approximately two million dollars in property damage. The riot grew out of the Civil War Draft Law's provision which allowed men to pay $300 for a substitute draftee. Since poor white laborers, many of them Irish and German immigrants, could not afford to buy substitutes, they bore the brunt of the draft. Blacks were ineligible (at the time) for the draft. In venting their frustrations over the draft law, the poorer laborers turned on the blacks, especially, whom they regarded as the principal inheritors of the jobs they would have to leave behind to enter the Army. During this period of racial tension, similar riots occurred in Boston, where twenty people were killed or wounded, and in Troy, New York, where a ship with black servants aboard had to be diverted to avoid an attack.

July 30. President Lincoln warned of retaliatory action if the Confederates continued to murder or enslave captured Negro soldiers.

————. The 54th Massachusetts Negro Regiment served a year without pay rather than accept discriminatory wages.

1864

April 12. Confederate forces under General Nathan Bedford Forrest captured Fort Pillow, Tennessee. Following the surrender, the Union's black troops were massacred.

June 15. Congress passed a bill equalizing salaries and supplies for Negro troops.

Emancipation Proclamation.

Relief of Colonel Robert Gould Shaw and the all-black 54th Regiment of Massachusetts at Fort Shaw, Montana. This regiment was the subject of the 1989 film Glory.

June 19. A Negro sailor, Joachim Pease, won the Congressional Medal of Honor for his role in the famous naval battle between the USS *Kearsage* and the USS *Alabama* off the coast of France.

October 4. The *New Orleans Tribune,* a black newspaper, began daily publication in French as well as in English.

———. Black Sergeant William Walker of the Third South Carolina Regiment was shot under order of a court martial for leading a protest against discriminatory pay for black soldiers.

1865

———. The "Black Laws" of Illinois were repealed. These laws, like similar ones in other Northern states, restricted the freedom of movement and limited the civil and political rights of free blacks. John Jones, one of the wealthiest blacks in America, led the fight for repeal. Jones was born free in Green City, North Carolina, in 1816. He was self-educated and became a tailor's apprentice, first in Memphis, Tennessee, before moving to Chicago in 1845. Jones opened a tailoring business there, from which he amassed a fortune. Using his wealth and influence, Jones led the successful fight against the prohibition of the immigration of free blacks into Illinois in 1853, the "Black Laws," and school segregation in Chicago. He was elected a Cook County commissioner in 1875 and served for two terms. Jones was also the first black elected to the Chicago Board of Education. Prior to the Civil War, he was also active in the abolitionist movement, his home being used as a station on the Underground Railroad. Jones died in 1879 leaving an estate valued at more than $100,000.

January 11. Robert E. Lee, with his armies at low tide, recommended the employment of blacks in the Confederate forces because it was "not only expedient but necessary."

March 3. Congress established, within the War Department, a Bureau of Freedmen, Refugees and Abandoned Lands. The Freedmen's Bureau was to help freed blacks survive, aid them in their contractual relationships, and begin educating them. The Bureau, in its five years of existence, issued more than twenty million rations, more than five million going to whites; established approximately fifty hospitals; resettled more than 30,000 people; set up 4,330 schools, enrolling 247,000 students; and aided in the establishment of such black colleges as Atlanta University, Fisk University, Hampton Institute, and Howard University.

March 3. The United States government chartered the Freedmen's Bank in Washington, D.C. to encourage financial responsibility among the former slaves. On April 4, 1865, the headquarters of the Freedmen's Bank opened in New York. Shortly thereafter, branches were established in Louisville, Nashville, New Orleans, Vicksburg, and Washington. By 1872 there was a total of thirty-four branches, all located in the South, with the exception of the New York and Philadelphia offices. Incompetency and inefficiency in the bank's operation appeared almost immediately. By the time Frederick Douglass was made president in March, 1874, the bank was already a failure. It closed its doors on June 28, 1874.

March 13. Confederate President Jefferson Davis signed a bill authorizing the employment of blacks as soldiers in the Confederate Army. The law culminated a long period of dispute in the South over the use of blacks as soldiers. While Southerners willingly used blacks for fatigue duties and personal service, the idea of black combat soldiers was generally repugnant to them. It seemed to invite slave violence and to make a mockery of the concept of Negro inferiority. The war ended before any blacks faced combat.

April 11. President Lincoln again conceded that Negro veterans and "very intelligent" blacks might be given the right to vote. He had suggested in a letter to Governor Hahn of Louisiana in 1864 that the "very intelligent" and those who had "fought gallantly in our ranks" should be considered for the franchise. At the time of Lincoln's death, no serious efforts had been made to grant suffrage to freed Negroes.

Former slaves at labor camp.

April 14. Abraham Lincoln was shot by John Wilkes Booth during a performance at Ford's Theater in the nation's capital. Lincoln died early the next morning.

May 29. President Andrew Johnson announced his program of Reconstruction. It required ratification of the Thirteenth Amendment, but did not guarantee Negro suffrage.

December 18. The Thirteenth Amendment, which prohibited slavery or involuntary servitude, except as punishment for a crime, was adopted. (See Appendix for the text of the Thirteenth Amendment.)

————. All-white legislatures, under the Johnson Reconstruction program, began enacting "Black Codes" which restricted the rights and freedom of movement of Negroes. These codes were patterned after the ante-bellum slave codes. Newer aspects of the laws imposed heavy penalties for vagrancy, "seditious speeches," "insulting gestures," and curfew violations.

1866

January 9. Fisk University, one of the most prestigious black colleges in the nation, opened in Nashville, Tennessee. The school was distinguished early by the music of its Jubilee Singers.

April 9. The Civil Rights Bill of 1866, granting to Negroes the rights and privileges of American citizenship, was passed by Congress. The law formed the basis for the Fourteenth Amendment to the United States Constitution and was passed over the veto of President Johnson.

May 1-3 A tragic race riot took place in Memphis, Tennessee. Forty-eight people, mostly black, were killed. Negro veterans were special targets, and at least five black women were raped during the disturbances. Schools and churches were burned.

July 30. A serious race riot occurred in New Orleans. At least thirty-five people were killed; more than 100 wounded. Anti-Negro attitudes and actions on the part of police officers allegedly sparked the outbreak of violence in that city.

————. The first blacks to sit in an American legislative assembly, Edward G. Walker and Charles L. Mitchell, were elected to the Massachusetts House of Representatives.

1867

January 8. Congress enacted a law giving the suffrage to blacks in the District of Columbia.

February 7. A delegation of Negroes, led by Frederick Douglass, visited President Johnson and urged that the suffrage be given to all qualified blacks.

February 18. An institution was founded at Augusta, Georgia which was later to become Morehouse College, following its relocation to Atlanta. Morehouse College is one of the most prestigious black colleges in the nation.

March 2. The Congress began passing a series of Reconstruction Acts which laid the foundation for Negro political participation in the South. The former Confederate states were required to ratify the Fourteenth Amendment which guaranteed civil rights to blacks, before being readmitted to the Union.

April 1. The first national convention of the Ku Klux Klan, a violent anti-Negro group, was held in Nashville, Tennessee.

May 1. Howard University, "the capstone of Negro education," opened in Washington, D.C. The school was established under the auspices of the Freedmen's Bureau and named for General Oliver O. Howard, head of the Bureau.

————. Atlanta University, the first all-black American graduate school, received its charter. The University began as an undergraduate institution, but became an institution for post-baccalaureate studies in 1929.

————. The National Association of Baseball denied admission to any club with black players. An excerpt from the official statement follows:

"It is not presumed by your committee that any clubs who have applied are composed of persons of color, or any portion of them; and the recommendations of your committee in this report are based upon this view, and they unanimously report against the admission of any club which may be composed of one or more colored persons. . . . If colored clubs were admitted, there would be in all probability some division of feeling—whereas by excluding them, no injury could result to anybody."

1868

January 14. The new state constitutional conventions met in Charleston, South Carolina. Negro delegates were in a decided majority. Louisiana had an equal number of blacks and whites in its convention, while all other Southern states had white majorities. The magnanimity of the Negro delegates at Charleston can be seen in the words of black representative Beverly Nash: "I believe, my friends and fellow-citizens, we are not prepared for this suffrage. But we can learn. . . . We recognize the Southern white man as the true friend of the black man. . . . In these public affairs we must unite with our white fellow-citizens. They tell us that they have been disfranchised, yet we tell the North that we shall never let the halls of Congress be silent until we remove that disability." The state constitutions drawn up by the Southern constitutional conventions with black members in 1867 and 1868 included among their progressive features the abolition of property qualifications for voting and holding office, abolition of imprisonment for debt, and state abolition of slavery.

April. Hampton Institute, for a time the leading agricultural-industrial college for blacks, opened in Virginia. Samuel Chapman Armstrong, a former Union officer and an advocate of agricultural-industrial training for the freed blacks, was one of the founders and first head of the institution. Hampton Institute remains one of the most prestigious black colleges in the United States.

June 13. Oscar J. Dunn, a freedman, became lieutenant governor of Louisiana, the highest elective office ever held by a black American at that time. Dunn was an apprentice to a plasterer and house painter until age fifteen, when he escaped. Born in New Orleans in 1826, Dunn took a job with the Freedman's Bureau there at the close of the Civil War. (He had served as a captain in the Union Army during the War). As an agent of the Freedman's Bureau, Dunn checked the employment practices of planters who hired black laborers. He found that the freedmen were often cheated of their minimum $15 a month earnings, and thus reported these and other abuses of the Freedman's Bureau wage-contract system. Dunn was one of the forty-nine blacks who attended the Louisiana Constitutional Convention in 1867–1868. As lieutenant governor, Dunn presided over the state senate and signed some of the laws emanating from the new state constitution. In 1871, he was named chairman of the Republican State Convention. Since Dunn was a skillful politician, some consideration was given to nominating him for governor or U. S. Senator before his untimely death in 1871. Two other Negroes, C.C. Antoine and P.B.S. Pinchback, served in the same office in Louisiana. Antoine was a freeborn Creole Negro whose father fought under Andrew Jackson at New Orleans in 1814 and who himself organized a black regiment in Louisiana during the Civil War and served as its captain. After the war, he became a grocer and later a politician in Shreveport. Prior to becoming lieutenant governor, Antoine served in the Constitutional Convention of 1867–1868, and the state senate. Blacks also served as Reconstruction lieutenant governors in Mississippi and South Carolina.

July 6. The South Carolina Legislature met in Columbia, the state's capital. More than half of the lawmakers were black (87 Negroes and 40 whites), making South Carolina the only state legislature in American history to have a black majority. The whites, however, controlled the state senate, and by 1874 there was a white majority in the lower house. At all times there was a white governor. There were two lieutenant-governors, Alonzo J. Ransier in 1870 and Richard H. Gleaves in 1872. Two blacks, Samuel J. Lee and Robert B. Elliot, served as Speaker of the House between 1872 and 1874. One of the most accomplished South Carolina black officeholders was Francis L. Cardozo. Cardozo, educated in London and Glasgow, Scotland, served with distinction as secretary of state (1868–1872) and state treasurer (1872–1876).

July 28. The Fourteenth Amendment, which made blacks American citizens and gave them constitutional guarantees, was adopted. All persons born or naturalized in the United States were defined as American citizens as well as citizens of the states in which they resided. No state could make or enforce laws denying such persons the rights and privileges of citizens or to fail to give them the equal protection of the laws. (See Appendix for the text of the Fourteenth Amendment.)

September 22-October 26. A series of race riots developed in Louisiana. Such disturbances occurred in New Orleans on September 22; in Opelousas on September 28; and in St. Bernard Parish on October 26.

June 7. Marie Laveau, the "Queen of the Voodoos," was dethroned because of old age. Marie, the most famous and most powerful of all of the Voodoo queens, was born in New Orleans circa 1796 as a free woman. A beautiful mulatto and a professional hairdresser, Marie worked in the homes of some of New Orleans' most prominent white women. She was also reportedly a procuress for white men. Marie became the chief Voodoo queen succeeding the old Sanite "Dede," and subsequently dominated Voodooism in New Orleans for nearly forty years. Under Marie, Louisiana Voodooism was a mixture of West Indian fetishism and a distorted form of Catholicism. This unusual mixture served to increase the popularity of Marie's cult and to give it a degree of legitimacy. Marie's unusual power lay in her ability to convince blacks and whites alike that she could produce "good fortune" and stave off evil. Marie died in 1879 and was succeeded by Malvina Latour.

1870

February 2. Jonathan Jasper Wright, a well-educated Pennsylvanian, became associate justice of the South Carolina Supreme Court. Wright served for seven years as the highest black judicial officer in the nation. Although Wright was one of only three members of the Court, he exercised no influence on behalf of Negro rights. Yet white Democratic leaders sought constantly to have him removed on charges of corruption. Wright left the bench in 1877 as Black Reconstruction toppled in the state.

February 25. Hiram R. Revels of Mississippi took Jefferson Davis' former seat in the United States Senate, becoming the only black in the United States Congress. Revels, a former barber and preacher, was a reluctant politician. It is said that his fervent prayer before the Mississippi legislature in 1870 persuaded many to vote for his election to the Senate. Many of these Democrats opposed his selection to the Senate and argued vainly that he could not be legally seated, not having been a citizen before the Civil War. (Constitutionally, senators must be citizens of the U.S. for at least nine years). After retiring from politics, leaving an undistinguished legislative record behind him, Revels became president of Alcorn College for Negroes in Mississippi.

March 30. The Fifteenth Amendment, forbidding the denial of the right to vote to American citizens, was ratified. (See Appendix for the text of the Fifteenth Amendment.)

May 31, 1870-October 17, 1871. Congress and President Ulysses S. Grant made efforts to prevent intimidation of Negro voters. The Enforcement Acts (Ku Klux Klan Acts) and a presidential proclamation were the most important measures.

Hiram R. Revels sworn in as U.S. Senator from Mississippi, 1870.

December 12. Joseph H. Rainey of South Carolina was seated in the U.S. House of Representatives. Rainey was born to slave parents in Georgetown, South Carolina in 1832. His own freedom was purchased before the Civil War by his father, a barber. A rather well-educated mulatto, Rainey himself became a barber in Charleston, having learned much from listening to and observing his better educated, white customers. Even though a respected member of the Charleston black community, he was called to work on fortifications by the Confederates during the Civil War. Rainey refused and exiled himself in the West Indies, where he remained until the end of the Civil War. During Reconstruction, he returned to South Carolina and served as a delegate to the Constitutional Convention of 1868. In 1870 he was elected to the state senate, but soon resigned to accept the seat in the U.S. House vacated by B. Franklin Whittimore. Rainey was then elected to the four succeeding Congresses. As a member of the House, he frequently spoke in favor of education and other social advances for blacks. The House's first black member was also a consultant to President Rutherford B. Hayes and once received the president's personal commendation for sobriety and attention to duty. After returning from Congress in 1879, Rainey served as an Internal Revenue Service (IRS) agent in South Carolina and then entered business in Washington, D.C. He returned to Georgetown, South Carolina in 1886 and died there a year later.

1872

December 11. P. B. S. Pinchback, a former Union officer and lieutenant governor of Louisiana, was named temporary governor of the state, becoming the first black American to serve as governor of an American state. He served for forty-three days as the incumbent was impeached. Pinchback was the son of a white Mississippi planter and army officer, and a mulatto woman who bore nine other children. The father took all the children North for manumission. Young Pinchback received private tutoring at home and then formal schooling in Cincinnati, Ohio. After his father's death, he became a cabin boy on Mississippi river boats. During the Civil War, Pinchback organized a company of Union volunteers at New Orleans and became their Captain. He held sundry political offices during the Reconstruction of Louisiana, including United States senator. Pinchback earned a reputation as a shrewd, aggressive politician. (See also entry dated March 8, 1876.)

1873

November. The first black graduate of Harvard University, Richard T. Greener, was appointed to the faculty of the University of South Carolina. The university's white students and faculty left the college when it was integrated.

1874

July 31. Father Patrick Francis Healy, a black priest, became president of Georgetown University, the oldest Catholic college in the United States. Healy, the brother of James Augustine Healy, the first black American to become a Roman Catholic bishop, headed the institution until 1883. (See also entry dated April 6, 1830.)

1875

March 1. A Civil Rights Bill was passed by Congress which prohibited discrimination in places of public accommodation. Inns, public conveyances on land or water, theaters, "and other places of public amusement" were included among those accommodations to which "all persons within the jurisdiction of the United States" were entitled to enjoy, regardless of any previous condition of servitude. Because of economic deprivation and prickly legal arrangements, few blacks were able to take advantage of the law's provisions. The United States Supreme Court overturned the law in 1883. (See also entry dated October 15, 1883.)

March 15. Mississippi's second black senator, Blanche K. Bruce, took his seat in Congress. He was the only Afro-American to serve a full term in the U.S. Senate until the mid-twentieth century. Bruce was only thirty-five at the time. He was born a slave in Virginia. As a body servant for the son of a wealthy planter, he was allowed some education. When his young master took him to the Confederate Army as a valet, Bruce escaped in Missouri. There he established a school for blacks. Bruce later attended Oberlin College, where he spent two years in study. After the Civil War, he became a modestly wealthy Mississippi planter, taught school occasionally, and held minor political offices as a Republican before being elected to the Senate. Bruce's good reputation even won him a few votes from white Democrats in the Mississippi legislature. However, when Bruce's fellow senator (a white) from Mississippi refused to escort him to be sworn in, as was the custom, dapper Senator Roscoe Conkling of New York took the Negro's hand and led him to the front of the chamber. It was a well-publicized event and an historic moment.

1876

March 8. The United States Senate, following three years of debate and controversy, refused to seat P. B. S. Pinchback of Louisiana. In the fall of 1872, Pinchback was elected to the U.S. House of Representatives and later to the U.S. Senate in the winter of 1873. During the long debate over Pinchback's case, including almost the whole of an extra session of Congress, the affable Pinchback became a national political figure as well as a prominent name in Washington society. Opponents of Pinchback argued that he had not been properly elected or was qualified, but the real reason, some authorities insist, was that many senators' wives were opposed to social intercourse with Mrs. Pinchback and influenced their husbands' negative votes.

————. Undoubtedly the first Doctor of Philosophy degree to be awarded to an Afro-American by a major university was bestowed upon Edward A. Bouchet, a physicist, by Yale University.

July 8-October 26. Serious racial disturbances in South Carolina resulted in President Grant's ordering federal troops in to restore order. In Hamburg, five blacks were killed in July.

————. Meharry Medical College, the first all-black medical school in the United States (and still one of only three), was established in Nashville, Tennessee. In the beginning, Meharry was a branch of Central Tennessee College. In 1915, it became a separate corporate entity.

Thomas Nast illustration of Klansmen terrorizing Southern blacks.

Chapter 3
The Nadir, 1877-1900

1877

February 26. A conference was held at the black-operated Wormely Hotel in Washington, D.C., between representatives of presidential candidate Rutherford B. Hayes and representatives from the South. A complicated agreement was reached which led to the election of Hayes as President, and the removal of the last federal troops supporting Black Reconstruction in the South.

March 18. Despite opposition within his own party as well as much Southern opposition, President Hayes appointed Frederick Douglass marshal for the District of Columbia.

1879

————. Large numbers of Southern blacks, frustrated with discrimination and poverty in the South, emigrated to the West. Most were disappointed in the "Exodus of 1879" as they met white and Indian hostility in the West. The most prominent leader of the exodus, which led principally to Kansas, was Benjamin "Pap" Singleton. He was a former slave who, after a number of unsuccessful attempts, made his way to freedom in Canada. An unlettered mulatto, Singleton favored racial separatism and encouraged industriousness among blacks. Many of the better educated blacks were hostile to Singleton's movement, especially to his concept of a black community apart from white influence.

1881

April 11. Spelman College, an institution sponsored by John D. Rockefeller's family, opened for Negro women in Atlanta, Georgia. It became "the Radcliffe and the Sarah Lawrence of Negro education."

May 17. Frederick Douglass became recorder of deeds for the District of Columbia. This second important appointment for Douglass was made by President James A. Garfield.

May 19. President Garfield appointed former Senator Blanche K. Bruce of Mississippi Register of the Treasury.

July 4. Booker T. Washington opened the famed Tuskegee Institute in Alabama. The school was to become the leading Afro-American agricultural-industrial institution.

————. Tennessee took the lead in requiring segregation in railroad cars. By 1907, all of the Southern states required segregation in public accommodations.

1883

March 20. Jan E. Matzeliger, a black Massachusetts shoemaker, invented a complicated machine that manufactured an entire shoe. The invention, which was sold to the United Shoe Company, revolutionized the industry. Matzeliger was born in Paramaribo, Dutch Guiana, in 1852, the son of a black woman and a Dutch engineer. He began working in his father's machine shop at the age of ten. Later, Matzeliger worked his way to the United States as a sailor. Stopping at Philadelphia, he soon moved to Lynn, Massachusetts, where he learned the shoemaking trade. By 1880, machines were able to cut and stitch the leather, but not to shape and attach the upper portion of the shoe to the sole. This had to be done by hand, a slow and tedious process. Working in secret, Matzeliger tackled the "lasting" problem for ten years. In 1883, he received the patent for his perfected product, a "lasting machine," which could hold the shoe on the last, grip and pull the leather down around the heel, set and drive the nails and discharge the completed shoe. A shoemaker to the end, Matzeliger died in 1889.

October 15. The United States Supreme Court ruled that the Civil Rights Act of 1875 was unconstitutional. The Reconstruction Amendments, the Court reasoned, did not extend into the area of public accommodations. (See also entry dated March 1, 1875.)

November 26. Sojourner Truth, the second best known black female abolitionist, died in Battle Creek, Michigan. Truth was born a slave, with the name Isabella, in Hurley, New York in 1797. The mother of five children, she was separated from her husband prior to her freedom in 1827. After her statutory emancipation in New York in 1827, Truth went to work for a "religious fanatic" named Pierson in New York City. By 1843, she had become disillusioned with Pierson and left, proclaiming that her name was no longer Isabella, but Sojourner. She said that "the Lord gave [her] Truth, because [she] was to declare the truth to the people." She became a legendary "sojourner," as she travelled about espousing abolition, women's rights, and other reforms. She held steadfastly to the belief that she was a chosen messenger of God. Though unlettered, Truth made a substantial impression upon her audiences. On one occasion, when Frederick Douglass was speaking at Faneuil Hall in Boston, he said that blacks could not hope to find justice in America. Truth sought to counter this pessimism by asking "Frederick, is God dead?" A more hopeful atmosphere then pervaded the meeting. Truth also played a prominent role in the Second National Women's Suffrage Convention in Akron, Ohio, in 1852. During the Civil War, she supported the arming of the slaves and helped to care for wounded soldiers and freedmen. During the Reconstruction era and until the end of her life, she urged property ownership and education as keys to black advancement.

1884

————. T. Thomas Fortune founded the *New York Age*. Fortune, born in Florida in 1856 to mulatto parents, was the leading Afro-American journalist until the First World War. After the Civil War, he attended a Freedmen's Bureau school. Fortune's father, a tanner and shoe merchant, served several terms in the Florida legislature during Reconstruction and secured for his son an appointment as page boy in the state senate. The family's political activities and close social contacts with some whites created racial animosity among other whites that eventually forced the family from the capital to Jacksonville, where the father became town marshal. Fortune himself went to Washington, where he attended Howard University, partly from earnings secured as a special customs agent in Delaware. After leaving Howard, he taught briefly in Florida, but soon left for New York. In 1879, Fortune began his long newspaper career in New York City. His first paper was the *New York Sun*, one of the city's leading newspapers. He published three books—the well-known *Black and White* (1884), a historical essay on land, labor, and politics in the South, as well as *The Negro in Politics* (1885) and *Dreams of Life* (1905). He was active in Republican politics after the Civil War and advocated civil rights for blacks. Fortune closely identified with Booker T. Washington and his ideas, but in later years edited some of Marcus Garvey's black nationalist publications. During World War I, Fortune had helped to establish the 369th black regiment. He died in 1928.

Sojourner Truth

1886

June 12. The Georgia State Supreme Court sustained the will of the late David Dickson, thus making Amanda Eubanks the wealthiest Negro in America. Dickson, a former slaveholder, willed more than half a million dollars to Eubanks. White relatives of Dickson, a bachelor, had contested the will on the grounds that it was illegal for a white man to leave property to his black illegitimate children. The court disagreed.

1890

August 12-November 1. A constitutional convention in Mississippi adopted the literacy and "understanding" tests as devices to disfranchise Negroes. A poll tax of two dollars and a provision excluding voters convicted of bribery, burglary, theft, arson, murder, bigamy, and perjury were also included in the amendment. Before the convention, black delegates from forty counties had met and protested to President Benjamin Harrison their impending disfranchisement. The President declined to interfere. To avoid a fight over ratification, the white proponents of the disfranchising measures declared the amendment to be in effect after passage by the convention.

―――. The Colored Farmers' Alliance, a socio-economic-political organization dedicated to improving the lot of the black farmer, reached a membership of one million. The Alliance, founded in 1886, included twelve state organizations and many local chapters formed wherever black farmers were sufficiently numerous. There was for a time cooperation between the black group and the white farmers alliance, but this was ruptured when the black group called for a strike of Negro cotton pickers. Leonidas L. Polk, president of the National Farmers' Alliance, accused the blacks of attempting to better their condition at the expense of whites.

1891

January 22. The Lodge Bill, aiming to prevent infringements on the Negro's right to vote, was killed in the United States Senate.

July 10. A black jockey, "Monk" Overton, won six straight horse races at the Washington Park race track in Chicago. In 1907, another black jockey, Jimmy Lee, also won six straight races at Churchill Downs in Louisville. Prior to 1907, only two other jockeys had equalled the achievements of Overton and Lee, the Englishmen Fred Archer and George Fordham.

―――. Isaac Murphy, a black jockey riding "Kingman," became the first man to win three Kentucky Derbys. Murphy won his first Derby in 1884 on "Buchanan" and his second in 1890 on "Riley." Other black jockeys winning the Derby were: Oliva Lewis in 1875 on "Anstides"; Billy Wakers in 1877 on "Buden Baden"; Babe Hurd in 1882 on "Apollo"; Enoch Henderson in 1885 on "Joe Cotton"; Isaac Lewis in 1887 on "Montrose"; Alfie Clayton in 1892 on "Azra"; "Soup" Perkins in 1895 on "Haima"; Willie Sims in 1896 on "Ben Brush," and again in 1898 on "Plaudit"; Jimmy Winkfield in 1901 on "His Eminence," and again in 1902 on "Alan-a-Dale."

1892

―――. The Populist Party, which at first welcomed black support, became a viable political organization in the South.

―――. Sissieretta Jones, the "Black Patti," performed for President Benjamin Harrison at the White House. Jones, a soprano, was born in Virginia, spent her childhood in Providence, Rhode Island, and studied at the New England Conservatory. She first attracted the attention of critics in 1892 when she appeared at the Jubilee Spectacle and Cakewalk at Madison Square Garden in New York. One critic called her the "Black Patti," a comparison with the Italian prima donna Adelina Patti. According to some authorities, "Black Patti Jones" was sought for roles in *Aida* and *L'Africaine* by the

Metropolitan Opera, but the project was dropped, reportedly because the "musical world was not ready to accept black prima donnas." Jones made her grand tour of Europe in 1893. Upon her return to the United States, she organized an all-black company, "Black Patti's Troubadours," in which she was the featured soloist. Jones died in 1933.

1895

January 14. Blacks organized the National Steamboat Company in Washington, D.C. The company sailed a steamboat, the *George Leary,* between Washington, D.C. and Norfolk, Virginia. The luxury boat held a capacity of 1,500 passengers and included three decks, sixty-four state rooms, one hundred berths, and a dining room.

February 20. Frederick Douglass died in Anacostia Heights, in the District of Columbia. (See entry dated December 3, 1847, for further information about Douglass.)

June. W.E.B. Du Bois became the first Afro-American to receive a Harvard Ph.D. He immediately embarked upon a successful career of teaching and research, principally at Atlanta University.

W.E.B. Du Bois

September 18. Booker T. Washington, the principal of Tuskegee Institute, delivered his controversial "Atlanta Compromise" speech to the Cotton States International Exposition in Atlanta. Washington asked for economic and educational progress for blacks aided by whites while playing down political power and social equality.

1896

May 18. The United States Supreme Court upheld the concept of separate but equal public facilities for blacks in the case of *Plessy v. Ferguson*, stemming from a dispute over transportation facilities in Louisiana. The segregation of the races thus won the sanction of the highest national tribunal. Justice John Harlan, in a prophetic dissent, asserted that segregation laws fostered ideas of racial inferiority and would increase attacks against the rights of blacks. (See Appendix for an excerpt taken from *Plessy v. Ferguson*.)

June. Booker T. Washington received an honorary Master of Arts degree from Harvard University.

July 21. The National Association of Colored Women, led by Mary Church Terrell, was organized in Washington, D.C. Terrell was born in Memphis, Tennessee, at the close of the Civil War, to wealthy and well-educated parents. Terrell inherited a substantial fortune and received an Oberlin education. She probably would have become a teacher, but her father considered the occupation beneath her station. As Mary Church, she married Robert Terrell, a prominent Washington, D.C. educator, attorney, and judge. Terrell did become a feminist leader and a close associate of a number of white feminist leaders. She remained wedded to the goal of racial integration despite numerous disappointments.

————. W.E.B. Du Bois's *The Suppression of the African Slave Trade to America*, his Harvard dissertation, was published as the first volume in the Harvard Historical Studies Series. This work, along with *The Philadelphia Negro* (1899), *The Souls of Black Folk* (1903), and *The Atlanta University Publications* (1898-1914), helped to establish Du Bois's scholarly reputation.

1897

November 15. John Mercer Langston, Virginia soldier, educator, diplomat, and United States congressman, died. (See also entry dated 1855, for further information about Langston.)

1898

March 17. Former United States Senator Blanche K. Bruce died in Washington, D. C. After leaving the Senate, Bruce had served as register of the United States Treasury and had been a successful banker. (See also entry dated March 15, 1875, for further information about Bruce.)

July 1. Four black regiments participated in fighting around Santiago, Cuba during the Spanish-American War. Approximately twenty Afro-American regiments served in the conflict. Most of the black outfits had been activated shortly after the end of the Civil War for action against the Indians in the West. In the present conflict, blacks, like many of their white counterparts, were ill-prepared in terms of experience, equipment, and training for combat in a tropical zone. Yet in the end, the blacks won the praises of almost all their officers. At the beginning of the Spanish-American War, there was only one Negro commissioned officer, Captain Charles Young. At the close of the war, there were more than one hundred black officers, including Young, now a Brevet Major and commander of the Ninth Ohio regiment.

July. At least twenty-five black soldiers, members of the United States Tenth Colored Cavalry, participated in the famous charge up San Juan Hill in Cuba. The assault was a major engagement of the Spanish-American War.

Soldiers of the Tenth Colored Cavalry.

———. Will Marion Cook directed the sensational musical-comedy sketch, *Clorindy, the Origin of the Cakewalk,* on Broadway. Disregarding warnings that Broadway audiences would not listen to Negroes singing black opera, Cook composed music to lyrics written by the famed black poet Paul Laurence Dunbar, and assembled a company of twenty-six black performers. The performances of the first Negro musical-comedy sketch in New York were held at the Casino Roof Garden. Cook was born in Washington, D.C. in 1869. The son of a Howard University law professor, he was sent at age thirteen to the Oberlin Conservatory to study the violin. Cook later studied with the violinist Joseph Joachim in Berlin and with John White and Antonin Dvořák at the National Conservatory of Music. Cook made additional theatrical history when *In Dahomey* (1902), his satire on the American Colonization Movement's efforts to promote black emigration to Africa, opened on Times Square on Broadway. Other Cook successes were *In Abyssinia* (1906) and *In Bandana Land* (1907). Cook's lively shows left his audiences whistling and tapping their feet and helped to popularize the Cakewalk both in the United States and Europe. Cook died in 1944.

1899

———. Charles Waddell Chesnutt published a volume of tales called *The Conjure Woman,* which helped to establish him as the foremost Afro-American novelist of his time. *The Conjure Woman,* based upon the superstitions of North Carolina blacks, was probably his best work. Chesnutt was born in North Carolina in 1858, but spent much of his adult life in Ohio. After the Civil War, he taught in the public schools of North Carolina, then was principal of the Fayetteville State Teachers College. As segregation and discrimination intensified in the South in the 1880s, Chesnutt returned to the North, first to New York, where he worked as a journalist, then Cleveland, where he was a clerk and an attorney. Prior to the publication of *The Conjure Woman,* Chesnutt had contributed several short stories to American periodicals, including the *Atlantic Monthly.* Following the highly successful *Conjure Woman,* Chesnutt published *The Wife of His Youth* and *The House behind the Cedars,* both in 1900; *The Marrow of Tradition* (1901); and *The Colonel's Dream* (1905). In recognition of his literary and other achievements, the NAACP awarded him its prestigious Spingarn Medal in 1928. Chesnutt died in 1932.

1900

April 30. The famed steam locomotive driven by John "Casey" Jones collided with another train. The incident inspired the popular song, "Casey Jones." Two black men, Wallace Saunders and Sim Webb, were members of Jones's crew. At the time of the collision, Jones ordered Sim Webb to jump to safety, but remained with the train himself. When Jones's body was recovered, it was discovered that he had kept one hand on the airbrake and the other on the whistle. Saunders took the occasion to write a song immortalizing the noted engineer and his train.

July 24-27. Another serious race riot broke out in New Orleans. Black schools and homes were destroyed during the disturbance.

August 23-24. The National Negro Business League, sponsored by Booker T. Washington, was formed in Boston. More than four hundred delegates from thirty-four states had answered Washington's call to stimulate black businesses. Washington himself was elected the first president of the organization. After only one year of the League's existence, Washington reported a large number of new black businesses and by 1907, the national organization had 320 branches. Though service-related concerns were by far the most numerous, blacks engaged in various types and sizes of business enterprises. The North Carolina Mutual Insurance Company, founded in 1898, became the largest of black-owned firms.

Chapter 4
The Age of Booker T. Washington, 1901-1917

1901

January 16. Hiram R. Revels, former United States Senator from Mississippi, died at Holly Springs. (See also entry dated February 25, 1870, for further information about Revels.)

March 4. George H. White left Congress. It would be more than twenty years before any other Afro-American served in Congress. White was first elected to Congress from North Carolina in 1896 and was reelected in 1898. In a moving valedictory address, White attacked Jim Crowism and predicted that the Negro would return to the United States Congress.

October 16. Booker T. Washington dined with President Theodore Roosevelt at the White House. The dinner meeting was viewed by many whites, especially Southerners, as a marked departure from racial etiquette and was bitterly criticized. In the previous year, the publication of Washington's autobiography, *Up From Slavery*, had been hailed by Southern and Northern whites for its "reasonable" and nonvindictive attitude towards the South and the previous slave system. The book has become a classic in American letters primarily because of Washington's prominence.

————. William Monroe Trotter, a Phi Beta Kappa graduate of Harvard University, founded the *Boston Guardian,* a militant newspaper which opposed the accomodationist policies of Booker T. Washington and demanded full equality for blacks. Trotter was born in Boston in 1872. After earning a Bachelor of Arts degree from Harvard, he returned for his Master's, which was awarded in 1895. Trotter opened the *Guardian* offices in 1901 in the same building where William Lloyd Garrison had published the *Liberator* and where

Booker T. Washington (center), founder of Tuskegee Institute.

Harriet Beecher Stowe's *Uncle Tom's Cabin* was printed. Trotter announced that "propaganda against discrimination based on color" was a principal aim of his publication. In editing the *Guardian*, Trotter abandoned a promising career as an insurance executive because "the conviction grew upon me that pursuit of business, money, civic or literary position was like building a house upon sands; if race prejudice and persecution and public discrimination for mere color was to spread up from the South and result in a fixed caste of color . . . every colored American would be really a civil outcast, forever an alien, in the public life." Trotter confronted his foe, Booker T. Washington, at the Columbus Avenue African Zion Church in Boston on July 30, 1903 by heckling the preeminent black leader. He and his followers were arrested—Trotter was sentenced to serve thirty days in jail. He explained that he had to resort to a public confrontation with Washington because the "Tuskegee kingpin" held a monopoly on the American media and opposing views could not be heard. The treatment of Trotter in Boston inspired W.E.B. Du Bois to become more active in the opposition to Washington. Trotter collaborated with Du Bois in the organization of the Niagara Movement, but declined a position of leadership in the NAACP because of his distrust of whites.

Yet Trotter continued his career as a civil rights activist. In 1906, he protested President Theodore Roosevelt's discharge of the black soldiers involved in the

Brownsville, Texas riot. In 1910, Trotter led a demonstration against a performance of the anti-Negro play *The Clansman* in Boston. In 1913 he confronted President Woodrow Wilson at the White House, accusing the President of lying when Wilson denied that he was responsible for segregation in the government cafeterias of Washington, D.C. Two years later, Trotter landed in jail for picketing the showing of the anti-black film *Birth of a Nation*.

When the Paris Peace Conference convened in 1919, Trotter applied for a passport to attend in order to present the grievances of American blacks to this world forum. When the U.S. government denied his visa, Trotter obtained a job as a cook on a transatlantic ship and managed to reach Europe. As a representative of the National Equal Rights League and of the Race Petitioners to the Peace Conference, Trotter supported the Japanese motion to include a prohibition against discrimination in the Covenant of the League of Nations. The Western Allies, including the United States, opposed such a proviso. In his final years, his money and energy dwindling, Trotter continued to agitate for equal rights. He died in 1934. (See Appendix for Trotter's essay on President Woodrow Wilson's policy of segregation.)

1903

————. W.E.B. Du Bois's *The Souls of Black Folk* was published. The book crystallized black opposition to the policies of Booker T. Washington.

1905

July 11-13. A group of black intellectuals from across the nation met near Niagara Falls and adopted resolutions demanding full equality in American life. The meeting has become known to history as the beginning of the Niagara Movement. W.E.B. Du Bois and William Monroe Trotter spearheaded the movement.

————. The Atlanta Life Insurance Company was founded by Alonzo F. Herndon in Atlanta. It was once the first, and now the second, largest black-owned business in the United States. The distinction of the largest black-owned business was later acquired by the North Carolina Mutual Insurance Company of Durham, founded in 1898-99 by John Merrick, C.C. Spaulding, and others.

————. Robert S. Abbott began publication of the militant *Chicago Defender*. It became one of the most widely read and influential black newspapers in the country. Abbott was the son of a slave butler and a field woman who purchased their son's freedom. After his father's death, Abbott's mother married John Sengstacke, an editor, educator, and clergyman. Young Abbott worked on his stepfather's newssheet. He received his education at Hampton Institute, where he came under the influence of General Samuel C. Armstrong, who had also molded Booker T. Washington. In Chicago, Abbott began his newspaper with a staff of former barbers and servants as well as a few recently educated blacks. He attracted good journalists like Willard Motley and published the early poems of Gwendolyn Brooks. Abbott's scathing attacks on Southern racism coupled with his appeals for Northern migration enhanced the *Defender*'s prestige.

1906

February 9. Paul Laurence Dunbar, the black poet who made Negro dialect an accepted literary form, died in Dayton, Ohio. Dunbar was born in Dayton in 1872, the son of a former slave. Although he was senior class poet at Dayton's Central High School and editor of the school newspaper and yearbook, Dunbar began his career as an elevator boy. In 1893, he compiled a book of his verse which he sold to passengers on his elevator, which he operated for four dollars a week. In 1895, he published *Majors and Minors,* which received a very favorable review by William Dean Howells in *Harper's Weekly.* That review brought Dunbar national recognition. In the following year, Dunbar's *Lyrics of Lowly Life* appeared. Many of these earlier works were published by Orville and Wilbur Wright who were experimenting with printing newspapers on a homemade press. In 1897, Dunbar became an assistant at the Library of Congress, a position which he held only a year. During the last ten years of his life, Dunbar produced eleven volumes of verse, three novels, and five collections of short stories. Critics generally agree that Dunbar's best work is his poetry, particularly those written in Negro dialect. Despite his midwestern origins, Dunbar's poems dealt nostalgically with the pathos and humor of the Old South. The *Encyclopaedia Britannica* for 1911 described Dunbar's poetry "as a distinct contribution to American literature, and entitles the author to be called preeminently the poet of his race in America." William Dean Howells considered him to be the first Afro-American to feel an aesthetic appreciation of the life of his people and to express it lyrically. Dunbar's biographer, Benjamin Brawley, observed that Dunbar "soared above race and touched the heart universal. He came on the scene at a time when America was being launched on the machine age and when the country was beset with problems. . . . In a world of discord, he dared to sing his song about nights bright with stars, about the secret of the wind and the sea, and the answer one finds beyond the years. Above the dross and strife of the day, he asserted the right to live and love and be happy. That is why he was so greatly beloved and why he will never grow old."

No black writer before him had been so widely hailed by white and black Americans. The conflict between Dunbar's genius and the limitations of

American racism probably drove him to drink. Whiskey and tuberculosis brought him down at age thirty-four.

April 13. Serious racial disturbances involving white civilians and black soldiers occurred at Brownsville, Texas. The black soldiers who had retaliated for racial slurs and taunts by the whites, which resulted in the deaths of at least three white men, were dishonorably discharged by President Theodore Roosevelt. Roosevelt's handling of the matter convinced many blacks that there could be no appeal to him in the wake of increasing anti-Negro assaults. When Congress met in December of 1906, some Northerners, led by Senator Joseph B. Foraker of Ohio, protested that a full investigation and trial should have preceded the President's action. In January, 1907, such an investigation was launched by the Senate. After several months, the Senate Committee's majority report upheld the President's decision. Finally, in 1909 Senator Foraker won approval for a court of inquiry to pass on the cases of the discharged soldiers and to allow reenlistment for those deemed eligible.

June. John Hope assumed the presidency of Morehouse College. Hope, one of the most militant of early black educators, was the school's first Negro president and was the catalyst behind many of the programs which resulted in the institutions's favorable reputation. Hope was born in Augusta, Georgia, in 1868 to prosperous parents, a white father and mulatto mother. His relatively secure childhood was shaken by his father's death in 1876 and the subsequent loss of much of the family's wealth at the hands of callous executors and prejudiced whites. In the same year, Hope witnessed a violent racial clash in Atlanta. This incident, together with the infamous Atlanta riot of 1906, probably influenced his militancy. Hope denounced Booker T. Washington's "Atlanta Compromise" address and was the only black college president to join the militant Niagara Movement. Likewise, Hope was the only college administrator to attend the founding meeting of the NAACP in 1909 (see entry dated February 12, 1909). Hope was a founder and later president of the South's first biracial reform group, the Commission on Interracial Cooperation (the forerunner of the Southern Regional Council). The group was organized in 1919, and Hope assumed leadership in 1932. Hope was also president of Atlanta University from 1929 until his death in 1936.

September 22-24. A major race riot in Atlanta, Georgia left twelve dead. An irresponsible press and attempts to disfranchise blacks had increased racial tensions in the city. On September 22, newspapers reported four successive assaults on white women by black men. Many of the city's whites, joined by rural-folk in town for Saturday shopping, formed Negro-seeking mobs bent upon retaliation. Blacks who sought to arm themselves in defense were quickly arrested. The state of panic existed for several days until a group of level-headed blacks and whites could meet and plead for calm. The Atlanta Civic

League, an interracial organization dedicated to racial harmony, was formed in the wake of the riot.

1907

————. Alain Locke, one of the most brilliant of American Negro intellectuals, received a Rhodes Scholarship. No other Afro-American won this distinguished academic honor for more than half a century. Locke was born in Philadelphia in 1886. He obtained his Ph.D. degree from Harvard University in 1918. As a Rhodes Scholar, Locke studied at Oxford University in England from 1907 to 1910. He continued his studies at the University of Berlin from 1910 to 1911 and became Professor of Philosophy at Howard University in 1912, a position he held until his retirement in 1953. Locke published *Race Contacts and Interracial Relations* in 1916. His fame as a literary and art critic and interpreter of black culture rests largely on his anthology *The New Negro* (1925), a seminal work about the Harlem Renaissance. Locke died in 1954 prior to completing *The Negro in American Culture*. This work was completed by Margaret Just Butcher and published in 1956.

1908

August 14-19. A serious racial disturbance occurred in Springfield, Illinois. The shock of the riot near Abraham Lincoln's home prompted concerned whites to call for a conference which led to the founding of the NAACP.

1909

February 12. The National Association for the Advancement of Colored People (NAACP), was founded in New York City. White progressives and black intellectuals were the group's first leaders, including Jane Addams, John Dewey, W.E.B. Du Bois, Mary White Ovington, and Oswald Garrison Villard. Moorfield Storey of Boston was named president. The NAACP was for many years the nation's preeminent civil rights organization.

April 6. Matthew H. Henson, a black servant, accompanied Commodore Robert E. Peary to the North Pole. Henson, a Washington, D.C. mulatto, received a modest education, worked as a cabin boy, then later as a stock boy in a Washington clothing store. There he met Peary and was hired as his servant. After sharing Peary's great feat of discovering the North Pole, Henson served for many years as a messenger in the New York Customs House. In 1945, he received a medal for "outstanding service to the government of the United States in the field of science."

Arctic explorer Matthew Henson.

1910

April. The National Urban League (NUL), an organization designed to assist Southern black emigrants to the North, was established in New York City. It soon became a social relief organization for black urban dwellers in the North, West, and later in the South.

———. The NAACP's official organ, *The Crisis*, began publication. W.E.B. Du Bois was its first editor.

1912

September 27. A revolution in the music world occurred when W. C. Handy published his blues composition, "Memphis Blues."

1913

March 10. Harriet Tubman, "the Moses of her People," died in Auburn,

New York. (See entry dated July, 1849, for further information about Tubman.)

1915

June 21. The United States Supreme Court, in *Guinn v. the United States,* outlawed the "Grandfather Clauses" used by Southern states to deny blacks the right to vote. The Grandfather Clauses, which originated in Louisiana, was actually part of the state constitution. They restricted the ballot to descendants of the qualified voters as of January 1, 1867—prior to Black Reconstruction.

September 9. Professor Carter G. Woodson founded the Association for the Study of Negro Life and History (ASNLH). The group stood virtually alone for a time in attempting to properly portray the role of the Afro-American in United States history. Woodson, the son of former slaves, held a doctorate from Harvard University. He is sometimes called "the father of modern Negro historiography," having edited for many years the *Journal of Negro History* and other publications of the ASNLH, and having published a number of works on the Negro.

November 14. Booker T. Washington, the most noted black American between Frederick Douglass and Martin Luther King, Jr., died at Tuskegee Institute. He was succeeded by Robert Russa Moton of Hampston Institute. Moton was born in Virginia shortly after the Civil War. He was reared as a houseboy on a Virginia plantation, receiving secret instruction from his literate mother. Moton taught at Hampton Institute, his alma mater, before assuming the presidency at Tuskegee. He was one of the members of the Committee on the Welfare of Negro Troops sponsored by the Federal Council of Churches during World War I. While continuing, in the main, Washington's policies and practices at Tuskegee, Moton expanded the academic-classical curriculum at the institution and fought the efforts of white bigots to prevent black control of the Tuskegee Veterans Hospital.

————. The NAACP led the black outcry against the showing of D. W. Griffith's controversial film, *Birth of a Nation.* The film, based on the racist writings of Thomas Dixon, was the most technologically advanced motion picture produced at that time. It told an obviously distorted story of emancipation, Reconstruction, and black immorality, and glorified such anti-Negro organizations as the Ku Klux Klan.

————. Bishop Henry McNeal Turner, black Pan-Africanist leader and A.M.E. churchman, died. Turner was born free in Abbeville, South Carolina, in 1833. At an early age he was hired out to work in the field with slaves. Turner's first learning came from a white playmate. Making his way to Baltimore at age fifteen, Turner worked as a messenger and a handyman at a medical school, where he had access to books and magazines. He continued his self-education at the school until an Episcopal bishop consented to teach him. This was one of the influences which led Turner into the church, where he became an A.M.E. minister. During the Civil War, President Lincoln appointed Turner as Chaplain of the 54th Massachusetts Negro regiment. After the war, he worked with the Freedmen's Bureau in Georgia and became actively involved in Republican politics. Turner served in the Georgia constitutional convention of 1868 and was elected to the state legislature. Turner vehemently opposed the successful attempt of white Georgia lawmakers to expel the Black Reconstruction legislators. These and other experiences convinced him that the black man had no future in the United States. Turner became a colonizationist and Pan-Africanist. He was one of the sponsors of an ill-fated expedition of approximately two hundred blacks to Liberia in 1878. In spite of the failure of this venture, Turner continued his support of colonization. Prior to his death in 1915, Turner also served as director of the A.M.E. publishing house, editor of denominational periodicals, and chancellor of Morris Brown College, an A.M.E. school located in Atlanta, Georgia.

————. The war-time migration of Southern blacks to Northern industrial centers began. Millions of blacks left the South for better economic and social security.

1917

April 16. The United States entered World War I. Approximately 300,000 blacks served during this conflict; 1,400 blacks were commissioned as officers. Three Negro regiments received the *Croix de guerre* for valor. Several individual blacks were decorated for bravery.

July 1-3. A serious race riot occurred in East St. Louis, Illinois. At least forty blacks were killed, and martial law was declared. The riot resulted from the employment of blacks in a factory which held a contract with the federal government. In one of the most tragic incidents, a small black child was shot down and then thrown into a burning building. The Germans seized upon the riot in their campaign to attract Negro sentiment in the World War.

July 28. Approximately 10,000 Negroes participated in a silent march down Fifth Avenue in New York City to protest racial oppression. The march, organized by the NAACP, was largely motivated by the East St. Louis riot. The protestors asked for prayer for East St. Louis, and asked the President "Why not make America safe for Democracy?"

August 23. A serious disturbance between black soldiers and white civilians erupted in Houston, Texas. Two blacks and seventeen whites were killed. Thirteen blacks were later executed for participating in the melee.

November 5. Emmett J. Scott, former secretary to Booker T. Washington, was appointed special assistant to the Secretary of War. Scott was to serve as "confidential advisor in matters affecting the interests of . . . Negroes of the United States and the part they are to play in connection with the present war." Specifically, Scott was to work for nondiscriminatory application of the Selective Service Act; to formulate plans to build up morale among blacks, soldiers, and civilians; and to investigate complaints of unfair treatment of blacks. He also disseminated news concerning black soldiers as well as various related activities on the home front. In June, 1918, Scott called a conference of approximately thirty black newspaper publishers who pledged their support of the American war effort, but denounced anti-Negro violence and discrimination at home. The coalition also called for the recruitment of black Red Cross nurses, asked for the appointment of a black war correspondent, and requested the return of black Colonel Charles Young to active duty. Most of these requests were granted.

————. The Supreme Court, in *Buchanan v. Warley,* ruled unconstitutional a Louisville, Kentucky law which forbade blacks and whites from residing in the same block.

————. Harry T. Burleigh was awarded the Spingarn Medal, the NAACP's highest honor, for excellence in the field of creative music. Burleigh was born in

"Fighting 369th" Regiment marches up New York City's Fifth Avenue after return home.

Erie, Pennsylvania in 1866. Although he demonstrated an aptitude for music as a child, he did not receive formal training until many years later. In 1892, Burleigh began his studies at the National Conservatory of Music in New York, where he majored in orchestral as well as vocal music. During his sophomore year, Burleigh studied under the famous Czech composer Antonin Dvořák, who took the young black student as a protégé. Two years after entering the conservatory, Burleigh was well on his way in a singing career. He became the first black soloist at St. George's Episcopal Church in New York and at the Temple Emanu-El. His European tours included a command performance before King Edward VII in England. In his senior year, Burleigh became an instructor of voice at the Conservatory, a position he held for two years after his graduation.

Around 1900, Burleigh began to shift his attention from singing to composing. His first compositions were sentimental ballads; then he branched out into choral pieces, spirituals, and miscellaneous works. Among his better known compositions are "Six Plantation Melodies for Violin and Piano" (1901), "Southland Sketches" (1916), "The Prayer" (1915), "Little Mother of Mine" (1917), "Deep River" (1916), and "The Lovely Dark and Lonely One" (1935). Contemporary critics lauded Burleigh's "imagination" and his "masterly musicianship." Of his spiritual compositions, Burleigh wrote: "My desire was to preserve them in harmonies that belong to modern methods of tonal progression without robbing the melodies of their racial flavor." His determination "to capture the spirit of Negro folksong in composed music," according to Eileen Southern, "makes him a true disciple of his teacher, Dvořák. It was as an arranger of spirituals for the solo voice that Burleigh made a unique contribution to the history of American music."

In addition to the Spingarn Medal, Burleigh was the recipient of honorary degrees from Atlanta University and Howard University. The Harry T. Burleigh Association, a black performing company, was founded in his honor. Burleigh died in 1949.

Chapter 5
Between War and Depression, 1918-1932

1918

February 19-21. The First Pan-African Congress, led by W.E.B. Du Bois, met in Paris. The Congress met at the same time as the Paris Peace Conference, which ended World War I. There were about sixty delegates, including West Indians, Africans, and American blacks. The meeting focused attention on the fact that blacks all over the world were materially interested in the Paris Conference and specifically how they might benefit from it—the democracy for which many of them fought, they now said, should indeed become a reality. While this Congress accomplished very little, it stimulated subsequent and more fruitful assemblages of black people in later years.

July 13-October 1. Major race riots occurred across the nation in what James Weldon Johnson called the "Red Summer." More than 25 riots left over 100 people dead and more than 1,000 wounded. Federal troops had to suppress the disorders in some areas. Washington, D.C., Chicago, Illinois, and Longview, Texas were among the scenes of the disturbances.

July 25-29. Serious racial disturbances occurred at Chester and Philadelphia, Pennsylvania, with approximately ten killed and more than sixty injured.

July 29. The National Liberty Congress of Colored Americans asked Congress to make lynching a federal crime.

———. Eighty-three lynchings were recorded during the year.

1920

August 1-2. The national convention of the Universal Negro Improvement Association (UNIA), met in New York City. Marcus Garvey, the founder of the organization, spoke to approximately 25,000 blacks during a rally at Madison Square Garden. Garvey-type black nationalism was reaching its zenith. Garvey had begun his organization in his native Jamaica in 1914. In 1916 he arrived in the United States to organize a New York chapter of UNIA. By the middle of 1919 there were thirty branches of the organization in the United States, principally in the Northern ghettoes. Garvey founded a newspaper, the *Negro World,* to disseminate his ideas of race pride and to promote his back-to-Africa stance. His other auxiliary organizations included the Universal Black Cross Nurses, the Universal African Motor Corps, the Black Star Steamship Line, and the Black Eagle Flying Corps. In 1921 Garvey formally organized the Empire of Africa and appointed himself Provisional President. He appealed, unsuccessfully, to the League of Nations for permission to settle a colony in Africa and negotiated towards that end with Liberia. After these failures, he began planning a military expedition to drive the white imperialists out of Africa. This campaign, however, was never launched. In 1923 Garvey was arrested for mail fraud in his attempts to raise money for his steamship line.

————. Robert Nathaniel Dett, black composer, arranger, and conductor,

Marcus Garvey

was awarded the Bowdoin Prize by Harvard University for an essay entitled "The Emancipation of Negro Music." Dett was born in 1882 in the community of Drummondville, Quebec, which had been established by fugitive slaves before the Civil War. Inspired as a child by the Negro spirituals, Dett studied music at the American Conservatory of Music in Chicago, Columbia University, Harvard University, the Oberlin Conservatory, the Oliver Willis Halstead Conservatory in Lockport, New York, and the University of Pennsylvania. During his early career, Dett performed as a concert pianist while teaching and engaging in further study. Dett taught at Lane College, Texas (1908-11), Lincoln University in Missouri (1911-13), Hampton Institute in Virginia (1913-31), Sam Houston College in Texas (1935-37), and at Bennett College in North Carolina (1937). Under the leadership of Dett, the Hampton Institute Choir became internationally known, giving performances at the Library of Congress, Carnegie Hall in New York, and Boston's Symphony Hall. In 1930, the choir toured seven European nations. Meanwhile, Dett took some time off to study with Arthur Foote in Boston and with Nadia Boulanger at the American Conservatory at Fontainebleau. Among Dett's many notable compositions are *Magnolia* (five piano suites, 1912), *Music in the Mine* (1916), *The Chariot Jubilee* (oratorio, 1921), *Enchantment* (1922), and *The Ordering of Moses* (1937). In addition to the Bowdoin Prize, Dett was the recipient of the Francis Boot Prize for composition, the Palm and Ribbon Award of the Royal Belgian Band, the Harmon Foundation Award, and honorary degrees from the Eastman School of Music, Oberlin, and Harvard Universities. Dett died in 1943.

1921

————. Eubie Blake, along with Noble Sissle, produced the historic musical *Shuffle Along*. Blake was born in Baltimore in 1883. He began practicing music at age six, and during his adolescent years he played music in department stores and in "bawdy" and "sporting" houses. In 1899, Blake composed his first ragtime piece, "The Charleston Rag." Among his other compositions are "Chevy Chase" (1914), "Fitz Water" (1914), and "Bugle Call Rag" (1926). Even as late as 1970, Blake was still composing rags. He is often called "the leading exponent of the eastern school" of ragtime music.

1922

January 8. Colonel Charles R. Young, one of the highest ranking blacks in the United States Army, died in Nigeria. Young, the son of a former slave-soldier in the Union Army, was born in Kentucky. He entered West Point Academy in 1884, served with distinction in Cuba, Haiti, and Mexico, but always labored under the burdens of racial discrimination. During World War I, Young was called up for a physical examination and then retired due to "poor health." This action was an apparent subterfuge to prevent Young's promotion to General. After protests by blacks, (see entry dated November 5, 1917), Young was recalled, but was assigned only to relatively obscure duty in Illinois and in Liberia.

1922-1929. The Harlem Renaissance, a period of great achievement in Afro-American art and literature, begins. The writings of such poets as Claude McKay, Langston Hughes, Countee Cullen, James Weldon Johnson, and the novelists Walter White, Wallace Thurman, Nella Larsen, and Zora Neale Hurston, among others, drew critical attention and popular sentiments from both blacks and whites.

During this period, James Weldon Johnson and Alain Locke edited important anthologies of the works of black writers, *The Book of American Negro Poetry* (1925) and *The New Negro* (1925), respectively. Claude McKay, the first important figure in the Harlem Renaissance, was noted for his *Harlem Shadows* (1922), a collection of bitter but eloquent poems on the condition of the Negro in post-war America. Among Countee Cullen's better-known works was his volume of poems entitled *Color.* Its appearance in 1925 pushed the Harlem Renaissance to a new high.

Other notable works published during this period were poet Langston Hughes's *The Weary Blues* (1926), Walter White's *The Fire in the Flint* (1926), Nella Larsen's *Quicksand* (1928) and *Passing* (1929), and Wallace Thurman's *The Blacker the Berry* (1929).

1923

September 4. George Washington Carver of Tuskegee Institute received the Spingarn Medal, the NAACP's highest award, for distinguished research in agricultural chemistry. In 1939, Carver was awarded the Roosevelt Medal for distinguished achievement in science. Carver was born a slave in Diamond Grove, Missouri in 1864. He attended undergraduate school in Iowa and earned a Master of Science degree from Iowa State College. In 1896, Carver was appointed to the faculty of Tuskegee Institute, where he began a program of research in soil conservation and crop diversification. Often called by fellow blacks "the greatest chemist in the world," Carver's scientific fame rests largely in the 400 different products he produced from the peanut, potato, and pecan. He was a Fellow of the Royal Academy of England. A foundation and a museum have been established in his honor at Tuskegee Institute, where he died in 1943.

October 24. Black migration to the North continued as the Department of Labor estimated that some half-million Negroes left the South within the last year.

————. Garrett A. Morgan, a black inventor, developed the automatic traffic light. Morgan had earlier invented the gas mask used by American troops during World War I. The black inventor was born in Paris, Tennessee in 1875. In 1895 he moved to Cleveland, Ohio, where he produced in 1901 a belt fastener for sewing machines. In 1914 Morgan won the First Grand Prize at the Second International Exposition of Sanitation and Safety for the invention of a smoke inhalator. This inhalator was used in a successful rescue of workers trapped in a tunnel under Lake Erie in 1916. The city of Cleveland awarded Morgan a gold medal following the rescue. The patent rights to the traffic light were sold by Morgan to the General Electric Company for $40,000. Morgan died in 1963.

1924

July 1. Roland Hayes, who was born in a Georgia cabin in 1887, was named a soloist with the Boston Symphony Orchestra. Earlier, he had received the Spingarn Medal for "so finely" interpreting the beauty of the Negro folk song.

1925

January 10. Adelbert H. Roberts was elected to the Illinois state legislature—the first black to serve in a state assembly in at least twenty-five years.

May 8. The Brotherhood of Sleeping Car Porters, the trailblazing black labor union, was organized by A. Philip Randolph. Randolph, often called the dean of Negro leaders, was reared in Florida. He was the son of a minister and a seamstress, both of whom were former slaves. Randolph attended Cookman Institute in Florida and City College in New York. His intellectual interests and his practical experiences in Harlem evoked an intense hatred of racial bias and a zeal for economic and social justice. He joined the Socialist Party and attempted to organize black students and workers. Randolph founded the socialist periodical the *Messenger,* which became one of the best magazines in the history of black journalism. In later years he was prominent as an opponent of American intervention in foreign wars; an outspoken opponent of military segregation; the central figure in the 1941 "March on Washington"; a humanitarian; and a consultant to Presidents on matters of civil rights.

1926

June 30. James Weldon Johnson was honored for his careers as an executive of the NAACP, a member of the United States Consul, editor, and poet by the NAACP in New York City. Johnson was born in Florida in 1871 and was educated there. He continued his education at Atlanta University, New York City College, and Columbia University. Johnson began his professional life in Florida where he worked as a teacher, journalist, and lawyer before joining his brother J. Rosamond in New York as a writer of musical comedies. Johnson is best known as a writer of prose and verse; his most notable works include *God's Trombones* (1927), *The Book of American Negro Poetry* (1925), *Black Manhattan* (1930), *The Autobiography of an Ex-Colored Man* (1912), a novel, and his own autobiography, *Along This Way* (1933). Johnson's poem "Lift Every Voice and Sing," when set to music by his brother, became known as "the Negro National Anthem." The song still retains that characterization among blacks today. In New York, Johnson moved widely in interracial circles. These affiliations, along with his success as a writer and a diplomat and his "moderate" opposition to racial discrimination, made him a likely choice as the NAACP's first executive secretary. In this capacity, Johnson led the campaign to outlaw lynching in the United States, culminating in the Dyer anti-lynching bill of 1921 (which passed the House but died in the Senate). Before his death in 1938, Johnson also devoted a part of his career to a teaching assignment at Fisk University in Nashville, Tennessee. He has been called an "American Renaissance Man" in recognition of his multiple talents. (See Appendix for lyrics to Johnson's "Lift Every Voice and Sing.")

1927

March 7. The United States Supreme Court, in the case of *Nixon v. Herndon*, struck down a Texas law which excluded blacks from the Democratic primaries in that state. Texas managed, however, to erect new defenses against Negro voting. (See Appendix for an excerpt taken from *Nixon v. Herndon.*)

December. Marcus Garvey, after having been convicted in 1925 for mail fraud, was released from the Atlanta Federal Penitentiary and deported as an undesirable alien. Garvey was unsuccessful in keeping his black nationalist movement alive while in prison. (See also entry dated August 1-2, 1920, for further information about Garvey.)

1928

November 6. Oscar De Priest was elected congressman from Illinois. De Priest, the son of former slaves, was born in Alabama shortly after the Civil War. He was reared in Kansas, where he worked as a painter, but after moving to Chicago he became involved in real estate and politics, becoming Chicago's first black alderman. De Priest's activities with Republican ward politics was soon rewarded by local politicians with his nomination for Congress in 1928. When he first assumed office, some blacks considered him as an unscrupulous politician and an accommodationist on racial matters, but at the end of three terms in office he had won a reputation for outspoken militancy. De Priest was the first black from a non-Southern state to sit in Congress and the only Afro-American to serve in that body since George White left in 1901.

1929

January 15. Martin Luther King, Jr., called by many the greatest American of the twentieth century, was born in Atlanta. King's parents were members of the city's "black establishment," his father being one of the city's leading Negro ministers and his mother the daughter of a prominent preacher. King was educated at Morehouse College, Crozier Theological Seminary, and Boston University. He began his ministerial career as pastor of the Dexter Avenue Baptist Church in Montgomery, Alabama in 1954.

October 29. The New York stock market crashed, signaling the beginning of the Great Depression. During the Depression blacks complained that they were "the last to be hired and the first to be fired."

————. Albon Holsey of the National Negro Business League organized the Colored Merchants Association in New York. The group planned to establish stores and to buy their merchandise cooperatively. Blacks were urged to make their purchases from these merchants as a means for providing jobs for members of the race. The Depression forced the stores out of business within two years. By 1931, the "Jobs-for-Negroes" movement began in earnest in St. Louis, Missouri. The St. Louis chapter of the National Urban League launched a boycott against a white chain store whose trade was almost exclusively black but employed very few Negroes. This movement spread to Chicago, Cleveland, New York City, Pittsburgh, and other major cities. New York became the center of an intensive, sometimes bitter, campaign. The Citizens League for Fair Play launched a drive in 1933 to persuade white merchants to employ black sales clerks. They adopted as their motto: "Don't Buy Where You Can't Work." The campaign led to the employment of hundreds of blacks in Harlem stores and with public utility companies.

————. Lynchings were reported to be declining in the United States; ten were recorded for the year.

————. The New York City Board of Education issued a directive that the word "negro" should be spelled with a capital "N."

1930

March 31. President Hoover appointed Judge John J. Parker of North

Carolina, a known racist, to the Supreme Court. The NAACP launched a successful campaign against Parker's confirmation.

June 7. Respecting Negro demands, the *New York Times* announced that the "N" in the word "Negro" would be henceforth capitalized in its pages.

June 22. Mary McLeod Bethune, a Florida Afro-American educator, feminist leader, and civil rights spokesperson, was named one of America's fifty leading women by the historian Ida Tarbell. Bethune was born in Maysville, South Carolina in 1875. She studied at Scotia Seminary in North Carolina and at the Moody Bible Institute in Chicago. In 1904, Bethune founded the Bethune-Cookman College at Daytona Beach, Florida. A recipient of the Medal of Merit from the Republic of Haiti and the NAACP Spingarn Award, Bethune was president of the National Council of Negro Women and the Association for the Study of Negro Life and History. She was a principal advisor as well as a friend to President and Mrs. Franklin D. Roosevelt.

1931

April 6. Nine black youths accused of raping two white women of dubious reputation on a freight train went on trial for their lives in Scottsboro, Alabama. The case became a *cause célèbre*, with Afro-American organizations, liberal whites, and the Communist Party all vying to defend "the Scottsboro Boys." The defendants were hastily convicted, but by 1950 all were free by parole, appeal, or escape.

August 4. Daniel Hale Williams, pioneer heart surgeon and founder of Provident Hospital, a predominately black institution, died in Chicago. Williams was born in Philadelphia to a black woman and a white man. He received a medical education at the Chicago Medical College through the generosity of a former surgeon on General Ulysses S. Grant's staff. In 1913, Williams became the first black member of the American College of Surgeons. After withdrawing from Provident Hospital because of internal bickerings, Williams became the only black doctor on the staff of Chicago's St. Luke Hospital. His withdrawal from Provident Hospital and his marriage to a white woman subjected him to bitter attacks from fellow blacks in the latter years of his life. Prior to his death, Williams was seen as a bitter and frustrated man.

1932

November. Franklin D. Roosevelt was elected President of the United States, promising a "New Deal" to all in the Depression-ridden nation.

1932-1940. Faced with agricultural distress and racial oppression in the South, a new wave of black migration began into the major industrial centers of the North in search of economic and social opportunities.

Chapter 6
A New Deal—A New Life? 1933-1940

1933

March 15. The NAACP opened its attack on segregation and discrimination in American schools and colleges. On behalf of Thomas Hocutt, the NAACP sued the University of North Carolina. A black educator responsible for certifying the academic record of the applicant refused to do so, and the case was lost.

1934

November 7. Arthur L. Mitchell, a Democrat, defeated Republican Congressman Oscar de Priest of Chicago, becoming the pioneer black member of his party in Congress. Mitchell, like his predecessor, was born in Alabama to former slaves. He received his education at Tuskegee Institute, where he was Booker T. Washington's office boy, and at Talladega College in Alabama. Mitchell taught school in rural Alabama and served as an assistant law clerk in Washington. When he moved to Chicago, he became involved in Republican ward politics, but joined the Democrats with the shifting black party preference in the Depression years. In Congress, Mitchell professed to be a "moderate," thus drawing the ire of the black press and the NAACP. He did, however, sponsor the long and costly suit that led to an end to Jim Crowism in Pullman railroad cars. Mitchell served four terms in Congress. (See also entry dated April 28, 1941.)

———. Elijah Muhammad succeeded W. D. Fard as leader of the Black Muslim movement in the United States. Muhammad was born Elijah Poole in

81

Sandersville, Georgia in 1897. His father was a Baptist preacher, sawmill worker, and tenant farmer. Muhammad was a deeply religious and race conscious youth. While he was employed as a laborer in Georgia in 1923, a white employer cursed him and he decided to move North. While living on relief in Detroit during the Depression, Muhammad came under the influence of W. D. Fard or Wallace Fard Muhammad, a mysterious black silk peddler, who had been teaching blacks that they were members of a superior race, descendants of Muslims from Afro-Asia. Fard claimed to be a messenger from Allah sent to reclaim his lost people, to save them from the inferior race of "white devils" who had made their lives so miserable. Christianity, he asserted, was a false religion used by white people to keep blacks in subjection. Elijah Poole soon became Fard's closest associate and when Fard mysteriously disappeared in 1934, Poole, now known as Elijah Muhammad, took control of the group as "The Messenger of Allah to the Lost-Found Nation of Islam in the Wilderness of North America." Muhammad and his followers refused to bear arms for the United States during World War II; Muhammad himself was convicted of encouraging resistance to the draft and served three and a half years of a five year sentence in a federal prison. He was released in 1946. Meanwhile, Muslim membership dropped from a high of about 8,000 under Fard's leadership to 1,000.

1935

June 25. Afro-Americans received an emotional boost when the boxer Joe Louis defeated Primo Carnera, a white man, at Yankee Stadium in New York. Louis then began his great boxing career in earnest. Louis (born Joe Louis Barrow) was born in Lafayette, Alabama in 1914. Shortly thereafter, his family moved to Detroit, Michigan where Louis attended the Duffield Elementary School for a short time. After leaving school, he worked in an automobile plant and, in his leisure time, boxed. Louis became the heavyweight champion of the world in 1937 and held the title until 1949, interrupting his career to serve in World War II. A series of unsuccessful marriages and business ventures left Louis nearly penniless after his retirement from the ring.

1936

July 3. John Hope, now president of Atlanta University, was honored in New York City by the NAACP for his achievements as an educational and civil rights leader. Hope was a founder of The Atlanta University Center which comprises Morehouse College, an undergraduate school for men; Spelman College, an undergraduate school for woman; and Atlanta University, a co-educational graduate school which was founded in 1929. In later years, three other black colleges in Atlanta: Clark, Morris Brown, and a theological

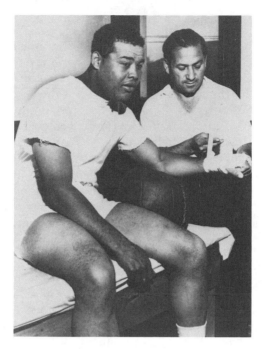

Boxing champion Joe Louis.

seminary (all co-educational), joined the complex, making it the largest educational center for Negroes in the world.

August 9. Afro-Americans reacted warmly to the news that Jesse Owens, a black track star, had won four gold medals at the Summer Olympics held in Berlin. Owens' first-place victories embarrassed Adolph Hitler, who championed the theory of Aryan racial superiority. Owens was born in Ohio in 1913. He began competing in track and field at the Fairmount Junior High School in Cleveland and continued through his years at Ohio State University. Owens was a student at Ohio State when he won the 100-meter dash, the 200-meter dash, the long jump, and anchored the victorious 400-meter relay at the 1936 Olympics. The Associated Press has designated Owens "the outstanding track athlete of the first 50 years of the 20th century."

December 8. The case of *Gibbs v. Board of Education* of Montgomery County, Maryland was filed by the NAACP. The decision set the precedent for equalizing the salaries of black and white school teachers.

————. President Franklin D. Roosevelt, continuing to organize his unofficial "Black Cabinet," appointed Mary McLeod Bethune director of the Division of Negro Affairs of the National Youth Administration. (See also entry dated June 22, 1930, for further information about Bethune.)

1937

March 26. William H. Hastie, a black lawyer, was confirmed as the first Afro-American federal judge. He served for two years on the District Court of the Virgin Islands. Hastie entered governmental service as an assistant solicitor in the Department of the Interior in the early part of the New Deal. His judicial appointment was supported by the NAACP and influential whites at the Harvard Law School. His nomination was approved over the vigorous opposition of Southern senators who labelled him a "leftist," primarily because of his support of civil rights activities. After his service in the Virgin Islands, Hastie returned to the Howard University Law School as its Dean, but was soon appointed to the "Black Cabinet" as a civilian aide to the Secretary of War by President Roosevelt. In 1941, Hastie resigned in protest against the failure of the War Department to act against segregation in the armed services.

June 22. Afro-Americans rejoiced as Joe Louis defeated James J. Braddock for the heavyweight championship of the world.

July 2. Walter F. White, an Atlanta-born writer and civil rights leader, was honored by the NAACP in New York City for his work as the organization's Executive Secretary, his investigations of lynchings, and his lobbying for a federal anti-lynching law. (In the latter instance, White continued the notable work of his predecessor, James Weldon Johnson, who actually persuaded Representative L. C. Dyer of Missouri to introduce an anti-lynching bill in the House in 1921. The bill passed in the House but was killed by a Southern-backed filibuster in the Senate.) White was successful in getting anti-lynching measures introduced in 1935 and 1940, but both died in the Senate. Although White, a black man, had blond hair and blue eyes, he totally identified himself with the black race after the 1906 Atlanta race riot. His pale complexion enabled him (with no threat of danger) to investigate atrocities against blacks in the South and later expose the perpetrators.

————. Issac Lane, Bishop and patriarch of the Colored Methodist Episcopal Church, and founder of Lane College in Tennessee, died. Lane was born a slave on a Tennessee plantation in 1834. While a slave, he was licensed to preach, but even after Emancipation, he had to supplement his income by raising cotton and selling firewood. Lane founded Lane College in 1882.

1938

December 12. In the case of *Missouri ex rel Gaines*, supported by the NAACP, the United States Supreme Court declared that states must provide equal, even if separate, educational facilities for blacks within their boundaries. The plaintiff, Lloyd Gaines, mysteriously disappeared following the Court's decision.

1939

March. Marian Anderson, whose voice Italian conductor Arturo Toscanini described as appearing once in a century, was refused permission to sing in Constitution Hall in Washington, D.C. by the Daughters of the American Revolution (DAR). Anderson, a black contralto from Philadelphia, had just completed a successful European tour. Eleanor Roosevelt, the nation's First Lady, resigned from the DAR in protest. The Secretary of Interior then provided the Lincoln Memorial for the Anderson concert, which drew an audience of 75,000 on Easter Sunday, 1939. Anderson was awarded the Spingarn Medal later in the year.

October 11. The NAACP Legal Defense and Educational Fund, pledging itself to an all-out war on discrimination, was organized. Charles H. Houston, a brilliant Amherst and Harvard-trained lawyer, spearheaded the effort to consolidate some of the nation's best legal talents in the fight against bias sanctioned by law.

1940

February. *Native Son,* the deeply-moving novel reciting the effects of racial oppression on black Americans, was published by Richard Wright and became a best-seller.

March. Black actress Hattie McDaniel was awarded an Academy Award for Best Performance by an Actress in a Supporting Role for her performance as "Mammy" in *Gone with the Wind,* becoming the first Negro ever to win an "Oscar." McDaniel also appeared in such films as *The Little Colonel* and *Showboat.*

April. The Virginia Legislature adopted black composer James A. Bland's "Carry Me Back to Ole Virginny" as the state song.

June 10. Marcus Garvey died in London. He was never able to revive his UNIA movement. (See also entry dated August 1-2, 1920 and December, 1927, for further information about Garvey.)

October 16. Benjamin O. Davis, Sr. was appointed brigadier general in the United States Army, becoming the highest ranking black officer in the armed services. Davis was born in Washington, D.C. in 1877 and studied at Howard University. He entered the Army as a first lieutenant in 1898 and served with the 8th Infantry during the Spanish-American War. Prior to the Second World War, Davis saw service in the Philippines, Liberia, and in Wyoming. He also taught military science at Wilberforce University in Ohio and Tuskegee Institute. In World War II, he served in the European Theater of Operations

*Hattie McDaniel receives an Academy Award for her perform-
ance in* Gone with the Wind, *1940.*

as an advisor on problems of black servicemen. He helped to implement the desegregation of armed forces facilities in Europe. At the time of his retirement in 1948, Davis was an assistant to the inspector general in Washington, D.C. His awards and decorations include the Distinguished Service Medal, the Bronze Star, the Croix de Guerre with Palm, and an honorary doctorate from Atlanta University. Davis' son, Benjamin, Jr., also had a distinguished military career.

Generals Benjamin O. Davis, Sr. (left) and George S. Patton.

Chapter 7
War Again, 1941-1945

1941

April 28. The Supreme Court ruled in a case brought by black Congressman Arthur Mitchell that separate railroad car facilities must be substantially equal.

June 18. Tuskegee scientist George Washington Carver was awarded an honorary Doctor of Science degree by the University of Rochester. (See also entry dated September 4, 1923, for further information about Carver.)

————. President Roosevelt held an urgent meeting with A. Philip Randolph, head of the Brotherhood of Sleeping Car Porters, and other black spokesmen, urging them to call off a march against employment discrimination and segregation in the national defense program scheduled for July 1. Randolph refused, and pledged that 100,000 Negroes would march.

June 25. President Franklin Roosevelt issued an Executive Order forbidding racial and religious discrimination in defense industries and government training programs. A. Philip Randolph then called off the march on Washington.

July 19. President Roosevelt established a Fair Employment Practices Committee to monitor discrimination against Negroes in defense industries. Blacks hailed the Committee and the preceding Executive Order 8802 of June 25 as revolutionary developments, perhaps the most significant executive action affecting them since the issuance of the Emancipation Proclamation. They were soon disappointed, however, when discrimination continued in spite of the Committee. The Committee became entangled in bureaucratic inefficiency and politics, and faced opposition in the South.

August 6. The first in a series of serious racial disturbances involving black soldiers, and white and black soldiers and civilians, occurred aboard a bus in North Carolina.

December 7. The Japanese attacked Pearl Harbor. President Roosevelt prepared to ask for a declaration of war. Doris (Dorie) Miller, a twenty-two year-old black messman aboard the USS *Arizona*, downed four Japanese planes with a machine gun after having moved his captain from the bridge to a place of greater safety. The next year, Admiral Chester W. Nimitz presented the Navy Cross to Miller. In 1943, Miller, a native of Waco, Texas, was listed as missing in action, and presumed dead, in the Pacific.

————. The United States Army established a school for black pilots at Tuskegee, Alabama. Some blacks opposed the establishment of segregated Air Force facilities, but most others seemed to view the move as a forward step, since no training schools had hitherto existed. While the pilots began their work at Tuskegee, ground crews were prepared at Chanute Field in Illinois. By the end of the year the 99th Pursuit Squadron was ready for action. About 600 black pilots received their wings during World War II.

Admiral Chester W. Nimetz awards Dorie Miller the Navy Cross for heroism during the Japanese attack on Pearl Harbor.

1942

June. A group of blacks and whites organized the Congress of Racial Equality (CORE) in Chicago. They committed themselves to direct, non-violent action. Their first major effort was a sit-in against discrimination at a Chicago restaurant. The national CORE was founded in June, 1943.

September 29. The *Booker T. Washington,* commanded by a black captain, Hugh Mulzac, was launched at Wilmington, Delaware.

November 3. William L. Dawson, for two decades the dean of black congressmen, was elected to the United States House of Representatives from Chicago. Dawson was the son of an Alabama barber. He received his education at Fisk University and at a Chicago law school. After service in the First World War, Dawson opened a law practice in Chicago and became interested in politics. He began as a precinct worker and soon won favor with the Thompson Republican machine. He won five terms (1933-43) in the City Council as a Republican before switching to the Democrats with the New Deal tide. Dawson became an important member of the Kelly and Daley Democratic machines during the Second World War. He served as "ward boss" in five Chicago districts, precinct captain, committeeman, vice-chairman of the Cook County Democrats, and vice-chairman of the Democratic National Committee during his long political career. He won a reputation as a shrewd political strategist. Dawson did not run for reelection in 1970 and died a year later.

1943

January 5. George Washington Carver died in Tuskegee, Alabama. A museum and a foundation were established there in his honor. (See also entries dated September 4, 1923, and June 8, 1841, for further information about Carver.)

May 12-August 2. A series of serious race riots occurred across the nation; approximately forty people were killed. United States troops were called out in Mobile and Detroit (where the clashes threatened defense production). Other incidents were in Beaumont, Texas, and in Harlem, New York.

1944

April 3. The United States Supreme Court ruled in *Smith v. Allwright* that the white primary, which had excluded Negroes from voting in the South, was unconstitutional. The decision paved the way for blacks to participate in Southern politics for the first time since Reconstruction, although many states were to enact new extra-legal devices to frustrate Negro voting.

April 24. The United Negro College Fund (UNCF) was founded to coordinate the fund-raising efforts of the private all-black institutions of higher learning in the nation. Many of these colleges were facing extinction due to inadequate finances.

August 1. Adam Clayton Powell, Jr., one of the most flamboyant and controversial politicians of the twentieth century, was elected U.S. Congressman from Harlem becoming the first black member of the House of Representatives from the East. Powell was the son of a famous Harlem minister and political leader. After being expelled from City College of New York, Powell received his education at Colgate University. After graduation, he became a vociferous minister and a publisher, and led Harlem ministers in a jobs-for-Negroes campaign in the 1930s. Powell began his political career in 1941 as the first black member of the New York City Council.

Powell chaired the powerful Education and Labor Committee from 1960 to 1967. He became famous for his Powell Amendments which aimed to deny federal funds for the construction of segregated schools. In 1967 he ran afoul of congressional ethics and was temporarily denied his seat in the House. Reelected by Harlem in 1968 despite the Congress's censure, he was defeated in 1970 by another black, Charles Rangel.

August 20. The SS *Frederick Douglass,* the first ship named in honor of a black man, was lost in European waters.

December 13. Black women were permitted to enter the Women's Naval Corp (WAVES).

1945

March 12. New York established the first state Fair Employment Practices Commission to guard against discrimination in the workplace.

June. The United Nations Charter was approved in San Francisco. Several blacks, including Mary McLeod Bethune, W.E.B. Du Bois, Walter White, Ralph Bunche, and Mordecai Johnson, attended the San Francisco conference.

September 2. The Japanese surrendered and the Second World War ended. More than one million blacks served in the conflict, again distinguishing themselves for valor, and paying the supreme price for devotion to duty.

September 18. A huge anti-integration protest took place in the schools of Gary, Indiana. One thousand white students walked out of classes. This massive walk-out, unparalleled at the time, would be a precedent for the integration troubles of the next two to three decades.

Chapter 8
The Attack against Segregation, 1946-1954

1946

May 1. Former federal judge William H. Hastie was confirmed as governor of the Virgin Islands. Hastie became the only Afro-American to govern a U.S. state or territory since Reconstruction.

May 1. Emma Clarissa Clement, a black woman and mother of Atlanta University President Rufus E. Clement, was named "American Mother of the Year" by the Golden Rule Foundation. She was the first Afro-American woman to receive the honor.

June 3. The United States Supreme Court, in *Morgan v. Virginia,* prohibited segregation in interstate bus travel. The case originated when Irene Morgan, a black woman, was arrested and fined ten dollars for refusing to move to the back of a bus running from Gloucester County, Virginia to Baltimore. She appealed her conviction. In practice, the case had little immediate effect; buses in Southern states continued segregation practices.

June 10. Jack Johnson, the first great Afro-American boxing hero, died in Raleigh, North Carolina. Johnson, a former stevedore from Galveston, Texas, gained pugilistic fame when in 1908 he became the first nationally prominent black champion.

August 10-September 29. Serious racial disturbances occurred at Athens, Alabama, and Philadelphia, Pennsylvania; nearly one hundred blacks were injured.

December 5. President Truman appointed a national Committee on Civil Rights to investigate racial injustices and make recommendations.

1947

April 9. The Congress of Racial Equality (CORE) sent "freedom riders" into the South to test the Supreme Court's June 3, 1946 ban against segregation in interstate bus travel. CORE, which was organized in 1942, had pioneered the sit-in tactic at segregated restaurants, but gained national attention with the "Freedom Rider" demonstrations. CORE is best known for the wave of "freedom rides" which began in May, 1961. These latter demonstrations eventually led to a firm anti-discrimination policy in interstate transportation.

April 10. Jackie Robinson, a Georgia-born athlete, joined the Brooklyn Dodgers. Robinson, the first Negro baseball player in the major leagues, became an outstanding player and a hero in the eyes of many Afro-Americans. He was the first black player to enter the Baseball Hall of Fame.

June 27. Percy Julian, a distinguished black research chemist who made important breakthroughs in the area of human reproduction, was honored in New York by the NAACP. Julian, the son of a Montgomery, Alabama railway

Brooklyn Dodger Jackie Robinson scores a run against the Cincinnati Reds.

clerk, graduated Phi Beta Kappa from DePauw University and did advanced work at Harvard and the University of Vienna. He taught at Howard and DePauw universities before becoming an industrial chemist in Chicago. He later established his own company, Julian Laboratories, and earned a reputation for manufacturing soya products, hormones and pharmaceuticals.

September 1. Charles Spurgeon Johnson began his administration as president of Fisk University, becoming the first black man to head the Nashville institution. Johnson was born in Bristol, Virginia in 1893 and was educated at Virginia Union University and the University of Chicago. From 1917 to 1919, he directed the division of research for the Chicago Urban League; was an investigator of Negro migration for the Carnegie Foundation in 1918; and served on the Chicago Committee on Race Relations from 1923 to 1929. When Johnson assumed the presidency of Fisk University, he had already become an eminent sociologist and writer. He founded and edited the National Urban League's house organ, *Opportunity* magazine in 1923 and sponsored literary contests for young black writers during the Harlem Renaissance. Johnson's major published works include *Shadow of the Plantation* (1934), *The Collapse of Cotton Tenancy* (1934), *The Negro College Graduate* (1938), and *Growing Up in the Black Belt* (1941). Johnson died in 1956.

October 29. The President's Committee on Civil Rights formally condemned racial injustice in the United States in its celebrated report called "To Secure These Rights." The biracial group also called for a positive program to eliminate segregation from American life.

1948

January 12. The United States Supreme Court ruled in *Sipuel v. University of Oklahoma* that a state must provide legal education for blacks at the same time it is offered to whites. The case stemmed from the application which Ada Sipuel filed in 1946 to attend the University of Oklahoma Law School. Sipuel sought relief in state and then federal courts after the University denied her admission. Despite the Supreme Court's decision, Sipuel did not enter the University of Oklahoma immediately. There were further legal proceedings, but meanwhile the University of Oklahoma failed to establish a law school for blacks. Finally, Sipuel did enter the University of Oklahoma and became one of its first black law graduates.

March 31. Negro labor leader A. Philip Randolph told a committee of the United States Senate that he would counsel black youths to refuse military induction unless segregation and discrimination were prohibited in the selective service system. In June, Randolph formed the League for Non-Violent Civil Disobedience Against Military Segregation.

May 3. The United States Supreme Court decided in *Shelley v. Kraemer* that the courts could not enforce restrictive housing covenants. This case was brought to the Court by J. D. Shelley and his wife Ethel, who bought a home in St. Louis, Missouri in August, 1945. It was located on a tract whose owner in 1911 had signed an agreement under which it was restricted against use and occupancy by "people of the Negro or Mongolian Race." The agreement provided that failure to comply with this restriction should result in the owner's loss of title to the property. Mr. and Mrs. Louis Kraemer led other owners on the tract in a suit against the Shelleys, and won an order from the Missouri Supreme Court which forced the blacks out of their home and forfeited their title because of their violation of the agreement. In 1947, the Shelleys appealed to the United States Supreme Court.

June 9. A modern breakthrough in Negro office-holding occurred in the South when Oliver W. Hill was elected to the City Council in Richmond, Virginia.

July 14. Several Southern delegates walked out of the National Democratic Convention after a strong civil rights plank was adopted. South Carolinians and Mississippians were in the vanguard of the movement which formed the "Dixiecrat" party.

July 26. President Truman issued an Executive Order which called for equality of treatment and opportunity for all Americans in the armed forces. This order was to pave the way for the gradual elimination of discrimination in the armed services.

September 13. Professor Ralph J. Bunche, a noted black political scientist, was confirmed by the United Nations Security Council as temporary UN mediator in Palestine. Bunche was born in a Detroit ghetto and reared by relatives in Los Angeles after his parents' death. He was educated at the University of California and at Harvard. Bunche began his career as a teacher at Howard University. He identified early with civil rights programs and became a staunch supporter of the NAACP. After receiving the 1951 Nobel Peace Prize, Bunche was elected president of the American Political Science Association and a member of the Board of Overseers at Harvard University.

October 1. The Supreme Court of California ruled that the state law prohibiting interracial marriages was unconstitutional. Two decades later, the United States Supreme Court sanctioned interracial marriage in all the states.

1949

October 3. The pioneer black-owned radio station, WERD, began operations in Atlanta.

October 15. William H. Hastie, former District Court judge and governor in the Virgin Islands, was appointed a Judge of the Third U. S. Circuit Court of Appeals.

1950

April 1. Charles R. Drew, the pioneer Afro-American hematologist who was often called the father of the "Blood Bank," died in Burlington, North Carolina. Drew was born in Washington, D.C. in 1904. A football and track star at Amherst College, he studied medicine at McGill University in Canada. Drew began his research into the properties of blood plasma while holding a General Education Board Fellowship at the Columbia University Medical School. During World War II, after discovering the method of preserving blood plasma for emergencies, he organized a blood-collection system for the British and U.S. governments. Drew served as a member of the faculty of the Howard University Medical School and was chief surgeon and chief of staff at Howard's Freedman's Hospital at the time of his death. Previously, Drew was the recipient of the NAACP's Spingarn Medal for outstanding contributions to human welfare.

April 3. Carter G. Woodson, pioneer black historian and one of the founders of the Association for the Study of Negro Life and History, died in Washington, D. C. (See also entry dated September 9, 1915, for further information about Woodson.)

May 1. Gwendolyn Brooks was awarded the Pulitzer Prize for poetry, becoming the first Afro-American to have received the honor. Brooks was born in Topeka, Kansas in 1917, but was raised in Chicago, where she attended Wilson Junior College. Some of her earliest works appeared in the Chicago *Defender*. Brooks's later works have appeared in such periodicals as *Harper's*, *Common Ground*, *Mademoiselle*, *Poetry*, and the *Yale Review*. Her first volume of poetry, *A Street in Bronzeville* (1945), won the Merit Award from *Mademoiselle*. *Annie Allen* (1949), Brooks's second volume of verse, captured the Pulitzer Prize.

June 5. The United States Supreme Court ruled in *Sweatt v. Painter* that equality in education involved more than identical physical facilities. Heman Sweatt of Houston was ordered admitted to the Law School of the University of Texas, the largest university in the South. Sweatt never attended.

June 5. The Supreme Court decided in *McLaurin v. Oklahoma* that once a black student is admitted to a previously all-white school, no distinctions can be made on the basis of race. McLaurin had been segregated within the University of Oklahoma.

June 27. The United States intervened in the Korean conflict. Thousands of blacks were among those fighting in the war.

September 22. Ralph J. Bunche was awarded the Nobel Peace Prize for mediating the Palestinian dispute. (See also entry dated September 13, 1948, for further information about Bunche.)

1951

April 24. The University of North Carolina joined a growing list of major Southern and border state universities in admitting black students.

May 10. Blacks continued to make political advances in the South with the election of Z. Alexander Looby, an attorney, to the city council in Nashville, Tennessee.

May 24. The Municipal Appeals Court in Washington outlawed segregation in District of Columbia restaurants. Mary Church Terrell, the black feminist leader, had been in the vanguard of the local anti-segregation movement.

June 21. Pfc. William H. Thompson of Brooklyn, New York received the Congressional Medal of Honor posthumously for heroism in Korea, the first such award to an Afro-American since the Spanish-American War. Private Thompson died at his machine gun after having refused to withdraw in the face of overwhelming Communist forces.

July 12. Governor Adlai Stevenson of Illinois ordered the National Guard to suppress a riot in Cicero, Illinois, as more than 3,000 whites protested the attempt of a black family to occupy a home in an all-white neighborhood. The riot was called by some the worst racial disturbance in the North since 1919.

October 1. The last all-Negro army unit, the 24th Infantry, was deactivated by Congress.

December 25. A new era of racist assassinations began with the bombing death of Harry T. Moore, a Florida NAACP leader, in Mims, Florida.

———. Ralph J. Bunche, educator, diplomat, and Nobel Peace Prize winner, was appointed Undersecretary of the United Nations, the highest ranking American in the UN Secretariat.

———. The NAACP argued cases in Kansas and South Carolina against the discriminatory effects of public school segregation.

1952

January 12. The University of Tennessee became the latest major Southern university to admit black students.

December 7. The Southern Regional Council, an interracial civil rights reporting agency, announced that racist bombings were increasing in the nation. About forty had been reported since January, 1951.

December 30. Tuskegee Institute reported that no lynchings occurred during 1952, the first such year in the seventy-one years the Institute had kept such tabulations.

1953

April 5. Fisk University received a chapter of Phi Beta Kappa, the prestigious scholastic honor society. In later years, only two other all-black schools, Howard and Morehouse, were awarded chapters.

June 8. The United States Supreme Court affirmed the opinions of lower courts that restaurants in Washington, D.C. could not refuse to serve blacks. In the case of *District of Columbia v. John R. Thompson Co., Inc.*, the Court said that well-behaved blacks must be served. It upheld an 1873 law that made it a criminal act for proprietors of public eating places to refuse to serve any person solely because of race or color.

June 19. Negroes protesting discriminatory treatment began a bus boycott in Baton Rouge, Louisiana.

August 4. Another serious riot erupted in Illinois in protest of integrated housing. One thousand law enforcement officers were called into the Trumbull Park apartments in Chicago.

December 2. The latest instance of black progress in Southern politics came with the election of Rufus E. Clement, president of Atlanta University, to the Atlanta Board of Education.

December 31. Hulan Jack, a native West Indian, was inaugurated as president of the Borough of Manhattan, the highest municipal executive post to be held by an Afro-American to that time.

Chapter 9
"The Second Reconstruction," 1954-1964

1954

March 4. President Dwight D. Eisenhower named J. Ernest Wilkins Assistant Secretary of Labor. Wilkins, a Phi Beta Kappa member who earned a Ph.D. from the University of Chicago at age twenty, had the distinction of being the top-ranking black person in the executive branch of the federal government.

May 17. The United States Supreme Court, in *Brown v. Board of Education of Topeka, Kansas*, ruled unanimously that racial segregation in public schools was unconstitutional. This historic decision overruled the findings in *Plessy v. Ferguson* (see entry dated May 18, 1896) and declared that separate educational facilities were inherently unequal. The NAACP legal team, headed by chief council Thurgood Marshall, represented the plaintiffs in this case, which marked their greatest victory in a series of recent judicial triumphs. (See Appendix for an excerpt taken from *Brown v. Board of Education*.)

July 24. Mary Church Terrell, a longtime leader of black club women and civil rights activist, died in Washington, D. C. (See also entry dated July 21, 1896, for further information about Terrell.)

September 7-8. Massive school desegregation began in the public schools of Washington, D. C and Baltimore, Maryland. This was the first widespread school desegregation since the U. S. Supreme Court decision of May 17.

October 27. Benjamin O. Davis, Jr., commander of the 15th Air Force bombers in their important attacks on Romanian oil fields during World War II, became the first black general in the United States Air Force. Davis, the son of the Army's General B. O. Davis, Sr., was born in Washington, D.C. in 1912.

He was educated at Western Reserve University, the University of Chicago, and the United States Military Academy at West Point. In 1936, Davis became the fourth black man to graduate from West Point. He received his wings from the Tuskegee Advanced Flying School in 1942 and became commander of the 99th Fighter Squadron at the Army Air Field at Tuskegee. He was ordered to North Africa in 1943. During and since the Second World War, Davis has seen service in Italy, Korea (where he served as commander of the 51st Fighter-Interceptor Wing during the Korean conflict), Japan, Formosa, Germany, and several U.S. mainland installations. Davis's awards and decorations include the Distinguished Service Medal, the Silver Star, the Legion of Merit, and the Distinguished Flying Cross. (See also entry dated October 16, 1940.)

October 30. Desegregation of the United States Armed Forces was completed as the Defense Department announced the final abolition of all-Negro units.

November 2. Charles C. Diggs, Jr. was elected to the U. S. House of Representatives. The thirty-three-year-old Diggs, the first black congressman from Michigan, joined Congressman William Dawson of Chicago, who was reelected in 1954 for a seventh term, and Congressman Adam Clayton Powell, Jr. of Harlem, who won his sixth term in 1954. Diggs's election marked the first time in the twentieth century that as many as three blacks served in the United States Congress. All were Democrats.

1955

January 7. Negro contralto Marian Anderson made her debut as Ulrica in Giuseppe Verdi's *Un Ballo in Maschera* (*A Masked Ball*) at the Metropolitan Opera House in New York City. She was the first black singer in the company's history.

March 21. Walter F. White, the second Negro to serve as executive secretary of the NAACP and leader of the organization during most of its judicial triumphs, died in New York. (See also entry dated July 2, 1937, for further information about White.)

April 11. Roy Wilkins became the third executive secretary of the NAACP. Wilkins, a journalist, had served as editor of the NAACP's magazine, the *Crisis*, and as assistant executive secretary of the organization.

Wilkins, a native of St. Louis, Missouri, was born in 1901. He studied at the University of Minnesota at Duluth and was editor of the *University Daily* there. Racial violence during his student days influenced his decision to work actively against discrimination. Similar experiences in Kansas City, where Wilkins was managing editor of the *Kansas City Call*, further inspired him to seek a career fighting for equal justice. Wilkins joined the staff of the NAACP in 1931. Within the NAACP, he played a leading role, representing the interests of blacks in the Philadelphia transit strike in 1943; and presided over the NAACP's efforts to implement the *Brown* school desegregation decision of 1954.

May 18. Mary McCleod Bethune, noted black female educator and political leader, died in Daytona Beach, Florida. She was one of the founders of the Bethune-Cookman College. (See also entry dated June 22, 1930, for further information about Bethune.)

May 31. The United States Supreme Court decreed that its May 17, 1954 school desegregation decision should be implemented "with all deliberate speed." The vagueness of the phrase would permit school segregation to continue in the nation for several more decades.

August 28. Lynchings were renewed in the South with the brutal slaying of a fourteen-year-old Chicago youth, Emmett Till, in Money, Mississippi. Till was alleged to have made indecent advances toward a white woman.

November 7. The United States Supreme Court prohibited segregation in recreational facilities in a Baltimore, Maryland case.

November 25. The Interstate Commerce Commission (ICC) prohibited segregation in public vehicles operating in interstate travel. The order also extended to waiting rooms.

December 1. Rosa Parks, a black seamstress in Montgomery, Alabama, refused to surrender her seat when ordered by a local bus driver. Her arrest (for violating Jim Crow ordinances) led to a city-wide bus boycott by blacks which began on December 5. Despite terrorist attacks, including the bombing of the homes of boycott leaders, legal harassment, massive arrests, and civil suits, the boycott continued until December 13, 1956, when the United States Supreme Court ruled that segregation on public buses in Montgomery was illegal. Another significant result of the boycott movement was the emergence of Martin Luther King, Jr. as a national leader.

December 5. Two black labor leaders, A. Philip Randolph and Willard S. Townsend, were elected vice presidents of the AFL-CIO.

1956

January 30. The home of Dr. Martin Luther King, Jr., was bombed in Montgomery, Alabama.

February 3. The desegregation of major Southern universities continued with the admission of a black coed, Authurine Lucy, under court order, to the University of Alabama. Lucy was suspended after a February 7 anti-Negro riot

Police officer places a segregation sign in front of the Illinois Railroad Station in Jackson, Mississippi despite ICC ruling.

at the school, and later expelled on February 29 for making "false" and "outrageous" statements about the university officials.

April 11. Racial tensions in the South continued to be explosive as witnessed by an attack on the popular Negro singer Nat "King" Cole in Birmingham, Alabama.

June 30. Mordecai Johnson retired as president of Howard University. Johnson was born in Paris, Tennessee in 1890. He was educated at Morehouse College, the University of Chicago, the Rochester Theological Seminary, and Harvard University. Upon receiving a Master of Sacred Theology degree from Harvard in 1923, Johnson attracted national attention for a speech entitled "The Faith of the American Negro." After teaching at Morehouse and Howard, he was named the first black head of the latter institution in 1926. When Johnson assumed the presidency, Howard, often called "the capstone of Negro education," consisted of a cluster of unaccredited departments. In 1928 Johnson was successful in getting a Congressional act allocating annual appropriations for the support and development of Howard University. At Johnson's retirement, Howard had ten schools and colleges; was a fully accredited institution; had an enrollment of more than 6,000 students, a few of them whites; and its School of Medicine was producing about half of the black doctors in the United States. Johnson was succeeded by James M. Nabrit, Jr., a law professor and civil rights attorney.

August 30-September 17. Anti-Negro protests and violence accompanied efforts to desegregate schools in Mansfield, Texas; Clinton, Tennessee; and Sturgis and Clay, Kentucky.

November 13. The Supreme Court upheld the decision of a lower court outlawing segregation on buses in Montgomery, Alabama.

December 20-21. The Montgomery bus boycott ended. Public buses in Montgomery were desegregated.

December 25-26. The home of black minister and civil rights activist F. L. Shuttlesworth was bombed in Birmingham, Alabama. The city's Negroes responded with a massive defiance of bus segregation regulations. At least forty people were arrested.

December 27. Segregation was outlawed on buses in Tallahassee, Florida. Blacks had boycotted the vehicles for more than six months.

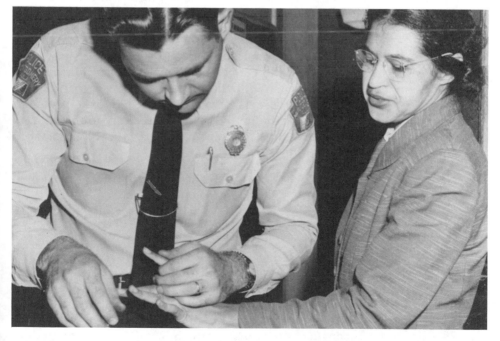

Rosa Parks is fingerprinted after her arrest for refusing to surrender her bus seat to a white passenger.

1957

February 14. The Southern Christian Leadership Conference (SCLC) was organized in New Orleans, Louisiana. Atlanta, Georgia was chosen as the site of the SCLC's national headquarters, and Martin Luther King, Jr. was elected its first president.

May 17. More than 15,000 Americans, mostly black, gathered at the Lincoln Memorial in Washington, D.C. to demonstrate support for a voting rights act. Martin Luther King, Jr. led the speakers shouting: "Give us the ballot!" It was the first large-scale black protest in Washington since the Second World War.

June. Blacks in Tuskegee, Alabama, began a boycott of white merchants in protest of the state legislature which had earlier thwarted their quest for political power by "gerrymandering": redividing the electorial districts of Tuskegee unfairly and making the black districts smaller. Charles G. Gomillion, a Tuskegee Institute sociologist, took the lead of the movement through the Tuskegee Civic Association.

August 29. The United States Congress passed the Voting Rights Act of 1957, the first major civil rights legislation since 1875.

September 9. Violence aimed at preventing school desegregation continued in the South. A Nashville, Tennessee school was bombed and the Reverend Fred L. Shuttlesworth was attacked in Birmingham, Alabama while trying to enroll his children in school.

September 24-25. After unsuccessfully trying to persuade Governor Orval Faubus of Arkansas to give up his efforts to block desegregation of a Little Rock school, President Dwight D. Eisenhower ordered federal troops into the city to halt interference with federal court orders. It was the most serious state-federal clash in modern times. Faubus and a mob of whites gave way to the military power, permitting nine black children to attend a desegregated high school on September 25.

December 5. New York City took the lead in local efforts against discrimination in housing by passing a Fair Housing Practice ordinance.

1958

June 30. The state of Alabama's attempt to cripple the NAACP by imposing a $100,000 contempt fine against it was stymied by the United States Supreme Court. In *NAACP v. Alabama*, the Court declared that it would not tolerate denial of constitutional rights through evasive application of obscure procedural rules. The fine had been imposed because of the NAACP's failure to produce its membership lists to an Alabama judge.

Troops escort Negro students from Central High School in Little Rock, Arkansas.

August 19. Members of the NAACP Youth Council began a new series of sit-ins at segregated restaurants. Lunch counters in Oklahoma City, Oklahoma were the latest targets.

September 20. Martin Luther King, Jr. was stabbed by a crazed black woman while autographing copies of his story of the Montgomery bus boycott, *Stride Toward Freedom*, in Harlem. King successfully recovered from the serious wound.

1959

March 11. *A Raisin in the Sun*, a play depicting a part of black life in the ghetto by the African-American playwright Loraine Hansberry, became a Broadway hit. Lloyd Richard, the play's director, was the first such black to appear on Broadway in more than fifty years.

April 25. Another Mississippi lynching was recorded with the death of Mack Parker of Poplarville.

1960

February 1. A wave of sit-ins at segregated lunch counters, led principally by black college students, began at Greensboro, North Carolina. Four students from North Carolina A and T College initiated the new movement.

In less than two weeks the drive spread to fifteen cities in five Southern states, and within two years had engulfed the South. The sit-ins were met by physical violence and legal harassment, including massive jailings, but most restaurants eventually desegregated voluntarily under court order or by legislation. The success of the sit-in technique encouraged blacks to use the method of non-violent direct action in other areas where discrimination persisted. Martin Luther King, Jr. assumed leadership of the widened movement.

February 25-27. On February 25, black students from Alabama State University conducted a sit-in demonstration at the County Courthouse in Montgomery. This was the first protest of this type in the capital of the Old Confederacy. Sheriff Mac Sim Butler and his deputies kept close watch on the demonstrators in the Courthouse's lunchroom while groups of white men, some armed with baseball bats, patrolled outside.

On February 27, a black woman was struck on the head and injured by a club-wielding white man. No arrests were made in the incident. Two days later, Alabama Governor John Patterson warned that there were not enough police officers in the country to prevent disturbances and offer protection if blacks continued "to provoke whites."

February 27. Black and white demonstrators were attacked in Nashville, Tennessee. The violence occurred in two of five stores where students had staged nonviolent lunch counter sit-ins. Police arrested about 100 people, mostly black demonstrators. Seventy-six of those arrested declined to pay fines or bonds pending trials. Those who chose jail were mainly black. Their attorneys said their decision was based on their reluctance to support "the injustice and immoral practices that have been performed" in their arrest.

February 29-March 6. On February 29, Martin Luther King, Jr. spoke to a crowd of more than 1,000 students in Montgomery, Alabama following three days of racial tensions occasioned by student sit-ins. King urged continued passive resistance to segregation. The students pledged to withdraw from their college, Alabama State University, *en masse* if any were expelled for previous as well as future sit-ins.

On March 1, blacks marched to the Old Confederate capitol building in Montgomery, where they prayed and sang the "Star Spangled Banner" during a non-violent demonstration against segregation. The next day, the State

A student sit-in at a segregated lunch counter.

Board of Education expelled nine of the participating students from Alabama State University.

On March 6, state, county, and local police stopped a march of nearly 1,000 blacks en route to a protest meeting at the Alabama state capitol. There were scattered fist fights between blacks and a mob of taunting whites, but police prevented large-scale violence. Two days later, Montgomery police broke up another protest demonstration on the campus of Alabama State University and arrested thirty-five students and at least one teacher. Thirty-three of the blacks were subsequently found guilty of disorderly conduct and fined $200 each.

March 4. Lunch counter sit-ins reached the Southwest as about one hundred students from Texas Southern University conducted nonviolent protests in Houston. Three days later four masked white men (in apparent retaliation) kidnapped a black man, Felton Turner, beat him, and carved the letters KKK on his chest and stomach.

March 16. President Dwight D. Eisenhower stated during a press conference that he was "deeply sympathetic" with the efforts of any group to enjoy Constitutionally guaranteed rights. The President did not endorse the lunch counter sit-in movement which was then sweeping the South, but called for biracial conferences in "every city and every community of the South" to help settle racial problems.

April 15-17. The Student Non-Violent Coordinating Committee (SNCC) was founded in Raleigh, North Carolina. The group became the nationwide

liaison for student sit-in activities.

April 19. The home of Z. Alexander Looby, a black Nashville, Tennessee city councilman and attorney for the NAACP, was demolished by a dynamite bomb. Looby and his family escaped injury. The bomb also damaged several homes in Looby's neighborhood and blew out hundreds of windows at the black Meharry Medical College in which several medical students were injured by flying glass. Looby served as chief counsel for more than a hundred students arrested in Nashville sit-ins since demonstrations began in the college town in February, 1960. After the bombing, more than 2,000 blacks marched on the Nashville City Hall protesting the police's failure to halt the racial violence. A black minister, the Reverend C. T. Vivian, accused Nashville mayor Ben West of encouraging the violence by permitting the police to use their authority with "partiality." West denied the accusation and claimed that he favored desegregation of lunch counters, but said that businessmen practicing segregation were acting within their rights.

May 6. President Dwight D. Eisenhower signed the Voting Rights Act of 1960. The law was designed to bolster the Voting Rights Act of 1957 which granted additional protections to blacks trying to obtain suffrage. Under the new law, federal courts would be authorized to appoint "voting referees" who would be empowered to register blacks in areas where racial discrimination against voters had been proven. Referees would be appointed only after (1) the Justice Department sued under the Civil Rights Act of 1957 to obtain an order requiring the registration of such persons unjustly disqualified by local registrars on racial grounds, (2) the Justice Department won the suits and then asked a judge to declare that a "pattern or practice" of discrimination had blocked blacks from voting. The referees could register all blacks who could establish their qualifications under state law, but who had been previously denied registration. The new law was invoked in the South for the first time on May 9.

July 31. Elijah Muhammad, leader of the Black Muslims, a religious-nationalist group, called for the establishment of an all-black state. Such a state, or group of states, later became a symbol and rallying cry for new supporters of black nationalism. (See also entry dated 1934, for further information about Elijah Muhammad.)

September 8. In his address to the annual meeting of the National Urban League in New York City, New York Governor Nelson A. Rockefeller considered the lunch counter sit-ins an "inspiring example" to the nation and maintained that the sit-in demonstrators personified the moral force and an "appeal to human conscience" which could solve civil rights problems.

October 19. Martin Luther King, Jr. and approximately fifty other blacks were arrested for sitting-in at an Atlanta department store restaurant. The arrest caused a Decatur, Georgia judge to revoke King's previous parole for conviction on a minor traffic violation. King was then sentenced to serve four months in Georgia's maximum security prison. Robert F. Kennedy and his brother, John F. Kennedy, the latter then a presidential candidate, assisted King's family in obtaining his release.

November 10. Andrew Hatcher was named associate press secretary by President-elect John F. Kennedy. Hatcher was for a time the highest ranking black appointee in the executive branch of the federal government.

November 14. Desegregation crept into the major industrial centers of the South with the admission of Negro children to schools in New Orleans. On November 10, U.S. District Judge J. Skelley Wright had prohibited implementation of Louisiana's anti-school-integration laws. On the same day, the New Orleans school board approved plans to admit five black children to two previously all-white schools. On November 13, the state legislature took control of New Orleans schools, fired the school superintendent, and ordered all schools closed on November 14. At the same time, Judge Wright issued a new order prohibiting interference by the state with the schools. Amid the jeering of angry white parents, four black children enrolled in the two schools on November 14. White protests, accompanied by a boycott, continued for much of the school year.

————. Membership in the Black Muslim cult reportedly reached 100,000. In 1959, the movement reported thirty temples and about 12,000 members. (Because of the secrecy of the organization, membership can only be estimated.) The rapid rise in membership can be attributed to the work of dynamic ministers like Malcolm X (born Malcolm Little) and publicity from the mass media. (See entry dated March 12, 1964, for further information about Malcolm X.)

1961

January 11. A riot resulted in the suspension of two recently admitted black students at the University of Georgia. The duo were reinstated under court order on January 16.

February 11. Robert Weaver, a black housing expert with a Harvard Ph.D., became administrator of the Housing and Home Finance Agency, the highest federal post ever held by an Afro-American to that time.

May 4. A contingent of white and black youths, sponsored by CORE, set out on a bus trip through the South to test desegregation practices. Despite court rulings and decrees set by the Interstate Commerce Commission (ICC), many Southern states refused to sanction non-discriminatory transportation. The biracial group was subjected to physical violence, including savage beatings and arson, and legal harassment. In the fall, the ICC reaffirmed its order prohibiting discrimination in transportation. Such discrimination gradually disappeared on vehicles themselves, but lingered in waiting-rooms and other facilities, especially in the rural South.

August 9. James B. Parsons was appointed by President John F. Kennedy as Judge of the District Court of Northern Illinois, the first such position for an African-American in the continental United States. Parsons, a fifty-year-old Chicago attorney, was serving as a judge on the Cook County Court at the time of his appointment.

September 1. Four high schools were peacefully desegregated by ten black children in Atlanta, Georgia. The orderly desegregation in the Deep South's largest city won praise from President John F. Kennedy, who hoped it would set a new precedent. Previously, desegregation had been marked by violence.

September 23. Thurgood Marshall, chief counsel for the NAACP, was appointed Judge of the Second Circuit Court of Appeals (New York, Connecticut, and Vermont) by President John F. Kennedy. Marshall, a native of Baltimore, Maryland, was fifty-three at the time of his appointment and had been with the NAACP for more than twenty years.

December 12-16. Martin Luther King, Jr. and his forces launched an all-out attack against segregation and discrimination in Albany, Georgia. The effort was frustrated by mass arrests and political maneuverings. The Albany debacle taught civil rights leaders valuable lessons for future massive direct-action assaults on segregation.

1962

January 18-28. Student protests at Southern University in Louisiana, the largest all-black state college in the South, resulted in the closing of the institution, a precedent for handling future student disturbances. Southern students had protested the expulsion of sit-in demonstrators. These expulsions were used by administrators at publicly supported black colleges to meet the demands of state authorities to quell sit-in and related activities.

September 9. Two black churches were burned in Sasser, Georgia. Burnings and bombings of black churches, especially those used for civil rights meetings, became common during the decade.

September 30. United States Supreme Court Justice Hugo Black ordered the admission forthwith of a black student, James H. Meredith, to the University of Mississippi. The governor of Mississippi, Ross Barnett, tried unsuccessfully to block Meredith's admission, and a tragic riot occurred on the day that U. S. Marshals escorted Meredith to the campus. Federalized National Guardsmen subsequently restored order on the riot-torn campus at Oxford. Meredith graduated from "Ole Miss" in 1963.

November 7-8. In elections across the country, Edward W. Brooke, an Afro-American lawyer from Boston, was elected attorney general for Massachusetts, becoming the highest-ranking black official in New England. Leroy Johnson, a black Atlanta lawyer, was elected to the Georgia State Senate, the state's only black legislator since Reconstruction, and in California, Augustus Hawkins became the first black to represent his state in the United States Congress.

November 20. Racial discrimination in federally-financed housing was prohibited by President Kennedy. The order was applied principally to housing projects and apartments but had little effect on homes which were not in commercially developed neighborhoods. Insured loans for home improvements from the Federal Housing Authority (FHA) were also excluded. In the event of violations, the government would first seek to obtain voluntary compliance. Administrative or court action leading to cancellation of loans or contracts would be taken in the event voluntary compliance could not be obtained.

1963

April 3. Civil rights forces, led by Martin Luther King, Jr., launched a drive against bias in Birmingham, Alabama. The city's police force, led by Commissioner Eugene "Bull" Connor, used high powered water hoses and dogs against demonstrators. The brutality of the repression and the legal harassments (including massive arrests) aroused public opinion, especially in the North. President Kennedy hoped to use the new public awareness to garner support for his civil rights proposals presented to Congress on March 1. The Birmingham protests continued until May 10 when an agreement was signed calling for gradual desegregation of public accommodations. The desegregation agreement was followed by bombings at the homes and businesses of black leaders, which led to hours of Negro rioting.

June 11. Two black students were admitted to the University of Alabama after an unsuccessful attempt by Governor George C. Wallace to block their entrance. President Kennedy ordered federalized National Guardsmen to insure the Negroes' enrollment. In a television address that night, Kennedy made an impassioned plea for an end to discrimination in the nation through moral suasion and legislative action. Congress continued to take no action on the President's civil rights proposals.

June 12. Medgar W. Evers, NAACP field secretary in Mississippi and a World War II hero, became the latest victim of assassination resulting from civil rights activity. Evers was gunned down by a sniper in Jackson. His alleged assailant, a white segregationist, was acquitted by a hung jury.

June-August. Civil rights demonstrations, protests, and boycotts occurred in almost every major urban area in the country. Boston and Harlem, for instance, were the scenes of protests in June by blacks demanding an end to discrimination in the construction industry and *de facto* segregation in the schools. Limited martial law was declared in July in Cambridge, Massachusetts, after black demonstrators and white segregationists clashed.

August 17. W.E.B. Du Bois, one of the most brilliant African-American intellectuals and a founder of the NAACP, died in Accra, Ghana. Du Bois, who became disillusioned with American racial attitudes and the democratic-capitalist system, emigrated to Ghana in 1961. (See also entries dated June, 1895; 1897; 1903; and July 11-13, 1905, for further information about Du Bois.)

August 28. The largest single protest demonstration in United States history

Alabama Governor George C. Wallace.

114

March on Washington, 1963.

occurred at the Lincoln Memorial in Washington, D.C., where 250,000 blacks and whites gathered to lobby for passage of sweeping civil rights measures by Congress. Martin Luther King, Jr. thrilled the crowd with his immortal "I Have a Dream" oration. President Kennedy received a delegation of civil rights leaders at the White House and promised to push ahead for anti-discrimination legislation. (See Appendix for the text of King's "I Have a Dream" speech.)

September 15. Racial tensions were renewed in Birmingham, Alabama, when four small Negro girls died in the bombing of the 16th Street Baptist Church. No serious disturbances followed the incident.

October 22. A massive boycott, involving nearly a quarter of a million students, was staged in Chicago to protest *de facto* school segregation.

November 22. Black Americans joined the world in mourning the assassination of President John F. Kennedy, who many blacks believed had been killed because of his advocacy of civil rights. Kennedy's civil rights measures were still being debated in Congress when he died.

December 7. Ralph J. Bunche and Marian Anderson were awarded Medals of Freedom, the highest civilian decoration, for outstanding contributions to the ideals of freedom and democracy by President Lyndon B. Johnson.

March on Washington, 1963.

1964

January 21. Black journalist Carl T. Rowan of Minnesota was appointed director of the United States Information Agency (UNIA) by President Johnson, one of Johnson's first of several high-ranking appointments of blacks.

January 23. The 24th Amendment to the Constitution prohibiting the denial or abridgement of the right to vote by "reason of failure to pay any poll tax or other tax" was adopted. The poll tax had been used by several Southern states as a means of discouraging black voters.

February 4. Austin T. Walden, a veteran civil rights lawyer and political leader, took the oath as a municipal judge in Atlanta, becoming the first black jurist in Georgia since Reconstruction.

March 12. Malcolm X, one of the most notable Black Muslim ministers, announced his withdrawal from Elijah Muhammad's Nation of Islam. Malcolm was born Malcolm Little in Omaha, Nebraska in 1925. His father was a Baptist minister from Georgia who had supported Marcus Garvey's "Back to Africa" movement in the early 1900s. His mother was a West Indian. Three of Malcolm's uncles were slain by whites, and by the time Malcolm was thirteen, his father was murdered and his mother committed to a mental institution. Malcolm himself was placed in a detention home for stealing. A school dropout, he made his living principally by illegal means. In February, 1946, Malcolm was sentenced to ten years in prison for burglary in Boston, where he later converted to Islam. Upon his release from prison in August, 1952, Malcolm drew closer to the movement. In the summer of 1953, he became Assistant Minister of the Detroit temple. In 1957, Malcolm founded the Muslim newspaper, *Muhammad Speaks,* and by 1959 had become one of the leading spokesmen for the Muslims. As Malcolm's charisma and media exposure brought him a larger following, Elijah Muhammad reportedly labelled him ambitious and dangerous. Following President John F. Kennedy's assassination in November, 1963, Malcolm referred to the killing as an example of "chickens coming home to roost." Muhammad immediately suspended Malcolm from his Muslim duties for this intemperate statement. This was the beginning of the end for Malcolm X. He left the movement on March 12, 1964, carrying only a few defectors with him. Malcolm was assassinated on February 21, 1965.

April 13. Sidney Poitier won an Academy Award for Best Actor for his role in *Lilies of the Field.* Poitier was the first Afro-American actor to receive the coveted award.

July 2. The United States Congress passed a sweeping civil rights act, including provisions prohibiting discrimination in public accommodations and discrimination in employment. The most important civil rights law since 1875,

Malcolm X

its passage was made certain after the Senate, for the first time in such a case, ended a Southern-sponsored filibuster by imposing cloture on June 10. President Johnson signed the bill in the presence of civil rights leaders, including Martin Luther King, Jr., immediately after its adoption. (See Appendix for an excerpt taken from the Civil Rights Act of 1964.)

President Lyndon B. Johnson signs Civil Rights Bill as officials (including Edward Brooke, Walter Mondale, and Thurgood Marshall) observe.

Chapter 10
"The Second Reconstruction" Wanes, 1964-1972

1964

July 18-August 30. Serious racial disturbances occurred in a number of American cities, beginning in the Harlem section of New York City. The Harlem riot followed after the shooting of a black teenager by white police officers. Several of the other riots were also sparked by clashes between blacks and white police officers. Other areas witnessing riots included Brooklyn and Rochester, New York; Jersey City, New Jersey; Chicago, Illinois; and Philadelphia, Pennsylvania. Injuries in the disturbances exceeded one hundred, property losses ran into the millions of dollars, and National Guardsmen had to be employed.

August 4. The bodies of three civil rights workers, James E. Cheney, Michael Schwerner, and Andrew Goodman, were discovered in a shallow grave on a farm outside of Philadelphia, Mississippi. The FBI accused nearly two dozen white segregationists of complicity in the murders. Included among them were law enforcement officers.

December 10. Martin Luther King, Jr., the champion of non-violent resistance to racial oppression, was awarded the Nobel Peace Prize in Oslo, Norway. King, at age thirty-five, became the youngest man in history and the second African-American to receive this prestigious award.

December. The United States Supreme Court upheld the constitutionality of that section of the 1964 Civil Rights Act which prohibited discrimination in public accomodations.

————. Reports from civil rights groups indicated that three people were

*Dr. Martin Luther King, Jr. receives the Nobel Peace Prize in
1964.*

killed, three wounded, eighty physically assaulted, over 1,000 arrested, and
thirty buildings bombed in Mississippi during the course of a year's civil rights
activity.

————. The United States Congress passed the Economic Opportunity Act in
the nation's "War on Poverty." The legislation was later to be severely
criticized by proponents and antagonists for inefficiency, but many blacks
benefited from it, especially through the Head Start program for pre-schoolers,
the Upward Bound program for high school students, and the college work-
study financial aid program.

1965

January 2-23. Civil rights forces led by Martin Luther King, Jr. opened a
voter registration drive in Selma, Alabama. Dr. King was attacked as he
registered at a formerly all-white Selma hotel, but was not seriously injured.
On January 19, Dallas County (of which Selma is the county seat) law
enforcement officers began arresting would-be black voters and their supporters. A federal district court issued an order on January 23 prohibiting interference with those seeking the right to vote.

Dr. Martin Luther King, Jr. joins hands with other black leaders while singing "We Shall Overcome" at a church rally in Selma, Alabama.

February 1-March 25. The drive to register black voters in Alabama developed into a nationwide protest movement as local whites in Dallas County stiffened their resistance and civil rights leaders intensified their efforts. More than seven hundred blacks, including Martin Luther King, Jr., were arrested on February 1.

On February 26, a black demonstrator, Jimmie L. Jackson, died from wounds received at the hands of state troopers in Marion, Alabama.

On March 7, several hundred protestors were routed by billy clubs, tear gas, whips, and cattle prods as they attempted to march across the Edmund Pettus bridge in Selma. President Lyndon B. Johnson, sympathizing with the demonstrators, denounced the incident. A white minister from Boston, the Reverend James Reeb (who assisted in the voting rights drive) died following an assault by three white men on March 11.

On March 17, a federal judge enjoined Alabama officials from interfering with a proposed march from Selma to the state capital at Montgomery, designed to dramatize the denial of voting rights. The fifty mile Selma to Montgomery march, under the protection of federal troops, occurred from March 21-25, 1965. Perhaps as many as 50,000 people appeared before the Alabama state capitol on March 25 to hear Martin Luther King, Jr. and others denounce

Alabama leaders for interfering with voting rights. Alabama governor George C. Wallace received a petition from the crowd. Viola Gregg Liuzzo, a white civil rights supporter from Michigan, was murdered that same night. Three Ku Klux Klansmen were later convicted of conspiracy to violate civil rights in Liuzzo's death.

February 21. Malcolm X, a black nationalist and former member of the Nation of Islam hierarchy, was assassinated in New York City. Three African-Americans were convicted of the murder in March, 1966.

Malcolm X, a former convict, was largely a self-educated man but became known as a persuasive orator with a fiery tongue. In recent years, a cult has been built around his memory by bitter young blacks. Malcolm told the story of his life in the posthumously published *Autobiography of Malcolm X*, written in conjunction with Alex Haley. The book has become a classic of twentieth-century black American literature. (See also entry dated March 14, 1964, for further information about Malcolm X.)

May 26. A new voting rights bill was passed by the United States Congress. The bill contained an anti-poll tax amendment designed to prevent certain states from using that tax to deny or abridge the right to vote. The bill also extended the right to vote to those who were unable to read or write English, but could demonstrate that they had an eighth grade education in a school conducted under the American flag. Federal registrars could enroll voters who had been denied the suffrage by local officials.

June 4. President Lyndon B. Johnson delivered a memorable speech at Howard University's commencement, in which he pledged an all-out effort to bring blacks into the mainstream of American society. He again quoted the title of a civil rights anthem, "We Shall Overcome," as a motto for action.

June 10-16. Blacks in Chicago, Illinois staged another round of demonstrations against school segregation. Entertainer Dick Gregory and the Congress of Racial Equality (CORE) director James Farmer were among those arrested. A specific target of the demonstrators was school superintendent Benjamin C. Willis, who blacks viewed as a segregationist. Willis was given a new one year contract on May 27. The next day a united front of civil rights groups, dissatisfied with the slow pace of school desegregation, announced that a public school boycott would be held to protest the rehiring of Willis. A federal judge issued an injunction on June 9 against the boycott. Nevertheless, the demonstrations began on June 10.

On June 11 the arrests began. Among the 225 arrested on that day were Farmer, Gregory, and nine clergymen. The protests continued through June 15, when Mayor Richard Daley sanctioned a downtown march and agreed to negotiate with civil rights leaders.

Dr. Martin Luther King, Jr. leads marchers on last leg of their Selma-to-Montgomery march.

July 13. Thurgood Marshall, an Appeals Court judge, was nominated as solicitor general of the United States by President Lyndon B. Johnson. This was the highest law enforcement position ever held by an African-American.

August 11-21. The most serious single racial disturbance in American history to that time erupted in the Watts section of Los Angeles, California. As in the riots of the previous year, a clash between blacks and white police officers triggered the disturbance. National Guardsmen assisted in quelling the disorder which left 34 dead, almost 900 injured, more than 3,500 arrested, and property losses near 225 million dollars. In the wake of the riot, federal, state, and local authorities sought ways to improve living conditions in the twenty-square mile ghetto of 100,000 people.

On August 20, President Lyndon B. Johnson denounced the Watts rioters and refused to accept "legitimate grievances" as an excuse for the disorder.

December 3-10. On December 3, a federal court jury in Alabama convicted Collie L. Wilkins of conspiracy to violate civil rights in the death of voting rights activist Viola Gregg Liuzzo. On December 10, another Alabama jury acquitted the whites accused of the murder of the Reverend James Reeb, a Boston minister, also slain in the Selma demonstrations. (See also entry dated February 1-March 25, 1965.)

1966

January 3. Floyd McKissick, a militant black civil rights leader from North Carolina, succeeded James Farmer as director of CORE. McKissick was to guide CORE into an aggressive, mostly black group dedicated to black liberation even if by separatist routes. McKissick, a forty-three-year-old Durham attorney, had served as CORE's national chairman since 1963. McKissick's announced plans included a program of community organization to help disadvantaged blacks living under "feudalism."

January 10. Julian Bond was denied his seat in the Georgia state legislature (after being duly elected), for opposing the United States's involvement in the Vietnam War. The vote against Bond in the Georgia House of Representatives was 184-12. On January 6, Bond, a native of Atlanta and the son of a former college president, had told journalists that he supported a SNCC policy statement that advocated civil rights and social service alternatives to the draft. Many white Georgia legislators interpreted his statements as reflecting an "un-American attitude." The seven other black members of the House voted to seat Bond.

January 13. Robert C. Weaver of Washington, D. C., one of the nation's leading authorities on urban housing, was appointed the first secretary of the new Department of Housing and Urban Development (HUD) by President Lyndon B. Johnson. Weaver became the first African-American to serve in a presidential cabinet in United States history and the highest ranking black in the executive branch of the government. The appointment climaxed a long, successful career for Weaver who had previously served as housing director for New York, a member of President Franklin D. Roosevelt's "Black Cabinet," and the highest ranking black in President John F. Kennedy's administration.

January 25. Constance Baker Motley, a former NAACP attorney, was appointed a federal judge by President Lyndon B. Johnson. She was the second black woman to hold such a post. Marjorie Lawson had been previously appointed by President John F. Kennedy.

March 7. The United States Supreme Court upheld the Voting Rights Act of 1965.

May 10. The California State Supreme Court ruled that a state constitutional amendment nullifying California fair-housing laws violated the United States Constitution. The state amendment, known as Proposition 14, had been placed on the general election ballot in November, 1964 and was approved by a 2-1 margin. It provided that no state or local agency could interfere with a real estate owner's "absolute discretion" in the sale and rental of property. The State Supreme Court's 5-2 decision held that it was "beyond dispute" that the Fourteenth Amendment's Equal Protection Clause secured the "right to acquire and possess property of every kind," without racial or religious discrimination. The court overruled a lower court's rejection of a complaint by Lincoln W. Mulkey, a black man, against apartment owners in Orange County. The lower court had ruled that the California open housing acts on which Mulkey's petition was based had been rendered "null and void" by the passage of Proposition 14. Six companion cases were also covered by the state court's order. Governor Edmund G. Brown, who had announced in March, 1966 that $200 million in federal urban-renewal funds had been withheld from California because of Proposition 14, promptly announced that the state court's decision would be appealed to the U. S. Supreme Court and that until then he would "continue to enforce" Proposition 14. State Attorney General Thomas C. Lynch said, however, that he would resume enforcement of the open-occupancy laws of 1959 and 1963 which Proposition 14 had invalidated. (See also entry dated June 9, 1966.)

May 16. Stokely Carmichael, an articulate West Indian-born youth, was named head of SNCC. Carmichael was to guide SNCC into a more militant organization, bent on achieving racial liberation, even if by employing a separatist route.

June 6. James Meredith, the black student who broke the color bar at the University of Mississippi in 1962, was shot but not seriously injured during his one-man pilgrimage "against fear" from Memphis, Tennessee to Jackson, Mississippi. A white segregationist was arrested for the attack.

June 7-26. The march begun by James Meredith resumed with civil rights leaders, including Martin Luther King, Jr. and Stokely Carmichael, taking the initiative. The demonstration ended with a rally of 15,000 people at the state capitol in Jackson. King, Carmichael, Meredith, and others addressed the crowd. It was during this march and rally that Carmichael and others began to freely employ the phrase "Black Power." The slogan was interpreted to mean many things, but all agreed that it denoted a more aggressive posture for its supporters.

June 9. The California State Supreme Court partially reversed a May 10, 1966 decision which invalidated a state constitutional amendment that had voided state open-housing laws. The new decision was based on a reconsideration of one of the seven cases covered by the earlier ruling. It declared that the owner of a single-family home not financed by federal funds was not covered by state open occupancy legislation and thus could refuse to sell or lease his home to blacks. The new ruling did not in any other way affect the earlier invalidation of the controversial constitutional amendment known as Proposition 14.

July 1-9. The national convention of CORE endorsed the "Black Power" concept. SNCC was also to adopt the slogan, while the SCLC shied away from it and the NAACP disassociated itself from the concept entirely.

July 10. Martin Luther King, Jr. addressed a predominately-black crowd of 45,000 in Chicago and launched a drive to rid the nation's third largest city of discrimination.

July 12-15. A dispute between police and black children over the use of a fire hydrant for recreation resulted in rioting in one of Chicago's black ghettoes. Two blacks were killed, many were injured, and 370 arrested. On July 15, Chicago mayor Richard Daley and Dr. Martin Luther King, Jr. announced new programs in recreation for Chicago blacks, a committee to study police-citizen relations, and closer cooperation between community residents and police.

July 18-23. A serious racial disturbance occurred in Cleveland, Ohio. The toll: four dead, fifty injured, 160 arrests, and widespread property damage. Shootings, firebombings, and looting were prevalent throughout the black ghetto of Hough on Cleveland's East Side. The incident which touched off the riot took place in a neighborhood bar. One version was that the bar's white management had refused to serve water to blacks; another was that a woman soliciting money for a friend's funeral had been ejected. Bands of blacks began roaming in the area after the incident. At least ten buildings were destroyed by fire.

August 5-6. Martin Luther King, Jr. was stoned in Chicago while leading a demonstration against discrimination in the city. King was not seriously hurt, but he left the city shortly thereafter. The Chicago campaign had been only partially successful.

October. The Black Panther Party was founded in Oakland, California. The two principal founders were Huey P. Newton, a native of Grove, Louisiana, and Bobby Seale, a native of Dallas, Texas. Newton and Seale grew up in California and met in 1960 while attending Merritt Junior College in Oakland. Inspired by examples of police brutality and other forms of white racism as well as the teachings of Malcolm X, the duo was very active in the college's African-American student association, but later withdrew and organized the Black Panther Party. The Black Panther Party adopted a ten-point program demanding full employment, restitution for past exploitation and oppression, education relevant to black needs and aspirations, release of all black political prisoners, decent housing, exemptions from military service for blacks, trial of blacks only by black juries, an end to police brutality, and black political and economic power. The Panthers insisted on "power to the people," advocated self-defense, called for a socialist economy, provided food and educational programs to young children, and published their own newspaper. They drew wide admiration, if not a large following, from young blacks in the Northern and West Coast ghettoes, and as their numbers and influence increased, so did clashes with law enforcement officers. (See also entry dated December 4-5, 1969.)

November 8. Edward W. Brooke, the attorney general of Massachusetts, was elected United States Senator from Massachusetts. Brooke, a Howard University graduate from Washington, became the first African-American to sit in the U. S. Senate since Reconstruction.

1967

January 8. Following a decision by the United States Supreme Court, Julian Bond was seated in the Georgia General Assembly. (See also entry dated January 10, 1966.)

January 9. Adam Clayton Powell was ousted as Chairman of the House Education and Labor Committee and denied his seat in the U. S. House of Representatives.

April 4. Martin Luther King, Jr. announced his unalterable opposition to the Vietnam War. King spoke first at a press conference at the Overseas Press Club in New York, and later that day at the Riverdale Church in Harlem, where he suggested the avoidance of military service "to all those who find the American

Bobby Seale (left) and Huey P. Newton (right), founders of the Black Panther Party.

course in Vietnam a dishonorable and unjust one." King compared the use of new U.S. weapons on Vietnamese peasants to that of the Nazis' testing of new medicines and use of torture on Jews in concentration camps during World War II. He proposed that the United States take new initiatives to end the war "in order to atone for our sins and errors in Vietnam." Many of King's supporters disagreed with his strong anti-war stance.

May 1-October 1. The worst summer of racial disturbances in American history occurred. More than forty riots were recorded and at least one hundred other incidents. The most serious outbreaks were in Newark, New Jersey (July 12-17), where twenty-six died and in Detroit (July 23-30), where forty died. New York City, Cleveland, Washington, Chicago, Atlanta, and others were also scenes of trouble. President Johnson appointed a National Advisory Commission on Civil Disorders to investigate them and make recommendations. The Commission, headed by Illinois governor Otto Kerner (commonly known as the Kerner Commission), conducted a series of hearings and investigations and reported its findings to the President in March, 1968.

May 12. H. Rap Brown, a militant black youth, was appointed the new chairman of SNCC. Brown was to have numerous brushes with the law. He disappeared in 1970 while awaiting trial on a charge of inciting a riot in Cambridge, Massachusetts.

H. Rap Brown stirs up a crowd.

July 1. Benjamin E. Mays retired as president of Morehouse College. Mays, the son of South Carolina tenant farmers, was educated at Bates College in Maine and at the University of Chicago. An ordained Baptist minister, Mays taught at Howard University and at Morehouse College, among other places, before becoming president of Morehouse in 1940. He expanded the programs begun by John Hope and the college produced an outstanding list of black business and professional men and civil rights leaders. Mays, like Hope, also became known as a militant civil rights advocate for his membership on the NAACP Board of Directors and his forthright speeches and writings demanding racial equality. In April, 1968, Mays delivered the eulogy at the funeral of Dr. Martin Luther King, Jr., (a Morehouse alumnus), in which he blamed America's racist society for King's assassination. Mays was elected president of the Atlanta Board of Education in 1969. Mays was succeeded by Hugh M. Gloster, Academic Dean at the Hampton Institute and a scholar in African-American literature.

September 21. President Lyndon B. Johnson appointed Walter Washington, an African-American, the first mayor of Washington, D.C. (the nation's largest predominately-black metropolis). Washington, the fifty-five-year-old chairman of the New York City Housing Authority, was officially "commissioner" of the newly reorganized municipal government of the District of Columbia. One interesting opponent of Washington's confirmation by the U.S. Senate was black militant Aketi Kimani, who stated that "any number of militant white men" could do a better job than "a house nigger" such as Washington.

November. The steady growth of the black population in the larger cities of the nation was reflected in the number of African-Americans holding important public offices. While blacks had substantial majorities in only a few cities, their numbers were large enough to, in conjunction with some whites, elect African-Americans in several localities. In 1967, Floyd McCree was elected mayor of Flint, Michigan. Carl B. Stokes and Richard B. Hatcher were elected mayor of Cleveland, Ohio and Gary, Indiana, respectively.

1968

January 16. Lucius D. Amerson began his tenure as sheriff of Macon County, Alabama, the first black sheriff in the South since Reconstruction. Three newly appointed deputies, one white and two blacks, were sworn in with Amerson.

February 8. Three black students died and several others were wounded by South Carolina law enforcement officers during a disturbance on the campus of South Carolina State College at Orangeburg. The protests had begun against segregation at a local bowling alley and had led to the mobilization of the National Guard and the closing of the school for two weeks. Some of the students had been jailed on charges of trespassing. The February 8 incident was preceded by an injury to a state trooper who was knocked down by a piece of wood. The Justice Department began an investigation of the incident on February 10. Later, a suit was filed against the owners of the segregated bowling alley charging them with violation of the Civil Rights Act of 1964. At the same time, action was filed against segregation and discrimination in Orangeburg hospital facilities. The courts upheld the anti-segregation complaints in both instances. Attempts to indict and prosecute the officers involved were unsuccessful.

March 2. The Kerner Commission reported that "white racism" was the principal cause of the disturbance that rocked the nation in 1967, and that the United States was headed toward two communities, "one white, one black, separate and unequal." (See also entry dated May 1-October 1, 1967.)

April 3. Martin Luther King, Jr. addressed a rally of striking garbage workers and their supporters in Memphis, Tennessee. King repeated his defiance of would-be assassins.

April 4. Martin Luther King, Jr., the most important black man in American

Aerial view of a Detroit neighborhood in flames during the 1967 Riot.

history, was assassinated in Memphis, Tennessee. The assassination was followed by a week of racial rioting in at least 125 localities across the nation.

April 9. Hundreds of thousands attended funeral services for Martin Luther King, Jr. in Atlanta. President Johnson decreed a day of national mourning. It was the most stately funeral ever accorded to an American civilian.

April 11. President Lyndon B. Johnson signed the Fair Housing Act, prohibiting racial discrimination in the sale and rental of most housing units in the country.

May 11. Ralph David Abernathy, successor to Martin Luther King, Jr. as head of the SCLC, led a motley array of blacks, poor whites, Native Americans, and Mexican-Americans to Washington, D. C. for a Poor Peoples Campaign. The drive, originally conceived by King, included lobbying and the erection of a campsite known as Resurrection City.

June 25. The SCLC-sponsored Resurrection City was disbanded, admittedly a failure. Poor weather, insufficient discipline, and an unreceptive Congress preoccupied with the war in Vietnam, limited the campaign's effectiveness.

July 23-24. A serious racial disturbance in Cleveland, Ohio left eleven people dead. A small band of armed "Black Nationalists" fought Cleveland police in the Glenville ghetto. This was followed by burning and looting which resulted in an estimated $1.5 million in property damage. Three white police officers and eight blacks died during the riot.

August 29. The name of Channing Phillips, an African-American minister from Washington, D. C., was submitted for the Democratic nomination as President of the United States. Phillips received only a handful of votes. The name of Julian Bond, the black Georgia legislator, was submitted for the Democratic nomination as Vice President. Bond received several votes before he withdrew his name, being too young to occupy the office, according to the U.S. Constitution.

September 8. Another result of the 1967 riots in black ghettoes was the strengthening of militant black self-defense groups such as the Deacons in the South and the Black Panthers in the North and West Coast. The Panthers, an avowedly revolutionary group, drew the ire of law enforcement officers and others. Several of their leaders were arrested, exiled, or killed. Huey P. Newton, a Black Panther leader, was convicted of manslaughter in California on September 8.

November 5. Shirley Chisholm, an African-American from New York, defeated James Farmer for a seat in the U. S. House of Representatives, becoming the first black woman ever to serve in Congress.

November 5. Eighty blacks were elected to political office in the South. There were now nearly 400 black elected officeholders in the eleven states that made up the Old Confederacy. By comparison, only seventeen blacks held political office in these states in November, 1965, after the new Voting Rights Act took effect. Most of the successful black candidates ran in districts with predominately-black constituencies. In primaries as well as in the general election, most black candidates lost when they challenged whites in predominately-white districts; voters generally balloted along racial lines. To black Southerners, the highlight of the November general elections was the election for the first time in this century of blacks to the legislatures in North Carolina, Florida, and Tennessee. Henry Frye, a Greensboro lawyer, won a seat in the North Carolina House. Joe Lang Kershaw, a Miami teacher, was elected to a seat in the Florida House. J. O. Patterson of Memphis and Avon Williams of Nashville were elected to the Tennessee Senate.

Across the South at this time there were more black city councilmen—126— than any other single type of office. The second highest was school board members, a position held by seventy-five blacks. According to figures released by the Voter Educational Project of the Southern Regional Council, Alabama led all of the South with 72 black elected officials, Arkansas with 45, Louisiana and Mississippi with 43, Georgia with 38, Texas and North Carolina each with 19, and Florida with 17. More than 3 million Southern blacks were eligible to vote in the November elections.

December 31. President Lyndon B. Johnson ended his last full year in office. Johnson made more appointments of blacks to high-level federal positions than any previous Chief Executive. Before leaving office, he appointed five black ambassadors, promoted Wade McCree from the U. S. District Court to a Court of Appeals, appointed Hobart Taylor to the Board of the Export-Import Bank, and named Andrew Brimmer as a governor on the Federal Reserve Board.

1969

January 8. The latest example of black student unrest on a predominantly-white campus occurred at Brandeis University in Waltham, Massachusetts. Sixty-five black students invaded Ford Hall, the Brandeis communications center, and barricaded themselves in the building. The students presented a "nonnegotiable" list of demands, including an African studies department: year round recruitment of black students by blacks; black directors of the Upward Bound and Transitional Year programs; the hiring of black professors; the establishment of an Afro-American student center; and ten full scholarships for blacks. Morris B. Abram, the recently appointed president of the University, offered temporary amnesty to the blacks and agreed to communicate with the barricaded students.

January 25. A mistrial was declared in the Mississippi murder trial of Ku Klux Klan leader Samuel H. Bowers, Jr. Bowers was one of thirteen men indicted in the fire-bomb slaying of black civil rights leader Vernon Dahmer in 1966. The thirteen were tried separately. While four defendants were convicted of murder, three of them received life sentences and the fourth was sentenced to serve ten years in prison. Including the Bowers trial, there were five additional mistrials when juries were unable to reach verdicts. In May, 1968, a mistrial was also reached in Bowers's trial for arson in connection with the Dahmer slaying. These efforts to prosecute white men who had committed violent acts against blacks was cited by the *Christian Science Monitor* and other publications as an important factor in deterring violence in Mississippi and the rest of the South.

January 27. The United States Supreme Court ruled that cities—like states—cannot enact ordinances or charter provisions which have the effect of establishing discrimination in housing.

The Court's decision involved a case filed by Nellie Hunter, a black housewife from Akron, Ohio. In 1965, Hunter attempted to buy a home on Akron's all-white West Side but was turned down by a real estate company on account of her race. Hunter filed a complaint with the Akron City Hall, requesting the protection of a 1964 ordinance which banned racial discrimination in housing. But city officials replied that local real estate interests had successfully waged a drive to amend the charter, nullifying the ordinance and requiring that any future fair-housing proposal be approved by a vote of the people.

The Supreme Court held that the Akron charter amendment "is no more permissible than denying racial minorities the vote on an equal basis with others." The city had placed, unconstitutionally, the Court reasoned, a "special burden" on its black residents by requiring bans against housing discrimination to have the approval of the majority of the city's voters. In effect, the Court's decision struck down the offending charter amendment and restored the original fair housing ordinance.

January-March. President Richard M. Nixon, elected without substantial black support, made only three top-level appointments of blacks to the Washington bureaucracy—James Farmer as Assistant Secretary of Health, Education and Welfare; Arthur A. Fletcher as Assistant Secretary of Labor; and William H. Brown III as chairman of the Equal Employment Opportunities Commission. President Nixon retained Walter Washington as mayor of Washington, D. C.

March 10. James Earl Ray, a white vagabond, was sentenced to ninety-nine years in prison for the assassination of Martin Luther King, Jr.

June 27. The United States Department of Labor issued guidelines for minority employment on federally-assisted construction projects. The guidelines, which had become known as "the Philadelphia Plan" (the plan was first imposed on the city of Philadelphia), required contractors on federally-assisted construction work exceeding $500,000 to hire a specific number of minority workers. Secretary of Labor George P. Schultz said on July 3 that the Philadelphia Plan was a "fair and realistic approach" toward eliminating racial discrimination in the construction industry. He added, however, that no contractor who failed to meet the standards set by the Labor Department would lose a federal contract if the contractor showed he had "made a good faith effort" to recruit the required number of minority workers.

July 16. Laurence H. Silberman, solicitor of the United States Department of Labor, announced that the Philadelphia Plan for minority hiring was legal under Executive Order No. 11246, which required equal employment clauses in all federal contracts. Republican minority leader Everett Dirksen of Illinois had asked President Richard Nixon on July 8 to hold up the plan because he thought it imposed a quota system in violation of the Civil Rights Act of 1964. Silberman, however, said the arrangement known as the Philadelphia Plan did not run counter to existing federal laws.

August 19. The FBI arrested Black Panther leader Bobby Seale for the torture-murder of Alex Rackley. Rackley was allegedly disloyal to the Panther organization and was burned to death on May 19 in New Haven, Connecticut. Francis J. McTernan, Seale's attorney, charged that the arrest was part of an organized campaign by the Justice Department to harass the Black Panther party. McTernan said that his staff had information that the Department had prepared a special file in connection with a program "of harrassment against leaders of the Black Panther party all over the country." Seale was arrested in California and later extradited for trial in Connecticut.

September. Harvard University moved to establish an Afro-American Studies program. An eight-person Faculty Committee on African and Afro-American Studies concluded in January that an Afro-American Studies program was needed in addition to the already-established African Studies program. The committee's report said: "We are dealing with 25 million of our own people with a special history, culture, and range of problems. It can hardly be doubted that the study of black men in America is a legitimate and urgent academic endeavor." Although not the first to establish an Afro-American studies program, the program at Harvard, one of the nation's most prestigious universities, was viewed as lending impetus to the establishment of such a field of study at other universities.

October 29. The United States Supreme Court ruled unanimously that school districts must end racial segregation "at once," and must "operate now and hereafter only unitary schools." The Court rejected the Nixon administration's appeal for a delay in desegregating thirty Mississippi school districts. The new ruling indicated that the Court had abandoned its fourteen-year-old standard of allowing desegregation to proceed "with all deliberate speed." In the current decision, the Court declared that "continued operations of segregated schools under a standard of 'all deliberate speed' for desegregation is no longer constitutionally permissible." The case known as *Alexander v. Holmes*, was the first major decision delivered by the Supreme Court under President Nixon's appointed Chief Justice, Warren E. Burger.

October 31. The United States Court of Appeals for the Fifth Circuit in New Orleans moved to implement the Supreme Court's October 29 decision on school desegregation by directing school districts in Mississippi to file desegregation plans by November 5, 1969. Meanwhile, NAACP attorneys said they would file motions in some 100 other school segregation cases pending in federal courts to press for "immediate integration."

November 4. Carl Stokes, the first black mayor of Cleveland, Ohio, was reelected. In other elections, Howard N. Lee was elected mayor of predominately-white Chapel Hill, North Carolina. In Fayette, Mississippi (a mostly black community) veteran NAACP leader and brother of the slain Medgar Evers, Charles Evers, was elected mayor. Blacks also took political control of the city of Tuskegee, Alabama.

December 4-5. On December 4, Black Panther Party leaders Mark Clark and Fred Hampton were killed in a raid by police in Chicago, Illinois. The pre-dawn raid on an apartment near the Illinois Black Panther Party headquarters resulted not only in the deaths of Hampton, the state party chairman, and Clark, leader of the Peoria, Illinois chapter, but in the wounding of four others, two of them women. The raid, according to police reports, was carried out on information that Hampton's apartment was being used to stockpile weapons. Police claimed that their knock on the door was answered by shotgun fire from a woman and contended that approximately 200 shots were fired during the ten-minute altercation. On December 5, spokesmen for the Black Panthers dismissed the police accounts of the raid and claimed that Clark and Hampton were "murdered" in bed by police. They purported to show that the only shooting in the apartment was done by police officers. State, federal, and congressional investigations were held. Neither Panthers members nor police officers were brought to trial in the wake of the controversial encounter. It did serve, however, to heighten tensions between the Panthers and law enforcement organizations and to help gain some additional sympathy among many Americans for the Panthers and their objectives.

1970

January 2. FBI Director J. Edgar Hoover said that black militant groups were "encouraged and inflamed from without" in violent attacks upon the government. In his report of FBI operations in 1969, Hoover also said that there were more than 100 attacks on police by "extremist, all Negro, hate-type organizations, such as the Black Panther Party" during the previous six months. He reported that seven police officers were killed and 120 injured during attacks by black militants.

January 3. Governor John Bell Williams of Mississippi announced in a statewide telecast that he would seek to help build a Mississippi private school system as a "workable alternative" to public school desegregation. Williams also urged white parents to peacefully accept the ruling of the Fifth Circuit Court of Appeals on November 6, 1969, which ordered thirty Mississippi school districts to desegregate. The governor said it was "a time when reason must outweigh emotion and calm must prevail over hysteria." Williams announced that he would resubmit to the state legislature a proposal to authorize income tax credits of up to $500 a year for those who donated to educational institutions. The legislature had previously rejected that request.

January 5. Statistics released by the Bureau of the Census confirmed earlier reports that nonwhite as well as white families were fleeing poverty areas in the cities. The Bureau said that whites had been leaving the urban poverty areas for years, but the nonwhite migration seemed to have occurred chiefly since 1966. As factors behind the exodus, the Bureau cited crime, educational problems, land clearance resulting from urban renewal, and the increased availability of low-income housing outside of poverty areas. Between 1960 and 1968, minority families living in urban poverty areas declined by 9 percent. In 1968, 2.5 million whites and 1.6 million blacks lived in urban poverty areas.

January 5-7. Black children were enrolled in formerly all-white public schools in three districts in Mississippi on January 5 under the watch of federal marshals. The federal officers were sent to the state to prevent violence and to look for signs of non-compliance as the government moved to implement the November 6, 1969 decision of the U. S. Fifth Circuit Court of Appeals which ordered thirty Mississippi school districts to desegregate. Three of the thirty districts under the desegregation order reopened classes for the second semester on January 5, 1970. The others were to reopen between January 7 and 12. There was no violence on January 5, but many white parents picketed the newly desegregated schools while other white parents boycotted the institutions. In Woodville, only two white children attended the district school where 1,400 black pupils had been registered. Two more Mississippi school districts reopened for the second semester on January 7, 1970 with desegregated student bodies. In Yazoo City, where white business leaders had asked parents to accept the school arrangements, nearly 1,500 white students attended the desegregated schools. In Petal, 4,000 white and 1,000 blacks went to classes together for the first time, despite a peaceful sit-in by 300 white parents at an elementary school. The whites were protesting a desegregation plan that assigned their children to classrooms as far as thirteen miles away.

January 6. Robert H. Finch, Secretary of Health, Education, and Welfare (HEW), expressed concern about the South's new private, all-white schools. He announced that there was a move within the Nixon administration to end tax exemptions for private schools established to avoid desegregation in public schools. Finch said he would request the U. S. Treasury Department to "reconsider the present policy" of granting tax-exempt status to such private schools. He estimated that as many as 400 private schools had opened in the South since the passage of the Civil Rights Act of 1964.

January 8. The Tennessee Supreme Court refused to consider a plea for a new trial for James Earl Ray, the white vagabond serving a ninety-nine year sentence for the murder of Dr. Martin Luther King, Jr. The court reasoned that there could be no legal basis for granting a new trial for the defendant who had pleaded guilty and fully understood what he was doing.

January 13. A three-judge federal district court in Washington, D. C. ordered the Internal Revenue Service to stop granting tax-exempt privileges to segregated private schools in Mississippi. The order did not affect the all-white private schools that had already been granted tax-exemptions. The newly chartered all-white private academies were being funded by white parents to avoid complying with the school desegregation taking place in Mississippi's public schools.

Under the court order, the Internal Revenue Service was to stop granting tax-exempt status to schools with applications then pending or yet to be filed, unless the private schools could show they were enrolling black children.

Also, on January 13, Mississippi Governor John Bell Williams asked the state legislature to grant financial assistance to the private academies in the form of state tax deductions to those who donated money to the all-white schools. He said his program would "strengthen the hands of Mississippians" in facing the government's desegregation orders.

January 14. The United States Supreme Court, in a brief unsigned order, overruled a decision by the U. S. Fifth Circuit Court of Appeals on December 1, 1969 which set September, 1970 as a deadline for student desegregation in Southern public schools. The Court thus rejected a U. S. Justice Department request that the September deadline be approved. The Court acted on an appeal filed by the NAACP involving fourteen school districts in five Southern states. The NAACP had requested a February 1, 1970 deadline and the Supreme Court's action affirmed this request.

January 15. Blacks and whites across the nation celebrated the forty-first anniversary of the birth of Martin Luther King, Jr., as the movement to make the day a national holiday gained momentum. Several governors, including Kenneth M. Curtis of Maine, Frank K. Licht of Rhode Island, and Nelson Rockefeller of New York declared "Martin Luther King, Jr. Day" in their states. In some cities, including Baltimore, Maryland; Kansas City, Missouri; New York; and Philadelphia, Pennsylvania, public schools were closed in tribute to the slain civil rights leader. In Atlanta, Georgia, King's hometown, four hundred people heard the city's new mayor, Sam Massell, eulogize King at a memorial service. Following the service King's widow, Coretta Scott King, dedicated Atlanta's new Martin Luther King, Jr. Memorial Center, which comprised King's birthplace, church, and crypt.

January 19. Florida Governor Claude R. Kirk, Jr. personally told the United States Supreme Court that his state was "financially and physically unable" to meet the Court's January 14, 1970 decree ordering immediate school desegregation. Kirk announced that he had instructed Florida school districts to change their school calendars during mid-term. The governor also asked the Court for a re-hearing of its January 14 order and requested a delay in the February 1 school desegregation deadline. Kirk said that Florida stood ready to comply with the Court's orders, but was presently simply unable to do so. Attorneys for two Louisiana school districts also appeared before the Court with similar pleas. The Supreme Court listened to the arguments then ordered the desegregation to proceed as scheduled.

January 20. Federal district Judge Manuel L. Real in Los Angeles ordered the Pasadena, California school district to submit a desegregation plan for its public schools by February 16, 1970. The plan, covering all the schools in the suburban Los Angeles district, would take effect in September. The Pasadena case was the first of the federal government's suits against non-Southern school districts to be acted upon. The judge ruled that the plan submitted by the school officials should not produce any school with a majority of nonwhite students. Judge Real also ordered that the plan should cover new teaching assignments, hiring and promotional practices, and the construction of new school buildings.

January 21. A coroner's jury in Chicago, Illinois concluded that the deaths of Black Panther Party leaders Fred Hampton and Mark Clark, slain by a police raiding party on December 4, 1969 (see entry above), were justifiable. The special inquest was assembled on January 6 after Panther leaders had charged that Hampton was "murdered in his bed." The foreman of the six-man jury said the verdict was reached "solely on the evidence presented." Chicago detectives who participated in the pre-dawn raid had testified that one or more persons in Hampton's apartment opened fire on the police. Seven other members of the Black Panther Party were arrested following the raid. The attorneys representing the families of the two slain Panthers did not call any witnesses during the hearing. They indicated that they did not want to reveal their plans for the defense of the seven Panthers who faced possible trial for attempted murder. A Cook County (of which Chicago is the county seat) Grand Jury was also investigating the incident.

January 24. In a report released in Saigon, South Vietnam, Army investigators found that "all indications point toward an increase in racial tension" on military bases throughout the world. The investigation, which had been ordered by General William C. Westmoreland, Army Chief of Staff, was presented to the Joint Chiefs of Staff in Washington in the fall of 1969 and then sent to congressmen and military commanders in the United States and abroad. The report said that "Negro soldiers seem to have lost faith in the Army system," and predicted increased racial problems unless "aggressive command action, firm but impartial discipline, and good leadership can prevent physical confrontation of racial groups." The study concluded that the Army had "a race problem because our country has a race problem." Yet there were conditions within the Army that possibly contributed to unrest among black soldiers. For instance, according to the report, the number of black junior officers were decreasing although there were more black non-commissioned officers of lower rank. The report also found that on European bases, where one out of eight soldiers was black, one out of four non-judicial punishments (minor penalties fixed without trial) was imposed on a black soldier.

January 27. Judge G. Harrold Carswell of Florida told the United States Senate's Judiciary Committee "I am not a racist. I have no notions, secretive or otherwise, of racial superiority." Senators questioned Carswell during the first day of confirmation hearings on his nomination to the United States Supreme Court on a "white supremacy" speech that he made during a political campaign in Georgia back in 1948. Carswell said that "the force of 22 years of history" had changed him as well as the South.

On January 21, the NAACP had urged the Senate to reject Carswell because of his pro-segregation record. NAACP Board chairman Bishop Stephen G. Spottswood noted that the NAACP and 124 other organizations had opposed Carswell's appointment to the U. S. Court of Appeals for the Fifth Circuit in May, 1969.

On January 23, Ralph David Abernathy, president of the SCLC, announced that he had sent a telegram opposing Carswell to Senate leaders. Abernathy said the rejection of Carswell "would provide some reassurances to the black community that there is still some understanding and support among government officials for our needs." The Senate later rejected the Carswell nomination.

January 29. President Richard M. Nixon expressed concern over his administration's failure to gain the confidence of the nation's black citizens. The President said that he could improve his standing among blacks by using phrases and slogans, but that he eschewed such tactics because it would only serve to widen the gap between the government and African-Americans. Nixon said he was more concerned with deeds than words, and that approval of his legislative proposals against crime and for increased job opportunities would serve to end the performance gap and inspire trust in his administration.

January. Blacks gained a degree of political control over the city of Atlanta, Georgia. Five African-Americans were elected or reelected to the eighteen-member Board of Aldermen (city council), three were elected or reelected to the ten-member Board of Education. A young black lawyer, Maynard Jackson, was elected vice mayor and president of the Board of Aldermen. The venerable black educator, Benjamin E. Mays, was named head of the School Board.

February 1. Southern school officials in twenty districts in Alabama, Georgia, and Mississippi defied federal court orders calling for total school desegregation and refused to implement federally-designed school desegregation plans. Some administrators closed their schools temporarily while others supported boycotts by white parents and students. In two Alabama districts the court orders were ignored. The February 1 deadline for desegregation was set by the U. S. Supreme Court on January 14. Of the forty school districts under court orders, only a few implemented desegregation plans. These included three in Louisiana, two in Mississippi, and one in Florida. Many of the officials in the twenty districts that disobeyed the orders arbitrarily closed the schools to await further appeals for delays.

In Bessemer, Alabama, school officials flatly stated that they would not comply with the desegregation orders. Black lawyers filed a suit on February 1 requesting that the Bessemer school board be found in contempt of court. In Burke County, Georgia, the schools reopened under a "freedom of choice" arrangement, even though the courts had previously invalidated such a scheme. Panama City, Florida was one of the few districts to fully comply with the court orders. About 1,000 of its 17,500 students were transferred to new schools to achieve a more racially-balanced system.

February 26. According to a *New York Times* report, efforts to increase black enlistments in the National Guard had proved largely unsuccessful. A survey conducted by the Guard revealed that there were 5,487 blacks in the Air and Army units at the end of 1969 out of a total enlistment of nearly 500,000 men. Blacks constituted 1.15 percent of guardsmen in 1969 as compared to 1.18

percent in 1968. Congress had refused a request for $6.5 million to recruit blacks into the Guard in 1969, and the Defense Department did not renew the request in 1970.

February 28. A confidential memorandum from Daniel P. Moynihan, domestic advisor to President Richard Nixon, proposed that "the time may have come when the issue of race could benefit from a period of 'benign neglect'" was made public. Moynihan, a "liberal" Democrat, explained later that all he meant was that blacks could fare better if extremists on both sides of the political spectrum would lower their voices. He asserted that his memorandum had been written with a twofold purpose: to bring the President up to date on the "quite extraordinary" progress of blacks in the last decade, and to suggest ways in which these gains could be "consolidated" in the future. (See also entry dated March 5, 1970.)

March 3. A mob of angry whites wielding ax handles and baseball bats stormed buses transporting black school children to a formerly all-white school in Lamar, South Carolina. About 100 South Carolina State police officers dispersed the mob with riot clubs and tear gas after the crowd of approximately 200 white men and women rushed the buses and smashed the windows at Lamar High School. Thirty-nine black students were aboard the buses. Several children received minor injuries from flying glass and the effects of tear gas. Although no one was arrested at the scene, state and federal officials later moved to apprehend the mob's leaders.

March 5. Twenty black civil rights leaders, authors, legislators, and educators issued a statement describing Daniel Moynihan's "benign neglect" memorandum to President Nixon as "symptomatic of a calculated, aggressive and systematic" effort by the Nixon administration to "wipe out" nearly two decades of civil rights progress. The signers included Professor Nathan Hare, Michigan Congressman John Conyers, Jr., and civil rights leader Bayard Rustin.

March 13. The United States Senate voted to extend the Voting Rights Act of 1965 for five additional years. The act would now expire in 1975. Among the provisions of the act was a ban on literacy tests as a qualification for voting and permission for one to vote in presidential elections if residency in a locality at least a month before election day was established.

March 14. United States District Court Judge Charles R. Weiner in Philadelphia upheld the constitutionality of the Labor Department's controversial Philadelphia Plan which sought to increase minority employment in the construction industry. Judge Weiner rejected a request for an injunction against the plan which was requested in a suit filed on January 6, 1970 by the Contractors Association of Eastern Pennsylvania. Judge Weiner said the pilot job program did not in any way violate the Civil Rights Act of 1964 which forbade racial quotas in employment. The jurist reasoned that "it is fundamental that civil rights without economic rights are mere shadows." The Philadelphia Plan did not violate the Civil Rights Act of 1964, the judge said, because it "does not require the contractor to hire a definite percentage of a minority group." The contractors had only to make "good faith" efforts to hire a certain number of blacks and other minorities. (See also entry dated June 27, 1969.)

May 12. Six black men died as a result of racial rioting in Augusta, Georgia. All died at the hands of local police.

May 14. Mississippi law enforcement officers killed two black youths during a racial disturbance at Jackson State College in the capital city.

May 29. The conviction of Black Panther party leader Huey P. Newton for manslaughter was reversed by a California Court of Appeals. Newton was convicted on September 8, 1968 in the fatal shooting of an Oakland, California police officer. Newton was also implicated in the wounding of another police officer and the kidnapping of a black motorist. In his 1968 trial, Newton was defended by attorney Charles A. Garry. A major contention of the defense was that Newton laid unconscious from a gunshot wound at the time the Oakland police officer was shot. The California court found procedural errors in the original trial and ordered the conviction overturned.

June. Charles Rangel, a black Harlem politician, defeated incumbent Adam Clayton Powell, Jr. for his long-held seat in the U. S. House of Representatives. Eight African-Americans sat in the House during 1970, including the venerable William L. Dawson (who was, at the time, on the verge of retirement), Charles C. Diggs of Michigan, Augustus F. Hawkins of California, Robert C. Nix of Pennsylvania, Shirley Chisholm of New York, Louis Stokes of Ohio, and the youthful John Conyers of Michigan.

June 29. The chairman of the NAACP's Board of Directors, Bishop Stephen Gill Spottswood, charged the administration of President Richard M. Nixon with being "anti-Negro" and accused it of implementing a "calculated policy to work against the needs and aspirations of the largest minority of its citizens." In his keynote address to the NAACP Annual Convention in Cincinnati, Ohio, Spottswood indicted the administration for, among other things, a retreat on school desegregation; the nomination of "conservative" Southerners Clement Haynsworth and G. Harrold Carswell to the United States Supreme Court; and the administration's memo calling for "benign neglect" of blacks. The statement marked a significant break between the largest and oldest black civil rights organization and the national administration. Because of this fact, and the NAACP's reputation as a "moderate organization," the administration quickly responded, calling the charges "unfair" and "disheartening," and, at the same time, pointing out positive contributions such as the administration's support of the extension of the Voting Rights Act of 1965.

July 1. Kenneth Gibson, a city engineer, became the mayor of Newark, New Jersey. At the time, Gibson was the only African-American mayor of a large Eastern city. By 1970, there were more than 500 elected black officeholders in the nation.

July 7-31. Racial rioting occurred in several Northern cities. On July 7, a curfew was imposed in Asbury Park, New Jersey, following four days of violence; forty-three people were shot during the rioting. The curfew was lifted on July 10. Calm was restored in the New Jersey resort town after Mayor Joseph Mattice agreed to consider a list of demands presented to him by a coalition of black organizations. William Hamm, a spokesperson for the black community leaders, presented the mayor with a list of twenty-two demands, including requests for better housing, more jobs, and increased efforts at halting narcotics traffic. On July 12, following four nights of racial disturbances, a curfew was imposed in New Bedford, Massachusetts. On July 31, a curfew was imposed in Hartford, Connecticut following three days of rioting by African-Americans and Puerto Ricans.

July 10. The Internal Revenue Service (IRS) announced that the tax-exempt status of private schools practicing racial discrimination in their admission policies would be revoked. The action came as the government sought to respond to the growing number of all-white private schools in the South. Most of the schools had sprung up in the wake of desegregation of the public schools.

July 29. United States District Court Judge Frank M. Johnson, Jr. ordered seven Alabama state agencies to stop discriminating against blacks in their hiring practices and to give immediate job consideration to sixty-two black applicants who were denied positions earlier. The federal judge directed state authorities to take steps in eliminating all future racial discrimination in hiring practices. He ordered them to submit a report to the court within thirty days on what had been done to comply with his order. In reviewing the case, which was filed by the U. S. Justice Department in 1968, Johnson noted that Alabama was the only state that had still refused to adopt a resolution formally prohibiting racial discrimination and providing for a system of redress in such cases. Johnson also directed the seven agencies to hire blacks and to appoint them to positions other than custodial, domestics, or laborers, when such applicants were listed as qualified and eligible.

August 1. The United States Department of Defense reported that the percentage of black soldiers killed in Vietnam had declined substantially during the first three months in 1970. The Pentagon report said that for the first time, the percentage of black soldiers killed in action in Southeast Asia had fallen below the percentage of blacks among the U. S. forces there. The government's data showed that as of March 31, 1970, blacks serving in Indo-China represented about 10 percent of the total American military presence in the area. During the same three months, black fatalities accounted for 8.5 percent of the combat deaths in Southeast Asia, in contrast to 9.5 percent in 1969. The Defense Department cited no specific effort in decreasing the casualty rates among black servicemen in Vietnam.

August 7. Four people died during a courthouse shootout in San Rafael, California when three black convicts attempted to escape. A judge, two of the convicts, and another black youth who was aiding the convicts were killed. Angela Davis, a former black American professor at the University of California at Los Angeles, was implicated in the incident and fled the state in order to avoid arrest.

August 17. Chicago detective James A. Alfonso, a member of the city's police gang intelligence unit, died from wounds he incurred on August 13 when a rifleman fired a shot into his unmarked police car on the city's South Side. Alfonso, age thirty, was the fourth Chicago police officer slain in the city's black neighborhoods since mid-June. The next day, Chicago police said that they had arrested four members of the "Main 21," the ruling body of the Black P. Stone Nation, a confederation of sixty black street gangs based on the old Blackstone Rangers. One of those held, Charles E. Bey, age twenty-three, identified himself as vice president of the "Nation" and a member of the "Main 21." Some Chicago blacks contended that the recent wave of violence grew out

Black soldier holding captured Viet Cong flag.

146

of a widespread pattern of police brutality and a series of incidents in which the police had slain blacks, including members of the Black Panther Party.

August 19. The administration of President Richard M. Nixon announced that it would soon terminate a contract with a Pennsylvania contractor for failure to comply with its "Philadelphia Plan" designed to train and employ blacks and other minority workers on construction jobs. It was the government's first enforcement action against a contractor charged with violation of a job agreement. Secretary of Health, Education, and Welfare Elliott L. Richardson notified Edgeley Air Products, Inc. of Levittown, Pennsylvania, that his Office for Civil Rights intended to cancel a contract and bar the company from future federal contracts on the grounds of noncompliance. The government's contract with the Edgeley Company was for sheet metal work on a building at the University of Pennsylvania. Leonard Nucero, the president of Edgeley, denied that the company practiced discrimination and said the company would appeal the termination of the contract. (See also entry dated March 14, 1970.)

August 26. A federal court in Washington refused a request by the Nixon administration to dismiss a suit pending against federal tax exemptions for the private all-white academies in the South. The court also denied a request by civil rights groups who brought the suit that all such academies have their tax-exempt status revoked immediately. The administration's lawyer told the court that the IRS would no longer grant tax-exempt status to private schools practicing racial discrimination in admissions policies, but that for now the government had relied on the word of the schools in determining whether they were willing to desegregate.

August 27. David L. Rice, minister of information for the National Committee to Combat Fascism, surrendered to police in Omaha, Nebraska, in connection with the August 17 death of a local police officer. Rice, a black man, was sought in the slaying of Officer Larry D. Minard, age twenty-nine, who was killed when he touched a satchel that police said was filled with an explosive and rigged as a booby trap. Seven other Omaha police officers were also injured. The eight officers were called to a vacant house in Omaha's predominantly-black North Side district to investigate a report of a woman in distress. Rice was charged with illegal possession of explosives.

August 29. Poindexter E. Williams, a black soldier killed in Vietnam during a mortar barrage, was buried in a formerly all-white cemetary in Fort Pierce, Florida. The cemetary had refused to bury the soldier since August 20. On August 27, a federal judge ordered the cemetary to accept Williams's body for burial. Williams was buried in a gravesite donated to his family by a white woman. Other whites, citing the Caucasians-only clause in lot purchase contracts, opposed the burial. Following Williams's interment, some whites who owned plots in the Hillcrest Memorial Gardens threatened to remove their relatives' remains.

August 29-31. In Philadelphia, one police officer was killed and six others were wounded in a series of gun battles between police and members of black militant organizations, including the Black Panthers. Police Commissioner Frank L. Rizzo blamed the incidents on a group called "The Revolutionaries," which he said had plotted to murder police officers, and the Black Panther Party of Philadelphia. The altercation with the Panthers resulted from an early morning raid on August 31 at the Panther Information Center on Philadelphia's North Side. Police said they were searching for a suspect in connection with an earlier shooting.

August 31. More than 200 school districts across the South that had resisted desegregation since the U. S. Supreme Court Order in 1954 reopened peacefully with newly desegregated classrooms. Nearly 300,000 black children from Virginia to Louisiana began classes with whites as threatened school boycotts by white parents failed to materialize. Despite the massive compliance, 175 other districts continued to hold out for segregation. Most of these were involved in litigation on the controversial issue of student busing. Some were involved in negotiations with governmental officials aimed at ending segregated school systems.

Also on August 31, the Supreme Court's Chief Justice Warren E. Burger announced that the Court would consider the broad aspects of remaining school desegregation problems when the new court term began on October 12. Many blacks and whites had raised questions concerning the legality of busing, the concept of racial balance, and the definition of a unitary school system.

August 31. Lonnie McLucas, the first of eight Black Panthers to stand trial for the 1969 slaying of a New York party member, was convicted of conspiracy to murder by a jury in New Haven, Connecticut. McLucas, age twenty-four, was acquitted on three other charges involving kidnapping resulting in death, conspiracy to kidnap, and binding with intent to commit a crime. He faced a maximum sentence of fifteen years in prison. The three other charges on which Lucas was acquitted all carried heavier penalties, including the death sentence for kidnapping resulting in death.

McLucas and seven other Panthers, including National Chairman Bobby Seale, were charged with conspiracy to murder Alex Rackley, whose body was found near Middlefield, Connecticut in May, 1969. The state had charged in the original indictments that Rackley was slain because he had been suspected by the party of being a police informant. McLucas' attorney, Theodore I. Kossoff, contended that the order for Rackley's murder originated from George Sams, Jr., a Panther member, whom the defense alleged was responsible for the torture and murder of Rackley. (See also entry dated August 19, 1969.)

August 31. John S. Martin, superintendent of public schools in Jackson, Mississippi, resigned, citing the federal courts and the pressures of school desegregation. According to the *New York Times*, Martin joined at least 200 other school superintendents in the South who had resigned in the past two years because of the problems and tensions resulting from desegregation in their districts. William Dunn, superintendent of schools in Louisiana, predicted that the federal government's latest attempt to desegregate schools in the South would lead to a wave of resignations from experienced educators. The rate of turnover among superintendents in Alabama, Louisiana, and Georgia since 1968 was nearly 40 percent, almost double the rate in any previous two-year period. Louisiana led the South in the rate of turnovers. In two years, there had been thirty-nine turnovers among the sixty-six district superintendents.

August. Huey P. Newton, one of the founders and leader of the Black Panther Party, was released on a $50,000 bond after serving more than two years in a California prison for a manslaughter conviction in the death of an Oakland, California police officer. Earlier, the California Court of Appeals reversed the conviction on the grounds that the trial judge erred in instructing the jury and opened the way for Newton's release pending a new trial (see entry dated May 29, 1970). Charles Garry, Newton's attorney, charged that the bail was excessive, but acquiesced. Newton was greeted by a crowd of about 300 upon his release. He shouted: "The people have the power! All power to the people!"

September 1. A federal grand jury in Augusta, Georgia, indicted two white police officers on charges of violating the civil rights of two black men who were shot May 12 during a night of racial rioting that left six blacks dead and sixty others injured. Officer William S. Dennis was charged with the fatal shooting of John W. Stokes, and Officer Louis C. Dinkins was accused of wounding Louis N. Williams. The grand jury began its inquiry into the shootings on August 24 and found cause for indictment in only one of the six deaths. After the biracial jury handed down the indictments, the decision was denounced by Georgia Governor Lester Maddox. The "national government, from the President on down," he said, "is only worrying about agitators."

September 1. The Justice Department announced that a federal judge in Cleveland, Ohio had issued a consent decree requiring Roadway Express Company, the nation's third largest trucking concern, to implement an equal employment program. The order ended the department's first efforts to enjoin job discrimination throughout a company's nationwide operation. Judge Thomas D. Lambros specifically enjoined Roadway from engaging in any act or practice that had the purpose of denying blacks equal employment opportunities in hiring, upgrading, and promotions. The decree also ordered Roadway, which had freight terminals in twenty-eight states, to offer job opportunities on a first available vacancy basis to 105 individuals with seniority and other benefits for forty-five of them. The Justice Department had filed suit against

Roadway in May, 1968, charging that blacks had been discriminated against in job placement and other opportunities.

September 2. In Baltimore, Maryland, United States District Court Judge Frank A. Kaufman rejected the appeal of William H. Murphy, Jr., a member of the Nation of Islam, who contended that he should be exempted from military service as a conscientious objector. Kaufman ruled that the Nation of Islam represented a political rather than a religious objection to war.

September 3. Representatives of nine black colleges charged the Nixon administration with failure to support black higher education. The educators, meeting in Detroit, Michigan, under the leadership of president Lucius H. Pitts of Miles College (Birmingham, Alabama), called for increased government and private funds to strengthen the more than 100 black colleges and universities. Vivian Henderson, president of Clark College in Atlanta, Georgia, accused the Nixon administration of an "utter lack of sensitivity" to the needs of black colleges and that this fed "the flames that already roar in the hearts of many black students." About two billion dollars was cited by Vernon Jordan, head of the United Negro College Fund (UNCF), as the minimum aid necessary to maintain black colleges. White House Press Secretary Ronald L. Ziegler, in a letter to Dr. Pitts, reminded the educators of a July 23 pledge by the administration to increase support for their colleges.

September 5-7. The Black Panther Party and members of the Women's and Gay Liberation movements held the first session of their "Revolutionary People's Constitutional Convention" in Philadelphia. Despite tensions over the August 29 slaying of a Philadelphia police officer and the subsequent arrest of fourteen people at three Black Panther offices, the three-day conference was conducted in a peaceful manner. The Panther Party had organized the convention in order to rewrite the U. S. Constitution, which according to the group, did not go far enough in protecting the rights of oppressed people. Approximately 6,000 people participated in the meeting. Among the Panther's delegation were co-founder Huey P. Newton and Panther Chief-of-Staff David Hilliard. The second session of the convention was slated for November 4, 1970 in Washington, D. C.

September 9. Another round of school desegregation in the South began and was marked by stiffening white resistance to federal orders and confusion over new student assignments. More disruptions were recorded with the reopening of schools than had occurred when most of the South's schools desegregated peacefully on August 31. White parents in Mobile, Alabama resisted desegregation efforts by enrolling their children in their formerly segregated schools and by boycotting their newly assigned schools. On September 10, the NAACP charged that the Mobile school board had discriminated against black children in the inner city by its deployment of 225 school buses. The board replied that it had neither the time nor funds to buy more buses to handle inner city children. On September 14, the Justice Department accused the same school board of repeated violations of desegregation orders. Federal Judge Daniel H. Thomas commanded the board to cease circumventing the school orders. There was little resistance in the Charlotte-Mecklenburg, North Carolina school system, one of the largest in the South, as the system reopened under a court-ordered desegregation plan that required extensive busing of children. The plan had aroused much community opposition in Charlotte, yet school officials said that 80 percent of the high school students reported to their classes. The school superintendent in Bogalusa, Louisiana closed the public schools on September 14 after police used tear gas to end a fight between black and white students at a recently desegregated school. Police Chief Thomas Mixon, Jr. estimated that 600 high school students were involved in the two hour altercation. Fourteen students were arrested.

September 11. The Internal Revenue Service (IRS) revoked the tax-exempt classification of five all-white private academies in Mississippi after the schools refused to enroll black children. The cancellations brought a total of sixteen all-white academies in the South that had lost their tax-exempt status since the IRS prohibited tax deductions for segregated schools (see entry dated July 10, 1970). The sixteen schools, and the five in Mississippi were among those in the South (forty-one of them in Mississippi) named in a court order directing governmental officials to revoke tax-exempt status for all-white private schools practicing racial discrimination in admission policies.

September 12. Governor Ronald Reagan of California signed into law a bill prohibiting the busing of students "for any purpose or any reason without the written permission of the parent or guardian." The law was to take effect in November. The California branch of the NAACP announced that it would test the constitutionality of the measure in court.

September 13. Eldridge Cleaver, exiled Black Panther Party leader, presided over the opening of the party's first "international section" in Algiers. The Algerian government, which had broken off diplomatic ties with the United States in 1967, had formally accorded the Panther party the status of a "liberation movement."

September 14-15. One black youth was killed and twenty-one others injured during a day-long gun battle between police and blacks in a New Orleans housing project. The incident began on September 14, when two black undercover police officers who successfully infiltrated the National Committee to Combat Fascism (NCCF), a branch of the Black Panther Party, were discovered and beaten. The officers escaped when the NCCF turned them over to a crowd of about 100 blacks for a "people's trial." Later, police returned to the project to investigate reports of a burning automobile. Police officers and fire fighters were fired upon and the melee broke out in full force. Fourteen blacks, most of them from the NCCF, were arrested during the disturbance and charged with attempted murder.

September 18. Lonnie McLucas, the first of eight Black Panther Party members to stand trial for the slaying of Alex Rackley, was sentenced to 12-15 years in prison by a New Haven, Connecticut court. McLucas was convicted of conspiracy to murder in the Rackley case on August 31, 1970 (see entry above). Superior Court Judge Harold M. Mulvey assessed the maximum term allowed under Connecticut law for the crime of conspiracy to murder. McLucas' attorney, Theodore I. Kossoff, immediately filed notice of appeal.

September 28. Cleveland L. Sellers, Jr., a black activist, was convicted by a biracial jury in Orangeburg, South Carolina of participating in a riot on the campus of South Carolina State College in 1968, in which three black students were killed by state highway patrolmen (see entry dated February 8, 1968). Sellers, a former national program secretary for SNCC, was sentenced to the maximum term of one year in prison and a fine of $250. Sellers was released on a $5,000 appeal bond by State Circuit Court Judge John Grimball, who said that the young black activist could leave the state in order to attend college. On September 26, Judge Grimball had ordered a directed verdict of acquittal of two other riot charges against Sellers, citing the fact that the prosecution had failed to prove that Sellers had incited the Orangeburg students to riot. During the 1968 riot, 27 blacks were wounded, including Sellers, in addition to the three students slain.

September 28. For the first time, a Health, Education, and Welfare (HEW) hearing examiner ruled that a Northern school district was illegally segregating its pupils according to race. The Ferndale, Michigan school district was deprived of $275,000 in federal aid because of its segregated elementary schools.

September 30. The Race Relations Information Center in Nashville, Tennessee reported that there were only three black executives among the 3,182 senior officers of the top fifty American corporate firms. These were Robert C. Weaver of the Metropolitan Life Insurance Co., Clifton R. Wharton, Jr. of the Equitable Life Assurance Society, and Thomas A. Wood of the Chase Manhattan Bank. All three held the position of corporate director.

October 1. J. Stanley Pottinger, director of the Office of Civil Rights of the Department of Health, Education and Welfare, reported that federal school monitors in the South had found extensive in-school segregation of black pupils. Pottinger said his office had investigated 120 desegregated school districts since the fall term began and found patterns of in-school segregation in at least half of them. The matter of segregation by classrooms received much attention from the Senate Select Committee on Equal Educational Opportunity throughout the summer of 1970. Pottinger announced that the Nixon administration intended to move against the new form of segregation but only after it had solicited the advice of educators. He promised to develop guidelines by the spring semester of 1971.

October 1. A federal court in Buffalo, New York ruled unconstitutional a New York statute that had made it illegal for appointed school boards to reshuffle pupil assignment plans to achieve racial balance without the consent of parents. The law, which was enacted in May, 1969, was challenged by a group of black and white parents in Buffalo. School administrators in the South had hailed it as a means of forestalling school desegregation. The court found the law contrary to the Fourteenth Amendment, in that it served to continue segregation in the schools and involved the state in racial discrimination.

October 1. Elliot L. Richardson, Secretary of Health, Education, and Welfare, announced a thirty percent, or $30 million, increase in federal aid to predominantly-black colleges. This increased the total aid from HEW to $129 million a year. Secretary Richardson noted that the increase was in response to recent appeals by black educators for more aid. Blacks complained that matching provisions of the fund grants and early deadlines for applications made it difficult for most African-American institutions to qualify.

October 5. The Internal Revenue Service reported that nine all-white private academies in Mississippi had agreed to admit black students. In the same announcement, the IRS said it had removed fourteen other all-white academies from its list of schools eligible for tax-exempt status. These suspensions brought to thirty-eight the number of private schools in the state which had lost their tax-exempt status.

October 5-November 8. Violent racial clashes connected with school desegregation occurred in three cities in both the North and South. Four white boys and one black youth were shot and wounded in two apparently related incidents on October 5 and 7 outside a desegregated high school in Pontiac, Michigan. A second black student was struck down by a car near Pontiac Central High School on October 7 as white and black students continued in their two day battle with rocks and bottles. Tensions had run high in Pontiac following a recent court decision ordering desegregation of Pontiac's public schools. Public schools in Trenton, New Jersey were closed for two days, October 29-30, due to racial disorders stemming from the school board's decision to implement a student busing plan. On November 1, the board voted to reopen the schools, and a dusk-to-dawn curfew that was imposed on the city on October 29 was ordered relaxed by Mayor Arthur J. Holland. The trouble started on October 29 when fighting began between one hundred black and white students in a predominantly-Italian section of the city. Fighting spread into the downtown area when bands of black youths surged into the district hurling bottles at police officers and breaking windows. More than 200 people were arrested during the three days of disorder. The fighting was apparently triggered by the school board's decision to implement a busing plan to achieve racial balance in the schools. The plan called for the cross-town busing of fifty-five black and one hundred white students. Four days of sporadic sniper fire and burnings erupted in Henderson, North Carolina, November 5-8, in the aftermath of a dispute over the county's school desegregation policies. Police jailed 101 people during the melee. Blacks in Henderson had been engaged in a long protest over a decision by school officials to reopen an all-black school in the community. The blacks charged that the board of education was trying to evade desegregation by reopening the school. The National Guard was called to help restore order. By November 9, the school board had agreed to close the school in contention and bus its pupils to desegregated schools. The National Guard remained on duty.

October 12. The United States Commission on Civil Rights reported a major breakdown in the enforcement of the nation's legal mandates prohibiting racial discrimination. The Commission urged President Richard Nixon to use "courageous moral leadership" and, within the White House, to establish committees to oversee enforcement of court decrees, executive orders, and legislation relating to civil rights. Rev. Theodore M. Hesburgh, the chairman of the Commission, said the findings were based on a six-month study of the executive departments and agencies charged with enforcing the nation's civil rights laws. The report, entitled "The Federal Civil Rights Enforcement Effort," asserted that "the credibility of the government's total civil rights efforts" had been "seriously underminded." Hesburgh warned that "unless we get serious about this, the country is on a collision course."

October 12-14. The United States Supreme Court heard arguments on student busing and racial balance in the schools of the South. The arguments were heard by the Court as part of appeals filed by attorneys representing school districts in Charlotte, North Carolina, and Mobile, Alabama. Attorneys for the NAACP Legal Defense and Educational Fund, Inc., representing black children, argued on October 13 that each black child had a constitutional right to be enrolled in a school that was not recognizably black. The lawyers contended that any desegregation plan that did not eliminate every all-black school should be adjudged as inadequate. The NAACP lawyers told the court that the *Brown v. Board of Education* decision of 1954 would be undermined if the Court now permitted some Southern school districts to maintain some recognizably black schools. Solicitor General Ervin N. Griswold, representing the Justice Department, rebutted the NAACP argument on October 12 and 14. The Solicitor General contended that the NAACP's petition amounted to a demand for racial balance in the schools, something which the Constitution did not require. Lawyers for the school districts told the court on October 13 that the Brown decision is violated by court-ordered desegregation plans that assigned children to schools by race, and that the busing of school children to increase the incidence of desegregation was unconstitutional. The court promised a ruling during its present term.

October 13. Angela Davis, a twenty-six-year-old black professor at the University of California at Los Angeles, was apprehended by FBI agents in a New York City motel. Davis, who was the object of a two-month nationwide search for her alleged role in the murder of a California judge (see entry dated August 7, 1970) was arraigned on October 14 in federal court on a charge of unlawful flight to avoid prosecution on the California charges. The federal charge was later suspended when the California warrants charging Davis with the capital offenses arrived in New York. Federal authorities announced that it was customary in such cases for the state warrants to take precedence. Davis's attorney, John J. Abt, refused to waive extradition to California. Since Davis was being held for capital offenses, no bail was permitted. David R. Poindexter, Jr., age thirty-six, was released from jail on October 16 on a $100,000 bond, having been arrested with Davis and charged with harboring a fugitive.

October 19. The NAACP and the Washington law firm of Rauh and Silard filed suit against the Department of Health, Education, and Welfare (HEW) charging it with "general and calculated default" in its enforcement of federal school desegregation guidelines. The suit accused the federal agency of laxity in applying the cut-off of federal school funds to force recalcitrant school districts to comply with the law. It was the second time in two weeks that the government's enforcement of civil rights had been questioned. The U. S. Commission on Civil Rights reported on October 12, 1970, that there had been a "major breakdown" in the enforcement of the nation's law forbidding racial discrimination. HEW Secretary Elliot L. Richardson replied that his department was "committed faithfully to carry out both the letter and the spirit of the 1964 Civil Rights Act."

October 19. United States District Court Judge Julius J. Hoffman dismissed the government's conspiracy charges against Bobby G. Seale, chairman of the Black Panther Party, at the request of the U. S. Attorney in Chicago. William J. Bauer told the court that "it would be inappropriate to try Seale alone on a conspiracy charge." Seale was one of eight defendants charged with conspiracy to cross state lines with intent to riot at the 1968 Democratic National Convention in Chicago. Judge Hoffman had severed Seale's case after the Black Panther leader had bitterly denounced the manner in which the jurist handled the trial. Seale's co-defendants, all whites, were subsequently acquitted on the conspiracy to riot charges. Seale still faced a four year prison term on contempt of court charges in Chicago as well as charges of kidnapping and murder in the slaying of a New York Black Panther Party member (see entry dated August 31, 1970).

October 24-25. Violent clashes between blacks and police officers continued in Northern ghettoes. On the night of October 24-25, several car loads of armed blacks riddled the police station in Cairo, Illinois with hundreds of rounds of gunfire three times in six hours. No police officers were wounded and the attackers were repelled after each assault. It was the first outbreak in racially-tense Cairo since September, 1969, when disturbances broke out in the all-black Pyramid Housing Project. The October attacks began the evening of the 24th shortly after a white-owned grocery store located across from the housing project was burned. Cairo Mayor A. B. Thomas called the incident an "armed insurrection." In Detroit, on October 24, one black police officer, Edward Smith, was killed and another wounded in an altercation with members of the National Committee to Combat Fascism. The policemen were felled by shotgun blasts from the NCCF's headquarters, according to police accounts. Fifteen blacks were arrested after a day-long confrontation around the NCCF offices. The seven men and eight women were charged with murder and conspiracy. The disturbance was triggered by an incident involving the sale of Black Panther Party literature on a Detroit street corner. The NCCF claimed that two policemen beat two youths distributing the literature and that police fired the first shots in the melee.

October 28. Edward A. Poindexter and David L. Rice, leaders of the National Committee to Combat Fascism, were ordered to stand trial in Omaha, Nebraska, on murder charges in connection with the August 17, 1970 slaying of an Omaha police officer. The two blacks, who had been in custody since August, were to remain in jail without bond. (See also entry dated August 27, 1970.)

November 20-22. More than 500 inmates reportedly took part in a racial disturbance at the sprawling 16,000 acre Cumming prison farm, 90 miles southeast of Little Rock, Arkansas. The fighting stemmed from inmates' demands for separate quarters for black and white prisoners. Commissioner of Corrections Robert Sawer reported that state troopers were called in after the violence reached riot proportions; some of the prisoners had armed themselves with knives, pipes, and broomstick handles. Prison guards broke up the fighting with tear gas.

December 11. The Justice Department filed suit in a federal district court in Alabama charging that the United States Steel Corporation, the United Steelworkers of America, the AFL-CIO, and twelve union locals had violated the Civil Rights Act of 1964 which prohibits discrimination in employment. U.S. Steel operated plants in the Birmingham area. On December 14, the Chairman of the Board of U. S. Steel Corporation announced that the Justice Department had demanded that the company allocate fifty percent of its office and clerical jobs in its Fairfield, Alabama plant to blacks in the next five years and that blacks make up 40 percent of all those promoted to management positions during the next five years.

December 11. A federal grand jury investigating the killing of two black youths at Jackson State College, Mississippi, on May 14, 1970 concluded its deliberations without returning any indictments. The jury also failed to submit a report.

December 27. The United States State Department invited fourteen leading Soviet scientists to attend the forthcoming murder trial of Angela Davis, former UCLA professor and avowed Communist, to assure themselves that she would receive a fair trial. The invitation was personally sanctioned by President Nixon. The offer was an apparent response to a cablegram sent by the fourteen scientists to the President asking him "to safeguard the life of Angela Davis and give her an opportunity of continuing her scientific work." According to U. S. officials, the government's quick response was due to the high regard in which the scientists were held by professional colleagues in the United States. Among the fourteen scientists were Igor P. Tamm, a Nobel Prize-winning physicist, and Pyotr L. Kapitsa, the dean of Soviet physicists. It was the first time that Soviet personalities had been invited to observe American judicial proceedings.

December 30. The United States Court of Appeals for the Third Circuit in Philadelphia ordered the Department of Housing and Urban Development (HUD) to "affirmatively promote fair housing" in considering applications for support of housing projects. The case involved HUD mortgage insurance and rent supplements in a predominantly-black neighborhood in Philadelphia. The court ruled that HUD must determine, through public hearings or by other means, whether such projects would increase or maintain segregation. According to the court, HUD could not support such housing unless it determined that the need for urban renewal or increased minority housing "clearly outweighs the disadvantages of increasing or perpetuating racial concentration." The court reasoned that after the passage of the 1964 and 1968 Civil Rights Acts, HUD could no longer "remain blind to the very real effect that racial concentration has had in the development of urban blight." Edwin D. Wolf, executive director of the Philadelphia office of the Lawyers Committee for Civil Rights, said on January 4, 1971 that the ruling was a landmark decision which could have an impact comparable to the Supreme Court's 1954 school desegregation decision.

December. Captain Curtis R. Smothers and six other black Army officers petitioned Secretary of the Army Stanley R. Resar for a court of inquiry and investigation of alleged racial bias against black soldiers in West Germany. The seven black servicemen complained of widespread housing discrimination and charged that the bias was going unchallenged because the United States government failed to press the West Germans to enforce the laws against discrimination. According to the blacks, "only an open court of inquiry convened by the Secretary of the Army could adequately determine the facts, assess the feasibility of alternative solutions and inquire into factors motivating the long-standing noncompliance with applicable laws and regulations." Under military procedures, a court of inquiry is usually convened when the issues involved were so complex that normal proceedings would not go far enough into them, or when charges were levied against high-ranking officers. Smothers, a military circuit judge in West Germany, was joined in the petition by Major Washington C. Hill, Lieutenant Edwin Dorn, Sergeant Willie Payne and three Specialists, 4th Class, Gregory Jones, Bobby Metcalf, and James Wilder. On March 13, 1971, Pentagon officials returned to Washington after discussing the December petition with Smothers in West Germany. Smothers was then summoned to Washington for further discussions. This latter event was seen by some sources as an attempt to persuade Smothers to withdraw his petition. On June 3, 1971 the black members of the U. S. House of Representatives announced that they were sending a staff member to Germany, Greece, Italy, and Turkey to investigate complaints of racism and discrimination in the U. S. Armed Forces abroad. Rep. Shirley Chisholm, chairman of the Black Caucus' Military Affairs Committee, said racial tension between the Germans and black enlisted men was reported very critical.

1971

January 1. James A. Floyd was named mayor of Princeton Township, an affluent, predominantly-white suburban community in west central New Jersey. Floyd became the first black mayor in the township's history. He was selected unanimously by the five-member Township Committee, Princeton's governing body. In December of 1970, the same committee had named Frederick M. Porter, a black police lieutenant, as chief of police.

January 4. The Reverend Leon Howard Sullivan, a forty-eight-year-old Philadelphia black minister, was elected to the board of directors of the General Motors Corporation (GM). Sullivan, pastor of Zion Baptist—Philadelphia's largest Protestant church—was the founder of Opportunities Industrialization Centers of America, a job-training program for blacks and other minorities, and a director of the Girard Trust Bank in Philadelphia. His election to the GM Board was interpreted as a move to placate demands that the company, the world's largest industrial corporation, give the public and minority groups a voice in corporate decision-making. At GM's annual stockholders meeting in May, 1970, a reform group, the Project on Corporate Responsibility, had criticized GM for not having a black director on its board.

January 5. Angela Davis was arraigned on charges of murder, kidnapping, and criminal conspiracy in a Marin County, California court for her alleged participation in the August 7, 1970 incident at the San Rafael Courthouse which resulted in the deaths of four men. Flanked by her attorney, Howard Moore, a black Atlantan, Davis declared her innocence and said she was the "target of a political frame-up." (See also entry dated December 27, 1970.)

January 5. A federal labor panel charged the Bethlehem Steel Corporation, the second largest steel producer in the United States, with discriminating against blacks through its seniority system. A report compiled by the panel was sent to Secretary of Labor James D. Hodgson, who would decide what sanctions, if any, to impose on the firm. The three member federal panel reached a unanimous decision against Bethlehem, but disagreed on what corrective measures should be taken. In a statement which accompanied the report, Bethlehem denied the charge but agreed to set new hiring, promotion and training quotas for blacks while studying the government's report. The action against Bethlehem was the second taken against one of the nation's major steel corporations. On December 11, 1970, the Justice Department had filed a suit against the U.S. Steel Corporation, accusing it of bias against blacks at its Fairfield, Alabama steelworks (see also entry dated December 11, 1970).

January 6. FBI Director J. Edgar Hoover issued his annual report in which he stated that the number of racial incidents in schools had declined during the year, but attacks on police by blacks had increased. The FBI chief said racial disorders in secondary schools declined from 299 in the first months of the 1969-70 year to 160 in the corresponding period of the new term. Hoover warned, however, that "the number of incidents of racial disorder that did occur in our cities and in secondary schools, along with the many unwarranted attacks on police, strongly indicated that we are far from the realization of racial harmony in the nation." Hoover said there was a "marked increase" in attacks on police officers by persons identifying themselves as Black Panthers. He said such persons were responsible for the deaths of six police officers and the wounding of twenty-two others and that in the previous two years, five police officers were killed and forty-two wounded under such circumstances.

January 11. The United States Supreme Court agreed to review the 1967 draft evasion conviction of former heavyweight boxing champion Muhammad Ali. The action assured that Ali, who won the championship under the name Cassius Clay, would be free to fight the recognized title holder, Joe Frazier, in March. (Frazier defeated Ali on March 8 in New York). Ali was convicted when the courts rejected his contention that he should be exempted from the draft because of his religious status as a Black Muslim minister. The current appeal was based largely on the Supreme Court's ruling in 1969 that conscientious objectors could base their claims on philosophical or moral objections rather than strictly religious grounds.

Muhammad Ali

January 14. The United States Supreme Court ruled that Southern states must obtain federal approval before making any changes in their election laws that might affect the rights of black voters as provided by the 1965 Voting Rights Act. The order came in a case brought by two black voters and six defeated black candidates in the 1969 municipal elections in Canton, Mississippi. The plaintiffs contended that the city in shifting polling places, annexing neighborhoods with white majorities, and changing to at-large elections of aldermen had discouraged and diluted the black vote. The Supreme Court returned the case to the district court to decide if the election should be reheld.

January 14. Secretary of Health, Education and Welfare Elliott L. Richardson announced in Washington that the Nixon administration would soon turn its attention to the task of increasing the rate of school desegregation in the North. The report cited a survey showing the percentage of blacks attending desegregated schools in the North and West rose from 27.6 percent to 27.7 percent in the period since 1968. This compared with a two year increase from 18.4 percent to 38.1 percent in the South. The administration concluded that a Northern drive was necessary because there were now more desegregated school systems in the South than in the North (see also entry dated June 18, 1971).

January 14. The Oregon Court of Appeals ruled that mental anguish was one of the effects of racial discrimination and could be compensated by a cash award. The court sustained the contention of Beverley A. Williams, a young black woman, who said she was discriminated against when Margaret C. Joyce refused to rent her an apartment in Portland. Williams's charge was earlier upheld by the Oregon state Bureau of Labor which assessed Joyce $200 for humiliating Williams and $140 to pay for her moving expenses, but the cash award for humiliation was overthrown by the state circuit court on appeal by Joyce. The Court of Appeals, in setting aside the circuit court's ruling, said that compensation for humiliation was proper.

January 16. Preliminary studies of the 1970 Bureau of the Census indicated very little racial integration of American suburbs during the 1960s, according to a *Washington Post* report. Specialists at the Census Bureau predicted that early trends showing little suburban integration would hold true even as more detailed analyses were completed. Meyer Zitter, assistant chief of the Bureau's population division, estimated that about 15 percent of the nation's blacks lived within metropolitan areas and outside the central cities. The figure for whites was nearly 40 percent. Census officials said that if the preliminary reports were sustained, it would again illustrate that whites were fleeing the inner cities to the suburbs. During the 1960s, there was a reported net loss of about 2.5 million whites from the inner city areas and an increase of about three million blacks. Two-thirds of the rise in the number of black inner-city dwellers was attributable to births. These preliminary reports came at a time when the Nixon administration was still shaping its policies regarding suburban desegregation.

January 17. A jury in Chicago acquitted seven members of the Black P. Stone Nation, a confederation of sixty black street gangs, of murder in the August 17, 1970 sniper slaying of a Chicago detective (see entry above). All were acquitted of charges of murder and conspiracy to commit murder in the death of Detective James A. Alfonso, Jr. The acquittal came three days after the biracial jury had begun deliberations. Those freed were Edward Bey, Lamar Bell, Tony Carter, Dennis Griffin, Ronald Florence, William Throup, and Elton Wriks. The alleged involvement of the black gangs in the murder had exacerbated tensions between the black community and Chicago police. Concomitantly, Chicago black leaders, including the SCLC's Operation Breadbasket leader, the Rev. Jesse Jackson, had criticized the black gangs for terrorizing the black communities.

January 20. The North Carolina Supreme Court sustained the state's policy of providing school buses for urban children involved in desegregation programs. As long as state funds were used to transport children from rural areas to their schools, the court reasoned, city dwelling children must have the same rights. The ruling struck down a lower court's prohibition on the use of state funds for busing. In effect, the court's decision gave the state legislature the choice of continuing busing for all children who required it or discontinuing the practice altogether. An assistant state attorney general expressed the view that the court's decision could not be appealed because it did not involve any constitutional issue.

February 1. Howard Jordan, Jr., the president of Savannah State College in Georgia, assumed duties as vice-chancellor of the Georgia State Board of Regents, becoming the first black so named. Dr. Jordan had served as president of Savannah State College since 1963. His new duties involved handling administrative matters for all state-run colleges and universities in Georgia.

February 1. The United States Court of Appeals for the Fifth Circuit in New Orleans ruled that local governments must provide such public services as road paving and sewers on a racially equal basis. The suit was filed by black residents of Shaw, Mississippi. According to the court, no compelling interests "could possibly justify the gross disparities in services between black and white areas of town."

February 4-5. Eight black federal employees charged in a suit filed February 4 in the United States Court in Washington, D. C. that the Federal Service Entrance Examination, the principal test that must be passed by qualified college graduates for civil service posts, was "culturally and racially discriminatory." The eight plaintiffs, employees of the Department of Housing and Urban Development's (HUD) Chicago regional office, alleged that the examination violated the equal opportunity guarantees of the Fifth Amendment. They also charged that it violated, among other things, the 1964 Civil Rights Act. The suit asked the court to prevent the use of the examination until its alleged discriminatory aspects were eliminated, and that the use of other testing procedures be stopped until a determination could be made of their relation to specific job requirements. According to the plaintiffs, about 49 percent of the 100,000 applicants who took the test in 1969 finished with scores above seventy (the passing percentile) with "a disproportionately low percentage" of blacks and other minority group members passing. In another development involving blacks and examinations, Edward F. Bell, president of the National Bar Association (NBA), a predominantly-black lawyers' group, asked other lawyers' organizations on February 5 to ascertain whether bar examinations should be abolished as racially discriminatory. Bell said recent studies seemed to indicate that bar examinations discriminated against black law school graduates. The Detroit attorney cited lawsuits that were filed in several states by law students seeking to abolish the bar examinations because they did not test a graduate's legal knowledge.

February 5. The Justice Department filed a suit in the United States District Court in Atlanta charging the Clayton County, Georgia, school board with maintaining a dual public school system. The Clayton system was described by the department as one of fifty remaining recalcitrant school districts in the South. According to the suit, Clayton officials assigned its 1,479 black and 25,220 white pupils as well as their teachers to different sets of schools. The department requested a court order demanding that the county submit a desegregation plan immediately.

Judge Oren Harris of the U. S. District Court for the Eastern District of Arkansas issued an ultimatum to the officials of the Watson Chapel, Arkansas School District No. 24, warning them that they faced stiff jail terms if they continued to defy a court-ordered desegregation ruling. Harris said a fine of $350 a day would also be levied for each day they remained in contempt of court by ignoring the school order. Watson Chapel District, which included part of Pine Bluff, Arkansas, as well as the town of Watson Chapel, had about 4,000 students, almost half of them black. Judge Harris had ordered all children in grades one through four to attend three elementary schools, all of which would retain a substantial white majority.

The Justice Department, also on February 5, charged the Henry County, Virginia, school district with failing to execute a desegregation arrangement that it had earlier agreed to implement. In a suit filed in the federal district court in Danville, Virginia, the department accused the Henry County system of continuing to assign its high school pupils on a freedom-of-choice plan in violation of the 1964 Civil Rights Act. Henry County, according to the suit, had used the freedom-of-choice scheme to assign nearly 800 black pupils to an all-black high school.

February 6-9. National Guardsmen patrolled the streets of Wilmington, North Carolina, in the wake of four days of racial violence in which two people were killed. The unrest was linked to a boycott of Wilmington's high school by black students. Blacks were protesting the city's desegregation plans. The first of the two slayings took place on February 6 when a black youth was killed by a police officer who said the boy pointed a shotgun at him. Blacks in Wilmington asserted the youth was shot as he helped move furniture from a home threatened by a nearby fire. The second victim was a white man who was shot later outside of a black church which was being used as headquarters by the boycotting blacks. The white man was armed with a pistol. Local officers, aided by the 600 National Guardsmen, restored order on February 8, but remained on alert.

February 10. A Gallup Poll reported that American blacks continued to disapprove of the way President Richard Nixon was handling his job by a 2-1 ratio, the same ratio recorded in surveys the previous spring.

February 11. Scores of white high school students walked out of their school near Pine Bluff, Arkansas, to protest a court-ordered desegregation plan. They were greeted by their parents and other adult supporters. The mostly peaceful demonstration was the only incident on the day the school district began operating under the desegregation order. Watson Chapel School District No. 24 reluctantly implemented the plan after a federal judge warned the school board members that they faced stiff jail terms and fines if they continued to defy his orders.

February 16. Twenty-two whites were indicted by a county grand jury in Darlington, South Carolina on riot charges in connection with a March, 1970 incident in which a mob of angry whites overturned two school buses transporting black children to desegregated schools in nearby Lamar. Charges against twenty-one other whites, including a state legislator, were dropped by the grand jury.

February 17. Lucius D. Amerson, sheriff of Macon County, Alabama and the state's first black sheriff since Reconstruction, and one of his black deputies were arrested on a federal indictment accusing them of beating a black prisoner. Amerson and his deputy, Richard Coleman, Jr., posted bonds of $1,000 each on the charge of violating the civil rights of Wilbert D. Harris while acting under the cover of the law. Harris was arrested in Tuskegee, the county-seat of Macon County, in August, 1970 and charged with driving while intoxicated. The prisoner reportedly used a pistol to disarm two deputies and was also accused of firing at Amerson. Harris was subdued and charged with assault with intent to murder. The alleged beating by Amerson and Coleman reportedly took place after Harris was subdued. Conviction on the federal charge carried a penalty of up to a year in prison and a $1,000 fine. (See also entry dated January 16, 1968.)

February 17. The Carnegie Commission on Higher Education called for a tripling of federal aid to the nation's 105 black colleges and universities. In a report entitled "From Isolation to Mainstream: Problems of the Colleges Founded for Negroes," the Commission also urged increased funds from states, corporations, and foundations to allow black colleges to double their current enrollment of 150,000. The commission, headed by Dr. Clark Kerr, said that the black colleges were faced with special difficulties at a time of major transition as they emerged from their "historic isolation" into the mainstream of U.S. education. The report pointed out that at a time when other institutions were enlarging black enrollment and developing black studies programs, the black colleges had to compete for students, faculty, and financial resources. In addition, black colleges had to meet the special expenses of remedial training for poorly prepared students and financial aid for the 70 percent of their students who required some type of scholarly assistance.

March 3. The Bureau of the Census announced that contrary to earlier reports, the rate of black migration from the South to the North during the 1960s had remained unchanged from the pace of the two previous decades.

Earlier statistics had indicated that the number of Southern blacks moving North had dropped sharply during the 1960s to about half the levels of the prior twenty years. The new figures from the 1970 census showed that the migration pace through the 1960s was nearly the same as the high levels of the 1940s and 1950s. According to the Bureau's analysts, more than three-fourths of the 1.4 million blacks who left the South during the decade settled in five large industrial centers. New York had a Southern black influx of 396,000; California, 272,000; New Jersey, Michigan, and Illinois each gained about 120,000. The analysts said there were indications that the migration rate would continue to be high and might increase in the 1970s. The Bureau also reported an increased movement of whites to the South. This dual movement of blacks to the North and whites to the South was reportedly a continuation of a long-term trend toward distribution of the black population throughout the United States. According to the Bureau's report, the South still contained 53 percent of the nation's blacks, compared to 77 percent in 1940. Since 1940, the percentage of blacks in the Northeast and North Central states had risen from about 11 percent to 20 percent. Bureau analysts said that each of the eleven states of the Confederacy had lost residents. Mississippi and Alabama led with 279,000 and 231,000 respectively. Secretary of Commerce Maurice H. Stans speculated that the continued black Northern migration was due in part to the "higher welfare benefits" of the Northern states. He added, however, that he assumed that "greater job opportunities (in the North) would be the chief motivating factor." The Bureau statistics showed that there were about 22,672,570 blacks in the United States or about 11.2 percent of the population. In 1960, the figures were 18,871,831 or about 10.6 percent.

March 8. The United States Supreme Court ruled that employers could not use job tests that had the effect of screening out blacks if the tests were not related to ability to do the work. According to the Court, the employment bias section of the 1964 Civil Rights Act involved the consequences of employment practices, not simply whether the practices were motivated by racial bias. The Court imposed limits on the use of general educational and aptitude tests and said that "any tests used must measure the person for the job and not the person in the abstract." The case stemmed from the application for promotion by thirteen black workers at the Duke Power Company's generating plant in Draper, North Carolina. The NAACP, the Justice Department, and the federal Equal Employment Opportunity Commission had sought the ruling.

March 8. FBI files stolen from a Bureau office in Media, Pennsylvania and released to the public revealed several documents relating to black activist groups. One of the FBI memoranda was a November 4, 1970 dispatch from Director J. Edgar Hoover ordering an investigation of all groups "organized to project the demands of black students." The dispatch said that "increased campus disorders involving black students" posed a definite threat to the nation's "stability and security" and indicated a need for an increase in both the quality and quantity of intelligence information on Black Student Unions and similar groups. The memorandum went on to say that such groups were targets for influence and control by the "violent-prone Black Panther party and other extremists." (Black Student Unions and other such groups had sprung up on mostly predominantly-white campuses during the past five years. Their origins stemmed from the increased enrollment of black students at such schools and the bias which they allegedly encountered on the campuses. Sometimes their organized protests bordered on violence. See, for example, the entry dated January 8, 1969). The memoranda also contained a report of a 1970 convention of the National Association of Black Students at Wayne State University in Detroit, reports of surveillance of black student activities at Swarthmore College in Pennsylvania, of the Philadelphia Black Panthers, and the National Black Economic Conference held in Philadelphia during 1970. Muhammad Kenyatta, who headed the Philadelphia conference and was mentioned prominently in several of the FBI documents, stated on March 24 that he had received copies of the memoranda relating to him before they were published. He would not identify his sources. On March 23, Attorney General John Mitchell denounced the thefts and the publication of the records. He warned that the information could "endanger the lives" of "persons engaged in investigative activities on behalf of the United States."

March 11. Whitney M. Young, Jr., executive director of the National Urban League, died in Nigeria. Young and a group of other Americans, white and black, were in Lagos attending an African-American conference designed to bridge the gap between Africans and Americans, particularly black Americans. Young drowned while swimming with a party which included former U.S. Attorney General Ramsey Clark. Young left his position as Dean of the School of Social Work at Atlanta University in 1961 to become head of the nation's leading black economic and social reform agency. He made the organization more effective and increased its influence. During the height of the Civil Rights Era, Young became, with Martin Luther King, Jr., Roy Wilkins and James Farmer, one of the movement's "Big Four" leaders. President Nixon expressed personal sorrow at the news of his death. The President commented: "I have lost a friend, Black America has lost a gifted and commanding champion of its just cause."

March 23. The Reverend Walter E. Fauntroy, a Baptist minister and a Democrat, was elected the District of Columbia's first non-voting Congressional delegate in this century. Fauntroy captured 58 percent of the vote to defeat Attorney John A. Nevins, a white Republican, Julius W. Hobson, a black independent, and three minor independent candidates. Fauntroy's salary, $42,500 per year, would equal that of other members of the House of Representatives and he would be permitted to sit on the House District Committee, vote in other committees, but could not vote on the House floor.

The black members of Congress immediately selected Fauntroy as the thirteenth member of the so-called Black Caucus.

March 24. The NAACP filed a suit challenging the legality of zoning laws that prohibited the construction of apartment buildings in suburban communities. It was the first time the NAACP had gone to court against suburban zoning laws. The action was taken in the federal court in Brooklyn, New York, against the town of Oyster Bay, New York. The NAACP charged that the town's zoning laws had "foreclosed black and other non-white minorities from obtaining housing in the town," with results that "intensify and harden patterns of racial ghetto living" in the city of New York. Roy Wilkins, executive secretary of the NAACP, said black workers employed in Oyster Bay often could not find suitable housing. He said forty-five new industries had located in Oyster Bay since 1965, but that workers earning less than $17,000 a year could not afford to buy houses in the town because of the minimum lot sizes prescribed by the zoning laws.

March 24. The Southern Regional Council issued a report in Atlanta which said that for the first time desegregation in the South's public schools was the rule rather than the exception. This transformation had occurred, the Council said, despite the proliferation of all-white private academies in the region and the continued operation of some all-black schools. At the same time, the Council accused the Nixon administration of "playing a deceptive game of numbers" by using misleading figures about the extent of actual desegregation. Despite the recent gains, the Council asserted that the South was "a far cry" from the final dismantling of the dual [school] system." Desegregation in 1970 and in 1971, according to the Council, was less successful than the administration asserted in its figures, but "more successful than policies of [the] government gave it any right to be." The Council's report was entitled "The South and Her Children: School Desegregation, 1970-71."

March 25. President Richard Nixon met with a group of black members of the U.S. House of Representatives to receive a list of sixty grievances presented on behalf of black Americans. The so-called Black Caucus asked for reforms in welfare, job discrimination and job placement, social justice, school desegregation, etc. The President appointed five White House staff members to work on the list of recommendations. The meeting, first proposed in 1969, was set up soon after the black members of the House boycotted the President's State of the Union Address in January. The group charged that the President's failure to meet with them up until that time constituted a flagrant disregard for the opinions of black Americans.

March 31. Admiral Elmo R. Zumwalt, Jr., Chief of Naval Operations, announced the formation of a six-man team (including three admirals) to oversee a five-year program to recruit more black officers and enlisted men for the Navy. The aim of the recruiting drive was to bring the numbers of black Navy personnel up to the level of the nearly twelve percent black representation in the total U.S. population. Black recruiters were added to the staffs of the thirty-seven recruiting stations across the nation. New Navy Reserve Officer Training Corps units were added at Savannah State College in Georgia and Southern University at Baton Rouge, Louisiana. These were to supplement the sole existing black Navy ROTC unit at Prairie View A and M College in Texas. The Navy said it would also increase the number of black midshipmen at the Naval Academy at Annapolis, Maryland. On June 2, 1971 Samuel L. Gravely, Jr. was named the first black admiral in the Navy. Vice Admiral Raymond Peet performed the ritual known as "frocking" which promoted Gravely from captain to admiral. Gravely became director of naval communications in Washington, D.C.

April 6-13. Warren Widener, a Berkeley, California black city councilman, was elected mayor of the city. Widener defeated Wilmount Sweeney, described as a moderate black, by fifty-six votes. Widener was considered to be aligned with the so-called radical coalition which sought to take political control of the town. Two black lawyers, also called "radical," D'rmy Bailey and Ird T. Simmons, were elected to the city council. Bailey said a description of their politics as "radical" was misleading and suggested instead the term "progressive." The election results pointed to a "radical-moderate" control of the city council. In other spring municipal elections, James E. Williams, Sr. was elected the first black mayor of East St. Louis, Illinois, on April 6 and John Franklin, a Chattanooga, Tennessee, educator and businessman, was elected the first black commissioner in the city's history on April 13.

April 12. A federal jury in New York City acquitted David R. Poindexter of harboring and concealing the identity of black militant Angela Davis while she was the target of a nationwide police search. Poindexter was arrested in New York on October 13, 1970 along with Davis, who was at that time one of the FBI's ten most wanted fugitives. She was being sought in connection with the murder of a California judge during a courtroom shootout on August 7, 1970. During the trial, the prosecution presented more than forty witnesses in an effort to prove that Poindexter had moved through several cities with Davis under assumed names and must have known that she was being sought under federal warrant. The defense summoned no witnesses, relying on the argument that the prosecution had failed to prove its case beyond a reasonable doubt. Following the verdict, Poindexter commented that his trial " was a minor skirmish in a big war. The major battle is in California over Angela."

April 13. The Internal Revenue Service announced that the Fayette Academy in Somerville, Tennessee, was notified that contributions for its operation were no longer tax deductible because it had failed to adopt non-discriminatory admissions policies. The action was the first time the IRS had suspended tax privileges for an all-white private school outside of Mississippi.

April 15. Approximately 2,000 black and white students gathered at the home of the president of the University of Florida at Gainesville protesting what they called the school's "racist" policies and demanding the resignation of President Stephen C. O'Connell. Earlier the same day, sixty-seven blacks, members of the school's Black Student Union, were arrested during a sit-in outside O'Connell's office. The blacks and their white allies called for increased black enrollment at the university by recruiting five hundred new students. There were at the time about three hundred blacks out of a 22,000 total enrollment. In a television address to the students, President O'Connell said "we have made remarkable racial progress," but he rejected the black recruitment demands calling them "a racial quota" and "racism in reverse." Nearly one hundred black students subsequently withdrew from the university in further protest of the school's policies.

April 16. Carl B. Stokes, the first black mayor of Cleveland, Ohio, announced that he was leaving office at the end of his current term in 1971. He said he would help develop a "people's lobby" to bring pressure on the two major political parties toward "responsive" presidential candidates in 1972 and toward a reordering of the nation's priorities. Stokes was first elected in 1967 as the first black mayor of a major American city, and was reelected in 1969.

April 19. The United States Bureau of the Census released a study compiled from federal and private sources which revealed that black women, on the average, had fewer illegitimate births in the late 1960s than they did in the earlier part of the decade. Meanwhile, the white illegitimacy rate was climbing. According to the report, the black illegitimacy rate, which was ten times higher than the white rate in 1961, had dropped to about seven times in 1968, the last year considered in the study. The raw figures for 1968 alone were 184,000 black and 155,000 white illegitimate births. The report, entitled "Fertility Indicators: 1970," was developed by Campbell Gibson of the Census Bureau.

April 20. The United States Supreme Court, in a series of unanimous decisions, told the Charlotte-Mecklenburg County, North Carolina joint school system and all the other school districts of the nation that busing children as a means of dismantling a racially dual school system was constitutional. The rulings ended the final legal efforts by Southern school boards to prevent the busing of students to achieve more desegregation in schools. Chief Justice Warren E. Burger wrote the opinions of the Court in the four cases on which it ruled. In addition to upholding the school desegregation plan, which included busing for the Charlotte-Mecklenburg district, the Court struck down an anti-busing law enacted by the North Carolina Legislature, ordered school officials in Mobile, Alabama to use "all available techniques" to correct segregation in their schools, and overruled a Georgia Supreme Court order that had said certain desegregation efforts in the city of Athens were unconstitutional. The High Court reasoned that "desegregation plans cannot be limited to the walk-in school." The justices held that busing school children was proper unless "the time or distance is so great as to risk either the health of the children or significantly impinge on the educational process." The Court added that at times busing was an indispensable method of eliminating "the last vestiges" of racial segregation. The Court made it clear, however, that the rulings did not apply to *de facto* segregation caused by neighborhood housing patterns, as is found most often in the North. The landmark decision has become known to history as *Swann v. Charlotte-Mecklenburg.*

April 23. The United States Court of Appeals for the Third Circuit upheld the legality of the Nixon administration's pilot job plan for minorities, known as the "Philadelphia Plan." The plan, devised by the Labor Department in 1969, required contractors bidding on federal or federally-assisted projects to hire a fixed number of minority group members by a certain date (see entry dated June 27, 1969). A number of groups, foremost among them building and construction organizations had sought in a number of courts to stop the plan on the grounds that it was unconstitutional. In this case, the Court of Appeals was asked by the Contractors Association of Eastern Pennsylvania to declare the plan illegal. They contended that the plan denied the group equal protection of the laws and violated the 1964 Civil Rights Act because it required racial "quotas." The court reasoned that the plan did not violate the 1964 Civil Rights Act because the contractors were not, in fact, required to hire a "definite percentage" of a minority group.

April 28. The Joint Center for Political Studies in Washington reported that the number of black elected officials in the U.S. rose 22 percent during 1970. Despite these gains, however, black public officials still represented only about .3 percent of all officeholders in the nation. The center's director, Frank D. Reeves, commented that the 22 percent rise showed that "blacks are gaining clout more and more in the nation's electorial systems." The report also revealed that 1,860 blacks held office as of April, 1971. By comparison, in 1967 only 475 blacks held elective offices. Nearly three-fifths of the blacks in office were Southerners. According to the report, 711 blacks held office in the eleven states of the Old Confederacy, a 26 percent rise above the 1970 figure of 563.

May 4. In another spring primary election, Richard B. Hatcher was renominated to a second four-year term as mayor of Gary, Indiana. Hatcher won 59 percent of the vote cast and was heavily favored to win the general election over the Republican nominee, Theodore Nering. In the primary Hatcher, who was first elected mayor in 1967, defeated Dr. Alexander Williams, the black Lake County Coroner, and John Armento, the president of the city council.

May 4. United States District Judge William P. Gray ordered David Hilliard, Chief of Staff of the Black Panther Party, released from federal custody after the government refused to divulge wiretap logs of conversations involving Hilliard. Hilliard was charged with threatening the life of President Richard Nixon during an anti-war speech in November, 1969. When U.S. Attorney James Browning told the court that he was not authorized to make the wiretap logs available to Hilliard's lawyers, Judge Gray ordered the indictment dismissed and the case dropped.

May 5. A riot involving mostly black youths occurred in the Brownsville section of New York City. Hundreds of youths set scores of fires and fought police. One police officer was shot and fourteen others were injured during the melee. Police arrested twenty-five people on charges of larceny or malicious mischief. At the height of the rioting, marauding bands of young people looted stores and battled police with rocks, bricks, and bottles. The rioting began after thousands of angry Brownsville (Brooklyn) residents closed off dozens of streets in their neighborhood with abandoned cars and trash piles to protest state budget cuts affecting welfare assistance, anti-narcotics programs, Medicaid, educational facilities, and the food stamp program. The legislation was signed by Governor Nelson A. Rockefeller on April 15. Organizers of the peaceful protest disavowed the actions of the rioting youths, and the disturbance was brought under control by late evening.

May 5. The United States Labor Department announced that it would impose mandatory racial hiring quotas on federally-sponsored construction projects under way in San Francisco, St. Louis, and Atlanta. The established plans for the three cities varied slightly in their formats. Overall, however, they required contractors bidding on federal or federally-sponsored projects to agree to hire a fixed percentage of minority group members by a certain date. Washington and Philadelphia were the only other two cities to have such job plans. (See also entry dated April 23, 1971.)

May 10. The United States Commission on Civil Rights reported that the Nixon administration had shown some signs of progress in enforcing civil rights laws but considerable strides needed to be made. The new commission report came seven months after it issued a harsh indictment of the administration asserting that there had been a "major breakdown" in the enforcement of the rights laws. The commission singled out for praise George P. Shultz, director of the Office of Management and Budget and Leonard Garment, a presidential counselor, for what it termed their efforts at "active intervention" in seeking compliance with Civil Rights laws. The report also cited other signs of progress:

1. President Nixon, in his fiscal 1972 budget recommendations, had sought

more funds for the Office of Federal Contract Compliance and the Equal Employment Opportunity Commission.

2. The Army, among other departments, had set up a program to establish goals for minority employment in its own offices.

3. The Justice Department had announced that it would add six lawyers to its office to coordinate efforts to enforce Title VI of the 1964 Civil Rights Law, which forbade discrimination in federally-assisted programs.

May 13. The United States Army announced that it had nominated three black colonels for promotion to the rank of brigadier general. The three black officers were among 80 colonels approved by President Nixon for promotion to the one-star rank. The three blacks promoted were Colonels Alvin W. Dillard, James F. Hamlet, and Roscoe C. Cartwright. Their nominations would bring the number of black Army generals to four. The Air Force also had one black general while the Navy nominated its first black admiral on April 28, 1971.

May 14. The Department of Health, Education and Welfare (HEW), complying with the Supreme Court's ruling which upheld school busing to achieve greater desegregation, recommended "extensive" crosstown busing as part of a plan to desegregate the public schools in Austin, Texas. The desegregation proposal was the first made by the government since the Supreme Court in *Swann v. Mecklenburg* (April, 1971) rejected the administration's objections to busing and declared the method constitutional as a means of dismantling dual school systems. Austin, the sixth largest city in Texas, had about 56,000 students in fifty-six elementary schools, nineteen junior high schools and eight high schools. About 15 percent of the students were black and about 20 percent Mexican-American. The city had two high schools and seven elementary schools with virtually all-black enrollments.

May 17. An all-white jury in Opelika, Alabama acquitted black Macon County Sheriff Lucius Amerson and his deputy, Richard Coleman, Jr. of a federal charge that they had beaten a prisoner in their custody (see entry dated February 17, 1971). Amerson commented that the verdict reaffirmed his belief that he could receive a fair trial at the hands of an all-white jury in the South.

May 18. In a 115-page report, President Richard Nixon told the Black Caucus of the House of Representatives that his administration would continue to support "jobs, income, and tangible benefits, the pledges that this society has made to the disadvantaged in the past decade." The President was responding to a list of sixty grievances the black congressman had asked him to consider in a meeting on March 25, 1971 (see entry above). The President announced that he agreed with the Caucus' welfare reform proposals but limited his guaranteed annual income figure to $2,400, compared to the $6,500 a year figure proposed by the blacks. In almost all of the recommendations, the

President differed with the Caucus in amounts and scope of reform programs. For instance, the black legislators suggested one million summer jobs for youths. The President promised 500,000 with some 300,000 more being made available through private sectors. The Black Caucus received the report through the office of its Chairman, Representative Charles C. Diggs, Jr. from Michigan. After studying the report, the Caucus issued a 76-page reaction that expressed "deep disappointment." They called the President's message "a mere codification of slim efforts" rather than "massive immediate aid for minorities and the poor." In the end, the blacks charged, the administration "lacked a sense of understanding, urgency and commitment in dealing with the critical problems facing black Americans." It was pointed out that only one of the sixty demands was fully agreed on by both sides—the formation of a task force to study the problems of black soldiers and veterans.

May 21-26. Racial violence erupted in Chattanooga, Tennessee, after a black musician failed to perform at a rock concert in the city auditorium. When some of the black youths did not get refunds for their admission fees, they began vandalizing the building. The disorder later spread into the streets. On May 24, Governor Winfield Dunn ordered 2,000 National Guardsmen into the city after local police were unable to contain the arson and sniping which was centered in the black neighborhoods located on the outskirts of the downtown area. On May 25, a young black man was killed by police who said they fired after the man hurled bricks at them. Black witnesses said the victim, Leon Anderson, was apparently drunk, and charged that police shot him without provocation. The incident increased tensions, but did not lead to heightened violence. On May 26, a rigid dusk-to-dawn curfew was lifted in the city and Governor Dunn announced that guardsmen would be gradually withdrawn.

May 25. Judge Harold H. Mulvey of the Connecticut State Court in New Haven dismissed all charges against Black Panther Party members Bobby Seale and Ericka Huggins. The two were on trial for six months for the murder of former Black Panther member Alex Rackley in May, 1969 (see entry dated August 19, 1969). Judge Mulvey ordered the charges dropped after the jury in the case told him it was hopelessly deadlocked. The judge declared a mistrial and announced that the "massive publicity" about the case had made it too difficult to select an unbiased jury to try the pair again. Seale was chairman and co-founder of the Black Panther Party, Huggins was a party member from Connecticut. Throughout the trial the state, led by state attorney Arnold Markle, sought to prove that Seale had ordered a group of party members to murder Rackley after he was accused of treason against the party. The state's principal witness, George Sams, Jr., testified that Seale had given him the orders. Seale's defense counsel, Charles R. Gary, countered consistently that Sams ordered Rackley's death. Sams, a member of the party, had already pleaded guilty to second-degree murder in the case. The dismissal of charges brought to an end another chapter of violence and legal proceedings connected with the Black Panther Party.

May 25. Racial tension was sparked anew in Mississippi as Jo Etha Collier, an eighteen-year-old black girl, was shot dead in Drew, Mississippi. Collier was felled by a bullet from a passing car as she stood with other young blacks on a street corner in her hometown. The incident occurred less than an hour after the young black girl graduated from desegregated Drew High School and was designated the student with the best school spirit. Three white men were arrested and charged with the killing on May 26. On June 14, Allen Wilkerson of Memphis and Wayne and Wesley Parks of Drew, Mississippi, were arraigned on charges of murder before circuit Court Judge Arthur B. Clark in Indianola, Mississippi. The three pleaded innocent. The swift arrests, arraignments, and the sympathetic attitude of local white officials served to help calm tensions in the community.

May 30. Three police officers were injured in a gun battle in Cairo, Illinois, one of the most racially tense cities in America. Cairo mayor Albert B. Thomas blamed the shootings on the United Front, a predominantly-black organization that had led a boycott of the town's white merchants. The United Front declined to comment on the incident. (See also entry dated October 24-25, 1970).

June 4. Arthur A. Fletcher, assistant secretary of labor, announced that the Labor Department was withdrawing its support of Chicago's voluntary equal hiring plan for federal construction projects and would impose mandatory racial quotas on federally-assisted projects throughout the city. Chicago's voluntary plan failed after being in operation for eighteen months. The plan called for the hiring and training of some 4,000 minority group members. But by June 4, 1971, only 885 blacks and Hispanic-Americans were enrolled for training, and only a few had obtained membership in the city's construction unions. The Labor Department said it would replace the Chicago plan with the now standard formula known as the Philadelphia Plan, under which a certain number of minority group members should be employed on federal projects exceeding $500,000.

June 4-22. Racial tensions in Columbus, Georgia, the state's second largest city, erupted into violence. The trouble began on May 31, 1971 when seven members of the African-American Police League, including its executive director, were fired from the police department for picketing police headquarters and removing the American flag shoulder patches from their uniforms. The blacks were protesting alleged racial discrimination in the police department. Police department officials accused the blacks of conduct unbecoming to an officer and said they "ripped" the flag from their uniforms. The officers said they gently removed the emblems. On June 3, the Muscogee County Grand

Jury announced that complaints of discrimination against black officers were unfounded. The jury said it found no basis for charges of the use of unnecessary force in the arrests of blacks but instead criticized both the African-American Police League, which made the charges of discrimination and police brutality, and the Fraternal Order of Police, a union. On June 19, Hosea Williams, national program director for the Southern Christian Leadership Conference (SCLC) and Chairman of the Georgia statewide Black Leadership Coalition, led more than 500 blacks on a fifteen-block march in Columbus, then issued a five-point ultimatum to city and county officials. The Coalition demanded the reinstatement of thirteen black policemen, promotion of the thirty-eight blacks still on the force, desegregation of jail facilities, a biracial "citizens police review board," and increased hiring of black police officers. On June 21, Columbus mayor J. R. Allen declared a state of emergency following a weekend of racial strife. A total of twenty-six fires attributed to arsonists were set in the city and a black man was fatally wounded by police. The City Council gave the mayor broad powers to order a curfew, shut down stores selling alcoholic beverages, stop the sale of firearms, and curtail gasoline sales. Meanwhile, the African-American Police League called for a city-wide boycott of white businesses.

June 7. The United States Supreme Court ruled that states are not required to carve out separate legislative districts for urban blacks or any other racial or ethnic group. The Court held in an apportionment case from Indiana that core-city blacks may be lumped with more populous suburban white voters into one large district that is represented by a number of legislators elected at large. The 5-3 ruling upset a federal district court's finding that Indianapolis blacks were the victims of racial gerrymandering and were entitled to their own district with state legislators elected by and responsible to them. The five-man judicial majority, led by Justice Byron R. White, said there was no evidence that the Indianapolis blacks did not have an equal say in choosing legislative candidates or that they were not allowed to register or vote. The majority reasoned that "the mere fact that one interest group or another concerned with the outcome of Marion County elections have found themselves outvoted and without legislative seats of its own provides no basis for invoking constitutional remedies." No explanation was given of the different result that was reached on May 31 when the Court ordered Hinds County, Mississippi, which included the capital city of Jackson, to be divided into single-member districts so that black voters would have a chance to elect their own representatives. Had the Supreme Court established the Jackson principle consistently, blacks and other inner-city residents would have been assured of larger representation in state legislatures.

June 11. Black legislators from nine Southern states met in closed sessions in Atlanta to talk about black representation in reapportioned legislatures. The major problem concerning the group centered around recent decisions of the

U.S. Supreme Court, which black lawmakers felt pointed in opposite directions. In one decision, the Supreme Court ruled that one-representative legislative districts are allowable in Mississippi (see entry directly above). In another decision, the Court declared that multi-member districts are allowable in Indiana. The black legislators said that they were confused and concerned about what the Supreme Court intended, and concluded that they had a better chance for election in the South if they were candidates in districts where more than one representative is elected. There were forty black legislators in the eleven Southern states. Only Arkansas was without a black lawmaker.

June 11. President Richard Nixon promised to enforce federal laws prohibiting racial discrimination in housing but said the government would not force introduction of low cost housing for blacks or whites into suburban communities that did not want it. The President's fifteen-page report sharply distinguished between economic segregation and racial segregation, and the government's authority to deal with each situation. Nixon said that his administration would seek to carry out all requirements of federal law and judicial decisions involving housing but that it would take no action to go beyond them. "Racial discrimination in housing is illegal and will not be tolerated," the President affirmed, but the issue of public housing projects for the poor was another matter. Although predominantly-white and affluent suburbs would be encouraged to accept them, the ultimate decision about the location of the housing projects would be made at the local level.

June 12. Charles Evers, the black mayor of Fayette, Mississippi, began his campaign for governor on the eighth anniversary of his brother Medgar's death (see entry dated June 12, 1963). Surrounded by ten armed black men acting as security guards, Evers returned to his hometown of Decatur, Mississippi to campaign as an independent. Evers was the first black to seek the governorship since Reconstruction. He told a crowd of 300 supporters at the Newton County Courthouse that it was time for members of both races to work together for common goals.

June 12. David Hilliard, Chief of Staff of the Black Panther Party, was found guilty of assault but innocent of attempted murder in connection with a 1968 shootout with police. Hilliard contended that he was not involved in the Panther-police altercation on April 6, 1968. That gun battle resulted in the death of Panther Party member Bobby Hutton, the wounding of two police officers, and criminal charges against Panther Minister of Information Eldridge Cleaver, who later jumped bail and fled to Algeria (see entry dated September 13, 1970). Hilliard was charged with two counts of attempted murder and another dual count of assault on a police officer. The trial was held in the Alameda County Superior Court in Oakland, California before Judge William J. Hayes. Frank Vukota prosecuted Hilliard, who was defended by Attorney Vincent Hallinan.

June 13. The latest in a series of race riots on military bases occurred at Sheppard Air Force Base, Texas. A midnight battle between white and black airmen left twenty injured. According to a military spokesman, the two-and-one-half hour fight started when a black and white airman clashed in the base's club. The fight then escalated among young trainees, and was eventually halted by base police. Major General Jerry Page, the base commander, said no arrests would be made until an investigation of the incident was completed.

June 14. Owen B. Kiernan, executive secretary of the National Association of Secondary School Principals, told the United States Senate's Equal Educational Opportunity Committee that a survey of eleven Southern and two border states had revealed that more than 1,200 black school principals lost their jobs to whites after public school desegregation began in the South. Dr. Kiernan claimed that the problem of the elimination, displacement and demotion of black public school principals had reached such serious proportions that it required the intervention of the federal government.

June 14. The Justice Department announced the filing of a suit in St. Louis against Black Jack, Missouri, a St. Louis suburb, charging the town with illegally blocking a desegregated housing development. The action came on the heels of President Nixon's policy statement on housing issued on June 11, 1971. The issue arose when a nonprofit corporation made detailed plans in late 1969 to build a housing development for people of limited income. It was widely known that the project would be desegregated. The federal suit charged that the residents of Black Jack incorporated their community to gain zoning power and then used that power to block construction of the project. This action, the suit said, violated federal civil rights laws and the U.S. Constitution.

June 14. The United States Supreme Court ruled 5 to 4 that officials may close swimming pools and other public facilities to avoid desegregating them. The closings are not unconstitutional since blacks and whites are treated equally, Justice Hugo L. Black reasoned in the Court's rare recent setback for blacks. The ruling went against blacks in Jackson, Mississippi, who tried to force the city to reopen public swimming pools. They were closed after a district court ruled they could not remain segregated. In announcing the majority opinion, Justice Black cautioned that the decision did not signal approval of any subterfuge for desegregation. "We want no one to get any hope that there has been any retreat," he said. In one of three dissenting opinions, Justice Thurgood Marshall reasoned that the city's actions were unconstitutional and that "the fact that the color of [a black's] skin is used to prevent others from swimming in public pools is irrelevant."

June 15. Vernon E. Jordan, Jr., former Atlanta attorney and executive director of the United Negro College Fund, (UNCF) was named executive director of the National Urban League. Jordan succeeded Whitney Young, Jr.

who drowned on March 11, 1971, in Lagos, Nigeria (see entry above). Jordan was director of the Voter Education Project (VEP) of the Southern Regional Council in Atlanta until 1969. As head of the VEP, he helped organize massive voter registration campaigns across the South to help blacks win political power. In January, 1970, Jordan became head of the UNCF, which raises funds for more than thirty black colleges across the country.

June 16. The Race Relations Information Center (RRIC) of Nashville, Tennessee announced that predominantly-black public colleges were in "imminent danger of losing their identity through integration, merger, reduced status, or outright abolition." In a report entitled "The Black Public Colleges—Integration and Disintegration," the RRIC said "the prevailing pattern is one of racially separate and qualitatively unequal higher education." The 1970-71 academic year marked the first time in their history that the nation's thirty-three black state-supported colleges enrolled more than 100,000 students. During the past decade, enrollment at the institutions increased 75 percent. The report said the figures suggested thriving institutions, "but a closer look tells another story." In fact, the death knell of the black state-supported colleges has already been sounded, according to the report. There were originally thirty-five public colleges created for blacks—two of them are now predominantly white. Those two, Maryland State College and Bluefield State College located in West Virginia, were joined by two more, West Virginia State and Lincoln University (Missouri). The RRIC said three other institutions—Delaware State, Bowie State (Maryland), and Kentucky State—"appear likely to become majority-white before long." Of the twenty-six remaining schools, fourteen were in direct competition with a predominantly white college. The RRIC speculated that most of these would eventually lose their identity, perhaps even be completely abolished.

June 17. The United States Fifth Circuit Court of Appeals ordered complete desegregation in eighty-one Southern school districts. The court reversed a U.S. District Court decision of April 22, 1970, which exempted some districts (mostly in Georgia) from full desegregation compliance on the grounds that such compliance would produce educationally unsound school systems. The Appeals Court said that the District Court must apply the Singleton decree to the eighty-one school districts in the areas of faculty and staff desegregation, school construction, site selection, and school attendance outside the system. The decree, issued in 1970 by the Fifth Circuit Court in the case of *Singleton v. Jackson,* required that the faculty of each school have approximately the same racial ratio as the entire school system, and that decisions regarding school construction and selection of school sites be made without evidence of racial discrimination. The New Orleans-based court also said the eighty-one school systems must comply with the U. S. Supreme Court's decision in *Swann v. Charlotte-Mecklenburg* (see entry dated April 20, 1971), which held that busing could be used as a tool to dismantle a dual school system. The eighty-one school districts have been under federal court jurisdiction since December, 1969. The latest appellate ruling in the case stemmed from the intervention by Charley Ridley, Jr., a black student from Gray, Georgia, in the blanket desegregation suit filed against Georgia and the State Board of Education in 1969.

June 17. Jacksonville police officers armed with riot equipment dispersed a crowd of 400 black youths in a second night of racial violence in that Florida city. Three youths were arrested and charged with looting. Several police officers were slightly injured by rocks and bottles during the melee. Sheriff's Captain E. W. Hartley said police went into the black neighborhood to protect its many elderly black residents in the wake of the rock and bottle hurling. Deputies reported that two supermarkets in the black business district were looted and set afire, but there was no gunfire. Black youths were angered by an earlier slaying of a young black man by Jacksonville police.

June 17. NAACP executive secretary Roy Wilkins called the Nixon administration's policy on housing discrimination a "timid tightrope walking act of the greatest kind." Wilkins challenged President Nixon to exert more "positive federal power" to help blacks move to the suburbs in search of employment. "The issue of the 1970s now appears to be whether the black population will be able to move into the suburbs in pursuit of jobs that are moving to the suburbs," Wilkins declared. "The 15-page statement issued last week by the White House had done nothing to solve that problem." President Nixon had announced on June 11 that he would enforce federal laws preventing racial discrimination in housing, but would not force communities to accept low-cost housing for blacks or whites (see entry above). According to an *Atlanta Constitution* report, Wilkins also said that "Mr. Nixon ought to stop going around saying he does not want to enforce integration of the suburbs, because he is using the language and nomenclature of those who simply do not want Negroes in the suburbs." Wilkins made his criticisms of the President at a panel discussion on "The Status of Civil Rights in 1971" at the annual meeting of the black National Newspapers Publishers Association in Atlanta.

June 18. The Department of Health, Education, and Welfare (HEW) completed and released the most detailed study of school desegregation in the nation's history. According to the report, the only significant gains in school desegregation in the nation's largest school districts during the past two years have occurred in the South. The 38 Southern school districts among the country's largest districts accounted for almost all of the desegregation gains in urban areas while 26 of the 63 districts in Northern and Western states showed a decrease in desegregation. The figures reflected the amount of desegregation based on the number of black children in predominately-white schools, the statistical yardstick favored by most civil rights groups. Of the 756,000 black pupils who moved from largely black into predominately-white schools during the past two years, a total of 690,000 lived in the South. The national desegregation comparison was the result of an eight-month survey conducted by HEW. The preliminary results of the study were revealed on January 14, 1971.

June 22. The Department of Health, Education and Welfare (HEW) announced that letters were forwarded to thirty-nine school districts in eleven Southern and border states suggesting that they must further desegregate by the fall of 1971. HEW was attempting to bring all school districts in line with the Supreme Court's ruling in the *Swann* case in North Carolina (see also entry dated April 20, 1971). Recent action was taken in Nashville, Tennessee, Norfolk, Virginia, and Austin, Texas. The latest action included such diverse localities as Wilmington, Delaware; Paducah, Kentucky; Gulfport, Mississippi; Fayetteville, North Carolina; Amarillo, Texas; and Martinsville, Virginia. HEW told the districts that they must prove that the presence of heavily black schools is not discriminatory.

June 23. School officials and civil rights leaders in Jackson, Mississippi, the largest school district in the state, agreed on a plan for desegregating the city's elementary schools through busing and educational parks. Both parties, in the first such compromise they had ever reached, agreed that the plan would remain in effect for three years without a court challenge. Dr. Harry S. Kirshman, acting superintendent of schools, announced that the agreement would affect about 18,000 to 19,000 elementary school children, with approximately 8,000 to 9,000 being bused to classes. The educational park concept is built on clusters of modules around a common center. Each module is to accommodate the equivalent of four traditional classrooms with 30-1 pupil-teacher ratios. Black enrollments in the schools would range from 41 to 70 percent.

June 25. Agents from the Bureau of Alcohol, Tobacco, and Firearms arrested three black men in Columbus, Georgia, and charged them with possessing firebombs in the racially tense city. The agents said they confiscated enough material at the People's Panther Party headquarters to make more than fifty firebombs. Two of the three arrested men were soldiers stationed at nearby Fort Benning, and the third was a former Army private. The agents arrested William Craig Garr, Jesse Reed, Jr., and Anthony L. Brewer less than a week after the outburst of new racial disorders, which included firebombings. Garr was identified as the president of the People's Panther Party, an organization described by a federal official as a training group for the Black Panther Party. Meanwhile, white police officers in Columbus presented a petition to Mayor J. R. Allen urging him not to give in to black demands. The petition was prompted by black charges of racial discrimination in the city's police department and a subsequent announcement by the mayor that the department would be investigated. Earlier, black police officers had told the mayor, in response to his plea to them to help "cool" the black community, that they would protect the black community "from the white cops" (see also entry dated June 4-22, 1971).

June 28. The United States Supreme Court overturned the 1967 draft evasion conviction of former heavyweight boxing champion Muhammad Ali. In an unanimous 8-0 opinion (Justice Thurgood Marshall did not participate), the Court ruled that the Justice Department had erred in contending that Ali's objection to military service was based on political rather than religious beliefs. The Court said it was "indisputably clear . . . that the Department was simply wrong as a matter of law in advising that Ali's beliefs were not religiously based and were not sincerely held." Ali, who is a Black Muslim, exclaimed "Thanks to Allah!" when he learned of the Court's decree. "I thank the Supreme Court for recognizing the sincerity of my belief in myself and my convictions," he said.

June 28-July 8. Court action and out-of-court settlements continued in an effort to desegregate the nation's schools. On June 28, a federal district judge in Nashville, Tennessee approved a cross-town busing plan designed to desegregate the Nashville-Davidson County public school system. Judge L. C. Morton adopted, with modifications, a plan drawn up by the Department of Health, Education, and Welfare which required the daily busing of about 47,000 students, an increase of approximately 13,500 over those bused in 1970-71. The number of black children required to ride buses would almost double while the number of whites to be transported would increase by only one-third. The Nashville-Davidson County school system had an enrollment of about 95,000 pupils. Judge Morton ordered the plan implemented in September, 1971. On July 8, the NAACP's Legal Defense Fund and the Mobile, Alabama school board agreed upon a school desegregation plan that would allow at least ten of Mobile's public schools to retain virtually all-black student bodies until the fall of 1972. Attorneys for the blacks said they accepted the school board's suggested course of action only to avoid another year of litigation before a federal district judge they regarded as hostile to desegregation.

June 30-August 8. Throughout the summer of 1971, members of the Black Panther Party were continuously engaged in legal disputes of various kinds. On June 30, a jury in Detroit acquitted twelve party members of charges that they murdered a police officer and of conspiracy to murder in a gun battle with police at the party's local headquarters in October, 1970. Three party members, however, were convicted of felonious assault in the case. This trio, Erone D. Desansser, Benjamin Fandrus, and David Johnson, faced a maximum penalty of four years imprisonment. The Detroit jury, consisting of ten blacks and two whites, returned its verdict after four and a half days of deliberations. On July 2, David Hilliard, the Black Panther Party's Chief of Staff, was sentenced to a one-to-ten year prison term by an Oakland, California judge for assault in connection with a gun battle with police in April, 1968. Hilliard, who was convicted on June 12, was denied a retrial and remanded to custody. On August 6, a biracial jury of ten blacks and two whites acquitted twelve Black Panther Party members of the attempted murder of five New Orleans police officers in a gun battle at a local housing project in September, 1970. The biracial jury, which received its instructions from a black judge, Israel M. Augustine, reached its verdict after only thirty minutes of deliberation. If convicted, the blacks could have faced terms of twenty years in prison on each of the five counts. During the trial, nine of the black defendants participated in an uprising involving thirty-four inmates at the Orleans Parish Prison, where they were held. The uprising was staged to protest what the blacks called the prison's "corrupt judicial system." The protest, which was held on July 26, ended after almost eight hours as the inmates released two black guards they had been holding hostage. On August 8, Superior Court Judge Harold B. Hove declared a mistrial in the second manslaughter trial of Huey P. Newton, co-founder of the Black Panther Party, in Oakland, California. A lone white housewife held out for the acquittal of Newton, who had been charged in connection with the killing of an Oakland police officer in October, 1969.

July 5-6. Members of the National Conference of Black Lawyers and the Black American Law Students Association distributed leaflets accusing the American Bar Association of excluding blacks from its major policy making organs and of emphasizing the "order" side of the law and order issue. The leaflets also called for an end to bar exams which allegedly excluded blacks. Similarly, Judge Edward F. Bell, president of the black National Bar Association (NBA), speaking before his group's annual convention, urged the abolition of bar exams, claiming that they did not reflect the potential for a successful practice and that they discriminated against minority applicants (See also entries dated February 4-5, 1971 and November 15, 1972.)

July 5-9. Bishop Stephen G. Spottswood, board chairman of the NAACP, remarked during the group's 62nd Annual Convention in Minneapolis that the Nixon administration had taken steps during 1971 to dispel the image that it was "anti-Negro." Without being very specific, Spottswood said that the President had taken certain steps and announced certain policies which had "earned cautious and limited approval among black Americans." A year before, at the NAACP's convention, Spottswood portrayed the Nixon administration as anti-black. Some NAACP leaders apparently disagreed with Bishop Spottswood's new assessment of the Nixon policies. NAACP Labor Director Herbert Hill characterized the administration's racial policy as "criminal negligence," a posture even worse than "benign neglect." Hill specifically accused the administration of failure to enforce laws forbidding discrimination by federal contractors which resulted, in his view, in a high unemployment rate among blacks. Similarly, NAACP Executive Secretary Roy Wilkins told the delegates that President Nixon could increase his influence among black voters in the 1972 elections if he made more jobs available to black voters. (See also entries dated February 10, 1971, March 25, 1971, and May 10, 1971.)

July 6. Louis (Satchmo) Armstrong, the black jazz trumpeter, died in New York. The seventy-one-year-old Armstrong had reshaped the development of American music by introducing the black folk music of New Orleans into mainstream American culture. His distinctive abrasive voice and innovative solos were trademarks of his long career which began in small Southern nightclubs at the close of the World War I. President Nixon eulogized Armstrong as "one of the architects of the American art form."

July 7. Professional baseball commissioner Bowie Kuhn announced that veteran black player Satchel Paige, who pitched for twenty-five years in the "Negro Leagues" and the Major Leagues, would be given full membership in the Baseball Hall of Fame at Cooperstown, New York. Originally, it was intended that Paige and other black players be honored in a separate division of the Hall of Fame which was established for players in the old "Negro Leagues." In response to criticism by baseball fans of the separate division of the shrine, the decision was made to give Paige full honors.

July 11. President Nixon signed a five billion dollar education appropriation bill, the largest of its kind in history. Among the features of the bill was a provision which prohibited the use of any of the funds to force school districts considered already desegregated under the Civil Rights Act of 1964 to bus students, abolish schools, or to set attendance zones against parents' wishes or as a stipulation for receiving federal funds.

July 13. A coalition of 126 civil rights groups held a Leadership Conference on Civil Rights in Washington, D.C. The coalition attacked President Nixon's housing policies as insufficient to the needs of minorities and the poor. The President's policy, which was outlined on June 11, 1971, was "disastrous and chaotic," according to the group's spokesperson Bayard Rustin. The coalition urged the federal administration to require localities to provide for low-income housing needs or risk losing all federal aid. The civil rights groups also urged the Justice Department to take action against any local zoning laws erected to block housing for low and moderate income families. (See also entry dated March 24, 1971.)

July 18-20. United States District Judge Jack Roberts refused to accept a Department of Health, Education, and Welfare (HEW) school desegregation plan for Austin, Texas schools which would have required extensive cross-town busing. Instead, the judge accepted a desegregation plan filed by the local school board which established learning centers in fine arts, avocations, and social and natural sciences which would be open to elementary pupils of all races for a portion of the school day. Students could be bused, if necessary, to these learning centers. The plan also assigned black junior high school students to schools which were not "identifiably Negro." In a related matter, on July 20, HEW officials announced that they had told sixty-four school districts in Southern and border states that they would have to alter their school desegregation plans for the fall of 1971 so as to achieve greater racial desegregation. An HEW representative said that most of the sixty-four districts were in small and rural areas and that each contained one or more all-black schools.

July 21. Blacks in Passaic, New Jersey began a long boycott against downtown merchants protesting alleged police brutality. The boycott grew out of a series of incidents of "police harassment" and "brutality" which culminated in an incident on the night of July 20 between police and eight blacks. During the altercation a black man was beaten and shots were fired. The Rev. Calvin McKinney, leader of the black Urban Crisis Council, protested that the town's all-white City Council ignored black pleas for protection against police harassment. The FBI did, however, agree to investigate the blacks' charges.

July 26. Federal analysts studying the 1970 Census returns concluded that despite a decade of general progress, black Americans remained far behind whites in terms of economic prosperity, social gains, and educational advancement. The study, compiled by the Bureau of the Census and the U. S. Bureau of Labor Statistics and entitled "The Social and Economic Status of Negroes in the United States, 1970," found that 28.9 percent of every one hundred black families were headed by women. Many analysts saw this proportion of female-headed households as an important indicator of black social progress. (That view was disputed immediately by Dr. Robert B. Hill, a research analyst for the National Urban League, as he appeared before the League's annual convention.) The percentage of fatherless white families in the 1960s remained at about 9 percent. Other statistics showed that blacks increased their median income by 50 percent during the 1960s, but that their incomes were still only three-fifths of that earned by whites, and that about half of the all-black occupied housing units in rural areas were substandard in 1970 as compared with only 8 percent of white rural housing.

July 27. Frank W. Render, second deputy assistant secretary of defense, announced that almost a dozen military officers were relieved of command, transferred to new assignments, or reprimanded for failing to adequately enforce the Defense Department's guidelines for racial equality in the armed services. The unidentified officers were said to rank from general down to company grade.

July 28. Vernon E. Jordan, Jr., executive director designate of the National Urban League, told the closing session of his group's annual convention in Detroit that the Nixon administration had compiled a "record of ambiguity" toward black Americans. He accused the administration of allowing federal civil rights laws to "languish in dusty books." The remarks were a part of

Jordan's first major address to the Urban League since he was named its director, succeeding the late Whitney M. Young, Jr. (See also entry dated June 15, 1971.)

August 2. The Reverend Jesse Jackson of Chicago, leader of the Operation Breadbasket unit of the Southern Christian Leadership Conference (SCLC), accused the newly reorganized U. S. Postal Service of discriminating against blacks. Jackson, speaking to postal workers in Washington, D.C., said the Postal Service had begun laying off a number of workers as part of its reorganization plan and that since the majority of the black postal employees were in the lower job categories, they were the first to be fired. The black civil rights leader also accused the Postal Service of discrimination by placing new postal service offices in all-white suburban areas, where blacks could not obtain services or jobs.

August 3-11. President Nixon disowned a school desegregation plan drawn up by the Department of Health, Education, and Welfare (HEW) which would have required extensive crosstown busing in Austin, Texas. The President also took the occasion to reaffirm his strong opposition to any busing designed to achieve a racial balance in the schools. The President further directed HEW Secretary Elliott L. Richardson to aid individual school districts as they attempted to "hold busing to the minimum required by the law." The President, however, reasserted the duty of his administration to enforce orders of the federal courts, including those calling for busing to achieve desegregation. On August 11, the White House announced that President Nixon had warned administrative officials that they risked losing their jobs if they pushed for extensive busing as a means of desegregating the nation's schools. The President reaffirmed his stated policy of August 3 that the busing of children for purposes of school desegregation should be kept to the "minimum required by the law."

August 3-12. In an August 3 announcement, the United States Commission on Civil Rights (USCCR) charged that Air Force officials in southwest Texas were seeking to continue the "illegal busing" of school children on a military base to a predominantly white school nearby. The busing permitted 850 children to bypass the closer San Felipe school district that was largely Mexican-American in order to attend the mostly white Del Rio schools. In July, the Texas Education Agency had advised the Del Rio district that it could no longer accept the Air Force children because of a federal court ruling that the transfers were illegally perpetuating segregation. The Air Force, denying that it was seeking to perpetuate segregation, contended that the San Felipe school district did not have sufficient educational facilities to handle the 850 children from Laughlin Air Force Base and hence the plea for continued busing. On August 12, the USCCR maintained that President Nixon's directives to keep busing for racial desegregation to a minimum would undermine efforts to desegregate the nation's schools. The transportation of students, according to the commission's unanimous report, "is essential to eliminating segregation."

August 4. The nation's black federal, state, and municipal judges attending the 46th annual meeting of the black National Bar Association (NBA) in Atlanta announced the formation of a judicial court through which they would work for legal reform. Judge Edward Bell of Detroit, president of the NBA, said the new council would seek to return to the idea that the courts belong to all of the people, poor as well as rich, black as well as white. The judges also pointed out the absence of black federal judges in the South. At the time of the meeting, there were 285 black judges in the country, representing slightly more than 1 per cent of 20,000 jurists in the nation.

August 12. The United States Court of Appeals for the Ninth District declined to grant a delay in the implementation of a citywide elementary school desegregation program scheduled to take effect in San Francisco on September 8, 1971. The desegregation program involved the transfer of 48,000 children and had been ordered into effect on April 28, 1971 by U. S. District Judge Stanley A. Weigel.

August 16. The school board of Richmond, Virginia, told Federal District Court Judge Robert R. Merhige, Jr., that it was unable to reduce the large number of black students attending its public schools without a merger with the Henrico and Chesterfield county school systems. The board asked the court to order such a merger. The Richmond officials reported to the judges that they were not able to fully comply with his previous desegregation orders which involved widespread crosstown busing. This feature of the desegregation plan had been offset because too many white families had moved to the suburbs. The plight of the Richmond school board was typical of that of many urban school districts trying to desegregate with large black populations in the inner cities and predominantly or all-white suburban populations. Suburban residents expressed strong opposition to the school board's proposal, and demonstrated outside the home of Judge Merhige, who was protected by United States marshals.

August 18. A Jackson, Mississippi police officer was killed in a gun battle which broke out when local police raided the headquarters of the Republic of New Africa (RNA) in order to serve three of its members with fugitive warrants. Another Jackson police officer and a FBI agent were wounded during a twenty-minute exchange of gunfire. On August 23, 1971, eleven members of the black separatist group were accused of murdering Lieutenant W. L. Skinner. Previously, the eleven were charged with treason for allegedly engaging in armed insurrection against the state of Mississippi. Among those arrested was Imari A. Obadele, president of the RNA. Obadele expressed regret over Skinner's death but criticized the Jackson Police Department and the FBI for raiding the office. He declared that his group would receive any warrant peacefully, provided one or two black lawyers were present.

August 18. Governor George C. Wallace of Alabama ordered two of his state's school boards to ignore federal court-ordered desegregation plans. Wallace directed the school boards in Calhoun County and the city of Oxford to disregard the orders of a federal judge that an all-black school in Hobson City be paired with two predominantly-white schools in Oxford. Governor Wallace contended that his actions were consistent with President Richard Nixon's anti-busing declaration of August 3. The Governor's actions followed by only two days federal district Judge Sam C. Pointer Jr.'s declaration that such action was "legally meaningless." Mississippi Governor John Bell Williams was one of those, however, who announced immediate support for Wallace's anti-desegregation tactics. Wallace, Williams said, had "drawn a line in the dust and I stand fully with him."

August 18-September 8. As the fall school term approached, additional legal skirmishes concerning desegregation took place across the South. On August 18, the Justice Department filed a brief with Associate Supreme Court Justice Hugo Black which supported the Corpus Christi, Texas school board's request for a stay of a federal court order to desegregate the school district. The court-approved plan had called for massive busing of students.

On September 2, Supreme Court Justice Potter Stewart refused to stay a court order requiring extensive busing to achieve desegregation in the Nashville-Davidson County, Tennessee school system.

On September 4, Supreme Court Chief Justice Warren E. Burger refused to halt the busing of students to achieve desegregation in Arlington, Virginia. And on September 8, the Mobile, Alabama school board implemented a plan which called for the massive busing of students to desegregate schools.

August 20. U.S. Attorney General John Mitchell rejected a plan for reapportioning the legislative districts of Louisiana, contending that the plan would discriminate against blacks.

August 23. The Internal Security Committee of the U.S. House of Representatives issued a report declaring that while the Black Panther Party posed a physical danger to the nation's law enforcement officers, they were totally incapable of overthrowing the United States government by violent means. The four Republican members of the committee, John M. Ashbrook of Ohio, John G. Schmitz of California, Fletcher Thompson of Georgia, and Roger H. Zion of Indiana, objected to the panel's findings, contending that the majority view did not give "a clear understanding of the Black Panther Party as a subversive criminal group using the facade of politics as a cover for crimes of violence and extortion."

August 24. Fourteen law enforcement officials, including Illinois state attorney Edward U. Hanraham, chief prosecutor for Chicago, were named in a long-suppressed indictment handed down in Chicago on charges of conspiracy to obstruct justice by trying to suppress or thwart criminal prosecutions of eight police officers who participated in the December 4, 1969 raid of an apartment rented by a Black Panther party member (see entry above). The indictment was made public on orders issued by the Illinois Supreme Court. Judge Joseph A. Power of the Illinois Criminal Court had kept the indictment sealed since April, 1971, when it was first prepared. Power had refused to accept the indictment, contending that the grand jury had not heard all the pertinent witnesses and that it was pressured into returning true bills. Among others named in the indictment were an assistant state attorney, the police superintendent of Chicago, eight police officers who took part in the controversial raid, and four other officers who later conducted departmental investigations into the affair.

August 26. The Office of Civil Rights of the Department of Health, Education, and Welfare (HEW) reported that black student enrollment in the nation's colleges and universities had increased at a rate five times greater than white student enrollment since 1968. Black enrollment grew from 303,397 in 1968 to 379,138 in the fall of 1970, a 24 percent increase. According to the HEW report, 44 percent of all black undergraduates were enrolled in colleges with black minorities. The largest increase in black enrollment, 47 percent since 1968, came in the eleven states comprising the Deep South. Nevertheless, blacks still represented only 6 percent of the undergraduates in the nation.

August 26. A federal court in Washington, D. C. refused a request by the administration of President Nixon to dismiss a suit pending against federal tax exemptions for private all-white academies in the South. The court also denied a request by civil rights groups who brought the suit that urged all such academies have their tax-exempt status revoked immediately. The administration's lawyer told the court that the Internal Revenue Service would no longer grant tax exempt status to private schools practicing a policy of racial discrimination in admissions, but that for now the government had relied on the word of the schools in determining whether they were willing to desegregate.

August 30-September 8. As the nation's schools reopened for their fall terms, the stiffest resistance to court-ordered racial desegregation in public education was seen in the North and West. In Pontiac, Michigan, eight white students and one black pupil were injured on September 8 as fights erupted during protests against a school busing plan. On August 30, 1971, arsonists in Pontiac had set firebombs which destroyed ten school buses to be used for implementing desegregation plans. The protests in Pontiac were among the most violent seen in the country. White parents, carrying American flags, marched in front of the school bus depot on September 8 daring bus drivers to run them down. In San Francisco, Chinese-American spokesmen announced that they intended to resist a court-ordered busing plan scheduled to be implemented on September 13, 1971. The Chinese-Americans acted in response to Supreme Court Justice William O. Douglas's rejection of their anti-busing appeal on August 29, 1971. Under the plan, upheld by the courts, approximately 6,500 Chinese-Americans were to be included among 48,000 students to be bused in order to achieve further school desegregation. In Boston, Massachusetts, parents of about 300 children who were assigned to a new racially desegregated school refused to enroll their children there on September 8. Instead, the children were returned to their previous neighborhood schools. A similar defiance of court-ordered desegregation occurred in Evansville, Indiana. By contrast, most newly desegregated schools reopened quietly in the South, although many were faced with new busing plans.

August 31. Warren E. Burger, Chief Justice of the United States Supreme Court, announced that he was afraid that federal judges were misinterpreting the high Court's decision on busing which was delivered on April 20, 1971. Burger feared that judges were assuming that the order required racial balance in every school. In a ten-page opinion (an unusual length in denying a stay), which denied a stay of enforcement of a court-ordered busing plan for the schools in Winston-Salem-Forsyth County, North Carolina, Burger said the unanimous court ruling in April did not require a fixed racial balance or quota in order to legally desegregate schools. A school district's racial balance could be used as a point of beginning to determine "whether in fact any violation [of law] existed." On the same day, Secretary of Health, Education, and Welfare Elliott L. Richardson reported that he agreed with President Nixon's announced policy of limiting school busing to achieve racial desegregation. Richardson denied that he had considered resigning after the President repudiated a school desegregation plan which his department had drawn up for the Austin, Texas school district, a plan which required extensive crosstown busing.

September 13. More than 1,000 state troopers, prison guards, and sheriff's deputies stormed the Attica State Prison in New York, ending a five-day strike by inmates. Forty-three people, including nine guards held as hostages, were killed in the most disastrous prison tragedy in United States history. Most of the slain prisoners were black. The troubles at Attica were sparked by a misunderstanding between two inmates who were playing touch football and a guard who believed they were fighting. Rumors spread through the prison that the inmates, one black and one white, were beaten by guards.

September 13. Approximately 45 percent of the school children in San Francisco, California refused to attend classes as a new school desegregation plan calling for the busing of 48,000 children was put into effect. (See also entry dated August 12, 1971).

September 22. Alabama Governor George C. Wallace signed a bill passed by the Alabama legislature which permitted parents to send their children to their neighborhood schools if they felt that busing to achieve desegregation would be harmful to their children.

September 23-25. On September 23, Associate Supreme Court Justice John M. Harlan, citing reasons of health, retired from the bench after sixteen years of service on the high Court. Hugo L. Black, who retired from the United States Supreme Court as an Associate Justice after thirty-four years of service on September 13, 1971, died on September 25. Harlan and Black had participated in many of the historic decisions concerning civil rights and legal protections for minorities and the poor. During his last years on the Court, Justice Black was accused of inconsistency and "turning his back on blacks," yet the justice, a native Alabamian and one-time Ku Klux Klansman, replied: "I haven't changed a jot or a tittle." Black was eulogized by the popular black news magazine *Jet* as "a real American."

September 26. The United States Bureau of Labor Statistics released a study which showed that 27.9 percent of the blacks employed across the country held white collar jobs during 1970. In 1960, 16.1 percent of the white collar jobs were held by blacks.

October 6. A black man and a white woman were married officially for the first time in North Carolina. Lorraine Mary Turner and John A. Wilkinson took their vows in Durham County, North Carolina.

October 9. The Ford Foundation announced in New York a six-year $100 million program to aid black private colleges in providing individual study awards to various minority students. About twenty of the nation's better known black private colleges, including Hampton and Tuskegee Institutes, Benedict College, Fisk University, and the six schools comprising the Atlanta University Center complex of black institutions, were chosen to receive awards averaging as much as $300,000 annually. In a closely related matter, Morris Brown College announced that it might withdraw from the famous Atlanta University Center and reject the Ford funds. Morris Brown officials objected to a proviso in the Atlanta grants which called for a reorganization of the Atlanta University Center, so as to effect closer cooperation.

October 15. Elton Hayes, a seventeen-year-old black youth, was killed by police officers in Memphis, Tennessee. The slaying of Hayes was followed by five days of racial violence in Memphis. Nine local law enforcement officers, including a black police lieutenant, were later charged with murder in the brutal death of the youth.

October. Ralph David Abernathy, president of the Southern Christian Leadership Conference (SCLC), returned to the country from a European tour which took him, among other places, to Russia and East Germany. Abernathy preached to approximately 7,000 people in the Russian Orthodox Cathedral. In East Germany, the veteran civil rights leader was awarded the Peace Medal of the German Democratic Republic.

October. President Richard M. Nixon nominated William Rehnquist of Phoenix, Arizona, and Lewis F. Powell of Richmond, Virginia, to the United States Supreme Court. Both nominations were opposed by many blacks. Black judge George W. Crockett of the Detroit Recorders Court assailed the President for his refusal to consult black lawyers on the appointments. The chief criticisms coming from blacks were that Rehnquist was a "rational reactionary" and that Powell was associated with private clubs and law firms in Virginia which discriminated against African-Americans. Both nominees denied anti-black attitudes and practices. Rehnquist, at the time, employed a black secretary in his office where he was an Assistant U. S. Attorney. The United States Senate subsequently confirmed both appointees with a minimum of difficulty.

October. A lively controversy arose among black and white politicians after Senator Edmund Muskie from Maine, a likely candidate for the Democratic nomination for President in 1972, stated that a black vice presidential candidate, regrettably, would be a handicap to the Democratic ticket. (Muskie himself was the Democratic vice-presidential candidate in 1968.) Vice President Spiro Agnew, former black Assistant Secretary of Labor Arthur Fletcher, both Republicans, and black Democratic National Committeeman Hobart Taylor, Jr. were among those disagreeing with Muskie. Former Georgia Governor Lester Maddox claimed he would vote for the "right" black vice-presidential candidate, but Alabama Governor George C. Wallace, himself a presidential candidate, said that Muskie's position was "probably right."

November 2. In general elections across the country, blacks were elected mayors in four additional American cities and were named to various other local and state offices. In Englewood, New Jersey, the Reverend Walter S. Taylor was elected the city's first black mayor. Gilbert H. Bradley, Jr. was elected mayor of Kalamazoo, Michigan. In Benton Harbor, Michigan, Charles Joseph became the town's first black mayor. Richard B. Hatcher was easily reelected to a four-year term as mayor of Gary, Indiana. Two blacks, Henry Owens and Saundra Graham, were elected to the City Council in Cambridge, Massachusetts, and a third black, Charles Pierce, was selected to the city's School Board.

In Mississippi, Fayette's black mayor Charles Evers was defeated in his bid for governor, but state Representative Robert Clark, the only black legislator in

Mississippi, was returned to his seat. Blacks also won seven county supervisor posts, one circuit court clerk's position, and about twenty other county offices. Almost 300 blacks campaigned for offices in Mississippi during the November elections.

Also in the elections, former heavyweight boxing champion Jersey Joe Walcott was elected sheriff of Camden, New Jersey. Blacks were elected to the City Council in Indianapolis, Indiana, Davenport, Iowa, Burlington, Iowa, Memphis, Tennessee, and Miami, Florida. In Memphis, black councilman Fred Davis was elected chairman of the thirteen-member city council. In Miami, the Reverend Edward Graham managed to retain his seat on the city council, although black mayoral candidate Tom Washington was defeated.

Defeated in the Mississippi state legislature race were veteran civil rights leaders Fanny Lou Hamer and Aaron Henry. Voters in Cleveland, Ohio rejected a second black mayor in Arnold R. Pinkney's candidacy. Although Thomas I. Atkins, a black city councilman in Boston was defeated in his bid for mayor, he was appointed secretary of the Department of Communications and Development, the highest position held by an African-American in Massachusetts state government.

November 16. The United States Commission on Civil Rights again criticized the administration of President Richard M. Nixon, charging that it had failed to adequately enforce civil rights laws and regulations.

November. Alonzo G. Moron, the first black president of Hampton Institute in Virginia, died in San Juan, Puerto Rico. Moron had recently served as deputy director of the Department of Housing and Urban Development in San Juan.

December 15. Huey P. Newton, co-founder of the Black Panther Party, was declared free after manslaughter charges against him were dismissed. Newton was imprisoned for nearly two years for the 1967 death of an Oakland, California police officer, and was tried three times on the manslaughter charge. His latest trial ended in a hung jury when the jury reported that it was "utterly unable to reach a verdict." (See also entries dated September 8, 1968, and May 29, 1970.)

December. United States District Court Judge Sam C. Pointer declared an

Alabama anti-busing law unconstitutional. The judge ruled that the stature "is but a freedom-of-choice option dressed in slightly different colors," and such options, he said, were illegal.

December. Two veteran champions of Negro rights died before the close of the year. Arthur B. Spingarn, the NAACP's president since 1940, succumbed at his home in New York at age ninety-three. Spingarn, a white civil rights lawyer, once headed the NAACP's National Legal Committee. The NAACP's annual meritorious award, the Spingarn medal, was named in honor of the long-time civil rights leader. NAACP executive secretary Roy Wilkins eulogized Spingarn as one who had challenged "the sanctioned institutions of Jim Crow" and characterized his death as "a great loss to the Negroes in particular and the liberal social movement in general." Ralph J. Bunche, undersecretary general of the United Nations, Nobel Peace Prize winner, scholar, and civil rights activist, died at age sixty-seven in New York. Bunche, who was a familiar figure in international councils as well as on civil rights battlefields, and a key figure in Martin Luther King, Jr.'s Selma to Montgomery March in 1965, was eulogized by United Nations Secretary General U Thant as "an international institution in his own right." (See entry dated September 13, 1948, for further information about Bunche.)

1972

January 3. A United States District Court in Montgomery, Alabama ordered the implementation of a new reapportionment plan that would split the Alabama legislature into single-member districts. The decision could put as many as twenty additional blacks in the Alabama state legislature. There were, at the time, only two black members of the Alabama legislature. The new districts would represent the decennial population count based upon the enumerated districts of the United States Census.

January 10. United States District Court Judge Robert R. Merhige, Jr. ordered the merger of the predominately-black schools of Richmond, Virginia with those of two suburban counties with nearly all-white enrollments in order to promote school desegregation. Judge Merhige directed that the new metropolitan school district be formed as the only "remedy promising immediate success" to end segregated education based upon separate housing patterns. The order required the merger of the 70 percent black Richmond city schools with the 90 percent white schools of Henrico and Chesterfield counties.

January 25. Representative Shirley Chisholm from New York, the first black woman ever to serve in the United States Congress, announced that she would seek the Democratic presidential nomination. Representative Chisholm said that her candidacy would help repudiate the notion that the American people would not vote for a qualified black or female candidate.

January 27. Mahalia Jackson, one of the world's foremost gospel singers, died at age sixty in Evergreen Park, Illinois. Jackson was largely responsible for spreading gospel music from black churches in the Deep South to concert halls throughout the world. Her 1946 recording of "Move On Up a Little Higher" sold at least one million copies. President Nixon eulogized Jackson as "an artist without peers."

February 11. About fifty members of the Congress of Racial Equality (CORE) went to the office of black Democratic Congressman Augustus Hawkins from California demanding that black opponents of busing to achieve school desegregation be given a voice in national black meetings. Victor A. Solomon, leader of the CORE contingent, said his group advocated separate but "really equal" schools under community control. The NAACP and other black organizations had supported busing as a necessary tool to achieve school desegregation.

March 24. Z. Alexander Looby, one of the first blacks elected to the Nashville, Tennessee City Council (1951-1971) and a veteran civil rights activist, died at age seventy-two in Nashville. (See also entries dated May 10, 1951 and April 19, 1960, for further information about Looby).

March 27. An all-white jury in San Francisco, California acquitted Fleeta Drumgo and John Cluchette—the so-called Soledad Brothers—in the slaying of a Soledad Prison guard in 1970. Black communist Angela Davis was charged with plotting to free Drumgo, Cluchette, and the late George Jackson, her alleged lover, in the famous Marin County Courthouse shoot-out on August 7, 1970 (see entry above). In the Soledad Brothers trial, the prosecution was unable to produce witnesses who actually saw any fatal blows delivered or who had seen the defendants toss a guard over a third floor tier. The defendants had denied that they were present at the scene of the slaying.

April 4. Adam Clayton Powell, Jr., United States Representative from Harlem for more than twenty years (1945-1969) and one-time chairman of the influential House Education and Labor Committee (1960-67), died at age sixty-three in Miami, Florida. Powell was surrounded with controversy in death, as in life, as two women fought over the disposition of his body and his estate. On April 10, Powell's body was cremated and the ashes scattered over the island of Bimini in the Bahamas. (See also entries dated August 1, 1944 and January 8, 1967, for further information about Powell).

May 19. The National Education Association (NEA) reported that over 30,000 black teachers had lost their jobs in seventeen Southern and border states because of segregation and discrimination since 1954. 21 percent of the teachers in these states were black in 1954, but by 1970 that percentage had dropped to nineteen. The percentage of black job losses was lowest in Alabama, and highest in Kentucky, Missouri, and Delaware.

May 19. The National Black Political Convention issued a 58-page "Black Agenda" that had been adopted at its founding meeting in March in Gary, Indiana. Although a special committee had modified provisions on school busing and on black attitudes toward Israel, these statements continued to arouse opposition. Partly because of these provisions, the NAACP, as well as other black organizations and individuals, criticized that part of the report which called for the "dismantling" of Israel and which condemned that nation's "expansionist policy." The school provision which also provoked controversy called busing "racist" and "suicidal." In their modified forms, the Israeli statement embraced the condemnations of Israel contained in numerous resolutions of the Organization of African Unity and the United Nations Commission on Human Rights, while the school provision criticized the Nixon administration's busing policies and demanded that blacks retain control of any busing program. Despite the modifications, however, the NAACP announced its continued opposition and withdrawal on May 16. NAACP assistant executive director John A. Morsell called the "Agenda's" Israeli and busing statements "particularly outrageous."

May 21. Professor David J. Armor, a white Harvard University professor, released a study of school desegregation programs in six Northern cities in which he concluded that there was no improvement in either academic achievement among black students or racial cooperation. While no significant academic differences were found among black students who had been bused for desegregation purposes and those who remained in black ghetto schools, the desegregated students tended to reveal declines in educational and career aspirations and in self-esteem. Professor Armor did, however, recommend the continuation of "voluntary" programs of busing to achieve desegregation, because those bused students tended to get better opportunities for higher education. The study was conducted in Boston, Massachusetts, White Plains, New York, Ann Arbor, Michigan, Riverdale, California, and Hartford and New Haven, Connecticut.

May 23. The annual convention of the National Congress of Parents and Teachers adopted a resolution requesting governmental and educational authorities "to search for solutions that would by rational means reduce racial isolation through transportation." The resolution passed by a vote of 303-296. The National Congress has eight and one-half million members.

May 24. The United States Senate passed and sent to the House of Representatives a final version of an omnibus higher education-desegregation aid bill with an anti-busing provision. The bill would delay all new court-ordered busing until appeals had been exhausted, or until January, 1974. Federal funds could not be used to finance busing to achieve desegregation unless specifically requested by local authorities. Federal officials would be prohibited from encouraging or ordering school districts to spend state or local funds for busing in cases where such busing endangered the health or education of students involved, "unless constitutionally required." John Ehrlichman, President

Nixon's chief assistant for domestic affairs, described the bill as falling "far short" of what was necessary to control busing to achieve desegregation.

June 2. Former SNCC leader H. Rap Brown was sentenced to five years in prison and fined $2,000 for a 1968 conviction on a federal weapons charge by United States District Court Judge Lansing L. Mitchell in New Orleans. Brown was flown to New Orleans from New York City where he had been held since his capture by New York police during an alleged robbery attempt in October, 1971. Brown was wounded by police in that altercation and his attorneys protested against the trip to New Orleans, claiming that it endangered their client's health.

June 3. United States District Court Judge Alfonso J. Zirpoli of San Francisco ordered David Hilliard, Chief of Staff of the Black Panther Party, cleared of perjury charges after the Justice Department refused to disclose wiretap evidence requested by the jury. Hilliard was accused of filing a false declaration of poverty in 1971. At the time of his latest trial he was serving a prison sentence for assaulting a police officer. (See also entry dated June 12, 1971.)

June 4. Black Communist Angela Davis was acquitted on all charges of murder, kidnapping, and conspiracy by a Superior Court jury in San Jose, California. An all-white jury deliberated for thirteen hours before announcing their verdict. Davis reacted to the acquittal by at first proclaiming that the "only fair trial would have been no trial," but later added that the verdict was a victory for the people. Praise for the verdict was generally heard in the black and white "liberal" communities of the nation and overseas, including Moscow. (See also entries dated August 7, 1970, October 13, 1970, December 27, 1970, and January 5, 1971.)

June 6. United States Senator James O. Eastland, a Democrat from Mississippi, was renominated for a sixth term with 70 percent of the vote over two challengers, including James H. Meredith, the first black to enroll at the University of Mississippi (see entry dated September 30, 1962). Eastland had earned a reputation for supporting anti-Negro policies.

June 6. The Fourth U. S. Circuit Court of Appeals in Richmond, Virginia, overruled a federal district court order that called for the merger of the school districts of Richmond and two suburban countries, which would have involved the busing of thousands of children to achieve desegregation. The court held that U. S. District Court Judge Robert R. Merhige, Jr. had excessively interpreted the Fourteenth Amendment when he earlier ordered the "metropolitan desegregation" plan into effect (see entry dated January 10, 1972). The Richmond Board of Education announced that it would appeal the court's 5-1 ruling to the United States Supreme Court where, along with a similar case from Denver, Colorado, it was expected to bring a new crucial ruling in the annals of school desegregation. The appeal to the Fourth Circuit Court was sponsored by the U. S. Department of Justice. The NAACP, the National Education Association (NEA), and the American Civil Liberties Union (ACLU) opposed the appeal to the Circuit Court.

June 8. The United States House of Representatives approved and sent to President Richard Nixon for his signature an omnibus higher education-desegregation aid bill which would, among other things, delay all court-ordered busing to achieve desegregation until all appeals were exhaustive or until January 1, 1974. (The United States Supreme Court has held since 1969 that busing to achieve desegregation had to be implemented immediately when ordered by federal district courts.) The bill also prohibited federal funds for busing unless requested by a community and where there was no danger to student "health, safety, or education." Federal officials were not to require or encourage busing to achieve desegregation "unless constitutionally required." The bill further appropriated $2 billion over a two-year period to aid school districts with the desegregation process. Although the Nixon administration had criticized the bill as inadequate, HEW Secretary Elliott Richardson announced that it embodied "the heart" of the President's "higher education initiative." Nixon signed the bill into law on June 23.

June 12. The United States Supreme Court ruled in a 6-3 decision that a state could grant a liquor license to a private club which practiced racial discrimination. The Court ruled against the petition of K. Leroy Irvis, black majority leader of the Pennsylvania House of Representatives. Irvis had been denied service in the restaurant of the lodge of the Loyal Order of Moose in Harrisburg, Pennsylvania. Justice William H. Rehnquist wrote that the authority to grant liquor licenses did not "sufficiently implicate the state in the discriminatory guest policies" of private clubs. Justices Douglas, Brennan, and Marshall dissented from the majority view.

June 14. United States District Court Judge Stephen J. Roth ordered a massive busing program to desegregate the city and suburban schools in the Detroit, Michigan area. It was the most extensive desegregation plan ever ordered by a federal court. Under the plan, 310,000 of 780,000 students in Detroit and fifty-three suburban school districts would be bused to achieve desegregation. The Detroit schools had, at the time, 290,000 students, 65 percent black, while 29 of the 53 suburban districts had all-white enrollments and the rest were predominately-white. On June 22, President Nixon voiced complete disagreement with the court's decision and reiterated his appeal for congressional action on a strong anti-busing law. The President called the Detroit order "perhaps the most flagrant example that we have of all the busing decisions, moving against all the principles that I, at least, believe should be applied in this area." On July 21, the Sixth United States Circuit Court of Appeals issued an order delaying the implementation of Judge Roth's order until it could hear the merits of the case on August 24, 1972.

June 26. A bloc of black delegates to the Democratic National Convention led by Representative Walter E. Fauntroy from Washington, D.C., endorsed the presidential candidacy of South Dakota Senator George McGovern. Fauntroy announced that ninety-six previously uncommitted black delegates would now vote for McGovern. McGovern predicted that the black bloc might be enough to give him the nomination on the first ballot. A later recount by all parties confirmed that the black bloc really numbered only about sixty votes, not enough to assure McGovern a first ballot victory. Senator McGovern had won favor among blacks for his "positive" attitude as exhibited in his support of parts of the programs of the Black Congressional Caucus, the Black National Convention, and his pledge to appoint blacks to high-ranking positions in any administration which he should head.

June 29. The United States Supreme Court, in a 5-4 decision, ruled that the death penalty as it was usually enforced violated the Eighth Amendment prohibition against cruel and unusual punishment. The high Court order overturned the conviction of two Georgia blacks, Henry Furman, a convicted murderer, and Lucius Jackson, a convicted rapist, and a Texas black, Elmer Branch, also a convicted rapist. All of the victims in the crimes were white. Of the 600 men and women awaiting execution at the time of the ruling, 329 were black while 14 belonged to other minority groups. Justice William O. Douglas wrote that the disproportionate number of minority and poor felons sentenced to death were victims of unconstitutional discrimination.

July 3-7. During its annual convention held in Detroit, Michigan, the NAACP again criticized the Nixon administration for its attitude towards black people. The 2,632 delegates passed an emergency resolution condemning the administration for its school busing policies. On July 6, NAACP Labor Director Herbert Hill reiterated his criticism of the administration's record on black employment. Black officials in the Nixon administration, including Assistant Secretary of Housing and Urban Development Samuel Jackson, defended the Nixon program and claimed support for the President even among NAACP board of directors.

July 6. James E. Baker, a career black foreign service officer, was appointed economic and commercial officer at the United States embassy in Pretoria, South Africa, becoming the first black American diplomat to gain a permanent assignment in that nation. The Department of State expressed confidence that Baker would be accepted in South Africa without restrictions, despite that nation's racist apartheid policy.

July 12. South Dakota Senator George S. McGovern, with widespread support from black delegates, won the Democratic presidential nomination on the first ballot in Miami Beach, Florida. Representative Shirley Chisholm from

New York, the first black woman ever to seek a presidential nomination, received 151 of the more than 2,000 votes cast.

August 2. The United States Circuit Court of Appeals for the Fifth District countermanded desegregation orders of lower courts for the school districts in Austin and Corpus Christi, Texas. In Austin, the lower court had rejected plans for crosstown busing of students, but the appellate court counselled against the total rejection of the busing tool and ordered new plans from all of the concerned parties. In the Corpus Christi case, the appeals court overturned a crosstown busing plan, instructing the lower court to examine all neighborhood-oriented tools before resorting to busing to achieve desegregation.

August 3-8. In fall primary elections, State Senator James O. Patterson, Jr. was nominated for a congressional seat in the new Fourth Congressional District (Memphis) of Tennessee. Patterson thus became the first black to win a major party congressional nomination in the state's history. In Georgia, a former aide to Dr. Martin Luther King, Jr., Hosea Williams of Dekalb County, placed a distant third in the Democratic race for United States senator and, in the same state, another former aide to King, Andrew Young of Atlanta, won the Democratic nomination from the Fifth Congressional District. Five blacks were also elected to the ten-person City Council in Selma, Alabama, the scene of violent voting rights demonstrations in the 1960s. This group, elected from predominately-black wards rather than at-large, were the first of their race to win seats on the local council.

August 25-October 28. Black civil rights and political leaders campaigned in behalf of the presidential nominees of both parties. On August 25, Georgia State Representative Julian Bond told an audience at Columbia University in New York that black Americans ought to "come together to drive Richard Nixon from the White House." Bond predicted that Nixon's opponent, Senator George McGovern from South Dakota, would capture 90 percent of the nation's black vote. On October 28, Floyd McKissick, former national director of the Congress of Racial Equality (CORE) and developer of the new town of Soul City in North Carolina, told an Atlanta audience that he supported the reelection of President Nixon because blacks should belong to both political parties and because Nixon had done more for blacks than Senator McGovern. Veteran Atlanta civil rights leader William Holmes Borders, another Nixon supporter, cited the administration's aid to Howard University in Washington, D.C., Tuskegee Institute in Alabama, sickle-cell anemia research, and job retraining programs as evidence of the President's concern for blacks.

August 26. United States District Court Judge L. Clure Morton ordered the Nashville, Tennessee school board to obtain thirty additional school buses in order to meet the court's desegregation requirements. Nashville's mayor and city council had hesitated to release the necessary funds for the new buses. Judge Morton, however, told city officials that they must acquire the additional buses immediately so that his year-old busing order could be made effective.

August 26. Dr. Thomas A. Shaheen, an advocate of busing to achieve racial desegregation in the public schools, resigned under board pressure as superintendent of schools of San Francisco. Shaheen directed the first massive busing plan to achieve desegregation in a major Northern or Western city in September, 1971, when more than half of San Francisco's 40,000 elementary school children were ordered to be bused by the federal courts. Shaheen predicted that "rocky days" were ahead for proponents of desegregation in American education. He was succeeded by Dr. Stephen Morena, assistant chancellor of the San Francisco Community College District. (See also entry dated August 12, 1971).

August 26. John LeFlore, a veteran civil rights leader and journalist in Mobile, Alabama, was officially certified as the first black candidate for the United States Senate in Alabama since the Reconstruction era. LeFlore was certified by Alabama Secretary of State Mabel Amos under the banner of the mostly black national Democratic party of Alabama (NDPA). Other candidates in the senate race were Democratic incumbent John Sparkman and Republican W. M. Blount, former Postmaster General of the United States.

August 30. Three Meridian, Mississippi whites were freed from a federal prison after serving slightly more than two years of their three-year sentences on charges of slaying three civil rights activists in Neshoba County, Mississippi, in 1964. Jimmy Arledge, Jimmie Snowden, and Horace Doyle Barnette were convicted in 1967 on conspiracy charges following the deaths of Andrew Goodman, Michael Schwerner, and James E. Chaney near Philadelphia, Mississippi (see entry dated August 4, 1964). Chief Deputy U. S. Marshal Charles T. Sutherland said the convicted trio were approved for release in the spring of 1972 after receiving time off of their sentences for "good behavior."

September 1. A group of black parents asked for federal protection for their children attending desegregated schools in Oklahoma City, Oklahoma. The blacks vowed not to return their children to the schools—scenes of continued outbursts of racial violence—without protection. The black parents presented their requests to the local school board and to the offices of the United States Attorney and U. S. Marshal. They suggested that federal officers board school buses and patrol the schools.

November 2. Racial tensions flared in Lavonia, Georgia, after a black man was slain in a gunbattle with police. Police Chief Joe Foster said Ollis Hunter was killed after he opened fire on officers attempting to serve him with a peace warrant at his home. Lavonia patrol officer Freddie Smith was wounded in the exchange of gunfire. Blacks contended that the slaying of Hunter could have been avoided. Almost immediately, the town's black population began a boycott of downtown merchants, demanding, among other things, that better streets be provided in their communities, more black school bus drivers and police officers, and the firing of Chief Foster. Mayor Herman Ayers and the city council took the demands under advisement. On December 8, 1972, a gunman rode through the black residential area of Lavonia firing shotgun blasts into two homes, two restaurants, and a church. Police said one of the homes belonged to the head of the local chapter of the Southern Christian Leadership Conference. There were no injuries in the incident and no immediate arrests.

November 7. Richard M. Nixon was reelected President of the United States by one of the largest majorities in the nation's history. As in 1968, the President failed to win substantial support from black voters. Preliminary estimates gave Nixon only about 30 percent of the black votes cast in the election.

The fall elections also saw the selection of two additional black women for seats in the United States Congress and the election of the first black representative from the South since Reconstruction days. The new black congresswomen are Yvonne Braithwaite Burke from California and Barbara Jordan from Texas. Andrew Young, formerly a top aide to the late Dr. Martin Luther King, Jr., was elected congressman from Georgia's Fifth District (Atlanta).

November 11. Black syndicated columnist Carl T. Rowan was elected to membership in the Gridiron Club, a prestigious organization of Washington journalists. Rowan became the first black member of the club, which was established in 1885.

November 14. Thirteen blacks, members of the Dallas, Texas chapter of the Southern Christian Leadership Conference, were arrested on charges of disrupting a public meeting after they staged a sit-in demonstration in the chambers of the Dallas City Council. George Holland, spokesperson for the SCLC group, read a list of demands which included the resignation of Dallas Mayor Wes Wise, Police Chief Frank Dyson, and City Attorney Alex Bickley; the arrest of three officers who were recently cited but exonerated, in the slaying of local blacks; and a percentage (24) of city jobs commensurate with that of the city's black population. Police officers arrested the group before Holland could finish reading his demands.

November 15. Private Billy Dean Smith, a black soldier, was acquitted by a military court in San Francisco of the "fragging" slaying of two officers in South Vietnam. Smith later stated at a news conference, which was attended by black Communist Angela Davis, that "the system of military justice is still riddled with injustice." Smith said the only fair trial in his case would have been "no trial at all."

November 15. The black National Bar Association (NBA) announced that it will co-sponsor a federal court suit protesting the failure of all black applicants in the last semi-annual Georgia Bar examination. Atlanta City Councilman Marvin S. Arrington, deputy regional director of the NBA, said that none of the fifty-five black applicants received a passing grade and charged that "there is conscious and invidious discrimination" on the part of the bar examiners in Georgia. He pledged to call on the U. S. Department of Justice and Georgia Governor Jimmy Carter to conduct investigations into allegations of discrimination. Georgia Bar Examination Board Chairman Trammell Vickery denied that discrimination existed against black applicants and cited the fact that applicants are not identified by race. (See also entries dated February 4-5, 1971, and July 5, 1971.)

November 16. The Reverend Theodore Hesburgh, chairman of the United States Civil Rights Commission (USCCR) since 1969 and a member since its inception in 1958, resigned. Hesburgh, president of Notre Dame University, has led the USCCR in a constant stream of criticism of the Nixon administration's commitment to civil rights progress. Maurice Mitchell, chancellor of the University of Denver, also announced his resignation. Mitchell had charged that President Nixon ignored the Commission and its work.

November 16. Two black students at Southern University in Baton Rouge, Louisiana, were killed during a confrontation between black students and law enforcement officers. High ranking police officials had denied in their first statements following the shooting that their men had fired the fatal shots. Some suggested that there might have been accidental firings. Spokespersons for the students charged intentional shooting by law enforcement units. Louisiana Governor Edwin Edwards immediately requested State Attorney General William J. Guste, Jr. to investigate the incidents. Guste subsequently appointed a biracial committee consisting of police officers, university administrators, students, elected officials, and private citizens. Some blacks expressed distrust of the official committee and vowed to assemble a group of their own to look into the altercation.

Southern University, one of the nation's largest all-black colleges, has been the scene of student protests in recent years. The students have generally charged the school's administration, backed by the power of the state government, with being unresponsive to academic and social change.

November 17. United States District Court Judge John H. Pratt ruled in Washington, D.C. that efforts made by the Department of Health, Education, and Welfare (HEW) to obtain voluntary compliance with the 1964 Civil Rights Act had been largely unsuccessful and that HEW should withhold funds from school districts still practicing segregation. U. S. Attorneys announced that they would appeal the ruling, claiming that there appeared to be serious errors in the judge's decision. They did not specify the errors.

November 18. Fayette, Mississippi Mayor Charles Evers called for a federal investigation into problems faced by small Southern cotton farmers. The black mayor told Secretary of Agriculture Earl Butz in a telegram that many farmers, black and white, had come to him with their problems.

November 18. United States District Court Judge Edward T. Ginouz set a limit on the contempt-of-court sentence that may be ordered for the "Chicago 7" defendants and their lawyers and ordered contempt charges against Black Panther leader Bobby Seale entirely dropped. The contempt charges arose from the actions of the defendants and the lawyers in the courtroom of Judge Julius J. Hoffman, who heard the case after disturbances during the 1968 Democratic National Convention in Chicago. The charges against Seale were dropped at the government's request. An Appeals Court had ruled earlier that if Seale were prosecuted, the government would have to reveal the contents of electronic surveillance logs. The prosecution refused, claiming such disclosures would "endanger the national security."

November 22. The Louis Harris Poll, a major survey of public opinion, announced that the sharpest division in the 1972 presidential election was according to race, with blacks voting 79-21 percent for Senator George McGovern while whites voted 67-33 percent in favor of President Nixon. The survey went on to say that in terms of their political inclinations and in their outlook on American issues, blacks and whites have rarely been so far apart. The survey cited such examples as the blacks' overwhelming preference for racially desegregated schools (78-12 percent) as against a plurality of 46-43 percent among whites. While roughly 50 percent of the black population endorsed busing to achieve school desegregation, only 14 percent of the nation's whites approved of this method to dismantle separate schools. Also, nearly 80 percent of the nation's blacks sympathized with the plight of the poor, while no more than 46 percent of whites supported increased federal assistance for poverty-stricken Americans. The Harris Survey reflected racial attitudes as of Thanksgiving Day, 1972.

November 27. H. Rap Brown, former secretary of the Student Non-Violent Coordinating Committee (SNCC), went on trial on charges of robbery, attempted murder, and possession of an illegal weapon. There was speculation, however, that the trial might be further delayed by legal arguments over the effect of a magazine article dealing with one of the arresting officers. Brown was arrested after a New York robbery on October 16, 1971. The trial finally got under way after Brown's lawyers, William Kuntsler and Howard Moore, Jr., both famed civil liberties attorneys, failed in an effort to have the case transferred to the federal courts. (See also entry dated June 2, 1972.)

November 29. President Nixon nominated Peter J. Brennan, the president of the Building and Construction Trades Councils of New York, to be his new Secretary of Labor. Many blacks voiced opposition to the nomination, claiming that Brennan was a representative of a segment of organized labor which had been desegregated "minimally" and, generally, at government insistence.

December 4. Black poet Imamu Amiri Baraka (born LeRoi Jones) told the representatives at the triennial general assembly of the National Council of Churches that the nation's major religious organizations must support the "revolution" of the poor or cease to exist. Baraka, an influential resident of Newark, New Jersey, called for the destruction of capitalism, claiming it was part of a "cruelly primitive social system" subjecting the poor to misery in this country and abroad. Observers of the American Jewish Committee, Rabbi A. James Ruden and the Reverend Gerald Strober, voiced "deep chagrin" at Baraka's appearance and accused him of "anti-white racism and vicious anti-Semitism." Many other delegates stood to applaud the black poet.

December 7. The Reverend W. Sterling Cary, the black administrative officer for approximately ninety United Church of Christ congregations in New York City, was unanimously elected president of the National Council of Churches at the group's annual meeting in Dallas, Texas. Cary, the first black American to head the group, was originally a Baptist minister before he began preaching at Presbyterian, Congregational, and interdenominational churches in a ministerial career spanning twenty-four years. The newly elected president of the "liberal" religious group told his fellow delegates at Dallas that American churches preach but do not practice integration. He said that as president of the National Council of Churches he would promote efforts to achieve decent housing for the poor, better employment opportunities for racial minorities, and an overhaul of the welfare system.

December 9. Lieutenant Edward Kerr, a black police officer with fifteen years of service, was nominated director of the Newark Police Department, the largest in the state of New Jersey. Kerr, a native of Willacoochee, Georgia and a student at Rutgers University, was slated to succeed John Redden, a white police officer, who resigned after becoming embroiled in a controversy over whether a black-sponsored housing project ought to be built in a white community. The white members of Newark's biracial city council asked black mayor Kenneth Gibson not to accept Redden's resignation. Gibson refused to heed their plea.

December 11. Soul singer James Brown was arrested and charged with disorderly conduct in Knoxville, Tennessee. The arrest of Brown, an idol of rock and soul fans and a political supporter of President Nixon, sparked a heated controversy in which lawyers for the singer threatened to sue the city of Knoxville for one million dollars. Brown said he was talking with a group of children about drugs and the importance of school attendance when he was arrested by Knoxville police. The police charged Brown with disorderly conduct by creating a scene and failing to move on. On December 12, Knoxville

Mayor Kyle Testerman said the arrest of Brown apparently resulted from a misunderstanding and promised to meet with Brown's attorney, Albert G. Ingram, in an effort to resolve "differences brought about by this incident." Following his meeting with the mayor on December 18, Ingram announced that the matter still had not been satisfactorily resolved.

December 14. The United States Supreme Court, in a unanimous opinion, ruled that the Civil Rights Act of 1964 authorized the residents of "white ghettos" to file lawsuits aimed at ending racial discrimination in their own apartment developments. The opinion, which was written by Justice William O. Douglas, said residents of both races who lived in discriminatory housing developments could sue because they may suffer specific "individual injury" when deprived of the social, professional, and business "benefits" available in integrated communities. The decision was rendered in a San Francisco case involving an apartment complex formerly owned by the Metropolitan Life Insurance Company. The NAACP applauded the court's decision because it said it lacked the personnel and resources to fight widespread housing discrimination.

December 14. Black Communist Angela Davis announced plans to form a national defense organization to help "black and brown political prisoners of the government." Davis, in a news conference held in Harlem, said that the new group would provide legal aid to the oppressed.

December 15. Fifty special sheriff's deputies and police officers patrolled the Escambra High School in Pensacola, Florida, after a day of fighting between black and white students which left several persons injured and forty-seven arrested. The 38 whites and 9 blacks were subsequently released when school officials dropped trespassing charges against them. The fighting apparently began in the school's cafeteria and spread to other parts of the large school. The deputies who broke up the melee said they seized bicycle chains, belts, and knives used as weapons by the students.

December 17. George Wiley, black director of the National Welfare Rights Organization (NWRO) since 1965, announced his resignation in Washington, D.C. Wiley said he was leaving the NWRO, the nation's leading group of welfare recipients, to form a broader-based organization to help the nation's poor. Wiley ran the NWRO since its founding in 1965.

December 21. Horace Mann Bond, formerly dean of the School of Education at Atlanta University and former president of Fort Valley State College and Lincoln University (located in Georgia and Pennsylvania, respectively), died in Atlanta. The seventy-year-old educator was a pioneer in black scholarship, publishing distinguished books and articles in the fields of black education and history. He was the father of Georgia State Representative Julian Bond, whose name was placed before the 1968 Democratic National

Convention as a vice-presidential candidate. The *Atlanta Constitution* eulogized the black scholar as one who had "a full and fruitful life of achievement."

Chapter 11
"The Second Reconstruction" Betrayed, 1973-1990

1973

January 4. U. S. Attorney General Richard Kleindienst announced that the Civil Rights Division of the Justice Department would have to conduct a careful examination of a report by the FBI on the killings of two students at black Southern University in Baton Rouge, Louisiana before deciding whether to call a federal grand jury into the case. The two black youths were slain by law enforcement officers on the Southern campus during student protests on November 16, 1972 (see entry above).

January 29. U.S. District Court Judge Jon O. Newman ordered the city of Bridgeport, Connecticut to hire blacks and Puerto Ricans to fill 50 percent of the vacancies on the police force until the two minority groups constituted at least 15 percent of the force. The judge's order was designed to correct racial imbalances in Bridgeport's law enforcement.

May 29. Thomas Bradley, a veteran Los Angeles city councilman, was elected mayor of the city of Los Angeles, California. Bradley defeated incumbent mayor Sam Yorty who was seeking a fourth four-year term. The new black mayor, who lost to Yorty in 1969, won about 56 percent of the vote cast, although the city's total black population was about 18 percent. Yorty's campaign rhetoric had pictured Bradley as a fellow-traveler of left-wing radicals. Bradley assessed his victory as a rejection of racism in the election.

July 1. Alonzo A. Crim, former superintendent of schools in Compton, California, assumed his duties as the first black superintendent of the public schools in Atlanta, Georgia, one of the Deep South's largest predominantly-black school systems. Crim's selection resulted from a compromise desegregation plan worked out between local black and white business and political leaders in which the blacks agreed to desist from further pressures for busing to achieve desegregation and the whites agreed to the hiring of a black superintendent and other black school administrators. The plan, reminiscent of the famous "Atlanta Compromise" of 1895, in which Booker T. Washington urged blacks to shun social equality for economic advancement, was denounced by the national NAACP leadership in New York. They felt the agreement set a bad precedent and would hamper future efforts to achieve massive desegregation of the nation's schools. Although local NAACP leaders who assented to the pact argued that massive desegregation was impossible in Atlanta, a city with a 55 percent black population and an 80 percent black school-age population, they were suspended and eventually expelled from office for their support of the desegregation agreement.

July 2. The National Black Network (NBN), the nation's first black-owned and operated radio news network, began operations with hourly newscasts to forty affiliated stations. Although based in New York City, the NBN planned to provide news stories of interest to blacks everywhere.

July 29. The Bureau of the Census released a report of six Northern urban areas which showed that Southern-born black males living in those areas were more likely to be employed and living with their wives than Northern-born blacks living in the same areas. The study, which was based upon data from the 1970 Census, reported that about 65 percent of the black men born in New York City were employed. The figure rose to 78 percent for Southern-born blacks who migrated north before 1965 and to 85 percent for those who moved north since 1965. The study also revealed that 70 percent of Southern-born black men were living with their wives as compared with 51 percent of the blacks born in Illinois. Robert Hill, the National Urban League's research director, said the report refuted the widely held view that Southern blacks migrated to the North to obtain higher welfare benefits.

August 15. The National Black Feminist Organization (NBFO) was founded in New York City, with chapters in several other localities, including Chicago, Cleveland, and San Francisco. Eleanor Holmes Norton, a member of the New York City Human Rights Commission and a founder of the feminist group, accused the nation of expecting black women to suppress their aspirations in deference to black males. Another founder, Margaret Sloan, said the new group would remind "the black liberation movement that there can't be liberation for half a race."

August 15. Ralph David Abernathy announced that he would remain as president of the Southern Christian Leadership Conference (SCLC) after the civil rights group's board of directors refused to accept his resignation during the SCLC's sixteenth annual convention in Indianapolis, Indiana. The board,

208

however, agreed to try to remedy some of the complaints which led Abernathy, successor to Martin Luther King, Jr. to offer his resignation—inadequate financing and insufficient staff. The board pledged increased fund raising efforts, the hiring of more full-time staff, and the creation of five regional offices to assist in administrative functions.

September. Henry C. Ponder, vice president of academic affairs at Alabama A and M College, assumed the presidency of Benedict College in Columbia, South Carolina. W. Clyde Williams, acting president of Miles College in Birmingham, Alabama, since 1971, was inaugurated as the tenth president of the historically black institution.

October 10. Richmond Hill, a sixty-eight-year-old black mortician and mayor pro tempore of Greenville, Georgia, was elected mayor of his city and became the first black mayor in Georgia's history. Hill, who had previously worked as a farmer and then a businessman, defeated a white opponent in a town with a population of about 1,500, 40 percent of whom were black.

October 14. The famed African-American blues singer B. B. King was awarded an honorary doctor of humanities degree from Tougaloo College in Mississippi, making him the first blues musician ever to receive an honorary doctorate for his contributions to the music world. George A. Owens, president of the college, conferred the degree during the celebration of the 104th anniversary of the founding of Tougaloo, the state's most prestigious private black college.

October 16. Maynard H. Jackson, a thirty-five-year-old attorney and vice mayor of the city of Atlanta, was elected mayor of the Deep South's largest city. Jackson defeated incumbent mayor Sam Massell in a campaign marred by Massell's injection of the race issue. Jackson ousted the city's first Jewish mayor to become the city's first black mayor.

Jackson, the son of a minister and a college professor, was educated at Morehouse College and North Carolina Central University Law School. He had run unsuccessfully for the United States Senate in 1968 before being elected vice mayor in 1969. Jackson's election signaled a swing of political power from white to black in Atlanta as African-Americans achieved equality on the eighteen-member city council and a slight majority on the nine-member school board. Slightly more than 50 percent of the population of Atlanta was black at the time of Jackson's election, but whites held a slight edge in voter registration. Although opposed by many whites for his forthright opposition to alleged police brutality in Atlanta, Jackson appealed to voters of both races and captured at least 20 percent of the white vote cast in the election.

October 26. Vernon Jordan, Executive Director of the National Urban League, told an audience at Clark College in Atlanta that the Nixon Administration left "unfinished" the economic improvement of black Americans after a decade of advancement in civil rights. Jordan said the steady flow of congressional action, executive orders, and federal court decisions in the 1960s did for blacks what the New Deal had done for whites and organized labor, but the Nixon Administration allowed this "Second Reconstruction" to expire uncompleted. Jordan's remarks reiterated a continuing theme among black American leadership—criticism of President Nixon's failure to recognize the legitimate needs of black citizens.

October. Seven members of the Republic of New Africa (RNA), including its president, Imari A. Obadele, were convicted in the U. S. District Court in Biloxi, Mississippi, on charges resulting from a shootout at RNA headquarters in Jackson, Mississippi in 1971 (see entry dated August 18, 1971). Two black women and five men were charged with illegal possession of weapons and assault on a federal officer. Two of the defendants, Wayne M. James and Thomas E. Norman, were already serving life sentences for convictions in state courts. In the federal trial Obadele received a twelve-year sentence; the other defendants received sentences ranging from three to twelve years. Attorneys for the RNA indicated they would file a motion for a rehearing of the cases.

October. Robert Threatt, president of the Georgia Association of Educators, assumed duties as president of Morris Brown College in Atlanta, Georgia. Threatt succeeded John A. Middleton, a black member of the Atlanta Board of Education, who resigned because of the school's deteriorating financial condition, a situation which appeared to worsen as the school withdrew from the Atlanta University Center complex of black colleges. Threatt, a graduate of Morris Brown and the University of Oklahoma, was also a professor of education at Fort Valley State College in Georgia prior to becoming, at forty-six years of age, the youngest president in the history of Morris Brown.

October. As the 1973 professional baseball season closed, black centerfielder Willie Mays ended his long, outstanding career. Mays won national acclaim for his fielding heroics and for his powerful bat during nearly twenty years of play with the New York and San Francisco Giants and the New York Mets of the National Baseball League. Upon his retirement, New York City honored Mays in special ceremonies at Shea Stadium on September 25. Mayor John Lindsay issued a proclamation of celebration as 55,000 fans cheered the black star. The Alabama-born Mays was also presented with a honorary LL.D degree from his home state's Miles College during the ceremonies.

In a related development, Reggie Jackson of the world champion Oakland Athletics was unanimously selected as the World Series's Most Valuable Player (MVP). Four other black players had won the MVP award in previous years: Roberto Clemente of the Pittsburgh Pirates in 1971; Brooks Robinson of the Baltimore Orioles in 1970; Bob Gibson of the St. Louis Cardinals in 1967 and 1964; and Frank Robinson of the Baltimore Orioles in 1966.

October. Jesse W. Lewis, a founder and former director of Industrial Bank in Washington, D. C., died in Washington. Industrial Bank was one of the nation's first black financial institutions, having been founded during the Great Depression of the 1930s.

Lewis was born in 1902 in Richmond, Virginia, and was educated at Shaw University in North Carolina and New York University. He began his career as a teacher at Howard University, where he taught for nineteen years. In 1934, Lewis joined Jesse H. Mitchell and other black financial leaders to form the Industrial Bank. He was also a lawyer, a real estate broker, and a trustee of Virginia Union University.

November 6. Michigan State Senator Coleman Young was elected mayor of Detroit, Michigan. With only about 10 percent of the white blue-collar votes going for him, Young won with an overwhelming vote in black precincts and some support from white middle-income voters. He defeated former white police commissioner John F. Nichols, becoming the "Motor City's" first black mayor.

Young, a native of Tuscaloosa, Alabama, would preside over the nation's fifth largest city, but one plagued with crime.

Black political power in Detroit was also measurably increased by the election of State Representative James Bradley as the first black city clerk, the second highest elective position in the city, and by the fact that four of the nine city councilmen were black.

By the end of 1973, blacks would hold mayoral positions in almost 100 of the nation's 18,000 local governments, including such major cities as Los Angeles, Washington D.C., Newark, Cincinnati, and Atlanta.

November 9. An eight-member biracial committee, which included Georgia's Secretary of State Ben Fortson and Clarence A. Bacote, veteran professor of history at Atlanta University, met at the request of Georgia Governor Jimmy Carter to select the portraits of three outstanding black Georgians to be displayed in the rotunda of the Georgia State Capitol in Atlanta. It was agreed almost immediately that the portrait of slain civil rights leader Martin Luther King, Jr. would be one of those selected. Tennessee had previously honored blacks by placing the portraits of blues musician W. C. Handy and Memphis political leader and writer George Washington Lee in its capitol building at Nashville.

November 23. United States Representative Yvonne Braithwaite Burke, a California Democrat and one of the first African-American women to serve in the U. S. Congress, gave birth to a baby girl in Los Angeles, becoming the first member of Congress to give birth while in office. Burke was granted maternity leave by House Speaker Carl Albert.

November 26. The United States Department of Justice filed fifteen civil rights suits to desegregate twenty-four bars, liquor stores, and pool halls in seven Southern states—Arkansas, Florida, Georgia, Louisiana, South Carolina, Tennessee, and Texas. The civil suits charged the owners and operators of the establishments with violating the public accommodations section of the 1964 Civil Rights Act. A Justice Department representative said it was the largest number of civil rights suits filed in one day within memory.

November. George Washington Carver, the famed black scientist from Tuskegee Institute who won acclaim for developing hundreds of uses for the peanut, was elected to the Hall of Fame of Great Americans at New York University. Carver's bust will be placed in the Hall of Fame along with 100 other great Americans, including Tuskegee's founder Booker T. Washington, who was elected in 1945. Candidates for election to the Hall of Fame must have been deceased for at least twenty-five years and must have been American citizens who made significant contributions to the nation. Carver's selection was sponsored in the Hall of Fame by black educator Benjamin E. Mays, an elector since 1958. (See also entries dated September 4, 1923, June 18, 1941, and January 5, 1943, for further information about Carver.)

December 2. Two United States District Court judges, in separate decisions, ordered the city of San Francisco to implement quota systems for the employment of minorities in its police and fire departments. Judge Robert F. Peckham directed the police department to hire three minority persons (defined by Peckham as blacks, "Latinos," and "Asians") for every two whites at the patrolman's level until minority representation reached 30 percent. The department was also instructed to adopt a one-to-one ratio in appointments to the rank of sergeant until 30 percent of those officers were from minorities. The judge outlawed a hiring and promotion test which had been used by the city's Civil Service Commission. He found the test to be discriminatory and ordered that any future tests be submitted to him for approval. In the second decision, Judge William T. Sweigert ordered the San Francisco Fire Department to fill half of its more than 200 vacancies with members of racial minorities.

December 3. The United States Supreme Court refused to overturn the contempt conviction of eighty-one Columbus, Georgia blacks who were convicted of violating a city ordinance prohibiting the gathering of more than twelve people in a group. The blacks were part of a larger movement formed to protest local police hiring practices in June, 1971.

December 4. The United States Court of Appeals for the Sixth Circuit upheld a desegregation plan for the Memphis, Tennessee school system.

Although the plan involved some crosstown busing, the NAACP opposed it because it allowed too many all-black schools. In rejecting the NAACP's contentions, the court said there was a "necessity of tolerating some one-race schools because minority groups concentrate in urban areas." The Appeals Court also agreed with a lower court that the city of Memphis had acted improperly by cutting its transportation budget in an attempt to circumvent an order for busing to achieve desegregation.

December 19. United States District Court Judge Frank Gray, Jr. ruled that the Department of Health, Education, and Welfare's (HEW) refusal to consider applications for transportation aid had "impeded" a court-ordered busing plan for the public schools in Nashville, Tennessee. Gray called the action illegal and ordered HEW to review within thirty days its earlier refusal to grant the city of Nashville funds to purchase buses to transport about half of its 95,000 students.

December 20. The Department of Labor announced that it had prepared and presented a plan to increase the employment of minorities on federally-aided construction projects in the Chicago area. The plan set goals and timetables and provided penalties, including contract cancellations and ineligibility for future contracts, if companies failed to demonstrate "good faith" efforts to comply. The Labor Department imposed its plan in Chicago after voluntary efforts to end bias failed.

1974

January 7. The Department of Justice announced that it had obtained a consent decree whereby the state of Maryland agreed to hire more blacks and women for the state police and assign them on a nondiscriminatory basis. The state police stipulated that it would set a goal for a force which would be 16 percent black within a five year period and that it would no longer use a pre-employment test that had been adjudged discriminatory to blacks and women. The Maryland agreement was made in response to a suit filed by the Justice Department on January 4, 1974.

January 11. United States Senator William Proxmire, a Wisconsin Democrat and chairman of the congressional appropriations subcommittee which oversees funds for the National Aeronautics and Space Administration (NASA), ordered the space agency to double the fiscal 1975 budget of its equal employment office and to report to his subcommittee every three months on progress in hiring minorities and women. Proxmire's action was prompted by reports that NASA, as of mid-1973, had the lowest percentage of minority and female employees of any federal agency, and that two-thirds of these workers were in lower-level jobs. NASA officials also admitted that the agency had failed to act against project contractors who had not met minority employment goals.

January 11. The Bureau of the Census reported that as of July 1, 1973, the black population in the United States had increased to 23.8 million, up 1.2 million from the 1970 census. The Bureau also reported a continuing pattern of black youthfulness, in comparison to the general population. According to the latest statistics, the median age of blacks was 22.9 years; the median age for the total population was 28.4 years.

January 15. The United States Supreme Court, in a 6 to 3 decision, ruled that a group of seventeen blacks and two whites from Cairo, Illinois could not obtain injunctions against local judges and prosecutors who, the plaintiffs claimed, were engaged in a pattern of setting excessive bail and harsher punishments for blacks than whites. The Court held that the complaints did not constitute a real case of controversy, hence they did not meet the necessary test for receiving relief from the federal courts. Five members of the six-justice majority also ruled that the plaintiffs would not have been entitled to injunctions even if they had been able to prove discrimination, for such a procedure would be tantamount to "an on-going audit of state criminal proceedings" in violation of the principle of federalism—federal-state harmony. The majority opinion was supported by Justices Burger, White, Powell, Stewart, Rehnquist, and Blackmun. In a dissent, Justice William O. Douglas said that the record of the case demonstrated "a more pervasive scheme for suppression of blacks and their civil rights than I have ever seen." The majority's decision, Douglas added, "will please the white superstructure, but it does violence to the conception of even-handed justice envisioned by the Constitution." Cairo was the scene of angry clashes between blacks and whites since 1969.

January 17. The Department of Health, Education, and Welfare (HEW) reported that racial discrimination still existed in the Topeka, Kansas school system. The Board of Education of Topeka was a defendant in the landmark Supreme Court decision, *Brown v. Board of Education*, which outlawed school segregation in 1954. HEW said that it found a substantial number of schools which had disproportionate minority enrollments and that attendance zone transfers had impeded desegregation. Most of the black junior high and elementary pupils, HEW discovered, attended schools where the facilities were generally inferior to those at predominantly-white schools. The department began its investigation of Topeka's schools in December, 1973 after being named a party in a new suit against the city. As a result of its inquiry, HEW ordered Topeka school officials to submit corrective plans.

January 20. Dr. Peggy Sandy, a University of Pennsylvania anthropologist, released a study which indicated that whites scored higher than nonwhites on intelligence tests because of environmental factors rather than genetic differences between races. The study was conducted in the Pittsburgh public school system and financed by a grant from the Department of Health, Education, and Welfare (HEW). Dr. Sandy concluded that test score differences were a function, among other factors, of "middle-class social integration" and that her study, combined with data from other investigations, suggested that I.Q. differences between racial groups were "exclusively a matter of environment" while differences within racial groups were determined by both genetics and environment. These findings ran counter to the theories of Dr. William Shockley, a Nobel Prize-winning physicist at Stanford University, who had held that intelligence was largely inherited and that the disadvantaged social position of American blacks was caused more by heredity than environment. Shockley's views had become increasingly controversial by late 1973, when he was prevented from speaking on several college campuses by protesters who contended that giving him a public forum would lend dignity to racist theories.

January 21. The United States Supreme Court upheld a lower court ruling approving a school desegregation plan for Knoxville, Tennessee. Under the approved plan, 59 percent of the city's black students would be placed in nine schools where the black enrollment would be 64 percent or more. Justices Powell and White dissented. Justice Marshall did not participate.

January 24. The United States Department of Justice filed a suit in the federal court in Boston accusing the city of Boston of discrimination in the hiring of black and Spanish-surnamed as firemen. The Justice Department cited that out of 2,100 firemen in Boston, only sixteen were black and three had Spanish surnames, although these minorities constituted 16 percent and 4 percent of the city's population, respectively. These facts demonstrated, the department said, that the city had failed or refused to hire minorities on an equal basis with whites, and had employed tests and other qualifications that had "not been shown to be required by the needs of the fire department or predictive of successful job performance." The suit asked the District Court to order city officials to begin an active recruiting program and to hire enough black and Spanish-surnamed firemen to compensate for individuals who had taken fire department examinations but had been unfairly denied positions. In a closely related matter, the Justice Department also reported that a job-bias suit against Montgomery, Alabama was resolved by a consent decree filed on October 3, 1972. This action, the department said, substantially expanded job opportunities for blacks in Montgomery's city government.

January 28. United States District Court Judge Jack B. Weinstein of New York City ordered federal, state, and local housing authorities, along with the city departments of police, parks, and transportation, to cooperate with city school officials in formulating plans to desegregate a junior high school in Brooklyn. As of 1973, the school in question had an enrollment of 43 percent black, 39 percent Hispanic, and only 18 percent white. In his order, Weinstein told housing officials to develop a joint plan "to undo the racial imbalance" in the public housing near the school. He said all levels of government had failed to take appropriate and available steps to counter trends toward segregation in both housing and education and ruled that "federal complicity in encouraging segregated schooling through its housing programs" was unconstitutional. In his order, Weinstein directed housing authorities to include in their plan "advertisements and inducements" directed at the white middle class so as to "stabilize" the district's population. He also directed the city's department of transportation to develop busing plans for the immediate balancing of the school's enrollment. The police department was ordered to submit plans for the adequate protection of children in the area and the parks department, whose facilities were used frequently by the school, was directed to develop a desegregation plan. Weinstein set a March 1, 1974 deadline for submission and a September deadline for implementation of the joint desegregation program. The ruling, said to be the first decision of its kind, resulted from a suit filed by attorneys for the NAACP.

January 31. A federal court in Atlanta ordered the Georgia Power Company, the state's largest utility corporation, to pay retroactive wages and pension benefits amounting to almost 2.1 million dollars to black employees who had been denied equal job rights. The ruling also required the company to increase black employment to 17 percent of the total work force within five years. At the time of the court's decision, 9.3 percent of the company's 8,278 workers were black. The ruling resulted from a suit filed by the U. S. Department of Justice in 1969.

February 4. The Voter Education Project (VEP) reported that 363 blacks had won elective offices in the South in the 1973 off-year elections. Of these victories, 253 were in elections for local councils and commissions, sixty-three were for school boards, nineteen were new black mayors, fourteen were election commissioners, and two were selected to state legislatures. The VEP, a privately-funded political study group, reported from its headquarters in Atlanta.

February 13. The American Association of University Professors (AAUP) issued a statement condemning both students and faculties at American colleges who prevented research and debate on the race-intelligence issue which recently had been brought into focus by Stanford University's William Shockley. The AAUP accused some of its own members of "undermining the integrity of the academic community by attempting to suppress unpopular opinions." Nevertheless, on February 18, the student-controlled Political Union at Yale University cancelled a scheduled debate between Shockley and Roy Innis, national director of the Congress of Racial Equality (CORE), after protest from various student groups. (See also entry dated January 20, 1974.)

February 15. The *San Francisco Chronicle* reported that two black escaped convicts had been identified as leaders of the Symbionese Liberation Army (SLA). The head of the interracial group of radical revolutionaries, which received notoriety for their alleged kidnapping of newspaper heiress Patricia Hearst, was said to be Donald D. DeFreeze, age thirty. DeFreeze, who called himself Field Marshall Cinque on tapes sent to the Hearst family, was listed as an escapee from the minimum security area of the Soledad State Prison in California on March 5, 1973. The other black SLA leader was identified as Thero M. Wheeler, age twenty-nine, an escapee from the medical facility at Vacaville State Prison in August, 1973. The report traced Wheeler and DeFreeze's association with the SLA to their memberships in the Black Cultural Association (BCA) at Vacaville State Prison. The BCA was described as an inmate group which sponsored cultural activities, educational programs, and pre-release preparation projects for prisoners. Russell Little, Jo Ann Little, and William Wolfe, all white, reportedly gained control of the BCA while working as tutors at the prison. DeFreeze was listed as a teacher of a BCA course entitled "Insight" which was designed to increase the racial consciousness of black inmates.

March 15-17. The second National Black Political Convention met in Little Rock, Arkansas. The 1,700 delegates approved several resolutions, including (1) the creation of a black "united fund" of about $10 million to further convention agenda items, local organization within the United States, and to develop projects to aid African nations; (2) the condemnation of black congressmen who had voted for military aid to Israel while "ignoring" the plight of Palestinian refugees; and (3) support of African "liberation movements." The delegates rejected a resolution calling Israel a "major instrument" of an American supported "world strategy of monopoly," and another which sought to establish an all-black political party. Opponents of the latter resolution argued that the convention had not done enough local organizational work to effectively build such a party. The convention was seriously split, as it had been in 1972, between those arguing for a black separatist approach to political organization and those who favored a continuation of ties with existing political structures. Black elected officials, such as Mayor Richard B. Hatcher of Gary, Indiana and Democrat Congressman Ronald V. Dellums of California, led those who urged the convention to remain an "inclusive" organization, embracing and tolerating different ideologies. Black separatist spokesmen, lead by Newark's Imamu Amiri Baraka, accused the more conservative delegates of espousing "neocolonialism" and "opportunism." Baraka said blacks should build an anti-capitalist "revolutionary ideology" and operate as a separate political force. NAACP leaders again boycotted the convention and drew the ire of the co-chairman Mayor Hatcher. Many black elected officials, including veteran Congressman Charles C. Diggs of Michigan (co-chairman of the 1972 convention), were also criticized for being conspicuously absent.

(See Appendix for an excerpt taken from Mayor Richard Hatcher's Address to the National Black Political Convention.)

March 17. United States District Court Judge Luther L. Bohanon ordered an end to racial segregation at the Oklahoma State Prison at McAlester, Oklahoma. Observing that he had "no idea of the deep cruelty inmates were subjected to," the judge also ordered prison officials to stop mistreating convicts. Bohanon found that since the riots that had occurred at the prison in the summer of 1973, inmates were not provided with proper food, bedding, or heat, and that they were subjected to arbitrary punishments with chemical mace and tear gas. The judge noted that black inmates had received worse treatment than whites.

March 31. The United States Department of Justice announced that it had reached an agreement with the city of Jackson, Mississippi calling for an increase in the number of blacks on municipal jobs and granting back pay up to $1,000 for blacks currently employed who had been denied promotion opportunities. The five-year plan set a goal of a 40 percent black work force, approximately the same percentage of blacks as in the city's population. At the time of the agreement, about 800 of Jackson's 3,000 municipal workers were black, most of these serving in the lowest-paying job classifications. Both the police and fire departments were affected by the accord.

April 8. Atlanta Braves baseball star Henry (Hank) Aaron hit his 715th career home run, thus becoming the all-time leading home run slugger. Aaron broke the record, previously held by the immortal Babe Ruth, at Atlanta Stadium. The Braves star had tied Ruth's record on April 4, 1974 in Cincinnati. The record-breaking pitch was thrown by a Los Angeles Dodgers pitcher, Al Downing.

April 8. United States Circuit Court Judge William E. Doyle ordered the desegregation of 70,000 students in the Denver public school system during the 1974-75 school year. The desegregation was to be accomplished mostly through the redrawing of attendance boundaries or zones and the pairing of black, white, and Mexican-American pupils so that they might share classrooms on a half-day basis. The order further provided that elementary schools would have between 40 percent and 70 percent white enrollment and that white enrollment in high schools would be between 50 and 60 percent. Judge Doyle rejected the school board's plan to close twelve of the public schools. He saw his move as a tactic "to avoid adoption of a desegregation plan." He also ordered the merger of two high schools and the introduction of bilingual programs in schools with large numbers of Mexican-American pupils. The United States Supreme Court had first ordered a desegregation plan to be drawn up by Denver in 1973.

April 8. The Reverend C. Shelby Rooks was named the first black president of the predominantly-white Chicago Theological Seminary, an affiliate of the United Church of Christ. Rooks, age forty-nine, was executive director of the Fund for Theological Education in Princeton, New Jersey at the time of his new appointment.

April 15. The United States Departments of Labor and Justice and the Equal Employment Opportunities Commission (EEOC) announced that nine major steel companies had agreed to a five-year plan for ending job discrimination against women and minorities, and would grant back pay of more than $30 million to the victims of such bias. The companies directly involved were the Allegheny-Ludlum Industries, Inc., Amco Steel Corporation, Bethlehem Steel Corporation, Jones and Laughlin Steel Corporation, National Steel Corporation, Republic Steel Corporation, United States Steel Corporation, Wheeling-Pittsburgh Steel Corporation, and Youngstown Sheet and Steel Company. Together, they employed 347,000 employees in 249 plants at the time of the agreement. The steel companies vowed to restore more than $30 million in back pay to 34,000 black and Spanish-surnamed male employees and to 5,599 women who were adjudged to be victims of job bias. The back pay settlements ranged from $250 to $3,000 per person, depending upon length of service.

April 18. Peter Holmes, Civil Rights Director of the Department of Health, Education, and Welfare (HEW), reviewed the progress of school desegregation in the nation on the eve of the 20th anniversary of the historic *Brown v. Board of Education* decision and the 10th anniversary of the enactment of the Civil Rights Act of 1964. Holmes told a group of Washington journalists that there were virtually no blacks in school with white students in the eleven Southern states in 1964. By 1968, he noted, a total of 18.4 percent of the black pupils in the South were in majority white schools. This rose to 39.1 percent in 1970 and 44.4 percent in 1972. Perhaps of greater significance, Holmes said, was the fact that the black pupils in all-black schools decreased in the South from 68 percent in 1968 to 14.1 percent in 1970, and to 9.2 percent in 1972. On the other hand, Holmes noted that while current school year figures were not available, there was likely to be an increase in segregation in Northern metropolitan school districts. (See Tables A and B in Appendix for data compiled by the Department of Health, Education, and Welfare (Office of Civil Rights).)

April 20. The *New York Times* reported a sixth anniversary assessment of black studies in predominantly-white colleges and universities. Since the student protests in the 1960s, which helped to give impetus to black studies as a legitimate academic enterprise, 1,272 institutions of higher learning have offered at least one course in the area. Although the tumult which surrounded the initiation of black studies movement has ceased, the controversy over the validity, viability, and aims of the programs continues. One of the more vocal critics of the programs has been Professor Martin Kilson, a black political scientist at Harvard University. He has called them "distinctly anti-intellectual and anti-achievement in orientation." Others see them differently. Professor Barbara A. Wheeler, of the City University of New York, supported black studies as different from traditional studies in that they are organized around the black experience rather than around the subject matter. This allows the black person to see the impact of the event on his own life. Professors Elias Blake, head of the Institute for Services to Education; Henry Cobb, dean of Southern University at Baton Rouge; and Tobe Johnson, director of under-graduate African-American studies programs for the Atlanta University Center, completed an analysis of twenty-nine black studies programs for the U.S. Office of Education just prior to the *Times* report. Blake told the *Times* that the ideological questions had been settled. "God knows," he said, "we need more study on black Americans. The issue is how do you build a good program." The Blake-Cobb-Johnson team found that only carefully struc-tured programs were likely to survive in an era when colleges were undergoing financial retrenchment.

April 22. The Joint Center for Political Studies, a privately funded research organization, reported from Washington that 2,991 blacks held political office in forty-five states and the District of Columbia, a gain of more than 300 between 1972-73 and a jump of more than 1,000 from 1969. The Center noted that most of the gains during 1973 had resulted from municipal elections. For example, 1,080 out of the latest total were city councilmen, and 108 were mayors. Michigan led in the number of black elected officials with 194, followed by Mississippi with 191. Other states with 150 or more black officeholders included New York, New Jersey, Illinois, Alabama, Arkansas, and Louisiana. (See Table C in Appendix for date compiled by the Joint Center for Political Studies.)

April 25. United States District Court Judge Alfonso J. Zirpoli in San Francisco ruled that the San Francisco police had violated the constitutional rights of 600 black men they had stopped for questioning in their investigation of the so-called "Zebra" killings ("Operation Zebra" was the police code used in the dragnet which officers conducted in their probe of the random slayings of twelve whites). Zirpoli issued an injunction prohibiting their profile of the Zebra killer, a slim-built young black man, as the sole basis for stopping men for questioning. The suit was filed by the American Civil Liberties Union (ACLU).

April 26. The United States Department of Justice rejected a Mississippi act eliminating party primaries and replacing them by a single open primary in which no candidate could be elected with less than a majority vote. The Justice Department said that such a system would discriminate against independent candidates, and thus against blacks, since most of the successful black candi-dates in recent general elections had run as independents. The Mississippi legislature was seeking to repeal current statutes which required a majority vote to win the separate party primaries, but which allowed independents to run in the general election and win with only a plurality. Under the Voting Rights Act of 1965, states like Mississippi, where a pattern of voter discrimination had been found, were required to submit changes affecting the suffrage to the Justice Department for approval.

April. The United States Circuit Court of Appeals for the Fourth District ordered the Nansemond County, Virginia School Board to rehire 56 black teachers who the court said were arbitrarily discriminated against in the administration of a national teaching test. The Appellate Court directed the United States District Court in Norfolk to reexamine the circumstances surrounding the dismissal of the teachers, a practice which was begun in 1971. The court also enjoined the school board from any further discrimination.

May 1. United States District Court Judge Albert Henderson in Atlanta ruled that the city's school system had done all it could to desegregate public education. Attorneys for the American Civil Liberties Union (ACLU) and the NAACP had argued for increased desegregation in the system, which only had an 18 percent white enrollment. The ACLU argued for more desegregation through a merger of the Atlanta city schools with surrounding suburban systems. The NAACP wanted more desegregation within the bounds of the current Atlanta system. Judge Henderson rejected both appeals and allowed previous court decisions approving the "Atlanta Compromise" school desegregation plan to stand. That controversial program required a minimum of school integration. Attorneys for the ACLU and NAACP filed notices of appeal to the 5th Circuit Court of Appeals in New Orleans. (See also entry dated July 1, 1973.)

May 7-14. In primary elections held in the spring, Southern blacks continued to increase their numbers in major posts in state governments and blacks continued to hold the mayor's office in major American cities. Fourteen blacks were assured election to the Alabama House of Representatives in the May 7 primary. Those victories could mean a total of 17 black representatives. Two blacks were assured election to the Alabama State Senate, with the possibility of one other also being selected. In North Carolina, three blacks won state house seats and one a post in the state senate in the May 7 primary. A black was elected to a municipal judgeship in Nashville, Tennessee. Another was elected a constable in Cleveland, and still another won an alderman's seat in Ripley, all in Tennessee. Three blacks led in contests for seats in the Texas legislature. Kenneth A. Gibson won an easy victory in his second bid for mayor of Newark, New Jersey on May 24. Gibson, the first black mayor of a major northeastern city, claimed that his victory showed that "Newark had come up from its past." He noted that the racial issue which divided the city during the 1970 mayoral election was not a major factor in the current campaign. Gibson won the support of about 65 percent of the 118,000 registered voters in defeating State Senator Anthony Imperiale. Also, in the May 7 Alabama primary, Alabama Governor George Wallace made a direct appeal for black votes for the first time. Estimates of the number he actually received ranged from about 10 percent to as much as 30 percent. Wallace won important backing from several black Alabama politicians, including Mayor Johnny Ford of Tuskegee. Despite criticism from fellow blacks throughout the nation, Ford stood by his support for Governor Wallace. The young mayor justified his actions on the fact that Wallace had been responsive to the economic problems of Tuskegee and had aided the city in receiving state and federal grants. In connection with the spring elections, a joint report issued by the Voter Education Project in Atlanta, the Joint Center for Political Studies, and the Lawyers Committee for Civil Rights Under Law in Washington, showed that implementation of the 1965 Voting Rights Act led to a 169 percent increase in the number of black elected officials in the South between 1969 and 1974 alone. According to the report, there were 299 black elected officials in the six Southern states covered by the act—Alabama, Georgia, Louisiana, Mississippi, South Carolina, and Virginia—in 1969. By 1974, the number had risen to 815, a 169 percent increase. (See Table D in Appendix for data compiled by the Voter Education Project.)

May 8. Southern Democratic Congressmen, reportedly concerned about a major increase in black registered voters, joined with Republicans to defeat a bill (by a vote of 204 to 197) which would have allowed voters to register for federal elections by postcard.

May 16. Four young black men were indicted in the random "Zebra" killings of whites which left the city of San Francisco tense for five months. Indicted on various charges of murder, robbery, and assault with a deadly weapon were Manuel Moore, J. C. Simon, Larry C. Green, and Jessie Cooks. All but Cooks were arrested during a massive manhunt by police on May 1, known as "Operation Zebra." Cooks was already serving a prison term for murder. Twelve murders and six assaults were attributed by police to the Zebra killers. During "Operation Zebra," San Francisco police blanketed the city stopping and searching young black males. A federal judge subsequently ruled the searches unconstitutional. (See also entry dated April 25, 1974.)

May 16. The United States Senate approved a bill to limit court-ordered busing to achieve school desegregation but allowed judges to issue such orders as they see fit. The principal new limitation provided that pupils should not be bused beyond the next nearest school to their homes. The legislation also required the consideration of alternatives to achieve desegregation before any busing could be required. These included such things as construction of new schools, revision of attendance zones, and permission for students to transfer to schools in which their race was a minority. The bill also stated that the new limitations were not intended to inhibit the courts from ordering busing if such measures were necessary to enforce the equal rights provisions of the United States Constitution.

May 17. In a speech at Emory University in Atlanta, Dr. Alvin Poussaint, a black psychiatrist affiliated with the Harvard School of Medicine, gave a major assessment of the growing incidence of homicide among blacks. Poussaint said that 23 percent of the deaths among black males aged seventeen to twenty-five were the result of homicide, and that the matter should be treated as a health problem. Among the causes of homicide among blacks, according to Poussaint, is "black racism" or low self-esteem, which is evidenced by the use of racial epithets before a homicide is committed and by an inner battle by black men to preserve their self-respect in a racist society. Another contributing factor is that "black life has not been valued." Because of this, Poussaint said, some police officers do not follow up on solving crimes in black neighborhoods and the media fail to give much attention to homicide unless it involves whites. Poussaint contended that the American black community was "in a state of despair and demoralization," partly because of its failure to realize some of the dreams of the Civil Rights era and partly because of governmental corruption. When such corruption goes unpunished, he said, a "jungle mentality is created and people begin to believe that they can do whatever they can get away with." Reduction of crime among blacks, Poussaint suggested, required the development of new values and psychological as well as political approaches. He called for the regulation of violence depicted in the media, particularly as portrayed in black "exploitation" films; the establishment of homicide prevention centers to help potential criminals before they commit murder; the control of handguns; increased black employment, particularly among black youths; and the promotion of black pride or black consciousness programs. Although the matter was defined by Poussaint as a black health problem, he concluded that it would take interracial cooperation to solve it. Poussaint is the author of *Why Blacks Kill Blacks (1972)*.

May 17. The twentieth anniversary of the historic Supreme Court decision, *Brown v. Board of Education*, which outlawed school segregation, was observed in the nation. In assessing the impact of the decision, the editors of the *Atlanta Constitution*, the South's leading daily newspaper, admitted that even after a generation, racial prejudice and discrimination have not been eliminated. This fact gave credence, in the editor's opinion, to the view that one cannot legislate morals. Yet, the *Constitution* said, "there is no denying that tremendous progress has been made in race relations in our country since 1954. . . . The progress, the vast changes in education, in employment, in housing, in politics, was the result of a struggle for civil rights that was given a decisive impetus on the day the Supreme Court ruled in the case of *Brown v. Board of Education of Topeka* in 1954." The noted black syndicated columnist Carl Rowan, in his assessment of *Brown* twenty years later, found that "we are still a racist society," and that the historic school decision did not deliver justice to the black plaintiffs of 1954, or even to their children. "Some of the litigants in that 1954 decision," he said, "never saw a day of desegregated education. They saw evasion, circumvention, massive resistance and a generation of litigation." One of the plaintiffs, Linda Brown Smith (the "Brown" in the famous 1954 case) is now a grown woman with children of her own. Before a meeting of the Association of Social and Behavioral Scientists (ASBS), a mostly black professional group, in Atlanta in April, 1974, she recalled her family's motivations for permitting her to become a plaintiff. The family was incensed by the fact that their children had to wait in oft-times inclement weather to be taken to black schools in Topeka when a white school was within walking distance from their home. Ironically, Smith said she now opposes crosstown busing to achieve racial desegregation in the schools.

May 18. Benjamin L. Hooks, the only black member of the Federal Communications Commission (FCC), called for increased participation by whites in the NAACP. Although Hooks acknowledged that there was a difference between being born black and being born white, in that those "born black live in the valleys while those born white live on the mountain tops," he also said "We made a mistake when we close the doors on our white brothers." Hooks also urged more blacks to join the organization as he spoke to the 38th Annual NAACP Freedom Banquet held in Port Huron, Michigan. Hooks was appointed to the FCC by President Nixon in 1972. Other blacks, including the late Harlem congressman Adam Clayton Powell, Jr., had repeatedly asked the NAACP to purge itself of white influence.

May 22. United States District Court Judge Frank M. Johnson, Jr. in Montgomery, Alabama rejected crosstown busing as a remedy for the desegregation of some predominantly-black schools in Montgomery County and instead ordered a new desegregation plan, one which allowed, with some exceptions, elementary school children to attend neighborhood schools. He endorsed the creation of a biracial committee to help the school board carry out the program.

May 24. Edward Kennedy "Duke" Ellington, one of America's greatest musician-composers, died in New York at age seventy-four.

Described as a musical genius, Ellington began playing the piano at age seven, composed his first song at seventeen, and began playing professionally at eighteen. He wrote more than 1,000 compositions, including "Take the A Train," "Don't Get Around Much Anymore," "Satin Doll," and "Caravan." In later years he composed several orchestral pieces, tone poems, jazz masses, film, television, and ballet scores, and several operas. His orchestra was one of the few of the "big bands" to thrive after the 1940s. Some of the members of his orchestra remained with him for more than forty years.

Among Ellington's numerous awards were the NAACP's Spingarn Medal, the

French Legion of Merit (France's highest honor), and America's highest civilian honor, the Medal of Freedom, bestowed upon him in 1970 by President Richard M. Nixon. The President had told Ellington in February 1974 that "There'll never be another you."

The NAACP responded to Ellington's death by noting: "Few composers have attained the greatness of stature that was the Duke's at the time of his death. Prolific, versatile, and popular, the Duke claimed the hearts of a wide range of followers, black and white, rich and poor. He was indomitable." Although sometimes criticized for not taking on an active role in the Civil Rights Movement, Ellington himself claimed that "protest and pride in the Negro have been the most significant themes in what we've done." His composition of "My People" was a musical salute to African-Americans.

May 25. A federal grand jury paid a personal visit to Southern University at Baton Rouge, Louisiana, to inspect the site where two students, Denver Smith and Leonard Brown, were shot to death on November 16, 1972 (see entry above). The jury was investigating the slaying of the youths by law enforcement officers during a student demonstration to determine whether or not their civil rights had been violated.

May 27. About 1,000 orderly demonstrators marched through downtown Atlanta, Georgia demanding the ouster of the city's controversial police chief, John Inman. The marchers were led by veteran protester Hosea Williams, formerly a top aide to slain civil rights leader Martin Luther King, Jr. Many Atlanta blacks had labelled the white police chief a racist and had long sought his removal. Atlanta's black mayor, Maynard Jackson, attempted to fire Inman on May 3, 1974 for administrative inefficiency and insubordination, but was prohibited from doing so by a Dekalb County Superior Court judge. The marchers reaffirmed their support of the efforts to oust Inman.

June 4. James Meredith, the first officially recognized black student to attend the University of Mississippi, led a field of five candidates for the Democratic congressional nomination in the Fourth District of Mississippi. Meredith, a forty-three-year-old business man, had previously ran for the United States Senate in 1972 and the Jackson City Council in 1973. 44 percent of the population of the Fourth District was black at the time of the election. Meredith assessed his primary victory as a milestone in the black struggle for "self-determination and full freedom." He boasted that he had won the nomination without "white folks' money" and without "white folks' niggers, white folks' colored people, and white folks' Negroes."

June 6. The Washington *Star-News* reported that President Richard Nixon called the United States Supreme Court's only black justice, Thurgood Marshall, a "jackass" in a tape recording of a White House conference with then-counsel John W. Dean III on February 28, 1973. In the same conversation, the

President reportedly made other racial and ethnic slurs, particularly against Jews. The tape recording was one of many released to the public during the Watergate scandal.

June 16. The Reverend Lawrence W. Bottoms, a Decatur, Georgia minister, was elected as the first black moderator of the General Assembly of the Presbyterian Church of the United States at its 114th general meeting in Louisville, Kentucky. Bottoms, a sixty-six-year-old native of Selma, Alabama, had long experience as a pastor and leader of Georgia's black Presbyterians. A strong supporter of racial integration and toleration, Bottoms' election placed him at the head of that portion of the Presbyterian Church that broke with its national body to defend slavery before the Civil War.

June 17. A tour guide in the Georgia State Capitol in Atlanta reported that the portrait of slain civil rights leader Martin Luther King, Jr. was defaced with a red ink pen. Although the portrait was only slightly damaged, it was removed immediately and placed with the artist, Paul Mandus, for repairs. Two days later, Georgia Governor Jimmy Carter announced that a black woman who had a history of mental illness had marred the King portrait. The woman told state officials that she scribbled on the painting to show her respect for Dr. King. The incident was reminiscent of the stabbing which King suffered at the hands of a crazed black woman in 1958. The King portrait was the first of a black Georgian to hang at the state capitol.

June 21. The United States Department of Health, Education, and Welfare (HEW) accepted university system desegregation plans from nine states, eight of them in the South. The HEW action stemmed from an order issued in February, 1973, by U. S. District Court Judge John H. Pratt in Washington, D.C., which required the department to increase efforts to assure that the states were in compliance with the Civil Rights Act of 1964. States winning approval of their desegregation plans were Arkansas, Florida, Georgia, Maryland, North Carolina, Oklahoma, Pennsylvania, and Virginia. The HEW rejected Mississippi's plan and announced that it would initiate a law suit against that state. Louisiana refused to submit a plan and was promptly sued by the HEW. Louisiana officials had protested attempts by federal authorities to force a merger of the state's black and white universities.

At the time, black educators and civil rights leaders across the country had become increasingly divided over the question of desegregation in higher education. Many blacks feared losses of jobs, social status, and aspects of their cultural heritage through desegregation plans which involved merger. Black students, particularly those in state-supported institutions, formed a nationwide coalition called "Save Black Schools" to protest school mergers or other actions which might destroy the racial identification of their colleges. On the other hand, many civil rights leaders continued to clamor for desegregation at all costs.

In approving the new desegregation plans, Peter E. Holmes, HEW Civil Rights Director, remarked, "We have seen the development of consciousness, a sensitivity and an awareness to the problems of predominantly-black institutions and minority students that was absent in these states in previous years."

June 21. United States District Court Judge Robert McRae, Jr. began a preliminary hearing in Memphis, Tennessee to determine whether or not James Earl Ray, the confessed assassin of Dr. Martin Luther King, Jr., should receive a new trial. Ray was sentenced in 1969 to a term of ninety-nine years for the slaying of King on April 4, 1968. He was serving his time in the Tennessee State Prison at Nashville. Ray had sought a new trial on the grounds that he was pressured into pleading guilty by his original attorneys, Percy Foreman and Arthur Haynes, Sr. because of their alleged financial relationships with William Bradford Huie, author of one of the first books to be published about King's death. Ray's new attorney, Robert Livingston, had also charged that his client was innocent of King's murder and that two professional assassins hired by four "wealthy, socially prominent Americans" had killed the Nobel Prize-winning civil rights leader.

June 21. United States District Court Judge W. Arthur Garrity, Jr. ruled in Boston, Massachusetts that the Boston public school system was "unconstitutionally segregated" and ordered the implementation of a desegregation plan, including the busing of several thousand school children in the fall of 1974. The order prohibited enrollments of 50 percent or more nonwhites in any school. There were 95,000 pupils attending Boston public schools at the time of the decision. The Boston edict stemmed from a suit filed on behalf of black parents by the NAACP in the spring of 1972. The blacks contended that Boston operated a dual school system and asked the court to dismantle it. (See also entry dated December 28, 1988.)

June 22. Senator Hubert H. Humphrey, a Minnesota Democrat, introduced a bill in Congress providing for the placing in the United States Capitol of the portraits and statues of individuals from minority groups who had made significant contributions to the nation's history. Humphrey said that the statues and paintings now existing in the Capitol building "do not properly reflect the ethnic, cultural, and racial diversity of the people of the United States who have made outstanding contributions to our country."

June 22. The United States Navy reported that its investigation showed no basis for accusations of racial discrimination made by a group of black sailors who refused to return to the aircraft carrier USS *Midway* when it left the Yokosuka Naval Base near Tokyo, Japan, the previous week. Eight of the fifty-five sailors involved called for the U. S. Congress to investigate conditions aboard the ship and demanded replacement of the ship's captain, Richard J. Schutte. They complained of torture in the brig, long duty hours, and dangerous work, which they said they were forced to perform. Naval officials reported that twenty-two of the absentees had returned to their base by June 22 and that the remaining thirty-three were listed as "unauthorized absentees." The Navy reasoned that since the complaint of racial bias was found to be unsubstantiated, the men were "being misled by private organizations" trying to exploit them for "their own purpose." There was no further elaboration. The *Midway* incident was the latest in a series of racially related events involving black armed forces personnel. Although Naval officials had announced new and far-reaching policies to combat bias as early as 1971, this branch of the service has also continued to experience racial problems.

June 26. Atlanta police officers armed with clubs broke up a march of about 250 blacks and arrested fourteen people, including the demonstration's leader, Hosea Williams, president of the local chapter of the Southern Christian Leadership Conference (SCLC). Seven people, including three police officers, were injured in the disturbance. The violent conflict, the first in Atlanta since the riots of the 1960s, came as the marchers sought to protest the killing by police of a seventeen-year-old black youth the previous weekend and to continue their demand that the city's police chief, John Inman, be removed from office. The blacks arrested were charged with parading without permits.

The controversial police chief defended the force used against the marchers, but the city's black mayor, Maynard Jackson, described it as excessive. The latest incident occurred as the Georgia Supreme Court was considering whether the city of Atlanta could legally fire Inman, who was viewed by many of the city's whites as a staunch defender of "law and order," but by many blacks as a racist. (See also entry dated May 27, 1974.)

June 29. Robert Livingston, the Memphis, Tennessee attorney handling the legal appeals of James Earl Ray, the convicted assassin of Martin Luther King, Jr., told newsmen he was convinced that a conspiracy existed in the slaying of the civil rights leader. The attorney said he was contacted on March 22, 1974 by an intermediary for the gunmen actually hired to kill King. The intermediary and two other men were prepared to testify before a grand jury that they were hired to kill King by four prominent black and white men, according to Livingston. The theory of a conspiracy in the assassination of the famed civil rights leader had been previously discounted by law enforcement officials. They continued to insist that James Earl Ray acted alone. (See also entry dated June 21, 1974.)

June 30. A young black man interrupted the worship services at Ebenezer Baptist Church in Atlanta with gunfire, killing Mrs. Martin Luther King, Sr., mother of the slain civil rights leader, and church deacon Edward Boykin.

Another worshipper, Mrs. Jimmie Mitchel, was wounded. The alleged gunman, identified as Marcus Chenault of Dayton, Ohio, was subdued by other worshippers, including Derek King, grandson of the slain woman. Chenault told Atlanta police that he had orders from "his god" to go to Atlanta and kill the Reverend Martin Luther King, Sr., father of the Nobel Prize-winning civil rights leader. Instead, he allegedly fired upon Mrs. King and others as the sixty-nine-year-old matriarch of the King family played "The Lord's Prayer" on a church organ.

The accused slayer was described as an Ohio State University dropout who became deeply involved in a small religious cult which claimed that blacks were descendants of the original Jews. Chenault was said to have taken the name "Servant Jacob" and discarded his original name. The cult reportedly believed that black Christian ministers deceived African-Americans and hence were the cause of many of the social and economic woes of blacks.

Mrs. King, Sr. was born Alberta Williams, the daughter of the Reverend Adam Daniel Williams, one of the founders of the historic Ebenezer Baptist Church. Her husband, a powerful religious and political figure in Atlanta for more than twenty-five years, succeeded Williams as pastor of the church. Dr. Martin Luther King, Jr. was serving as co-pastor of the church at the time of his assassination in April, 1968. Another son, the Reverend A. D. Williams King, drowned in 1969.

Reacting to the tragedy, Atlanta Mayor Maynard H. Jackson compared the deaths of the King family to those of the family of the late President John F. Kennedy, stating "Never have I seen a family suffer so much for so long and yet give such brilliant leadership."

June 30. The *Atlanta Journal-Constitution* reported that the state of Alabama was moving toward total compliance with a federal court order issued in 1972 which required that racial discrimination in hiring be eliminated. When the suit was filed in 1970, only a few blacks were on the state's payroll, most of these in janitorial and other low-paying jobs. As of June 30, 3,000 of the state work force of 21,000 were black. At that rate of hiring, the state was about four years away from reaching the court-assigned goal of a 25 percent black work force. At the upper levels, a black executive assistant had been hired by the head of the Public Service Commission and the Attorney General had selected several black assistants. Alabama Governor George C. Wallace, according to the report, had named several blacks to positions on various governmental boards, commissions, and committees, but had not hired a single black to an administrative position. The report quoted an unidentified "black leader" as saying that Alabama "will someday have the most model race relations program of any state in the Union."

July 1. The *Atlanta University Center Digest* reported that the largest single gift ever donated by a black organization was received by the United Negro College Fund (UNCF). UNCF executive director Christopher F. Edley announced that the $132,000 gift came from the Links, Inc., a national black woman's social organization. At the time, the Links had more than 130 chapters in thirty-five states across the nation. Helen G. Edmonds, a North Carolina Central University history professor and president of the Links, said that her organization "recognized the absolute importance of higher education to black people at this point in history and [agreed] wholeheartedly with the UNCF slogan, 'A Mind is a Terrible Thing to Waste'."

July 3. More than 600 mourners, including First Lady Betty Ford, Mrs. Nelson Rockefeller, Georgia Governor Jimmy Carter, and Atlanta Mayor Maynard H. Jackson, attended funeral services for Mrs. Martin Luther King, Sr., mother of the slain civil rights leader in Atlanta, Georgia. Mrs. King was murdered by a gunman on June 30, 1974. (See entry above).

July 4. Several thousand protesters, led by black Communist Angela Davis and SCLC president Ralph David Abernathy, marched on the North Carolina state capitol in Raleigh to call for an end to the death penalty in that state. The march, which was organized by the National Alliance Against Racist and Political Repression, was called by its organizers "a rebirth of the civil rights movement of the 1960s, but on a higher level." During the march, twelve picketers representing the American Nazi Party, the Ku Klux Klan, and similar groups stood alongside the route holding signs urging segregation forever as well as support for Governor George Wallace of Alabama as President of the United States. Raleigh police kept the two groups apart amid jeering and shouting. There were no major incidents or arrests. The crowd of four to five thousand protesters were invited to the city by its black mayor, Clarence Lightner.

July 5. Approximately 200 blacks marched about seven miles along Highway 41 in Talbot County, Georgia to protest the shooting of a young black man by the white police chief of Woodland. Willie Gene Carraker, a twenty-five-year-old black resident of Woodland, died from gunshot wounds on June 29, 1974. The black man's family accused Police Chief Doug Watson of aggravated assault and murder in the slaying of Carraker. These charges were subsequently dismissed by a local Justice of the Peace. In the march on July 5th, black protesters, led by SCLC field secretary Tyrone Brooks, demanded the prosecution and removal of the Chief. During the demonstration Brooks told the crowd: "We are sick and tired of white folks shooting down our young men every weekend. We are sick and tired of being treated like second class citizens." Woodland City Attorney George R. Jacobs defended the dismissal of charges against Chief Watson and advised that the matter could be considered by the county Grand Jury in November, or by a specially called grand jury.

July 6. The *Atlanta Constitution* reported that the United Methodist Church had abolished districts which were racially segregated. According to the report, the last all-black districts, ones in Mississippi and South Carolina, were abolished in June, 1974. At the same time, Methodist officials announced that 37 of its 530 districts in the United States are now headed by ethnic minority persons, including 34 blacks.

July 7. In a special supplement to *Time* magazine, fifteen blacks were among 200 people named who seem destined to provide the country with a new generation of leadership. *Time* said the principal criterion for inclusion on its list was that the persons selected have the capability to achieve "significant civic or social impact." Eligibility was restricted to individuals forty-five years old and younger. The blacks named included: State Senator Julian Bond of Georgia; Congresswoman Yvonne Brathwaite Burke of California; Congressman Ronald V. Dellums of California; Marian Wright Edelman of the Children's Defense Fund; Mayor Kenneth A. Gibson of Newark, New Jersey; Earl G. Graves, founder of *Black Enterprise* magazine; Mayor Richard Hatcher of Gary, Indiana; Mayor Maynard Jackson of Atlanta, Georgia; Congresswoman Barbara C. Jordan of Texas; Vernon E. Jordan of the Urban League; John Lewis of the Voter Education Project; Eleanor Holmes Norton, Chairman of the New York City Commission on Human Rights; Congressman Charles Rangel of New York; Bill Russell, coach of the Seattle Supersonics; and Congressman Andrew Young of Georgia.

August 19. The Joint Committee on Congressional Operations, which handles hiring requests for members of Congress, began an investigation to determine whether one Senator and nineteen Congressmen were duped or actually have been practicing racial or religious discrimination in seeking staff personnel. The Fort Worth *Star Telegram* reported on August 18, 1974 that it had obtained copies of the hiring forms with varying discriminatory requests from Senator William Scott from Virginia and members of the House of Representatives. Senator Lee Metcalf from Montana, chairman of the Joint Committee, said that some of the request forms contained such notations as "no minorities," or "white only," or "no Catholics," or "no Blacks." While most of the congressmen disclaimed responsibility for the biased forms, Senator Metcalf said it was "possible that (discriminatory) limitations expressed were those of the staff persons placing the request or a misunderstanding by the office staff."

August 23. Franklin W. Morton was elected chief legal Advisor for the Veterans of Foreign Wars (VFW). He is the first black person to hold a national leadership position in the organization.

August 25. Robert C. Weaver, former Secretary of Housing and Urban Development (HUD) and the first black to serve in a presidential cabinet, said during a news conference in Atlanta that the federal government had a "laissez-faire attitude" that threatened efforts for equal opportunity in housing. Weaver said the attitude was based on the revenue-sharing policy of allowing federal funds to be allocated at the local level and the lack of responsibility for social issues on the federal level. He said: "Federal funds (for housing) without strings attached are used for other things. . . . Sophisticated and concerned people must be watchful and vigilant to see that there is equitable participation and involvement in access to housing. . . . The federal government can make an impact." Weaver, president of the National Committee Against Discrimination in Housing (NCADH) made his remarks as he prepared to address the Southern Regional Conference of the NCADH.

August 29. The U.S. Department of Labor announced that in 1973 the unemployment rate in poverty areas of metropolitan centers was almost twice that in the non-metropolitan poverty areas, 9 percent as opposed to 4.7 percent. The report also revealed that 70 percent of the blacks living in poverty areas were in metropolitan centers. The total unemployment for blacks in all poverty areas was 10.8 percent as opposed to 4.6 percent for whites. The Labor Department defined a poverty area as a census tract in which at least one-fifth of the residents had income at or below $4,540 (based upon a non-rural family of four).

September 7. Owners of the Black National Network (BNN), the nation's first black oriented, owned, and operated radio network, announced plans to expand its coverage with a black news service. The 24-hour-a-day service was expected to be fully operational by March 1, 1975, employ 25 reporters, and use the resources of the networks' 68 affiliates in 68 major cities.

September 7. Public officials and spokesmen for civil rights groups criticized Secretary of Health, Education, and Welfare Casper Weinberger's latest pronouncement on school desegregation. On September 6, during an interview, Weinberger said that the cutoff of federal funds for education, which had been used in the past to coerce recalcitrant southern school districts into compliance, would serve to increase segregation in the North. Secretary Weinberger denied that his department was "footdragging" on the question of desegregation, but admitted that "we are dealing with a very fierce public opposition to desegregation." Ruby Hurley, Southeastern Regional Director of the NAACP, disagreed with Weinberger's assessment that a cutoff of funds would be counterproductive and compared the conciliatory approach to northern school desegregation with the more forceful tactics in the South. According to Hurley, "Public school systems are often poor even without federal money. Officials who run segregated school systems will think twice if they are faced with a cutoff. . . . If you wait for people to change their minds on a problem like this without leverage, you'll wait a long time. . . . It's a lot easier to clean up somebody else's back yard than your own."

Atlanta School Superintendent Alonzo Crim responded to Weinberger's statement by declaring that: "The law should be applied with equal force in all parts of the country . . . quite often segregation is intensified by these delays."

Margie Hames, an attorney for the American Civil Liberties Union who has handled many desegregation cases, expressed the belief that "segregation in the South was more open and easy for us to deal with. I don't think the North has accepted the fact yet that they have more subtle forms of segregation." In defense of Weinberger, Peter Holmes, director of HEW's office for civil rights enforcement, pointed out that the cutoff of funds and other legal actions are more complex in the North than in the South since segregation was not legalized in the North.

September 12. Marcus Wayne Chenault of Dayton, Ohio, was convicted and sentenced to death for the murder of Mrs. Martin Luther King, Sr., mother of the slain civil rights leader. Mrs. King was killed, along with Deacon Edward Boykin, during a worship service at the Ebenezer Baptist Church in Atlanta on June 30, 1974 (see entry above.) Chenault was identified as the gunman who interrupted that service with bullets. The Fulton County Court jury rejected Chenault's plea of insanity in delivering their verdict.

September 12-October 31. The city of Boston, Massachusetts began a program of busing to achieve school desegregation which sparked boycotts and demonstrations reminiscent of the early, vehement opposition to school integration in the South. In June, 1974, U.S. District Court Judge W. Arthur Garrity had ordered the busing of about 18,200 of the city's 94,000 public school pupils as part of a plan to dismantle Boston's dual school system. Opposition arose immediately.

On September 9, 1974, Senator Edward M. Kennedy was heckled and splattered with a tomato as he tried to address an angry group of anti-busing demonstrators. The crowd, estimated at between eight and ten thousand shouted insults, called for the impeachment of the Senator, and sang "God Bless America" when Kennedy stepped to a microphone. After preventing Senator Kennedy from speaking at the John F. Kennedy Memorial Building, the demonstrators—most of them white women—marched to the federal building. They stopped in front of the office of Judge Garrity and shouted, "Garrity must go." Kennedy, an advocate of peaceful school integration, said he was disappointed that he had not been able to speak, but assessed this treatment as milder than that he received at the hands of anti-war demonstrators.

On September 11, 1974, Boston School Superintendent William Leary said that everything possible had been done in the time allowed to prepare for desegregation. Yet, he added, "I know there will be problems. I ask the public for patience." Boston Mayor Kevin White, on the eve of the scheduled desegregation, appealed for calm but warned that "swift and sure punishment" would be meted out to those who resorted to violence. When the desegregation began on September 12, many white and black parents kept their children at home. Black children attending some of the schools, particularly in the white neighborhoods of South Boston, Hyde Park, and Dorchester, were subjected to jeers from angry white parents.

On September 16, a crowd of white teenagers and mothers clashed with police officers at South Boston High School. Twenty-two people were arrested during the confrontation. Police ordered the closing of bars and liquor stores in the area for the next two days.

Violence continued in Boston for the next several weeks. Four white students were injured in skirmishes with black students at the Washington Irving Junior High School in Roslindale on September 18. None of them required hospitalization. After the incident, forty black children walked out of the school. Police made no arrests. Eleven people, including three teachers, were injured on October 2 at the racially tense South Boston High School. A number of weapons were confiscated during the incident in which two black girls who allegedly pulled a knife on a police officer were arrested. Fighting broke out during an assembly of ninth graders at the Hart Deah Annex of South Boston High School on October 21. After this incident 30 of the 40 white pupils walked out of the school; most of the 130 black pupils remained.

On October 26, Matt Koehl, national commander of the American Nazi Party, demonstrated in front of the Boston federal building, protesting Judge Garrity's desegregation orders. He bore a sign reading, "White Power." Koehl was arrested and charged with impeding access to a federal building. Koehl's arrest followed by three days that of three other Nazi Party Members who were charged with attempting to incite a riot as they distributed anti-black literature in South Boston. Those charges were later reduced to disorderly conduct. John W. Roberts, Director of the Civil Liberties Union of Massachusetts, decried the arrests, saying that the state charges were a violation of the Nazis' constitutional rights. In a final decree, issued on October 30, 1974, Judge Garrity told the Boston school committee to complete the total desegregation of its schools by the fall of 1975. The final order authorized Boston school officials to use "any known desegregation techniques," including busing (although this was to be minimized), changing school districts and voluntary transfers. The judge promised a new order at a later date dealing with minority recruitment and hiring of school teachers and administrators.

The traumatic experience of desegregating schools in Boston highlighted the growing manifestation of white opposition to massive school desegregation in the North. It also struck many observers as a sign of retrogression in American race relations.

September 17. The United States Senate approved amendments to a $39.9 billion appropriations bill which prohibit the use of federal funds for busing to achieve school desegregation. According to the anti-busing amendment, which was approved by a vote of 45-42, federal funds could not be used for transporting students to achieve racial balance in schools. The practical effect of the bill, however, would be minimal, since very little federal money is used for such purposes.

September 21. White voters are reluctant to vote for black candidates for mayor in cities where blacks constitute a majority of the population, according to a study appearing in the September issue of *Psychology Today*. In comparing recent mayoral elections in Los Angeles (a white majority city) with Detroit and Atlanta (black majority cities), the article's author, Professor Howard Schuman of the University of Michigan Institute for Social Research, found that Los Angeles was the only major city where close to a majority of whites voted for a black candidate (Thomas Bradley) in preference to a white candidate (Sam Yorty). Los Angeles, Schuman said, apparently separated the question of the candidate's own race from the issue of which race would "control the city." By contrast, in Atlanta and Detroit, where whites were becoming the minority population, the elections became "full scale battles over which race would run the city."

In a previous study, Professor Schuman had found that about 60 percent of the whites in fifteen cities which had been surveyed said they would be willing to vote for a qualified black mayoral candidate of their own party. Yet, he pointed out, successful black mayoral candidates like Maynard Jackson of Atlanta and Coleman Young of Detroit received far less than half of the white vote.

Schuman concluded that while whites are becoming more liberal, they are still opposed to basic, structural changes in society. At the same time, he observed, blacks are becoming more open in their criticism of whites and are more distrustful of whites than in the past.

Schuman's study is entitled "Are Whites Really More Liberal?"

September 27. U. S. District Judge Albert V. Bryan, Jr., in Richmond, Virginia ordered the American Tobacco Company and Local 182 of the Tobacco Workers' International Union to allow blacks and females to "bump" white employees with less seniority. Having found Local 182 and the American Tobacco Company's two Richmond plants guilty of racial and sexual discrimination in violation of the Civil Rights Act of 1964, Judge Bryan directed the company to freeze hiring and promoting white male supervisors and adjust retirement and pension plans in order to halt discrimination. Any white employees who were displaced would be allowed to retain their present rates in the lower classifications. Litigation in the case began in March, 1973. It is believed to be the first instance in which a court has sanctioned "bumping" in a civil rights case. At the time of the decision, the tobacco company employed more than 1,000 production workers at its two plants in Richmond. Of that number 239 were black and 441 were female.

September 28. The *Atlanta Inquirer* reported a study by the Southern Regional Council (SRC) which showed that the South, the historic home of black Americans, was going through a whitening process despite increasing black concentrations in the urban areas of the region. All Southern states, except Texas, were losing more blacks than were being replaced by the birthrate and the "reverse migration" of young blacks from the North. According to the study, the black exodus from the South continued at such a steady pace that the region's black population, as shown in the 1970 Census, was down to 20 percent—the same percentage recorded in 1790. The loss of black populations was particularly acute in the rural areas. In Georgia, two-thirds of the state's 152 counties were losing blacks; in Mississippi 90 percent of the counties had declining black populations. A similar story was told for Alabama, South Carolina, and Arkansas, all of which had 80 percent or more of their counties losing blacks. Conversely, 51 percent of the population of Atlanta was black. Augusta, Georgia had a 50 percent black population, and New Orleans, Charleston, and Savannah boasted black populations of 45 percent or more. In sum, the study reports, there were ten metropolitan areas in the 11 southern states where the black population was 40 percent or more.

The SRC report's authors, Jack Tucker of Atlanta University and Everett S. Lee of the University of Georgia, concluded that:

The growth of the black population lags behind that of whites. So year by year, "the South becomes increasingly white. Losses of black population are frequent and heavy in rural counties, so Southern blacks are increasingly concentrated in metropolitan areas. And within the metropolitan areas, blacks are clustered in central cities with relatively few making their way into the more affluent suburbs."

"Generally," the report says, "people move from one area to another for one of two reasons, either the attractiveness of destination outweighs that of origin or there are so many negative features at the point of origin that any place seems better." Migration thus becomes a movement of the upper socio-economic classes to seek better opportunities and of the lower economic classes to escape oppression that can no longer be endured.

October 3. Frank Robinson, the only man in baseball history to be named Most Valuable Player in both the American and National Leagues, was named baseball's first black manager by the Cleveland Indians. During a press conference held to announce the appointment, Robinson said: "To say that this is a proud day for me would be an understatement. . . . If I had one wish in the world today, that wish would be to have Jackie Robinson here to see this happen. . . . I don't think I could have stood the pressure or have gone through what Jackie had to." Jackie Robinson (no relation to Frank) became the major league's first black baseball player in 1947. He died in 1972. Frank Robinson, as a professional player, had accumulated nearly 3,000 hits, including 574 home runs, before breaking the 105-year-old managerial color-line.

October 3. A bronze plaque was placed upon the then-unnoticed and unattended grave of ragtime composer Scott Joplin, who died in 1917. Joplin began composing ragtime in 1899 with "The Maple Leaf Rag." Ragtime music, however, was largely ignored until it regained popularity through the soundtrack of a 1974 film, *The Sting*. The plaque on Joplin's grave, located in St. Michael's Cemetary in Queens, was purchased by the American Society of Composers, Authors, and Publishers (ASCAP).

October 4. Money for research dealing with blacks has diminished, according to an assessment given by Professor Charles Hamilton of Columbia University. Although Hamilton decried the lack of money "for research on blacks or for blacks to do . . . research," he added, "it may affect our budgets, but never our integrity or our legitimacy." Hamilton, co-author of the widely acclaimed book, *Black Power*, spoke to more than 400 black professors and students at the W.E.B. Du Bois Conference on the American Black in Atlanta.

October 12. Frank L. Stanley, Sr., owner and publisher of the *Louisville Defender* and veteran civil rights activist, died in Louisville, Kentucky, at age sixty-eight. Stanley, the son of a butcher, was born in Chicago. At the age of six, his family moved to Louisville. He attended Atlanta University, where he was an all-American quarterback and captain of the football and basketball teams, and the University of Cincinnati. He received honorary doctorate degrees from several universities, including the University of Kentucky. In 1933, Stanley went to work for the *Louisville Defender* as a reporter. Three years later he became editor, general manager, and a part owner. During the years that he published the *Defender,* it received more than thirty-five awards in journalism, including the President's Special Service Award of the National Newspaper Publishers' Association (NNPA) in 1970, and the coveted Russwurm Award in 1974. He was a co-founder of the NNPA and was elected its president on five separate occasions.

Stanley drafted the legislation which led to the desegregation of state universities in Kentucky by its General Assembly in 1950. Ten years later he wrote the bill that created the Kentucky Commission on Human Rights, and was one of the original members of that body. His influence on race relations in Kentucky was noted by the *Louisville Courier Journal* on the occasion of the 25th anniversary of the *Defender* in 1950. "Much of the credit," the newspaper said editorially, "for the even and amiable pace Kentucky has maintained in its working out of race relations problems must be given the *Defender.*" Stanley was the force behind the *Defender's* role in that achievement.

October 16. Dr. Berkeley G. Burrell, president of the National Business League (NBL), told the 74th Annual Convention of the NBL in Atlanta that black businessmen must develop hard strategies in this time of economic turmoil. "If we do not come out of this 74th convention with a sound assessment of the situation and a unified front of committed allies to guarantee the continued survival of the black community and its economic resources," Dr. Burrell said, "a severe blow will be dealt to the potential economic independence of our people." The whole range of minority businesses, from the black capitalists to the Nation of Islam, were represented at the 74th Annual NBL Convention.

October 26. Fire swept through three black-owned businesses in the heart of downtown Sparta, Georgia. Police suspected arson in the blazes which destroyed a furniture store and damaged an adjacent warehouse and barber shop. Police also reported some attempted burglaries during the three-hour fight to bring the fires under control. On October 30, 1974, the *Atlanta Constitution* reported that the records of the furniture store burned on October 24 had been subpoenaed by a federal grand jury investigating the affairs of Hancock County's foremost black political leader, John McCown. Local investigators, however, were unable to say whether the subpoenaed records were destroyed in the fire.

October 26. The *Atlanta Inquirer* quoted a report from the Department of Commerce which cited a trend of larger black insurance companies to purchase or merge with smaller ones to keep them from passing out of the hands of blacks. Overall, the number of black insurance companies had declined to thirty-nine, but the assets of these firms had increased within the past five years by $73 million. (See Table E in Appendix for data compiled from the United States Department of Commerce.)

October 29. James Earl Ray, convicted assassin of Dr. Martin Luther King, Jr., insisted during a federal court hearing in Memphis, Tennessee that he did not slay the Nobel Peace Prize-winning civil rights leader. Ray admitted that he had purchased the gun which killed King and that he rented the room in the building from which the shot was fired, but said he did not pull the trigger. Ray referred to a mysterious figure he called "another party" as the possible slayer in a conspiracy to murder the civil rights leader. Prosecuting attorneys faced difficulties in their efforts to elicit further details from Ray because of a ruling from presiding Judge Robert McRae that only questions about what he told his previous lawyers and not about what he failed to tell them could be admitted. Ray was seeking his freedom or a new trial on the grounds that his original lawyers misled him into a guilty plea at the time of his 1968 trial. Those lawyers, Ray now contended, conspired with author William Bradford Huie for such a plea so that Huie could write a financially profitable book on King's assassination. (See also entries dated June 21, 1974 and June 29, 1974.)

October 29. Muhammad Ali regained the heavyweight boxing championship by defeating George Foreman in Kinshasa, Zaire. Ali, a thirty-two-year-old Black Muslim, knocked out the title holder, Foreman, in the eighth round of a scheduled fifteen round match. Ali was stripped of his title in 1967 after being convicted for draft evasion. Four years later that conviction was overturned by the United States Supreme Court. The Zaire title fight was the richest contest in history, with both Ali and Foreman earning $5 million each.

October 30. A biracial group of citizens in Sparta, Georgia requested that the State Elections Board send officials to observe the conduct of the November General Elections in Hancock County. A committee of three persons sent to Hancock County under court order for the August primary elections reported widespread election abuses. That report, however, was ignored by the Hancock County Grand Jury in its September presentments. In the report on the August elections, the committee had said that the balloting was conducted in a "tense and undesirable atmosphere" caused partially by the presence of armed men in the polling places. Hancock County is the only county in Georgia with a black-run government. It has often been the scene of racial and political strife.

October 31. The Voter Education Project (VEP) in Atlanta reported a record number of 118 blacks were seeking major public office in the November 5th general elections in nine Southern states. Seven blacks were seeking congressional seats, 14 were candidates for state senate seats, and the remaining 97 blacks were candidates for state houses. The VEP predicted that at least 31 of the candidates for state legislative seats would be successful. In 1962, when the VEP first began monitoring and promoting black political participation in the South, there were no black members in any Southern legislature. The black political progress continued despite "repulsive national political scandals and severe economic problems," according to VEP executive director John Lewis. "The black gains in state legislative posts in 1974, and the possible addition of at least one black member of Congress from the South will be yet another milestone in a steady progression of black political gains in the past few years," Lewis concluded.

November 2. Huey P. Newton, co-founder of the Black Panther Party, was being sought for murder. Newton was accused of shooting seventeen-year-old Kathleen Smith in the head during a dispute on an Oakland street on August 6, 1974. She never regained consciousness. The results of the police investigation as to the cause of the dispute were not released. Newton jumped a bail of $55,000 and disappeared on August 23, 1974. The accusation of murder was the latest in a long history of altercations between Newton and the law.

November 5-6. Controversial Atlanta civil rights activist Hosea Williams, who has had numerous encounters with the law, was acquitted on charges of simple battery on a police officer and of carrying a concealed and unlicensed pistol by two separate Fulton County Criminal Court juries. Williams was accused of grabbing the genitals of Officer A.L. Bradfield during a demonstration at the Martin Luther King, Jr. Nursing Home on September 15, 1972 and of carrying a pistol into the Atlanta Hartsfield International Airport on March 9, 1974. Williams's attorneys claimed that he was the victim of political harassment. Williams himself responded to the verdicts by declaring: "I carry only the love of God in my heart."

November 15. Robert Dancz, associate professor of music and director of the marching band at the University of Georgia, announced that the University of Georgia Redcoat Band would not play "Dixie" at future university football games. In a campus referendum held several days before Dancz's statement, students had approved the playing of the song by a margin of 3,467 to 1,270. Despite this vote, however, Dancz said that his band would "under no circumstances play the song." It "brought out the worse in some people," he said, and "black people feel like it is a slap in the face. This isn't the same school it was 20 years ago and not many southern schools play 'Dixie' anymore." Dancz also said that playing of the Civil War melody exposed his band members to physical danger.

December 8. The Sixth U.S. Court of Appeals in Cincinnati upheld a lower court ruling that the Grand Rapids, Michigan schools were not segregated. The appealate court said that "a review of the evidence and statistics in this case makes it clear not only that Grand Rapids was not guilty of acts of intentional segregation, but that much progress has been made toward elimination of the de facto segregation resulting from housing patterns." The court rejected the contentions of black plaintiffs that discriminatory acts of other individuals and governmental agencies were sufficient to support a finding of *de jure* segregation.

December 21. Five black women were named among the forty most highly respected women in the United States, according to a poll appearing in the January, 1975 edition of *Good Housekeeping* magazine. The blacks were California Congresswoman Yvonne Braithwaite Burke, New York Congresswoman Shirley Chisholm, Texas Congresswoman Barbara Jordan, Coretta Scott King, widow of the slain civil rights leader, and actress Cicely Tyson. The blacks were selected from a slate of forty-seven prominent women presented to the readers of *Good Housekeeping* in the sixth annual Most Admired Women's Poll. In the poll, King ranked 19th (her name has been among the winners since 1970) to take the highest position among the five black women selected. The total number of black women named for 1974 was three more than in 1973.

1975

January 1. Samuel DuBois Cook assumed the presidency of Dillard University in New Orleans, Louisiana. Cook earned his bachelor's degree from Morehouse College and his master's and doctorate degrees from Ohio State University. Previously, he had taught at Atlanta University and Duke University, and served as a consultant to the U. S. Office of Education and the Ford Foundation. Cook was also a former president of the Southern Political Science Association and, at the time of his appointment, was serving as a trustee of the Martin Luther King, Jr. Center for Social Change. Cook succeeded Broadus Butler as president of the 105 year-old predominantly black college.

January 2-26. Several reports appeared in the nation's newspapers revealing a history of Central Intelligence Agency (CIA) and Federal Bureau of Investigation (FBI) spying on black individuals and organizations. The *New York Times* reported on January 2 that the CIA was collecting data on singer Eartha Kitt since 1956. According to the CIA files, Kitt had danced, at the age of twenty, with a group whose leader allegedly had "served as a sponsor or endorser of a number of Communist-front activities"; she was involved in "escapades overseas and her loose morals were said to be the talk of Paris" in 1956; she had "a very nasty disposition" and was "a spoiled child, very crude," with "a vile tongue;" and she "often bragged that she had very little Negro blood." The CIA file also revealed that in 1960 Kitt signed an advertisement in support of the civil rights activities of the late Martin Luther King, Jr., which was also endorsed by "a number of persons identified in the past with the Communist party." However, the CIA report concluded that there was no evidence of any foreign intelligence connections on the part of Kitt. The detailed investigation of Kitt, according to the *Times,* was also possibly related to remarks which she made during a White House luncheon in January, 1968. At that time, Kitt shouted that the nation's youth were in rebellion because they were being "snatched off to be shot in Vietnam." Both President and Mrs. Lyndon B. Johnson were reportedly upset by the singer's remarks.

In response to the investigation of Kitt, the *Atlanta Constitution*, on January 6, 1975 published an editorial which stated that "nobody in today's world should deny our government the right to protect itself and us by keeping a close eye on potential threats, foreign or domestic. The question is, who should do it and under what kind of controls and guidelines? The pursuit of national security should not lead us to a place where we jettison the Bill of Rights." Kitt responded, "I don't understand this at all. I think it's disgusting. . . . I've always lived a very clean life and I have nothing to be afraid of and I have nothing to hide."

On January 25, the *Washington Post* reported that the FBI had wiretapped the conversations of Martin Luther King, Jr., and other civil rights leaders during the 1964 Democratic National Convention in Atlantic City, New Jersey. The reports from the wiretaps, according to the *Post*, were delivered to President Lyndon B. Johnson.

These reports of government spying on blacks came in the wake of the Watergate scandals and newer accusations that governmental agencies had illegally invaded the privacy of American citizens.

January 3. The Swope Parkway National Bank, the only black operated bank in Kansas City, was declared insolvent by the Federal Deposit Insurance Corporation (FDIC). Officials, however, said that the bank, with total assets of $10.6 million, would be reopened on January 4 as the Deposit Insurance National Bank under FDIC receivership. The Deposit Insurance Bank stood ready to assume all of Swope's "insured and fully secure deposits." An FDIC spokesman said these moves were being taken "in recognition of both the practical and symbolic importance of the Swope Parkway National Bank to [Kansas City's] black community."

January 5. Professor Moses W. Vaughn of the University of Maryland-Eastern Shore announced that he was studying the nutritive value of some types of soul food—the popular name for a number of items, including chitterlings, pigs' ears, pig knuckles and feet, hog maws, neck bones and pigs' tails, said to be particularly favored by blacks. Vaughn said the study is expected to fill a gap in nutritional knowledge, for even the official Department of Agriculture handbook contains no mention of soul food pork products. Yet, according to Vaughn, consumer research organizations and the Agriculture Department have received numerous requests for information about these foods. Vaughn received a $175,000 federal grant for his two-year study.

January 8. The Federal Communications Commission (FCC) denied the Alabama Educational Television Commission renewals of licenses for all eight of its television stations because of racial discrimination. The FCC said that the Alabama Commission had, between 1967 and 1970, failed to meet the high standards which it expected broadcast stations to maintain. It found that the Alabama Commission had followed a racially discriminatory policy in its over-all programming practices and through its "pervasive neglect" of Alabama's black population. Furthermore, it had failed to adequately meet the needs of the public it served. Still, the FCC said the Commission could continue to operate the television stations on an interim basis pending a final determination of its future. The denial of license renewal is one of the FCC's most severe and most rarely used actions.

January 8. Students returned to school in South Boston, Massachusetts for the first time in four weeks as more than 400 police officers kept watch on the arrival and departure of school buses. Four schools in the South Boston area were closed since December 11, 1974 when a white student was stabbed at the

South Boston High School. As the students returned to school, officials announced a first day attendance of 876 out of a total of 3,000 pupils enrolled in the four affected buildings. Meanwhile, the Boston School Committee appeared before U. S. District Court Judge W. Arthur Garrity, Jr. with a new desegregation plan. The new plan, which omitted busing, was the means by which the committee hoped to avoid punishment for contempt of court for three of its five members. (See also entry dated September 12-October 31, 1974.)

January 10. A crowd of 3,000 people, most of them young blacks rushing to apply for 225 new public service jobs, crashed into the glass doors at the Atlanta Civic Center Auditorium. The job seekers had gathered in the pre-dawn hours in search of employment. In December, 1974, the unemployment rate in Atlanta had been 7.5 percent, but the jobless rate among blacks was 9.2 percent. The spectacle at the Civic Center Auditorium pointed up again the growing economic desperation of blacks during the current recession.

January 11. A committee of the Governor's Minority Affairs Council of Mississippi reported that it is investigating reports that highway patrol officers have been beating blacks. The council, composed of fifteen black citizens, met with Governor Bill Waller to inform him of its plan for the investigation.

January 12-15. Celebrations were held throughout the nation commemorating the forty-sixth birthday of slain civil rights leader Martin Luther King, Jr. Much of the activity was focused in King's hometown, Atlanta, Georgia.

On January 12, King's widow, Coretta Scott King, gave a major new assessment of the current civil rights struggle. Excerpts from her statement follows:

"What we are seeing in the South is a transformation. . . . You don't have the tension in the South that you had 10-15 years ago. The battleground is definitely in the North now . . . Detroit, Chicago, New York—most of these cities are sitting on a powder keg because of neglect. Urban America is where it is going to happen in the 70's and 80's. The problems in the major cities across the country are the problems of America in miniature. Every city is beset by problems of poverty, crime and housing. . . . Blacks always suffer more than any other group. . . .

[The Nixon administration was] totally unresponsive to the basic human needs of blacks and whites. . . . [In the Ford administration] the only thing is the climate is a little less oppressive. . . . I think that the people were so relieved to get rid of Nixon that they set Ford up as a kind of savior. I don't think that he's really a leader. . . .

In some instances we still have to march but not as much as we once did. . . . I think the movement has reached a more sophisticated state. Marches, picketing and boycotting are part of it, but we are at the stage now where we have some political power. We are the balance of power in many areas. . . .

We do have a lot to work on but I do believe Martin Luther King left us a great legacy and told us how we can achieve the American dream—a just and peaceful society."

King made her remarks during an interview with Walt Smith of United Press International.

Also in connection with the birthday celebration, a summit meeting of national civil rights and political leaders was held in Atlanta on January 13. The meeting called to discuss the Voting Rights Act of 1965 and its possible extension or renewal, was sponsored by the Martin Luther King, Jr. Center for Social Change. Participants included United States Senators Hugh Scott, a Michigan Republican, and Birch Bayh, an Indiana Democrat; U. S. Representatives Ronald Dellums of California and Andrew Young of Georgia (both African-Americans); Former U. S. Attorney General Nicholas Katzenbach; National Urban League director Vernon E. Jordan; veteran civil rights leader Bayard Rustin, executive director of the A. Philip Randolph Institute; John Lewis, executive director of the Voter Education Project; Georgia State Senator Julian Bond; and Atlanta Mayor Maynard Jackson.

In his remarks at the conference, Senator Bayh said that other minorities needed the extension of the Voting Rights Act to foster their causes, because there was substantial evidence that the protections provided by the act could aid Mexican-Americans, especially. The Nixon administration, according to Bayh, tried to "gut" the Voting Rights extension bill in 1970, but he didn't anticipate that the Ford administration would try to do the same.

Former Attorney General Katzenbach expressed the opinion that the Voting Rights Act freed Southern white politicians from campaigns of "race, race, race" and enabled them to seek office without reference to race. It also enabled blacks to seek national office for the first time in forty years, he said.

In his remarks, Rustin said that the issues of the turbulent 1960s were black issues—equality under the law and the end of segregation. But today the issues were broader and included blacks, other minorities and women, and are economic and political in nature. The agenda, he said, had now changed from getting the rights whites had to the things whites wanted—"a job, a house, a decent education."

On January 15, an ecumenical service was held at the Ebenezer Baptist Church where King pastored, with the Reverend Theodore Hesburgh, president of Notre Dame University and former chairman of the U. S. Commission on Civil Rights as the principal speaker. Other activities in King's hometown during the day included the dedication of the civil rights leader's birthplace as a national historic site and a "people's march" in the downtown area of the city.

January 15. John Lewis, executive director of the Voter Education Project (VEP), was awarded the Martin Luther King, Jr. Non-violent Peace Prize for 1975. The award is the highest prize of the Martin Luther King, Jr. Center for Social Change. The presentation was made by Mrs. Coretta Scott King, widow of the slain civil rights leader, who said of Lewis:

"We feel that this man exemplifies the life, the teachings, and the contributions of Martin Luther King, Jr., and certainly has brought about in his efforts the kind of non-violent social changes in our society that have moved us forward and will continue to move us toward the dream. . . . This young man is a very humble man, a deeply committed man, and a man whom I respect, admire, and love very deeply."

Lewis began his civil rights career as a member, and later executive secretary, of the Student Non-Violent Coordinating Committee (SNCC). He participated in the first Freedom Rides in 1961 and was a principal speaker at the March on Washington in 1963. He was a leader of the Selma-to-Montgomery Voting Rights Marches. It was during the first of these marches in 1965 that Lewis received a fractured skull after Alabama law enforcement officers charged the crowd of peaceful demonstrators. As head of the VEP, Lewis directs programs to advance, through nonpartisan action, minority political participation.

In receiving the award, Lewis said, "I am deeply moved and I hope that in the days, months, and years to come I will be worthy of this honor. As Dr. King said so many times, "We've come a distance, but we still have a distance to go."

January 16. Muhammad Ali, heavyweight boxing champion, was named the Associated Press' Athlete of the Year for 1974. In winning the award, as a result of a nationwide poll of sportswriters and sportscasters, Ali edged out another black, baseball's Hank Aaron, by a margin of 162 to 110. Ali became only the third fighter to win the AP award since it was initiated in 1931. Joe Louis, an African-American, won it in 1937 after he had knocked out heavyweight Jim Braddock for the title, and Ingemar Johansson of Sweden was selected in 1959 after he defeated Floyd Patterson for the heavyweight championship.

The AP award signaled a new acceptance of Ali by Americans. The champion had incurred widespread disfavor and was forced to take a three and one half year retirement from the ring when he refused induction into the Armed Forces in 1968. Ali began his comeback in 1971 after the United States Supreme Court overturned his conviction for draft evasion. His comeback fight was a third round knockout over Jerry Quarry in Atlanta, Georgia.

January 16-February 22. Blacks in DeKalb County, Georgia staged a number of demonstrations protesting what they called "the racist" DeKalb school system. On January 15 (the anniversary of the birthday of Dr. Martin Luther King, Jr.), sixty black parents and pupils picketed at the Columbia High School in Decatur. They accused the school system of, among other things, dishonoring the memory of Martin Luther King, Jr. by refusing to declare a holiday on his birthday. However, Joe Renfroe, an assistant superintendent of schools, said that special programs, rather than a holiday, would "make all students more aware of his (King's) contributions better than closing down which we do not do for the birthdays of other great men."

On February 20, about 100 black students at Columbia High School were arrested after they refused to obey an order from school authorities to leave the campus. The arrested students were part of a group of 170 blacks who had been suspended the previous week for staging a sit-down and walkout because the school failed to hold an assembly during Black History Week.

On February 22, more than 100 black students and parents marched from Columbia High School to the DeKalb County Courthouse in the continuing protest. According to one parent: "Our children have been coming home all this time telling us how bad the situation is and some of the things that the school officials up there do to them. . . . We see what they've been telling us is true."

Also on February 22, Columbia High School readmitted nearly all of the black students suspended during earlier demonstrations. DeKalb County, whose seat is the city of Decatur, is a part of the Metropolitan Atlanta area.

January 17. Stanley Scott, President Ford's chief black White House aide, said during a seminar on mass communications at the John F. Kennedy Center in Atlanta, Georgia that "fast buck operators" were threatening America's remaining black newspapers. He said wealthy whites were "buying out black-owned newspapers and franchising them like McDonald's hamburgers." The "black press should survive," Scott added, because the "majority white press" did not cover adequately all aspects of life in black communities. "I believe in integration," Scott continued, "but I think we should maintain and save some of our old institutions too." Scott estimated that of the 500 black-oriented newspapers in the country, "only about 30 or 35 are still black-owned." One of those was the *Atlanta Daily World*, a pioneer black daily, published by Scott's family.

January 22. In its latest report, the United States Commission on Civil Rights said that President Gerald Ford must exert leadership to insure "vigorous and effective enforcement" of school desegregation laws. The commission was also, as in the past, highly critical of the civil rights enforcement of several governmental agencies. Noting the continued resistance to school desegregation in Boston, Massachusetts and elsewhere, the commission said: "We are at a dangerous crossroads in connection with school desegregation. . . . We cannot afford—because of organized resistance in Boston or any other community—to turn back." It called for "extraordinary actions," including appointment by the President of "an appropriate federal official" who would have the responsibility of making certain federal agencies fully enforce civil rights laws.

In the new report, the commission charged that the Department of Health, Education, and Welfare (HEW), the Internal Revenue Service (IRS), and the Veterans Administration (VA) had failed to use existing federal laws to guarantee equal educational opportunities for racial minorities, non-English speaking people, and women.

The HEW, according to the commission, had "diminished its overall effectiveness and credibility" by interminable negotiations with segregated school districts, rather than cutting off their federal funds. It had also failed to tell school districts what they must do to comply with civil rights laws, including the degree of busing required to desegregate schools.

The IRS, the commission contended, had taken little action to make sure that private schools which received exemptions from federal taxes were operated without racial bias.

The VA, which was responsible for enforcing anti-bias laws regarding profit-making schools, apprenticeship programs, and on-the-job training programs remained "deficient in several areas," according to the commission. The VA, for example, had refused to examine possible discrimination in the hiring of faculty at certain schools.

The latest Civil Rights Commission document was the third in a series of reports assailing the degree of civil rights enforcement under the Nixon and Ford administrations.

January 22. The Voter Education Project (VEP) rendered an assessment of the political progress of blacks in the 1974 general elections. Georgia, according to the VEP, led the South in the number of blacks elected and reelected to public office. In elections from coroner to congressman, Georgia had 101 blacks elected out of the 525 successful black candidates in the region. Among the new black officeholders in Georgia were John White, the first African-American to represent Dougherty County in the state legislature, and Henry Dodson and J. O. Wyatt, the first black commissioners of Fulton County (of which Atlanta is the county seat).

Elsewhere, Harold Ford was elected to the U. S. Congress from Memphis, Tennessee; forty-six blacks were elected to state legislatures in Alabama,

Georgia, and South Carolina alone; and blacks were elected to 226 city councils and commissions. In the end, however, VEP Executive Director John Lewis said "the election of 525 blacks in a single year is a small but important step in the long march toward equity of representation in Southern politics." (See Table F in Appendix for data compiled by the Voter Education Project.)

January 24. J. Mason Brewer, possibly the best known writer of African-American folklore in the United States, died in Commerce, Texas at age seventy-eight.

Brewer wrote some of his stories and poems in black dialect "so ancient" that it was difficult for most people to read. Others were written in standard English. Prior to his death, Brewer had served as a vice president of the American Folklore Society and a member of the Texas Institute of Letters and the Texas Folklore Society. He was a lecturer at Yale University, the University of Southern California, and the University of Texas, and a Distinguished Visiting Professor at East Texas State University. The late J. Frank Dobie, himself a distinguished folklorist, once called Brewer "the best storyteller of Negro folklore anywhere in the world."

January 25. Nannie Mitchell, founder of the *St. Louis Argus* and a veteran black business and civic leader, died in St. Louis, Missouri at age eighty-eight.

In 1905, Mitchell, along with her late husband William and her brother-in-law, J. E. Mitchell, founded the We Shall Rise Insurance Company in St. Louis and began publishing a newsletter to be distributed to black churches in the area. This newsletter eventually became the *Argus*, a newspaper which has been published weekly since 1915.

January 25-February 15. George C. Wallace, a perennial symbol of resistance to civil rights for blacks, began his third term as governor of Alabama. At his most recent inauguration, Wallace observed that social changes had been effected so smoothly in Alabama that other states might want to emulate it. Fifteen black state legislators and the state's first black cabinet officer, Jesse Lewis, witnessed the ceremonies. Wallace had received more black support than ever before in his recent successful reelection campaign and his subsequent recognition by black organizations had been the source of considerable controversy in the black communities of the nation. John Lewis, Director of the Voter Education Project (VEP), who was assaulted during the famous Selma to Montgomery March, is one of those who oppose black support for Wallace. In an interview with Boyd Lewis of the *Atlanta Inquirer*, John Lewis said: "Black people giving Wallace an award is like the Anti-Defamation League giving a posthumous award to Hitler." Lewis also observed that "George Wallace, in spite of his condition remains a symbol of the most brutal forms of violence inflicted against poor and black people in Alabama. . . . There is no way you can erase that from the psyche of black people. . . . As we celebrate Black History Week, we must not forget. . . . I am troubled by this newly found admiration of a man like Governor Wallace."

January 29. Former Georgia State Senator Leroy R. Johnson was convicted in the United States District Court in Atlanta of submitting a false statement to the Internal Revenue Service (IRS) in connection with his 1969 and 1970 income tax returns. Johnson was acquitted of two other charges of willfully evading some $40,000 in taxes for 1969 and 1970. Johnson's lawyers announced that they would appeal the verdict. Johnson became the first black person elected to a Southern state legislature since Reconstruction days when he won a seat in the Georgia legislature in 1962. During his twelve years in the state legislature, he became one of the most powerful black politicians in Georgia and the South. Johnson was defeated for reelection in 1974, after an unsuccessful campaign for mayor of Atlanta, and with the tax charges against him still pending.

January 29. Atlanta Mayor Maynard H. Jackson appointed the first full-time black Municipal Traffic Judge and the first black Municipal Court Solicitor in the city's history. Edward L. Baety, a thirty-year-old attorney who graduated from Morris Brown College and Harvard University, was named judge. Mary Welcome, a thirty-one-year-old attorney who graduated from the Howard University Law School, was named Municipal Court Solicitor.

February 1. The results of a study of the public schools of Philadelphia, Pennsylvania showed that whether the race of the pupil and teacher was the same appeared unrelated to learning. The report also concluded that counseling and remedial education—given current rates of expenditure—had "no particular value" in increasing learning. The report said that optimal learning growth at the elementary level occurred in classes that were about half black and half white. In junior high schools, the achievement among blacks increased as the percentage of blacks increased. On the other hand, white junior high school students experienced a decline in learning in schools that were more than half black. The study, sponsored by the Federal Reserve Bank of Philadelphia, was co-authored by Anita Summers and Barbara L. Wolfe.

February 2. Sam Beard, head of the Development Council, announced in New York that minority-owned companies were moving into the economic mainstream and doing business with the industrial giants of the nation. According to Beard, "There was almost no history of minority business ownership prior to the Sixties," but in the last three years, his nonprofit organization had arranged 1,003 contracts totaling $141 million between minority-owned businesses and major corporations. Included among the Council projects are the financing of a health center in South Jamaica, a section of Queens, New York, where thirty black doctors had tried unsuccessfully for eighteen months to raise money for a medical facility to treat the community of

150,000; the funding of Soul City, the multi-racial town under construction in North Carolina; assistance to the Black Feet Indian Writing Company in Montana which now supplies pens to Atlantic-Richfield Company; and assistance to the black-owned Baldwin Ice Cream Company of Chicago which sells food to United Airlines. The Council, according to Director Beard, is not a charity organization. Instead, he said, "We're building long-lasting business relationships that will feed hundreds of thousands of dollars back into minority communities and create jobs."

February 3. Georgia State Representative Hosea Williams, head of the Atlanta chapter of the Southern Christian Leadership Conference, and three other men, including Socialist Workers Party presidential candidate Peter Camejo, were arrested during a demonstration in Atlanta outside of a hotel where President Gerald Ford was speaking. Williams and fifty other demonstrators demanded to see the President to ask for jobs for the poor. A presidential aide told them that Ford's schedule did not permit such a meeting. Amid jeering from hotel guests, the demonstrators were arrested and charged with trespassing and disorderly conduct.

February 4. The Opportunities Industrialization Centers (OIC) held its eleventh annual convention in Atlanta, Georgia. The OIC, a black self-help organization, was founded in Philadelphia, Pennsylvania by the Reverend Leon Howard Sullivan, the pastor of Philadelphia's Zion Baptist Church. Sullivan first received national attention in 1963 when, after increasing his church's membership from 600 to 5,000, he established a day care center, a federal credit union, a community center, an employment agency, adult education reading classes, several athletic teams, choral groups, and a family counseling service. For these and other things, Sullivan was cited by *Life* magazine as one of 100 outstanding young adults in the United States in 1963. During this same period he was named one of the ten outstanding young men of Philadelphia, won the city of Philadelphia Good Citizenship Award, the Silver Beaver Award of the Boy Scouts of America, the West Virginia State College Outstanding Alumnus Award, the Freedom Foundation Award, and the Russwurm Award.

In 1964, at the age of forty-one, Sullivan established the first OIC in an abandoned jailhouse in Philadelphia. Starting with almost nothing, Sullivan built OIC into a $4.5 million a year enterprise which has trained and found jobs for more than 200,000 people. A comparison of the OIC's expenditures with the number of people it had successfully trained over the past ten years showed that the organization was able to put trainees through its programs at an average cost of only $1,500 each. Secretary of Health, Education, and Welfare Caspar Weinberger stated that the OIC was more effective in training people and finding jobs for them than the vocational education programs in the nation's high schools.

During the eleventh annual convention, President Gerald Ford addressed the delegates and praised the work and enthusiasm of Sullivan. The OIC head responded: "Mr. President, we are glad you came. It is time someone came to us to give the poor and those who work with the poor, some encouragement and some hope. It is refreshing to know that now, at last somebody in the White House seems to care."

Also on February 4th, the OIC presented a State Government Award to Alabama Governor George Wallace. In presenting the honor, Connie Harper, the black executive director of the Central Alabama OIC, kissed the handicapped, formerly rabid segregationist on the cheek. A week later, however, Tyrone Brooks, public information officer for the Southern Christian Leadership Conference, resigned from the Board of Directors of the Atlanta OIC in protest of the award to Wallace. Brooks called the presentation "an insult to all of black Atlanta and black America."

February 12. United States District Court Judge Wilbur Owens, Jr., in Macon, Georgia, approved the Georgia State Board of Regents' plan for the desegregation of predominantly-black Fort Valley State College. The thrust of the plan called for upgrading academic programs, especially in agriculture, in order to attract more whites to Fort Valley State. Special education courses and a master's degree program in education were also parts of the plan. The suit against Fort Valley was filed in 1972 by a group of white citizens of the town who objected to a black state school existing in their midst while their children attended other state schools. It was also contended, by blacks, that the plaintiffs opposed the influence which the students helped blacks in Fort Valley to exert on local politics.

In his ruling, Judge Owens said "there is no magic way whereby this college can be transformed overnight." Yet, he continued, "the court feels the plan is real and it is designed to do what is necessary. The court believes the plan is evidence of an intention to attempt to do what the court says."

Black faculty members and students at Fort Valley announced that they would probably appeal the judge's ruling. Some of them had joined the case with a contention that the desegregation suit was in reality an attempt by whites to take control of the school. Thomas M. Jackson, attorney for the blacks, said some provisions of the plan were commendable, but that the "concept is most suspect that a college must be controlled or operated by whites in order to attract white students." One of the attorneys for the Board of Regents told Judge Owens that there was no justification for Jackson's fears. In his ruling, Owens himself noted that "there are some who will say the plan will result in the demise of this college but the court feels that those fears are unfounded. . . . If the plan is carried out by everyone involved the end result will be that students who attend—be they black, white or any other race—will get a good college education that they need, want, and ought to have!"

Even before Judge Owens' ruling, some white faculty members were transferred to the school from other colleges and some white students had enrolled. About 25 percent of the faculty and student body were white at the time of the decision.

The issues involved in the desegregation of Fort Valley State College were similar to those which have faced a number of predominantly-black colleges in the past decade. Federal law had dictated the dismantling of dual school systems. In most instances white controlled state boards of regents or trustees had recommended closing, merger, or transformation of predominantly black colleges as a principal means of accomplishing these objectives. Blacks, while generally not opposed to the principle of desegregation, had often contended that the plans for achieving it would destroy essential elements of their cultural heritage and place them at an unfair disadvantage in competition for positions in the newly desegregated schools.

February 13. Dr. Peter T. Singleton, Jr. of Atlanta, Georgia was awarded the Commendation for Excellence in Clinical Medicine and Human Relations at the Walter Reed General Hospital and Medical Center in Washington, D. C. The young black cardiologist graduated from Morehouse College and the Howard University Medical School.

February 15. Alameda County, California Superior Court Judge Lyle Cook ordered the city of Berkeley to promote eight white firemen who were passed over in favor of minority race candidates. Judge Cook ruled that the city's "affirmative action" program, introduced in 1972, was unconstitutional because it amounted to discrimination in reverse. According to the 1972 act, persons of minority races should be represented in the fire department in proportion to their population in the city. Whites, however, complained that they were discriminated against because non-whites were hired and promoted ahead of them on the basis of quota rather than merit. Judge Cook agreed that ignoring competitive examinations to hire and promote minority persons violated the Berkeley Charter, the Civil Rights Act of 1964, and the Fourteenth Amendment of the United States Constitution.

February 16. The Anacostia Neighborhood Museum, a branch of the Smithsonian Institute, announced that a travelling exhibit on black history will tour the country as part of the bicentennial celebration. The exhibit will include forty-six illustrated panels, along with artifacts and a written text. Among the characters and events in the exhibit are York, William Clark's slave; Mary Fields, a colorful Western pioneer; Benjamin "Pap" Singleton, an early black migrationist; Bill Pickett, a pioneer black cowboy; and Mary Ellen Pleasant, a pioneer civil rights leader.

York was a strapping, six-foot interpreter for the Lewis and Clark expedition of 1804-1806. His fluency in French and Indian dialects as well as English made him indispensable to the exploration. He was, in fact, seen as the leader of the expedition by the Indians. Because of his services, York was granted his freedom in 1805.

"Black Mary" Fields was born in slavery, but migrated to Montana after emancipation. She became a friend and confidante of the nuns of Cascade, a restaurant owner, and a mail woman, who often walked through the snow when it was too deep for horses, to insure that the mail got through.

Benjamin "Pap" Singleton, one of the earliest "Black Moses" led an exodus of blacks from the South to the West in 1879 (see also entry dated 1879). Between 1870 and 1890, a number of these Western migrations took place as blacks sought to escape racial oppression in the Post-Reconstruction South. Men like Singleton organized "colonies" to help the blacks move West, where they often faced legal and extra-legal moves to keep them out of the frontier territories. Once in the West, blacks founded all-black towns, worked on the railroads, and in cattle drives. It is estimated that there were at least 8,000 black cowboys during this pioneer era.

Among the most famous of the black cowboys was Bill Pickett, "the Dusky Demon" of the rodeo circuit. Pickett lost his life at age seventy-one, when he tried to make a comeback to the rodeo by roping and taming a wild horse.

Mary Ellen Pleasant was born a slave in Georgia, but also became a migrant to the West. She was one of San Francisco's first civil rights leaders and helped to finance the raid of John Brown at Harpers Ferry, Virginia in 1859.

February 25. Georgia Governor George Busbee urged his state legislature to pass a bill dictating increased state employment for blacks and women. Busbee told leaders of the House and Senate that an affirmative action plan was needed to prevent mandatory hiring quotas imposed by the federal government. In May, 1974 the Equal Employment Opportunities Commission had accused eleven state departments and agencies of racially and sexually discriminatory hiring practices. The federal government had earlier imposed hiring quotas on the states of Alabama and Mississippi.

February 25. Elijah Muhammad, leader of the Black Muslims, died in Chicago at age seventy-seven. Muhammad was born Elijah Poole, near Sandersville, Georgia in 1897. He moved to Detroit in the 1930s and met W. D. Fard, Founder of the Temple of Islam (Black Muslims). Muhammad himself erected a temple in Detroit, then, in 1934, moved to Chicago. Subsequently, 79 temples were erected in 70 cities. Jesse Jackson, head of Operation PUSH and one of the nation's most articulate black civil rights leaders, eulogized Muhammad as "the single most powerful black man in this country. . . . His leadership extended far beyond his membership. He was the father of black self-consciousness during our 'colored' and Negro days." Muhammad was succeeded by his son, the honorable Wallace D. Muhammad.

During the height of the Civil Rights Movement, Muhammad and his followers provoked the ire of white and black leadership alike for their preachings of racial separatism, racial pride, and self-defense. The increasing popularity of those teachings among blacks, however, was demonstrated in the scope of philosophies represented in the eulogies for Muhammad. Civil rights leaders, including Jackson and Tyrone Brooks of the SCLC, joined Julian Bond of Georgia, and traditional black Baptist ministers in extolling the virtues of the Black Muslim patriarch. (See also 1934 for further information about Elijah Muhammad. For excerpts taken from his essay, "Qualifications for Independence," and from the "Muslim Program," see Appendix.)

February 28. United States District Court Judge Robert M. McRae, Jr. in Memphis, Tennessee denied James Earl Ray's motion to withdraw his guilty plea and face a new trial on the charge that he murdered Dr. Martin Luther King, Jr. in 1968. McRae said Ray's original plea of guilty was "cooly and deliberately" submitted and that he found no violation of Ray's constitutional rights that would warrant a reversal of the plea and a full trial in state court. McRae rejected Ray's contention that he came to believe he had no choice but to plead guilty because of his former attorney's actions and rejected Ray's allegations that famed criminal lawyer Percy Foreman of Houston, Texas and attorney Arthur Hanes, Sr. of Birmingham, Alabama failed to take adequate steps to prepare a defense because they were more interested in promoting their royalties on the Ray story under contracts with Alabama author William Bradford Huie. McRae ruled groundless Ray's argument that Foreman, specifically, coerced him into the guilty plea. The judge said there was no "impermissable pressure" from the attorney. "On the contrary, the matter was discussed on numerous separate occasions over almost one month, at the least." Ray carefully considered and partially amended the lengthy stipulation of facts that formed the basis for accepting his guilty plea . . . and entered the plea in an open court where he spoke to correct the record as he thought appropriate," according to Judge McRae. Robert I. Livingston, one of Ray's new attorneys, announced an immediate appeal to the U.S. Court of Appeals for the Sixth Circuit. (See also entries dated June 21, 1974, June 29, 1974, and October 29, 1974.)

February. The Free Southern Theater presented the play *If the Opportunity Scratches, Itch It*, in Eutau, Alabama. It was the first time ever that live theater, other than high school plays, were performed in this predominantly black farm community in central Alabama. The occasion also marked the first time since 1969 that the Free Southern Theater had taken a show on tour, although this was its original purpose when it was established in 1962 as a cultural arm of the

Student Non-Violent Coordinating Committee (SNCC). The Free Southern Theater was viewed by some as the beginning of a modern renaissance of black culture that grew out of the civil rights and black consciousness movements of the 1960s and 1970s. The idea of a theater to dramatize the concept of black liberation had spread rapidly across the country, and most cities with a sizeable black population had some form of organized cultural activity. They included: The Fire Company in Birmingham, Alabama; the New African Company; the National Center of Afro-American Artists, and the Museum of Afro-American History in Boston, Massachusetts; the Ku Mba Workshop in Chicago, Illinois; the Karamu House Theater in Cleveland, Ohio; the Rapa House in Detroit, Michigan; Opera South in Jackson, Mississippi; Bodaciouis Buggerilla; the Mafandi Institute, and the Performing Arts Society in Los Angeles, California; the Black Theater Troupe and Umba Ujaama in Phoenix, Arizona; and the Kahero Cultural Gallery of Richmond, Virginia.

The aim of all of this activity was to allow blacks, who felt that they had been generally left out or misrepresented in America's cultural media, to interpret their own history, thought, ideas, strengths, weaknesses, and aspirations. In addition to theater, blacks were engaged in community writing, dancing, directing, designing, sculpturing, singing, and photography.

In interviews with the *New York Times* in February 1975, Kenneth E. Snipes, executive director of the Karamu House Theater, and Gilbert Moses, one of the founders of the New Orleans based Free Southern Theater, assessed the new movement. According to Snipes: "Blacks have more needs for certain kinds of programs to provide them with a sense of self-worth, more of the things that are appreciative of black people. There is a need to appreciate black people, to appreciate the role of blacks in the history of this country, to appreciate the work of the black playwright or the black dancer is doing today to eventually attain self-worth and self-esteem." Moses added that "it was more important that we develop our own artists, our own image. It had to happen."

March 2. Arthur Ashe, the nation's leading black tennis player, won the singles finals of the World Championship Tennis Green Group Tournament in Rotterdam. He defeated Tom Okker of the Netherlands 3-6, 6-2, 6-4, in a ninety-five minute match at the Ahoy Sports Palace.

March 14. United States District Court Judge John H. Pratt in Washington, D. C. ordered the Department of Health, Education, and Welfare (HEW) to quickly enforce school desegregation laws in 125 school districts in sixteen states where voluntary desegregation was in effect. The judge told HEW to begin proceedings against the school systems within two months and said that in the future only seven months would be granted for systems to formulate voluntary school desegregation plans. HEW had found within the past fifteen months that the school districts included in the order were "substantially

Arthur Ashe holding trophy following his victory.

disproportionate" in their racial composition. The affected districts were located in Arkansas, Delaware, Florida, Kentucky, Louisiana, Maryland, Mississippi, Missouri, North Carolina, Oklahoma, South Carolina, Tennessee, Texas, Virginia, and West Virginia. The ruling came as a result of a suit filed by the NAACP's Legal Defense Fund in 1971. Failure of any district to comply with HEW requirements could mean a cut off of federal funds.

March 17. The Reverend Jesse Jackson of Chicago, Illinois, head of People United to Save Humanity (Operation PUSH), said during a press conference in New York City that the National Collegiate Athletic Association (NCAA) was "racist" and warned that a black boycott of the college football bowl games may be the next target of civil rights groups. Jackson remarked that "the NCAA is not fair. . . . The colleges don't have black head coaches. They will select an assistant grudgingly but they don't consider the black man to be head coach or athletic director. . . . We found that the selection committees for various bowl games are almost totally white. This is a situation we intend to change."

Earlier, Jackson had met with Michael Burke, president of Madison Square Garden in New York City, and Peter Carlesimo of Fordham University on the issue of giving black colleges a role in the National Invitational Basketball Tournament (NIT). Jackson's organization had threatened to picket the NIT unless changes were made. Under an agreement reached with Burke and Carlesimo, two athletic directors from black colleges would be elected to the NIT Selection Committee (Jackson suggested the names of Earl Banks of Morgan State University and Eddie Robinson of Grambling University), at least one black institution would be invited to compete in future NIT events, and the New York branch of Operation PUSH would play a supportive role in the promotion of future tournaments. Jackson said that the pressure on the NIT was part of a national program to break down racial barriers which extended beyond the playing field.

March 17. The American Civil Liberties Union (ACLU) released documents indicating that the FBI had fabricated a threatening letter in order to persuade a black civil rights worker to leave Mississippi in 1969. A month after Muhammad Kenyatta received the letter, he returned with his family to Pennsylvania. The ACLU said that Kenyatta (formerly Donald W. Jackson) had come under the scrutiny of Cointelpro, the FBI's counter-intelligence unit, which the Bureau operated between 1956 and 1971 in an effort to disrupt groups it considered subversive. The letter in question, allegedly written by a group of Tougaloo (Mississippi) college students, warned Kenyatta to leave Mississippi or "we shall consider contacting local authorities regarding some of your activities or take other measures available to us which would have a more direct effect and which would not be as cordial as this note." The ACLU obtained the FBI documents in connection with a suit filed against the Bureau by Kenyatta, alleging a violation of his constitutional rights.

March 20. The April issue of *Redbook* magazine listed four black women among the forty-four American women qualified for top governmental positions, including cabinet officers, in the United States. The blacks included U. S. Representative Barbara Jordan of Texas, who was suggested as eminently qualified for Attorney General of the United States; Mrs. Martin Luther King, Jr., listed as qualified for chairperson of the Equal Employment Opportunity Commission; Eleanor Holmes Norton, Commissioner of Human Rights for New York City, listed as qualified for Secretary of Housing and Urban Development; and C. Delores Tucker, Secretary of State of Pennsylvania, seen as qualified for Ambassador to the United Nations. The list of qualified women was drawn up by Frances "Sissy" Farentold, chairperson of the National Women's Political Caucus, because she became convinced that women's abilities were underestimated when selections for high level jobs were made.

March 20. Kenneth Ivory, a seventeen-year-old black youth from Milwaukee, Wisconsin, was named national "Boy of the Year" in a White House ceremony attended by President Gerald R. Ford. Ivory, a senior at Lincoln High School in Milwaukee, was president of his student body and captain of the football, baseball, and basketball teams at the time of his selection as Boy of the Year.

March 24. Heavyweight boxing champion Muhammad Ali defeated Chuck Wepner in the final round of a 15-round title fight to retain his crown. Wepner went down in the last round from a right to the head and referee Tony Perez stopped the fight at the count of eight.

March 28. The *Washington Star* reported new evidence of governmental spying on black individuals and organizations. These included investigations of Marion Barry, a former SNCC activist and ex-president of the Board of Education of Washington, D. C.; Walter Fauntroy, Washington, D. C.'s delegate to the U. S. House of Representatives; the Reverend David Eaton, pastor of Washington's All Souls Unitarian Church; and Absalom Frederick Jordan, chairman of the Black United Front. According to the *Star*, Barry's file read, "subject referred . . . by FBI due to activities in SNCC, active in civil rights movement. Dislikes police." (See also entries dated January 2 and June 6, 1975.)

April 1. The Black Christian Nationalist Church (BCN) opened its Third Biennial National Convention in Atlanta, Georgia. The BCN was a movement dedicated to changing the condition of black people by changing their life-styles. According to the creed of the BCN, "Jesus, the Black Messiah, was a revolutionary leader, sent by God to rebuild the Black Nation, Israel, and to liberate Black people from powerlessness and from the oppression, brutality and exploitation of the white gentile world." The national chairman of the BCN, Jaramazi Abebe Agyeman (formerly the Reverend Albert Cleage) was lauded by Atlanta Mayor Maynard Jackson as "a master teacher." Coleman Young, mayor of Detroit, Michigan, where the BCN was founded, presented Agyeman with a certificate from his city council. Young said that the "BCN is a force to be reckoned with not only in Detroit but in the nation."

April 1. Poppy Cannon White, widow of the late NAACP Executive Secretary Walter Francis White, died by jumping off the terrace of her apartment in New York City. Walter White, whose marriage to the white author in 1947 created a mild controversy within the ranks of the NAACP, died in 1955. The NAACP issued an official statement of sorrow, however, upon the death of White.

April 2. Judge Dennis Jones of the DeKalb County, Georgia Juvenile Court dismissed charges against eighty black students arrested during a demonstration in February, 1975, at the Columbia High School in Decatur. Judge Jones did not specify his reasons for dismissing the charges. Assistant School Superintendent Joe Renfroe, who had brought charges against the blacks, said he was "shocked" by the judge's ruling, contending that the demonstrating blacks had disrupted the instructional and academic process at Columbia. Defense Attorney Roger Mills praised the judge's decision, calling it "amazing." The blacks were originally charged with juvenile delinquency by violation of public disturbance statutes during a series of protests aimed at what they called the "racist administration" of DeKalb County schools. (See also entry dated January 16-February 22, 1975.)

April 8. One of the last remaining barriers in professional sports fell as Lee Elder, a black golfer, began competition in the famed Masters Tournament at Augusta, Georgia. Elder was invited to participate in the prestigious Masters after winning the Monsanto Open in 1974. The black golfer was officially welcomed to Georgia by the state's governor, George Busbee. Elder was later disqualified in the preliminary rounds of the tournament.

April 9. The Georgia Supreme Court upheld the murder conviction and death sentence of Marcus Wayne Chenault for the slaying of Mrs. Martin Luther King, Sr., and Deacon Edward Boykin at the Ebenezer Baptist Church in Atlanta on June 30, 1974. Chenault was convicted by a Fulton County Court jury on September 12, 1974 (see entry above). Like the jury that convicted him, the State Supreme Court rejected Chenault's plea of insanity.

April 12. Josephine Baker, one of the most popular American singers in France for the past fifty years, died in Paris at age sixty-nine.

Baker began dancing and singing as a small child. She left her hometown of St. Louis, Missouri at age fifteen with a dance troupe and began regular performances at the Music Hall and the Plantation Club in Harlem. After Broadway rejected her as being "too ugly," she went to Paris, where in 1925 she became an instant success in the all-black "Blackbird Revue" at the Champs-Elysees theater. In the 1920s and 1930s, Baker also starred in the Folies-Bergere and the Casino de Paris. She became a French citizen in 1937. During the Second World War, Baker won the Croix de guerre and Resistance Medal for her dangerous assignments with French intelligence units.

Baker announced numerous retirements but kept coming out of them in order to raise money for the orphan home which she set up in the French countryside for children of all races and nationalities. Two days before her death, she celebrated the 50th anniversary of her first appearance in Paris with a gala performance of *Josephine*. Princess Grace of Monaco was one of the celebrities in the audience. French President Valéry Giscard d'Estaing sent a congratulatory telegram. During this performance, Baker said, "I have two loves, Paris and my own country." She collapsed two days later prior to going onstage. Baker once said "the day I no longer go on stage will be the day I die."

April 14. Preliminary legal motions were presented in the Beaufort County, North Carolina Superior Court in the celebrated murder case of Joann Little, a twenty-year-old black woman charged with murder after a Beaufort County Jail guard, Clarence Alligood, was found dead in her cell on August 27, 1974. Little pleaded self-defense on the grounds that the seminude Alligood had attempted to rape her. In the preliminary legal skirmishes, Little's attorneys, Jerry Paul and Karen Galloway, sought a change of venue and a delay of the trial. They argued that racist feelings and pretrial publicity had made it impossible for Little to get a fair trial in Beaufort County.

The Little case became a cause célèbre when civil rights groups and feminist organizations rallied to the young black woman's defense, claiming that the case typified the abuses which the Southern criminal justice system has long heaped upon blacks and women. By early April, thousands of dollars had been raised in behalf of the defense effort. Also, Representative Shirley Chisholm from New York had asked U.S. Attorney General Edward Levy to intervene in the case on Little's behalf. Rep. Chisholm said: "There are very few black people of either sex called to serve on juries in these eastern North Carolina counties. So this can really hurt Joann, who lives in a region where many, many Caucasian people hold the worst sort of prejudices against black women."

April 15. The Georgia Institute of Technology (Georgia Tech) announced that it had hired the first black assistant football coach in its history. Bill McCullough of Atlanta, a graduate of Fort Valley State College and Georgia State University, resigned from his position as Education Program Coordinator with the Georgia Department of Public Safety to accept the position at Tech.

April 23. Thirteen people, including self-avowed Communist and Black Panther Party leader Ron Carter, were arrested during a demonstration outside the office of Georgia State Labor Commissioner Sam Caldwell. The protest centered on demands for an extension of unemployment benefits, a minimum $75 per week payment, and reduction of "red tape" in connection with unemployment aids. The arrests came after the demonstrators refused to clear the halls outside of Caldwell's office. Labor Department officials had told the protesters that they could picket on the sidewalk outside the building.

April 23. Racial fighting erupted at the Boca Raton High School in Boca Raton, Florida. Three students and a police officer were injured. Two white students were arrested on charges of disorderly conduct. Police said the melee began about seven a.m. when several buses carrying black students from Delray Beach arrived at the school. The blacks discovered a racial slur on the wall, became incensed, and the fight was on. The school, located in a resort area for millionaires, was first desegregated in 1971. At the time of the racial incident, it had 225 black and 1,050 white students.

May 1. A new ten-cent commemorative stamp honoring the African-American poet Paul Laurence Dunbar went on sale. Dunbar, the son of ex-slaves, was born June 27, 1872 in Dayton, Ohio, and the first-day issue of the stamp was sold there.

Dunbar, best known for his humorous poems in black dialect, published several volumes of verse, three novels, and five collections of short stories. He died in 1906.

Coincidental with the issuance of the Dunbar stamp, the United States Postal Service opened a special exhibit called "Black Americans on U. S. Postage Stamps" at the Museum of African Art in Washington, D. C. At the conclusion of the special showing in Washington, the exhibit toured various post offices throughout the nation.

June 5. Attorneys for Joann Little, accused of murdering a North Carolina jail guard, announced that they were filing a $1 million damage suit against the estate of the man whom Little accused of attempting to rape her in a Beaufort County jail, where she stabbed him to death. The suit claims that the deceased guard, Clarence Alligood, acting under the color of North Carolina law, inflicted cruel and unusual punishment on Little and invaded her privacy in the alleged sexual attack. Little was being held in the Beaufort County Jail on a charge of breaking and entering at the time of the alleged assault. The suit, sponsored by the Southern Poverty Law Center in Montgomery, Alabama, also asked the Federal District Court in New Bern, North Carolina to protect all female inmates from sexual abuse by male attendants at the Beaufort County Jail. The class action portion of the suit claims that women prisoners are largely supervised by males who can see them as they bathe, undress, or use restroom facilities; that women inmates "are confined in such a manner that male trustees, jailers, and other male persons given free run of the jail expose their genitalia . . . and make vulgar and obscene remarks and gestures against the will and beyond the control" of the female inmates; that bail bondsmen are allowed access to the women's cells to conduct bonding business and at times have "made lewd and vulgar sexual propositions" to the female prisoners; and that prior to the slaying of Alligood, the women inmates were under 24-hour surveillance by closed-circuit television cameras which anyone in the jailer's office could watch. Although the cameras were removed after Alligood's death, they could be reinstalled. Little's suit was filed as she awaited trial for the murder of Alligood. (See also entry dated April 14, 1975.)

June 6. News reports of FBI spying on black individuals and organizations appeared in the *Atlanta Constitution*. According to the newspaper, the FBI had spied on the Afro-American Patrolmen's League since its founding in Chicago in 1968. The report quoted the Patrolmen's League founder, Renault Robinson, as saying that the FBI shared its information with Army intelligence units and with the intelligence division of the Chicago Police Department. The Afro-American's Patrolmen's League was organized to voice the particular racial grievances of black police officers in the United States. (See also entries dated January 2, 1975 and March 28, 1975.)

June 10. Harvard University announced that it had negotiated an agreement under which 20 percent of the university's $228 million in group life insurance was to be insured by the North Carolina Mutual Life Insurance Company and the Atlanta Life Insurance Company, the two largest black-owned insurance companies in the nation. The total amount involved in the deals was approximately $45 million, with one half going to each company. A spokesman for Harvard, Walter J. Leonard, said "the agreement is a mutually beneficial one. . . . Our joint venture will not only enhance North Carolina Mutual Life Insurance Company's and the Atlanta Life Insurance Company's images as growing and strong companies, but it will, simultaneously, radiate Harvard's concern for the development and growth of stable and strong black business enterprises."

June 12. Judge Dan M. Russell of the United States District Court in Jackson, Mississippi declared a mistrial in the tax evasion trial of Fayette, Mississippi mayor Charles Evers after an Internal Revenue Service (IRS) agent suggested from the witness stand that Evers might have "pocketed" campaign contributions. The questionable remarks were made by IRS agent William Jack Sykes when asked about possible sources of taxable income which Evers allegedly failed to report. Sykes said, "Well, he did run for Congress." Defense attorney Michael Fawer objected to the agent's remarks on the ground that the government's attorneys had agreed not to bring up the 1968 campaign as a source of more than $161,000 in taxable income that Evers allegedly concealed between 1968 and 1970. Although he declared a mistrial, Judge Russell refused to agree to a defense motion to dismiss the indictment against Evers.

June 14. The United States Department of Justice announced in Washington that it had asked a federal court in Mississippi to order that state to adopt a new reapportionment plan for its legislature that would meet federal standards prior to the 1975 elections. The Justice Department asked the court specifically to prohibit the use of a reapportionment plan drawn up by the Mississippi legislature during its 1975 session and to forbid the implementation of any plan that is not cleared in advance as having met federal standards. The Voting Rights Act of 1965 requires that such advanced clearance be obtained either from the U.S. Attorney-General or the U.S. District Court in Washington, and that any political change in an affected Southern state must meet the test of whether it would have the intent or effect of diminishing the voting rights of minorities.

June 22. In an interview on the second anniversary of his electoral victory in Los Angeles, California, Mayor Tom Bradley said that race was not a factor in his administration. Excerpts from Bradley's statements follows:

"I don't think that race is a significant factor in my administration. In part this is because I have tried to serve all the people of the city in the best way I know how. We've tried to bring in the advice of all segments of the city: the business community, homeowner groups, and just grassroots citizens. That kind of openess has created the atmosphere of acceptability that has made possible the view of my service without regard to color. I have not run across a single incident of bigotry. In fact, the usual expression I hear is: "Well, I didn't vote for you, but I think you're doing an excellent job and commend you and I'd like to help."

Bradley's remarks were in response to a question from Paul Finch of the Associated Press. (See also entry dated May 29, 1973.)

July 3-August 25. On July 3, attorneys for the NAACP, the NAACP Legal Defense and Educational Fund (LDEF), and the Center for National Policy Review (CNPR) filed a suit in the United States District Court in Washington, D. C. to compel the federal government to require Northern and Western states to end school segregation or to face the termination of their school aid, as had been done in the South. The suit was filed on behalf of the children of eighteen families in eight Northern and Western school districts and as a class action representing the interests of minority children in thirty-three states outside of the South. The suit charged that Secretary of Health, Education, and Welfare (HEW) Caspar W. Weinberger had not performed his legal obligation to be certain that no federally funded school system segregated students and teachers by race or national origin. The complaint also charged that HEW had failed to act even when evidence came to its attention suggesting segregation, and that protest proceedings tended to drag on indefinitely. The suit asked that HEW make findings of noncompliance, seek voluntary compliance on a prompt basis, and then cut off federal aid if all else failed.

On August 13, 1975, officials at HEW responded to the suit by calling for a meeting in Cleveland, Ohio, to plan stepped-up enforcement of school desegregation in Northern districts.

July 24-28. On July 24, the United States Senate voted 77 to 12 to extend the Voting Rights Act of 1965 for an additional seven years. On July 28, the U. S. House of Representatives voted 346 to 56 to approve the same measure.

The act of 1965 allowed federal registrars and the Department of Justice to assist thousands of blacks to register and vote in the South. The new law was even supported by a few Southern Senators and scores of Representatives from the region. Some of the Southerners had failed earlier in an attempt to extend the coverage of the law from the South to the entire nation.

July 30. United States District Court Judge James F. Gordon ordered the full desegregation of the Louisville, Kentucky public schools. The judge's order called for the busing of 22,600 pupils to achieve the desegregation. Judge

Gordon's ruling climaxed four years of litigation by civil rights groups. The order affected a city-county system of 140,000 pupils, including about 20,000 blacks. Judge Gordon said that all of the Louisville-Jefferson County schools were to be desegregated and each should have a black enrollment of at least 12 percent. No school could be more than 40 percent black. Gordon also warned those "who would resort to public disorder and violence" to oppose the desegregation to "think twice."

August 6-15. Racial violence continued in Boston, Massachusetts, the scene of sporadic incidents ever since busing to achieve school desegregation was ordered in the city in 1974. On August 6, racial fighting erupted at the Charles Street Jail and 150 police officers were called in to put down the disturbance involving seventy-five to one hundred inmates. Martin Whitkin of the Sheriff's Office said the trouble apparently started in the lunchroom with a fight between a white man and several blacks, then escalated into a full-scale brawl throughout the jail.

On August 10, black and white swimmers threw rocks and bricks at one another on South Boston's Carson Beach. About 500 blacks were at the beach in the predominantly-white section of the city in response to a request by black leaders who urged them to "reassert the rights of all Boston residents to use all public facilities." There were no reports of injuries.

On August 13, police patrols were increased in the predominantly black Roxbury section of the city after young blacks had made sporadic attacks on passing whites for three days.

On August 15, three people were slightly injured during incidents of stone throwing in the city. A sixteen-year-old black youth was arrested during the melee in the Roxbury section. Meanwhile, Massachusetts' black U. S. Senator Edward Brooke, joined local leaders in an attempt to ease racial tensions. Brooke said, "I think the polarization in the community is unfortunate, but it seems to be building."

August 8. Julian "Cannonball" Adderley, a "prophet of contemporary jazz," died in Gary, Indiana. Adderley was born in Tampa, Florida, in 1928, the son of a jazz cornetist. Known primarily as an alto saxophonist, Adderley also played tenor sax, trumpet, clarinet, and flute. He studied brass and reed instruments in a Tallahassee, Florida, high school from 1944 until 1948 and formed his first jazz group there with the school's band director as advisor. Because of his hearty appetite, fellow students nicknamed him "Cannibal," which later became "Cannonball." From 1948 until 1956, Adderley was music director at the Dillard High School in Fort Lauderdale, Florida. At the same time, he directed his own jazz group in southern Florida. He served for three years as a member of the 36th Army Dance Band and later studied at the Naval School of Music in Washington, D. C. Adderley's first big break came in New

York in 1955 when he appeared with Oscar Pettiford. The next year he signed his first recording contract with EmArcy Records. Adderley later recorded for Capitol Records and other companies, and became famous for such albums as *Black Messiah*, *Country Preacher*, *Fiddler on the Roof*, *Walk Tall*, and *Quiet Nights*. His last album was *Phoenix*. Until 1957, Adderley toured with his brother, Nat, a cornetist. In 1957, he joined the Miles Davis group. After a tour with George Shearing, he formed his own quintet, including his brother Nat, in 1959. Charles Suber, publisher of *Down Beat* magazine, which named Adderley New Alto Star of the Year in 1959, described the "Cannonball" as "a helluva musician. . . . He was one of the best alto players in recent years." During his eulogy of Adderley before 2,000 mourners in Tallahassee, Florida, the Reverend Jesse Jackson, director of People United to Save Humanity (PUSH), said the "Cannonball" had "his greatness and his fame, but he did not use it, abuse it, or lose it. He expanded it. . . . When he blew his saxophone you felt a little ease in the troubled world and the savage beast had to hold his peace."

August 10. Emory O. Jackson, editor of the *Birmingham World*, was laid to rest in Birmingham, Alabama. Jackson was born on September 8, 1908, in Buena Vista, Georgia. He moved with his parents to Birmingham in 1919. He graduated from Morehouse College in 1932, after which he taught school in Dothan and Jefferson counties, Alabama. After serving in World War II, Jackson became managing editor of the *Birmingham World*—a position he held from 1943 until his death. Jackson was one of the founders of the Alabama Conference of NAACP Branches and was a leader of several other political and civil rights organizations. In his eulogy of Jackson, the Reverend Samuel Pettagrue of the Sardis Baptist Church of Birmingham proclaimed that "the presses in heaven have stopped. A new edition was on the street and its headline read: 'The paper's top foreign correspondent, Emory O. Jackson, after serving 67 years away has returned home to serve out his assignment eternally.'" In another eulogy, Benjamin E. Mays, president of the Atlanta, Georgia, Board of Education and president-emeritus of Morehouse College, said the late editor was "born a free man. He walked like one; talked like one and looked like one."

August 15. A jury of six whites and six blacks in Raleigh, North Carolina acquitted Joann Little, a twenty-one-year-old black woman, of the August 27, 1974 murder of white guard Clarence Alligood. The murder case became a *cause célèbre* for feminist and civil rights groups after Little claimed she stabbed Alligood while defending herself against a sexual attack. (See also entries dated April 14, 1975 and June 5, 1975.)

August 16. United States District Court Judge Robert DeMascio rejected the busing of students to achieve school desegregation in Detroit, Michigan. He ordered the Detroit Board of Education to seek an alternate plan to better balance the races in the schools. C. L. Golightly, president of the city's school board, called the judge's decision "a victory for the school children of Detroit."

Lawrence Washington of the Detroit branch of the NAACP expressed disappointment, commenting, "We're right back where we started five years ago."

September 1. Lieutenant General Daniel "Chappie" James, Jr. became the first African-American to be promoted to the rank of four star general in the U.S. Armed Forces. The Pentagon announced that James, a veteran of nearly 200 combat missions in Korea and Vietnam, was also appointed chief of the North American Air Defense Command (NORAD).

James, age fifty-five, was born in Pensacola, Florida and graduated from Tuskegee Institute. He was one of the original black pilots in the U. S. Army Air Corps, predecessor to the present-day Air Force. He achieved a great deal of notoriety for his speeches on Americanism and patriotism. With the appointment of James, there were now twenty-one black generals and admirals in the Army, Air Force, and Navy out of a total of about 1,200 in the U. S. Armed Services.

November 19. James B. Adams, associate deputy director of the FBI, told the United States Senate's Intelligence Committee that there was no legal justification for the twenty-five separate attempts by the Bureau in the 1960s to discredit the late Dr. Martin Luther King, Jr., as a civil rights leader. The FBI, he continued, was led to investigate King because of the possibility that Communist influences were being brought to bear on him and the Civil Rights Movement. No such evidence, however, was ever uncovered. During its spying on King, the FBI installed a total of sixteen electronic bugs and eight wiretaps in an attempt to collect damaging evidence against the civil rights leader and even sent his wife an anonymous letter and tape recording which King reportedly interpreted as a suggestion for suicide. (See also entries dated May 29-June 3, 1978, and November 17, 1978.)

November 19. Former Black Panther Party leader Eldridge Cleaver arrived in California in federal custody to face charges of attempted murder. Cleaver, age forty, was to be charged in connection with a shootout with Oakland police on April 6, 1968, in which Panther Bobby Hutton, age seventeen, was killed and a police officer was wounded. Cleaver had earlier ended his seven years of exile abroad to have his "day in court." After having lived in Cuba, Guinea, Algeria, North Korea, and France, Cleaver said his voluntary return was prompted by his belief that the United States "had changed" to the extent that he could now receive a fair trial. Cleaver's *Soul on Ice*, revealing intimate details of his life in the ghetto and imprisonment, had become a minor classic in revolutionary literature. (See also entry dated September 13, 1970.)

November 21. John Calhoun, age thirty-eight, a former Foreign Service Officer and deputy special assistant to President Gerald R. Ford, was appointed special assistant to the President for Minority Affairs. Calhoun succeeded

Stanley Scott, another black man, who resigned. Calhoun, at the time of his new appointment, had been a member of the White House staff since 1973.

1976

January 20. The U. S. House of Representatives voted by voice vote to authorize an appropriation of $25,000 for the creation of a bust of the late Martin Luther King, Jr., and to install it in the Capitol. King will be the first black person ever so honored, if the bill is passed by the U.S. Senate. The House measure noted King's contribution to the civil rights movement and his winning of the Nobel Peace Prize. The House's Administration Committee had said that the tribute was appropriate "because of Dr. King's prominence in American history and because of all the black Americans who have done so much to contribute to this country's greatness, [yet] not one is now honored among the 681 works of art in the Capitol."

January 21-May 31. Racial violence erupted in Boston, Massachusetts, amid protests by whites against court-ordered school desegregation.

On January 21, black and white students at Hyde Park High School fought with fists and chairs. Across the city in East Boston, approximately three hundred whites tried to block a major Boston Harbor tunnel during the morning rush hour. Five people, including a Boston police officer and the mother of a student, received minor injuries at Hyde Park. Seventeen people were arrested in the two incidents.

On February 15, about two thousand people fought the police near South Boston High School, "the focus of opposition to federal court ordered desegregation." Between forty and fifty police officers were injured in the mob attack. There "was no estimate of the number of civilians injured." Thirteen people, three of them juveniles, were arrested. Boston Police Commissioner Robert J. Di Grazia called the twenty-minute melee (during a so-called "Father's March") "an obvious conspiracy" by "an element of hoodlums."

On May 30, a fire was set next to the replica of the *Beaver*, a two-masted sailing ship, which was moored at a bridge which leads into South Boston. Although the ship was unharmed, $75,000 worth of damage was done to an adjoining gift shop and ticket office. The Fire Department said the blaze was "of suspicious origin." The next day United States Attorney General Edward H. Levi announced that the Department of Justice would not intervene in an appeal of the Boston desegregation orders to the Supreme Court. Some whites had urged the administration of President Gerald Ford to side with them in their anti-busing stance before the high court, while civil rights leaders had urged the federal government to stay out of the Boston desegregation controversy.

At the time of this violence and controversy, Boston was in the second year of a school desegregation program ordered by U.S. District Court Judge W. Arthur Garrity. The program had been periodically marred by fighting in schools as well as scattered attacks on blacks in white neighborhoods and of whites in black sections of the historic city. (See also entries dated September 12-October 31, 1974, and January 8, 1975.)

January 23. Paul Robeson, athlete, actor, singer, and civil rights activist, died in Philadelphia, Pennsylvania at age seventy-seven.

Robeson was born on April 9, 1898 in Princeton, New Jersey, to William, a minister, and Maria Louisa Bustill Robeson. William Robeson was a former slave from North Carolina who worked his way through Lincoln University in Pennsylvania. In 1915, young Paul entered Rutgers University after earning an academic scholarship in a statewide competition. When he joined the football team, where he became an all-American, Robeson was once nearly mangled on the playing field by white bigots. The scholar-athlete graduated with Phi Beta Kappa honors in 1919.

Robeson scorned his father's wishes that he follow him into the ministry, but after a brief career in law, he grudgingly accepted his wife Eslanda's urgings to use his rich baritone voice in singing and acting. She helped persuade her husband to accept a role in *Simon the Cyrenian* at the Harlem YMCA in 1920. "Even then," Robeson later recalled, "I never meant to [become an actor]. I just said yes to get her to quit pestering me."

The Harlem performance, however, did launch the remarkable stage career of Robeson. In 1922, he made his first Broadway appearance as Jim in *Taboo*. He also made his debut in London in the same year in *Taboo*, which was retitled *The Voodoo*.

Upon his return to New York in late 1922, Robeson joined the Provincetown Players, a Greenwich Village group that included dramatist Eugene O'Neill, and took the role of Jim Harris in O'Neill's *All God's Chillun Got Wings*. This led to another successful appearance as Brutus Jones in *The Emperor Jones*, another play by O'Neill which had been especially revived for Robeson.

The Provincetown Players also sponsored Robeson's first major concert in 1925, which consisted of a collection of spirituals. Between 1925 and 1928, he had a triumphant performance in *The Emperor Jones* and a heralded portrayal of Joe in *Show Boat*, in which he sang "Ol' Man River," both in London, England, as well as in an appearance as Crown in George Gershwin's *Porgy and Bess* on Broadway.

Between 1928 and 1939, Robeson lived mostly abroad, particularly in London, where he found fewer color barriers than in the United States. One of his most spectacular successes in London occurred in 1930 when he played the lead in Shakespeare's *Othello*. To many, the *New York Times* stated, Robeson's performance was "an unforgettable experience." Following these latest triumphs, Robeson toured the major cities of Europe both as a recitalist and an actor.

Robeson's political consciousness was first jolted in 1928 when writer George Bernard Shaw asked him what he thought of socialism. Robeson later recalled, "I hadn't anything to say. I'd never really thought about Socialism." In 1934, Robeson visited the Soviet Union where he was warmly received. He was also impressed "by the absence of racial prejudice among Soviet citizens" (in Germany, Robeson was subjected to racial slurs by a Nazi soldier). Later, Robeson began to publicly express a belief "in the principles of scientific Socialism" and his "deep conviction that for all mankind a Socialist society represents an advance to a higher stage of life."

In the late 1930s, Robeson sang for the Republican troops and for members of the International Brigades who were fighting the fascist dictator Francisco Franco in Spain. That experience led him to see "the connection between the problems of all oppressed people and the necessity of the artist to participate fully" in the struggle for human rights. It also convinced him to return to the United States to continue his work.

On October 19, 1943, Robeson became the first black actor to play the title role of *Othello* (with a white supporting cast, including Jose Ferrer and Uta Hagen) before a Broadway audience. The next year, the NAACP bestowed upon him its highest award, the Spingarn Medal.

Meanwhile, Robeson increased his political activity. He led a delegation to national baseball commissioner Kenesaw Mountain Landis which urged him to remove "the racial bias" in baseball. Robeson called on President Harry S. Truman to extend civil rights to blacks in the South. He was also a co-founder and chairman of the Progressive party, which nominated former Vice President Henry A. Wallace for President in 1948. Then, at a World Peace Conference in Paris in 1949, Robeson declared, "It is unthinkable that American Negroes will go to war on behalf of those who have oppressed us for generations against a country [the Soviet Union] which in one generation has raised our people to the full dignity of mankind." Although Robeson later asserted that this statement had been taken "slightly out of context," adding that he had really spoken for 2,000 students "from the colonial world" who had requested him to express their desire for peace, his words stirred widespread opposition in the United States. In August, 1949, veterans' groups and "right wing extremists" attacked crowds who were arriving for one of his concerts in Peekskill, New York. Subsequently, professional concert halls were closed to him and commercial bookings "grew scarce." Robeson's income reportedly dropped from $100,000 in 1947 to $6,000 in 1952.

Beginning in 1948, Robeson was called before Congressional committees on several occasions in which he was usually asked if he was a member of the Communist party. He always refused to answer, invoking his Fifth Amendment rights. The *New York Times,* however, reported that Robeson maintained "privately . . . that he was not a member." Nevertheless, in 1950 the United States State Department cancelled his passport on "the ground that he had refused to sign the then-required non-Communist oath" for travelling abroad. Robeson had contended that "the Government had no right to base his freedom of travel on his political beliefs or a lack of them." He sued the State Department over the issue, and in 1958, the United States Supreme Court, in a related case, ruled that Congress "had not authorized the department to withhold passports because of applicants' 'beliefs and association[s]'."

Once Robeson received his passport, he departed immediately for Great Britain, declaring, "I don't want any overtones of suggestion that I am deserting the country of my birth. If I have a concert in New York, I will go there and return to London." He did return permanently to the United States in 1963, where he lived quietly, first in a Harlem apartment and then with his sister, Marian Forsythe, in Philadelphia, Pennsylvania.

Despite his difficulties with Congress, the State Department, and many American organizations and individuals, Robeson became a hero to much of black America and to countless numbers of other peoples throughout the world. On his sixtieth birthday in 1958, he was given a thunderous ovation by a sold-out house at Carnegie Hall in New York City. It was his first New York recital in eleven years, and on the same day, birthday celebrations were held in many nations abroad, including India. There Prime Minister Jawaharlal Nehru called Robeson "one of the greatest artists of our generation [who] reminds us that art and human dignity are above differences of race, nationality, and color." In 1973, on his seventy-fifth birthday, another tribute in his honor was held at Carnegie Hall. Although the ailing actor-singer could not attend, he sent a recorded message to the crowd, which included many theatrical personalities.

Upon the occasion of Robeson's death, the official Soviet news agency Tass commented: "The persistent struggle for black civil rights and for stronger world peace won him recognition not only in the United States but also outside of it."

January 27. The National Urban League (NUL), in its annual "The State of Black America" Report, contended that "many of the gains blacks made over the past decade were either wiped out or badly eroded in 1975 and the portents for the future are not encouraging." The League warned that "the absence of overt discontent in the cities" did not mean that the problems did not continue to exist and that the future of the nation is "bound-up in how it deals with these problems."

As examples of how blacks lost ground in 1975, the NUL cited the following:

1. There was a further decline in middle-income black families, continuing a trend from 1973-74 that saw these families decrease from one-fourth to one-fifth of the total population for all black families.

2. The average black family income was only fifty-eight percent of that of average white family income, representing a decline from sixty-one percent in 1969.

3. The black unemployment rate remained virtually unchanged at 14.1 percent for the first three quarters of 1975.

4. In 1975, Congress failed to enact any substantial legislation that would "foster full employment."

5. The outbreaks of racial violence in Boston, Massachusetts, a city "long regarded, if incorrectly as the fountainhead of liberalism in this country, served notice that racism has no geographical limits and continues to exist in the American body politic."

In concluding the review, Vernon Jordan, executive director of the NUL, commented that "all across the board, black people lost out in 1975."

In order to alleviate the distress among blacks which the League cited, it recommended "a full employment policy that assures decent jobs for all; an income maintenance system that alleviates economic hardship and replaces the present welfare system; and housing, health, and education programs that go beyond rhetoric to bring our nation closer to a prosperity that includes all of its citizens."

January 28. Vivian W. Henderson, president of Clark College in Georgia, died during heart surgery in Atlanta, at age fifty-two.

Henderson, a native of Bristol, Virginia, was born on February 10, 1923. He received a bachelor's degree from North Carolina College in Durham (later North Carolina Central University), and M.A. and Ph.D. degrees in economics from the University of Iowa. In 1948, Henderson began his teaching career in Texas at Prairie View A and M College, but returned to his alma mater, North Carolina College, the following year as a professor of economics. In 1952, Henderson moved to a similar position at Fisk University in Tennessee where he eventually became chairman of the Department of Economics. Henderson was named president of Clark College in 1965.

In addition to his roles as a teacher and an administrator, Henderson achieved distinction as one of the nation's most foremost African-American scholars in economics. He was the author of *The Economic Status of Negroes* (1963), co-author of *The Advancing South: Manpower Prospects and Problems* (1959), and contributing author of *Principles of Economics* (1959). He also contributed to *Race, Regions and Jobs,* edited by Arthur Ross and Herbert Hill in 1967. His work, according to the *Atlanta Journal,* "is considered to have had an important impact in convincing industry and business of the buying power of the black American community."

Outside the academic world, Henderson was a member of the boards of directors of the Atlanta Community Chest (later the United Way), the Atlanta chapter of the American Civil Liberties Union, the Atlanta Urban League, the Ford Foundation, the National Sharecroppers Fund, the Institute for Services to Education, the Martin Luther King, Jr. Center for Non-Violent Social Change, and the Voter Education Project (VEP), among others. He was also chairman of the board of the Southern Regional Council (SRC) and chairman of the Georgia advisory committee of the U. S. Commission on Civil Rights (CCR).

Henderson's governmental activities included serving as a member of the advisory committee of the Atlanta Charter Commission, co-chairman for education of the Georgia Goals Commission, advisor to former President Lyndon Johnson, and member of the Manpower Advisory Committee of the U. S. Department of Labor.

Former Atlanta mayor Ivan Allen, Jr., called Henderson's death "a great loss to the city. . . . He left a vital and lasting impact. . . ." Atlanta mayor Maynard H. Jackson added that the educator was a man "never too busy to accept the call to service."

January 30. John L. LeFlore, black legislator and civil rights activist, died of an apparent heart attack in Mobile, Alabama. He was serving his first term as a member of the Alabama house of representatives.

Prior to being elected to the legislature, LeFlore had spent thirty-eight years as a civil rights activist, much of it as executive secretary of the Mobile Branch of the NAACP. He helped lead the successful challenge to Alabama's Democratic White Primary in 1944. LeFlore was also a member of the Alabama Advisory Council to the United States Civil Rights Commission.

January 31. A plan that involved a limited amount of busing to achieve school desegregation was initiated in the Detroit, Michigan, school system—the nation's fifth largest. The implementation of the desegregation plan climaxed a court battle that began in 1970. The NAACP filed suit against the Detroit system in 1970 after the Michigan legislature overruled the city's first desegregation plan. In 1972, a federal district court ordered the integration of the primarily black schools of Detroit with those of surrounding, predominantly white suburbs. But in an important decision in July, 1974, the United States Supreme Court struck down the provision relating to suburbs and ordered the district court to draw up a plan relating to Detroit only.

The Detroit plan, which was ordered by U.S. District Court Judge Robert De Mascio, permitted a total of 21,800 pupils in kindergarten through the eighth grade to be bused. Another 4,700 were transferred to schools within walking distance. In addition, 1,500 ninth and tenth graders were transferred to other schools, but they had to provide their own transportation.

In sum, approximately 160 schools exchanged pupils in order to achieve enrollments of about half black and half white. The city's remaining 140 schools remained all black.

The NAACP opposed the Detroit plan on the grounds that it did not go far enough, but urged compliance with the court order.

February 5-26. Racial violence erupted in Pensacola, Florida, over the issue of whether athletic teams at a local high school would be called "Rebels" or "Raiders."

On February 5, 1,500 people rioted at the Escambia High School. Four white students were wounded by gunfire, six others were also injured, and at least nine people were arrested. One of these was a twenty-three-year-old black man who was suspected in the shootings. Subsequently, crosses were burned on the lawns of school board members, a bullet was fired through the window of a black school board member, and the homes of a human relations council member and a state legislator were burned by arsonists. Blacks began a boycott of the school.

On February 9, one hundred of the six hundred blacks enrolled in Escambia High School attended classes, but they were met with taunts from whites. Nearly one thousand white students also remained out of class "apparently in anticipation of violence." The school had a total enrollment of 2,523 students. The only incident of the day, however, was the arrest of a fifteen-year-old white youth who was brandishing a foot-long chain "equipped with a bolt-type grip."

On February 21, the home of Teresa Hunt, a member of the Pensacola-Escambia Human Relations Commission and the county school board Citizens Advisory Committee, was set afire with diesel fuel. Four nights later, the home of State Representative R. W. Peaden, a block away from Hunt's residence, was destroyed when a flammable liquid was poured on its floors and ignited. Both Hunt and Peaden had been involved in the controversy over the school name.

The Escambia Chapter of the Southern Christian Leadership Conference

(SCLC) continued to urge black parents to keep their children away from the school, warning that they would be unsafe there. The chapter's president, F. L. Henderson, remarked, "We'd rather see a child held back in school than see them in the morgue." He asked Florida Governor Reuben Askew to provide "as much protection as within his power" for black students.

The controversy over the school's nickname first arose in 1973 when black students, who had been attending the school since 1969, protested both the name and the flying of the Confederate flag at athletic events and other functions. They said both symbols were a direct insult to them. After several protests, some of which were accompanied by violence, a U.S. District Court, on July 24, 1973, permanently enjoined the use of the rebel name, the flag, "and related symbols on the grounds that they were 'racially irritating'." Students then chose the name "Raiders" to represent the school. But after an appeal by a group of white students and school board members, a U.S. Court of Appeals overturned the injunction and returned the matter to the school board "to make its own decision on the name." On February 4, 1976, an election was scheduled at Escambia High to allow students to choose between "Raiders" and "Rebels". The riot erupted the next day.

March 20. Rubin "Hurricane" Carter and John Artis were released from prison in New Jersey after serving nine years for murder. Carter, a former middleweight boxer, and Artis, his "casual friend," had been convicted in 1967 for allegedly participating in the fatal shootings of three people in a Patterson, New Jersey tavern on June 17, 1966. The shootings occurred at a time of heightened racial tensions in the city and the two black men were convicted largely on the testimony of two ex-convicts who claimed "they had seen the defendants at the murder scene with guns." But the defendants maintained their innocence and many blacks believed they were being prosecuted and persecuted because of their race.

In September, 1974, the *New York Times* reported that Alfred Bello and Arthur Bradley, the former convicts, had recanted their testimony and claimed that "they had been pressured to lie" by Passaic County (of which Patterson is the county seat) detectives.

On March 17, the Supreme Court of New Jersey unanimously reversed the convictions of Carter and Artis because "evidence beneficial to the defense had been withheld" at the original trial. This evidence "included secret promises by detectives" to Bello and Bradley "that they would be aided in unrelated criminal cases if they testified for the prosecution."

On March 20, pending new trials, Carter was released on $20,000 bail and Artis was set free on $15,000 bail. Some of the bail money was provided by heavyweight boxing champion Muhammad Ali, a supporter of the campaign by the Carter-Artis Defense Committee to win a new trial for the men.

April 3. Samuel DuBois Cook, former professor of political science at Duke University in North Carolina, was inaugurated as the sixth president of Dillard University, a historic black institution located in New Orleans, Louisiana.

Cook, a native of Griffin, Georgia, received a bachelor's degree from Morehouse College and master's and doctorate degrees from Ohio State University. He had previously taught political science at the Atlanta and Southern Universities, the University of Illinois, and the University of California at Los Angeles.

At Duke University, Cook won an Outstanding Professor Award. He also received a Citation of Achievement from Duke University, a honorary Doctor of Laws degree from his alma mater, Morehouse College, and was a member of Phi Beta Kappa.

June 16. The Reverend Richard Allen Chapelle of Jacksonville, Florida, was elected general conference secretary of the African Methodist Episcopal (A.M.E.) Church during the Fortieth Quadrennial General Conference of the Church in Atlanta, Georgia. Chapelle succeeded the Reverend Russell S. Brown of Chicago who at seventy-eight was at the age of retirement. More than 30,000 participants, representing more than one million members of the denomination from eighteen districts in the United States, Africa, Central America, and the Caribbean attended the meeting.

June 25. The United States Supreme Court voted 7-2 to prohibit private schools from excluding blacks on the basis of their race. The private school case stemmed from a suit filed by the parents of two black children who were turned away from the Fairfax-Brewster School and Bobbe's Private School, both in the Virginia suburbs of Washington, D.C. The two schools had denied that they discriminated and said they had not had previous black applicants. They contended, however, that they had a right to discriminate if they so chose.

The Council for American Private Education, which represents about 90 percent of the nation's private school enrollment, and the Department of Justice supported the black children in their suit, but the Southern Independent Schools Association, which represents 395 schools, and President Gerald R. Ford opposed judicial relief for the blacks. President Ford did say that he personally disapproved of discrimination against blacks by such schools. According to the Court, racial discrimination by private schools was a "classic violation" of the Civil Rights Act of 1866 which prohibited, among other things, discrimination in the enforcement of contracts. The Court continued: "It may be assumed that parents have a First Amendment right to send their children to educational institutions that promote the belief that racial segregation is desirable, and that the children have an equal right to attend such institutions. . . . But it does not follow that the practice of excluding racial minorities from such institutions is also protected by the same principle."

In reacting to the ruling, Andrew Lipscombe, an attorney for the Fairfax-Brewster, Virginia schools, said: "Parents are not going to be able to have the associations for their children that they wish, even in private situations which in small, private schools are intimate."

The Court's majority opinion was written by Justice Potter Stewart. In their dissents, Justices Byron R. White and William H. Rehnquist said the Act of 1866 prohibited only discrimination imposed by state law; hence the majority had gone too far in outlawing bias in the private schools.

June 25. The United States Supreme Court ruled unanimously that victims of so-called reverse discrimination have the same rights as blacks to sue in federal courts if they have been terminated from their jobs. The high Court said that the Civil Rights Act of 1964 was "not limited to discrimination against members of any particular race."

The Court ruled in a case from Houston, Texas, where two white employees of the Santa Fe Trail Transportation Company had been fired because they allegedly misappropriated ten cases of antifreeze. A black employee who was also charged in the incident was not terminated. The whites charged that their employer had discriminated against them on the basis of race and that their labor union had acquiesced in the bias by failing to represent one of them properly. The Supreme Court agreed with the petitioners and returned the matter to a lower court. (See also entries dated July 3, 1978, July 2, 1986, June 12, 1984, January 23, 1989, June 5, 1989, and January 12, 1989.)

July 15. Jimmy Carter, former governor of Georgia, accepted the Democratic nomination for president of the United States at the close of his party's national convention in New York City. The convention ended with the singing of the anthem of the Civil Rights Movement, "We Shall Overcome," and a benediction by Martin Luther King, Sr., father of slain civil rights leader Martin Luther King, Jr., and one of Carter's strongest supporters during the presidential primary campaigns.

July 26. The United States Court of Appeals for the Sixth Circuit ruled that each of the 68 public schools of Dayton, Ohio, "must reflect roughly the same black-white population as the entire state school system." The order would require a black-white student population in each school that "reflects within 15 percent" the racial composition of each school district. The Dayton Board of Education said it would appeal the ruling to the United States Supreme Court.

August 28. Haile Selassie, former emperor of Ethiopia and also known as "King of Kings," "The Conquering Lion of Judah," and "Elect of God," died of prostrate gland problems in Addis Ababa, Ethiopia, at the age of eighty-three.

Selassie had been a hero for many African-Americans since 1936 when he made an impassioned plea and took a firm stance for Ethiopian self-determination before the League of Nations following the invasion of his country by fascist Italy. Selassie last visited the United States in 1969 and laid a wreath on the grave of slain civil rights leader Martin Luther King, Jr. Five years later, the emperor was deposed in a military coup after ruling the African nation (one of human civilization's oldest countries) for fifty-seven years. Selassie was "the world's longest serving monarch."

September 10. Mordecai Wyatt Johnson, former president of historically black Howard University, died in Washington, D.C., at age eighty-six.

Johnson was born on January 12, 1890, the son of a Baptist minister. He received undergraduate degrees from both Atlanta Baptist College (now Morehouse College) in 1911 and the University of Chicago in 1913, a Bachelor of Divinity degree from Rochester (New York) Theological Seminary in 1920, and a Master of Sacred Theology degree from Howard University in 1932.

After serving nine years as pastor of the First Baptist Church of Charleston, West Virginia, Johnson assumed the presidency of Howard University in 1926 and held the position until 1960. Under his leadership Howard grew from a mostly black school to an international university in its student body, faculty, and scope of its academic programs. During this period, the student population increased by 250 percent, seventeen new buildings were constructed, and the annual budget increased from $700,000 to $6 million.

Johnson also gained a reputation as a champion of human rights and a spellbinding orator. After addressing the North Atlantic Treaty Organization (NATO) in June, 1959, the French newspaper *Le monde* reported that the "650 delegates heard the most courageous exposé that one might be able to hear at such a meeting," and the *New York Post* remarked that "many were moved (by the address), some with annoyance, but at its end, the applause lasted for five minutes."

In commenting on Johnson's death, the current president of Howard University, James Cheek, said that "love and dedication to Howard University will long be remembered by thousands of persons whose lives he touched throughout the world."

September 19. William "Bill" Lucas, a former baseball player for the Milwaukee and Atlanta Braves of the National Baseball League, was named director of player personnel by the Atlanta Braves club. The position is the highest ever held by an African-American in professional baseball.

After leaving the playing field in 1964, Lucas joined the Braves' executive staff in sales and promotions. The following year he worked in public relations, and then, in 1962, was named assistant farm director and director of player development.

Of his new appointment, Lucas said that it held no special meaning. Wayne Embry, also an African-American, held a similar position for the Milwaukee Bucks of the National Basketball League. Another prominent black baseball figure, Hank Aaron, also formerly of the Atlanta Braves, led a campaign to get more blacks into "front office" jobs in baseball and other professional sports.

September 20. Matthew Simpson Davage, former president of Clark College in Georgia, died in New Orleans, Louisiana, at age ninety-seven.

Davage was born in 1879 in Shreveport, Louisiana. He earned a B.A. degree from New Orleans University (now Dillard University) in 1900 and immediately joined the faculty there as an instructor in mathematics. He remained on the faculty until 1905 and, at the same time, pursued graduate studies at the University of Chicago.

Between 1905 and 1915, Davage was business manager of the *Southwestern Christian Advocate*, a Methodist publication. In 1915, he returned to education as president of the George R. Smith College at Sedalia, Missouri. After only one year at Sedalia, he assumed the presidency of the Haven Institute at Meridian, Mississippi, which he quickly left to assume the presidency of Samuel Huston College (now Huston-Tillotson College) in Austin, Texas. In the spring of 1920, Davage was elected president of Rust College in Holly Springs, Mississippi, where he became the first black to head the fifty-four-year-old historically black institution. In 1924, he became the sixteenth president of Clark University, as it was then called. Davage was the second black person to head the institution, the first having been his predecessor, William Henry Crogman.

During his seventeen-year tenure at Clark, Davage presided over the removal of the institution from southeast Atlanta to its present location near the city's other black institutions of higher education, and he helped to provide new financial strength and vitality for the school, even during the Depression years.

In 1939, Davage became one of the first blacks to speak before the all-white Atlanta Rotary Club. Because of the Jim Crow laws and customs of the time, he could not eat lunch with the Rotarians and had to wait in an adjoining room until the meal was finished. Then he gave a speech entitled "The Negro's Place in Atlanta's Life." In it, he said, "Some day we may hope, the thinking people of both races will translate that mutual respect and trust into some concrete work. . . . They may meet and work on the same critics trying to say they are seeking to tear down a social order."

September 28. Muhammad Ali won a hard-fought bout to retain his world heavyweight championship title in New York City. 42,000 people paid a total of 3.5 million dollars (a record for a title fight at that time) to see Ali defeat challenger Ken Norton in a unanimous fifteen-round decision. Ali employed his usual wiggling style, known as the "rope-a-dope," while Norton was only able to land several solid blows with both hands. The previous largest gate in a heavyweight title fight was 2.6 million when Gene Tunney fought Jack Dempsey in Chicago in 1927.

October 4. President Gerald R. Ford accepted the resignation of Secretary of Agriculture Earl L. Butz, who had made uncomplimentary remarks about African-Americans. The President said it was "one of the saddest decisions" of his presidency.

Butz, in a private conversation following the Republican National Convention in August, 1976, had accused blacks of laziness and shiftlessness. The "off-color" remarks were traced to the secretary in September, 1976.

African-American civil rights leaders and Democratic presidential candidate Jimmy Carter, among others, had roundly criticized Butz for his racial slurs and Ford for not immediately firing him.

October 25. Clarence "Willie" Norris, "the last of 'the Scottsboro Boys'," was pardoned for a 1931 rape conviction. The order was signed in Montgomery, Alabama by Governor George C. Wallace.

Norris, age sixty-four, was among eight black men convicted of raping two white women near Scottsboro, Alabama, and sentenced to death in 1931. The original conviction was later overturned by the U.S. Supreme Court, and a subsequent guilty verdict was set aside after one of the alleged victims recanted her previous testimony. Although the eight were also convicted at a third trial, all but Norris, who escaped while on parole in 1946, had already been pardoned.

The NAACP, along with the Communist Party and other organizations, had waged celebrated protests as well as legal actions on behalf of "the Scottsboro Boys" over the years, and announced after the pardon that it was interpreting it "as a total absolution for Norris. . . . [He] has been absolved of any wrongdoing. We will interpret this as applying to the others." All of the other "Scottsboro Boys" were, however, presumed to be dead at the time of Norris's release. (See also entry dated April 6, 1931.)

November 15. The congregation of all-white Plains Baptist Church in Plains, Georgia, voted 120-66 to admit black worshippers as members. The church's racially exclusionary policy had been under attack since October, 1976, when Clennon King, a fifty-six-year-old black minister from Albany, Georgia, announced that he would seek to join the congregation. The Plains

Baptist Church had at various time included among its membership President-elect Jimmy Carter, his wife, Rosalyn, and his mother, Lillian. After the motion to admit blacks was approved, Carter remarked that he was "proud of my church, God's church."

December 8. The United States Supreme Court, in a 7-2 decision, ruled against "a sweeping desegregation plan" for the city of Austin, Texas. The Court sent the case back to the U. S. Court of Appeals for the Fifth District to review "in light of" its decision last June that "government acts are not unconstitutional simply because "they have [a] disproportionate effect on blacks."

The Court also contended that "school desegregation plans should be tailored to correct only the amount of segregation caused intentionally by school officials." They argued that the courts cannot impose "sweeping orders" designed to correct all school segregation which may result "from racial and ethnic housing patterns." The dissenting Justices, William J. Brennan and Thurgood Marshall, believed the appellate court had "decided the case correctly."

December 16. President-elect Jimmy Carter announced the nomination of Georgia Congressman Andrew Jackson Young as U.S. Ambassador to the United Nations. The nomination marked the first time an African-American had ever been asked to lead the American delegation at the world peace organization. The position also carries cabinet-level status in the United States government.

Young, the first black congressman from Georgia since 1871, was serving his second term in Washington at the time of the nomination. (See also entry dated January 30, 1977, for further information about Young.)

December 23. President-elect Jimmy Carter completed the nominations for his Cabinet. The cabinet nominees included two blacks, Georgia Congressman Andrew Young as U. S. Ambassador to the United Nations, and Washington, D. C. attorney Patricia Roberts Harris as Secretary of Housing and Urban Development (HUD).

1977

January 17. Shirley Creenard Steele, a black attorney, was appointed Assistant Attorney General for the state of Iowa. Steele, a native of Salisbury, North Carolina, graduated from Livingstone College in North Carolina in 1974 and received a Doctor of Jurisprudence degree from the Drake University School of Law in Iowa.

In her new position, Steele will be responsible for representing the state in civil rights legislation and criminal appeals. She is the first black woman ever to serve in such a position in Iowa's history.

January 19. Clifford Alexander, Jr., a forty-three-year-old black attorney, was named Secretary of the Army by President-elect Jimmy Carter.

Alexander, who served one year as a private in the Army during 1958 and 1959, was Chairman of the Equal Employment Opportunities Commission (EEOC) under President Richard M. Nixon, but resigned in the middle of a five-year term because of policy disagreements with the Republican administration. He had also served as an assistant district attorney in New York City and a White House aide under Presidents John F. Kennedy and Richard Nixon.

Alexander practiced law in Washington, D.C. for more than six years and ran an unsuccessful mayoral campaign in that city in 1975. Alexander's appointment marked the first time in United States history that a black American had served as Secretary of the Army.

January 20. Jimmy Carter, former governor of Georgia, took the oath of office of the President of the United States at the Capitol in Washington, D.C. A black woman from his native state was overheard in the crowd murmuring, "Yes, Lord!" Black voters had supported Carter overwhelmingly in his campaign for the nation's highest executive office.

January 26. The United States Supreme Court, in a 6-3 decision, returned a plan involving the busing of black students to surrounding predominantly white school districts in Indianapolis, Indiana, to a lower federal court for reexamination. The effect of the high court's ruling was to nullify the busing plan to achieve further desegregation which the lower court had already ordered.

January 27. U. S. Attorney General Griffin Bell selected Drew Days, a thirty-six-year-old black lawyer, to be assistant attorney general in charge of civil rights in the U. S. Department of Justice.

Days, a Florida native, graduated from the Yale University Law School in 1966. In 1970, he took a position as an attorney with the NAACP Legal Defense Fund (LDF), which handles legal matters for the parent organization. The appointment made Days the first black person ever to oversee civil rights enforcement and also the first black assistant attorney general in American history.

January 30. Andrew Jackson Young, an African-American congressman from Georgia, took the oath of office as United States Ambassador to the United Nations (UN), the highest diplomatic post ever held by a black

American. The appointment also carried cabinet rank in the administration of President Jimmy Carter.

Young was born in New Orleans, Louisiana on March 12, 1932, the son of a dentist and a school teacher. He received a bachelor's degree from Howard University in 1951 and a Bachelor of Divinity degree at the Hartford Theological Seminary in Connecticut in 1951. Young was then ordained a minister in the United Church of Christ. His early pastorates were in Marion, Alabama, and Thomasville and Beachton, Georgia. After a brief period of service at the National Council of Churches, Young joined the staff of the Southern Christian Leadership Conference (SCLC).

In 1964, Martin Luther King, Jr. named Young executive director of the SCLC, and in 1967 he became its executive vice president. In these roles, Young was one of the principal negotiators "with recalcitrant white leaders" who were just "beginning to understand the moral and political power of nonviolent protest."

Young entered national politics in 1970 when he ran unsuccessfully for Congress from Georgia's Fifth District. Two years later, the majority white district in the Atlanta area had undergone reapportionment. Young was then elected as the first black Georgia congressman since the Reconstruction era. Although whites retained a slight voting edge in his district, Young was returned to Congress in 1974 and 1976.

In commenting on the appointment of Young, President Carter said the congressman "did not want or ask for this job. It was only with the greatest reluctance on his part that he finally agreed to accept [it] for me and for our country." Young himself remarked: "Through many dangers, toils and snares we have already come, the faith that brought us safe thus far will lead us safely on."

February 3. The "Roots" miniseries, based on Alex Haley's novel of the same title in which he traced his ancestry to Africa and slavery, ended eight nights of presentations on the ABC television network. The Sunday night finale achieved the highest single ratings ever amassed by a television production. The previous top television presentation had been the epic Civil War drama, *Gone with the Wind*. During the eight nights of programming, "Roots" was watched by more than 130 million viewers.

February 17. The Department of Health, Education, and Welfare (HEW) announced that it was cutting off funds to the public schools of Chicago, Illinois because of alleged violations of civil rights laws. The alleged violations included an "inadequate bilingual program and too many black teachers in schools with overwhelming black student populations." The order was to become final within twenty days unless the school district appealed or made "appropriate changes to comply with the law." It was estimated that $100 million of the district's annual budget of $600 million came from the federal government.

HEW Secretary Joseph A. Califano, Jr., in his first formal statement on civil rights, stated: "We have no desire ever to cut off funds to any school district or other educational institutions. But the way to insure compliance with civil rights laws is to make clear that we will order funds cut off if we must."

March 2. Joseph E. Lowery, chairman of the board of the Southern Christian Leadership Conference (SCLC), was named acting president of the civil rights organization. He succeeded the Reverend Ralph David Abernathy, who resigned to run for a congressional seat in Georgia's Fifth District. Lowery was appointed to serve until the SCLC Convention in August, when he or some other person would be confirmed as permanent president.

March 3. Lester Kendel Jackson, minister and civil rights leader, died in Chicago, Illinois.

Jackson, the son of tenant farmers, was born in Fort Gaines, Georgia, in 1895. He earned a Bachelor of Divinity degree at the Virginia Theological Seminary and a Doctor of Divinity from Union Theological Seminary in New York. Jackson pastored Baptist churches in Hollins, Lynchburg, and Danville, Virginia; Passaic and Long Branch, New Jersey, and Gary, Indiana. At the time of his death, he was the pastor of the St. Paul Baptist Church in Gary. All totaled, he spent fifty-five years of life in the Christian ministry.

Jackson also served as executive secretary of the Hunter Branch YMCA in Lynchburg, Va., Professor of Religious Education, Educational Secretary and General Manager, and trustee of Virginia Theological Seminary. In addition, he was a member of the Board of Directors of the National Council of Churches in the United States.

Jackson was a leader of civil rights protests in both Long Branch, New Jersey and Gary, Indiana. His activities in Long Branch resulted in a court decision which permitted blacks to bathe on local beaches and his work in Gary led to the hiring of hundreds of blacks by banks, savings and loan associations, and public utilities companies.

In September, 1973, more than 250 people, including the Rev. Martin Luther King, Sr., father of slain civil rights leader Martin Luther King, Jr., attended a tribute for Jackson in Gary. Jackson called that occasion the "most joyful moment" in his life.

March 9. A group of armed Black Muslims took hostages at three sites in Washington, D.C.; one man was slain. The attacks occurred at the offices of the Jewish organization B'nai B'rith, an Islamic center, and the Washington city hall. At city hall, Maurice Williams, a twenty-two-year-old radio reporter, was killed and at least eleven others were wounded. Washington's Mayor Walter Washington barricaded himself inside his office.

The gunmen demanded that the premiere of the film *Mohammad, Messenger of God* be cancelled because they said it "ridiculed the Prophet." United Artists immediately cancelled showings of the film in New York City. Another gunman, however, said the attacks were a reprisal for the slaying in Washington four years ago of seven Hanafi Muslims. The Hanafis were allegedly killed by members of a rival Muslim sect.

March 14. The United States Senate adopted a resolution praising Alex Haley, the author of *Roots*, for "his exceptional achievement." The unanimous resolution, sponsored by Senator John Glenn from Ohio, said the historical novel and its television adaptation had "contributed to the cause of a better racial understanding in the United States."

March 15. B.L. Perry, Jr. resigned as president of Florida A and M University, one of the nation's largest historically-black institutions of higher education. Perry, who left because of personal reasons, was an alumnus of Florida A and M. Before departing, he told faculty and students that the university "must remain as an institution, changed of course by the social and

Alex Haley (right), displays the historical marker designating his boyhood home. At left is Samba M. B. Fye, Director of Tourism (North America), for the Gambia.

legal evolutions it institutionalized, as a force for providing higher education to a discernible segment of the population, and providing hope and inspiration to thousands who look upon it as a model for pursuing pluralistic ideals in a multi-ethnic, multi-cultural, and multi-racial society." Perry had been president of Florida A and M since 1968.

March 31-April 18. On March 31, Rust College, a black school in Holly Springs, Mississippi, was closed and all of its 800 students were ordered off campus following a demonstration and fire on campus. The fire, of unknown origins, caused an estimated $500,000 damage to the college's administration building.

Students blamed the school's president W.A. McMillan for the disturbance. Some said that he exercised "strict discipline," had failed to communicate with them, had alienated them and "forced them to action." George Dupont, a sophomore student, called the president "a stubborn dictator, deceitful, unreaching. We want him out. . . . He runs this place like a penal institution."

The damaged building, a replica of Independence Hall in Philadelphia, was constructed on the small, church-related liberal arts campus in 1947.

On April 18, Rust College reopened to students and faculty. In a statement, W.A. McMillan, who had been asked by twenty of his faculty members to resign, stated: "I am disappointed, but not discouraged. Rust has a heritage that a disruption or a fire cannot destroy. We will heal our wounds and get to the business of making Christian higher education better than ever at Rust College."

April 2. U.S. District Court Judge John Pratt ruled in Washington, D.C., that the Department of Health, Education, and Welfare (HEW) had violated civil rights laws by failing to order "adequate racial desegregation" in the higher educational institutions of six Southern states. The judge ordered HEW to solicit new desegregation plans from Florida, Georgia, North Carolina, Arkansas, Oklahoma, and Virginia, but he warned that the plans "must preserve the status of their historically black colleges."

Under Pratt's order, HEW was given ninety days to set guidelines for which the states must comply. The states would then have sixty days to submit detailed plans on the "best way to balance the proportion of black and white students in schools that receive federal aid." HEW would then have an additional 120 days to accept or reject the states' plans.

In 1972, Pratt had found Louisiana, Maryland, Mississippi, and Pennsylvania, in addition to the aforementioned slates, guilty of violating the Civil Rights Act of 1964. They were not included in the most recent order, however, because they were involved in civil rights suits elsewhere. (See also entries dated June 21, 1974 and September 6, 1977.)

April 14. William H. Hastie, the first black person appointed to a United States Court of Appeals, died after collapsing on a golf course in Philadelphia, Pennsylvania, at the age of seventy-one.

Hastie, the son of a federal clerk, was born in Knoxsville, Tennessee. He graduated *magna cum laude* from Amherst College in 1925 and taught junior high school in New York before enrolling in Harvard Law School. He was admitted to the bar in 1930.

Between 1939 and 1946, Hastie was dean of the law school of Howard University. While at Howard, President Franklin D. Roosevelt asked him to join his "Black Cabinet" (a group of African-American advisors) as a civilian aide to Secretary of War Henry Stinson. In 1943 Hastie resigned from the War Department in protest against what he called the "reactionary policies and discriminatory practices" of the Air Force. At that time, he said "the simple fact is that the air command does not want Negro pilots flying in and out of various fields, eating, sleeping, and mingling with other personnel. . . ." These and other actions led some persons to regard him "as one of the pioneers in the civil rights movement in the United States."

After leaving the War Department, Hastie further served the federal government as the first black on the District Court of the Virgin Islands and later governor of the United States possession from 1946 to 1949. In 1949, President Harry S. Truman elevated Hastie to a position of justice of the United States Court of Appeals for the Third Circuit. He retired from that court as chief judge in 1971 but retained the position of senior judge until his death.

Upon learning of Justice Hastie's death, the U. S. Supreme Court's Chief Justice Warren Burger called it "a great loss to the judiciary and to the country." (See also entries dated March 26, 1937, May 1, 1946, and October 15, 1949, for further information about Hastie.)

May 5. About 150 students continued their demands calling for the resignation of Prince Jackson, Jr. as president of predominantly black Savannah State College in Georgia. The students' grievances included decreased alumni financial support because of "several scandals involving college staff members," alleged diversion of scholarship monies to other purposes, and alleged illegal diversion of student government association funds to "pay a deficit in the athletic program." President Jackson did not make an immediate public response to the students' allegations.

Savannah State was one of several historically black colleges that experienced student protests recently over questionable internal practices.

May 16. Muhammad Ali retained his world heavyweight boxing championship with a unanimous decision over twenty-two year old Alfredo Evangelista after fifteen rounds in Landover, Maryland. Evangelista, a native of Uruguay who had been heralded as "the Spanish Rocky," never caught Ali with a solid punch during the entire fight. He fought a mostly defensive contest. Ali received $2.75 million for the victory, $200,000 of which had been used to buy tickets for disadvantaged youths to attend the fight.

It was the ninth time in his second reign as champion that Ali had defended his title. He had been beaten only twice, by Joe Frazier and Ken Norton in 56 career bouts.

May 19. A three-day statewide festival honoring Alex Haley, the Pulitzer Prize winning author of the novel *Roots*, began in Henning, Tennessee, the author's hometown. Haley said that he was inspired by his grandmother's tales of his family's struggles in slavery and freedom. By the spring of 1977, *Roots* had sold more than 1.6 million copies in the first six months after publication and was translated into 22 foreign languages.

June 1. The oldest known identified photographs of African slaves in the United States were published in the June issue of *American Heritage Magazine*. The photographs were discovered eighteen months previously in an otherwise empty cabinet in an attic of the Peabody Museum at Harvard University by Elinor Reichlin. The daguerreotypes, were taken in Columbia, South Carolina in 1850 "for scientific study," by J.T. Zealy, whom Reichlin traced as a photographer in Columbia until 1880.

Professor Stephen Williams, director of the Peabody Museum, asserted that the photographs were "the oldest examples of rare pictures of American slaves born in Africa." At least four of the seven subjects shown in several poses were identified on the prints by first name, African nation or tribe of origin, and by slave owner. Among them was a man named Alfred, identified as a Foulah, a West African tribe, and owned by an I. Lomas of Columbia, South Carolina, and Jack and Renty from Guinea and the Congo, respectively, owned by a B.F. Taylor, also of Columbia. Nude photos of African women were not released by the Peabody Museum.

August 1. Elias Blake, Jr., forty-seven-year-old president of the Institute for Services to Education (ISE), became the new president of Clark College in Atlanta, Georgia. Blake succeeded Vivian W. Henderson, who died during heart surgery on January 28, 1976.

Blake, a native Georgian, received Bachelor and Master's degrees from Paine College in Augusta, Georgia in 1951 and Howard University in 1954, respectively, and a doctorate from the University of Illinois in 1960. He came to Clark

College from the Institute for Services to Education in Washington, D.C., where he was a consultant to governmental and private educational agencies.

August 1. Ethel Waters, African-American singer and actress, died of apparent heart failure in Chatsworth, California at age seventy-six.

Waters was born on October 31, 1900 in Chester, Pennsylvania. She first appeared on stage at age seventeen and later toured with jazz groups where she became "a leading theater and cafe personality." But after a religious conversion, Waters gave up singing in nightclubs and turned to spirituals.

After her talents were more widely recognized, Waters made her Broadway debut in *Plantation Revue of 1924*. In this production, she scored one of the greatest song hits ever when she introduced the piece "Dinah." From Broadway she began making motion pictures and was cast in *As Thousands Cheer, At Home Abroad*, and *Rhapsody in Black*. In 1950, Waters was nominated for an Academy Award for her role in *Pinky*. Her last motion picture was *The Sound and the Fury* in 1958. By this time, however, Waters began appearing on such television programs as "The Tennessee Ernie Ford Show," "Daniel Boone," and "Route 66."

In her later life, Waters turned increasingly to singing, becoming noted particularly for blues renditions of "Am I Blue" and "Stormy Weather" as well as Negro spirituals. She was, according to an article in the *Atlanta Constitution*, "the first woman ever to sing 'St. Louis Blues'" and thrilled millions around the world with her rendition of "His Eye Is on the Sparrow" with the Billy Graham Evangelical Crusade. She had been singing with the Crusade for fifteen years at the time her death. Waters's autobiography, also entitled *His Eye Is on the Sparrow*, was published in 1951 and became a best seller.

In the 1960s, stricken with diabetes and heart problems, it was revealed that Waters had lost much of her wealth and was subsisting on Social Security. She admitted her financial difficulties but said "if half the people that owed me money paid it back, I'd be a rich woman." Yet she refused to make television commercials in order to earn more money. Instead, she exclaimed "I couldn't be happier because I'm at peace with the Lord."

In an editorial published after Waters's death, the *Atlanta Constitution* commented that "few American entertainment figures have had careers as varied and memorable as Ethel Waters."

August 1. Joseph N. Gayles, Jr., program director of the Medical Education program at Morehouse College, assumed the presidency of Talladega College in Alabama. Gayles succeeded Herman Long, who died in office in 1976.

Gayles, a *Summa Cum Laude* graduate of Louisiana's Dillard University, received a Ph.D. degree in chemical physics from Brown University in Rhode Island. He was previously a professor of chemistry at Morehouse College.

September 1. Cleveland L. Dennard, president of the Washington Technical Institute in Washington, D.C. assumed the presidency of historically black Atlanta University in Georgia.

Dennard, a native of Sebring, Florida, was educated at Florida A and M University, the University of Colorado, and the University of Tennessee, from which he earned a Ed.D. degree. Prior to becoming president of the Washington Technical Institute in 1967 he had been principal of the George Washington Carver Vocational School in Atlanta (1960-1965), and Deputy Commissioner for Manpower and Program Management in the New York City Human Resource Administration (1965-1967). Dennard had also lectured in sixteen foreign countries under the auspices of the United States Information Agency (USIA).

September 5-7. On September 5, Kenneth Wilson, a seventeen-year-old white youth wearing a Nazi armband, shot into a crowd of about 200 blacks attending a Labor Day church picnic in Charlotte, North Carolina before killing himself. One black man, Roosevelt Davis, aged twenty-nine, was killed in the attack. On September 7, a second victim, Jo Ann Terry, a twenty-eight-old widow, died of wounds received two days earlier. Two other black victims survived the assault.

September 6. Governor Mills E. Godwin announced that the state of Virginia would not comply with "federal racial quotas" ordered by the Department of Health, Education, and Welfare (HEW) to desegregate its colleges and universities. In a letter to HEW, Governor Godwin stated: "All our accomplishments to date signal one thing—Virginia's intention to provide access, for all of its citizens regardless of race, to higher education which is as diverse and as excellent as it can possibly be." But he said the state would not surrender its "administrative responsibilities to the federal government."

Alabama, Florida, Georgia, North Carolina, Oklahoma, and Virginia were under orders to submit revised desegregation plans to HEW by the week of September 5. Louisiana had previously refused to submit any plan to HEW and Mississippi had submitted an unacceptable one. Both states were still in federal courts for their actions.

Virginia, which did not fully comply with the HEW desegregation guidelines, faced the possible loss of an estimated $40 million in federal funds. (See also entries dated June 21, 1974, and April 2, 1977.)

September 8. A study by scholars at the Case Western University in Cleveland, Ohio confirmed that homicide was "the leading cause of death nationally among black men aged 25-34." Although the research team focused their study on Cleveland, they also used a federal government report entitled "Homicide Trends in the United States," to draw nationwide conclusions. In Cleveland, however, between 1958 and 1962 20 blacks died of homicide for every white, and from 1963 to 1974, 12 blacks for every white. Nationwide, in 1975, 1,913 blacks between the ages of 24 to 34 died of accidental causes; 3,256 from disease; 439 from suicide; and 2,506 from homicide. The study was published in the September, 1977 issue of the *New England Journal of Medicine*. (See also entry dated March 15, 1989.)

September 9. Claire Ford, an eighteen-year-old student at Memphis State University, was crowned "Miss Black America" for 1977 in Santa Monica, California. Mary Denise Bentley, "Miss Indiana," was the first runner-up.

Ford, who entered the pageant as "Miss Tennessee," won $10,000 in prize money, an acting role in the television mini-series "Roots: The Next Generation," and screen tests at both NBC and Universal Studios. Ford later revealed that she wanted to become a lawyer.

September 11. The epic television mini-series "Roots," based on Alex Haley's novel about his family in Africa and America, swept the Nineteenth Annual Emmy Award presentations in Los Angeles, California. Among the top Emmys awarded were: Outstanding Lead Actor for a Single Appearance in a Drama or Comedy Series: Lou Gossett, Jr., who portrayed the smooth survivor "Fiddler;" Outstanding Writing in a Drama Series: Ernest Kinoy and William Blinn; Outstanding Directing in a Drama Series: David Greene; and Outstanding Single Performance by a Supporting Actor and Actress in a Drama or Comedy Series: Edward Asner and Olivia Cole, respectively. The drama also garnered the Outstanding Limited Series award.

"Roots," the most successful mini-series in television history, was broadcast over eight nights on the ABC television network in January and February, 1977.

October 3. Ten members of the United States House of Representatives signed a resolution calling for the impeachment of Andrew J. Young, the first African-American Ambassador to the United Nations (UN). Most of the charges stemmed from public statements made by Young before and since his appointment to this position. The document cited twenty actions by Young that warranted his impeachment, including his depiction of Great Britain and Sweden as racist nations. The resolution also accused Young of failing to oppose the admission of Vietnam to the United Nations and of "seeking to transfer the governing power in the anti-communist nation of Rhodesia to the pro-Marxist guerilla coalition."

October 18. Reggie Jackson, African-American outfielder for the New York

Yankees of the American Baseball League, hit three home runs in a single World Series game, the first time in history that such a feat had been accomplished. The Yankees went on to defeat the Los Angeles Dodgers of the National Baseball League 8-4 and to capture the 1977 World Series title.

Dodgers manager Tom "Tommy" Lasorda called Jackson's achievement "the greatest performance that I've ever seen in a World Series." Jackson himself commented, "It's a nice feeling, but I'm beat. I know there's a God in heaven."

October 29. Muhammad Ali retained the World Heavyweight Boxing Championship with a unanimous decision in fifteen rounds, over challenger Earnie Shavers. The pattern of the fight was "one of Shavers stalking and looking to throw the big right hand that had enabled him to knock out 52 of his first 60 opponents, while Ali looked for ways to nullify the challenger's power." Ali, using "jabs, hooks and flurries of punches with both hands to the head," was the most successful. At the end of the New York City fight, Shavers cried, "They robbed me! They robbed me!"

November 13. The Associated Press reported that since taking office in January, 1977, President Jimmy Carter had appointed four blacks as United States Attorneys (chief prosecutors). They were: G. William Hunter of San Francisco, California, Hubert H. Bryant of Tulsa, Oklahoma, James R. Burgess, Jr. of East St. Louis, Illinois, and Henry M. Michaux of Greensboro, North Carolina. During the administrations of Presidents Richard M. Nixon and Gerald R. Ford, there was only one black U.S. Attorney, Frederick Coleman in Cleveland, Ohio.

November 18. Robert Edward Chambliss, a seventy-three-year-old former Ku Klux Klansman, was convicted of first degree murder in the 1963 dynamite bombing of the Sixteenth Baptist Church in Birmingham, Alabama. The blast killed four young black girls who were attending Sunday School. Chambliss was convicted specifically for the death of eleven-year-old Carol Denise McNair. He was immediately sentenced to a term of life imprisonment.

November 30. The *Atlanta Constitution* reported increased enrollments in many of the nation's historically-black colleges and universities. The ten black colleges with the largest enrollments in 1977 were: 1.) Howard University, Washington, D.C. (9,752); 2.) Texas Southern University, Houston (9,552); 3.) Southern University, Baton Rouge (9,002); 4.) Jackson State University, Mississippi (7,844); 5.) Norfolk State College, Virginia (7,263); 6.) Morgan State College, Baltimore (6,424); 7.) Florida A and M, Tallahassee (5,837); 8.) North Carolina A and T State University, Greensboro (5,515); 9.) Tennessee State University, Nashville (5,348); 10.) Prairie View A and M University, Texas (5,146).

December 10. Barbara Jordan, African-American Congresswoman from

Texas, announced that she would not seek reelection. She denied rumors of poor health and said she would not seek a seat on the federal bench. She did say "the longer you stay in Congress, the harder it is to leave. . . . I didn't want to wake up one fine sunny morning and say there is nothing else to do."

Jordan had gone to Congress from Houston's Eighteenth District in 1972 after serving in the Texas State Senate, where she became president pro tempore (the first African-American to preside over that body). During the impeachment hearings for President Richard Nixon in 1974, Jordan caught the attention of the nation with an eloquent condemnation of the President's involvement in the Watergate burglary scandal and an equally eloquent defense of the Constitution of the United States. At the 1976 Democratic National Convention held in New York City, she "electrified what had previously been a dull gathering, speaking with a precise, clipped delivery."

1978

January 13. Hubert Horatio Humphrey, who served as Senator from Minnesota, Vice President of the United States under Lyndon Johnson, and a key leader in the fight for passage of civil rights legislation in the 1960s, died of cancer in Waverly, Minnesota, at age sixty-one.

Commenting on Humphrey's death, African-American civil rights activist John Lewis said "In this century, we lost two great Americans. . . . One was Dr. Martin Luther King, Jr., the other was Hubert Humphrey, who was the champion for the rights of all people. His life should be an inspiration to us all." (See also entry dated June 22, 1974.)

January 15. Walter Payton, African-American running back for the Chicago Bears, was named the National Football League's Most Valuable Player for 1977. Payton received 57 of 87 votes cast by sportswriters and broadcasters, three from each league city. Quarterbacks Bob Griese of the Miami Dolphins and Craig Morton of the Denver Broncos were the runner ups with ten votes each.

Payton, a graduate of Jackson State University in Mississippi, led the League in rushing with 1,852 yards during the 1977 season, his third year in the NFL (a League record). He ran for 275 yards in one game (November 20 against the Minnesota Vikings), which surpasses the record set by African-American O.J. Simpson. Payton also exceeded Simpson's record of 332 carries with 339 of his own. Finally, Payton's 1,852 yards rushing was third only to Simpson's 2,003 and the African-American Jim Brown's 1,863 during a season.

January 17. In its third "State of Black America" report, the National Urban League (NUL) stated that 1977 was "a year of continued depression, with unacceptably high unemployment and a widening income gap" for African-Americans.

In remarks accompanying the presentation of the report, NUL director Vernon Jordan said the group was "disappointed" in President Jimmy Carter. He added, "the administration must face up to two basic realities. First— more, much more, is needed by way of federal actions to assist poor people and the cities. . . . Second, it must recognize that the priority of balancing the budget by 1981 cannot be reconciled with more pressing priorities."

February 15. Leon Spinks, a black former Marine, defeated Muhammad Ali for the heavyweight boxing championship of the world. The championship was given to Spinks, age twenty-four, after fifteen rounds on a split decision by ring officials. The thirty-six-year-old Ali bled from the mouth during most of the fight. Both men were former Olympic light heavyweight champions—Spinks in 1976 at Montreal, Canada and Ali in 1960 in Rome, Italy.

Spinks's victory represented one of the biggest upsets in "world heavyweight title history" since Ali, an 8-1 underdog himself at the time, dethroned the late Sonny Liston in 1964. It also ranked alongside Jim Braddock's upset over Max Baer in 1935, Jersey Joe Walcott's defeat of Ezzard Charles in 1951, and Ingemar Johansson's win over Floyd Patterson in 1959. Spinks received $350,000 for his victory; Ali made $3.5 million in defeat.

February 25. Daniel "Chappie" James, the only four-star black general in the U. S. Armed Forces, died of a heart attack in Colorado Springs, Colorado at age fifty-eight.

James, a graduate of Tuskegee Institute, grew up in Pensacola, Florida during a period of rigid racial segregation. His mother, Lillie A. James, who founded her own school for black youths, encouraged him to dream of higher things. James emerged from pushing a coal dolly in a Pensacola gas plant to one of the nation's most influential military leaders. Of his mother's influence, James once stated: "My mother used to say, 'Don't stand there banging on the door of opportunity, then, when someone opens it, you say, 'Wait a minute, I got to get my bags.' You be prepared with your bags of knowledge, your patriotism, your honor, and when somebody opens that door, you charge in."

James, who served in three wars with the Air Force, retired on January 26, 1978. He wrote on a portrait of himself which now hangs in the Pentagon: "I fought three wars and three more wouldn't be too many to defend my country. . . . I love America and as she has weaknesses or ills, I'll hold her hand."

February 27. The United States Supreme Court ruled that the federal government does not have to help pay the costs of court-ordered busing to achieve racially desegregated public schools. The justices rejected without comment an appeal by Kentucky Governor Julian M. Carroll, who sought permission to ask for federal help in paying for the busing of school children in Louisville and surrounding Jefferson County, Kentucky. A school desegregation plan, which was in effect in the area, required the busing of approximately 23,000 students daily.

In his appeal, Governor Carroll had said that "the drain on state and local funds [was] quite real and devastating." Thus, he challenged the constitutionality of three federal laws which prohibited federal funding of busing to achieve desegregation.

March 3. Syed Riaz Hussain Shah, a horticulturist who formerly taught at Miami-Dade Community College, pleaded guilty in federal court in Miami, Florida to "holding a person in involuntary servitude." Shah admitted that he and his wife, Isharad Majed Shah, an anesthesiologist, bought a ten-year-old African girl from her mother and employed the child "for at least two years as a house slave." During most of her enslavement, the girl, Rose Iftony, had only one dress to wear, ate rice from a tin plate, and drank from a broken glass.

Iftony was ten years old in 1974 when she arrived in the United States from Sierra Leone, where the Shahs paid her mother $200 and promised to educate her. Both of the Shahs, at the time, were registered aliens from Pakistan.

FBI agent Joseph Bell called the girl's bondage "the first classic case of slavery in this century [that] the FBI knows of. . . . That's what used to happen before the Civil War."

March 3. Cleveland Leon Dennard was inaugurated as the eighth president of historically black Atlanta University. The new president of the 112-year old institution formerly served as president of the Washington Technical Institute in the District of Columbia.

March 5. A study of death row inmates financed by the Southern Poverty Law Center showed that very few blacks and no whites received the death penalty for the killing of blacks. In the three Southern states surveyed, Florida, Georgia, and Texas, 45 percent of the death row inmates were blacks who killed whites, while only 5 percent were blacks who killed blacks. 50 percent were whites who killed whites. There were no white inmates on death row who killed blacks.

Morris Dees, director of the Poverty Law Center (based in Montgomery, Alabama), claimed that the study "proved that blacks still make up a far greater proportion of the death row population than are represented in the general population. . . . But the real clincher is that death is reserved for those who kill whites."

The death penalty study was conducted by William J. Bowers, a Northwestern University professor, who published *Executions in America* in 1974.

March 14. The National Catholic Educational Association reported that while the overall attendance in Roman Catholic parochial schools dropped in 1977, the percentage of minority students "increased sharply." The exact percentage of minority students enrolled in both Catholic elementary and secondary schools over the six year period, 1971 to 1977, increased from 10.8 percent to 16 percent. Among black students in elementary schools alone, the increase was from 5.1 to 7.6 percent. The figures were contained in the Catholic Educational Association's 1978 edition of "Catholic Schools in America."

March 15. President Jimmy Carter presented Anthony Owens, a seventeen-year-old African-American youth from Austin, Texas, with a plaque naming him "Boy of the Year." Owens won the distinction in a competition sponsored by Boys' Clubs of America.

March 17. The *Atlanta Constitution*, quoting from the *New York Times*, reported that the Central Intelligence Agency (CIA) recruited African-Americans to spy on members of the Black Panther Party in the United States and Africa in the late 1960s and early 1970s. The *Times* based its information on "sources with first-hand knowledge of the operation." The activities of the black agents included "following and photographing" suspected Black Panther Party members in the United States and infiltration of Panther groups in Africa. One agent even "managed to gain access to the personal overseas living quarters of Eldridge Cleaver, the exiled Panther leader who set up a headquarters in Algeria in the late 1960s."

The CIA had said "repeatedly that the goal of the agency's domestic spying program was to determine whether anti-war activists and black extremists were being financed and directed by Communist governments," but "one longtime operative with direct knowledge of the spying said . . . that there was an additional goal in the case of the Black Panthers living abroad: to 'neutralize' them; to try and get them in trouble with local authorities wherever they could."

The *Times* sources further revealed that the CIA conducted at least two major operations or programs involving the use of African-Americans at the time that the Black Panther Party was "attracting wide public attention" in the 1960s and 1970s. One of the programs, directed by the CIA Office of Security, was operated in the Washington, D.C. area with the code name "Merrimac." In this operation, black agents attended rallies and even funerals, "in hopes of identifying members of the Black Panther Party." In the second program, centered in North and East Africa, "carefully recruited" African-American agents who were sent to Algeria, Kenya, and Tanzania, "among other places, to keep close watch on American black radicals."

Details of the clandestine activities against the Panthers were considered among the CIA's "most sensitive and closest held information," according to the *Times* sources, "because of fears that disclosures about the program would arouse a public backlash." (See also entry dated June 30-August 8, 1971.)

March 22. Joseph A. Califano, Jr., Secretary of Health, Education, and Welfare (HEW), announced that he would withhold some federal funds for public universities in North Carolina because that state had "failed to submit an acceptable plan to eliminate the vestiges of segregation." At the same time, the HEW Secretary "initiated formal administrative action" that could result in a withdrawal of all federal funds for the sixteen universities in North Carolina, which were once legally segregated. At the time of this action, eleven of the schools were still predominantly white (91.2 percent) and five predominantly black (91.6 percent).

On February 3, 1978, HEW had rejected North Carolina's plan to desegregate its universities but accepted a proposal for its 57 community colleges. North Carolina was one of six Southern states under a federal court order to submit an acceptable plan to HEW by February 3. It was the only one of the six states which did not fully comply. (See also entries dated June 21, 1974, April 2, 1977, and September 6, 1977.)

March 24. Bill Kenny, "whose tenor voice helped make the original Ink Spots one of the world's best known singing groups in the 1940s," died of a respiratory ailment in New Westminster, British Columbia, at age sixty-three.

Kenny, together with Charles Fuqua, Orville Jones, and Ivory Watson, formed the Ink Spots in 1939. He was the last survivor of the group and continued performing almost up to his death. Kenny's most recent album was entitled *Bill Kenny Is Back*.

April 15. Horace T. Ward, the first black person to sit on the Fulton County (Georgia) Superior Court, was presented the 1978 Northwestern University Alumni Merit Award for "outstanding contributions to his profession" in Evanston, Illinois.

After receiving undergraduate and graduate degrees from Morehouse College and Atlanta University and serving a three year stint in the United States Army, Ward earned a Doctor of Jurisprudence degree from Northwestern in 1959. He enrolled at Northwestern only after having been denied admission, possibly because of his race, to the School of Law at the University of Georgia.

In 1964, Ward became one of the first blacks elected to the Georgia State Senate since Reconstruction. He was reelected to the Senate four times, ending his service there in 1974. He also served as a deputy city attorney for Atlanta

(1969-70), and assistant attorney for Fulton County (of which Atlanta is the county seat).

In 1974, Georgia Governor Jimmy Carter appointed Ward to the Civil Court of Fulton County and three years later Governor George Busbee elevated him to the Fulton Superior Court, where he became one of eleven judges of the Atlanta circuit.

Ward was an active civil rights attorney during the height of the Civil Rights Movement in Georgia. He participated in bus desegregation cases in Augusta; the Martin Luther King, Jr. case in Dekalb County; and the desegregation of the University of Georgia at Athens.

April 17. James Alan McPherson, Jr., African-American author, was awarded a Pulitzer Prize in fiction for his volume of short stories, *Elbow Room*. The book characterized "various aspects of the black experience."

McPherson, a thirty-four year old native of Savannah, Georgia, received a bachelor's degree from Morris Brown College in 1965, and an LL.B degree from the Harvard University Law School in 1968. A year later he earned a master's of fine arts degree from the University of Iowa. McPherson taught writing in the college of law at Iowa before joining the faculty at the University of California at Santa Cruz from 1969 until 1970.

The new Pulitzer Prize winner had also been a contributing editor of *Atlantic Monthly* magazine and a contributor to *Black Insights, Cutting Edges,* and *New Black Voices*. He also wrote *Hue and Cry,* a collection of short stories, and edited *Railroad: Trains and Train People in American Culture* in 1969 and 1976, respectively.

In 1970, McPherson won the National Institute of Arts and Letters literature prize, and in 1972 and 1973 he was awarded Guggenheim fellowships.

At the time of his receipt of the Pulitzer Prize, McPherson was an Associate Professor of English at the University of Virginia.

The Pulitzer Prize, considered by many "the most prestigious award that can be bestowed in the literary arts and journalism," carries a stipend of $1,000 and is administered by the trustees of Columbia University.

April 24. The Liaison Committee on Medical Education, the official accrediting agency for medical schools in the United States, announced provisional accreditation for the School of Medicine at Morehouse College in Atlanta. The decision paved the way for the opening of the first new predominantly black medical school in the United States in 100 years. The other two black medical schools are Meharry Medical College in Nashville, Tennessee and Howard University in Washington, D.C.

In September, 1978, the new medical school planned to enroll a class of twenty-four students in a two-year program. By 1983, the institution planned to begin graduating four-year medical students. Until that time, under an arrangement with four other medical schools, Emory University (also in Atlanta), the Medical College of Georgia in Augusta, and Meharry and Howard, Morehouse students would go elsewhere for their final two years of training.

Discussions about a possible medical school at Morehouse College began in the 1960s, but it was not until February, 1973, when the institution received a federal grant of almost $100,000 to study the feasibility of such a school, that "intensive efforts" got under the way.

Medical officials had consistently pointed out the "great need" for more black doctors in the United States. Of the 370,000 physicians in the United States in 1976, only 6,600 or 1.8 percent, were black.

In response to the news of provisional accreditation, Dr. Louis Sullivan, dean of the medical school, remarked: "As we look to the future, we are confident that, with continued broad support from both public and private sources, we will train those primary-care physicians needed for our undeserved rural areas and inner cities in Georgia, the Southeast and the nation."

May 9. The Martin Luther King, Jr. Center for Non-Violent Social Change announced that Kenneth D. Kaunda, president of the Republic of Zambia, would receive the annual Martin Luther King, Jr. Nonviolent Peace Prize. The announcement was made in Atlanta by Mrs. Coretta Scott King, Jr.

Kaunda led his country's transition from colonial rule under the British to self-determination in 1964 without resorting to violence. Prior to achieving independence, Zambia had been known as Northern Rhodesia. Since independence, Kaunda, who was imprisoned several times by British authorities, has been the only president to serve the country.

Mrs. King said that Kaunda was chosen for the peace prize because he exemplified her husband's "ideals in searching for peaceful and meaningful methods of bringing about social and political justice. . . . Kenneth Kaunda's leadership in preparing his people for self-government and in resisting the forces of violence and hatred is truly a model for all countries to follow."

May 29-June 3. On May 29, Joseph Lowery, president of the Southern Christian Leadership Conference (SCLC) urged the FBI to release "all the facts" in the Bureau's "attempt to discredit Dr. Martin Luther King, Jr. during the 1960s." At the same time, while refusing "to comment specifically on the alleged FBI excesses," King's widow, Coretta Scott King, said "J. Edgar Hoover's monstrous acts refuse to leave the stage. He is dead, but his despicable legacy lives on."

Lowery's comments came in response to a recent report that "a prominent black leader worked with the FBI in its undercover campaign to replace King as head of the civil rights movement." He said the new report was "another in a long line of FBI attempts to smear black leadership. . . . This is a terrible shadow to be holding over the head of black leadership. . . . I find it incredible [that] any prominent black leader would cooperate to destroy the movement." Lowery added that civil rights leaders had always "had reason to believe" that FBI informants were working within the movement.

On June 3, the *Atlanta Daily World* published an article which reported "claims that Roy Wilkins, former head of the National Association for the Advancement of Colored People (NAACP) was the black collaborator who sided with the Federal Bureau of Investigation in an attempt to discredit the late Dr. M. L. King, Jr." Lowery gave a "blistering" response to these new allegations. Excerpts from Lowery's statement follows:

"Black folks in particular and the nation in general must see through this vicious effort to shift a portion of the blame for attacks on Dr. King to the black community. . . .

We (SCLC) in no way condone nor place any credence in attempts to vilify Roy Wilkins, whose distinguished career in civil rights speaks for itself. We condemn the continued attempts of the FBI to discredit black leaders and impede the civil rights movement. . . .

The fact that Wilkins had conversation[s] with the FBI in no way indicates that he collaborated with them to discredit Dr. King and the movement. The failure of the FBI to substantiate the fantastic claim that a black leader collaborated with them is evidence that the FBI's intent is to discredit, divide, and destroy. . . .

[Referring to an FBI memo which described the so-called collaborator as 'young and ambitious,' and since the collaboration was alleged to have taken place in 1964] I hardly consider a man in his mid-60s [as Wilkins was in 1964] as 'young and ambitious.' . . .

We're all aware . . . that in the mid-60's Mr. Hoover had a fierce determination to discredit Dr. King and thereby weaken the civil rights movement by establishing the Communist influence or by any other means." (See also entry dated November 19, 1975.)

June 3. Several hundred people gathered at a hotel in Atlanta, Georgia to pay tribute to Ruby Hurley, southeastern regional director of the NAACP, on the occasion of her retirement after more than three decades of service to the nation's "oldest, largest, and most respected" civil rights organization.

Hurley, a native of Washington, D.C., joined the NAACP after heading a committee "that sought to establish singer Marian Anderson's right to sing" at Constitution Hall in the capital in 1939 (see entry dated March, 1939). Because of white opposition, the famed opera star had to perform her concert at the Lincoln Memorial instead. In 1943, Hurley joined the NAACP as National Youth Director. In her eight years as Youth Director, the NAACP's membership tripled to 92 college chapters and 178 youth councils, enrolling 25,000 members.

Following her success in the Youth Division, Hurley was sent into the Deep South to coordinate membership campaigns and reactivate dormant branches. Out of these activities, the Southeastern Regional Office, embracing the states of Alabama, Florida, Georgia, Mississippi, North Carolina, South Carolina, and Tennessee, was established. It became the largest region of the entire NAACP.

Hurley began her work in the South in 1951, the same year that a Christmas night bomb killed Harry T. Moore, the NAACP's Florida coordinator, and his wife, Harriett. Hate and violence, then, became her constant companions for the next twenty-seven years.

In an interview with the *Atlanta Constitution* on May 30, 1978, Hurley, who said she "never found time to sit down and worry about the obscene telephone calls, threats against her life, and 'never say die' pro-segregation politicians," recalled her life's work and commented on present and future trends. For example, Hurley recalled her attempts to gather information about the murder of black teenager, Emmett Till, in 1955, by posing as a field hand at several Mississippi plantations:

"I must have been crazy. Young people talk about what they would have done if they were living during those times. . . . But they wouldn't have done anything. They couldn't have done any more than their elders. . . .

I started worrying about black young people when I heard them saying they're black and they're proud. But just being black is no reason to be proud. . . . My feeling is that if you're going to be proud, you ought to have some knowledge (about the history of the black race) to build a basis to be proud. You won't have to go bragging that you're black and proud. . . .

As long as there are black people and white people, there will be conflicts. . . .

There is still a lot of work to be done, and I'm too old to do it. I can't keep up with the pace and maintain sanity anymore. I'll leave that to someone else."

June 9. The Bureau of the Census reported that the number of black youths attending colleges and universities in the United States rose from 282,000 in 1966 to 1,062,000 in 1976, an increase of 275 percent. The number of black women in college rose more than four fold, while the number of black men tripled. In 1976, the number of black women college students exceeded the number of black men by 84,000. Despite the increases, the proportion of blacks aged eighteen to twenty-four years of age enrolled in colleges was only 20 percent in 1976, considerably less than the 27 percent of whites in the same age group. At the time, 74 percent of blacks completed high school by their mid-twenties, compared to 86 percent of whites. In addition, of those blacks who enrolled in college, only about 39 percent actually graduated as compared to 57 percent of whites. The new enrollment statistics, however, raised the black percentage of all college students to 10.7 percent, up from 4.6 percent in 1966. At the time, blacks made up 11.6 percent of the population of the United States.

June 25. Abraham Lincoln Davis, a founder of the Southern Christian Leadership Conference (SCLC) and the first black city councilman in New Orleans, Louisiana, died there at age sixty-three.

Davis, pastor of the New Zion Baptist Church in New Orleans for forty-three years, met there with Martin Luther King, Jr. and other civil rights activists in 1957 to organize the SCLC. King was chosen the group's first president and Davis vice president. Davis was elected to the New Orleans City Council in January, 1975.

July 1. The *Atlanta Inquirer*, quoting a study by Beverly Howze, a University of Michigan psychologist, reported that suicides among blacks had increased by 97 percent since the mid-1950s. In Wayne County, Michigan, (of which Detroit is the county seat), the focus of the Howze study, the increase was 187 percent, compared with less than 23 percent for whites. The greater proportion of black suicides, as for white ones, was among black youth aged 15 to 34. The new statistics represented "a complete reversal for the black race . . . which has a history of rarely resorting to suicide," Howze claimed.

As a result of her study among 300 black and 41 white teenagers in the Detroit area, Howze found "an alarming pattern of alienation and self-destructiveness. . . . While these traits were strongest among black youths in the low income group, they were also evident among . . . young people in general. . . . Many showed feelings of very low self esteem and self confidence. They admit difficulty in dealing with day to day stress and frustration, yet they are extremely hesitant to ask for help—even from their own families. Blacks, particularly black males, insist on handling their problems alone."

The study also revealed "striking differences between blacks and whites and between males and females. White males were more capable of admitting varied feelings, like sadness and frustration. Females mentioned seeking consolation from a parent or close friend. But the black males were the most likely to close themselves off. 'I wouldn't feel anything, only emptiness;' they would claim."

July 3. The United States Supreme Court upheld a plan that used racial and sex quotas to end job discrimination. The Court denied, without comment, an appeal protesting a quota system adopted by the Bell Telephone System. (See also entries dated June 25, 1976, July 2, 1986, June 12, 1984, January 23, 1989, June 5, 1989, and June 12, 1989.)

August 19. Lydia Monice Jackson, a nineteen-year-old music student from Willingboro, New Jersey, was crowned Miss Black America for 1979 in Philadelphia, Pennsylvania. The lyric soprano was selected over twenty-nine other young women from twenty-seven states, the District of Columbia and Puerto Rico.

August 20. The *Detroit Free Press* published details of documents obtained by the American Civil Liberties Union (ACLU) which showed that the FBI passed along information about two Freedom Rider buses to a Birmingham, Alabama police sergeant who was "a known Ku Klux Klan agent" in 1961. The actual documents consisted of approximately 3,000 pages of letters, memoranda, and teletype.

The documents indicated that the FBI knew that Sgt. Thomas Cook of the Birmingham Police Department's intelligence unit was passing the information which the Bureau gave him to the "top leadership" of the Ku Klux Klan. The papers also showed that the chief of the FBI office in Birmingham called Cook to inform him of the progress the buses were "making through the racially tense" South and when they arrived at terminals in Birmingham. They further revealed a plan under which the Birmingham police agreed to get to the terminals 15 or 20 minutes after the arrival of the buses in order to give Klansmen enough time to attack Freedom Riders. (See also entry dated May 4, 1961.)

The documents were released to ACLU attorneys for Walter Bergman, aged seventy-eight, a former professor at Wayne State University in Detroit who had filed suit against the FBI alleging that he was partially paralyzed from a beating he suffered at the hands of Ku Klux Klansmen when they intercepted a Freedom Riders' bus in Anniston, Alabama (fifty miles east of Birmingham). On the same day, a similar Klan assault occurred in Birmingham. In commenting on the documents, Howard Simon, executive director of the Michigan ACLU, said that they showed that the FBI's "failure to provide protection provoked" the assaults on the Freedom Riders.

August 20. The Reverend Clennon King, a black Albany, Georgia minister, interrupted worship services at the Americus Fellowship Baptist Church, where President Jimmy Carter and his eighty-year-old mother Lillian were among the worshippers. The outburst was a continuation of King's efforts to agitate the president on the question of desegregation of churches. He had previously tried to join the all-white Plains Baptist Church, where the

President and his mother previously attended services. Mrs. Carter had withdrawn from that church after its deacons reaffirmed a decision to continue prohibiting black membership.

In his outburst, King accused the President of preventing him from building a new church across from the all-white, Plains Maranatha Baptist Church that "was formed by a group which split from Plains Baptist." He asserted that he loved "the President and he loves me, but he is listening to the wrong Negroes." Although Secret Service agents surrounded King, he was not removed from the church. Of the incident, President Carter said "I hope he gets his church. . . . I didn't know anything about it." (See also entry dated November 15, 1976.)

August 20. Lee Elder, one of the few professional black golfers in the United States, won the Westchester Golf Classic in Harrison, New York. The triumph resulted in a purse of $300,000. The forty-four-year-old Elder won with a 274, ten under par on the 6,603-yard Westchester County Club course. In the previous month, he had won the less prestigious Milwaukee Open. Elder called the Westchester victory "a little more significant to me personally" than his historic feat of four years ago, when he became the first black to compete in the Masters Tournament held in Augusta, Georgia.

September 1. The *Atlanta University Center Digest* reported that 74 percent of blacks participating in a national survey "favored integration," but only 29 percent of them felt that it was "the best method for overcoming racial discrimination." A larger proportion, 45 percent, felt that although integration was "desirable, blacks should have an equal voice in the control of schools and housing first."

The poll, conducted by Lee Slurzberg Research, Inc. for the National Urban League, questioned more than 2,000 black men and women in the spring of 1978. Other results of the poll showed: 1.) Employment/economic development were the principal black concerns. 77 percent cited it "as a priority issue and 46 percent mentioned it as their first priority"; 2.) Education/youth were cited second in importance. 64 percent called it a priority issue and 20 percent mentioned it as their first priority; 3.) 77 percent of blacks felt that American society had "serious problems" and thirty-six percent called for "sweeping changes." Only 20 percent felt that "the American way of life was superior to that of any other country." This attitude was greatest among blacks fifty-five and older, those living in the South, and those with less than a high school education.

September 7. The Southern Christian Leadership Conference (SCLC) office in Jacksonville, Florida reported that within the preceding week it had received 22 complaints from black soldiers of "abusive treatment" at Fort Stewart-Hunter near Savannah, Georgia. The head of the Jacksonville SCLC office said white officers and non-commissioned officers were harassing blacks, who were being "inflamed by harsh treatment and harsh words." Black soldiers said the whites used the derisive epithet "nigger" and other such inflammatory words.

The Fort Stewart-Hunter incidents followed an announcement in August, 1978 by Army Chief of Staff Bernard Rogers that a year-long study would be launched to find out "why a greater percentage of black soldiers" were "being punished and dishonorably discharged than whites." In a letter to commanders of major Army installations across the country, Rogers described the situation as a "disturbing trend" that was "worsening." Rogers based his comments on a recent Army equal opportunity report which showed that blacks received 54 percent of all dishonorable discharges during the fiscal year 1976 and nearly 57 percent during the 1977 fiscal year. Those figures were about twice the rate for white soldiers. In addition, blacks were "charged with more serious offenses than white soldiers."

September 9. United States Supreme Court Justice Lewis F. Powell refused a new request by opponents of busing to achieve school desegregation to delay a wide-spread busing plan scheduled to take effect the following week in Los Angeles, California. A similar request had been denied earlier the same day by Justice William H. Rehnquist. The desegregation plan had been previously upheld by the California State Supreme Court.

September 15. Muhammad Ali regained the World Boxing Association's (WBA) heavyweight boxing championship in a unanimous decision over Leon Spinks, age twenty-five, in New Orleans. The thirty-six-year-old Ali thus became the first heavyweight boxer to win the championship three times. A crowd of 70,000 witnessed the match in the Louisiana Superdome. (See also entry dated February 15, 1978.)

October 7. Democratic Congressman Charles Diggs from Michigan was convicted in a federal district court in Washington, D.C. of using the mails to defraud and file false payroll vouchers. The latter charge stemmed from "a scheme to require his staff members to give him money from their padded pay raises so he could pay off huge personal debts."

Diggs, a veteran black congressman and a founder of the Congressional Black Caucus (CBC), had just been overwhelmingly reelected by his Detroit, Michigan constituents in the past week. (See also entry dated November 2, 1954, for further information about Diggs.)

November 17. Two agents of the Federal Bureau of Investigation (FBI), Charles D. Brennan and George C. Moore, testified before the Select Committee on Assassinations of the U. S. House of Representatives that the Bureau's eleven-year surveillance of Dr. Martin Luther King, Jr. "was based solely" on the late FBI Director J. Edgar Hoover's "hatred of the civil rights leader." The two agents added that "neither the surveillance ordered under the guise of communist influences on King nor that supposedly linking King's efforts with radical violent groups could be justified." However, the two witnesses did not link the FBI directly to the murder of King.

Another FBI agent, Arthur Murtaugh, had told the U. S. Senate's Select Committee of Intelligence in 1975 that another agent, James J. Rose, who worked with him in the Bureau's Atlanta Office, was "overjoyed" when he heard of King's murder. Murtaugh added, "I never heard anyone say anything favorable about Dr. King in . . . 10 years. . . . It just defies reason to say that the same people who have engaged in a 10-year vendetta against Dr. King should investigate his murder." But the Bureau did just that, and within twenty-four hours after King's assassination the FBI concluded "that there was no conspiracy and its investigation was basically in search of the fugitive [James Earl] Ray," according to Murtaugh.

In a syndicated column published in the *Atlanta Constitution* on September 11, 1978, Jesse L. Jackson, one of the civil rights leaders who was with King when the fatal bullet struck him on April 4, 1968, said "circumstantial evidence" suggested that the FBI was "deeply implicated" in King's assassination. (See Appendix for an excerpt taken from Jackson's column, entitled "The FBI and Dr. King's Assassination." See also entries dated October 29, 1974; November 19, 1975; and May 29-June 3, 1978.)

1979

August 15. Andrew J. Young, the African-American United States Ambassador to the United Nations, resigned, asserting that he "could not promise to muzzle himself and stay out of controversies that might prove politically embarrasing to President [Jimmy] Carter." The President accepted the ambassador's resignation with regret. Young indicated that he didn't "feel a bit sorry for a thing I have done. I have tried to interpret to our country some of the mood of the rest of the world. Unfortunately, but by birth, I come from the ranks of those who had known and identified with some level of oppression in the world . . . . By choice," Young said, "I continued to identify with what would be called in biblical terms the least of these my brethren. . . . I could not say that given the same situation, I wouldn't do it again, almost exactly the same way."

Because of his unorthodox approaches to diplomacy, Young's brief career as the first black UN Ambassador was marked by continued controversy. He had made American relations with African nations a priority of his mission while at the same time condemning such leading Western democracies as Great Britain and Sweden as racist. His downfall occurred after he held an unauthorized meeting in July, 1979 with a representative of the Palestine Liberation Organization (PLO), a group which the United States government considered a terrorist organization. Young was also accused of first failing to inform the State Department about the talks and then of giving "only a partial and inaccurate version of events when he was asked."

Following the disclosure of Young's unauthorized meeting with the PLO representative, many influential Americans, including Robert C. Byrd, majority leader of the United States Senate, called for his removal from office. Yet African-American civil rights leader Jesse L. Jackson defended the former ambassador and accused President Carter of sacrificing "Africa, the third world, and black Americans," adding, "I think it's tragic." (See also entries dated January 30, 1977, and October 3, 1977.)

1980

May 18. At least fifteen people died after two nights of racial rioting in Miami, Florida. The disturbances were the worst in the nation since the black ghettos of Watts and Detroit erupted in the late 1960s. The Miami riot began in the wake of a controversial verdict in a case of alleged police brutality.

The violence began on May 17 after the announcement that not guilty verdicts had been returned in Tampa, Florida against four white deputy sheriffs from Dade County (of which Miami is the county seat). The four former deputies were charged with beating Arthur McDuffie, a black insurance executive, to death and then covering up the beating to make it appear that McDuffie had died in a motorcycle accident. The all-male, all-white jury was empaneled in Tampa because Dade Circuit Court Judge Lenore Nesbitt had ruled that the case was "a racial time bomb" in Miami. In the wake of the rioting, U. S. Attorney Atlee Wampler III said that evidence already assembled by the FBI in the McDuffie case would be presented to a federal grand jury in Miami on May 20, 1980.

During the riot, snipers shot at cars, civilians, and police. Three Miami police officers were wounded by gunfire on May 18. At least two of the rioters were shot dead by police. Florida Governor Bob Graham called up 1,100 National Guardsmen, 300 highway patrol officers, four helicopters, and an armored personnel carrier to assist local law enforcement authorities. At least 216 people were injured in the rioting and widespread looting and property damage were reported.

The disturbances occurred in a section of northwest Miami known as "Liberty City." Black leaders in the area said they "had seen the violence building for months," and blamed the unrest on a long series of accusations of police brutality against blacks, "none of which resulted in significant action against the accused white officers"; the conviction and suspension of leading black officials on "corruption charges"; and a "new wave of Cuban refugees, sharpening the economic competition" that had "left blacks on the margin of the city's economy" since the first black workers came to Miami in the 1920s to work in the city's new resort hotels.

As the riot progressed, Miami Mayor Maurice Feree received a set of eleven demands from a grassroots black organization. Feree said he thought at least nine of the demands, including hiring and promotions of blacks, could be readily met. He also said he would consider granting amnesty to all of those accused of looting, but could not agree with the demand to fire State Attorney Janet Reno, the prosecutor in the McDuffie case.

October 26. The ten black Roman Catholic bishops in the United States issued a pastoral letter proclaiming that "the black Catholic community has come of age within the Church and must seize the initiative to 'share the gift of our blackness with the church in the United States'." The 15,000 word letter, entitled "What We Have Seen and Heard," was the first time the ten black bishops had spoken collectively and it emphasized both "the strengths blacks bring to the Church" as well as "the 'stain' of racism" that they claimed still existed in "Catholic structures."

At the time that the letter was written, there were an estimated one million black Roman Catholics in the nation, less than 2 percent of the country's approximately 52 million Catholics. Within the Church hierarchy, in addition to the ten black bishops mentioned above, there were approximately three hundred black priests and seven hundred black religious women. (See also entry dated March 15, 1988.)

December 22. President-Elect Ronald Reagan named Samuel Riley Pierce, Jr., an African-American lawyer, Secretary of Housing and Urban Development (HUD). He was the only black or minority person selected to join the new President's cabinet.

Pierce was born on September 6, 1922 in Glen Cove, Long Island, New York. He played football at Cornell University and graduated with Phi Beta Kappa honors. After service in World War II, Pierce obtained a law degree from Cornell and began work as an assistant district attorney in New York City. In later years, he was appointed, on two separate occasions, to court vacancies in Manhattan borough by then-Governor Nelson Rockefeller, yet in 1959 he was defeated in a bid for election to a Manhattan judgeship.

Pierce entered governmental service at the federal level in 1955 when President Dwight Eisenhower named him an assistant to the Under Secretary of Labor. He was the first African-American ever appointed to this position. In 1970, President Richard M. Nixon made him the first black to serve as a general counsel to the Treasury Department. At the time of his appointment to the

Reagan cabinet, however, Pierce had left government and was serving as a partner in a prestigious New York law firm.

Of Pierce's cabinet appointment, Barbara Penn Wright, Pierce's wife and a physician with the Metropolitan Life Insurance Company remarked, "He's never been adverse to accepting a challenge. And he's always been able to handle them."

1981

April 15. Thomas (Tom) Bradley was reelected to a third term as mayor of Los Angeles, California. Bradley, a sixty-three-year-old African-American, defeated his perennial opponent, former Mayor Sam Yorty, age seventy, by a margin of 64 to 32 percent to gain four more years as mayor of the nation's third largest city.

August 1. Benjamin F. Payton assumed the office of president of Tuskegee Institute. Payton succeeded Luther H. Foster, who retired after twenty-eight years as president of the historic and predominantly black university founded by Booker T. Washington in 1881.

Payton was program officer for education and public policy at the Ford Foundation at the time of his appointment to Tuskegee. He had previously taught and directed the Community Service Project at Howard University, directed the Commission on Religion and Race and the Department of Social Justice at the National Council of Churches in the U.S.A., and was a president of Benedict College in South Carolina.

November 16. President Ronald Reagan fired Arthur S. Flemming, the seventy-six-year-old chairman of the United States Commission on Civil Rights (CCR). Sources told United Press International (UPI) that the White House was "angered by the Commission's and Flemming's strong advocacy of affirmative action, voting rights, and . . . busing to achieve school desegregation." This was the first time in the twenty-four-year history of the commission that "an incoming administration [had] changed [the CCR's] membership, a restraint underlining a bipartisan commitment to civil rights." Flemming, a former Secretary of Health, Education, and Welfare (HEW) in the administration of President Dwight D. Eisenhower, was appointed to the commission in 1974 by President Richard M. Nixon. He had recently said that the Reagan administration's views on school desegregation were "in conflict with the Constitution."

Reagan appointed Clarence Pendleton, a fifty-year-old black Californian, to replace Flemming as chairman of the CCR. Pendleton, "a conservative Republican," had supported Reagan in the 1980 elections. He had previously been chairman of the San Diego Transit Corporation and head of the San Diego Urban League. Pendleton became the first black chairman of the Civil Rights Commission.

1982

February 21. United States District Court Judge Aubrey E. Robinson, Jr. of the District of Columbia ruled that the federal Drug Enforcement Administration (DEA) must give black special agents preference in promotions and pay them for the period they suffered from a discriminatory promotions policy. The order required a payment of about $2 million to be shared among 200 and 300 black DEA agents, according to their attorney. The ruling also meant that one black agent for every two whites would have to be promoted to the sixth highest, or a higher federal pay grade. Those ranks carried salaries of $33,586 to $47,500 at the time.

Judge Robinson had ruled in 1981 that the drug agency discriminated against black agents with respect to salary, entry grades, work assignments evaluations, discipline, and promotion during the period 1972 to 1981. The new order set the amount of back pay and provided a remedy for "eliminating the effect of the discrimination in the future." The judge said the preferential promotions for blacks must continue either for five years or "until the percentage of blacks in the six highest pay grades reached 10 percent."

February 27. Wayne Williams, a twenty-three-year-old black entertainment "talent scout," was convicted of murder in the slayings of Jimmy Ray Payne, age twenty-one, and Nathaniel Cater, age twenty-seven, in Atlanta, Georgia. Payne and Cater were two of the twenty-eight young blacks, mostly males, who were slain in Atlanta in a twenty-two month period beginning in 1979. Most of the victims were strangled. The serial murders became known as "the Atlanta Child Murder Cases," since most of the victims were under twenty-one years of age.

The case began on July 27, 1979 when the first two bodies were found, but it was July, 1980 before the police publicly linked the two cases. By that time, eleven black children had disappeared or were found slain. The police action came after an organization of parents, the Committee to Stop Children's Murder (STOP), led by the mother of one of the victims, was formed in May, 1980 to show linkages in the cases.

During the twenty-two months when black children's bodies were being found periodically in the metropolitan Atlanta area, President Ronald Reagan committed $1.5 million in federal funds and scores of FBI agents to the case. Heavyweight boxing champion Muhammad Ali pledged $400,000, and hundreds of thousands in additional dollars were donated by other athletes and celebrities or raised in benefit concerts. The state of Georgia and citizens throughout the nation gave thousands of dollars to help with the investigation or for a reward fund. Some of the donations went to STOP or directly to the mothers of the slain youths.

The Guardian Angels, a group of New York City youths who had patrolled the subways of their city to deter crime, went to Atlanta to teach local youths how to defend themselves. A vigilante group of blacks armed with baseball bats in the Techwood Housing projects formed a "Bat Patrol" to protect black children. In addition, psychics, writers, civil rights activists, and others offered theories on the motives and identities of the killer or killers. Many were convinced that Ku Klux Klansmen or other white supremacists, bent on genocide, were responsible for the murders. And, since most of the victims were young black males, the idea that a homosexual committed the crimes also emerged.

On May 22, 1981, law enforcement officers on stake out along the Chattahoochee River in north Atlanta heard a loud splash. Shortly thereafter, other officers questioned and detained Wayne Williams after he was noticed driving slowly with his headlights dimmed across the James Jackson Parkway Bridge over the Chattahoochee. Two days later, the body of twenty-seven year old Nathaniel Cater was found floating in the river. On June 21, 1981, Williams was arrested and charged with the murders of Cater and Jimmy Ray Payne.

Williams, who took the stand in his own defense during the trial, vigorously denied that he had committed the murders. He and his attorneys refuted suggestions of a homosexual motive and denied any acquaintance with most of the seven victims in whose company prosecution witnesses had placed him. The prosecution, however, had also presented fibers taken from clothing and other fabrics and bloodstains found in William's car as evidence. On February 27, 1982, after eleven hours of deliberations, a majority black jury found Williams guilty of two counts of murder. The presiding judge, Clarence Cooper, also an African-American, sentenced Williams to two consecutive life terms in prison. The defense promised an immediate appeal.

The "Atlanta Child Murder Cases," involved one of the largest searches for a killer in the nation's history and Wayne Williams was convicted as America's first major black serial murderer.

March 17. Reuben M. Greenberg, a thirty-two-year-old deputy director of the Florida Division of Criminal Justice Standards and Training, was named the first black police chief of Charleston, South Carolina by Mayor Joseph Riley. The South Carolina Criminal Justice Academy also announced that Greenberg's appointment made him "the first black police chief in modern South Carolina history."

March 20. Ernest "Dutch" Morial was reelected mayor of New Orleans, Louisiana. The city's first African-American chief executive defeated Ron Raucheux, a white legislator, 71,231 (56 percent) to 55,814 (44 percent) with 75 percent of the vote counted. Although New Orleans had a majority black population at the time of the election, more whites were registered to vote than blacks. Morial was expected to need "about fifteen percent of the white vote to win . . . . Racial issues" had "played [only] a minor role in the campaign."

March 23. The City Council of Houston, Texas confirmed Lee P. Brown as the city's first black police commissioner. Brown, age forty-four, had recently been the second black police commissioner in Atlanta, Georgia. During his tenure in Atlanta, the city was the site of the murders of twenty-eight young black people over a period of twenty-two months. The murders were linked in 1980 and in the following year, Wayne Williams, a young black man, was accused of the serial slayings (see entry dated February 27, 1982). He was convicted and sentenced to two consecutive life terms in prison less than one month before Brown resigned from the police department. Although Brown was variously praised and criticized for his department's handling of the "Atlanta Child Murder Cases," he denied that his resignation was connected with the infamous case. Brown, a former head of the police department in Portland, Oregon, said it was simply time for him to seek a new challenge. Brown was the first person chosen from outside the department to head Houston's police force. The department was frequently under criticism by some of the city's blacks for alleged brutality.

May 6. Loretta Glickman, a thirty-six-year-old African-American investment counselor, was elected mayor of Pasadena, California, by the city's Board of Directors. Glickman, who had also been a teacher and singer, became the first black woman to become mayor of a major city in the United States. In response to her election, Glickman said that Pasadena was a place "where dreams can and do come true."

June 23. Coleman Young, the first African-American mayor of Detroit, Michigan, was elected president of the U. S. Conference of Mayors at its 50th annual meeting in Minneapolis, Minnesota, succeeding Helen Booalis of Lincoln, Nebraska. The new president announced immediately after his selection that he would ask mayors to return soon for a special meeting to recommend ways to strengthen their local economies.

June 30. The United States Supreme Court, in a 5-4 decision, overturned an initiative from the state of Washington which prohibited the voluntary assignment of students to schools beyond their neighborhoods. In an opinion written by Justice Harry Blackmun, the Court said the statewide vote in the state of Washington violated the "equal protection" guarantee of the U.S. Constitution because it "imposed an unfair burden on minority groups" who were "singled out" to "be dealt with at the state level, which is more remote than the local school board." The high Court also said the initiative burdened "all future attempts to integrate Washington schools in districts throughout the state by lodging decision-making authority over the question at a new and remote level of government." Justices Lewis F. Powell, Jr., William H. Rehnquist, Sandra Day O'Connor, and Chief Justice Warren Burger dissented. Justice Powell considered the ruling an "unprecedented intrusion into the structure of a state government. . . ." It deprived "the state of Washington of all opportunity to address the unsolved questions resulting from extensive mandatory busing."

The case stemmed from a voluntary plan which the Seattle school board adopted in 1977. It involved the busing of some 7,000 students. In 1978, the state's voters approved Initiative 350 to end the busing. A lower federal court, in a suit filed by the school board, upheld the plan and declared the referendum unconstitutional. Thus, the case reached the Supreme Court on further appeal by opponents of busing.

July 5. The United States Supreme Court ruled that "nonviolent boycotts, organized to achieve constitutional rights goals," are protected by the First Amendment guarantees of free speech. The decision reversed a ruling by the Supreme Court of Mississippi which held that the NAACP and ninety-one black citizens were liable for business losses caused by a boycott of local merchants in Port Gibson, Mississippi, which began in 1966.

The Port Gibson boycott was launched by blacks to achieve desegregation in schools and public facilities, to encourage the hiring of black police officers, and to improve lighting, sewers, and the paving of streets in black neighborhoods. The Mississippi Court, however, citing evidence of coercion and violence during the boycott, declared the protest "to be an illegal conspiracy" and ordered it ended.

Yet the U.S. Supreme Court, in an opinion written by Justice John Paul Stevens, ruled that "the presence of some illegal threats and violence" did not mean that all of the business losses, in the seven-year period, were attributable to the "illegal" aspects of the boycotts.

August 21. Calvin Simmons, the thirty-two-year-old African-American conductor of the Oakland (California) Symphony Orchestra, was presumed drowned in Lake Placid, New York. Witnesses said he never surfaced after his boat capsized in about 23 feet of water on Connery Pond. Simmons was considered "one of the nation's most promising young black Conductors."

October 27. Richard T. Rives, senior judge of the United States Court of Appeals for the Eleventh Circuit, died of an apparent heart attack in Montgomery, Alabama, at age eighty-seven.

Rives had served on the Court of Appeals for the Fifth Circuit since 1951 and served as that court's chief judge from 1959 to 1966. He became senior judge of the Eleventh Circuit Court after it was split from the Fifth Circuit at the time of his death.

Rives and Judge Frank M. Johnson rendered the historic decision in 1955 that declared discrimination on Montgomery, Alabama buses unconstitutional. The ruling was later upheld by the United States Supreme Court. (See also entry dated December 1, 1955.)

November 5. Bernice King, daughter of slain civil rights leader Martin Luther King, Jr., accepted a posthumous award for her late father from the United Nations General Assembly in New York City. The award recognized the late civil rights leader's work against apartheid in South Africa. In 1965, King had called for an international boycott against South Africa. He predict- ed that "the day is fast approaching when people of good will all over the world will rise up in nonviolent solidarity with freedom fighters in Africa."

December 4. Herschel Walker, African-American running back for the University of Georgia, won the Heisman Trophy, football's highest collegiate award, in New York City. Walker, a native of Wrightsville, Georgia, became the seventh person to capture the Heisman in his junior year. He had previously been named to the football writers All-America team on three occasions.

In the balloting for the Heisman, Walker received 525 first place votes, followed by Stanford University (California) quarterback John Elway with 139 first place votes, and Southern Methodist University (Texas) running back Eric Dickerson, with 31 first place votes.

December 16. The United States Court of Appeals for the Fifth Circuit ordered approval of a system of promotions on the New Orleans police force that would make it half black at every level. Under the ruling, blacks would be promoted to forty-four new positions immediately, then blacks and whites would be promoted on a one-to-one ratio. In addition, the police department was ordered to recruit more blacks, make it more difficult for a black police cadet to fail, set up $300,000 as a back-pay fund, and pay the fees of the plaintiffs' lawyers.

The suit which resulted in this ruling was filed by thirteen black New Orleans police officers in 1973. They claimed that the city, its Civil Service Commission, and various officials discriminated against them. The suit was dismissed "for failure to prosecute" in 1978, but was later reopened.

December 16. James C. White, a thirty-four-year-old accountant, was named Commissioner of the Department of Revenue for the state of Alabama.

White, a resident of Birmingham, was appointed to the position by Governor George C. Wallace, formerly a staunch segregationist.

White, a native of Montgomery, Alabama, earned a Bachelor's degree in accounting from Dillard University in Louisiana. In May 1973, he co-founded Banks, Finley, White, and Company Certified Public Accountants, "the largest minority CPA firm in the nation."

White's appointment as revenue commissioner made him the highest-ranking black in the executive branch of Alabama government and one of the few blacks to hold such a position in the nation.

December 28-29. A new wave of racial violence erupted in Miami, Florida after a Hispanic police officer, Luis Alvarez, shot and killed twenty-one-year-old Nevell Johnson, a suspected black looter. The altercations in the Overtown section of the city left two people dead and twenty-seven wounded. Dozens of businesses were destroyed or damaged. Forty-three people were arrested in the area.

During the melee, up to 200 people participated in rampages throughout the Overtown section, but the disturbances did not reach the proportions of racial rioting in Miami's Liberty City area in 1980, when eighteen people died during three days of violence. (See also entry dated May 18, 1980.)

1983

January 6. United States District Court Judge Milton Shadur upheld the constitutionality of a new desegregation plan for the public schools of Chicago, Illinois. The plan pledged that by September, 1983, no school would be more than 70 percent white. It relied largely on "magnet schools" and voluntary transfers, with 180 programs from which students of all races and ethnic groups could choose. The plan also defined a desegregated school as one containing at least 30 percent white and 30 percent minority students including blacks and Hispanics in one "minority" group, and placed "no undue burden" for desegregation on black students. At the time of the ruling, there were only 16.3 percent of white students in the public schools of Chicago and more than 100,000 of 435,000 students were in "desegregated settings."

January 11. Carl Ellis, a twenty-year-old unemployed African-American from Harrisburg, Pennsylvania, won the Pennsylvania State Lottery. Ellis's winnings assured him of payments of $1,000 per week for the rest of his life.

January 15. Martin Luther King, Sr., father of slain civil rights leader Martin Luther King, Jr., and Richard Attenborough, the British filmmaker who produced and directed the epic motion picture *Gandhi*, were named co-recipients of the Martin Luther King, Jr. Non-Violent Peace Prize. The awards were presented by Coretta Scott King, president of the Martin Luther King, Jr. Center for Non-Violent Social Change and widow of the slain civil rights leader, at ceremonies marking the 15th annual observance of King Jr.'s birthday in Atlanta, Georgia. Each man was given a medal inscribed with a quote from a King, Jr. speech: "Now the judgment of God is upon us, and we must all live together as brothers or we will all perish together as fools." They were also presented checks for $1,000.

Upon receipt of his award, Attenborough recalled that in the Gandhi Museum in New Delhi there is one picture in "the great hall," the picture of Martin Luther King, Jr. "That is fitting," he said, because "no one—and there are many who claim to—followed his teachings more closely than Dr. King. . . . I feel more touched now than I can ever remember on any occasion in my life." King, Sr. thanked his family "for helping him through" the deaths of his two sons and his wife, and thanked "God for what He left me."

January 19. In its annual report on the "State of Black America," the National Urban League (NUL) claimed that blacks ended 1982 "in worse shape than in 1981" and expressed concern that "an economic recovery would bypass many minority Americans." The League added that blacks had continued to be hurt by the severity of the current economic recession and by federal cut backs in domestic social service programs. "Vital survival programs were slashed at the same time that the black economy was plunged even deeper into depression. The result was to drive already disadvantaged people to the wall," according to John Jacob, president of the NUL. Jacob also contended that many black Americans would not benefit from an economic "up turn." "We've never fully participated in post recession recoveries," Jacob said. He also noted that black employment was concentrated in automobile and other "heavy industries" that were hit hard by the recession, and he predicted that those industries would never employ as many people as in the past. "A major question facing the nation in 1983 is whether the inevitable restructuring of the American economy will include black people," Jacob asserted.

Jacob also claimed that President Ronald Reagan didn't "understand the effects" his economic policies were "having on the nation's poor.... He is looking at the world through rose-colored glasses, both of which are painted black."

The NUL maintained that federal programs serving the poor had been cut by $10 billion in 1972. As a result, welfare rolls had fallen by one million people, the federal school lunch program was serving about one million fewer children, one million people weren't getting federal food stamps any longer, and 200,000 infants and pregnant women weren't receiving federal nutrition aid.

The NUL recommended that Congress pass "a broad job-training and job creation program" and that it resist efforts by President Ronald Reagan to decrease money for several federal civil rights enforcement agencies. It also urged the Reagan administration not to reduce Social Security benefits in "an attempt to bolster the nation's financially beleaguered retirement system." The League report concluded: "We are not recommending a 'welfare state,' but certainly some better way has to be found to take care of our people than we presently practice."

The administration of President Reagan continued to reject suggestions by the NUL and other civil rights groups and leaders that its policies were "unfair or insensitive to the concerns of minorities." Yet criticisms continued from these as well as other sources. The *Atlanta Constitution,* "the South's standard newspaper," for example, in an editorial on December 15, 1982, had made sharp and specific attacks on the Reagan administration's civil rights policies. (See Appendix for an excerpt taken from the editorial "The South Doesn't Want to Go Back.")

January 25. The United States Supreme Court refused to hear a challenge to a busing plan to achieve school desegregation in Nashville, Tennessee. The plan required elementary school pupils to be bused rather than attend neighborhood schools. It had been opposed by the Department of Justice which contended that "busing does not work." After the Court's action, Assistant Attorney General William Bradford Reynolds remarked that the decision "in no way indicates that the legal issue of mandatory busing is closed. . . . We see no reason for a change of this administration's position of advancing alternatives to mandatory transportation to remedy intentional school segregation." But the decision pleased Avon N. Williams, Jr., a civil rights lawyer who had fought segregation in Nashville's schools for over 25 years. Williams stated: "I think all right-thinking people were or should have been shocked that the Justice Department, for the first time in several decades, intervened on the side of segregation and discrimination."

February 12. Eubie Blake, African-American ragtime pianist-composer, died of natural causes in Brooklyn, New York, after having celebrated his 100th birthday on February 7th.

Blake, the son of former slaves, was born in Baltimore, Maryland. At the age of four, he wandered into a music store while his mother was shopping and began to play a pump organ. A salesman convinced his mother that the boy had "a God-given talent" and she purchased the $75 instrument. Blake learned about ragtime "by tagging after" black funeral processions, where he heard "melodies played as dirges" on the way to the cemetary and "ragged" on the way back. In his biography *Eubie Blake* by Al Rose, he recalled the processions and exclaimed, "Oh how they'd swing."

Like most young black musicians of his time, Blake began his career as a pianist playing in a local bordello. He was fifteen at the time and his mother, Emily Blake, "a deeply religious woman, was mortified when she found out." His father, however, convinced her to allow him to continue to play, especially since he contributed a portion of his "substantial earnings" to the family.

Blake wrote his first composition, "Charleston Rag," in 1899 (although it was not notated until 1915). Yet Blake observed in his memoirs that "it ain't until modern times that I ever really looked at it as a piece of music." His biographer Rose also observed that Blake "considered most of what he composed a mere point of departure for his personal improvisations. The music on the paper wasn't designed to be played literally. In fact, it would change in each rendition."

After 1915, Blake collaborated with bandleader Noble Sissle, who served not only as a lyricist but also a business agent. Then, in 1921, Blake composed *Shuffle Along*, one of the first black musicals to appear on Broadway. It played for 504 performances and helped launch the careers of Josephine Baker, Florence Mills, and Paul Robeson, among others. The song "Love Will Find a Way" made musical history depicting blacks "as people with a full range of emotions." *Shuffle Along* was such a success that police had to make 63rd Street in New York into a one-way thoroughfare in order to handle the crowds. After Broadway, the show toured the country in three companies.

Another of Blake's shows, *Blackbirds* (with lyrics by Andy Razaf), became a big hit in 1930. It featured John Bubbles, Buck Washington, and Ethel Waters and such famous tunes as "Memories of You" and "You're Lucky to Me."

Blake's popularity began to wane during the Great Depression of the 1930s and he himself fell into a state of dejection and depression following the death of his wife of twenty-eight years, Avis, in 1939. He emerged to play in USO camps and military hospitals during World War II. In 1945, Blake married Marion Tyler, a former show girl and secretary, who helped him put his personal life and business affairs back in order. But it was not until the 1960s, with the increased awareness of Scott Joplin and ragtime, (furthered by the emergence of the black consciousness and black studies movements) that Blake became known to new generations of music lovers. In 1969, Columbia Records signed him "to a massive recording project." At the time, Blake was "the oldest living exponent of ragtime," and scores of fans hummed "I'm Just Wild About Harry," the hit tune from *Shuffle Along*, and the song that also became the theme song for Harry Truman's 1948 presidential campaign.

February 16. Luis Alvarez, a police officer in Miami, Florida, was indicted by the Dade County (of which Miami is the county seat) Grand Jury for manslaughter in the shooting death of Nevell Johnson, Jr., a twenty-one-year-old black man, on December 28, 1982 (see entry above). The killing of Johnson had sparked two days of racial rioting in the Overtown section of Miami.

317

Garth Reeves, editor of the *Miami Times*, a black newspaper, said the indictment of Alvarez would probably satisfy "the black communities, although he had expected a harsher charge." He added: "For so long, police killings have gone unindicted. So this is a small victory of sorts."

February 23. Former African-American congressman Harold Washington won the Democratic primary election for mayor of Chicago, Illinois. Washington defeated incumbent Mayor Jane Byrne by 32,810 votes in a race that drew "a record" 1.2 million voters.

Washington's election came after a bitter and racially divisive campaign. While the African-American candidate appealed to whites for their votes, he built the foundation of his quest on turning out a solid bloc of black voters. Washington repeatedly told them that "it's our turn. . . . We don't need to apologize for it, and we're not going to waste a lot of time explaining it. . . . It's our turn—that's all." In the end, Washington garnered about 85 percent of the votes cast by blacks.

The new Democratic nominee was born in Chicago, the son of an attorney and a Democratic precinct captain. He attended Roosevelt College in Chicago and the Northwestern University Law School. Before his election to the U.S. Congress, Washington was a city prosecutor, an arbitrator for the Illinois Industrial Commission, a state legislator, and a Democratic precinct captain in Chicago. The sixty-year-old-nominee had also served in the Army Air Corps during World War II.

February 23. Herschel Walker, the African-American collegiate football player who received the Heisman Trophy in December, 1982, signed "the biggest contract in football history" with the New Jersey Generals of the United States Football League. The value of the three-year contract was estimated at more than $8 million. Walker, a resident of Wrightsville, Georgia, passed up his senior year at the University of Georgia in order to join the Generals.

March 4. Coretta Scott King, president of the Martin Luther King, Jr. Center for Non-Violent Social Change, was awarded the Franklin D. Roosevelt Freedom Medal at Hyde Park, New York. King was cited for epitomizing the late President's four freedoms—"worship, speech, from want, and from fear."

April 4. Twenty-two school districts in St. Louis County, Missouri agreed to a desegregation plan to begin the "nation's first widespread voluntary school busing between a major city and its suburbs." The accord came just before a deadline imposed by United States District Judge William L. Hungate in an eleven-year-old desegregation suit.

Under the plan, all transfers would be voluntary. Predominantly-white suburban school districts agreed to accept black students from the city of St. Louis until "their racial balance was at least 15 percent, but no more than 25 percent, black." In order to achieve the ratios, 15,000 black students would have to be bused to suburban schools in the fall of 1983. White suburban students would be encouraged to attend "magnet schools" in the city and city schools would be improved. Teachers were also to be reassigned to achieve more racial balance.

April 7. As the nation marked the 15th anniversary of the assassination of Dr. Martin Luther King, Jr. with memorial services across the country, Hodding Carter III, one of the nation's leading journalists and a correspondent for the PBS network, gave a broad assessment of King's meaning for America, then and now, in the April 7, 1983 edition of the *Wall Street Journal*. (See Appendix for an excerpt taken from Carter's essay, "Martin Luther King, Jr.: A Dream Deterred.")

April 12. Former African-American congressman Harold Washington defeated Republican lawyer Bernard Epton to become the first black mayor of Chicago, Illinois. Washington, a Democrat, captured 636,136 votes (51.5 percent) to 595,694 (48.2 percent) for Epton, totaling 96 percent of 2,914 precincts. Washington's victory was made possible by a very heavy turnout of black voters, strong Hispanic support, and from some support from middle class whites, although the election had been marked by serious racial divisions. On March 27, for example, an angry white crowd forced Washington to curtail a campaign appearance at a Catholic church in a white area of the city. The group waved signs in support of candidate Epton, who later denounced the incident. (See also entry dated February 23, 1983.)

April 19-20. On April 19, about 100 black students prayed and sang in front of the administration building at the University of Mississippi at Oxford in a protest against the use of the Confederate flag as a symbol of the university. During the previous night, several hundred white students had waved the flag and sang the Confederate battle song, "Dixie," in front of a black fraternity house on the campus. Charles Griffin, a black student, told reporters that the whites also yelled "nigger night" and "save the flag."

In the fall of 1982, some black students at the university had called for the banning of the rebel flag, the display of the Colonel Reb cartoon mascot, and the singing of "Dixie" at athletic games. John Hawkins, the first black varsity cheerleader at the university, refused to wave the flag as he lead cheers at football games. The protesting blacks said the Confederate symbols were both "racist and offensive."

On April 20, Porter Fortune, chancellor of the University of Mississippi, announced that the Confederate flag would no longer be used as a school symbol. But black students complained because the statement did not ban individuals from continuing to wave the flag on campus or at athletic contests, nor did it prohibit the use of the Colonel Reb mascot or the singing of "Dixie." A group of white students cheered the chancellor's announcement and waved Confederate flags.

May 12. Louis Gossett, Jr. won an Academy Award as Best Supporting Actor for his role as a Marine Corps drill sergeant in the film *An Officer and a Gentleman.* He became the third black actor or actress to win an Oscar in the fifty-five-year history of the awards. The first black person to win the coveted honor was Hattie McDaniel (Best Supporting Actress) for her work in *Gone with the Wind* in 1940. Sidney Poitier was named Best Actor for his lead role in the 1963 film *Lillies of the Field.*

Gossett, age forty-four, had won an Emmy Award in 1977 for his role as "Fiddler" in the ABC miniseries "Roots." As Gossett received his Oscar, blacks demonstrated outside the Hollywood Music Center calling the Academy Awards "a racist affair." In reaction to the protest, Gossett commented: "You shouldn't call anything racist if [it is] improving." He expressed the hope that his award would "catch on like measles" and lead to the creation of more roles for black actors and actresses in Hollywood. (See also entries dated March, 1940, March, 1964, and September 11, 1977.)

May 24. The United States Supreme Court, in an 8-1 decision, ruled that the federal government cannot grant tax exemptions to private schools that practice racial discrimination. Chief Justice Warren Burger, writing for the majority, stated that "it would be wholly incompatible with the concepts underlying tax exemption to grant the benefit of tax exempt status to racially discriminatory educational entities." Justice William H. Rehnquist was the lone dissenter.

The Court's ruling upheld a policy of non-exemption for discriminatory private schools which the Internal Revenue Service (IRS) had adopted in 1971, but which the administration of President Ronald Reagan had tried to abandon in 1982. Under the original policy, Bob Jones University in Greenville, South Carolina, lost its tax-exempt status in 1975 because it prohibited interracial dating or marriage among its students and the Goldsboro Christian Schools of Goldsboro, North Carolina, which refused to admit blacks, also lost its tax-exempt status for 1969 through 1972. Both schools subsequently sued the IRS, but lost in both federal district and appellate courts. Both cases reached the Supreme Court on appeal from the lower court.

June 17. Nelson W. Trout, the sixty-two-year-old professor and director of minority studies at Trinity Lutheran Seminary in Columbus, Ohio, was elected Bishop of the American Lutheran Church's South Pacific District (located in

California), becoming the first black person ever elected to full-time office among North American Lutheran Church bodies.

The members of the Lutheran Church in the United States have been historically concentrated among Scandinavian and Germanic ethnic groups in the East and Midwest and had little success in attracting large members of blacks to the denomination. Election of blacks to positions of "prominence in predominately-white denominations has been a way of returning the church's focus to black concerns," according to the *National Leader,* a black-oriented news digest. Trout himself said of his election, "It's the one exception that defies the rule. It does not mean that the rapture has come or anything like that. It means that at a certain time and place the Lord was in our midst and He blessed us."

June 22. The State Senate of Louisiana repealed the last of the nation's racial classification laws. The unanimous senate action followed a 90-4 vote for repeal in the Louisiana House of Representatives on June 9, 1983. The racial classification law had defined a black person as anyone "with one-thirty secondth 'Negro' blood."

The repeal effort gained impetus after an unsuccessful effort was made by Susan Guilliory Phipps of Sulphur, Louisiana, to have the racial designation on her birth certificate changed from black to white. A state court judge, however, had ruled that Phipps had not proved "beyond doubt" that she was not at least one-thirty-second black.

August 13. President Ronald Reagan vetoed a bill which allocated $20 million to implement a school desegregation program in Chicago. The desegregation had been ordered by United States District Court Judge Milton I. Shadur on June 30, 1983. In that order, the judge said that the federal government should allocate more than $14 million for desegregating Chicago's schools in 1983-84 and set aside $250 million more for possible distribution in the next five years. Pending resolution of the case, Shadur also ordered that $55 million allocated for other education programs across the nation be frozen. But in July, 1983, he freed $6.5 million of the amount.

In his veto message, President Reagan said: "The Chicago court's ostensible purpose in issuing this order was to provide a source of funds for the implementation of its decree. . . . Congress hoped by the passage of this legislation to induce the court to release the funds that were impounded by the court. But I believe that the better course is to seek swift reversal of the district court's order." The President added that the government would pay the money mandated by the court if the decision were upheld, but he claimed that it was "inappropriate . . . for a court to withhold millions of dollars worth of unrelated and necessary education programs to enforce its orders." (See also entry dated January 6, 1983.)

August 20. A *Chicago Sun Times* survey revealed that more than 600,000 new black voters were expected to register in nine Southern states—Alabama, Arkansas, Georgia, Louisiana, Mississippi, North Carolina, South Carolina, Tennessee, and Virginia—in time for the 1984 presidential election. The survey's projections were derived from interviews with election officials in six states, who based their estimates on "current and anticipated registration trends." In the other three states—Alabama, Arkansas, and Tennessee—the figures were provided by independent black organizations. By August of 1983, 190,000 new black voters had already been added to voter rolls in the Southern states.

The new black voters were expected to have a "potent" and "perhaps decisive" impact not only in the upcoming presidential contest, but also in many local elections. One potential presidential candidate, Jesse Jackson, a black minister and civil rights leader, had set a goal of two million new black voters in the South by 1984. The attainment of this goal was viewed as "a key to his decision" whether or not to pursue the Democratic presidential nomination.

August 21. The Bureau of the Census reported that "the traditional migration of blacks from the South to the urban centers of the North and West ended" in the 1970s. "Between 1975 and 1980, about 415,000 blacks moved to the South, whereas (in the more recent period) only about 220,000 left, thereby reversing the longstanding black exodus from the South."

In 1980, 53 percent of the nation's blacks lived in the South—the same proportion as in 1970, yet approximately 60 percent of the nation's black population lived in central cities—an increase of approximately 13 percent. The new demographic data was contained in a report entitled "America's Black Population: 1970 to 1982." It was based on data from the Census Bureau, the U. S. Labor Department and other governmental agencies.

The Census Bureau's report also noted that: (1) The number of blacks in the civilian labor force increased by 2.7 million or 31 percent between 1972 and 1982, and the number of employed blacks grew by 1.4 million, or 19 percent. However, the number of blacks who were unemployed rose 140 percent, from 900,000 in 1972 to 2.1 million in 1982. The unemployment rate for blacks continued at more than double the rate for whites. In 1972, when the unemployment rate for whites was 5 percent, the unemployment rate for blacks was 10.3 percent. In 1982, the unemployment rates for both blacks and whites were the highest for any period since the second World War. (2) The median income for black married couples increased 6.9 percent between 1971 and 1981. Such families, however, made up only 55 percent of all black families in 1982, compared with 64 percent in 1972. (3) For all black families, median income, after adjustment for inflation, declined by 8.3 percent since 1971, with a 5.2 percent drop occurring between 1980 and 1981. This decline was attributed to the increase in the number of single-parent black families headed by females. In 1982, these families totaled 2.6 million—up 32 percent from 1972. Female-headed households made up 41 percent of all black families and 70 percent of all poor black families. (4) The poverty rate for blacks remained steady at 34 percent, though there were one million more poor blacks in 1980 than in 1970—nine million compared with eight million.

August 23. Clarence Thomas, the black chairman of the Equal Employment Opportunity Commission, told a group of faculty and staff at Clark College in Atlanta, Georgia that black colleges had become "the victim" in the effort to desegregate the nation's colleges. He added that the "threat" to black colleges stemmed "from a misguided philosophy of desegregation that focuses on numbers rather than quality education for blacks. . . . If the goal of desegregation is to have every black student sit next to a white student then there is no room in education for black colleges," he said. "If the goal is for quality education," Thomas asserted, "then there is plenty of room."

Thomas also said that as the former assistant secretary for civil rights in the Department of Education, he became " 'terrified' by the prospective effects of desegregation on black colleges," but added "they were not the ones doing the discriminating." (See also entries dated June 21, 1974, and September 6, 1977.)

August 24. The Southern Christian Leadership Conference (SCLC) opened its 26th Annual Convention in Washington, D.C. In one of the opening addresses, the Reverend Joseph E. Lowery, president of the SCLC, asserted: "We are being told still that America cannot afford freedom and justice for all of our citizens. . . . Two decades of hard-fought progress are in danger of erosion through budget cuts. . . . Federal agencies have callously abdicated their mandated responsibility to enforce anti-discrimination laws. . . . Those rights we fought for dearly are being eroded."

The SCLC was founded in 1957 by Dr. Martin Luther King, Jr. and other Southern civil rights leaders. The focus of the 1983 convention was "Jobs, Peace, and Freedom."

September 1. Luther Burse, former interim president of Cheyney State College in Pennsylvania, assumed the presidency of Fort Valley State College in Georgia.

Burse was born June 3, 1937 in Hopkinsville, Kentucky. He received a bachelor's degree from Kentucky State University in 1958 and a master's degree from the University of Maryland in 1969. He was also a research assistant at the University of Maryland from 1966 to 1969.

Prior to accepting the presidency of Fort Valley State, Burse had also taught at Elizabeth City State University in North Carolina (1960-66), and served as coordinator of Graduate Studies in the division of Applied and Behavioral Sciences (1969-1981), and was interim president of Cheyney State from 1981 to 1982.

September 17. Vanessa Williams, a twenty-year-old African-American woman from Millwood, New York, was crowned "Miss America" for 1984. It was the first time in the history of the sixty-year-old pageant that a black woman had won the title. Indeed, for half of the pageant's history, black females were barred from entering the competition.

Williams, a junior at Syracuse University, entered the pageant as "Miss New York." She cried as she walked down the runway after receiving the crown.

October. Hundreds of scholars, teachers, and students attended a major conference on the Study and Teaching of Afro-American History at Purdue University in West Lafayette, Indiana. The meeting, which assessed the latest studies and trends in African-American life and history, was sponsored by the American Historical Association and directed by Darlene Clark Hine, a Purdue University history professor.

In one of the keynote addresses at the conference, John Hope Franklin, professor of history at Duke University and one of the premiere scholars in African-American history, described a fourth generation of practitioners of African-American historical scholarship. He said the approaches of the recent generation of scholars, "the largest and perhaps the best trained [ever] were greatly stimulated by the drive for equality [during the 1950s and 1960s]." He also said that they had kept the subject "alive and vibrant."

Another keynote speaker, African-American labor historian William H. Harris (also the president of Paine College in Augusta, Georgia), suggested that scholars needed to do "more work" on the black working class. He also indicated that "the quest for a change in perspective" by historians would "improve overall the range of history and the level of our understanding of the numerous black experiences that have been lived in America."

October 27. John Lewis, civil rights activist, was presented the Martin Luther King, Jr. Award for his contributions to voter education and registration by the Voter Education Project (VEP), at ceremonies commemorating the organization's 21st anniversary in Atlanta, Georgia. During its twenty-one year history, the VEP had helped register at least four million black voters across the South.

Lewis, who was beaten unconscious four times and arrested at least forty times during the Civil Rights Movement of the 1960s, served as executive director of the Voter Education Project from 1970 to 1977. In accepting the VEP's highest honor, Lewis said "it means a great deal to me, but this isn't so much an honor for me as it is for the thousands of people who have worked in the voter registration movement. . . . I think we're on the way to a biracial democracy in the South."

November 2. President Ronald Reagan signed a bill at the White House establishing a federal holiday in honor of slain civil rights leader Martin Luther King, Jr. The President also paid personal tribute to King, saying his words and deeds had "stirred our nation to the very depths of its soul." Reagan continued: "Dr. King made equality of rights his life's work. . . . Often he was beaten, imprisoned, but he never stopped teaching nonviolence. . . . If American history grows from two centuries to 20, Americans and others will still remember King's 'I Have a Dream' speech." The President warned, however, that "traces of bigotry still mar America. . . . So each year on Martin Luther King Day, let us not only recall Dr. King, but rededicate ourselves to the commandments he believed in and sought to live every day. 'Thou shalt love thy God with all thy heart and thou shall love thy neighbor as thyself'."

Many Americans, including soul singer Stevie Wonder (who composed and recorded a birthday song honoring King) and Coretta Scott King, the martyred civil rights leader's widow, had lobbied for the holiday (which was to begin on the third Monday in January, 1986) since King's assassination in 1968. At the White House ceremonies at which the president signed the holiday bill, Mrs. King remarked: "Thank God for the blessing of his [King's] life and his leadership and his commitment. What manner of man was this? May we make ourselves worthy to carry on his dream and create the [beloved] community." (See also entry dated January 18, 1986.)

November 11. Representatives from the United States Congress and the Reagan Administration reached an agreement to extend the life of the United States Commission on Civil Rights (CCR). Under the new accord, the six-member body would be reorganized into an eight-member one. The President and Congress would each name four members to serve staggered six-year terms and can only be removed "for cause, thus eliminating the possibility of firings for political reasons."

Earlier, President Reagan had tried to replace but eventually fired three Democratic members of the Commission "who did not share his administration's views in opposing busing to achieve school desegregation and broad affirmative action relief in job-discrimination cases." Many Congressmen complained that Reagan was attempting to destroy "the commission's independence and integrity." Congress refused to appropriate funds for the extension of the Commission on September 30, 1983.

Under the agreement of November 11, two Democratic Commissioners, Mary Frances Berry (an African-American) and Blandina C. Ramirez (a Hispanic), would be reappointed by Congress. The two women were among the three Commissioners released by Reagan.

The CCR, an advisory group, investigates reports of discrimination and recommends steps for Congress and the President to take in remedying it. It was established in 1957. (See also entry dated November 16, 1981.)

November 24. An A.C. Nielson survey reported that blacks spent more time watching television (35 percent) than whites, and "that their prime-time choices" were different. The top ranked television program among whites was the CBS news program "60 Minutes," which ranked 18th among black viewers. The top rated program among blacks was the drama "Dynasty," which ranked sixth among whites. Television programs with largely black casts, "The A Team," "Gimme a Break," and "The Jeffersons" ranked second, third, and fourth among blacks; among white viewers they were 23rd, 64th, and 24th, respectively.

1984

January 2. W. Wilson Goode, the forty-five-year-old son of North Carolina sharecroppers, was inaugurated as mayor of Philadelphia, Pennsylvania. Goode became the first African-American chief executive in the city's 301 year history. At the time of his inauguration, about 40 percent of Philadelphia's 1.6 million people were black.

In an eight minute inaugural address, Goode, who served in the cabinet of former Mayor William Green, said that his election "might have been thought an impossible dream" for a black person, "but in America dreams can come true."

January 4. Robert O. Goodman, Jr., a black Navy Lieutenant, was welcomed by President Ronald Reagan and others at the White House after having been freed from captivity in Syria. The release was negotiated by the African-American Democratic presidential candidate Jesse L. Jackson. At the White House, Reagan declared, "This is a homecoming, and a very happy and welcomed one. . . . We are very proud of him."

Goodman had served a month as a prisoner in Syria after an A-6E Intruder jet, on which he was serving as bombardier-navigator, was shot down during an American air strike against Syrian anti-aircraft positions in Lebanon on December 4, 1983. The pilot of the plane, Mark Lange, was killed in the attack.

Goodman's release was made possible by "a moral appeal" which candidate Jackson, also a national civil rights leader, made to Syrian President Hafez Assad. Jackson's intervention into the realms of American foreign policy had been the subject of both praise and criticism, yet President Reagan said following Goodman's release, "You don't quarrel with success."

January 6. Benjamin E. Mays, former president of Morehouse College and the Atlanta, Georgia school board, was inducted into the South Carolina Hall of Fame. Mays, age eighty-nine, a native of South Carolina and the son of former slaves, was cited for his long career in education and civil rights.

Since Mays was hospitalized with pneumonia, the plaque recognizing his induction was presented to him in Atlanta by former President Jimmy Carter, a longtime friend. Carter called the black educator "a credit to Georgia and South Carolina, he's a credit to the Southland and he's a credit to the United States of America and to the world." In his response, Mays commented: "I was born a little stubborn on the race issue. . . . I felt that no man had a right to look down on another man. Every man, whether he's on the right of you, the left of you, certainly in back of you—it makes no difference—is still a man."

January 6. Robert N. C. Nix, Jr. was inaugurated as Chief Justice of the Pennsylvania Supreme Court, becoming the first African-American to sit on a state Supreme Court bench since the Reconstruction era.

Nix was born on July 13, 1928, the grandson of a college dean and the son of Robert N. C. Nix, Sr., Pennsylvania's first black Democratic congressman. He received a bachelor's degree from Villanova University in Pennsylvania and a law degree from the University of Pennsylvania.

After serving as deputy attorney general of Pennsylvania in 1956-57, Nix spent ten years in private practice. In 1968, he returned to public life to serve on the Philadelphia Court of Common Pleas. He was elected to the Pennsylvania Supreme Court in 1971.

Nix hoped that his appointment as chief justice would "inspire confidence in the legal system," and saw it as a reaffirmation of those principles upon which "American democracy was founded."

January 16. The American Music Awards presented the Award of Merit to African-American pop singer Michael Jackson at its eleventh annual ceremonies. The award recognized Jackson's "outstanding contributions over a long period of time to the musical entertainment of the American public." Previous African-American winners of the award included Berry Gordy, Jr., founder of Motown Records, and singers Ella Fitzgerald and Stevie Wonder.

January 22. Marcus Allen, African-American running back for the Los Angeles Raiders, was named Most Valuable Player (MVP) of the 28th Annual Super Bowl in Tampa, Florida. Allen gained a record 191 yards rushing on 20 carries and scored two touchdowns, one on a five-yard run, the other on a 74-yard run. The Raiders defeated the Washington Redskins 38-9.

February 2. Mobile County Circuit Court Judge Braxton Kittrell sentenced Ku Klux Klansman Henry Hays to death for the 1981 strangulation murder of Michael Donald, a nineteen-year-old black youth whose body was found hanging from a tree in downtown Mobile, Alabama. Hays, age twenty-nine, was convicted of capital murder by a jury of eleven whites and one black on December 10, 1983.

In sentencing Hays to death by electric chair, Judge Kittrell ignored the recommendation of the jury for a life sentence in prison. But Mobile County District Attorney Chris Galanos said there was only "one chance in a million" that the death penalty would stand up on appeal since Donald (who was beaten, slashed across the throat, and found hanging across the street from Hays's house) had been killed four months before Alabama law permitted judges to give a stiffer penalty than that recommended by jurors.

February 7. United States District Court Judge Richard Enslen in Kalamazoo, Michigan, awarded a judgement of $50,000 to Walter Bergman, an eighty-four- year-old former Freedom Rider, who was beaten by Ku Klux Klansmen at an Alabama bus station in 1961.

On May 31, 1983, Judge Enslen had decided that there was a "preponderance of evidence" to indicate that the FBI knew the Klan planned to attack Bergman and other Freedom Riders as they rode through Anniston and Birmingham, Alabama during the height of the Civil Rights Movement. The Bureau, he added, "had specific information" that the Klan "would be given free reign" by police in the two cities "to attack the Freedom Riders." Thus, he ruled, it could be sued for damages.

At the time of Judge Enslen's decision, Bergman, a former Wayne State University professor from Grand Rapids, was confined to a wheelchair from injuries suffered in the 1961 attack. He had asked for $2 million from the FBI for himself and the estate of his late wife, Frances. (See also entries dated May 4, 1961 and August 20, 1978.)

February 28. The United States Supreme Court, in a 6-3 decision, ruled that federal law prohibiting racial or sexual discrimination by schools and colleges extends only to the affected program or unit, not to the entire institution.

The case came to the high Court from Grove College in Pennsylvania which had refused to sign a required "assurance of compliance" with Title IX of the Education Amendments of 1972. The federal government then began proceedings to disqualify the college from receiving federal scholarship aid. The college and four of its students brought suit in a U. S. District Court in Pennsylvania challenging the government's actions. Although the District Court sided with the college, the U. S. Court of Appeals for the Third Circuit ruled that despite the limited nature of the federal assistance received by Grove College, the law applied to the entire institution. The Supreme Court's majority disagreed. Justices Lewis Powell and Sandra Day O'Connor wrote that the case presented "an unedifying example of overzealousness on the part of the Federal government" in its previous interpretation of Title IX.

While the administration of President Ronald Reagan applauded the decision, many congressmen, women's rights, and civil rights groups reacted with alarm. For while the issue presented by Title IX of the Education Amendments of 1972 focused on sex discrimination, the broader provisions of the landmark Title VI of the omnibus Civil Rights Act of 1964 contained almost identical language. Thus, these groups feared its application too might be restricted by the Supreme Court's decision in the Grove College case. (See also entries dated March 16, 1988, March 20, 1988, and March 22, 1988.)

March 15. The College Board, promoters of the Scholastic Aptitude Test (SAT), reported that the average SAT scores for blacks had risen 22 points since 1976. While the national SAT verbal average decreased 6 points between 1976 and 1983, the average for blacks increased by 7 points verbally and 15 points in mathematics during the period. The report said that the black SAT score increases had occurred "in all regions of the country." But among blacks students who took the SAT in 1983, those enrolled in private schools had average scores 43 points higher in verbal and 24 points higher in mathematics than those in public schools. The new results of black SAT scores, overall, represented a reversal of a trend of falling test performances.

The new statistics on black SAT performances were included in a report entitled, "Profiles, College Bound Seniors," published by the College Board in New York City. (See also entry dated September 11, 1989.)

March 28. Benjamin Elijah Mays, educator and civil rights spokesperson, died of heart failure in Atlanta, Georgia, at age eighty-nine.

Mays was born August 1, 1894 in Epworth, South Carolina, the youngest of eight children of Hezekiah and Louvenia Carter Mays, former slaves and tenant farmers. After graduating valedictorian from the high school department of South Carolina State College in Orangeburg, he entered Virginia Union College in Richmond, where he earned a straight "A" average. A year later Mays transferred to Bates College in Lewiston, Maine, from which he graduated with honors in 1920. While a graduate student at the University of Chicago, Mays taught mathematics at Morehouse College in Atlanta, Georgia. He completed a doctorate degree at Chicago in 1935. In the interval, Mays had also pastored the Shiloh Baptist Church in Atlanta (1921-24), taught English at South Carolina State College (1925), served as executive secretary of the Tampa, Florida Urban League (1926-28), served as national student secretary of the Young Men's Christian Association (YMCA) (1928-30), directed a study of black churches under the auspices of the Institute of Social and Religious Research (1930-32), and began a career as dean of the School of Religion at Howard University in Washington, D.C. (1934-40).

In 1940, Mays was elected president of Morehouse College (a prestigious all-black, all-male institution) which was faltering in a weakened Depression economy and which had lost much of its student body to war-time employment. One of his earliest students was young Martin Luther King, Jr., who came to the school in 1944 from the eleventh grade of high school. King soon became a protégé of the college president.

Through his skills as an orator and a fund-raiser, Mays restored the viability and prestige of Morehouse College and when he retired in 1967, the school had just been awarded a chapter of Phi Beta Kappa, the country's oldest and most prestigious academic honors society. Only two other black institutions of higher education in the nation, Fisk and Howard Universities, had previously earned such a distinction.

Following his retirement as president of Morehouse, Mays won a seat on the Atlanta Board of Education in 1969. The next year he was elected the first black president of the city's school board and was subsequently reelected six times over the next twelve years. During Mays's tenure as head of the school board, a group of black and white leaders adopted the so-called Atlanta Compromise Plan for school desegregation. With the approval of federal court judges, the blacks agreed to abandon pressures for cross-town and cross-jurisdictional busing to achieve further school desegregation, while whites consented to black administrative control of the school system. As a result of the pact, Alonzo Crim became the first black superintendent of the Atlanta Public Schools in 1973.

Mays began his civil rights activities as early as 1942 when he filed a successful suit challenging separate black and white dining cars on railroads. Between 1950 and 1970, he wrote hundreds of essays in magazines and newspapers (including a column in the *Pittsburgh Courier*), scholarly articles, and books denouncing segregation and discrimination and pleading for racial justice and racial harmony. Among these were *A Gospel for the Social Awakening* (1950), *Seeking to Be Christian in Race Relations* (1957), *Disturbed About Man* (1969), and his autobiography, *Born to Rebel* (1971). He gave an invocation and remarks at the historic March on Washington in 1963 and preached the principal eulogy at the funeral of Martin Luther King, Jr. in 1968. During that sermon Mays said, "God called the grandson of slaves and said to him, 'Martin Luther, speak to America about war and peace, speak to America about social justice, speak to America about racial discrimination, about its obligation to the poor'."

In commenting on Mays's death, Charlie Moreland, president of the Morehouse College Alumni Association, remembered one of Mays's favorite quotations: "It must be born in mind that not reaching your goal is not tragic. The tragedy lies in not having a goal to reach." (See also entries dated July 1, 1967, and January 6, 1984.)

April 26. William "Count" Basie, African-American band leader, died of cancer in Hollywood, Florida, at the age of seventy-nine.

Basie grew up in Red Bank, New Jersey, and began taking .25¢ music lessons at age eight. Despite his protests, Basie's mother insisted that he was "going to learn how to play the piano if it kills you."

Basie began playing professionally with Walter Page's Blue Devils group in Kansas City, Missouri in the late 1920s and later joined Benny Moten's band in 1929. When Moten died six years later, Basie took over and began the Count Basie Band. The group was not really "discovered" until 1935 when John Hammond, a jazz impresario who had brought Billie Holiday to prominence, saw Basie's ten-piece band in Kansas City. He was so impressed that he urged Basie to increase the size of his ensemble and booked its first national tour.

It was also in Kansas City that Basie acquired the famous nickname, "Count." A radio announcer discussing the "royal family" of jazz, which included "Duke of Ellington" and "King of Oliver," struck upon the idea of a "Count of Basie," yet Basie never really liked the title. He said in 1982, "I wanted to be called Buck or Hoot or even Arkansas Fats," all silent-film heroes. By 1936, Basie and his band had garnered a reputation far beyond Kansas City and it travelled widely throughout the country, with its residency at the Roseland Ballroom in New York City. It "delivered several seminal improvisers to the world of jazz." Most notable were Buck Clayton, Herschel Evans, and Lester Young, "whose logical flow of melody became the standard for horn players of subsequent generations."

The Basie band began recording in 1937 and such tunes as "One O'Clock Jump" became "studies in call-and-response phrasing in which the saxophones often trade simple blues riffs with the brass." The group's early albums included *Basie's Back in Town, Blues by Basie,* and *Super Chief.*

The Basie band began to pare down in the 1950s, collaborating with blues singer "Big" Joe Williams in what "was widely considered a creative peak" for both Basie and Williams.

The demeanor of Basie, who was influenced by the legendary "Fats" Waller, was perhaps best described by Whitney Balliett, a jazz critic, in his book *Night Creature* (1980). Balliett said the band leader "pilots his ship from the keyboard with an occasional raised finger, an almost imperceptible nod, a sudden widely opened eye, a left-hand chord, a lifted chin, a smile, and plays background and solo piano that is the quintessence of swinging and taste and good cheer, even when almost nothing happens around it."

331

Basie's last performance was on March 19, 1984 at the Hollywood Palladium in California. He was completing more than fifty years as a jazz artist.

In commenting on Basie's death, blues singer Joe Williams said "we have just lost a national treasure but the happiness that his music gave us will live." (See also entry dated February 26, 1985.)

June 12. The United States Supreme Court, in a 6-3 decision, ruled that employers may not eliminate seniority plans that favor white men in order to protect "affirmative action gains by minorities and women when hard times hit." The Court also ruled that special preferences to remedy past discriminations were available only to persons who could prove they had been victimized by such bias, and not to "a class of people such as all blacks in an employer's work force." The decision arose from a Memphis, Tennessee case when the city protected blacks from possible layoffs or demotions during an economic crisis in 1961. The Court's action was seen as a major defeat for civil rights advocates. (See also entries dated June 25, 1976, July 3, 1978, July 2, 1986, January 23, 1989, June 5, 1989, and June 12, 1989.)

July 17. The Center for the Study of Social Policy, a Washington, D.C. research group, released a study which revealed that "the gap between the average incomes of whites and blacks" was as wide in 1984 as it was in 1960. The group blamed the disparity on the increase in the proportion of black families headed by females, from one-fifth to nearly one-half, and a sharp drop in the number of jobs held by black men.

In 1984, 14 percent of white families with children were headed by women, whereas 47 percent of black families fell in that category, an increase of 8 percent since 1950 and 21 percent since 1960. In 1984, only 55 percent of black men over the age of sixteen were employed, compared to 74 percent in 1960. As a consequence, the Center's study disclosed the median income of black families in 1981 was 56 percent of the whites' median, compared to 51 percent in 1960, but "the difference of one percentage point is statistically insignificant."

The report concluded: "Despite the fact that black Americans have made some gains since the civil rights movement, the economic gap between blacks and whites remains wide and is not diminishing. On measures of income, poverty, and unemployment, wide disparities between blacks and whites have not lessened or have even worsened since 1960."

July 27. C. L. Franklin, minister and civil rights leader, died in Detroit, Michigan at the age of sixty-nine. Franklin, who was also the father of soul singer Aretha Franklin, had been in a coma for five years after having been shot by robbers in his home.

Franklin was pastor of the New Bethel Baptist Church in Detroit for thirty-eight years and recorded more than twenty albums of his sermons, including *The Eagle Stirred Its Nest.* On some of his recordings, he was joined by the New Bethel Baptist Church Choir and his daughter Aretha.

Just months before the famous March on Washington in 1963, Franklin led a civil rights march in Detroit which attracted thousands of people. Jesse Jackson, one of the nation's most prominent civil rights leaders, and also a minister, eulogized Franklin as "the high priest of soul preaching."

August 4-11. At the Summer Olympic Games held in Los Angeles, California, several African-American athletes captured the coveted gold medal, indicating first place finishes.

On August 4, Carl Lewis won the finals of the prestigious 100-meter dash in track and field. Lewis defeated Sam Graddy by finishing in 9.99 seconds. Graddy won the silver medal for his second place finish in 10.19 seconds. Lewis's winning margin of two-tenths of a second was the largest in Olympic history for the event. It was also the first gold medal in track and field for the United States in the 1984 Olympics and the first for the U.S. in the 100-meter since 1968, when Jim Hines set a world record of 9.95 in the high altitude of Mexico City. Still, Lewis's 9.99 represented the fastest 100 meters ever run at sea level in the Olympics.

On August 5, Evelyn Ashford set an Olympic record of 10.97 seconds while winning the women's 100-meter finals, and Edwin Moses won the 400-meter intermediate hurdles in 49.75 seconds.

On August 11, Carl Lewis completed his sweep of four gold medals by running the last leg of the U.S. 400-meter relay team. He went 100 meters in 8.94 seconds, enabling the Americans to set the first track and field record of the 1984 Games, 37.83 seconds. Earlier, Lewis had won gold medals in the 100-meter dash, the 200-meter dash, and the long jump.

Lewis's feats in the 1984 Olympics equalled those of Jesse Owens, the African-American who won four gold medals in the same events in the 1936 Olympics in Berlin, Germany. Of his achievements, Lewis told news reporters "It is an honor. Two years ago, everyone in the world said it couldn't be done. Even a year ago, I said I couldn't do it." He added, "I was looking for Ruth Owens [Jesse Owens's widow]. Jesse has been such an inspiration to me. I wanted to dedicate one medal to her." (See also entry dated August 9, 1936.)

November 6. Ronald Reagan was reelected President of the United States by the biggest margin in recent history. Reagan captured at least 58 percent of the more than 50 million votes cast, while his Democratic challenger, former Vice President Walter Mondale, received approximately 41 percent. Reagan's landslide victory was comparable to that of Franklin D. Roosevelt's over Alf Landon in 1936; Lyndon B. Johnson's defeat of Barry Goldwater in 1964; and Richard Nixon's defeat of George McGovern in 1972. Reagan, who was frequently attacked by civil rights leaders during his first term for alleged insensitivity toward black issues, received only 20 percent of the African-American vote by most estimates, including media exit polls.

November 11. Martin Luther King, Sr., minister, civil rights activist, and father of slain civil rights leader, Martin Luther King, Jr., died following a heart attack in Atlanta, Georgia at age eight-four.

King, Sr. was born Michael Luther King to a sharecropper and cleaning woman in Stockbridge, Georgia on December 19, 1899. He changed his name "to honor" the famous German theologian Martin Luther in 1934.

King moved to Atlanta and became a minister at age seventeen. He also attended Morehouse College, where he graduated in 1930. A year later King succeeded his deceased father-in-law, the Reverend Adam Daniel Williams, as pastor of the Ebenezer Baptist Church, one of Atlanta's largest black congregations. He remained as pastor or co-pastor of the church until 1975.

Even before King assumed the pastorate at Ebenezer Baptist Church, he had become active in political and racial affairs in Atlanta. He was one of the black leaders who "successfully lobbied" for the construction of the Booker T. Washington High School, the first secondary school for blacks in the city, in 1924. In 1936, King was a leader in a voting rights march to Atlanta's City Hall and participated in protests against segregated cafeterias in the city and helped negotiate an agreement for their desegregation in 1961.

The elder King accumulated considerable wealth as well as political and social influence. He was a director of Citizens Trust Company, the city's black bank, and a member of the board of directors or trustees of SCLC, Morehouse College, the Morehouse School of Religion, and the Carrie Steele-Pitts Orphans Home. In 1972, he was named "Clergyman of the Year" by the Atlanta Chapter of the National Conference of Christians and Jews. A year before his death, King was awarded the Martin Luther King, Jr. Non-Violent Peace Prize.

Although King lost his famous son to an assassin's bullet in 1968 and his wife to another assassin in 1974, he continued to insist "I don't hate. . . . There is no time for that, and no reason either. Nothing that a man does takes him lower than when he allows himself to fall so low as to hate anyone."

In commenting on King's death, Marvin Arrington, the black president of the Atlanta City Council, remarked, "We've lost one of our patriarchs."

November 14. The Wonder Woman Foundation presented its first "Eleanor Roosevelt Woman of Courage Award" to Rosa Parks, the black woman who sparked the famous Montgomery, Alabama bus boycott in 1955. Parks, age seventy-one, recalled her experience in accepting the award in New York. She said, "I am not going to move," when a bus driver told her to give up her seat to a white man. Parks added, "I stand before you full of new courage and determination not to retire, as long as I feel I can be of some assistance to troubled people. . . ."

The Wonder Woman Awards were established in 1981 to highlight the 40th Anniversary of "Wonder Woman," the comic book heroine created by William Moulton Marston. (See also entry dated December 1, 1955.)

December 15. Miles Davis, the fifty-eight-year-old African-American jazz trumpeter, was awarded the Sonning prize for musical excellence in Copenhagen, Denmark. Davis was also presented with $9,000 in cash.

December 31. The United Negro College Fund (UNCF), a coordinating fund-raising organization for most of the nation's private black colleges and universities, announced that it had raised more than $14.1 million in pledges during a national telethon. The event, the first of its kind carried on national television, was hosted by singer Lou Rawls and had a goal of $15 million. (See also entry dated April 24, 1944.)

1985

January 7. Lou Brock, African-American outfielder for the St. Louis Cardinals of the National Baseball League, was elected to the Baseball Hall of Fame at Cooperstown, New York. Brock received 315 of the 395 ballots cast (79.5 percent) by members of the Baseball Writers' Association of America. He was only the fifteenth ballplayer to be elected in his first year of eligibility.

Brock played in the major leagues from 1961 until 1975. He began his career with the Chicago Cubs, but spent most of it with the St. Louis Cardinals. At the time of his election to the Hall of Fame, Brock still lead all players in the number of bases stolen with 938; held the National League record of 118 bases stolen in one season (1974); and held the highest batting average for World Series games (.391) in 21 games.

January 7. The United States Supreme Court, in a 6-3 decision, upheld the use of affirmative action plans by states that grant special employment preferences to minorities. The Court rejected arguments by fifteen prison guards in New York who contended that their chances of being promoted to captain were unlawfully diminished when state officials added points to promotion test scores of blacks and Hispanics. The guards sued the New York Civil Service Commission in 1982 after eight minority guards, whose promotion test scores had been upgraded, were added to a list of candidates for the rank of captain. At the time, there were no minority officers holding permanent positions as captain in any prison in the state of New York.

January 11. Reuben V. Anderson was appointed to the Mississippi Supreme Court, becoming the first black person ever to sit on the bench of that state's highest court. Anderson, who was previously a state Circuit Court Judge, was named to the high court by Mississippi Governor Bill Allain to fill the unexpired term of Justice Francis S. Bowling, who retired on January 1. Bowling's term runs to the fall of 1986.

Anderson, an attorney practicing in Mississippi since 1967, recalled that he never thought of the possibility of sitting on Mississippi's highest court. "When I first started practicing law," Anderson said, "I had to take my diploma with me wherever I went. Judges would not allow black lawyers to practice in a lot of courts in this state. . . . Back then many court houses had separate facilities for blacks and whites. . . . It makes you proud, so proud that Mississippi has come so far."

January 23. The National Urban League (NUL) said that 1984 was a year of "survival and hope" for African-Americans, despite attempts by the administration of President Ronald Reagan "to be a Rambo-like destroyer of civil rights gains."

In 1984, the NUL reported that most black children lived in poverty; black unemployment had declined to 15 percent, but was still three points above the black average since 1975 and more than double the white rate; and although black family incomes rose, the gap between black and white incomes had "grown wider for every type of family except those with two earners." The statistics and observations were included in the NUL's eleventh annual "State of Black America" Report.

In commenting on the Report, John Jacob, president of the NUL, said that President Ronald Reagan's citation of Martin Luther King, Jr.'s call for "a colorblind society" in 1963 was "obscene" and used "as a justification for trimming 'measures like affirmative action [that] move us toward a racially neutral society by opening opportunities that help black people enter the mainstream'."

February 26. Several African-American entertainers received awards during the presentations of the 1984 Grammys, the highest honors for recording artists. Tina Turner, the "Queen of Rhythm and Blues," won three Grammys, including Record of the Year and Song of the Year for "What's Love Got to Do With It?" Three Grammys also went to Prince for Best Rock Performance by a Group and Best Original Film Score for *Purple Rain*. For his songwriting efforts, Prince won Best New Rhythm and Blues Song for "I Feel for

You." Lionel Richie's *Can't Slow Down* was named Album of the Year, and Chaka Khan was awarded a Grammy for her recording of "I Feel For You." Jazz trumpeter Wynton Marsalis, the Pointer Sisters, and Shirley Caesar also won two Grammys each. Marsalis won in the Jazz and Classical categories, the Pointer Sisters in Pop, and Caesar in Gospel. Michael Jackson won an award for his video *Making Michael Jackson's 'Thriller'* and the late Count Basie was awarded a Grammy for his orchestra's *88 Basie Street*.

March 21. The Joint Center for Political Studies (JCPS), a Washington, D.C. research firm, reported that the 1984 elections increased the number of black mayors serving in the United States to 286. Thirty-one new black mayors were elected in 1984 in such cities as Battle Creek, Michigan, Gainesville, Georgia, Union Springs, Alabama, Pasco, Washington, Peekskill, New York, and Portsmouth and South Boston, Virginia. The increases in black mayors during 1984 was the largest "one-year increase yet recorded." Since 1975, the number of black mayors in the country had more than doubled from 135 to 286.

May 5. The historic Apollo Theater in the Harlem section of New York City reopened to celebrate its 50th anniversary. The theater, which was once the premiere showplace for America's black entertainers, had been closed for fifteen months and had undergone more than ten million dollars in refurbishings. More than 1,500 people attended the reopening celebrations while another 2,000 stood outside.

The Apollo opened on 125th street in Harlem in 1916 as an unnamed storefront and began offering showcase talent in 1935. Its earliest performers included comedians Jackie "Moms" Mabley and "Pigmeat" Markham. At the reopening ceremonies, many of the biggest names in black entertainment returned for an appearance, including comedian Bill Cosby, and singers and dancers Patti LaBelle, Gregory Hines, Wilson Pickett, Little Richard, Stevie Wonder, and the Four Tops.

During the ceremonies, Percy Sutton, the chairman of the Inner City Broadcasting Company who was "the prime mover behind the renovation," said "this theater is legendary to the thousands of performers who appeared on its stage, to the millions of people who attended its shows, and to the entertainment industry, which has been influenced by the innovations that occurred on the stage for five decades."

July 30. The United States General Accounting Office (GAO) agreed to pay $3.5 million in back pay to about three hundred "present and former" black employees who were denied promotions because of racial discrimination. Under the terms of the arrangement, thirty-two black evaluators would be promoted immediately and the GAO would then change its "competitive selection programs, including the preparation of an affirmative action plan to increase the percentage of minority people in upper-level positions."

The settlement resulted from class action suits filed by two GAO employees from Washington, D.C. and San Francisco, California in 1980 and 1983, respectively, which claimed that whites were favored over blacks in promotion to supervisory positions from 1976 through 1983. In 1984 the Equal Employment Opportunity Commission (EEOC) found that the GAO's use of two different promotion systems had, indeed, "resulted in racial discrimination against many of its black employees."

November 7. The Bureau of the Census reported that the number of black-owned businesses in the United States had increased forty-seven percent over a five year period. In 1982, there were 339,231 black-owned firms, compared to 231,203 in 1977.

The majority of black-owned companies were service and retail businesses with gross receipts totaling $12.4 billion in 1982. That was an increase of nearly forty-four percent from $8.6 billion five years earlier.

The largest segment of black firms were "miscellaneous retail businesses," 53,981, with total receipts in 1982 of $993 million. Black automotive dealers and service stations accounted for the largest dollar volume, however, $1.3 billion for 3,448 firms in 1982.

Small, sole proprietorships firms totalling 322,975 accounted for more than ninety-five percent of all black businesses in 1982, while corporations made up only 1.8 percent.

November 19. Veteran African-American actor Lincoln Theodore Andrew Perry, better known as Stepin Fetchit, died of pneumonia and congestive heart failure in Woodland Hills, California. He was eighty-three years old.

Perry, a native of Key West, Florida, began his acting career in the 1930s, appearing in such films as *Steamboat Round the Bend*, and was best known for his roles as "a shuffling, head-scratching" servant. He took his stage name from a race horse on which he had won some money in Oklahoma before leaving for Hollywood in the 1920s. Perry was the first black performer to appear on film with such movie stars as Will Rogers and Shirley Temple.

Perry's film characters were viewed by many blacks as negative stereotypes of their race, but Perry himself often bristled at such criticism and defended his "contributions." He once said that "when I came into motion picture, it was as an individual. . . . I had no manager, and no one had the idea of making a Negro a star. . . . I became the first Negro entertainer to become a millionaire. . . . All the things that Bill Cosby and Sidney Poitier have done wouldn't be possible if I hadn't broken that law [the race barrier]. I set up thrones for them to come and sit on."

After the CBS television documentary entitled "Of Black America" characterized him as a "stupid, lazy, eye-rolling stereotype" in the 1960s, Perry sued the network for $3 million, alleging that he had been held "up to hatred, contempt, [and] ridicule." A federal judge dismissed the suit in 1974.

1986

January 16. A bronze bust of Dr. Martin Luther King, Jr. was placed in the United States Capitol building. The statue was the first of any black American to stand in the halls of Congress. The bust, which depicts King in a meditative mood with a slightly bowed head, was created by John Wilson, a black artist at Boston University. After being displayed in the rotunda of the Capitol building for six months, the bust was to be moved to Statuary Hall to stand beside the statues of other famous Americans on display there.

The bust was unveiled by King's widow, Coretta Scott King. Among those who spoke at the ceremonies were Senator Charles Mathias from Maryland, who said "today, Martin Luther King, Jr. takes his rightful place among the heroes of this nation." Representative Mary Rose Oakar from Ohio added: "No other American of my generation affected the course of American history more than Dr. King." (See also entry dated June 22, 1974.)

January 18. A group of whites marched in downtown Raleigh, North Carolina, to honor the birthday of Confederate General Robert E. Lee and to protest the first federal holiday honoring Dr. Martin Luther King, Jr. Glenn Miller, leader of the White Patriots Party and a former Ku Klux Klansman, said that he was "nauseated and sickened" by the national tribute to King. Miller added, "We're down here to tell the world that we will never accept a birthday honoring a black communist. Never!"

The Raleigh demonstration was one of several protests and acts of vandalism directed at the first annual King holiday. During the week, vandals in Buffalo, New York painted a bust of King displayed in a city park white, while several muncipalities and states refused to recognize the holiday altogether.

January 20. The nation celebrated the first national holiday in honor of slain civil rights leader Dr. Martin Luther King, Jr. In Atlanta, Georgia (King's birthplace), Vice President George Bush attended a wreath laying ceremony at King's crypt and an ecumenical service at Ebenezer Baptist Church, where King pastored at the time of his death. Other political leaders attending the services were Senators Bill Bradley from New Jersey, Robert Dole from Kansas, Mack Mattingly and Sam Nunn, both from Georgia. Housing and Urban Development Secretary Samuel Pierce, Representative Newt Gingrich from Georgia, and Georgia Governor Joe Frank Harris were also in the audience, as was Rosa Parks, whose refusal to give up her bus seat to a white man sparked the famous Montgomery, Alabama bus boycott in 1955.

The celebrations also included the first national Martin Luther King, Jr. Holiday Parade held in Atlanta. Atlanta Police Chief Morris Redding stated that the parade yielded "probably the largest turnout we've ever had" for such an event in the city.

The Martin Luther King, Jr. national holiday was the first such honor ever extended to an African-American in United States history. (See also entry dated November 2, 1983.)

January 20. The 1986 Martin Luther King, Jr. Non-Violent Peace Prize was awarded to Bishop Desmond Tutu, a leader in the struggle against apartheid in South Africa. The award was presented on behalf of the King Center for Non-Violent Social Change by its president and King's widow, Coretta Scott King. She said that Tutu, like King, possessed "faith that dissipates despair." Also, like King, Tutu repeatedly encouraged those "who are denied fundamental human, civil, and political rights never to doubt that they will one day be free."

In his acceptance speech, Tutu, winner of the 1984 Nobel Peace Prize, said he trembled as he stood "in the shadow of so great a person" as King. He added, "I receive [the award] on behalf of those languishing in jail, sentenced to terms of life imprisonment because they have the audacity to say, 'All we want for ourselves is what white people want for themselves'."

January 28. Ronald McNair, an African-American astronaut, died aboard the *Challenger* space shuttle shortly after its lift-off from Cape Canaveral, Florida. McNair, a thirty-five year old physicist, was the nation's second black astronaut. He was one of a crew of seven aboard the *Challenger* when it exploded in the skies.

In one of the eulogies for McNair, actress Cicely Tyson remarked, "Ron and his crewmates touched . . . us. . . . They touched the other side of the sky for us."

February 8. Lorimer Douglas (L.D.) Milton, one of the nation's leading black bankers, died in Atlanta, Georgia, at age eighty-seven.

Milton was born on September 3, 1898 in Prince William County, Virginia, to Samuel Douglas and Samuella Anderson Milton. He was raised in Washington, D.C. and attended Brown University in Massachusetts on an ROTC scholarship. After receiving bachelor's and master's degrees in business from Brown in the 1920s, he began a long teaching career at Morehouse College and Atlanta University in Georgia. He retired as director of the Graduate School of Business Administration at Atlanta University in 1955.

In 1921 Milton began working in the Citizens Trust Bank of Atlanta, one of the nation's oldest and largest black financial institutions. He was elected president of the bank in 1930 and served in that position until 1971. At the time of

African-American astronauts from NASA's Space Shuttle program (left to right): Col. Guion S. Bluford, Jr., Dr. Ronald E. McNair, Col. Frederick D. Gregory, and Lt. Col. Charles F. Bolden, Jr.

Milton's retirement, Citizens Trust Bank had assets totalling $30 million and had established "a reputation for having opened the doors of the credit market to blacks."

Milton had served on a number of federal banking committees, including the advisory board of the Commodity Credit Corporation, which had responsibility for financing the government's farm price-support program. He also served on the President's Committee for the White House Conference on Education in 1955; the Federal Advisory Council's Social Security Board; and the National Commission of Economic Development in 1963. In addition, Milton was a former chairman of the board of trustees of Howard University.

March 2. City Councilman Sidney Barthelemy defeated state senator William Jefferson to become the second black mayor of New Orleans, Louisiana. Barthelemy garnered 93,054 votes (58 percent) to Jefferson's 67,668 (42 percent) of the vote to succeed Ernest "Dutch" Morial, New Orleans's first black mayor.

Barthelemy, age forty-three, told his supporters after his victory "This is like a dream! . . . Let us close ranks and fight the real problems."

In the New Orleans municipal elections held on March 2, two African-

Americans were also elected to the city council, giving blacks a majority on the seven-member body for the first time in that city's history. (See also entry dated March 20, 1982.)

June 30. A U. S. Department of Defense survey revealed that more than 400,000 black Americans were serving in the Armed Services during 1986. (See Table G in Appendix for data compiled by the Department of Defense.)

July 2. The United States Supreme Court, in two separate rulings, upheld affirmative action programs in hirings and promotions. In one case, the justices approved by a vote of 6-3 a plan from Cleveland, Ohio which reserved about half of the promotions in its fire department for "qualified minority candidates." In the other ruling, the Court declared by a margin of 5-4 that a union representing sheet metal workers in New York state and New Jersey must double its non-white membership.

In the majority opinion, Justice William Brennan wrote, "We . . . hold that [federal law] does not prohibit a court from ordering in appropriate circumstances, affirmative race-conscious relief as a remedy for past discrimination." (See also entries dated June 25, 1976, July 3, 1978, and June 12, 1984.)

September 30. Edward Perkins, a veteran diplomat, was named United States Ambassador to the Republic of South Africa, becoming the first African-American ever to serve in that position. At the time of the appointment, the U.S. Senate was considering whether or not to override President Ronald Reagan's veto of "harsh" economic sanctions against the white-minority government of South Africa. However, a "senior White House official" told news reporters that the "nomination was not made with the expectation of winning any converts in the Senate."

Perkins was currently serving as United States Ambassador to Liberia when President Reagan appointed him to the South African post.

October 15. A special Gallup Poll commissioned by the Joint Center for Political Studies in Washington, D.C., revealed that President Ronald Reagan's approval rating among blacks tripled between 1984 and 1986. The approval rate climbed from only eight percent in 1984 to 25 percent in 1986. In 1984, 82 percent of African-Americans polled disapproved of the President's performance. By 1986, however, the negative rating had dropped to 66 percent. The highest approval rates for Reagan (30 percent or better) came from blacks who were male, blue-collar workers, political independents, urban Southerners and individuals younger than thirty years of age. The poll was based on a national survey of 868 blacks.

October 18. The NAACP, one of the oldest and most prominent of the nation's civil rights organizations, dedicated its new national headquarters in

Baltimore, Maryland. The group, which was founded in 1909 "to fight discrimination and injustice," moved to Baltimore from its original headquarters in New York City, partially because "it could not afford the high rent and taxes." Baltimore was chosen for the new headquarters largely because of "its majority black population and long history in promoting civil rights."

October 23. Five white students dressed in Ku Klux Klan-type attire broke into the room of Kevin Nesmith, a black cadet at The Citadel in South Carolina. The five students taunted Nesmith and left a charred paper cross in his room. Nesmith said that he slept through most of the incident.

November 14-17. A black cadet at The Citadel who was harassed by five white students on October 23 (see above), resigned, and a South Carolina State Commission issued a report on the original incident.

On November 14, Kevin Nesmith resigned from the South Carolina military college because he felt he had been "made the villian" in the hazing incident, but added "the villians remain at Citadel." Nesmith also said that "anger and frustration built up, and I felt mentally drained and no longer wanted to subject myself to this humiliation."

The five white cadets who cursed Nesmith in the October incident were suspended from the college, but the suspensions were "stayed on the condition they not get into any more serious trouble during the school year." They were also restricted to campus for the remainder of the school year and "given additional marching tours." But some black leaders in the state contended that the five should have been expelled. The NAACP filed an $800,000 lawsuit against The Citadel, alleging that Nesmith's civil rights had been violated and that the school historically had "tolerated and sanctioned" racial bigotry. On November 17, civil rights leader Jessie Jackson met with Nesmith and later requested a congressional investigation of race relations at the college.

On November 16, the South Carolina Human Affairs Commission issued a report stating that a "minimal black representation" on the campus created "an environment lacking in ethnic diversity and cultural sensitivity." They recommended, among other things, that the school increase its black enrollment from 6 percent to 10 percent in two years and incorporate "mandatory human relations and cultural sensitivity classes" into the leadership training curriculum.

December 10. United States District Court Judge R. Allan Edgar dismissed a school segregation suit against the Board of Education of Chattanooga, Tennessee, which was first filed in 1960. Edgar commented: "Based upon their conduct for many years, there is no indication that the defendants [the school board] will take any steps to reinstitute vestiges of segregation." He ruled that the Board had finally met the court order "to racially integrate students and faculty."

At the time of Edgar's ruling, there were nearly 23,700 students, 51.26 percent of them black, enrolled in Chattanooga's public schools. Most recently, the school board had reassigned 185 teachers in order that the faculty at each school in the system match approximately the 60-40 white-to-black teacher ratio systemwide.

The desegregation suit, filed by black real estate agent James Mapp, was "the longest to linger" in the federal court in Chattanooga. But Mapp, whose home was bombed in 1970, said, "I think the past effects of state-imposed racial discrimination and segregation have not been completely done away with." He cited several local schools that were still either "almost 100 percent black or white."

December 20-23. One black man was killed and two others injured after a gang of white youths attacked them in the predominately-white Howard Beach section of Queens, New York. Michael Griffith, a twenty-three-year-old construction worker from Brooklyn, was hit by a car and killed on a highway while attempting to escape his attackers. Another black man, Cedric Sandeford, age thirty-seven, was beaten with a baseball bat. The three blacks were attacked outside a pizza parlor after being taunted with racial slurs.

The three blacks, whose car had experienced mechanical problems, had gone into the pizza parlor to call for help when they were confronted by a gang of whites yelling racial epithets and asking "'What are you doing in this neighborhood'," according to a statement by New York Police Commissioner Benjamin Ward. New York Mayor Edward Koch posted a $10,000 reward "for information leading to the arrests of the assailants."

On December 23, three white teenagers were ordered held without bond on second-degree murder charges in connection with the attack. Meanwhile, a group of blacks in the Jamaica section of Queens, chanting "Howard Beach! Howard Beach!" chased and beat a white teenager who was walking to a bus stop. Mayor Koch condemned the apparent retaliation.

The Howard Beach incident was another in a series of ugly racial confrontations which had occurred in various parts of the country this year. The first major encounter took place in Raleigh, North Carolina, on the eve of the first national holiday honoring Dr. Martin Luther King, Jr. (See also entry dated January 18, 1986.)

1987

January 2. Marion Barry, Jr. was inaugurated for an unprecedented third term as mayor of Washington, D.C. In his inaugural address, the former black civil rights activist asserted: "Nobody's going to turn us around from educating every person who wants to learn, employing every person who wants to work, housing every person who needs shelter, helping every person who needs new hope." (See also entry dated September 24, 1987.)

January 14. The National Urban League (NUL) said that black Americans were "besieged by a resurgence of violent racism, economic depression, and a national climate of selfishness marked by a retreat from civil rights" during 1986. In its annual "The State of Black America" report, the NUL noted that 15 percent of the black work force was unemployed and that black family income "over the past dozen years" had decreased by $1,500 "while economic need increased."

In presenting the report, NUL president John Jacob said, "We can't forget that for six years and more, Americans have been told that racism is a thing of the past. That poverty is caused by habits of the poor. . . . The result is a national climate of selfishness and a failure of government to take a positive role in ending racism and disadvantage."

The League's recommendations for solving the maladies which it identified included a "broad-based" attack on violent racism and a call for congressional action to toughen and tighten civil rights laws.

Larry Speakes, spokesman for the administration of President Ronald Reagan (which was harshly criticized in the report), said although he had not read the document, "Certainly we would share a concern with the Urban League over any increase or, for that matter, a single incident of racial intolerance or racial violence that would occur in this country."

January 17. Ku Klux Klansmen and other white supremacists threw rocks and bottles at a group of ninety civil rights marchers in Forsyth County, Georgia. The 400 counter-demonstrators also shouted racial slurs at the protestors, who had gathered on a state road about two miles outside of the city of Cumming. There were no serious injuries, but eight of the supremacists were arrested on charges including disorderly conduct, trespassing, and carrying a concealed weapon.

The aborted march was led by Dean Carter, a white martial arts instructor from Hall County, Georgia, and veteran civil rights leader Hosea Williams. Most of the marchers were blacks from Atlanta, thirty miles south of Forsyth County. Williams, an Atlanta City Councilman, commented: "In 30 years in the civil rights movement, I've never seen it worse than this," as he responded to the violence. He also added, "In 1987, who would believe this kind of racial violence in America?"

The march had been planned after the cancellation of a previous "brotherhood walk" which Carter had organized, partially to honor the memory of assassinated civil rights leader Martin Luther King, Jr. The event was cancelled after the organizers were threatened.

January 24. More than 20,000 people marched for "brotherhood" and against racism in Forsyth County, Georgia. The biracial demonstrators were protected by 3,000 state and local police officers and National Guardsmen. There were a few minor injuries and sixty people, mostly white counter-demonstrators, were arrested. It was "the largest civil rights demonstration in two decades."

The march was organized after a similar, smaller protest a week earlier had been broken up by white counter-demonstrators who threw rocks and bottles. That "brotherhood" march, also designed to honor the memory of slain civil rights leader Martin Luther King, Jr., was led by veteran civil rights activist and Atlanta City Councilman Hosea Williams and Dean Carter, a white marital arts instructor. Coretta Scott King, widow of the assassinated civil rights leader, was among the leaders of the January 24th march, as was

"Brotherhood Anti-Intimidation March" in Forsyth County, Georgia.

Williams, Carter, and civil rights leaders Benjamin Hooks of the NAACP and Joseph Lowery of the SCLC.

All of the speakers during the demonstration denounced the racist attack on the earlier protesters and called for a renewal of the commitment to racial justice. Hosea Williams, a leader of the January 17th march called the January 24th march "the greatest."

January 31. About 1,000 people rallied in Louisville, Kentucky to protest the burning of a picture of slain civil rights leader Martin Luther King, Jr. by Ku Klux Klansmen and what they called a resurgence of racism and racist violence in the United States.

February 19-20. On February 19, about 200 blacks ran through the streets throwing rocks and setting fires in Tampa, Florida. The disturbances began one night after a twenty-three-year old black man died after police had tried to "subdue him by using a 'choke hold'—applying pressure to his carotid artery."

On February 20, isolated incidents involving rock and bottle throwing by black youths continued, but there were no injuries. Two people were arrested. Meanwhile, black leaders and other volunteers walked the streets urging residents to remain calm.

Before the most recent incidents, another black man had been killed by police, and other incidents involving blacks and law enforcement officers had occurred in December, 1986, including the arrest of the New York Mets' star pitcher Dwight Gooden. Gooden had been charged with "battering police officers." A report released on February 19, 1987 by City Attorney Michael Fogarty, however, placed some of the blame for the Gooden incident on the police. The report also called on the city of Tampa to recruit more black police officers. At the time of these latest altercations, only 65 members of Tampa's 790 member police force were black, and the paucity of black police officers had been a constant complaint of local black leaders. (See also entries dated May 18, 1980, and December 28-29, 1982.)

February 26. Edgar Daniel "E.D." Nixon, "one of the fathers of the civil rights movement," died after prostate surgery in Montgomery, Alabama, at the age of eighty-seven.

Nixon was born July 12, 1899 in Montgomery. He received only about sixteen months of formal education. Between 1923 and 1964, he worked as a Pullman porter on a Birmingham-to-Cincinnati train and was a long-time member of the Brotherhood of Sleeping Car Porters. In 1949, Nixon was elected president of the Alabama state NAACP.

At the time that a Montgomery seamstress, Rosa Parks, refused to give up her seat on a segregated Montgomery bus to a white man, Nixon was still active in the state and local NAACP and was, according to another local NAACP official, "the most militant man in town." Parks was also secretary of the local NAACP at the time and a close acquaintance of Nixon's. After Parks's arrest, she called Nixon, but he was unable to learn more about the situation because Montgomery police told him he was an "unauthorized person."

Following his rebuff by the Montgomery police, Nixon phoned Clifford Durr, a white Montgomery lawyer sympathetic to blacks. Durr was able to obtain the specific charge against Parks, "failing to obey a bus driver," and urged Nixon to seek the services of NAACP lawyer Fred D. Gray. Durr further advised that the defense should be based on the unconstitutionality of the state law requiring segregation on city buses, rather than the Montgomery city ordinance relating to retaining and giving up seats. Such a defense, he suggested, could best provide "a test case" for bus segregation laws.

In addition to contacting Durr and Gray immediately after Parks's arrest, Nixon is also credited with posting bail for the seamstress; informing Martin Luther King, Jr. of the arrest; proposing the Montgomery bus boycott; and helping to choose King as president of the Montgomery Improvement Association, which directed the successful 381 day boycott. Nixon is quoted as once having told a friend, referring to King, "I don't know just how, but one day I'm going to hook him to the stars." He made the remark after hearing King preach.

Nixon is also credited with avoiding a potential major division at the beginning of the boycott by declining to aspire to the leadership of the movement. This move may also have helped keep one of his rivals, Rufus Lewis, a local funeral director, from seeking the presidency of the Improvement Association, opening the way for King, who had few partisan ties, to lead the boycott. Finally, it was also Nixon who publicly browbeated recalcitrant blacks and chided fearful ones into action. After some black ministers urged that the boycott be keep secret, Nixon asked, "What the heck you taking about? How you going to have a mass meeting, going to boycott a city bus line, without the white folk knowing it? You ought to make up your mind right now that you either admit you are a grown man or concede to the fact that you are a bunch of scared boys." He also told a crowd at a mass meeting, "Before you brothers and sisters get comfortable in your seats, I want to say if anybody here is afraid, he better take his hat and go home. We've worn aprons long enough. It's time for us to take them off." According to the Reverend Ralph David Abernathy, also one of the leaders of the Montgomery boycott, Nixon "wouldn't take any mess."

Nixon's home, which had a bomb tossed in its driveway during the height of the protests, is now an Alabama state historical landmark. Nixon himself was feted at a testimonial dinner in Atlanta, Georgia in 1985. At that time, he remarked: "Fifty thousand people rose up and rocked the cradle of the Confederacy until we could sit where we wanted to on a bus. . . . A whole lot of things came about because we rocked the cradle." (See also entry dated December 1, 1955.)

March 19. Alice Bond, estranged wife of former Georgia Senator and civil rights activist Julian Bond, told police in Atlanta, Georgia that her husband and other prominent Atlantans were either users or suppliers of cocaine. Andrew Jackson Young, the black mayor of Atlanta, was also drawn into the matter when his name appeared as one of those individuals allegedly named by Bond, and when he made a telephone call "to counsel" her after her allegations were revealed. The accusations led to investigations by the Atlanta police, the FBI, and the U. S. Attorney for the Northern District of Georgia. No formal charges, however, were lodged against Senator Bond, and after a lengthy federal grand jury investigation U. S. Attorney Robert Barr announced that there was "insufficient evidence" to prosecute Mayor Young for obstruction of justice.

April 16. A United States District Court jury in New York City found that the *New York Daily News*, considered the nation's largest general newspaper, was guilty of retaliation against copy editor Causewell Vaughan, reporters Steven Duncan and David Hardy, and editor Joan Shepard because they complained of unfair treatment. The four black journalists had filed suit against the *Daily News* claiming they had been denied salaries comparable to their white colleagues and were given fewer promotions. At the time of the trial, only 6.5 percent of the nation's journalists were members of minority groups. In praising the jury's verdict in the *Daily News* case, Albert Fitzpatrick, president of the National Association of Black Journalists (NABJ), commented that "Blacks are under-represented in all areas of the media."

August 24. Bayard Rustin, the African-American civil rights activist who directed the 1963 March on Washington, died in New York City at the age of seventy-seven. In addition to being chief organizer of the 1963 march, Rustin was also responsible for "many of the tactics and much of the strategy" used by Martin Luther King, Jr. and other leaders of the Civil Rights Movement. During the 1960s and 1970s he was often criticized by "more radical blacks" because he advocated better education as the best means for blacks to gain racial equality and because he was an apostle of non-violent protest. Yet Rustin continued to oppose nationalist and separatist ideas among African-Americans.

Rustin's pacifist ideology extended at least back to World War II when he spent more than two years in jail as a conscientious objector. In the 1960s, he became an early vocal opponent of American involvement in the war in Vietnam.

At the time of his death, Rustin was co-chairman of the A. Philip Randolph

Institute, a social-reform lobbying group, and had recently travelled to Cambodia and Haiti investigating "violence and injustice."

In its tribute to Rustin published on August 26, 1987, the *Atlanta Constitution* said that he "devoted his life to the fight for human rights, freedom and justice, not just in [the United States], but around the world. . . . His commitments to human rights and peace were neither trendy nor shallow. . . . America is indebted to Bayard Rustin. It is a better nation because of him."

September 13. Thurgood Marshall, the only African-American ever to sit on the United States Supreme Court, said in a televised interview that President Ronald Reagan ranked at "the bottom" among presidents in "protecting and advancing civil rights." "Honestly," Marshall said, "I think he's down with [Herbert] Hoover and that group—[Woodrow] Wilson—when we [blacks] really didn't have a chance. Marshall went on to say that Reagan "as the 'gatekeeper' of fairness and justice in America, had neglected his job. . . . I don't care whether he's the president, the governor, the mayor, the sheriff, whoever calls the shots determines whether we have integration, segregation, or decency. . . . That starts exactly with the president." Marshall's remarks were broadcast on television stations affiliated with the Ganett Broadcasting Company.

Marshall's off-the-bench criticisms were rare both for him and for any Justice of the United States Supreme Court. When excerpts were published in newspapers prior to the actual telecast, President Reagan's advisor for domestic affairs, Gary Bauer, called them "outrageous." He said President Reagan's policies had permitted blacks and other minorities to "enter the economic mainstream of the country." He specifically cited the president's endorsement of the 1986 tax reform act, which he claimed removed the federal tax burden from millions of poor people, and the President's proposals to help low income families buy public housing and to receive cash vouchers to pay for their children's tuition at better schools.

Justice Marshall's criticisms echoed those of other African-American leaders who had complained for several years that the President had "tried to undercut minority hiring programs, school busing to achieve integration, the Voting Rights Act, and other efforts to prevent discrimination and advance the social and economic conditions of minorities." The Justice Department, for example, had joined several cases in federal courts to argue against affirmative-action in employment, contending that employers should exercise total "colorblindness" in hiring and promotions. The government also took the side of the Norfolk, Virginia School Board in a case challenging the use of busing to achieve racial desegregation in public schools.

While domestic advisor Bauer had defended "a colorblind approach," saying "if people are looking for us to meet certain quotas all the time, they're going to be very disappointed," B.J. Cooper, a White House deputy press secretary, countered that Reagan's critics overlooked "the administration's crackdown on cases of racial violence and its commitment to enforce fair employment and fair housing laws." He claimed that the administration had prosecuted 55 cases of racial violence involving 137 defendants, including 75 Ku Klux Klansmen, since it took office. "That compares," Cooper added, "with 22 cases involving 52 defendants, of whom 35 were Klansmen, in the previous Democratic administration of President Jimmy Carter."

September 24. Members attending the annual convention of the National Black Alcoholism Council, Inc. (NBAC) in Atlanta, Georgia, declared that alcoholism was a serious threat to the continued welfare of Black America. Although figures varied, it was estimated that between 10 million and 24 million Americans were alcoholics in 1987. However, a recent government study showed that blacks were twice as likely to die from cirrhosis than whites and that esophageal cancer among blacks was ten times higher than among whites.

Maxine Womble, chairwoman of the nine year old NBAC, said that the impact of alcoholism among blacks could be seen in "the large number of single-parent households, the prevalence of poverty, youth gangs, violence," high dropout rates from schools, teenaged pregnancies, and "black-on-black crime." Some studies, for example, have suggested that alcohol and drugs are involved in between 50 percent and 70 percent of the black homicides in the United States. "A lot of what we're doing is about images and education," Mrs. Womble said. "People in these [black] communities must realize only they can save themselves."

September 24. The Congressional Black Caucus (CBC) issued a report which charged that black elected officials are "victims" of harassment by various prosecutorial branches of government and the white-controlled media in disproportionable numbers. The report concluded that while the number of black elected officials has almost doubled since 1977 and "some of the names in the drama have changed . . . the circumstances remain essentially unchanged." The CBC contends that while black officials should rightfully be scrutinized, their "scrutiny . . . too often issues from ignoble motives; it is designed not to protect the public interests but to prevent the public's interest from being represented by persons of the public's choosing."

An appendix to the report listed 78 cases of "harassment" against black elected officials, but almost half of the cases occurred before 1977, and several did not involve investigations by government or the press. For example, Lloyd Edwards, who ran for president of the St. James Parish in Louisiana in 1983, and Katie Jackson Booker, who ran for mayor of Ditmoor, Illinois in 1985, were not included because of cross-burnings on their lawns.

The report did include, however, at least a dozen cases of black politicians who were either brought before grand juries and never indicted or who were indicted and later acquitted since 1977. These included Kenneth Gibson, the former mayor of Newark, New Jersey, whom the study says was indicted in 1982 on 146 counts of "conspiracy misuse of funds and misconduct" and was acquitted of all the charges; Mayor Marion Barry of Washington, D. C., who has been the target of an investigation of cocaine use and whose administration has been probed extensively by the FBI and the U. S. Attorney's Office for alleged corruption in the letting of contracts to minority businesses; and that of Mayor Andrew Young of Atlanta, Georgia, who appeared before a federal grand jury investigating whether he "tampered" with a witness during a probe into allegations of drug abuse by several well-known Atlanta citizens (see entry dated March 19, 1987). Of Young, the report said "for him even to have become the subject of an investigation, was widely perceived as a totally inappropriate and abusive use of prosecutorial discretion by the U. S. Attorney."

The CBC report also claimed that the harassment of black officials has occurred through audits and investigations by the Internal Revenue Service (IRS); electronic surveillance, burglaries, and covert disruptive activity by various intelligence agencies; and grand jury investigations and indictments by criminal justice agencies.

However, John Russell, a spokesman for the U. S. Department of Justice, labelled the CBC report "nonsense." He said "I don't think those allegations can be substantiated in any way." Jackie Greene, regional director for the National Association of Black Journalists and director of editorial services at *USA Today* in Washington declared "I think that black politicians should be held to the same scrutiny that any other politician faces by the media. . . . For the most part that is being done."

The CBC report was written by Mary Sawyer, a professor of religion at Iowa State University, who wrote a similar report in 1977, and was published by Voter Registration Action Inc. in Washington, D. C.

October 27. John Oliver Killens, author and teacher, died in New York City. Killens was born in Macon, Georgia, but left the South at age seventeen and lived most of his life in the North. Like many other blacks who left the South in the first half of the twentieth century, Killens was "reluctant to return" to his native region. His first extended visit to his hometown occurred in 1986, when he spent two weeks as a lecturer and writer-in-residence in the Middle Georgia city.

Killens' major novels included *Youngblood* (1954), *And Then We Heard the Thunder* (1963), and *The Cotillion, or One Good Bull Is Half the Herd* (1971). *Youngblood* was a story of "powerful courage" among ordinary black folks in a small Georgia town, while *The Cotillion* was a "hilarious satire [of] social-climbing" black Northerners.

Some critics contended that Killens's later works "lacked the power" of his first two novels, *Youngblood* and *And Then We Heard the Thunder*. But at least one reviewer, Tina McElroy Ansa, asserted that if literary historians are looking for the quality of "power . . . they should also look to the man. There, they will find the power they seek. The power of his teaching, the power of his courage, the power of his generosity, the power of his gentleness, the power of his example, the power of his life."

Killens is known to have inspired a generation of young black writers, including Wesley Brown, Nikki Giovanni, Richard Perry, Janet Tolliver, and Brenda Wilkinson. His own philosophy was that "the responsibility of the writer is to take the facts and deepen them into eternal truth. Every time I sit down to the typewriter, put pen to paper," he once said, "I'm out to change the world."

Killens was an original member of the Harlem Writers Guild and worked on Paul Robeson's newspaper, *Freedom*. He held fund raisers during the Civil Rights Movement for Dr. Martin Luther King, Jr. and travelled to Africa, China, and the Soviet Union. During his tenure on the faculty of Columbia University, Killens achieved a reputation for opening his home at night to students "for talk, food, and sometimes, shelter."

November 3. In municipal elections throughout the country, Baltimore, Maryland elected its first black mayor; the black mayor of Philadelphia, Pennsylvania was reelected; and the black mayor of Charlotte, North Carolina was defeated.

In Baltimore, Kurt Schmoke, an attorney, prosecutor, and Rhodes Scholar, gained 100,923 votes (78.5 percent) to defeat his Republican challenger Samuel Culotta, who had 27,636 votes.

In Philadelphia, Mayor W. Wilson Goode, the city's first black mayor, gained 331,659 votes (51.1 percent) to defeat former mayor Frank Rizzo who had 317,331 votes (48 percent) with 99.13 percent of the vote counted. Goode scored heavily among blacks who made up 40 percent of the 1.6 million residents of the nation's fifth largest city, despite lingering opposition to his decision to bomb a house occupied by MOVE, a radical black group in 1985. The sixty-seven-year-old Rizzo continued to labor under accusations that he was a racist, and had permitted police brutality against blacks while he served police commissioner and later as mayor.

In Charlotte, Sue Myrick, a white Republican and former City Councilwoman, defeated mayor Harvey Gantt, the first black mayor of the city, 47,311 to

46,296. Myrick had accused Gantt of failing to solve the city's traffic congestion problems. Her campaign was also aided by the support of North Carolina Governor Jim Martin. Sixty-four percent of the registered voters in Charlotte were white at the time of the election.

November 25. Harold Washington, the first African-American mayor of Chicago, Illinois, died of an apparent heart attack at Northwestern Memorial Hospital. Washington was six months into his second term as mayor when he collapsed while working in his City Hall office.

Washington was first elected mayor of Chicago in 1983 after "a bitter, racially-charged election." He had once said he wanted to serve the city for twenty years. Washington won reelection in April, 1987 after campaigning on a theme of "uniting the city's diverse racial and ethnic groups." His first term was marred by racial divisiveness among black and white aldermen and by white, ethnic opposition to his policies on the city council.

President Ronald Reagan lead those expressing grief at Washington's death. The President observed that "Harold Washington will truly be missed, not only by the people of Chicago but also by many across the country for whom he provided leadership on urban issues." Massachusetts Senator Edward Kennedy called Washington's death "a tragedy for Chicago and for civil rights. . . . He was an outstanding congressman and an outstanding mayor, and the civil rights movement in America has lost one of its greatest and most respected leaders." Representative William Gray from Pennsylvania, the most powerful black in Congress, said Washington's death was "a real great tragedy." Finally, Richard Daley, Cook County state's attorney and the son of the legendary Chicago Mayor Richard J. Daley remarked, "Mayor Washington had a deep love for his city, which has suffered a tremendous loss with his passing. His name will loom forever large in the history of Chicago, and rightfully so." (See also entry dated February 23, 1983.)

December 1. James Baldwin, African-American writer and civil rights activist, died of cancer in St. Paul de Venece, France, at age sixty-three. Baldwin had moved to France in 1948 to escape what he felt was "the stifling racial bigotry" of the United States.

Baldwin, the son of "an autocratic preacher who hated his son," was born in the Harlem section of New York City in 1924. He began writing while a student at the DeWitt Clinton High School in the Bronx and by his early twenties was publishing essays and reviews in such publications as the *Nation,* the *New Leader, Commentary,* and *Partisan Review.* Baldwin also began socializing with a circle of New York writers and intellectuals, including William Barrett, Irving Howe, and Lionel Trilling.

A prolific author, Baldwin published his three most important collections of essays—*Notes of a Native Son* (1955), *Nobody Knows My Name* (1961), and *The Fire Next Time* (1963) during the height of the Civil Rights Movement. Some critics, the *New York Times* reported, "said his language was sometimes too elliptical, his indictments sometimes too sweeping. But then [his] prose, with its apocalyptic tone—a legacy of his early exposure to religious fundamentalism—and its passionate yet distanced sense of advocacy, seemed perfect for a period in which blacks in the South lived under continued threats of racial violence and in which civil rights workers faced brutal beatings and even death."

Other important works by Baldwin included *Go Tell it On the Mountain* (1953), his first book and novel; *Giovanni's Room* (1956) and *Another Country* (1962), which contains a frank discussion of homosexuality; and the drama *Blues for Mister Charlie* (1964). In the preface to *Blues for Mister Charlie*, Baldwin noted that the work had been inspired "very distantly" by the murder of Emmett Till, a black youth in Mississippi in 1955. He wrote:

"What is ghastly and really almost hopeless in our racial situation now is that the crimes we have committed are so great and so unspeakable that the acceptance of this knowledge would lead, literally, to madness. The human being, then, in order to protect himself, closes his eyes, compulsively repeats his crimes, and enters a spiritual darkness which no one can describe."

During the Civil Rights Movement, Baldwin not only wrote about the struggle, but helped raise money for it and organized protest marches. He was also an early opponent of the United States's involvement in the Vietnam War and a critic of discrimination against homosexuals. Baldwin's writings and activism were recognized by many groups both in this country and abroad. Perhaps the most distinguished of these was the Legion of Honor, France's highest national award, which was presented to him in 1986.

Among those eulogizing Baldwin were a fellow African-American novelist, Ralph Ellison, who commented, "America has lost one its most gifted writers." Henry Louis Gates Jr., a literary critic and professor at Cornell University, said Baldwin "educated an entire generation of Americans about the civil rights struggle and the sensibility of Afro-Americans as we faced and conquered the final barriers in our long quest for civil rights."

December 15. Septima Poinsetta Clark, African-American civil rights activist, died on John's Island, South Carolina, at age eighty-nine.

Clark was born to a former slave in Charleston, South Carolina in 1898. She received a bachelor's degree from Benedict College in her native state and a master's from Hampton Institute in Virginia. Clark began her teaching career in a public school on John's Island in 1916. In 1918, she transferred to Avery Institute in Charleston and in that same year Clark led a drive to collect 20,000 signatures on a petition to have black teachers hired by the Charleston County

School District. The law barring their employment was changed in 1920. When Clark moved to Columbia in 1927, she aided a campaign to equalize salaries for black and white teachers.

After returning to Charleston several years later, Clark was dismissed from her teaching job for being a member of the National Association for the Advancement of Colored People (NAACP) in 1955.

In the late 1950s, Clark worked at the Highlander Folk School in Tennessee, where she developed a program to teach illiterate blacks so that they could pass literacy tests and quality to vote. She later became a director of the school, a supervisor of teacher training for the Southern Christian Leadership Conference (SCLC), and a national lecturer for voting and civil rights.

In recognition of her contributions to the Civil Rights Movement, Martin Luther King, Jr. selected Clark to accompany him to Norway in 1964 when he was presented the Nobel Peace Prize. In 1974, she was elected to the Charleston County School Board. Five years later, President Jimmy Carter presented to Clark a Living Legacy Award. In 1982, she received the Order of the Palmetto, South Carolina's highest civilian award.

Clark told the story of much of her life in her autobiographies, *Echo in My Soul* (1962) and *Ready From Within: Septima Clark and the Civil Rights Movement* (1987). The latter won an American Book Award.

Upon learning of Septima Clark's death, South Carolina Governor Carroll A. Campbell, Jr. said "the state has lost not only a leading civil rights activist but a legendary educator and humanitarian."

1988

January 6. The City Council of Jackson, Mississippi voted unanimously to declare a local holiday in honor of the late Dr. Martin Luther King, Jr. The vote in Jackson raised the number to seven of Mississippi localities commemorating the birth of the slain civil rights leader. The state of Mississippi is one of twenty other states who do not honor King. The state does, however, allow time off for its employees on the third Monday in January in tribute to the birthday of Confederate General Robert E. Lee.

The action of the Jackson City Council followed that of the governing body of Clarksdale, a Mississippi Delta town, by just one day and also followed "disparaging remarks" which New York City Mayor Ed Koch had made about the South, in general, only a few days earlier. Koch, in noting a recent racial attack in New York, said such an incident was "something he expected to see in the Deep South," but not in his region. Several Mississippi mayors had written

Koch in protest. After the Jackson vote, Councilman Louis Armstrong declared, "I think this will send a clearer message to the Mayor Koches of the world that Mississippi has changed." E.C. Foster, the black president of the Jackson City Council who introduced the motion to honor King, added, "Dr. King had those values most Americans shared."

January 18. Political, civil rights, and religious leaders throughout the nation led commemorations of the third national holiday in honor of civil rights leader Dr. Martin Luther King, Jr. They generally urged Americans to renew King's struggle against injustice and intolerance of any kind.

In Phoenix, Arizona, thousands marched through the downtown area demanding that the King holiday be restored. In 1987, Governor Evan Meacham had repealed the state's observance of the holiday. This action was the first of many that led to an effort to remove him from office. During the demonstration, Phoenix Mayor Terry Goddard observed that "it is time to stop having the rest of the country think of us as the site of a three-ring circus."

In Los Angeles, California, celebrities and politicians led a group of singers, marching bands, and floats down a boulevard named for King to Exposition Park.

In Boston, Massachusetts, Edward Kennedy, the state's Democratic Senator, commented that it was a "national disgrace that social justice [was] in retreat." He added, "Bankrupt national policies have spawned a national environment that encourages discrimination and repudiates opportunity."

In Gretna, Florida, Governor Bob Martinez led 250 marchers in a driving rain through the streets of a poverty-ridden black neighborhood. The Republican governor told the crowd that he had felt the efforts of King's work himself. Martinez recalled that he had been told years ago that he could never become mayor of Tampa because he was both Roman Catholic and Hispanic.

At Yokota Air Base in Japan, 150 black airmen and civilians gathered on a baseball field to re-enact King's famous "I Have a Dream" speech. Jackie Chambers, a secretary at the base, recited the oration. During the ceremony Chambers stated that King "gave me the opportunity to get an education, and he's always given me the opportunity to progress." Sergeant Earl Richard, a native of New Orleans, Louisiana, commented, "I think he made a difference in everybody's life, no matter who you are, if you are an American."

In Philadelphia, Pennsylvania, Rosa Parks, who King once called "the great fuse" of the civil rights movement for her role in the Montgomery, Alabama bus boycott of 1955, was given a replica of the Liberty Bell during ceremonies honoring King in that city.

Finally, in Memphis, Tennessee, a wreath was laid at the steps of the Lorraine

Motel where King was mortally wounded in 1968. Blues musicians played "When the Saints Go Marching In," and Jacqueline Smith, a motel resident who has refused to leave to make way for the construction of a civil rights museum on the site, was generously applauded when she simply said "Happy birthday, Dr. King."

As of 1988, forty-three states observed the national King holiday. Only Arizona, Hawaii, Idaho, Montana, New Hampshire, South Dakota, and Wyoming continued to refuse to recognize the event.

January 18. Hundreds of Americans, black and white, attended the 20th annual ecumenical services honoring the birthday of slain civil rights leader Martin Luther King, Jr. at the Ebenezer Baptist Church in Atlanta, Georgia. The services also celebrated the third observance of the national holiday in honor of King. Among those in attendance were two Democratic presidential candidates, the Reverend Jesse L. Jackson and Senator Paul Simon from Illinois; National Security Advisor Lieutenant General Colin Powell; Senators Lowell Weicker, Jr. from Connecticut and Sam Nunn from Georgia; Congressman John Lewis and Newt Gingrich, both from Georgia; comedian Dick Gregory; and Martin Luther King III, a Fulton County, Georgia Commissioner and son of the martyred civil rights leader.

One of the speakers at the services, Ebenezer's pastor Joseph L. Roberts, called King a "visionary" and "our general of peace," and urged the crowd to continue King's work. Senator Weicker told the congregation that King's death would not be in vain if Americans remembered the ideals for which King stood. Weicker asserted: "Martin Luther King, Jr. did not wait for the multitude. He talked and wrote and marched through the intimidation, through the violence. . . . And in the end, even his death was an ally, and his example lives as powerfully as the man." Another speaker, the Rev. Joseph Lowery, president of the Southern Christian Leadership Conference (SCLC), cautioned that "the holiday cannot lose sight of the holy day and close the curtain before the crowning victory is won. . . . The holy day reminds us that the holiday honors an individual but also a struggle and a people who are on fire for justice and liberty."

Later in the day, more than 200,000 people from throughout the United States and abroad stood in a drizzle in downtown Atlanta to watch the third annual Martin Luther King, Jr. National Holiday Parade. Floats and banners in the procession included "Free South Africa," "Prejudice Is a Handicap," "Civil Rights/Gay Rights. Same Struggle, Same Fight," and "Stop the Death Penalty."

The Atlanta Constitution conducted an informal poll of children along the parade route, asking "Who was Martin Luther King, Jr.?" A third grader, Michael Paisant of Duluth, Georgia, responded typically, "He was a peacemaker."

January 22. The *Atlanta Constitution* reported that Tabatha Foster, a three-year-old African-American child, had become the longest survivor among American children who had received multiple organ transplants. Tabatha had survived nearly three months after she received the organs of a baby killed in an automobile accident in October, 1987. Other children who were recipients of multiple organ transplants had survived no longer than three days. Yet, at the time of the newspaper report, Tabatha remained hospitalized in serious condition.

January 23. Jon Lester, a white teenager, was sentenced in New York City to serve a prison term of ten to thirty years for his part in the beating death of a black man in the Howard Beach section of Queens in December, 1986. The assault of three black men in the predominantly-white neighborhood inflamed racial tensions in the city and led to several days of protest demonstrations. Lester was the first of three convicted white teenagers to be sentenced.

Lester's attorney, Bryan Levinson, said after the sentencing that his client should not have been sentenced "so harshly because this was a reckless act, not an intentional act." However, Justice Thomas Demakos, who sentenced the youth to the maximum term under the law, commented that Lester showed "no remorse, no suggestion of guilt," but instead demonstrated a "pretty close to craven indifference to life." The judge also added that the three black victims were attacked "just because they [were] black. . . . Make no mistake. . . . There are no ifs, ands, or buts about it: This was racial violence." The Reverend Al Sharpton, the civil rights activist who had led demonstrations against the assault, said "the stiff sentencing vindicated those who pressed for appointment of a special prosecutor to investigate the case." Sharpton also contended that Lester's sentence was "an affirmation that racism and racist violence will not have a place in our society." (See also entries dated December 20, 1986, and February 11, 1988.)

January 31. The *Atlanta Journal-Constitution* reported the results of a poll which showed that 75 percent of Alabama's white residents favored the continued flying of the Confederate flag over the state capitol at Montgomery.

In December, 1987, the Alabama NAACP announced a campaign to remove the flag from the statehouse, and the organization's state director, Thomas Reed, said he would climb the flagpole and tear it down. Yet Alabama Governor Guy Hunt assured that the flag would remain unless a majority of Alabamians wanted it removed.

The poll also revealed that 63 percent of the 400 people queried believed that the Confederate flag should fly over state office buildings. But among whites, 75 percent wanted the flag to continue to fly, while 53 percent of blacks said the flag should be removed.

In 1988, Alabama and South Carolina were the only two southern states that continued to officially fly the Confederate flag. Mississippi and Georgia incorporated the Confederate symbol into their state flags. Some blacks in these states have periodically protested the use of the Confederate symbol by public agencies and institutions. They contended that its identification with the pro-slavery states in the American Civil War made it a racist emblem.

January 31. Doug Williams, the African-American quarterback of the Washington Redskins, was named the Most Valuable Player of the 22nd Annual Super Bowl. Williams, the first black quarterback ever to start in a Super Bowl championship game, completed 18 of 29 passes totaling 340 yards and four touchdowns. The Redskins defeated the Denver Broncos of the American Football Conference 42-10.

Of Williams's achievements, Redskins Coach Joe Gibbs commented: "I think it's a great success story. . . . He's had some tough experiences in life, and in football. He saw the downs, but he's the type of man who has overcome them." Redskins owner Jack Kent Cooke added, "this is a tribute not only to a black quarterback, but to a very great quarterback." Williams, a graduate of predominantly black Grambling University in Louisiana, remarked, "I didn't come here with the Washington Redskins as a black quarterback. I came here as a quarterback with the Washington Redskins to play a football game."

February 11. New York State Supreme Court Justice Thomas Demakos sentenced Jason Ladone, age seventeen, to five to fifteen years in prison for his part in the December 20, 1986 death of Michael Griffith, a twenty-three-year-old black man, in the Howard Beach section of Queens, New York City (see entry above). In imposing the light sentence for manslaughter and assault, Demakos rejected the defense's appeal for mercy because of Ladone's age. The judge said that on the night of the incident, the otherwise exemplary Ladone had become a "violent person." Ladone was the only defendant in the Howard Beach assaults to plead for mercy and the only one to apologize to the victim's mother, Jean Griffith. He told Mrs. Griffith "I am sorry . . . for your senseless loss." (See also entry dated January 23, 1988.)

February 19. Several hundred students at the University of Massachusetts at Amherst held a demonstration against racism at the institution. Shouting "Hey, hey, ho, ho, racism has got to go," the students were specifically supporting an agreement which had just been reached between minorities and the school's administration after a six-day takeover of a campus building. The demonstrators also called for a two-day moratorium, beginning March 22, on attending classes. The moratorium was aimed at denouncing racism, sexism, and an alleged attack against three Puerto Rican students on February 17.

Racial tensions on the Amherst campus had increased after at least 200 black, American Indian, and Hispanic students took over the New Africa House on

February 12 to protest alleged assaults and racial slurs by white students. The occupation of the building ended on February 17 after an agreement was reached which stipulated that Chancellor Joseph Duffey would expel students who repeatedly committed acts of racial violence and that he would also promote multicultural education.

About seven percent of the university's 18,000 undergraduates were African-Americans at the time of the incidents.

February 20. Alfred Jewett, the dean of Harvard University in Cambridge, Massachusetts, warned students on his campus that anyone involved in racial incidents would be subject to expulsion and other disciplinary measures. Jewett's warning was published in the student newspaper, the Harvard *Crimson,* a week after a group of students took over a building at the University of Massachusetts at Amherst (see entry directly above), to protest campus racism. These events were the latest in a series of racially-related campus outbreaks which have disturbed American educators throughout the nation.

February 20. Attorneys for Boston University asked a Suffolk Superior Court judge to order Coretta Scott King to release tapes of conversations between her late husband, Dr. Martin Luther King, Jr. and others which were secretly recorded by federal investigators. The motion also asked for release of correspondence between King and his colleagues.

This action was the latest round in a legal battle between the school and Mrs. King over an estimated 83,000 documents relating to her husband that are now held at Boston University. Mrs. King had filed suit earlier, contending that the documents belonged in the Martin Luther King Jr. Center for Non-Violent Social Change in Atlanta, Georgia. She further claimed that the university had "mishandled or lost some of the papers."

The tapes sought in the suit included those reportedly sent anonymously to Mrs. King in the 1970s, after the FBI had bugged hotel rooms where Martin Luther King, Jr. was staying. Some of these tapes implicating King in alleged extramarital sexual activities were made available also to President Lyndon Johnson, members of Congress, and news reporters.

Melvin Miller, a Boston University trustee whose law firm is handling the suit for the school, refused to say why the university wanted the tapes in connection with the litigation. (See also entries dated November 19, 1975, and May 29-June 3, 1978.)

February 25. Associate Judge Stuart Nudelman of the Cook County (Illinois) Circuit Court sentenced James Kalafut, a twenty-one-year-old white man, to 200 hours of community service for his role in an assault on three blacks in the Gage Park neighborhood in 1987. Kalafut, who had stated that he had been "taught to hate black people," was also ordered to report to the judge's chambers once a month for a year.

Edward McClellan, executive secretary of the NAACP's South Side Chicago branch, responded to the sentencing by declaring that Judge Nudelman had "opened up a completely new approach to dealing with an old American problem: racism."

The sharp increase in the number of racist attacks on blacks in the 1980s has led many African-American leaders to link the civil rights policies of President Ronald Reagan to such incidents, contending that the Reagan administration has been hostile to civil rights advances.

February 27. A United States Court of Appeals in Washington, D. C., in a 2-1 decision, ruled that "an affirmative action plan aimed at increasing the number of black firefighters" in the District of Columbia was unconstitutional. The court said that "preferential treatment" for black firefighter applicants was not needed because blacks had not been discriminated against. The Washington city government had set aside six out of every ten new positions in the fire department for black applicants. In 1984, when blacks first complained about tests being used to "screen applicants for entry-level" firefighter jobs, only 38 percent of the members of the D. C. Fire Department were black. Only 26 percent of the higher ranking officers were black at the time. The population of the city was 70 percent black. Judge Kenneth Starr wrote in the majority opinion, however, that it "was undisputed that the Fire Department [had] consistently hired from the entire Washington metropolitan area," where the black population was only 29.3 percent.

March 1. Experts on race and urban affairs, some of whom worked with the Kerner Commission in producing the 1968 Report of the President's Commission on Civil Disorders, announced that the prediction of the Commission twenty years ago that the United States was moving toward two societies—one white and affluent, the other black and impoverished—was becoming a reality.

A new report, published after a seven month study following widespread racial rioting in the summer of 1987, proclaimed that "segregation by race still sharply divides American cities in both housing and schools for blacks, and especially in schools for Hispanics." It also contended that the nation was being torn apart "by quiet riots": unemployment, poverty, crime, and housing and school segregation. It claimed that "less than one percent of the federal budget is spent for education, down from two percent in 1980" and that "the gap between rich and poor has widened, and there is a growing underclass."

One of the former members of the original Kerner Commission, former Senator Fred Harris of Oklahoma, and the co-chairman of the new panel, former Justice Department official Roger Wilkins, offered comments on the new report at a news conference in Washington, D.C. as the new study was presented. Harris said that "twenty years later, poverty is worse, more people are poor. . . . It is harder to get out of poverty now." Wilkins added that the "quiet riots" of 1987 were caused "by racism in American culture" and economic discrimination. The original 1,400 page Kerner Report had also said that "white racism" was largely responsible for the "explosive mixture" of "poverty and frustration" in the black communities that erupted in violence. Both Harris and Wilkins blamed the administration of President Ronald Reagan for "cutting back funds on social programs and not taking a stronger stand for equal rights in employment and housing."

The new report concluded its findings with this statement: "We know what should be done. . . . Jobs are the greatest need. Full employment is the best anti-poverty program." (See also entry dated March 2, 1968.)

March 5. Governor Michael Dukakis of Massachusetts moved closer to winning the Democratic nomination for President of the United States after a "decisive victory" over his African-American rival, the Reverend Jesse Jackson, in the Wisconsin primary. As a result of the balloting, Dukakis took 43 of the state's 81 Democratic delegates, while Jackson captured 27 and Senator Albert Gore from Tennessee won 11. Before the Wisconsin primary, Dukakis led Jackson in delegates only by a margin of 691 to 682.

Although Wisconsin had a black population of only 3 percent at the time of the balloting, Jackson was expected to run very well among white blue collar workers and white liberals in the state. Yet, in the end, while Jackson won nearly all of the black vote, he lost the white blue collar vote to Dukakis and garnered only about 25 percent of the total white vote, according to exit polls conducted by the media.

March 12. The Reverend Jesse L. Jackson, African-American candidate for the Democratic party's presidential nomination, won precinct caucuses in the state of South Carolina. In the caucus election, Jackson acquired approximately 55 percent of the delegates; 20 percent were uncommitted, 17 percent went to Tennessee Senator Albert Gore, 6 percent to Massachusetts Governor Michael Dukakis, and two other candidates shared the remaining 2 percent. Kevin Gray, Jackson's campaign manager in South Carolina, estimated that his candidate would eventually be awarded about 25 of the 44 national convention delegates at stake in the South Carolina balloting. Although Jackson was a resident of Chicago, Illinois, he was a native of Greenville, South Carolina, had "the status of a favorite son" as well as the almost solid support of the South's second largest black population, and had a campaign organization that worked hard with the state's 4,000 black churches to turn out the vote. Before the South Carolina caucuses, according to figures from the Associated Press, Jackson trailed Governor Dukakis in the delegate count 459.5 to 400.5.

March 15. Chevene Bowers "C.B." King, the first black person to run for governor of Georgia since the Reconstruction era, died of cancer in San Diego, California, at age sixty-four.

King, who was also an attorney and civil rights activist, represented Martin Luther King, Jr., Ralph David Abernathy, and other civil rights leaders as well as student sit-in demonstrators during the tumultuous civil rights movement in Albany, Georgia in 1962. He was beaten on the steps of the Dougherty County courthouse (of which Albany is the county seat) during the demonstrations.

Prior to running for governor in 1970, King had also ran unsuccessfully for Congress in 1964. In the governor's race, he received 70,424 votes (8.82 percent) in the Democratic primary. The victorious candidate for governor was Democrat Jimmy Carter, who was later elected President of the United States. Reacting bitterly to his defeat, King blamed it on "little black political puppets who have exploited politics for their own selfish ends" and on blacks who still had "social and psychological hangups" about voting for a candidate of their own race.

March 15. Pope John Paul II appointed Eugene Antonio Marino, a black Josephite priest, as the archbishop of Atlanta, Georgia. It was the first time that an African-American was named an archbishop in the American Roman Catholic Church.

Marino, age fifty-three and a native of Biloxi, Mississippi, studied at St. Joseph's Seminary in Washington, D.C. from 1956 to 1962 and earned a master's degree in religious education from Fordham University. From 1962 to 1968, he taught in and directed training activities in the archdiocese of Washington, D.C. On July 13, 1971, Marino was elected to a four-year term as vicar general of the Josephite Fathers. Prior to being named archbishop of Atlanta, Marino was the auxiliary bishop of Washington, D.C. and secretary of the National Conference of Catholic Bishops. He was one of only twelve black bishops in the United States at the time of his appointment as archbishop.

In 1985, Marino was one of the ten black bishops who called on the National Conference of Catholic Bishops to create "a preferential option for black Americans" to help forestall "potential explosive racial strife in our country" which was "as immediate a threat as a nuclear holocaust."

Marino's appointment made him the spiritual leader of 156,000 Roman Catholics in sixty-nine counties in North Georgia, comprising the Archdiocese of Atlanta, of which ten thousand are blacks (most of whom were members of seven churches, including three predominantly-black ones, in the city of Atlanta). In the United States, 1.3 million of the Church's 52 million members were black in 1988.

Marino described his appointment to the highest office of any black American Roman Catholic as "a great sign of hope to all minorities." (See also entry dated October 26, 1980.)

March 16. President Ronald Reagan vetoed a civil rights bill which was designed to reverse a 1984 U. S. Supreme Court decision and restore the impact of four federal laws which prohibited discrimination on the basis of race, age, handicap, or sex. The high Court's ruling had limited "the liability for discrimination only to offending programs or activities that receive federal funds, not to an entire institution or entity."

Reagan objected to the bill, which passed 75-14 in the U. S. Senate and 315-98 in the House of Representatives, because he felt it "proposed unwarranted federal intervention in the affairs of corporations and institutions with religious affiliations." But supporters of the bill contended that its provisions adequately exempted small businesses, church institutions, and farmers. Nevertheless, Reagan said the bill failed "to eliminate invidious discrimination and to ensure equality of opportunity for all Americans while preserving their basic freedoms from governmental interference and control." Instead, he offered an alternative—a slight expansion on a previous version that had been rejected in both houses of the Congress—which he said would "protect civil rights and at the same time preserve the independence of state and local governments, the

Archbishop Eugene Antonio Marino of Atlanta, Georgia.

freedom of religion, and the right of America's citizens to order their lives and businesses without extensive federal intrusion."

Massachusetts Senator Edward M. Kennedy, one of the sponsors of the legislation, called Reagan's veto "shameful." (See also entries dated February 28, 1984, March 20, 1988, and March 22, 1988.)

March 16. After finishing second in the Democratic presidential primary in Illinois on March 15, African-American presidential candidate Jesse Jackson had won an estimated 460.5 delegates. Jackson's total placed him four delegates behind the Democratic frontrunner, Massachusetts Governor Michael Dukakis, who had 464.5 delegates at the time. A total of 2,082 votes were required to capture the Democratic nomination.

With almost half of the Democratic delegates chosen by March 16, Jackson had obtained more popular votes than any other Democratic contender and had combined the largest number of first and second place finishes in the balloting held in thirty states thus far.

March 20. The U.S. House of Representatives voted 315-98 to overturn a U.S. Supreme Court ruling that limited four laws banning discrimination based on age, race, sex, or handicap. The same measure had been approved by the United States Senate on January 28, by a vote of 75-14.

The legislation, known as the Civil Rights Restoration Act, requires that any institution or entity receiving federal funds, including school systems, corporations, and health facilities, must comply with civil rights statutes. It allows limited exemptions for small businesses and for institutions controlled by religious organizations.

The Supreme Court, in a 1984 case involving Grove City College in Pennsylvania, had ruled that only a program or activity receiving federal funds was subject to the federal anti-bias laws. Although the case focused on a 1972 law which prohibited sex discrimination in education, the Court's decision also applied to three other civil rights laws that contained the same language at issue in the Grove City College case. After the decision, federal agencies had dropped or limited hundreds of civil rights cases.

In October, 1987, a federal court of appeals rejected a lawsuit by a group in Alabama, which had been joined by the federal government against the state school system. That court held that only the "allegedly discriminatory program could be sued."

March 20. Mike Tyson knocked out challenger Tony Tubbs to retain the world heavyweight boxing championship in Tokyo, Japan. The thirty-year-old Tubbs collapsed in the second round of the scheduled fifteen round fight in the Tokyo Dome; his cornermen asked referee Arthur Mercante to stop the fight. Tyson improved his record to 34 wins (30 by knockout) with no losses. The twenty-one-year-old Tyson was guaranteed $5 million for defending his title.

March 22. The United States Congress overrode President Ronald Reagan's veto of the Civil Rights Restoration Act. The vote in the Senate was 73-24 and in the House of Representatives 292-133. The new law was designed to reverse a decision of the United States Supreme Court in 1984 which had limited the enforcement of previous civil rights acts. In that decision, the Court, in a case involving Grove City College in Pennsylvania, had ruled that some earlier civil rights laws "did not cover entire school systems, businesses, local governments or other entities, but only the programs receiving federal aid." The new law specifically extended coverage to entire institutions, although exemptions were provided for small businesses, churches, farmers who received price supports, and welfare recipients. President Reagan had objected on the grounds that the exemptions were inadequate and that religious freedoms were being threatened.

After the veto was overridden, Republican Senator Lowell Weicker from Connecticut, one of the sponsors of the measure, exclaimed: "[This] is as important a day as any of us have ever experienced or will experience in the near future. It has the potential of being a restatement . . . of our national commitment to equal opportunity for all." (See also entries dated February 28, 1984, March 16, 1988, and March 20, 1988.)

March 25. The *Chronicle of Higher Education* reported that a study by the American Council on Education and the Education Commission of the United States had concluded that America must renew its commitment to the advancement of minority groups or jeopardize the future prosperity of the nation. The Council and Commission report stated that "America is moving backward—not forward—in its efforts to achieve the full participation of minority citizens in the life and prosperity of the nation."

The report, entitled "One Third of a Nation," also documented that "in education, employment, income, health, longevity, and other basic measures of individual and social well-being, gaps persist—and in some cases are widening—between members of minority groups and the majority population. . . . If we allow these disparities to continue, the United States inevitably will suffer a compromised quality of life and a lower standard of living. . . . In brief, we find ourselves unable to fulfill the promise of the American dream."

"One Third of a Nation" emerged from a project established in 1987 by the American Council on Education and the Education Commission of the United States because of concern over a series of racial incidents on college and university campuses and the declining proportion of minority students in college. The report noted specifically that in 1986, 31.1 percent of the nation's blacks and 27.3 percent of its Hispanics had incomes below the poverty level—nearly three times the rate for whites. Also, in 1986, 20.1 percent of whites over age 25 had completed at least four years of college. For blacks, the completion rate was only 10.9 percent and for Hispanics, only 8.4 percent. In the same year, blacks were twice as likely to be unemployed than were whites.

As a result of its findings, the report recommended, among other things, that colleges and universities, particularly:

1. Recruit minority students more aggressively.

2. Create an academic atmosphere that nourishes and encourages minority students to stay enrolled and to succeed.

3. Create a campus culture that values the diversity minorities bring to institutional life—one that responds powerfully and forthrightly to the recrudescences of racism that have occurred too often on campus in recent years.

4. Place special emphasis on inspiring and recruiting minority candidates for faculty and administrative positions.

5. Work with educators at the primary and secondary levels to improve the education, training, and preparation of minority students.

March 31. African-American novelist Toni Morrison won a Pulitzer Prize for Fiction for her book, *Beloved*. The novel depicts the agonizing reminiscences of a former slave in post-Civil War Ohio. Morrison's work had provoked a controversy in the fall of 1987 when it failed to win the prestigious National Book Award. In January, 1988, forty-eight black writers had written an open letter to the *New York Times Book Review* protesting that failure as well as the fact that Morrison had never won the even more prestigious Pulitzer.

Responding to the announcement of the award, Morrison said, "I think I know what I feel. . . . I had no doubt about the value of the book and that it was really worth serious recognition. But I had some dark thoughts about whether the book's merits would be allowed to be the only consideration of the Pulitzer committee. The book had begun to take on a responsibility, an extra-literary responsibility, that it was never designed for."

An excerpt from a review of *Beloved* by author and critic Margaret Atwood in the *New York Times*, September 13, 1987, follows:

"In *Beloved*, Ms. Morrison turns away from the contemporary scene that has been her concern of late. The new novel is set after the end of the Civil War, during the period of the so-called Reconstruction, when a great deal of random violence was let loose upon blacks, both the slaves freed by emancipation and others who had been given or bought their freedom earlier. But there are flashbacks to a more distant period, when slavery was still a going concern in the South and the seeds for the bizarre and calamitous events of the novel were sown. The setting is similarly divided: the countryside near Cincinnati, where the central characters have ended up, and a slave-holding plantation in Kentucky, ironically named Sweet Home, from which they fled 18 years before the novel begins. . . .

Beloved is written in an antiminimalist prose that is by turns rich, graceful, eccentric, rough, lyrical, sinuous, colloquial, and very much to the point."

June 5. Clarence M. Pendleton, chairman of the U. S. Civil Rights Commission (CCR), died of an apparent heart attack in San Diego, California at age fifty-seven.

Pendleton was born on November 10, 1930 in Louisville, Kentucky, but grew up in Washington, D. C., where his father was the first swimming coach at Howard University and an assistant director of the District of Columbia's recreation department. He received a Bachelor of Science degree from Howard in 1954 and worked briefly for the D. C. recreation department before joining the U. S. Army. After his release from the Army in 1957, Pendleton returned to Howard and became an instructor of physical education.

In 1970, Pendleton became a director of the urban affairs department of the National Recreation and Parks Association. Two years later he moved to San Diego to take a position as director of the Model Cities program there. By 1975, Pendleton had become head of the San Diego Urban League. He was the only one of more than 150 officers in the League to support the presidential candidacy of former California Governor Ronald Reagan.

By 1980, Pendleton had abandoned what he called his "bleeding-heart liberalism" and switched to the Republican party. On November 16, 1981, President Reagan appointed him chairman of the CCR (see entry above). As CCR chairman, Pendleton followed President Ronald Reagan's desires and led the commission toward a "color-blind" approach to matters of civil rights. He opposed busing to achieve school desegregation and called affirmative action a "bankrupt policy." Civil rights leaders, some political leaders, and even some members of the CCR itself expressed shock at the stances which the commission's first black chairman took. Congress responded by cutting the CCR's budget from $11.6 million in 1985 to only $7.5 million in 1986. These cuts caused a considerable slowing of activity at the CCR.

After Pendleton's death, William Bradford Reynolds, assistant Attorney General for Civil Rights, called him "a man who felt very deeply that the individuals in America should deal with one another as brothers and sisters totally without regard to race and background."

June 17. Alabama State Representative Thomas Reed, who also served as president of the state's NAACP, was indicted by a federal grand jury on charges of accepting more than $15,000 in cash and restaurant equipment to secure the early release of a convicted murderer, Anthony Chesser. According to the indictment, Chesser's family paid Reed to use his position as a member of the Legislature's Joint Prison Committee to get "the state Department of Corrections to place Chesser in a work release program and get the Board of Pardons and Paroles to move up his date for parole consideration by 5 ½ years." At the time, Chesser was serving a 40 year sentence in a 1984 conviction for murdering his wife.

Reed, age sixty, was one of fourteen black state legislators arrested February 2, 1988 when they tried to remove the Confederate flag from the Alabama state capitol at Montgomery. Reed, who was also a member of the Board of Trustees of Tuskegee University, refused to comment on his indictment except to reiterate his innocence.

July 1. William H. Harris, a forty-four-year-old black historian, assumed the presidency of Texas Southern University in Houston. Harris, a native of Fitzgerald, Georgia, had previously been president of Paine College in Georgia, and a professor of history and associate dean of the Graduate School at Indiana University in Bloomington. At the time of his selection to the Texas Southern presidency, Harris was also completing a three year term as president of the Association for the Study of Afro-American Life and History (ASALH).

At his inaugural ceremonies, which were attended by the new president's ninety-eight year old grandmother, Mary Graham, Harris commented, "we now begin to speak in one voice, play by one score and the theme of that voice and score will be academic excellence."

July 11. The *Atlanta Constitution* reported results of a poll which revealed that if the African-American presidential candidate Jesse Jackson was not offered the vice presidential nomination or did not signal his support for the presidential ticket, more than a third of the delegates to the Democratic National Convention indicated that they would be less likely to support the party in the 1988 presidential election. The poll showed a strong potential for disunity among Democratic party delegates as they headed to the National Convention in Atlanta, Georgia, on July 18. Another important result of the poll was that 20 percent of the delegates polled thought Jackson was "pulling the party too far to the left." Among delegates pledged to Massachusetts Governor Michael Dukakis, 24 percent expressed that sentiment, compared with only 5 percent of the Jackson delegates.

The poll was conducted from June 15 to July 7, 1988. It included interviews with 1,921 delegates and alternates pledged to Governor Dukakis, 935 pledged to the Reverend Jackson, and 447 who were "either uncommitted or technically committed" to other candidates who had dropped out of the presidential race. (See also entries dated March 5, 1988, March 12, 1988, March 16, 1988, and July 20, 1988.)

July 13. As the date for the 1988 Democratic National Convention approached, Massachusetts Governor Michael Dukakis had secured enough delegate votes to win his party's nomination over his closest rival, the African-American candidate Jesse Jackson. However, there were serious concerns within the Democratic party over whether Jackson and his forces would attempt to disrupt the convention and/or enthusiastically support the party nominees in the November general elections.

One of the major disputes between the Jackson and Dukakis camps was over Dukakis's selection of Lloyd Bentsen, U.S. Senator from Texas, as his choice as a vice presidential running mate. Jackson complained earlier that Dukakis "had not engaged him in their private meetings on substantial issues, such as the platform," his role in the fall campaign, and the vice presidency, yet indicated that he would not be adverse to a vice presidential nomination. The Jackson campaign was most angered, however, by the fact that Jackson had learned from news reporters that Dukakis had chosen Bentsen as his running mate a full hour before the governor called with the information. Although the Dukakis campaign insisted that "the slight had not been deliberate" and apologized for having caused Jackson any embarrassment, Ronald Brown, Jackson's campaign manager, said he "was flabbergasted by the fact" that the matter "wasn't handled in a better way than it was."

The Bentsen incident refueled speculation in the media and in the Democratic Party as to exactly what it would take to mollify or pacify Jackson and his supporters. In an article published in the *Atlanta Constitution* on July 13 entitled "A Letter to My Delegates on the Road to Atlanta," Jackson said it was "not what . . . Jesse wants . . . [but] a question of what we have built." (See Appendix for an excerpt taken from Jackson's "A Letter to My Delegates on the Road to Atlanta.")

July 19. Using the theme "Keep Hope Alive," Jesse L. Jackson, African-American Democratic presidential candidate, addressed 11,000 people at the Democratic National Convention in Atlanta, Georgia, on the eve of the balloting for the presidential nomination. The speech, in which Jackson said "America must never surrender to a high moral challenge," electrified the audience.

July 20. The quest of Jesse L. Jackson for the Democratic nomination for President of the United States ended in Atlanta, Georgia. Delegates at the Democratic National Convention there gave the party's nomination to Massachusetts Governor Michael Dukakis. Dukakis won the votes of 2,876.25

The Rev. Jesse Jackson with his family before delivering his speech to the 1988 Democratic National Convention in Atlanta, Georgia.

delegates; Jackson emerged second in the contest with 1,218.5 delegate votes. Five other candidates divided nine votes. The number needed for nomination was 2,082.

Jackson began his second attempt to win the Democratic nomination shortly after he failed to capture the position in 1984. He remained a visible spokesman for the civil rights of blacks, other minorities, and women, by using his organizations Operation PUSH and the Rainbow Coalition as bases. More recently, he also added the causes of labor and depressed farmers to his agenda.

Unlike his race in 1984, when several major black leaders publicly opposed his candidacy, Jackson won their support or at least neutrality in his latest quest. He was also able to persuade more whites to back his candidacy. He campaigned as a populist, championing the cause of the downtrodden, those in "the outhouse" who were not fully sharing in the nation's opportunities, political, social, and economic.

In the primary elections and caucuses prior to the Convention, Jackson won the votes of 92 percent of blacks and 12 percent of whites. Four years earlier he had captured 77 percent of the black vote, but only 5 percent of the white vote.

Jackson's achievements in the 1988 campaign established him as the most formidable black candidate ever to seek the American presidency.

July 31. Willie Stargell, a former African-American baseball star with the Pittsburgh Pirates of the National Baseball League, was inducted into the Baseball Hall of Fame in ceremonies at Cooperstown, New York. Stargell got 82.4 percent of the vote by being named on 352 of 427 ballots cast by the Baseball Writers Association of America. (In order to be elected, a player must be named on 75 percent of the ballots). Stargell, age forty-seven, became the first player to be selected on his first attempt since Lou Brock, another African-American, accomplished the feat in 1985.

Stargell's best seasons as a baseball player were in 1971, when he scored 48 home runs, batted in 125 runs, and had a total batting average of .295; and 1973, when he hit 44 home runs, batted in 119 runs, and ended with a batting average of .299. Stargell played in the 1971 and 1979 World Series and was named the Most Valuable Player in the 1979 Series.

August 2. Joseph "Big Lester" Hankerson, black civil rights activist, died of a heart attack in Atlanta, Georgia, at age sixty-three. Hankerson, a leader of the civil rights movement in Savannah, Georgia, often marched at the side of Martin Luther King, Jr. during the 1960s. Hankerson was about 6 foot 5 inches tall and weighed 280 pounds.

In one of the eulogies for Hankerson, Joseph E. Lowery, president of the SCLC, said "Hankerson was one of the earliest among the valiant field workers who was a heart and soul of the [civil rights] movement. They did the harsh and dangerous groundwork that made it possible for the captains and generals to claim the victory." Another veteran civil rights activist, Hosea Williams, remarked, "Big Lester was a true unsung hero. . . . He contributed as much to the street movement as Dr. King did in the suite movement. He didn't go to jail as many times as I, but no one took more beatings and no one shed more blood."

August 11. M. Carl Holman, president of the National Urban Coalition, died of cancer in Washington, D. C., at age sixty-nine.

Holman was born June 27, 1919 in Minter, Mississippi. He grew up in St. Louis, Missouri and was a *magna cum laude* graduate of Lincoln University. He earned master's degrees at the University of Chicago in 1944 and Yale University in 1954. After receiving his Chicago degree, Holman taught English at Hampton Institute and his alma mater, Lincoln University. Beginning in 1949, he began a long career in Georgia as a professor of English at Clark College.

While in Georgia, Holman was an advisor to the student sit-in movement in

Atlanta and helped to escort and protect Charlayne Hunter and Hamilton Holmes, when the two black students desegregated the University of Georgia in 1961. He was also editor of the *Atlanta Inquirer,* a black weekly newspaper, which was founded as a voice for civil rights demonstrators.

In 1962, Holman left Clark College to become information officer and later deputy staff director of the U. S. Civil Rights Commission (CCR) from 1962 to 1968. He then became a vice president of the National Urban Coalition, a study and advocacy group on urban issues and policies. Holman was named president of the Coalition in 1971.

August 14. Participants at the annual convention of the American Psychological Association in Atlanta, Georgia, concluded that "the increasing absence of black men in the work force, on college campuses and as heads of households" was a problem that threatened "the 'fabric of American society'." Statistics quoted at the meeting to substantiate the point included:

1. The leading cause of death among black males between the ages of 15 and 24 is homicide.

2. A black man has a 1 in 21 chance of being murdered, 6 times greater than that of other Americans.

3. The average life expectancy of 65 years for black men is less than what is was for white men more than 40 years ago.

4. Black men represent 6 percent of the country's population but more than 40 percent of the prison population.

5. A black man is more than twice as likely to be unemployed as a white man.

6. Black men are increasingly absent from the home, with almost 60 percent of all births to black women occurring out of wedlock.

August 27. More than 55,000 Americans marched in Washington, D. C. to commemorate the 25th anniversary of the historic March on Washington of 1963. The original march had drawn 250,000 people to push for passage of the Civil Rights Bill of 1964. The leaders of the new march included Democratic presidential candidates Jesse Jackson and Michael Dukakis, Benjamin Hooks of the NAACP, Coretta Scott King, widow of slain civil rights leader Martin Luther King, Jr., and Joseph E. Lowery, president of the SCLC. The themes of the gathering were a tribute to Martin Luther King, Jr. and his memorable "I Have a Dream" speech at the 1963 March as well as a protest against the civil rights policies of the administration of President Ronald Reagan. In addressing the latter topic, the SCLC's Lowery told the crowd, "We fought too long, we prayed too hard, we wept too bitterly, we bled too profusely, we died too young

to let anybody ever turn back the clock on racial justice. We ain't going back."
(See also entry dated August 28, 1963.)

September 1. William S. Sessions, director of the FBI, announced that he
had approved a five-year affirmative action program to hire and promote more
minority employees in the Bureau. The program included the hiring of an
advertising agency, assignment of some of the "most capable people" to serve
as recruiters, improvements in career development and training programs,
internal audits of promotion procedures, equal opportunity programs, and
complaint processes. Sessions also said that "from the beginning, I have tried
to make the FBI's policy against racism and discrimination crystal clear to
every member of the FBI, both by policy statements . . . and by personally
addressing employees."

As Sessions issued his declaration, there were only 417 blacks and 439
Hispanics among the 9,597 agents in the FBI. 311 of the Hispanic agents had
filed a class action suit contending that the FBI discriminated in the promotion,
discipline, and assignment of Hispanics, while a black agent, Donald Rochon of
the Philadelphia, Pennsylvania office, had filed a racial harassment charge
with the Equal Employment Opportunity Commission (EEOC). In July, 1988,
Gary Miller, a white agent in the Chicago, Illinois office, acknowledged that he
and some white colleagues had harassed Rochon. The EEOC also upheld
many of Rochon's complaints of actions against him while he served in the
FBI's Omaha, Nebraska office in 1983-1984 and in Chicago from 1984 to 1986.

September 6. City officials in Yonkers, New York paid a fine of $192,000 for
contempt of court for refusing to carry out a federal judge's order to desegregate
the city's housing.

September 12. United States District Court Judge William H. Barbour, Jr.
ruled in Jackson, Mississippi that Mississippi judges were "elected in a
discriminatory manner." The order divided some of the state's judicial districts
into subdistricts where the black majority would be 60 percent to 65 percent.
This division was designed to overcome what the judge said was the white
majority's bloc votes, which "usually defeat the minority's preferred candidate." As a result of the ruling, eight judicial subdistricts with large black
majorities were created. At the time of the ruling, there were only three blacks
among the 111 trial and appellate judges in Mississippi, although blacks
constituted 35 percent of the state's population. In 1985, the Fund for Modern
Courts, a Washington, D.C. research group, had reported that there were only
238 blacks among the 7,500 elected judges in the United States. At that time,
blacks constituted 12 percent of the American population.

September 13. President Ronald Reagan signed a bill strengthening enforcement of the open housing law Congress passed in the wake of the
assassination of Martin Luther King, Jr. in 1968. The law, which was passed

overwhelmingly by both the U. S. House of Representatives and the Senate, authorizes the federal government, for the first time, to seek fines of up to $100,000 against individuals or organizations found "to have engaged in a pattern of housing discrimination." Under the open housing provisions of the Civil Rights Act of 1968, the government could only mediate housing discrimination disputes. The act also extended anti-discrimination protection in housing to the handicapped and families with children.

President Reagan called the new housing law "the most important civil rights legislation in 20 years." He said that discrimination was "particularly tragic when it means a family is refused housing near good schools, a good job, or simply in a better neighborhood to raise children." (See also entry dated April 11, 1968.)

September 26. The *New York Times* reported that a seven-month New York state grand jury investigation had concluded that Tawana Brawley, a sixteen-year-old African-American, had "fabricated" her story of abduction and sexual abuse by a gang of white men in Wyspingers Falls, New York on November 24, 1987. Brawley, who disappeared from her home four days earlier, was found nude in a garbage bag with feces and racial slurs covering her body.

Within days of Brawley's disappearance, her case became a focal point of protests and racial tensions throughout the state. Leaders of the protest and advisors to Brawley included New York lawyers Alton H. Maddox, Jr. and C. Vernon Mason, and the Reverend Al Sharpton, a community activist. The three counselled the Brawley family not to cooperate with law enforcement authorities, whom they accused of perpetrating a "cover-up" in the case. The group even contended that law enforcement officials were involved in the alleged attack on Brawley.

Nevertheless, the grand jury's final report found "no evidence of any abduction, racial or sexual attack, or any other crime against Miss Brawley."

September 26. The International Olympic Committee (IOC) took Canadian Ben Johnson's gold medal in the 100-meter dash away after he tested positive for "performance-enhancing anabolic steroids." The medal, which he won in the Summer Olympic Games at Seoul, South Korea on September 24, was then presented to the second place finisher in the 100- meter, African-American Carl Lewis.

October 3. *Forbes Magazine* reported that Michael Jackson, a thirty-year-old African-American, had become the world's highest paid entertainer, earning an estimated $60 million during 1988. Jackson was ranked ninth in *Forbes'* Top 40 list of wealthiest celebrities in 1987. Jackson had made about $40 million from a recent worldwide tour. The rest of his earnings came from sales of his album *Bad*, his autobiography *Moonwalk*, music publishing, and endorsements and commercials he made for the Pepsi Cola Bottling company.

In 1987, the wealthiest entertainer was another African-American, comedian Bill Cosby. Cosby had an income of $84 million in 1986-87. Other African-Americans on the 1988 list were actor-comedian Eddie Murphy, talk show host Oprah Winfrey, and professional boxers Mike Tyson, Sugar Ray Leonard, and Michael Spinks.

October 26. S. B. Fuller, founder and president of Fuller Products Company and a "dean of black entrepreneurs," died of kidney failure in Blue Island, Illinois, at age eighty-three.

Fuller, a native of Ouachita Parish, Louisiana, left school after the sixth grade and lived in poverty until his mother, who died when he was seventeen, convinced him to become a door-to-door salesman. He sold cosmetics and built a national enterprise with more than 5,000 salesmen. In the 1960s, Fuller expanded his company into newspapers, appliance and department stores, as well as farming and beef cattle production. He is credited with teaching business acumen to John H. Johnson, publisher of the highly successful Johnson Publishing Company, and George Johnson, one of the nation's leading cosmetic manufactures, both of Chicago, Illinois.

November 4. Comedian and television star Bill Cosby announced his intention to donate $20 million to Spelman College, an institution for African-American women in Atlanta, Georgia. The contribution represented the largest individual gift in the 107-year history of the college and the largest such gift ever made by an African-American. In announcing the donation, Cosby told a group of 2,000 people attending an inaugural reception for Spelman's new president, Johnetta Cole, that "Mrs. Cosby and I wanted this woman to know how much we love this school." He also urged other blacks to do more in supporting historically black colleges. "I think we all understand that schools need money, but I think we accepted that white folks were going to keep them alive."

College officials indicated that Cosby's money would be used to construct a new academic building, establish endowed academic chairs in the fine arts, humanities, and social sciences, as well as to strengthen the school's $42 million endowment. (See also entry dated December 31, 1984.)

November 4. Dedication of the Martin Luther King, Jr. Federal Building was held in Atlanta, Georgia. U. S. Congressman John Lewis and members of the slain civil rights leader's family participated in the ceremonies. Lewis had sponsored the bill in Congress to rename the building for King, the first federal building in the nation to bear his name.

November 16. Toni Morrison, African-American novelist, won a 1988 Elmer Holmes Bobst Award in Arts and Letters for her "powerful and haunting" book, *Beloved*. *Beloved*, like Morrison's other works, draws heavily on the black oral tradition. The Bobst Awards, sponsored by New York University, include medals and $2,000 cash prizes. Previously Morrison had won a National Book Critics Award for *Song of Solomon*, and the coveted Pulitzer Prize for *Beloved*. (See also entry dated March 31, 1988.)

November 24. Two University of Chicago researchers reported that blacks "still encounter major barriers" to integrated housing in the nation's suburbs. In a report entitled "Suburbanization and Segregation in U.S. Metropolitan Areas," Douglas S. Massey and Nancy A. Denton found that Asians and Hispanics had "greater contact with other races" as they moved out of larger American cities than did blacks. They concluded that "two decades after the Civil Rights Act of 1968, which, in theory, banned racial discrimination in the sale and rental of housing, blacks have still not achieved equal access to housing in American cities and suburbs." The study was published in the November, 1988 issue of the *American Journal of Sociology*.

December 19. An internal report on equal opportunity released by the United States Navy found "widespread but subtle bias against blacks and Hispanic sailors and other minorities in its ranks." Among the shortcomings cited in the report were "failure to direct recruiting ads to minority-dominated areas; enlist highly qualified blacks; instill a sense of racial and ethnic equality in training; and guide minorities equitably into technical fields." The study also found that black and Hispanic sailors were promoted "less quickly" than whites, "though rates of promotion varied from grade to grade."

In response to the report, Admiral Carlisle Trost, chief of naval operations, instructed naval officers "to maintain a climate in the Navy that provides the opportunity for our people to perform and achieve realistic goals."

December 20. Max Robinson, the first black news anchorman on American network television, died of complications relating to AIDS in Washington, D.C. at age forty-nine. Robinson, who had worked as a news anchor at WTPO TV in Washington, became a co-anchor with Peter Jennings and Frank Reynolds on the ABC-TV Network's "Evening News" in 1978.

Carl Bernstein, chief of the ABC News bureau in Chicago, said Robinson was "deliberately excluded from any decision-making related to the newscast." In a speech at Smith College in February, 1981, Robinson accused ABC of racism. Two years later after the death of Frank Reynolds, Jennings was named sole anchor of the "Evening News" and Robinson was "relegated to weekend anchor stints and news briefs." The next year he left ABC and joined WMAQ-TV in Chicago, Illinois. In June, 1985, Robinson entered a hospital suffering from "emotional and physical exhaustion." He never returned to full-time news reporting.

In commenting on Robinson's death, Roone Arledge, president of ABC News, said "he made an important contribution to ABC News for which we will always be grateful."

December 28. Widespread discussion began in African-American communities throughout the United States over the proper ethnic designation for Americans of African origins. Former Democratic presidential candidate Jesse L. Jackson, leaders of the NAACP, and others had agreed during a conference in Chicago that "African-American" was the preferable term and should replace "black," which gained prominence during the Civil Rights Movement of the 1960s. Jackson said the term African-American "[places] us in our proper historical context." The Reverend B. Herbert Martin, head of the Human Relations Commission in Chicago, and others disagreed. Martin said a change in nomenclature from "black to African-American amounted to little more than semantics."

December 28. The School Committee of Boston, Massachusetts voted 10-1 to allow parents to choose a public school for their children closer to home. In 1974, U. S. District Court Judge W. Arthur Garrity, Jr. had imposed a desegregation plan on the city of Boston which gave parents "little choice as to which schools" their children would attend. Garrity's latest orders in the case, however, required "only that a racial balance be maintained," which freed the School Committee to devise a plan of its own.

The new plan, which was subject to final approval by the State Board of Education, divided the Boston public school system into three zones of 14,000 students each, and parents could choose any school within the zone, "provided it did not upset the school's racial balance." A lottery would determine assignments in "oversubscribed" schools. (See also entry dated June 21, 1974.)

1989

January. Andrew F. Brimmer, former African-American governor of the Federal Reserve Board, was installed as president of the Association for the Study of Afro-American Life and History (ASALH). Brimmer, who had also served as president of the nation's oldest black history organization in 1969, returned to the leadership of the group at a time when it was just beginning to recover from severe financial difficulties. Administrative problems and a declining membership had seriously curtailed the association's ability to provide programs and deliver services in the 1980s. These financial straits had led to suspension of its two principal publications, the *Journal of Negro History* and the *Negro History Bulletin*. Just prior to Brimmer's installation, the *Journal of*

Negro History, the oldest and most prestigious of black scholarly journals, was revived through the assistance of Morehouse College, the base of its editorial operations. Leroy Keith, Jr., the newly inaugurated president of the college, had made the pledge to ressurect the periodical soon after taking office. Upon assuming the leadership of ASALH anew, Brimmer pledged to make a similar effort on behalf of the entire association and those it served.

January 14. Coretta Scott King announced her resignation as president of the Martin Luther King, Jr. Center for Nonviolent Social Change in Atlanta, Georgia, having been president of the Center since its founding in 1974. She also announced that her successor would be her twenty-seven year old son, Dexter Scott King, whom she described as "uniquely qualified to assume the civil rights mantle." Mrs. King, however, said that she would remain as chief executive officer and spokesperson for the Center.

January 15. On the eve of his departure from office, President Ronald Reagan criticized civil rights leaders for allegedly exaggerating "the degree of racism in America." The President suggested that black leaders were striving "to keep their cause alive and to maintain their own prominence." In an interview with the CBS television network news program "60 Minutes," Reagan specifically said: "Sometimes I wonder if they really want what they say they want. . . . Because some of those leaders are doing very well leading organizations based on keeping alive the feeling that they're victims of prejudice."

During his eight years in office, Reagan had been constantly attacked by black leaders for allegedly seeking to "roll back progress in civil rights." But in the interview, Reagan defended his position on civil rights. He pointed out that as governor of California he had "appointed more blacks to executive and policy-making positions in government than all the previous governors of California put together." Reagan confessed that "one of the great things that I have suffered in this job is this feeling and this editorializing comment that somehow I'm on the other side" of the struggle for civil rights.

January 16. President-elect George Bush praised the life and work of slain civil rights leader Martin Luther King, Jr. and promised to make King's "dream of racial equality" his mission in the White House. In a speech to the American Bicentennial Presidential Inaugural Afro-American Committee in Washington, D.C., Bush said that King had "lived a hero's life. He dreamed a hero's dreams. And he left a hero's indelible mark on the mind and imagination of a great nation. . . . So today we remember the man; we pay tribute to his achievements, and we pledge once more our nation's sacred honor in continuing pursuit of his dream."

In his remarks, Bush characterized King as a "'great gift' from God to the nation," adding, "What becomes of Martin Luther King's dreams is up to us.

We must not fail him. We must not fail ourselves. And we must not fail the nation he loved so much and gave his life for. I understand that five days before becoming president of the United States of America."

Bush concluded his comments by vowing to pursue equality, freedom, justice, and peace so "that bigotry and indifference to the disadvantage will find no safe home on our shores, in our public life, in our neighborhoods or in our home, and that Reverend King's dream for his children and for ours will be fulfilled. . . . This must be our mission together. It will, I promise, be my mission as president of the United States."

The administration of Bush's predecessor, Ronald Reagan, in which the president-elect served as vice president, had faced constant criticism from black leaders for alleged insensitivity to civil rights issues. A few days before Bush's speech, one such leader, the Reverend Jesse L. Jackson, had offered that Reagan "may be the worst civil rights president we've had in recent memory."

January 23. The United States Supreme Court, in a 6-3 decision, ruled that a program in Richmond, Virginia which required contractors in city construction project to "set aside" at least 30 percent "of the value of the project" for companies "at least half-minority owned" unconstitutional. The high Court said "the quota" was "an unlawful form of reverse discrimination." Justice Sandra Day O'Connor said local and state government could no longer rest on the "amorphous claim" that quotas were necessary remedies for past racial discrimination, adding "it is sheer speculation" to claim that if past discrimination had not occurred, there would be more minority firms. Justice O'Connor further commented: "The dearth of minority firms might have a number of explanations. For example, whites and blacks may simply make different 'entrepreneurial choices'." In any event, she wrote, if quotas were not "realistically tied to any injury suffered by anyone," they were not permitted by the equal protection clause of the Constitution's 14th Amendment. Justice O'Connor concluded that it was "disingenuous" to include "Spanish-speaking, Oriental, Indian, Eskimo or Aleut persons" in the affirmative action program, because no member of that "random inclusion of racial groups" had ever suffered from discrimination in Richmond.

The *City of Richmond v. J. A. Coson Co.* case stemmed from a 1983 ordinance which required the 30 percent "set asides." At the time, although 60 percent of the population of Richmond was black, minority-owned business had received less than 0.6 percent of the $25 million awarded in city contracts over the preceding five years.

The high Court's ruling was one of the most far reaching attacks on the notion of affirmative action since the *Regents of University of California v. Allan Bakke* decision in 1978. (See also entries dated June 25, 1976, July 3, 1978, June 24, 1984, and July 2, 1986.)

January 24. The Episcopal Church approved the election of Barbara Harris, a fifty-eight-year-old African-American, as the first female bishop in the "2,000-year tradition of apostolic succession, a line of bishops dating from Jesus and his apostles." Harris was assigned to the post of suffragan, or assistant bishop in the Diocese of Boston.

Harris was first ordained an Episcopal priest in 1980, four years after the Church first approved women as priests. She had studied theology through correspondence courses and with tutors. Prior to her elevation to the bishopric, Harris was also the head of the Episcopal Church Publishing Company.

February 1. The Bureau of the Census projected that the black population of the United States would grow 50 percent by the year 2030, but the growth of the "other races" population (primarily Native Americans, Asians, and Pacific Islanders) was expected to "be the fastest of any of the racial groups." These groups had tripled in size in the past seventeen years, increasing from 2.6 million in 1970 to 7.9 million in 1987, and are expected to be 50 percent larger by the year 2000, "double the present size by 2015, and triple its size by the year 2040." By 2040, the "other races" population could reach almost 25 million larger than it was in 1987. On the other hand, the black population, which was 29.9 million in 1987 (seven million more than in 1970) was expected to change relatively little after 2030.

February 24. William Lucas, an African-American attorney from Detroit, Michigan, was named assistant attorney general for civil rights by President George Bush. This appointment also made him director of the Civil Rights Division of the Department of Justice.

Lucas, a 1962 graduate of the Fordham University School of Law, first joined the Justice Department in 1963 and represented the government in efforts to desegregate the public schools of Tuskegee, Alabama. He also served on the New York Police Department, sheriff and executive of Wayne County, Michigan (of which Detroit is the county seat), and ran on the Republican ticket for governor of Michigan in 1986.

The appointment of Lucas was applauded by conservative groups. Patrick B. McGuigan, a leader of the Free Congress Foundation, "a conservative research organization" in Washington, D.C., called the selection "brilliant," adding that Lucas was "a fine, courageous man who, in his career, has been willing to put himself on the line." The appointment also drew expressions of concern from national civil rights organizations, however, because Lucas had indicated "that he generally opposes quotas to advance the interests of minority groups" and because of his long absence from federal service. Elaine R. Jones, an attorney with the NAACP Legal Defense and Educational Fund, Inc., charged that "it doesn't appear at first glance that he has had any substantial experience in this area in 20 years."

February 25. Mike Tyson retained his heavyweight boxing championship with a knockout of British fighter Frank Bruno in the fifth round of a scheduled 15-round bout. Bruno had a record of 32-3 and was the number one contender for the title at the time of the fight. Tyson went into the contest with a record of 36-0, with 32 knockouts. The African-American champion collected $8 million for the Las Vegas, Nevada appearance, bringing his total career earnings to approximately $48 million. Bruno was paid approximately $4 million.

February 28. Richard M. Daley, son of the legendary Chicago mayor Richard J. Daley, defeated acting Mayor Eugene Sawyer for the Democratic nomination for that city's executive office. Daley, who is white, captured 57 percent of the vote, compared to 43 percent for the African-American Sawyer. The vote was "marked by a sharp split along racial lines," but voter turnout in the black wards of the city were lower than usual.

As a result of the primary, the general election scheduled for April 11, 1989 was to be decided among three candidates: Republican Alderman Edward R. Vrdolyak, black independent Timothy C. Evans, and Daley. The winner of that election would serve the final two years of the late Harold Washington's term in office. Washington, Chicago's first black mayor, died of a heart attack in November, 1987. IIis death lcd to the election of Sawyer as acting mayor by the Chicago City Council.

Political analysts quoted by the *Atlanta Constitution* attributed Sawyer's defeat to: (1) a lack of charisma; (2) his alienating many blacks because of his support for the position of acting mayor by many of the same white aldermen who had opposed Mayor Washington's policies; (3) the looming candidacy of Evans, who was endorsed by the "Harold Washington slate"; (4) an antiquated campaign based largely on "grass roots" support; and (5) the political experience of Daley, who had served eight years as a state senator before becoming chief prosecutor of Cook County, of which Chicago is the county seat.

March 3. The Georgia Supreme Court, in a unanimous decision, declared the Atlanta Minority-Female Business Enterprise (MFBE) program unconstitutional. The Atlanta plan, one of the nation's oldest affirmative action programs, had set a 35 percent "minority participation goal" in all city contracts. It had been applauded nationally as a model device for insuring fair representation of minority and female businesses in public works. However, the Georgia Supreme Court contended that the plan "was too broadly drawn and failed to consider alternatives to the yearly goal." The Georgia decision was also based on the recent ruling by the United States Supreme Court which struck down an affirmative action program in the city of Richmond, Virginia. (See also entry dated January 23, 1989.)

March 6. The United States Supreme Court ruled against affirmative action programs in Florida and Michigan.

In the Florida case, the Court heard an appeal of a ruling from the U. S. Court of Appeals for the Eleventh Circuit which had upheld a set-aside plan for minorities in Dade County, Florida. Under the plan, which was adopted in 1979, in order to qualify for federal funds for a mass transit project, the county had to set aside 5 percent of construction contracts for minorities. But after a low bid on a construction project by the H.K. Porter Co. was rejected because the county did not meet the 5 percent goal, Porter sued. In light of its recent ruling in an affirmative action case from Richmond, Virginia, however, the Supreme Court vacated the decision of the appeals court and ordered it to reexamine the case of *Porter v. Metropolitan Dade County.*

In the Michigan case, the Court affirmed without a written opinion a ruling by the U. S. Court of Appeals for the Sixth Circuit which declared a Michigan law unconstitutional. That act, adopted in 1981, provided that 7 percent of state contracting expenditures should go to minority-owned businesses and an additional 5 percent to businesses owned by women. Although the state argued in its appeal of *Milliken v. Michigan Road Builders* that the set-aside percentages were carefully selected "to redress discriminatory practices by state agencies," the Supreme Court still ruled against it. (See also entry dated January 23, 1989.)

March 7. Lee Atwater, chairman of the Republican National Committee, resigned as a member of the Board of Trustees of predominantly-black Howard University in Washington, D.C. The resignation came as several hundred African-American students continued a sit-in that began as a protest against Atwater's selection to the Board.

During the demonstrations, which began on March 3, 1989, students took over the school's administration building. Although city police stormed the captured building on March 7, they left without removing or arresting any protestors at the request of Howard president James A. Cheek.

In announcing his resignation, Atwater remarked, "The opposition of some students to my service on the board appears to me to be counterproductive to Howard University and is a distraction to the work that I want to do in fulfilling George Bush's and my efforts to provide equal opportunity to all Americans. . . . I would never forgive myself if someone was hurt in one of these episodes."

Although Atwater's appointment to the Howard University Board of Trustees had been seen by some political analysts "as symbolic of his drive to broaden the Republican Party's appeal to blacks," others, including Democratic party and civil rights leaders, had accused the Republican leader of orchestrating "subtly racist appeals" during the 1988 presidential campaign. One Republican television ad, for example, featured Willie Horton, a convicted black rapist, in the party's attack on crime. Regina Davis, a twenty-year-old business management major at Howard, applauded Atwater's resignation, saying "if you're going to appoint someone, they should have the same views as the people they're going to represent."

But Atwater's resignation did not bring an immediate end to the protests, as students continued to press their demands for better housing and security, improvements in student services, and the appointment of more African-Americans to Howard's Board of Trustees.

March 8. The Bureau of the Census reported that 52 percent of the 19.7 million voting-age blacks went to the polls in the 1988 presidential election, as compared to 56 percent in 1984. White voter turnout also dropped from 61 percent to 59 percent, while the rate for Hispanics fell from 33 percent to 29 percent. Black voter participation was higher in the North and West (56 percent) than in the South (48 percent). Among whites, 60 voted in the North and West, and 56 percent in the South.

March 10. Louis Wade Sullivan, president of the Morehouse School of Medicine in Atlanta, was confirmed as Secretary of Health and Human Services (HHS) by the United States Senate. The confirmation came more than two months after President George Bush had nominated Sullivan for the position. Sullivan's nomination first ran into trouble on December 18, 1988, after the black physician told an *Atlanta Journal-Constitution* reporter that "while opposing federal funding for abortions," he supported a woman's right to have one. This view was incompatible with the President's outright opposition to abortion except in cases of rape or incest, or to save the expectant mother's life. The same position had been taken by several Republican senators and other leaders of the President's party.

On December 21, 1988, Sullivan began to back away from his pro-choice position. In a letter to the editors of the *Atlanta Constitution*, he wrote that he was "opposed to abortion, except in cases of rape, incest, and where the life of the mother is threatened. I am opposed to federal funding for abortions, except when the life of the mother is endangered. My position is entirely consistent with President-elect [George] Bush's position." Still, some pro-life activists were skeptical.

While Sullivan attempted to convince influential Republican senators in Washington of his correct position on the abortion question, President Bush announced on January 25, 1989 that Sullivan would carry out his abortion policies if confirmed by the Senate. On February 22, Sullivan confessed to the Senate Finance Committee that he had "misspoke" earlier when he said he supported a woman's right to an abortion. Sullivan's confirmation occurred the following month.

Sullivan was born on November 3, 1933 in Atlanta, Georgia, the son of Walter and Lubirda Elizabeth Priester Wade Sullivan. He graduated *magna cum laude* from Morehouse College in 1954 and earned a Doctor of Medicine degree (*cum laude*), from the Boston University Medical School. A respected hematologist, Sullivan taught at the Harvard Medical School (1963-64), the New Jersey College of Medicine (1964-66), and the Boston University Medical School before he was named dean of the new Morehouse School of Medicine in 1974. The next year, he became both dean and president of this institution. During his fifteen year tenure at Morehouse, the school emerged from being a two-year institution housed in two trailers, to a fully accredited, four-year institution comprised of three buildings.

March 10. James A. Goodman, executive vice president of the Morehouse Medical School, was named president of the predominately-black institution. The school's Board of Trustees selected Goodman, age fifty-five, who had served as an administrator there since 1980, to succeed Louis W. Sullivan, the school's first president. On the same day, Sullivan was sworn in as Secretary of the Department of Health and Human Services (HHS).

Goodman, who earned an undergraduate degree from Morehouse College and post-graduate degrees from the Atlanta University School of Social Work and the University of Minnesota, had previously served as a director of the Office of International Training for the Agency for International Development (AID) in the U. S. State Department. Goodman's teaching experience included tenures at the School of Social Work at the University of Minnesota and at the National Academy of Science's Institute of Medicine. At the time of Goodman's appointment, the Morehouse Medical School had an annual budget of $18 million and an enrollment of 144 students.

March 15. The federal government issued a report which showed that the life expectancy of African-Americans is continuing to decline. Major causes of premature deaths among blacks included homicide and AIDS. Blacks were also twice as likely to die in infancy as whites, because "pregnant black women receive early prenatal care far less than whites," and black children were "disproportionately" afflicted with influenza and pneumonia. The report also indicated that black men, "frequently the victims of drug-related violence," died at a 50 percent higher rate than white men in 1986, the last year for which comprehensive statistics were available. Also, a white child born in 1986 had a life expectancy of 75.4 years, an increase from 75.3 the previous year, while a black child, born at the same time, could expect to die at 69.4 years, down from 69.5 in 1985 and 69.7 in 1984.

In the period 1970 to 1986, the AIDS infection rate rose 51 percent among blacks, with a 74 percent increase among black women. In the same period, infant mortality among all groups was cut in half—from 20 deaths per 1,000 births in 1970 to 10.4 per 1,000 births in 1986, but in 1986 alone, the mortality rate for black infants was 18 deaths per 1,000 births compared with 8.9 per 1,000 births for whites.

Responding to the report, the African-American Secretary of Health and Human Services (HHS) Louis W. Sullivan said that "there is a disparity between the health of our white and black populations," and the nation needed to focus more attention "in such critical areas as prevention of AIDS, unintentional injuries, homicide, and suicide."

March 16. The United States Senate voted to try U. S. District Court Judge Alcee Hastings, the first African-American to be appointed to the federal bench in Florida, on all seventeen articles of impeachment adopted by the U. S. House of Representatives. The senators voted 92-1 to try Hastings on fifteen articles charging fraud, corruption, and perjury in a 1981 bribery conspiracy case for which he was acquitted in 1983. In voting against the articles, Senator Howard M. Metzenbaum from Ohio said he felt they placed Hastings in double jeopardy—the principle in American law that a person cannot be tried twice for the same offense—because of the previous acquittal. But Metzenbaum joined fellow senators in a unanimous vote for an article alleging "a pattern of misconduct and its harmful effect on the judiciary."

The Senate also created a special 12-member committee to hear testimony and collect evidence before it debated and voted whether to convict Hastings.

March 18. The *Atlanta Journal-Constitution* reported that there were 37 black-owned banks in the United States in 1989. Four of the institutions, including the number-one ranked IndeCorp, were located in Chicago, Illinois. The other Chicago banks, Seeway National, Highland Community, and Community Bank of Lawndale, were among the top twenty in total assets as ranked by *Black Enterprise* magazine. (See Tables H and I in Appendix for data compiled by *Black Enterprise* magazine, *Reuters*, the *Atlanta Journal-Constitution*, and the Sheshunoff Information Services, Inc.)

March 22. United States District Court Judge John Pratt declared that an 84-year old law prohibiting shoeshine stands on the streets of Washington, D.C. was unconstitutional. The case was brought to court on behalf of Ego Brown, a thirty-six-year-old black shoeshine vendor who had offered employment to homeless men until the city closed down his business in 1985. The suit was sponsored by the Landmark Legal Foundation Center for Civil Rights, which was based in Washington, D.C. The Landmark Center claimed that it provided "an alternative to the NAACP." Its director, Clint Bolick, charged that "the other major civil rights organizations are more worried about imposing racial quotas than protecting individual rights." The Brown case was the Center's first legal victory.

April 1. Bill White, a six-time All Star first baseman, was elected president of the National Baseball League, becoming the first African-American ever to head a major professional sports league in the United States.

White played baseball with the St. Louis Cardinals, the Philadelphia Phillies, and the New York and San Francisco Giants between 1956 and 1969. At the time of his appointment, White was a television announcer for the New York Yankees of the American Baseball League and a broadcaster with CBS Radio.

Henry "Hank" Aaron, vice president of the Atlanta Braves, who had been campaigning for more blacks in executive positions in baseball, applauded White's selection. He characterized White as "a baseball man. He knows baseball. There will be nothing that will be a surprise for him." White himself commented that "You just do the job whether you're red, yellow, purple, or whatever."

April 3. Twenty students occupied and barricaded the administration building at predominantly black Morris Brown College in Atlanta, Georgia. The demonstrators' demands included "a more lenient delinquent fees policy, a Pan-African studies program, better campus services (including a new cafeteria vendor) and (after a recent dormitory fire), an upgraded physical plant." The Morris Brown demonstration followed by one month a similar campus takeover at historically black Howard University in Washington, D.C. and by a week a black student takeover at predominantly white Wayne State University in Detroit, Michigan.

The campus demonstrations were reminiscent of similar protests on both black and white campuses during the 1960s, yet the young college students differed in both tone and manner from the radicals of earlier generations. For example, there was less damage to property in the current protests and little personal rage toward college administrators. At Morris Brown College, the students called their takeover "an act of love." The demonstrators did acknowledge, however, linkages to the 1960s through their quotations of both Martin Luther King, Jr. and Malcolm X, and their references to similar actions in the earlier period. Yet some observers saw the current demonstrators as having too much "reverence" for the "radicalism" of the 1960's "without a full understanding of the time in which the leaders worked."

Werner Sollors, a professor of Afro-American Studies at Howard University and author of a biography of black poet Amiri Baraka (one of the heroes of today's radicals), believed that the current campus protestors were "totally misreading the historical context of [the earlier movements], so what they're doing now seems pretty wacky."

April 6. The Bureau of the Census reported that African-Americans spent a larger share of their income on housing in 1985 than all other American ethnic groups. The median monthly housing cost for black households was $311 compared with $355 for all households. Because their incomes were lower, black households spent a median of 27 percent of their income for housing costs, compared with 21 percent for all U.S. households. Housing costs for homeowners include mortgage payments, real estate taxes, property insurance, utilities, fuel, and garbage collection. Renter costs were based on contract rent and the estimated cost of utilities and fuels, if these were paid in addition to rent.

The Census Bureau also reported that: (1) Black householders occupied 9.9 million housing units in 1985; 44 percent were homeowners compared with 64 percent of all households; (2) 16 percent of black householders lived in public or subsidized housing compared with 5 percent of all householders; and (3) There were five million black householders in single, detached homes. The median size of their unit was 1,337 square feet, or 487 square feet per person. The national average was 633 square feet per person.

The Census Bureau's data was compiled for its biennial report on housing.

April 29. Bobby Doctor, a member of the staff of the U.S. Commission on Civil Rights (CCR), told a state CCR meeting in Atlanta, Georgia that "federal agencies have gone to sleep on the question of civil rights enforcement." He also "attributed the ineffectiveness" of the Commission on Civil Rights "during the last decade to the anti-civil rights posture" of the administration of President Ronald Reagan.

The CCR, which was established in 1957, is responsible for monitoring such federal agencies as the Department of Housing and Urban Development (HUD) for possible discrimination in education, employment, housing, and other areas. According to Doctor, "for the past seven years we have not done that." He added that during the last decade, the budget of the CCR had been cut by at least 50 percent and seven of its ten regional offices were closed. "The agency has been teetering on the brink of annihilation," he added.

By not strongly enforcing civil rights compliance in federal agencies, Doctor accused the CCR of contributing to a national climate that condoned "hate activity" against minorities and such discriminatory practices as redlining, and other improper mortgage lending activities.

May 22. Oprah Winfrey, African-American national talk-show television host, received a Doctor of Humane Letters degree from Morehouse College in Atlanta, Georgia, and gave the all-male college a gift of one million dollars. She requested that the money be used to establish a scholarship fund to educate at least 100 black men in the coming decades. Morehouse, one of the country's most prestigious black colleges, was the alma mater of slain civil rights leader Martin Luther King, Jr.

Winfrey's gift represented a growing trend among black entertainers and athletes to lend their support to America's financially impoverished black colleges. Other recent donations included $800,000 to Meharry Medical College, $325,000 to Howard University, $1.3 million to Fisk University, and $20 million to Spelman College by comedian Bill Cosby; $500,000 to Tuskegee University by singer Lionel Richie; and $600,000 to the United Negro College Fund (UNCF) by singer Michael Jackson. (See also entries dated December 31, 1984, and November 4, 1988.)

May 23. The Committee on Policy for Racial Justice, a group of prominent African-American scholars, called for "smaller, more personal schools, significant parental involvement," and other steps that they said "would help black children achieve greater academic success." Sara Lawrence Lightfoot, professor of Education at Harvard University and a member of the committee, said "we believe it is the school's responsibility to overcome social barriers that limit academic progress." She added: "What we demand is this: that the schools shift their focus from the supposed deficiencies of the black child and the alleged inadequacies of black family life to the elimination of the barriers that stand in the way of academic success."

The committee's report (much of which was contained in its publication, *Vision of a Better Way: A Black Appraisal of Public Schooling*), also called upon black communities to make the improvement of public schools their main objective in the next decade. It further noted that the black middle class and such black institutions as churches and fraternal organizations had a special responsibility "to set expectations and support academic development among black children."

The committee's recommendations and suggestions included expanded funding for Head Start and Chapter I, the federal government's "major programs for at-risk and disadvantaged students, closer ties between schools and social services, recruitment of more black teachers, and an expanded curricular that recognizes the realities of black children's lives."

May 24. President George Bush met with seventeen members of the Congressional Black Caucus (CBC). It was the first time since 1981 that the Caucus, which had been critical of the civil rights policies of former President Ronald Reagan, was invited to the White House. Representative Ronald V. Dellums from California, who led the delegation, said that President Bush indicated that he was "ready to open up" and meet regularly with the CBC. Representative John Lewis from Georgia remarked, "there certainly is a new level of sensitivity at the White House."

May 31. Cito Gaston was named manager of the Toronto Blue Jays of the American Baseball League. The appointment made Gaston only the fourth African-American selected for a permanent managerial position in the major leagues.

Gaston began his major league career in 1967 with the Atlanta Braves of the National League. In 1968 Gaston was traded to the San Diego Padres. He played six years with the Padres and was selected to the National League All-Star team in 1970. In that year, Gaston hit 29 home runs, batted in 93 runs, and had a total batting average of .318. He returned to Atlanta in 1974 before being traded to the Pittsburgh Pirates in 1977. After being dropped by the Pirates in 1979, Gaston played two years in the Dominican League and the Mexican League before retiring. He emerged from retirement in 1981 as a minor league hitting instructor for the Atlanta Braves. He took a similar position with the Toronto Blue Jays in 1982, and the team improved its over-all batting average 36 points to 262.

Baseball Commissioner A. Bartlett Giammati, who had been a champion of equal opportunity for blacks in professional sports, applauded the choice of Gaston. Gaston said of his selection, "the organization doesn't see any colors. . . . I don't see any colors. I'm black, I'll always be black. When I stand here and look at you, I just see you as a person."

June 5. The United States Supreme Court, in a 5-4 decision, ruled that "when minorities allege that statistics show they are victims of bias, employers only have the burden of producing evidence that there is a legitimate reason for apparently neutral racial practices." Justice Byron White wrote that "the plaintiff bears the burden of disproving an employer's assertion that the adverse employment action or practice was based solely on a legitimate neutral consideration." He also added that an absence of minorities in skilled jobs is not necessarily evidence of bias if the absence reflected "a dearth of qualified non-white applications for reasons that are not [the employers] fault." In one of the dissenting opinions, Justice John Paul Stevens charged that the ruling retreated from eighteen years of court decisions "aimed at helping minorities victimized by discrimination that may be unintentional."

The case came to the Supreme Court from Alaska where a lower court had ruled in favor of Filipinos, Alaska natives, and Asians who claimed that they had been discriminated against by the Wards Cove Packing Co. and Castle and Cooke, Inc., owners of Alaskan salmon canneries. (See also entries dated June 25, 1976, July 3, 1978, June 14, 1984, July 2, 1986, and January 23, 1989.)

June 5. The United States Court of Appeals for the Tenth Circuit refused to close the landmark desegregation case, *Brown v. Board of Education*. The court said that the school board of Topeka, Kansas had still failed "to fully carry out" the Supreme Court's order of May 17, 1954. The Appeals Court ruling reversed a decision by a lower court that could have closed the case "that paved the way for nationwide school desegregation." In its decision, the appellate court concluded that "Topeka has not sufficiently countered the effects of both the momentum of its pre-Brown segregation and its subsequent acts in the 1960s."

The Brown case had been reopened in 1979 when a group of parents, including one of the original plaintiffs, Linda Brown Buckner, complained that the school system was not desegregated. (See also entry dated July 23, 1989.)

June 7. Joan Salmon Campbell, a fifty-year-old African-American from Philadelphia, Pennsylvania, was elected moderator of the Presbyterian Church, U.S.A. She became the sixth female and the first black woman to head the Church. The moderator presides at Assembly sessions and travels around the nation and the world promoting the programs of the 3 million member church.

Salmon Campbell had campaigned for the position of moderator on a platform of liberality and diversity. She said, "We must be liberal enough to include the rich diversity of God's family within our membership in its varied cultures, races, lifestyles, theological perspectives and economic status without restraint due to age, sex, or physical capacity."

June 12. The United States Supreme Court, in a 5-4 decision, ruled that workers "who are adversely affected by court-approved affirmative action plans may file lawsuits alleging discrimination."

The high Court's ruling came in a case from Birmingham, Alabama which had adopted an affirmative action plan, with federal court approval, in 1981 after blacks had filed suit "charging that the city had engaged in discriminatory hiring and promotions." However, white fire fighters challenged the plan, claiming that it denied them promotions because of their race. The Supreme Court agreed with the U. S. Court of Appeals for the Eleventh Circuit that, contrary to previous appellate court findings that prohibited "secondary attacks on court-approved affirmative action plans," the white fire fighters did have a right to sue. Chief Justice William Rehnquist wrote, "A voluntary settlement . . . between one group of employees and their employer cannot possibly settle, voluntarily or otherwise, the conflicting claims of another group of employees who do not join in the agreement." Justice Harry Blackmun, William Brennan, Thurgood Marshall, and John Paul Stevens dissented. Justice Stevens called the majority opinion "unfathomable" and said it would "subject large employers who seek to comply with the law by remedying past discrimination to a never-ending stream of litigation and potential liability." (See also entries dated June 25, 1976, July 3, 1978, June 12, 1984, July 2, 1986, January 23, 1989, and June 5, 1989.)

June 12. The United States Supreme Court, in a 5-3 decision, ruled that "the 300-day period that federal law allows for filing job discrimination lawsuits begins when . . . seniority plans [are] adopted." In a dissent, Justices Thurgood Marshall, Harry Blackmun, and William Brennan agreed with civil rights lawyers that such an interpretation was "unfair" because employees were often unaware of "the discriminatory effect" that a seniority system "may have on them for months or years." Justice Sandra Day O'Connor did not participate in the case and did not offer an explanation.

The case came to the high Court from Aurora, Illinois where three women filed suit in 1982 claiming that a change in the seniority system at the American Telephone and Telegraph Co. there caused them to lose seniority. However, federal courts in Chicago had held that the litigation (*Lorance v. AT and T Technologies, Inc.*) was filed too late. The U. S. Supreme Court agreed with the lower courts.

June 15. The United States Supreme Court unanimously reaffirmed a 1976 decision "that interpreted an 1866 Civil Rights law to permit lawsuits to remedy some forms of private discrimination." But the Court also ruled 5-4, that the 1866 law may "no longer serve as the bases for lawsuits alleging racial harrassment in the workplace." Civil rights attorneys said this latter ruling, written by Justice Anthony Kennedy, would make it almost impossible "to stop racial harrassment by supervisors or co-workers." Barry Goldstein, an attorney with the NAACP Legal Defense and Educational Fund, said the decision left "no effective legal remedy for racial harrassment in the workplace."

The Supreme Court's ruling came in the case of a black bank teller in North Carolina who had alleged that her supervisor at the McLean Credit Union had failed to promote her and then fired her on account of her race. A federal district court in North Carolina and a federal appeals court in Richmond, Virginia had said that she could not sue alleging harrassment. While the Supreme Court's decision ended the harrassment phase of the litigation, it sent the case back to the appeals court for another hearing on whether the woman could "prove that the company's reason for not promoting her was invalid." The case has become known to history as *Patterson v. McClean Credit Union*.

June 20. The Bureau of the Census reported that New York state had the largest number of African-American residents in 1985 while California had the fastest growing black population. New York state had a black population of 2.7 million, followed by California with 2.1 million. Fourteen other states had black populations of one million or more. These included Texas, Illinois, Georgia, Florida, North Carolina, Louisiana, Michigan, and Ohio.

The state with the largest proportion of blacks in its population was Mississippi with 36 percent, followed by South Carolina, 31 percent, and Louisiana, 30 percent. During the period 1980-1985, only West Virginia and the District of Columbia had declines in their black populations.

The Bureau's report also revealed that four out of every five blacks lived in metropolitan areas in 1985. Four metropolitan areas had black populations of one million or more. These included New York (Metropolitan New York also includes Long Island and portions of Connecticut and New Jersey, 3.2 million), Chicago (1.6 million), Los Angeles (1.2 million) and Philadelphia (1.1 million). The fastest growing metropolitan area in black residents was Atlanta, up 15.6 percent to 608,000 from 1980 to 1985, followed by Houston, up 13.6 percent to 641,000 in the same period.

The new calculations of the African-American population were the first detailed estimates of minorities by state since the 1980 census. They also showed that blacks remained the nation's largest minority at 28.9 million, or 11.8 of the estimated U. S. population. (See Table J in Appendix for data compiled by the United States Bureau of the Census.)

June 26. Two of the nation's oldest black institutions of higher education, Atlanta University and Clark College, merged. The new institution, Clark-Atlanta University, was created in response to severe financial problems at Atlanta University and a shortage of classroom space and research facilities at Clark College. Atlanta University was founded in 1867, Clark College was founded two years later.

The new university is expected to focus its activities on science and technology, foreign service careers, and teachers for rural areas, according to Thomas W. Cole, Jr., Clark-Atlanta University's new president. The university also hoped to offer six doctoral programs to "assist in curbing the shortage of blacks" holding doctorate degrees. In 1989, Clark-Atlanta University and Howard University in Washington, D.C. were the only two comprehensive historically black institutions in the nation which offered academic studies from undergraduate through graduate levels.

June 26. Moreland Griffith Smith, a retired architect and civil rights activist, died of heart failure in Atlanta, Georgia. Smith was born December 15, 1906 to Charles M. and Jennie Moreland Smith in Adrian, Michigan. He received a bachelor's degree from Auburn University in Alabama, a master's degree in architecture from the Massachusetts Institute of Technology, and did further study at the Ecole des Beaux-Arts in Fontainebleau, France.

In 1954, Smith went to the office of his friend, William "Tacky" Gayle, mayor of Montgomery, Alabama, to discuss what he termed "a simple matter of fairness," the issue of seating for blacks on city buses. The meeting occurred before Rosa Parks refused to give up her seat on one such bus and the launching of the famed Montgomery bus boycott. Two issues had already surfaced: Blacks were forced to stand on buses when "the white section" was nearly empty, and they had to pay their fares up front, exit, and reenter through the back door (sometimes the bus driver would pull away before they could do so). Smith urged Mayor Gayle to end both of these practices.

Because of his support for the demands of blacks regarding seating on buses, Smith was berated numerous times by whites. Among his detractors was Governor George C. Wallace, who allegedly tried to keep Smith from getting architectural jobs in the area. One bank, in fact, declined to extend a line of credit to Smith's architectural firm. Yet he "stubbornly" served on local civil rights committees and was a trustee at Tuskegee Institute. Smith hired many black architects and proposed some for membership in the American Institute of Architecture (AIA). These activities led to social ostracism among Montgomery's white community for Smith and his wife, Marjorie. In 1965, Smith lost the lucrative architectural business he had founded and built up over the years, and subsequently moved to Atlanta.

In 1987, the Atlanta chapter of the AIA honored Moreland Smith "for his conviction and courage during the tumultuous early years of the Civil Rights Movement."

July 10. African-American businessmen Bertram Lee of Boston, Massachusetts and Peter Bynoe of Chicago, Illinois purchased the Denver Nuggets of the National Basketball Association for $65 million. They became the first blacks ever to own a professional sports franchise.

After the purchase, Lee commented, "Do we overestimate the significance of a barrier coming down? A barrier that presumably had to do with other than people's abilities or their financial wherewithal? No, I don't think so. I think the analogy about Jackie Robinson is something that is very special to me. If breaking the color barrier in ownership is sort of put up there with that, I'm honored by it."

July 21. African-American heavyweight boxing champion Mike Tyson knocked out Carl "The Truth" Williams in the first minute and a half of the first round to retain his world title. It was the fifth fastest title bout in boxing history. Although Williams was on his feet at the count of seven (knockouts are usually declared at the count of ten), referee Randy Neumann declared him out in the Atlantic City, New Jersey contest.

July 23. A federal appeals court in Denver, Colorado, without explanation, withdrew its earlier ruling that the historic case of *Brown v. Board of Education of Topeka, Kansas* be continued. (See also entry dated June 5, 1989.)

August 1. The Judiciary Committee of the United States Senate voted 7-7 on whether to recommend the nomination of William Lucas, an African-American attorney, as U. S. Assistant Attorney General, to the full Senate. The tie vote meant a rejection of the nomination. Had Lucas been confirmed, he would have headed the civil rights division of the U. S. Justice Department. Some legislators and some civil rights leaders had cited Lucas's "inexperience," his opposition to racial quotas in employment and contracts, and his support of recent Supreme Court decisions severely limiting affirmative action programs for opposing Lucas's nomination. (See also entry dated February 24, 1989.)

August 7-13. On August 7, an airplane with the African-American Congressman Mickey Leland aboard crashed en route to the Fugnido refugee camp in Ethiopia. On August 13, the bodies of Leland and fifteen others were discovered. Other Americans aboard the ill-fated aircraft included Hugh A. Johnson, Jr., a staff member of the U. S. House Select Committee on Hunger, Patrice Y. Johnson, Leland's chief of staff, and Joyce Williams, a member of the staff of California Representative Ronald V. Dellums.

Leland, age forty-four, represented Texas and served as chairman of the House Select Committee on Hunger at the time of his death. He had made six previous trips to Africa to investigate and underscore famine conditions, particularly in war-torn Ethiopia.

After the congressman's body was discovered, Thomas S. Foley, Speaker of the U. S. House of Representatives, said "there will be a determination on the part of members of the House to work for those goals that Mickey Leland sought to achieve, the alleviation of hunger and suffering here and in Africa and elsewhere in the world."

August 8. Dexter Scott King, son of slain civil rights leader Martin Luther King, Jr., resigned as president of the Martin Luther King, Jr. Center for Non-Violent Social Change in Atlanta, Georgia. He had held the position for only four months. The *Atlanta Constitution* quoted sources as blaming "a power struggle" involving young King, his mother, Coretta Scott King, his aunt Christine Farris King, and his top aide, Barbara Williams-Skinner for the resignation. The King Center itself had "no comment" at the time of King's resignation. (See also entry dated January 14, 1989.)

August 8. A. W. Wilson, minister and civil rights activist, died in Montgomery, Alabama, at age eighty-seven. Wilson was the pastor of the Holt Street Baptist Church in Montgomery for fifty years. The church was the site of the first mass meeting of organizers of the famous Montgomery Bus Boycott in 1955. Many other rallies were also held at the church during the civil rights movement in Montgomery.

August 9. President George Bush told delegates to the 79th Annual Convention of the National Urban League (NUL) in Washington, D.C. that his administration would not "tolerate discrimination, bigotry or bias of any kind—period." He added, "your problems are my problems. . . . The 'great gulf' between black and white America has narrowed, but it has not closed."

President Bush also said that "race hate" still existed and as long as bigotry persisted, "our work is not over."

NUL president John E. Jacob said it was "significant" that Bush came to the meeting and made a vow to fight racial bias. It was, he thought, a first step in changing the "national atmosphere" of the preceding eight years. The previous administration of President Ronald Reagan was frequently criticized by the NUL and other civil rights groups for "insensitivity" to black issues and actually trying to "roll back" progress in civil rights. Former President Reagan never addressed a NUL Convention and rarely appeared before any civil rights group. Former President Jimmy Carter spoke to the NUL in 1977.

August 10. Army General Colin L. Powell was named chairman of the U. S. Joint Chiefs of Staff, the highest military position in the country. Powell, age fifty-two, became the first African-American ever to occupy the position. He is also the youngest man ever to lead the Joint Chiefs.

Powell, the son of West Indian immigrants, was born in the Harlem section of New York City on April 5, 1937. He received a bachelor's degree from the City College of New York in 1958 and a M.B.A. from George Washington University in 1971. In 1975-76, he attended the National War College.

Powell was commissioned a second lieutenant in the Army in 1958 and was promoted to full general in 1989. During the interval, he was a staff officer at the Pentagon (1974-75); brigade commander, 101st Airborne Division, (1976-77); senior military assistant to the deputy secretary of defense (1977-81); deputy commander of Fort Carson, Colorado (1981-82); deputy commander at Fort Leavenworth, Kansas (1982-83); senior military assistant to the secretary of defense (1983-86); commander, Fifth Corps U. S. Army, Europe (1986-87); deputy assistant and assistant to the President for national security affairs (1987-89). Prior to being named Chairman of the Joint Chiefs, he was commander in chief, Forces Command, Fort McPherson, Georgia.

After the "Iran-Contra" diplomatic scandal in 1987, Powell, then a lieutenant-general and national security advisor to President Ronald Reagan, "restored order" to the National Security Council (NSC). John Poindexter, a previous NSC advisor, had been implicated in the arms deal with Iran, with some of the profits allegedly illegally sent to rebels (Contras) in Nicaragua. After becoming chairman of the Joint Chiefs, Powell directed the American invasion of Panama, which led to the arrest of its leader, Manuel Antonio Noriega, on drug trafficking charges.

Former Secretary of Defense Caspar Weinberger, under whom Powell served in the Pentagon, once described the black general as "the quintessential soldier. He has a remarkable understanding of the great issues of our times, the problems in world affairs, and how our government operates."

Lt. Gen. Colin Powell

August 21. Fifteen people, including a four-month-old baby girl, were injured when a parcel exploded in the offices of the Southeast regional NAACP in Atlanta, Georgia. The injuries, mostly eye irritations and congestion, resulted from a tear-gas bomb but were not considered serious.

Georgia's black Congressman John Lewis, who was giving a speech nearby when the incident occurred, called the attack "another form of harassment and intimidation that seeks to have a chilling effect on individuals and organizations who may want to do something about racism." He added, "I thought it was over."

August 22. Huey P. Newton, a co-founder of the Black Panther Party, was shot to death in Oakland, California. He was forty-seven years old.

Since the demise of his racial activism in the 1960s, Newton continued to have numerous encounters with law enforcement and the criminal justice system. In 1974, he was charged with pistol-whipping his tailor, possession of a handgun, and of murdering a seventeen-year-old prostitute. Before his murder trial, Newton fled to Cuba but returned to face the charges in 1977. He was tried twice on the murder charge, but both trials ended in mistrials with the juries deadlocked in favor of acquittal. The charges were later dismissed in 1979. In 1978, Newton was convicted of possession of a handgun, but was acquitted on the charge of assaulting his tailor after the alleged victim refused to testify against him. Newton served nine months in California's San Quentin Prison on the gun charge in 1987. In March, 1989, Newton was sentenced to six months in jail after pleading no contest to charges of misappropriating $15,000 in public monies which had been given for a school the Black Panther Party had operated in the early 1980s.

At the time of his death, Newton, who had earned a Ph.D. degree in social philosophy from the University of California at Santa Cruz in 1980, was attempting "to rehabilitate himself from alcohol and drug abuse."

After Newton's death, Charles Garry, his attorney, called Newton the founder of "the renaissance of the black liberation movement." He said the Panther leader had "a very sweet side, a humane side, a dignified side, a man who was theoretically in favor of a better world." (See also entries dated September 8, 1968, December 15, 1971, and November 2, 1974.)

August 23. Yusef Hawkins, a sixteen-year-old African-American youth, was shot to death in the predominantly white Bensonhurst section of Brooklyn, New York. Hawkins and three friends had answered an advertisement for a used car when at least thirty whites wielding baseball bats, golf clubs, and at least one pistol attacked them. The whites allegedly thought that Hawkins and his companions had to come into the area to visit a white girl. Police quickly arrested six white youths in connection with the assault.

Following the Bensonhurst incident, the Reverend Al Sharpton and other local civil rights activists led two days of confrontational demonstrations though the largely Italian-American neighborhood. The furor was the largest and bitterest in New York since 1986, when a black man was killed while fleeing a white mob in the Howard Beach section of Queens.

August 26. About 30,000 people, many of the men dressed in black and women and children in white, staged a reenactment of the NAACP's famous "Silent March" of 1917 in Washington, D.C. The 1917 march down Fifth Avenue in New York City was held to protest lynching and racial segregation. The 1989 march sought to persuade the United States Congress to reverse recent decisions of the United States Supreme Court, which civil rights groups and others believed had weakened affirmative action laws and minority "set aside" programs. Many of the demonstrators wore signs reading "What the court has torn asunder, let Congress set right."

One of the speakers at a rally at the U. S. capitol, Joseph Lowery, president of the SCLC, told the crowd, "we declare here today in no uncertain terms that the path of progress has been filled with pain and suffering and sacrifice, and that we're fed up and fired up. . . . We don't intend to sit by and watch the meager gains washed away by a flood tide of insidious insensitivity nor invidious individualism. . . . In other words, we ain't going back."

August 28. Forty businesses and twenty cars were damaged in Vineland, New Jersey after 200 blacks rioted in protest of the slaying of Samuel Williams, a twenty-six-year-old black man, by police on August 27. Twenty-three people were arrested in the city of 54,000, located forty miles southeast of Philadelphia, Pennsylvania.

Williams, who was being sought by police on drug and weapon charges, allegedly attacked officers with a rod as they attempted to arrest him. No drugs or weapons were found on Williams's body. The state attorney general's office took over the investigation.

August 30. More than 300 mourners attended funeral services for Yusef Hawkins, an African-American youth slain in New York City. Another 1,000 persons who could not enter the church stood outside singing and listening to the eulogy. Hawkins had been shot to death on August 23 in the predominantly white Bensonhurst section of Brooklyn (see entry above).

The Reverend Al Sharpton, a civil rights activist who lead protests immediately following the killing, said in one of the eulogies, "We're not going to let you down. . . . They're going to pay this time, Yusef. It's time for us to change our ways. We can run a man for the White House, but we can't walk a child through Bensonhurst." Another speaker, Minister Louis Farrakhan, a leader of the Nation of Islam, proclaimed: "We say, as the Jews say; Never again, Never again, Never again. . . . As long as white children can get away with killing black children, and white law enforcement does not know how to make examples of its own . . . then justice is far off." The church's pastor, the Reverend Curtis Wells, exhorted, "Let freedom ring from Howard Beach, Mr. Mayor" (addressing New York mayor Edward Koch). . . . "Let freedom ring from Bensonhurst. We're not going to take it anymore. We're going to walk where we want to walk." Mayor Koch, New York governor Mario M. Cuomo, and Republican mayoral candidate Rudolph W. Giuliani were heckled outside the church, and Koch left the ceremonies through a side door. Others attending the funeral included the African-American mayoral candidate David Dinkins and black filmmaker Spike Lee.

August 31. More than 7,000 people, chanting "No more!" and "Whose street? Our street!" marched through the downtown section of Brooklyn, New York in further protests of the killing of sixteen-year-old Yusef Hawkins. Hawkins, a black youth, was shot and killed in Brooklyn on August 23 (see entry above).

The march turned violent after reaching the Brooklyn Bridge, where police had set up barricades. The marchers ran through the barricade, shouting "take the bridge, take the bridge!'' Hand-to-hand battles erupted between demonstrators and police. The rioters also threw bottles and rocks at police officers, who freely wielded their nightsticks. At least 23 police officers were injured, only one seriously. There were no immediate reports of injuries to civilians.

September 3. Four people were injured (two by gunfire) and at least 160 were arrested during a confrontation between police and black college students in Virginia Beach, Virginia. An estimated 10,000 people, mostly black collegians from Eastern colleges and universities, had gone to the resort city for Labor Day frolicking. The police department said that more than 100 businesses were looted in the riot. Some students who witnessed the melee said law enforcement authorities "overreacted" to their activities.

September 8. United States Supreme Court Justice Thurgood Marshall told a group of federal judges meeting at Bolton Landing, New York that a recent series of high Court decisions had "put at risk not only the civil rights of minorities but the civil rights of all citizens." The Supreme Court's only black justice was referring to several rulings during the 1989 term of the Court which struck severe blows to the notions of affirmative action programs and minority "set aside" laws. In a rare criticism of colleagues on the high bench, Marshall also said "it is difficult to characterize last term's decisions as the product of anything other than a deliberate retrenching of the civil rights agenda." But he warned, "we forget at our peril [that] civil rights and liberty rights [are] inexorably intertwined." (See also entries dated January 23, 1989, June 5, 1989, and June 12, 1989.)

September 11. *USA Today* reported new criticisms of the Scholastic Aptitude Test (SAT) for alleged bias against blacks and other minorities. The complaints against the SAT, the nation's best known college admission test, were contained in a book by John Weiss, Barbara Beckwith, and Bob Schaeffer entitled *Standing Up to the SAT*. The authors emphasized that the SAT employed vocabulary that "unfairly" penalized low income and minority students because they were unfamiliar with them. The *USA Today* report cited terms like regatta, melodeon, and heirloom as examples of such words. But Donald Stewart, the African-American president of the College Board, which conceived, developed, and owns the SAT, said "it's reverse racism that holds certain assumptions about a race or a gender and what they should know. . . . That's an insult. . . . If there is a bias in the test, its the same bias we have in American education." (See also entry dated March 15, 1984.)

September 11. After recent racial tensions and violence, including the killing of young blacks in predominantly-white neighborhoods in New York City, a *USA Today* poll found that 60 percent of America's blacks encounter racism "at least occasionally." Higher-income African-Americans reported that they experienced racism more than poor blacks. Blacks who reside in

Southern states reported less racism than blacks in other regions of the country. Another finding was that 71 percent of the blacks surveyed would like to live in integrated neighborhoods, although 53 percent live in largely black areas.

USA Today also asked a number of prominent African-Americans to offer solutions to the nation's racial problems. Eleanor Holmes Norton, a professor of law at Georgetown University and former chairperson of the Equal Employment Opportunity Commission (EEOC), suggested that "there needs to be a continuing public, conciliatory dialogue between racial and cultural groups so that those who continue to harbor racial prejudice feel isolated. We need to talk these things out, not act them out. . . . Black-white relations between average Americans are not hostile—they simply are not close enough. The kind of integrated society that has been hypothesized simply has not yet been achieved." Tony Brown, executive producer and host of PBS's "Tony Brown's Journal," remarked: "It doesn't surprise me that southern blacks find less racism. If blacks had marched in Bensonhurst and Howard Beach 30 years ago instead of Selma [Alabama], then the whites in Bensonhurst and Howard Beach would be as sensitive today to racism as whites in Selma are. . . . What blacks must do is through our achievements, through our own unity, through faith in ourselves, through sharing our resources, we must make these gains that will destroy the environmental supports [of racism]." Charles Moody, Sr., vice president for minority affairs at the University of Michigan and founder of the National Alliance of Black School Educators, suggested that "the first thing that people have to do is come to grips with the fact that racism does exist and not be so quick to try to rationalize it away or justify it, but to accept the fact that its there and begin to do something about it. . . . I think people as individuals can do something about it by looking at themselves and trying to change that part of the institution or community that they have control over."

September 16. Debbye Turner, a twenty-three year old black veterinary student at the University of Missouri, was crowned "Miss America" at the 68th Annual Miss America pageant in Atlantic City, New Jersey. Turner, "a born-again Christian," became the third African-American woman to hold the beauty and talent title. Of this achievement, Turner stated: "Being black is the very least of who I am. I had nothing to do with it, and that's not a landmark. I just came that way." (See also entry dated September 17, 1983.)

September 16. *Forbes* magazine estimated that African-American pop singer Michael Jackson would make $65 million in 1989 and would remain "the world's highest paid entertainer." The magazine placed his total earnings for 1988-89 at $125 million.

Other African-Americans on the *Forbes's* list of the highest paid entertainers for 1988-89 were actor-comedian Bill Cosby ($95 million); boxer Mike Tyson ($71 million); actor-comedian Eddie Murphy ($57 million); talk-show hostess and actress Oprah Winfrey ($55 million); boxer Sugar Ray Leonard ($42 million); and recording artist Prince ($36 million).

September 19. Gerald Turner, chancellor of the University of Mississippi, apologized to officials at predominantly black Rust College after members of a fraternity at his university dumped two naked white pledges, whose bodies were painted with racial slurs, on the Rust campus. The two naked pledges of the Beta Theta Pi fraternity with "KKK" and "We Hate Niggers" painted on their chests ran into the Rust College security office in Holly Springs while escaping pursuing students. In addition to his own apology, Chancellor Turner had directed officers of the Beta Theta Pi fraternity to also extend an apology to Rust College. The black private school is located about 25 miles from the University of Mississippi campus at Oxford.

The incident at Rust College was one of a series of similar occurrences aimed at black students on high school and college campuses across the nation throughout 1989.

September 20. The employment and housing subcommittee of the Government Operations Committee of the House of Representatives voted unanimously to subpoena former Housing and Urban Development (HUD) Secretary Samuel R. Pierce, Jr. to testify about alleged influence-peddling and mismanagement at the department he headed for eight years during the administration of President Ronald Reagan. The subpoena was issued after Pierce demanded a third delay on the eve of his scheduled voluntary testimony on September 15. Pierce's attorney, Paul L. Perito, said the former secretary—who had appeared voluntarily before the subcommittee in May—was willing to testify but needed two additional weeks for preparation. But Representative Ted Weiss from New York, a member of the subcommittee, charged that "rather than coming forth and clearing the record . . . he is toying with the subcommittee in order to evade or avoid his responsibility." The subcommittee ordered Pierce to make his first appearance on September 26.

The former HUD Secretary, who served from 1981 to 1989, was the only African-American appointed to the cabinet of former President Reagan. (See also entry dated December 22, 1980.)

September 20. The Armed Services Committee of the United States Senate voted unanimously to approve the nomination of General Colin L. Powell as chairman of the Joint Chiefs of Staff. The vote cleared the way for Powell to become the first African-American ever to lead the joint military forces of the United States. (See also entry dated August 10, 1989, for further information about Powell.)

September 20. The *Atlanta Constitution* reported that two new national magazines targeted for African-American audiences were beginning publication. One of the periodicals, *Sazz*, was founded by Mary Anne Holley, the other, *Emerge*, by Wilmer Ames. Both are based in New York City. The new magazines were the first national black-oriented ones to surface since the mid-1980s, according to Samir Husni, a journalism professor at the University of Mississippi who specializes in new magazines. Both publications arose at a time, however, when the magazine industry in general was facing declining circulations, and black magazines in particular were "facing a 'tough battle' for advertising dollars." Both of the new publications were aimed at "upscale black readers," i.e., higher income and college-educated blacks. *Sazz* was to highlight women's fashions, while *Emerge* was to be a national news monthly.

Prior to the appearances of *Sazz* and *Emerge*, several other recent attempts at publishing national black magazines had failed. These included *Elan*, *Elancee*, *Excell*, *Modern Black Man (MBM)*, *Spice*, and *Black Teen*. The most successful black magazines continued to be three publications of the Johnson Publishing Co. based in Chicago, *Ebony*, *Jet*, and *Ebony Man*, and *Essence*, geared toward women, and *Black Enterprise*, aimed at the black entrepreneur, both published in New York City. *Ebony* was founded in 1945 and had a circulation of 1.8 million in 1989; *Jet*, a news weekly, was founded in 1951 and reported a circulation of 892,000 in 1989. Both *Essence* and *Black Enterprise* were founded in 1970, and had circulations of 850,000 and 230,000, respectively, in 1989; and *Ebony Man*, which first appeared in 1985, had gained a circulation of 205,000 by 1989.

September 24. Thomas W. Cole, Jr., former president of West Virginia State College, was inaugurated as the first president of Clark-Atlanta University. The new institution resulted from a merger of historically black Clark College and Atlanta University in 1988. Cole had formerly been a professor of Chemistry and served as provost at Atlanta University. (See also entry dated June 26, 1989.)

October 2. The United States Supreme Court affirmed a decision of the United States Court of Appeals for the Eleventh Circuit which prohibited attorneys in civil cases "from striking jurors because of their race." Although the Supreme Court had barred criminal prosecutors from using their "preemptory challenges in a racially discriminatory fashion," in 1986, the Eleventh Circuit was one of the first courts in the nation to extend the rule to civil cases.

The case reached the Supreme Court from Richmond County, Georgia (of which Augusta is the county seat), where a black man sued a white deputy sheriff who had "accidentally" shot him while arresting him on suspicion of drugs. In 1982, an all-white jury found in favor of the defendants, Deputy Sheriff Frank Tiller and former Richmond County Sheriff J. D. Dykes. However the plaintiff, Willie Fludd, contended that the jury selection process was biased and appealed the decision.

October 3. Maynard Holbrook Jackson was elected to a new term as mayor of Atlanta, Georgia. Jackson scored a landslide victory over city councilman and veteran civil rights activist Hosea Williams to return to City Hall. Jackson won 82 percent of the votes to less than 20 percent for Williams. Jackson's victory had become all but certain after a more formidable candidate, Michael Lomax, the African-American chairman of the Fulton County Commission, withdrew from the race on August 8, 1989. When polls consistently showed that Lomax would also lose decisively to Jackson, the commissioner withdrew rather than jeopardize his seat on the county body.

Jackson was first elected mayor of Atlanta in 1973, becoming the first African-American to be elected mayor of a major Southern city since the Reconstruction era. He served two terms until 1982, when he became ineligible for another successive reelection. Between terms in the major's office, Jackson had served as a corporate attorney in Chicago, Illinois and Atlanta.

October 3. Art Shell, former lineman for the Oakland Raiders of the National Football League (NFL) and a member of the Professional Football's Hall of Fame, was named head coach of the Los Angeles Raiders. The appointment made Shell, age forty-two, the first black head coach in the NFL since Fritz Pollard was a player-coach for the Hammond (Indiana) Pros in 1923-25.

Shell's selection came just one day before the fifteenth anniversary of the appointment of Frank Robinson as the first black manager in major league baseball. Robinson was first hired by the Cleveland Indians. The first black head coach in professional basketball, which has had more blacks in this position than any other professional sport, was Bill Russell of the Boston Celtics, who served in 1966-67.

Shell called his appointment "an historic event," but did not believe that "the color of my skin entered into [the] decision."

October 6. Two former employees of Shoney's restaurants, one black, one white, filed a lawsuit in the Federal Court for the Northern District of Georgia, alleging that the restaurant chain practiced racial discrimination. The suit claimed that the managers of Shoney's franchises in the Metropolitan Atlanta area discriminated by limiting the type and number of jobs offered to blacks as well as their chances of promotion. It also alleged that the company retaliated against non-black employees "who [refused] to implement their racist policies."

The black plaintiff, Jackie Montgomery, claimed she was forbidden to work in a Shoney's dining room because of the restaurant's policy that "blacks should not be allowed out front," particularly in facilities located in predominantly white neighborhoods. The white plaintiff, Cylinda Adams, asserted that she complained to several supervisors about the alleged racism and was fired because of it.

The Atlanta suit was filed only four months after a similar allegation was brought before the courts in Florida and only two months after Shoney's executives signed an affirmative action agreement with the Southern Christian Leadership Conference (SCLC). In that accord, Shoney's promised to provide $90 million in jobs and minority business participation over the next three years. The agreement also included recruitment and training of blacks in managerial positions, and pledged to provide scholarships to African-American students interested in the food service industry. Shoney's Chief Executive Officer J. Mitchell Boyd had said that there was "no real connection" between the lawsuit filed in Pensacola, Florida, in June and the firm's agreement with SCLC.

Shoney's, based in Nashville, Tennessee, controls 1,600 restaurants in 30 states and had sales of $1.4 billion in 1988. Seven hundred of its restaurants are company-owned, the others, such as the ones involved in the Atlanta suit, are franchise operations.

October 10. The school board of White County, Georgia, voted unanimously to begin new desegregated bus routes, thus ending nine years of segregated busing in the area. The school board members claimed that they had only recently been made aware of the segregated routes. The board's chairman, Bob Owens said in a public apology "Our community has taken pride as a leader in public integration. For a black bus route to be scheduled into two predominantly-black communities and to be operated for an extended period of time is . . . unacceptable."

The dual busing system came to the board's attention after Jimmy Bolinger, the school system's new director of transportation, reported that nine of the 23 school routes were overcrowded with white students; while Andy Allen, the county's only black school bus driver, complained that she crossed the county to pick up black children, yet her bus was only half full.

October 11. The United States Court of Appeals for the Eleventh Circuit ruled that the Dekalb County, Georgia school board must dismantle its segregated neighborhood school system and must consider "forced busing" of students to achieve greater desegregation. The Court of Appeals also declared that Dekalb County must consider "drastic gerrymandering" or redrawing of school attendance zones and "dramatically expanded magnet schools" to expand its desegregation.

The court overturned a June, 1988 decision by United States District Court Judge William C. O'Kelley, that ruled the Dekalb school board had done all that it could to desegregate its schools. O'Kelley agreed with the board's argument that housing patterns were the primary cause of any remaining school segregation. The Appeals Court disagreed, and ruled that the Dekalb school system "may not shirk its constitutional duties by pointing to demographic shifts. . . . [The] system has a continuing constitutional duty to achieve the greatest possible degree of desegregation and to prevent segregation."

October 11. The Institute for Southern Study released a report which stated that African-Americans are nearly three times as likely as whites to be committed against their will to the 72 public psychiatric hospitals in nine southern states. The survey found that commitment rates for blacks and whites differed most in Florida, where blacks were 4.8 times as likely as whites to be committed. In Georgia, blacks were twice as likely as whites to be committed. Blacks in Mississippi and South Carolina were committed 1.8 times as often as whites.

Eric Bates, who supervised the study for the institute's *Southern Exposure* magazine, said there was "no simple answer why blacks are committed more than whites, but racism clearly plays a part."

October 11. J. Rupert Picott, educator and lobbyist, died of cancer in Washington, D. C., at age sixty-nine.

Picott, a native of Suffolk, Virginia, received his undergraduate training from Virginia Union University in Richmond, a master's degree in education from Temple University in Philadelphia, and a doctorate in education from Harvard University. In the 1940s, he became executive secretary of the black Virginia Teachers Association. After the decision of the United States Supreme Court in *Brown v. Board of Education* in 1954, when some school systems in Virginia attempted to fire some of their black teachers in the wake of desegregation, Picott "moved to protect the jobs" of the blacks. He became best known as executive director of the Association for the Study of Afro-American Life and History (ASALH) where he served between 1969 and 1985. In this position, Picott lobbied for the promotion of the study and celebration of African-American history and succeeded in getting both state and federal governments to proclaim February as Black History Month.

October 11-12. The principal and a student of Minor High School in Adamsville, Alabama were stabbed during a fight between black and white students.

Principal Judson Jones, who received a two inch knife wound to his stomach in the altercation, said tensions had escalated for several days, with several fights between blacks and whites in the previous week. In an effort to bring peace, he had called for additional police officers to patrol the grounds of the school and ordered all black students into the cafeteria and all whites into the gymnasium as they entered the school on October 11. But when Jones took a group of white students to the cafeteria to meet with the blacks, a fight erupted which quickly spread to other areas of the building.

Seven students were arrested at the school on October 11 on charges ranging from disorderly conduct to attempted murder. On October 12, two additional students were incarcerated on charges of possessing alcohol and weapons.

William James, a black senior at Minor High School, told newspaper reporters that the school's problems were not new. "There's always been racial trouble here. . . . They didn't want us here anyway."

These racial disturbances in Alabama were a part of the growing number of such encounters on high school and college campuses throughout the year.

October 12. A North Augusta, South Carolina restaurant owner, Rose Salter, announced that she would begin serving African-Americans in her establishment. Salter's declaration was made during a hearing before the South Carolina Alcoholic Beverage Control (ABC) Commission, which was considering revoking the liquor license of the Buffalo Room Restaurant and Lounge for barring six black government and NAACP officials from the premises in early September. As a result of the incident, both the NAACP and the Justice Department threatened to file suit against the restaurant's proprietors for illegal discrimination. During the investigation, it was revealed that the Buffalo Room had discriminated against blacks for the past twelve years. (See also entry dated October 24, 1989.)

October 12. Several of the nation's civil rights leaders sent a telegram to the Reverend Ralph David Abernathy, former president of the Southern Christian Leadership Conference (SCLC), urging him to repudiate sections of his published memoirs which claim that the late Dr. Martin Luther King, Jr., spent part of the last night of his life with two different women. The accusations were made in Abernathy's autobiography, *And The Walls Came Tumbling Down*, which had been released earlier in the month.

The civil rights leaders told Abernathy in a "message of pain and love" that "as friends and beneficiaries of the King dream, we are shocked and appalled by some of the statements in your new book." One of the signers of the telegram, John Hurst Adams, president of the National Congress of Black Churches, charged that the book was "riddled with gross inaccuracies and painful distortions." Another signer, NAACP executive secretary Benjamin Hooks, called the book "criminally irresponsible." Hooks took particular issue with Abernathy's account of an alleged encounter between Dr. King and a woman on the eve of the assassination. While Abernathy placed Dr. King in the woman's home at one a.m., Hooks recalled that he was with the civil rights leader at the Mason Temple in Memphis, where he had delivered his final sermon, at that hour.

Others who endorsed the message to Abernathy included United States Representatives Ronald V. Dellums, William H. Gray III, John Lewis, Floyd H. Flake, Alan D. Wheat, Walter D. Fauntroy, and former Representative Parren Mitchell, Southern Christian Leadership Conference president Joseph L. Lowery, Operation PUSH leader the Reverend Jesse L. Jackson, and Atlanta Mayor Andrew J. Young.

In his response, Abernathy asserted: "In including some of the things in the book, I have had to agonize, balancing my need to tell a complete and honest story with what I know to be my responsibility to respect the privacy and dignity of the living and the dead. . . . I can only say that I have written nothing in malice and omitted nothing out of cowardice." (See also entries dated October 24, 1989, and February 5, 1990.)

October 18. The White House revealed that President George Bush had accepted the resignation of William Barclay Allen as chairman of the U.S. Commission on Civil Rights. During his tenure, Allen, a California professor, had created repeated controversies which led to criticism of his leadership both within and without the Commission. The most recent controversy arose when he gave a speech entitled, "Blacks? Animals? Homosexuals? What is a Minority?" to the California Coalition for Traditional Values. (See also entry dated February 23, 1990.)

October 20. Alcee L. Hastings, a black United States District Court Judge from Florida, was convicted by the U. S. Senate on eight articles of impeachment relating to conspiracy and perjury. He became the sixth federal official in American history to be removed from office by impeachment. The vote to convict Hastings was 69-26.

Originally, Hastings was charged with seventeen articles of impeachment by the U. S. House of Representatives, but the Senate acquitted him on three of the articles and took no action on the others.

Hastings, age fifty-three, was appointed to the federal bench in 1979 by President Jimmy Carter. He was the first African-American ever to serve in this position in the state of Florida. After the verdict, Hastings remarked, "I don't accept this as a reading of Al Hastings the man. I didn't commit a crime. . . . There may be something about me—my outspokenness and what have you—that allows that maybe it's best that I'm out of this particular arena." He announced that he would later seek the Democratic nomination for governor of Florida. (See also entry dated March 16, 1989.)

October 23. Louis Farrakhan, Minister of the Nation of Islam, delivered his "Savior's Day Message" before a crowd of 12,000 people in Washington, D.C. Speaking on the theme "Stop the Killing," Farrakhan said the black people of Washington, D.C. were "brought to nothing in this society by their former slavemasters . . . and [were] being kept as nothing by the cruel hand of the government."

October 24. In a news conference in Washington, D.C., Abjua Abi Naantaanbuu, a civil rights activist from Memphis, Tennessee, and Bernard Lee, a veteran civil rights activist, disputed allegations made by Ralph David Abernathy in his autobiography *And the Walls Came Tumbling Down*, that Dr. Martin Luther King, Jr. may have engaged in extramarital affairs on the night before his assassination in 1968. Naantaanbuu and Lee, who were present when the alleged infidelity occurred, accused Abernathy of being drunk and asleep at the time.

The news conference was sponsored by the Coalition of Friends and Beneficiaries of the Martin Luther King, Jr. Dream which had taken strong exception to Abernathy's published views ever since they appeared earlier in the year. Members of the Coalition of Friends included civil rights leaders Dick Gregory, Benjamin Hooks, John Lewis, Jesse Jackson, Joseph Lowery, and Andrew Young. (See also entries dated October 12, 1989, and February 5, 1990.)

October 24. Despite the pledge of a North Augusta, South Carolina restaurant to end its barring of black customers, the South Carolina Alcoholic Beverage Commission revoked its liquor license. The Commission said the action to end discrimination was "very fragile and will likely continue only so long as official scrutiny is close at hand."

The Buffalo Room Restaurant and Lounge had been under scrutiny by federal and state governments and the NAACP since several blacks were turned away by its owners on September 5. Within weeks of this incident, the owners, Bruce and Rose Salter, announced that they would serve all people. (See also entry dated October 12, 1989.)

November 5. Thousands attended the dedication of a monument to martyrs of the Civil Rights movement in downtown Montgomery, Alabama. Among those in the audience were civil rights activist Julian Bond, Mrs. Ethel Kennedy, widow of slain Senator Robert F. Kennedy, and Carolyn Goodman, mother of Andrew Goodman, one of three young civil rights workers slain by Ku Klux Klansmen in Philadelphia, Mississippi in 1964. Forty names of martyred civil rights activists were inscribed in a great curving circle of black granite built by the Southern Poverty Law Center. Among those honored, in addition to Goodman, were James Chaney and Mickey Schwerner, who were killed with him; Medgar Evers, a Jackson, Mississippi NAACP leader assassinated in 1966; Emmett Till, a fourteen-year-old black youth murdered in 1955 for speaking to a white woman in Money, Mississippi; Jimmie Lee Jackson, a young black student slain in a civil rights demonstration in Marion, Alabama in 1965; and Martin Luther King, Jr., the last name on the stone. Some of King's words spoken at the March on Washington in 1963 were inscribed at the back of the monument by sculpturess Maya Lin, with water flowing over them:

"We will not be satisfied until justice rolls down like waters, and righteousness like a mighty stream."

November 7. David Dinkins, the sixty-two-year-old president of the Borough of Manhattan, was elected mayor of New York City, becoming the first African-American ever to occupy that office. Dinkins, a Democrat, won a narrow victory over the Republican challenger, Rudolph W. Giuliani, and two other candidates. Dinkins captured approximately 898,000 votes to Giuliani's 856,450.

After defeating Democratic mayor Edward I. Koch in the primary election on September 12, Dinkins ran a moderate campaign designed to "soothe, not excite." His campaign theme was an appeal to the city's ethnic diversity, what he termed "a gorgeous mosaic." Some analysts, however, including the *New York Times*, claimed that Dinkins's solutions to New York's problems were "often simple." For example, Dinkins's answer to the city's massive crime problem was to "double community patrol officers and put a cop on every subway train."

Despite the city's recent racial troubles, sparked by the killings of black men in

David Dinkins

predominately-white neighborhoods, Dinkins was able to build a biracial coalition which carried him to victory. At the time of the election, only 25.2 percent of New York City's eight million people were black.

Dinkins's mayoral campaign was also threatened by accusations of personal "financial laxity" and his friendship with former Democratic presidential candidate Jesse L. Jackson. Voters apparently overlooked his "fumbling on questions about his personal finances," while Jackson failed to return to New York after the primary election.

Dinkins, a former Marine, entered local politics in the 1950s as a Democratic precinct leader. In 1965, he was elected to the state Senate. Dinkins also served as city clerk in New York City before running for president of the borough of Manhattan in 1977. In his first two campaigns for this office, Dinkins lost by wide margins, but finally secured the office in 1985.

November 7. L. Douglas Wilder, lieutenant governor of Virginia, was elected the state's first African-American governor. The fifty-eight year-old Wilder, a Democrat, won a narrow victory over his Republican rival, J. Marshall Coleman. Of the more than 1.7 million votes cast, Wilder's margin of victory was only 7,000 votes. He garnered 888,475 ballots to 881,484 for Coleman (with all but two Virginia precincts counted). In addition to becoming Virginia's first black governor, the victory made Wilder the first black elected governor in American history.

Following his victory, Wilder sought to downplay any expectations that he would seek to become a major spokesman for African-Americans, stating "I don't see a confrontation with anybody. I'm not an activist. I'm not running for President."

November 7. Several African-Americans were elected or reelected mayors in major American cities during general elections. They included Michael White in Cleveland, Ohio, Coleman Young in Detroit, Michigan, Chester Jenkins in Durham, North Carolina, John Daniels in New Haven, Connecticut, and Norm Rice in Seattle, Washington.

In Cleveland, Michael White, a city councilman, became the city's second black mayor. He defeated a fellow African-American, city council president George Forbes 89,829 to 68,167.

In Detroit, Coleman Young won an unprecedented fifth term, defeating business executive Tom Barrow (a nephew of boxing champion Joe Louis) 138,175 to 107,195.

In Durham, Chester Jenkins won the mayor's office over Nelson Strawbridge 19,381 to 17,118.

In New Haven, Daniels captured 19,302 votes (69 percent) in his win over two opponents to become the city-s first black mayor.

In Seattle, Norm Rice, a Democrat, defeated a Republican, Doug Jewett by a margin of 93,901 to 67,575 to become the first black mayor of a city with only a 9.5 percent black population.

November 8-November 20. Political leaders, political analysts, journalists, and other commentators assessed the historic victories of L. Douglas Wilder as the nation's first elected black governor in Virginia, and the election of David Dinkins as New York City's first African-American mayor.

After Dinkins won the Democratic primary in September, 1989, syndicated columnist Carl Rowan suggested that Dinkins's victory was "desperately needed proof that resurgent racism in America can be stopped wherever political, business and other leaders ask the people to walk away from the dark side of man's animal impulses."

In an editorial on November 9, the *Wall Street Journal* said "There's irony in the failure of Republican candidates to learn the lessons of the Reagan Presidency: David Dinkins . . . and Virginia's Doug Wilder . . . ran as 'moderate' Democrats, promising to hold the line on taxes and spending." The newspaper also reported that Wilder "kept Mr. Jackson [civil rights leader Jesse Jackson] at

L. Douglas Wilder

arm's length during a year-long campaign that stressed his mainstream appeal to white voters. Wilder appealed for economic development, not economic empowerment, and talked about racial issues only under duress."

Cynthia Tucker, an African-American columnist for the *Atlanta Journal-Constitution*, wrote that "Mr. Wilder has apparently overcome the color question with a strong pro-choice position. . . . And, [he] has now provided a guidebook to other candidates of color who wish to serve beyond their traditional constituencies."

November 10. The Rhythm and Blues Foundation presented its first career achievement awards at the Smithsonian Institution in Washington, D.C. The impetus for the awards came from Howell Begle, a Washington attorney, life-long soul music fan, and admirer of blues singer Ruth Brown. After Begle discovered that Brown and dozens of other rhythm and blues artists had fallen into financial difficulties in the mid-1960s, he established the Rhythm and Blues Foundation to assist them, and later appointed blind blues singer Ray Charles chairman of the organization. The group eventually amassed an endowment of one and one half million dollars, donated mostly by Atlantic Records Company.

Several of the honorees performed for the audience, including Percy Sledge, whose "When A Man Loves a Woman," was the first soul recording to rise to the top of the pop music charts; Mary Wells, known for her recordings of "My Guy" and "You Beat Me To The Punch;" Charles Brown, who sang "Driftin' Blues" and "Black Night;" and Ruth Brown, often called "Miss Rhythm." In her remarks, Brown recalled the distressing segregated South. "Charles Brown nearly went to jail for me in Mississippi because they wouldn't let me use the bathroom at a gas station. . . . How many buses did we ride together? How many back doors did we go through together?"

Each winner of the Rhythm and Blues award received a check for $15,000 in order to right "some past wrongs" as well as recognizing lifetime achievement.

November 15. President George Bush signed into law a bill, HR-3318, to redesignate the Federal building located at 1990 Smith Street in Houston, Texas, as the George Thomas "Mickey" Leland Federal Building in honor of the late African-American Congressman from Texas who died in a plane crash in Africa on August 7, 1989. The bill, introduced by Democratic Representative Jack Brooks from Texas, became Public Law 101-152. (See also entry dated August 7-13, 1989.)

November 17. Gloria Naylor, African-American writer, won a Lillian

Smith Award for 1989. The award was presented for her third novel, *Mama Day*, which centers on cultural conflict in an all-black sea island community off the coast of South Carolina. The Smith awards were named for the late Georgia civil rights activist, who was also the author of *Strange Fruit*. They "recognize and encourage outstanding writing about the South." In 1983, Naylor had won an American Book Award for *The Women of Brewster Place*.

November 17. President George Bush met at the White House with leaders of the national Black Leadership Forum (BLF). The blacks told Bush that racism was "rising" in some areas of the country, "especially on college campuses." They urged him to set "a goal of bringing blacks to 'parity' with the rest of the population" in education, housing, and employment by the year 2000. President Bush made no commitments to the group and expressed surprise "to hear that there was [still] overt racism and he hoped it wasn't true." One of the leaders present, Dorothy Height, president of the National Council of Negro Women remarked, "I think the most significant thing was that [Bush] listened, that he showed a genuine interest." Other members of the BLF present at the meeting included Benjamin Hooks, executive director of the NAACP, Joseph Lowery, president of the SCLC, and Coretta Scott King.

————. Ron Walters, a professor of political science at Howard University, observed that "the key to victory for both these candidates (Dinkins and Wilder) was that, in terms of both style and substance, they ran mainstream campaigns tailored to the political realities of their respective jurisdictions. . . . But the new crossover black politics creates an ultimate irony for the black voter. Historically the black voter has laid the basis for the emergence of black politicians and has taken heart in their upward mobility. The danger is that the higher they go, the more restrained they will be in pursuing a black political agenda."

Hodding Carter III, a national political commentator, warned that "no one should minimize the distance yet to travel before the mountaintop is achieved. There is no excuse for complacency. But there is also no excuse for refusing to celebrate when, as with last week's election results, real cause for celebration is provided."

November 31. About 200 people gathered to protest racism at the Tuscaloosa campus of the University of Alabama and the school's financial investments in the Republic of South Africa. The protest was sparked by an incident that took place during a football game on October 14th, when Kimberly Ashely, the university's black homecoming queen, was subjected to jeers by spectators. The protestors also took offense at the prominent display of Rebel flags, symbols of the old Confederacy.

University officials contended that less than one percent of its total investments were in South Africa.

December 1. Alvin Ailey, African-American dancer and choreographer, died of a blood disorder in New York City at age fifty-eight.

Ailey was born in the rural town of Rogers, Texas, where he faced discrimination at a very early age. Yet by the time of his death, Ailey had received New York's Handel Medallion and the Samuel H. Scripps American Dance Festival Award for lifetime contributions to modern dance. In 1988, he received Kennedy Center honors in Washington, D.C. for lifetime achievement in the performing arts.

He founded the Alvin Ailey American Dance Theater in 1958 and choreographed seventy-nine ballets. In 1961, Ailey created his best known work, "Revelations," which was based on his childhood experiences in black Baptist churches. The dance became his company's "rousing signature piece."

Ailey also had a penchant for honoring the works of others whom he admired or with whose causes he sympathized. For example, he choreographed "For Bird with Love" as a tribute to jazz trumpeter Charlie "Bird" Parker, whose career was shortened by drug abuse. While Ailey refused to allow his company to perform in the Republic of South Africa, he choreographed in collaboration with jazz drummer Max Roach, "Survivors," in honor of the South African anti-apartheid activists Nelson and Winnie Mandela.

Although Ailey retired from performing twenty years before his death, he created "a choreographic style distinctly his own—a combination of modern, ballet, jazz, and ethnic [dance]." Professor Richard Long, author of *The Black Tradition in American Dance*, called Ailey, "the best-known American dancer in the world."

December 6. Nathan I. Huggins, a leading scholar of African-American culture, died of cancer in Boston, Massachusetts at the age of sixty-two. Huggins was the author of works on the black anti-slavery leader Frederick Douglass and on the Harlem Renaissance, the black cultural movement of the 1920s. Since 1980, he had been professor of history and Afro-American Studies and director of the W.E.B. Du Bois Institute for Afro-American Research at Harvard University.

December 7. Percy Snow, African-American linebacker for the Michigan State University Spartans, was awarded the Vince Lombardi trophy in Houston, Texas. The Lombardi trophy, named for the legendary coach of the Green Bay Packers, is awarded every year to the nation's top collegiate lineman. On December 5, Snow had also won a Dick Butkus Award for his outstanding feats as a linebacker. At the time, Snow held the Michigan State record of 164 tackles.

December 9. Craig A. Washington, a Houston, Texas attorney, was elected to the U. S. House of Representatives from the predominately-black 18th Congressional District. Washington defeated Houston city councilman Anthony Hall to take the seat formerly held by Mickey Leland, who died in a plane crash in Ethiopia on August 7, 1989.

December 11. A state appeals court in New York reversed the convictions of three white men who were found guilty in the 1986 death of Michael Griffith, a black man, in the Howard Beach section of Queens, New York. The unanimous ruling found that Thomas A. Demakos, the trial judge, had made two errors in his charge to the jury. He had, the higher court said, supplied the jury with verdict sheets that contained the charges against the defendants (which improperly described some of the alleged crimes) and he had improperly refused to instruct the jury on disorderly conduct, a lesser offense than the ones with which the defendants were charged.

The three defendants, William Bollander, Thomas Farino, and James Povinelli, all aged nineteen, were convicted in 1988 of second degree riot charges for their part in the racial attack on December 20, 1986.

December 16-19. On December 16, a mail bomb exploded in the home of Robert S. Vance, a judge on the U.S. Court of Appeals for the Eleventh Circuit, in Birmingham, Alabama. The Eleventh Circuit had handled many civil rights cases, including school desegregation ones, over the past decade.

On December 18, a mail bomb exploded in the office of Robert E. Robinson, an attorney in Savannah, Georgia who had represented the NAACP and other clients in civil rights cases.

The bombs, which were sent to Vance and Robinson in parcels addressed to them, killed both men instantly.

The FBI announced on December 18 that it suspected "white supremacists" in the mail bombings which killed a federal judge and a civil rights attorney.

Earl Shinhoster, Southeast Regional director of the NAACP whose office was the target of an earlier mailed tear-gas bomb, called the attacks "a very serious situation." (See also entry dated August 21, 1989.)

December 18-20. On December 19, a mail bomb was found and defused at the U.S. Court of Appeals for the Eleventh Circuit in Atlanta, Georgia. The Appeals Court had handled many of the South's civil rights suits over the past decade.

On December 19, a mail bomb found outside the headquarters of the Jackson-ville, Florida Chapter of the NAACP did not explode.

The FBI announced that the packages were mailed from Georgia, as were two other bombs which killed federal Judge Robert Vance and Savannah, Georgia attorney Robert Robinson on December 16 and 18. The FBI also said it suspected the same person (or persons) was responsible for all of the incidents.

December 21. A U.S. administrative law judge in Atlanta, Georgia, ordered Gordon C. Blackwell, a real estate broker, to pay $75,000 to a black couple whom he had discriminated against in the sale of a house. Judge Alan W. Heifetz also found that Blackwell, a sixty-six-year-old resident of Sandy Springs, Georgia, had flouted the civil rights of Terryl and Janella Herron by refusing to close the sale of a Stone Mountain, Georgia home. He also ordered the broker to complete the sale of the house.

The case was the first in the nation under the recently enacted federal law which "provides quicker and harsher penalties if bias is proved." Gordon H. Mansfield, Assistant Secretary for Fair Housing at the Department of Housing and Urban Development (HUD) said that the case was "a landmark in civil rights enforcement . . . making housing discrimination expensive as well as unlawful."

December 24. Ernest Nathan "Dutch" Morial, the first black mayor of New Orleans, Louisiana, died of an apparent heart attack in New Orleans at age sixty.

Morial was born in New Orleans on October 9, 1929 to Walter, a cigar maker, and Leonie Morial. He became the first black law school graduate of Louisiana State University in 1954.

Morial's public service career began in 1960 when he was elected president of the NAACP chapter in New Orleans. He worked with civil rights activist A.P. Tureard in filing suits against segregation in public facilities and institutions in the city. In 1965, Morial became the first black assistant U. S. Attorney in Louisiana, and in 1967 the first black legislator since the Reconstruction era. He also served as a member of the State House of Representatives from 1967 to 1970, and became the first black ever elected to Louisiana's 4th Circuit Court of Appeals in 1973.

In 1977, on the strength of a huge black vote, Morial became New Orleans' first black mayor. As mayor for two terms, he faced rampant floods in 1978, a police strike that crippled the city's annual Mardi Gras festival in 1979, and a financially-plagued World's exposition in 1984. Morial left office in 1986 following an unsuccessful attempt to amend the city charter to allow the mayor to serve a third four-year term.

Nationally, Morial had been a president of the National Conference of Mayors, a member of the Democratic National Committee (DNC) and one of the key black advisors to the Democratic presidential candidate Michael S. Dukakis in 1988.

After Morial's death, his predecessor, former mayor Moon Landrieu, remarked: "Dutch was the first black individual to achieve high public office in this state. . . . That alone I think is a very significant achievement."

1990

January 9. The National Urban League (NUL) said that in order "to close the economic gap" between black and white Americans, a $50 billion aid program, similar to the one that rebuilt Europe after World War II (the Marshall Plan) was needed. In the 15th Annual "The State of Black America" Report, the NUL contended that the fiscal and social policies of the administration of former president Ronald Reagan had helped "stall the efforts of blacks to achieve greater economic parity" with whites in the 1980s. The report added, however, that the "greater openness" of the administration of President George Bush had "inspired new confidence in the federal government's ability to 'complete our unfinished revolution for democracy and human rights.'"

January 10. Marcelite J. Harris, a forty-six-year-old native of Houston, Texas, was named brigadier general in the U.S. Air Force. She is the first African-American woman to hold this rank in that branch of the Armed Services.

Harris earned a bachelor's degree in business management from the University of Maryland. She was the Air Force's first female aircraft maintenance officer. In 1975 Harris was named personnel staff officer at Air Force Headquarters in Washington, D.C., where she also served as a White House aide to former President Jimmy Carter.

January 10. The Bureau of the Census reported that the proportion of blacks living in the Southern region of the United States increased from 1980 to 1988, the first such rise in this century. 56 percent of all blacks resided in the South in 1988, compared with 52 percent in 1980. The proportion had been declining since the beginning of the century when it was at 90 percent.

The Northeast was the only region in the 1980s to show a significant decline in the proportion of its black population, dropping from 19 percent to 17 percent. The proportion for the Midwest (19 percent) and West (8 percent), according to the Bureau, "did not change significantly."

The number of blacks living in the South in 1988 totaled 16.4 million, an increase of 2.8 million since 1980.

January 13. Lawrence Douglas Wilder was inaugurated as governor of Virginia, making him the first African-American elected chief executive of a state in American history. The only other black to occupy a governor's office was P.B.S. Pinchback, who served as acting governor of Louisiana for a month at the end of 1872.

Wilder, the grandson of slaves, was born in Richmond, Virginia in 1931, the seventh of eight children of Robert and Beulah Wilder. He received a bachelor's degree in Chemistry from Virginia Union University in 1951 and a law degree from the Howard University School of Law in 1959. Returning immediately to his Church Hill neighborhood in Richmond to open a law practice, Wilder "soon developed a reputation for flamboyance, driving convertibles and breezing into court, all smiles and trendy clothes, to take on difficult criminal cases." He also specialized in "lucrative personal injury cases."

Wilder's political career began in 1970, when he was elected to the Virginia state senate. There he spearheaded a campaign to make the birthday of Martin Luther King, Jr. a state holiday. The best he could achieve, however, was the addition of King's name to a holiday for Confederate generals Robert E. Lee and Thomas "Stonewall" Jackson. Although he had not been an active participant in the Civil Rights Movement of the 1960s, Wilder began his tenure in the senate with "a blistering attack" on the state song, "Carry Me Back to Old Virginny." He and other blacks objected to "the sentimental [melody] about a slave pining for the plantation," which included such lyrics as "There's where this old darky's heart am long'd to go. . . . There's where I labor'd so hard for old massa. . . ." Although the song was not removed, its playing at public functions was greatly diminished.

Wilder remained in the state senate until 1986, when he was lieutenant-governor. At the time, he was the only black serving in that position in the country, but gained increasing popularity in the state for his opposition to a sales tax increase. When Wilder began his campaign for governor, he changed his position against the expansion of the death penalty to support for its more frequent use. He also went from a vague position on a woman's right to an abortion to an enthusiastic supporter of that right, after "polls showed that some two-thirds of Virginians supported a woman's right to choose." Following his election, several analysts credited Wilder's strong "pro-choice" position for providing him the margin of his slim victory.

When Wilder took the oath of office as governor of Virginia, he declared, "I am a son of Virginia. . . . We mark today not a victory of party or the accomplishments of an individual but the triumph of an idea, an idea as old as America, as old as the God who looks out for us all. It is the idea expressed so eloquently from this great commonwealth by those who gave shape to the greatest nation ever known. . . . The idea that all men and women are created equal, that they are endowed by their Creator with certain inalienable rights: the right to life, liberty, and the pursuit of happiness. . . ."

February 3. Angela Davis, professor of ethnic and women's studies at San Francisco State University, told a crowd of 1,500 people at Spelman College in Atlanta that "we're moving to an era of intense activism, something that is going to make the '60s look like a tea party."

Davis was a controversial figure in the 1960s and 1970s as a black female activist who took "more radical" stances on issues than did leaders of the Civil Rights Movement like Martin Luther King, Jr. and Roy Wilkins, of SCLC and the NAACP, respectively. In 1972, at the age of twenty-eight, Davis was tried and later acquitted of aiding three black men who killed a judge during a shootout at the Marin County, California courthouse. In 1980, she was the vice presidential candidate of the American Communist Party.

In the 1980s, Davis, the late Malcolm X, and other black "radicals" of the 1960s and 1970s has enjoyed a resurgence of influence among young African-Americans, particularly on college campuses, as folk heroines and heroes. Their calls for "liberation by any means necessary" seemed to have new relevance to the problems of blacks in the current decades, in the eyes of the students.

February 4-7. Four black protesters were arrested after a melee in the mayor's office in Selma, Alabama on February 4. The blacks were protesting the earlier dismissal of Norward Roussell as the first black superintendent of the city's schools. The Selma Board of Education had said that Roussell's "managerial skills" were questionable. Among those arrested on February 4 were Rose Sanders and Carlos Williams, local attorneys, and Perry Varner, a Dallas County Commissioner.

On February 6, the Selma Board of Education offered to rehire Superintendent Roussell at least temporarily and asked the five black members of the board to return to their posts. The five blacks had resigned in December, 1989 after a racially divided school board voted against extending Roussell's contract. F. D. Reese, the black high school principal who had been named interim school superintendent on February 4, said he would relinquish the job to Roussell.

On February 7, despite the temporary reinstatement of Roussell as superintendent of Selma's schools, hundreds of demonstrators protested at City Hall. The demonstrators demanded a permanent reinstatement for Roussell and charged that Rose Sanders, an attorney arrested in a previous protest on February 4, had been brutalized by police. Meanwhile, the town's schools, which were 70 percent black, remained closed.

Since December, 1989, when the six white school board members rebuffed the five black ones and voted to oust Roussell as superintendent, black students had also boycotted several of the city's schools.

February 5. Abjuda Abi Naantaabuu, a Memphis, Tennessee woman who Ralph Abernathy implied had an extramarital affair with Dr. Martin Luther King, Jr., filed a $10 million suit against Abernathy and Harper and Row, the publisher of his autobiography, *And the Walls Came Tumbling Down*. The suit, which Naantaabuu brought to the United States District Court in New York City, charged that the defendants "falsely and maliciously . . . caused the readers of [the] book to believe that she had engaged in adulterous behavior and sexual relations with Dr. Martin Luther King on the last night of his life." King, Abernathy, and other civil rights activists had dinner at Naantaabuu's home the night before he was assassinated in Memphis on April 4, 1968. (See also entries dated October 12, 1989 and October 24, 1989.)

February 11. Nelson R. Mandela, the major symbol of the struggle for human rights in the Republic of South Africa, was released from prison after serving twenty-seven years. Mandela's release was ordered by Frederick W. de Klerk, the new President of South Africa. It was applauded by political and human rights leaders around the world, including the United States.

In 1986, the U. S. Congress had passed an Anti-Apartheid Act which imposed economic sanctions on the white minority government of South Africa. (President Ronald Reagan had vetoed the measure earlier.) The act stipulated that the sanctions could only be lifted after South Africa had freed all political prisoners (of which Mandela was considered the principal one); legalized the African National Congress (ANC) and other anti-apartheid groups; engaged in good faith negotiations on the nation's political future; lifted the state of emergency; and made substantial progress on dismantling apartheid, South Africa's system of racial segregation. President de Klerk lifted a thirty-year-old ban on the ANC on February 2, 1990.

Randall Robinson, executive director of Trans-Africa, the leading anti-apartheid group in the United States, expressed the great delight of most African-Americans upon the news of Mandela's release, but he warned that sanctions must remain in place and that "it would be a mistake . . . at this juncture for President Bush to invite President de Klerk to visit the U. S." (See also entry dated June 20-30, 1990.)

February 11. James "Buster" Douglas knocked out Mike Tyson in the tenth round of a Tokyo, Japan match to take the world's heavyweight boxing championship in "a major upset." Douglas, a twenty-four-year-old African-American from Columbus, Ohio, went into the contest against the champion with a 18-2-1 record, including fourteen knockouts, "mostly against lackluster opponents."

February 21-24. Students at historically black Tennessee State University in Nashville staged sit-ins and marches protesting "poor conditions" at the school. Targets of the protest were university president Otis Floyd, the state Board of Regents, the governing body for Tennessee's institutions of higher education. Several students were arrested for "violating school rules or criminal laws" during the demonstrations. Some of them, including Jeff Carr, the student body president, rejected offers of amnesty.

February 23. President George Bush named African-American businessman Arthur A. Fletcher to be chairman of the U. S. Commission on Civil Rights (CCR).

Fletcher, age sixty-five, had served with Bush when the President was U. S. Ambassador to the United Nations in 1971. Fletcher was an assistant secretary of labor in the administration of President Richard M. Nixon, and deputy assistant for urban affairs for President Gerald R. Ford. In 1978, he lost a contest for mayor of Washington, D. C. to Democrat Marion Barry.

Fletcher succeeded William Barclay Allen, who, as chairman of the CCR, had been embroiled in several controversies, even with fellow commissioners. After he delivered a speech in 1989 titled "Blacks? Animals? Homosexuals? What is a Minority?," the commission, by a vote of 6-1, condemned Allen's speech as "thoughtless, disgusting and unnecessarily inflammatory"(see entry dated October 18, 1989). Allen and his predecessor, the late Clarence Pendleton, both blacks, had also drawn the ire of some congresspersons and civil rights leaders for failing to aggressively champion civil rights enforcement. But the appointment of Fletcher drew praises. Benjamin Hooks, Executive Director of the NAACP, for example, described Fletcher as "a fair-minded, down-the-middle-of-the-road kind of person."

March 2. The Bureau of the Census estimated the African-American population at 30.6 million as of January 1, 1989, an increase of 462,000 from a year earlier. The total represented a growth of 1.5 percent during the year for blacks, which doubled the white increase of 0.8 percent. The annual growth rate of blacks had exceeded that of whites since 1950, according to the Bureau. Most of the gain for both groups came from "natural increase."

At the beginning of 1989, blacks made up 12.3 percent of the nation's population of 247.6 million. Whites comprised 84 percent of the total and other races (including Asians, Native Americans, Aleuts, Eskimos, and Pacific Islanders) made up three percent. The number of Hispanics rose by 3.4 percent and totaled 20.2 million or eight percent of the national total.

March 3. Walter H. Annenberg, former publisher of *TV Guide,* made a fifty million dollar pledge to the United Negro College Fund (UNCF). His gift was the largest single donation ever offered to the group, which serves as a coordinating fund-raising agency for more than forty private black colleges in the United States. In a statement released by Annenberg, he called black colleges "a major force for positive change. . . . As a society we cannot afford to waste our most valuable resources—our citizens. . . . Unless young blacks are brought into the mainstream of economic life, they will continue to be on the curbstone. The key to this problem is education." President George Bush applauded the gesture, remarking, "I think that generosity is a challenge . . . that will bring on well-deserved support from others. It's most generous and one of the most brilliant points of light I can think of."

In 1989, the UNCF had raised a total of $45.8 million for distribution to its member institutions. (See also entries dated April 24, 1944, November 4, 1988 and May 22, 1989.)

March 3. Carole Gist, a twenty-year-old African-American from Detroit, Michigan, was crowned "Miss USA" in Wichita, Kansas. Gist, a student at Northwood Institute, became the first black American to gain the beauty title. (Three blacks have held the older title of "Miss America.") Gist came into the contest as "Miss Michigan—USA." Of her selection, Gist said "there is so much more to me than my blackness, the color of my skin. . . . Never give up on your dreams." The new "Miss USA" received prizes totalling about $220,000, including $88,000 in cash. (See also entries dated September 17, 1983, and September 16, 1989.)

March 12. A group of African-American leaders met with Secretary of State James A. Baker III in Washington, D.C. for discussions involving the redistribution of foreign aid "from emerging East European democracies to needy African nations struggling for freedom." The group specifically requested an increase in aid to Namibia, from $7.8 million budgeted for 1991 to $25 million in 1990 and 1991, and a grant of $25 million to the African National Congress (ANC) "for its struggle to end apartheid in South Africa."

One of the blacks present at the meeting, Randall Robinson, head of TransAfrica, a lobbying group for U.S. foreign policy towards Africa, said there were "sharp disagreements" with Baker over increased aid to Namibia, as well as "continued covert aid" to rebels in Angola. Other blacks who attended the meeting included civil rights leader Jesse Jackson and Coretta Scott King, widow of slain civil rights leader Martin Luther King, Jr.

March 19. Harold Irwin Bearden, minister and civil leader, died after suffering a stroke in Atlanta, Georgia, at age seventy-nine.

Bearden was born in Atlanta on May 8, 1910 to Lloyd and Mary Da Costa Bearden. He obtained an A.B. degree at Morris Brown College and a B.D. degree from Turner Theological Seminary (both in Georgia). Bearden was ordained a deacon in the African Methodist Episcopal (AME) Church in 1930 and an elder in 1931. He pastored the Big Bethel AME Church, one of the oldest and largest congregations in Atlanta, from 1951 to 1964.

From 1960 to 1962, Bearden was an acting presiding elder of the A.M.E Church and in 1964, he was consecrated a bishop in Cincinnati, Ohio. Bearden's first assignments upon elevation to the bishopric were in Central and West Africa. While there, he was elected president of the board of trustees of Monrovia College in Liberia. Upon his return to the United States, Bearden had church district assignments in Ohio and Texas before being named bishop of the Sixth Episcopal District in his native Georgia in 1976. He was president of the AME Council of Bishops in 1973-74.

Bearden served as bishop in the Sixth Episcopal District of Georgia until 1980 and continued to serve on special assignments for his church until his retirement in 1984.

While Bearden was president of the Atlanta chapter of the NAACP in 1958-59, a suit was filed to desegregate the Atlanta public schools and a federal court ordered desegregation on the city's buses. Bearden was one of several black ministers who were arrested in 1957 for defying Georgia's bus segregation laws. He continuously used his Sunday radio broadcasts to chide both segregationists and black accommodationists about Jim Crow practices in Atlanta and the nation, and he supported student sit-in demonstrations in the city in the 1960s.

Bearden served as a director of the Atlanta University Center consortium of black colleges and was a chairman of the boards of trustees at both of his alma maters, Morris Brown College and Turner Theological Seminary. The state Senate of Georgia named him an outstanding citizen in 1978.

In one of the eulogies for Bearden, Jesse Hill, president of the Atlanta Life Insurance Company and a trustee of the Big Bethel Church, said "When the history of the turbulent '60s and the bi-racial progress of Atlanta is written, the name of bishop Harold I. Bearden, then the dynamic, fearless pastor of Big Bethel AME Church, has to be placed up front." John Hurst Adams, the current senior bishop of the AME's sixth episcopal district, remembers Bearden as "a major influence in the life of the community. He was active in community development, the civil rights movement, and all aspects in the advancement of the community and especially aspects of African-American community unity."

March 30. Thea Bowman, black Catholic educator, died of cancer in Jackson, Mississippi, at age fifty-two.

Bowman was the only African-American member of the Franciscan Sisters of Perpetual Adoration. She served as director of intercultural awareness for its

Jackson diocese and was a member of the faculty of the Institute of Black Catholic Studies at Xavier University in New Orleans, Louisiana.

In 1988, Bowman recorded an album, *Sister Thea: Songs of My People*, which consisted of fifteen black spirituals. The recording made the nun a popular figure at conventions and on college campuses across the nation. In that same year, she was featured on the CBS-TV news program "60 Minutes," which led to plans for a movie about her life and work.

She was widely honored for her educational work as well as her pioneering efforts to encourage black Catholics "to express their cultural roots inside the church." In 1989, she received the U.S. Catholic Award from *U.S. Catholic Magazine* "for furthering the cause of women in the Roman Catholic Church." In addition, the Sister Thea Bowman Black Catholic Educational Foundation was established in 1989 "to provide financial support for black students in Catholic primary and elementary schools and Catholic colleges and universities."

Upon her death, Joseph Houck, Bishop of the Diocese of Jackson, said, "She was an outstanding woman. She was proud of her heritage and totally dedicated to the vision of Jesus Christ for love and growth of all people."

April 4. Sarah Vaughan, African-American jazz singer known affectionately as "the Divine One," died of cancer in San Fernando Valley, California, at age sixty-six.

Vaughan was born on March 27, 1924 in Newark, New Jersey to Asbury, a carpenter and amateur guitarist, and Ada Vaughan, a laundry worker and choir singer. Sarah joined a Baptist church choir as a child and the gospel influence remained with her throughout her career. She occasionally included a version of "The Lord's Prayer" in her performances.

Ada Vaughan had wanted her daughter to pursue a career in classical music, and sent her to weekly organ and piano lessons, but young Sarah soon turned to a different path. At age eighteen, she won a talent contest at the Apollo Theatre in Harlem, New York with a rendition of "Body and Soul." She was soon singing and playing piano with the Earl Hines Band and later toured with Billy Eckstine.

Vaughan began a solo career in the 1940s. Between 1940 and her death, she performed before jazz audiences throughout the nation and recorded at least three Top 10 pop singles, including "Broken-Hearted Melody," which sold more than a million records. Other notable recordings included "Misty," *The Divine Sarah Vaughan, Gershwin Live*, and *Lover Man*.

Although Vaughan "did not swing as effortlessly as Ella Fitzgerald," according to Bo Emerson, music critic of the *Atlanta Constitution*, "nor bring to bear

Billie Holiday's intensity, the physical pleasure of [her] voice set her apart from most vocalists in any discipline." "She had the kind of voice that comes along once in a hundred years, once in a lifetime, maybe once in a thousand years," remarked jazz saxophonist and "elder statesman" Benny Carter.

At the 1989 Grammy Award ceremonies, Vaughan was presented with a Lifetime Achievement Award.

April 12. A *New York Times* /CBS Network News Poll revealed that African-Americans had given George Bush "the highest level of sustained approval" of any Republican president in thirty years. 56 percent of black Americans in the poll supported the way the President was doing his job. The survey was conducted by telephone from March 30 to April 2, 1990 and involved 403 blacks.

April 17. Ralph David Abernathy, minister and civil rights leader, died of heart problems in Atlanta, Georgia, at age sixty-four.

Abernathy was born on March 11, 1926 in Linden, Alabama to William L., a farmer and deacon, and Louiverney Valentine Abernathy. He was the tenth of twelve children. After his discharge from the U. S. Army in 1945, Abernathy enrolled in the Alabama State College in Montgomery, where he became both student body and class president. Abernathy led successful student protests against poor food in the cafeteria and inadequate living conditions for male students. He received a bachelor's degree from Alabama State in 1950. While attending graduate school at Atlanta University, Abernathy heard Martin Luther King, Jr. speak at the Ebenezer Baptist Church in Atlanta and developed an acquaintance with the young minister.

Prior to his involvement in the Civil Rights Movement of the 1950s and 1960s, Abernathy was a dean at Alabama State College and a part-time pastor of a church in Demopolis, Alabama. In 1948, he was named pastor of Montgomery's black First Baptist Church.

When Martin Luther King, Jr. went to Montgomery in 1954 to assume the pastorate of the Dexter Avenue Baptist Church, he received a warm welcome from Abernathy and their friendship was strengthened. King planned to spend two or three years getting himself established in the city before becoming active in civic affairs, while Abernathy wanted to return to his graduate studies in order to obtain, in his words, "the same kind of academic credibility" which his friend King had. Their plans were disrupted by the arrest of Rosa Parks and the subsequent Montgomery bus boycott of 1955-1956. Both men were thrust into the leadership of the protest; King as the major figure and Abernathy as his number one lieutenant.

For thirteen years, Abernathy remained King's closest aide, confidante, and supporter as they engaged in the civil rights struggles of Montgomery, Albany, Birmingham, Selma, Chicago, Memphis, and dozens of other cities, towns, and hamlets. After an assassin's bullet struck King on the balcony of the Lorraine Hotel on the evening of April 4, 1968, Abernathy cradled his fallen comrade in his arms and remained with him through his death and autopsy. He gave one of the principal eulogies at King's funeral ceremonies, on what he called "one of the darkest days in American history." Abernathy then succeeded King as president of the Southern Christian Leadership Conference (SCLC).

In his own right, Abernathy also led the "Poor People's Campaign" for jobs and freedom in Washington after King's death in 1968. He ran for Congress from Georgia's Fifth District in 1978 but received only 3,614 votes. Abernathy addressed the United Nations in 1971 and was a president of the World Peace Council. In 1980, he was one of the few national black leaders to endorse the Republican presidential candidate Ronald Reagan over President Jimmy Carter. Abernathy considered Carter's Presidency ineffectual and felt that Reagan would revive the economy and develop jobs for blacks. In 1984, he broke with some of his colleagues in the Civil Rights Movement, including former United Nations Ambassador Andrew Young, and endorsed another civil rights veteran, Jesse L. Jackson, for President of the United States.

April 27. A federal court jury in Memphis, Tennessee announced that it was unable to reach a verdict in the two-and-one-half month trial of Harold Ford, a black U.S. Representative. The forty-four-year-old Tennessee Democrat had been charged with nineteen counts of bank fraud, mail fraud, and conspiracy. He was specifically accused of taking more than one million dollars in "political payoffs disguised as loans" from bankers C.H. and Jake Butcher of Knoxville, Tennessee. Ford had consistently maintained his innocence and suggested that the charges against him were racially motivated.

May 4. Andrew J. Young, former U.S. Ambassador to the United Nations and mayor of Atlanta, Georgia, addressed the annual convention of the Rainbow Coalition held in Atlanta. The coalition was founded by former African-American Democratic presidential candidate Jesse L. Jackson. In the 1984 Democratic presidential contest, Young publicly opposed Jackson's candidacy and supported his rival, former Vice President Walter Mondale. In 1988 Young, citing his role as mayor of the host city of the Democratic National Convention, remained neutral. He once said that Jackson's presidential ambitions were "dangerous." But at the Rainbow Coalition Convention on May 4, 1990, Young drew applause when he described Jackson as the "only person in the Democratic Party who has dared to challenge" the administration of President George Bush. He also said that Jackson had "had the fire in his belly, the dream in his heart. He had the gleam and vision in his eyes." For his part, Jackson said "Young can win and deserves to win" his current quest for the Democratic nomination as governor of Georgia.

May 12. Joseph E. Lowery, president of the Southern Christian Leadership Conference (SCLC), held a workshop on race relations with four Ku Klux Klansmen in Birmingham, Alabama. The four were among a group of five Klansmen who had been sentenced to participate in the two hour meeting for their participation in a racial melee in Decatur, Alabama in 1979. Four people were wounded in an exchange of gunfire between blacks and whites after more than one hundred Klansmen tried to block a civil rights march. After the workshop, Roger Handley, a former grand dragon of the Alabama Ku Klux Klan, called the affair "a waste of two hours." Lowery, who preached patriotism, love, and brotherhood to the white supremacists, however, called it "heartwarming."

May 12. Governor L. Douglas Wilder of Virginia, ordered all of his state's agencies and institutions to divest themselves of business investments in companies not "substantively free" of economic activity in South Africa. Virginia officials estimated that such holdings amounted to more than $750 million. A large amount of this money was invested by the agency which paid pensions to retired state employees.

In announcing his actions, Governor Wilder said that the people of his state should support the efforts of South African blacks to break the chains of apartheid with the same vigor and enthusiasm that greeted the aspirations to freedom by people in China and Eastern Europe. He added: "If we are to participate in the extension to all peoples of the freedoms and liberties which we hold dear, we must take concrete actions which reflect our support." Wilder made his declarations in a commencement address at the predominantly-black Norfolk State University.

May 13. George Augustus Stallings was ordained the first bishop of the African-American Catholic Church. The forty-one-year-old black priest broke away from the Roman Catholic Church in June, 1989 after declaring that the Church failed to meet the needs of its African-American parishioners. On July 4, 1989, he was suspended for "founding an independent black congregation."

At the ordination of Bishop Stallings, African dancers and gospel singers performed before an audience of 1,000 people. Stallings "knelt on a decorated stage filled with elaborate banners, drummers, and icons" as six white bishops from the Independent Old Catholic Churches of California (which broke away from Rome in the 1870s) declared him "a suitable candidate for the office of bishop in the Church of God."

At the time of Stallings' assumption of his new post, his African-American Catholic Congregation had expanded from Washington, D.C. to Baltimore, Maryland, Norfolk, Virginia, and Philadelphia, Pennsylvania.

May 16. Sammy Davis, Jr., African-American entertainer and America's "Ambassador of Goodwill," died of cancer in Beverly Hills, California, at age sixty-four. He was born on December 8, 1925, in the Harlem section of New York City.

Davis was the consummate star, the epitome of versatility. He began performing at age three with his father, Sam, Sr., and his uncle, Will Mastin, in vaudeville. In his adult years, Davis's talents as a dancer, singer, and actor were revered on the stage, film, television, and in nightclubs. He made his Broadway debut in 1956 in the musical *Mr. Wonderful* and won a Tony nomination for his starring role as a cosmopolitan boxer in *Golden Boy*.

Davis's major recordings included "The Way You Look Tonight" (1946); "Hey There" (1954); "That Old Black Magic" (1955); "The Shelter of Your Arms" (1964); "I've Got to Be Me" (1969); and "The Candy Man" (1972).

In his recordings, as in his films, Davis often worked with his friends Frank Sinatra and Dean Martin. His first movie role was as a child in *Rufus Jones for President* (1933) with singer Ethel Waters. Davis also had major roles in *Anna Lucasta* (1958); *Porgy and Bess* (1959); *Oceans Eleven* (1960); *Robin and the Seven Hoods* (1964); and *Sweet Charity* (1969). Davis's last film appearance was in 1989 with dancer Gregory Hines in *Tap*.

Between 1956 and 1980, Davis appeared on almost every variety show and comedy series on network television; in 1966, he starred in his own television series, one of the first ever hosted by a black person.

Davis supported the Civil Rights Movement of the 1960s by singing at fund raisers, especially for Dr. Martin Luther King, Jr., and was with King at the end of the famous Selma to Montgomery voting rights march in Alabama. He also helped to raise money for the defense of Angela Davis, who was imprisoned for conspiracy to commit murder in the late 1960s. The entertainer was also the target of controversy; after being invited to an inaugural activity for President John F. Kennedy in 1961, he was later asked not to attend the affair because of fear that his presence there with his then-wife, Swedish actress Mai Britt, would "inflame Southerners." Davis also made headlines in 1972 at a function for President Richard M. Nixon during the Republican National Convention. He startled the President and many African-Americans, particularly, when he came up behind Nixon and gave him a big hug while flashing a wide, "cattish" grin.

The rise of Davis from demeaning, stereotypical roles in vaudeville and his early films to the highest place in the annals of American entertainment is documented in his autobiographies *Yes I Can* (1965) and *Why Me* (1989). At the time of his death, Davis had become, in the words of NAACP executive director Benjamin Hooks, "an American treasure that the whole world loved."

May 18. Joseph Fama, a nineteen-year-old New York City youth, was convicted of second degree murder in the 1989 slaying of Yusuf Hawkins, a sixteen-year-old black youth, in the Bensonhurst section of the city. The mob attack which led to Hawkins's death in an all-white neighborhood had been the focus of racial tension in the nation's largest city for more than six months. It was also frequently cited by some blacks as evidence of a resurgent racism in the United States.

May 25. A Gwinnett County, Georgia State Court Judge ruled that a thirty-nine-year old law which prohibited members of the Ku Klux Klan from wearing hooded masks in public was unconstitutional. Judge Howard E. Cook said that the state law was "overly broad" and violated the rights to "free speech, association, and [equal] protection" of the Klansmen. Although the Klan may "represent . . . hateful ideas, such ideas are still entitled to . . . protection," Judge Cook declared. Georgia state officials and civil rights leaders said they were "shocked" by the judge's decision and filed notice of appeal to the state Supreme Court "20 minutes after [the decision] was filed."

June 6. Harvey Gantt, the former African-American mayor of Charlotte, North Carolina, won his state's Democratic nomination for the United States Senate. Gantt gained 272,576 votes (57 percent) to defeat Michael Easley, a county district attorney. Easley received 206,397 votes (43 percent) with 99 percent of the state's precincts reporting. Gantt, a forty-seven-year-old architect, was the first black person in the history of the state of North Carolina to receive the Democratic Party's nomination for U. S. Senator. In 1963, he became the first black student to enroll in Clemson University in South Carolina and was the first black mayor of Charlotte. Of his nomination Gantt remarked, "There's a new day in North Carolina. This is a day where people are judged by what they can do and not by the color of their skin." In order to win election to the Senate, Gantt would have to defeat the veteran Republican Senator Jesse Helms in the November, 1990 general elections.

June 11. Judge Thaddeus Owens sentenced two nineteen-year-old white youths to prison for the August 23, 1989 shooting death of Yusuf K. Hawkins, a sixteen-year-old black youth, in New York City. Joseph Fama, who prosecutors and police authorities said actually shot Hawkins, was sentenced to thirty-two-and-two-thirds years to life in prison. He had been convicted of second-degree murder, inciting a riot, unlawful imprisonment, weapons possessions, and other crimes. Keith Mondello received a sentence of five-and-one-third to sixteen years in prison and a two thousand dollars fine. He was acquitted of murder and manslaughter, but convicted of inciting a riot, unlawful imprisonment, and discrimination. Mondello was identified as the ringleader of the mob which attacked Hawkins and three other blacks in the Bensonhurst neighborhood of New York City in 1989.

The family of the slain Hawkins and other blacks applauded the sentence handed down to Fama, but some threw rocks and bottles in Brooklyn when they heard that Mondello had been acquitted of the more serious charges.

June 12. Theo Mitchell, a black state senator, won the Democratic primary contest for governor of South Carolina. Mitchell gained 107,473 votes (61 percent) to 69,766 votes (39 percent) for Ernest Parsailaigue, a freshman senator (with 92 percent of precincts reporting). Mitchell would have to defeat incumbent Republican Governor Carroll Campbell in the November general elections to win the governor's office.

June 13. Marion S. Barry, Jr., mayor of Washington, D.C., announced that he would not seek a fourth term. At the time of the announcement, Barry, a former civil rights activist, was on trial in a federal district court in Washington. He was arrested on January 18, 1990 in a "drug sting" at a local hotel. The mayor had pleaded innocent to three felony counts of lying to a grand jury about his alleged drug use, ten misdemeanor cocaine possession charges, and one misdemeanor cocaine conspiracy charge. (See also entry dated January 2, 1987.)

June 17. About 850 people, mostly students, attended a march and rally sponsored by the National Collegiate Black Caucus (NCBC) in Washington, D.C. The organizers had expected a crowd of more than 5,000.

The demonstration was organized to coordinate the concerns of black collegians throughout the nation. In the past decade, black college students on both predominantly-black and predominantly-white campuses had demonstrated against racism and for a greater infusion of African and African-American studies into college and university curricula. The students at the Washington rally were also concerned about inadequate housing on their campuses and insufficient financial aid.

June 18. Kenny Leon, a thirty-four-year-old actor, was named artistic director of the Alliance Theater Company in Atlanta, Georgia. The appointment made him the second black artistic director of a major American theater. The only other African-American serving in such a position is Lloyd Richards, who announced his retirement from the Yale Repertory Theatre for June, 1991. Leon was associate artistic director at the Alliance Theater, where he gained popularity for his direction of such productions as *Fences, Gal Baby,* and *Joe Turner's Come and Gone.*

Leon, a graduate of Clark College in Georgia, will head one of the nation's largest theater operations, with 21,000 subscribers and an annual budget of $6.5 million. Yet the theater has yet to achieve real distinction in the artistic world after twenty-one years of operation. That task was handed to Leon.

June 20. The United States Department of Commerce reported that the percentage of black high school graduates increased between 1978 and 1988 and now approaches the percentage rate for whites. The report, based on national census data, indicated that in 1988, 75 percent of blacks and 82 percent of whites, aged eighteen to twenty-four, graduated from high school, compared with 68 percent for blacks and 83 percent for whites in 1978. There was apparently no change in the graduation or dropout rate for Hispanics during the same period.

June 20-30. Nelson Mandela, deputy President of the African National Congress (ANC) and the major symbol of the struggle for freedom in the Republic of South Africa, conducted a major tour of the United States. The ten-day foray was designed to convince Americans to maintain sanctions against the white-minority government in South Africa until its racial apartheid system was dismantled, and to raise money to assist the ANC's campaign for majority rule.

On June 20, Mandela was feted to a ticker tape parade in downtown New York City, where approximately 750,000 people lined the parade routes to greet him. He told crowds in the nation's largest city that apartheid in his country was "doomed," and added that with the aid of supporters in the United States, "We have made the government listen, and we have broken the walls of the South African jails."

On June 22, the South African freedom fighter addressed the United Nations (UN) in New York City. He cautioned the world body that "nothing which has happened in South Africa calls for a revision of the position that this organization has taken in the struggle against apartheid." During the almost three decades that Mandela was in prison, the UN consistently adopted resolutions opposing South African apartheid and the many speeches by delegates and others against the system usually ended in the refrain, "Free Mandela."

Mandela was in Boston, Massachusetts on June 23, where his hosts included Jacqueline Kennedy Onassis, widow of slain President John F. Kennedy, and the late President's brother, Massachusetts Senator Edward "Ted" Kennedy. Mandela told audiences in Boston, "We lower our banners in memory of Crispus Attucks [an African-American], the first victim to fall in your Revolutionary War," and "given the illustrious history of this city, it is only natural that we consider ourselves as visiting our second home." He also looked forward to a South Africa which was "free from all forms of racism and sexism. We do not seek to dominate whites in our country. We intend to live true to this principal to the end of our day."

On June 25, Mandela arrived in Washington, D. C., where he was greeted by, among others, Randall Robinson, head of TransAfrica, the principal anti-apartheid organization in the United States.

The South African leader met President George Bush on June 26. While Bush hailed Mandela's freedom and again denounced the apartheid system, he asked that "all elements in South African society . . . renounce the use of violence in armed struggle, break free from the cycle of repression and violent reaction that breeds nothing but more fear and suffering." In making his plea, President Bush quoted the slain civil rights leader Martin Luther King, Jr.: "Let us not seek to satisfy our thirst for freedom by drinking from the cup of bitterness and hatred." In his response, Mandela offered that the remarks that Bush made were "due to the fact that he has not yet got a proper briefing from us." He added that when a government prohibits free political activity, "then the people have no alternative but to resort to violence."

After a three hour meeting with the American President, Mandela emerged to say that the two had reached substantial agreement on most issues.

Before leaving the capital, Mandela addressed a joint session of the United States Congress on June 26. He invoked the names of Frederick Douglass, Thomas Jefferson, Joe Louis, and other American heroes, and repeated his plea for a continuation of sanctions against the white-minority government in South Africa. He received several thunderous standing ovations.

On June 27, Mandela visited Atlanta, Georgia, "the capital of the Civil Rights Movement," where he laid a wreath at the tomb of slain civil rights leader Martin Luther King, Jr., received honorary degrees from about a third of the nation's historically black colleges, and addressed a rally of more than 50,000 people. In his brief remarks to the mostly black crowd, Mandela, who made frequent references to King, said, "We are . . . conscious that here in the southern part of the country, you have experienced the degradation of racial segregation. We continue to be inspired by the knowledge that in the face of your own difficulties, you are in the forefront of the anti-apartheid movement in this country." Then, drawing upon King's famous "I Have a Dream" oration, Mandela declared "Let Freedom ring, Let us all acclaim now, 'Let freedom ring in South Africa. Let freedom ring wherever people's rights are trampled upon.'"

On June 28, Mandela made brief visits to Miami Beach, Florida, where he spoke to the annual convention of the American Federation of State, County, and Municipal Employees (AFSCME), and to Detroit, Michigan, where he addressed a rally of 50,000 people. In Miami, he repeated his call for continued sanctions against South Africa and thanked the American labor unions which had refused to handle materials destined for South Africa and lent financial support to his struggle. About 250 anti-Castro Cubans and Cuban-Americans protested Mandela's visit, however, because he had expressed gratitude for the Cuban dictator's support of the anti-apartheid movement and refused to denounce him during an appearance on a special "Nightline" segment on the

ANC leader Nelson Mandela and his wife, Winnie, place a wreath at the crypt of Dr. Martin Luther King, Jr., in Atlanta, Georgia, as King's widow, Coretta Scott King, observes.

ABC television network. A crowd of 2,000 demonstrators, mostly black, chanted to the beat of an African drum and waved colorful flags in support of Mandela. There were only a few minor clashes between the two groups.

In Detroit, Mandela met Rosa Parks, the Alabama seamstress who sparked the famed Montgomery bus boycott. While visiting the Ford Rouge plant, one of the oldest automobile factories in the country, he told members of the United Auto Workers, another anti-apartheid union, that he was their "comrade . . . your flesh and blood." Later that evening, Mandela and his entourage were honored at a rally held at Tiger Stadium.

On June 29-30, Mandela ended his American tour in California, with stops in Los Angeles and Oakland. He spoke to a crowd of 80,000 people at the Los Angeles Memorial Coliseum, after declaring that he was on the "last leg of an exhausting but exhilarating tour." He also told his Los Angeles audiences that "our masses in action are like a raging torrent. We are on freedom road, and nothing is going to stop us from reaching our destination."

As he prepared to leave the United States, Mandela indicated that he would probably return to the country in October 1990 to receive a $100,000 award from the Gandhi Memorial International Foundation in New York and to meet with several Native American leaders. He declared that he was "very disturbed" about the condition of the Native American and that it was "but natural" that he "should respond to them by seeing them. . . ."

While some Americans either expressed grave concern or opposition to Mandela's views, particularly his refusal to denounce Colonel Qaddafi, Libya's "pro-terrorist" leader, Yassar Arafat, leader of the Palestine Liberation Organization (PLO), and Cuban dictator Fidel Castro, and his unwillingness to abandon the use of violence in his struggle, the South African leader was very warmly received by most Americans on his tour. In New York, eighteen-year-old Tanera Ford remarked, "I'm glad to see so many black people here. . . . To have all these people together for something positive, it just makes me feel great." In Atlanta, Joseph E. Lowery, president of the SCLC, told Mandela "we reject the constant nagging that you have experienced about denouncing violence." Finally, in Detroit, Quirita Quates, a young dancer, said the South African anti-apartheid leader was "just the greatest man in the world." (See Appendix for a list of monies raised for the ANC by Mandela.)

June 25. Mollie Lewis Moon, the founder of the National Urban League Guild (NULG), died from an apparent heart attack in Long Island City, Queens, New York, at age eighty-two.

Moon founded the NULG in 1942 to raise money for Urban League programs "for racial equality and amity." Under her leadership, the guild grew to eighty units, with thirty thousand volunteers in the United States. A major guild event, over which Moon presided for almost half a century, was the annual Beaux Arts Ball. It began at the old Savoy Ballroom in the Harlem section of New York City in 1942, but moved downtown in 1948. In that year, Winthrop Rockefeller, a New York financier and philanthropist, arranged for the ball to be held in the Rainbow Room atop Rockefeller Center. Moon later recalled that the invitations for the event were sent out in both her name and that of Rockefeller. "Nobody was going to buck the landlord," she said, "that's how we broke the color barrier."

On April 23, 1990, which marked the beginning of National Volunteer Week, David Dinkins, the new black mayor of New York City presented an award for "dedicated and innovative volunteerism" to Moon on behalf of President George Bush.

June 27. Oscar L. Prater, vice president for administrative services at Hampton University in Virginia, was named president of Fort Valley State College in Georgia. Prater, a fifty-one-year-old African-American, succeeded Luther Burse, who left office in August, 1988.

Prater, a native of Sylacauga, Alabama, did his undergraduate work at Talladega College (Alabama) and received a doctoral degree from the College of William and Mary in Virginia. At Hampton University, he had been a professor of Mathematics and an administrator for eleven years. Prater was also active in community affairs in both Hampton and Williamsburg, Virginia, particularly the Head Start program for disadvantaged youth.

Appendix

Excerpts taken from Virginia Slave Laws, 1660-1669

I. On Running Away with Negroes (March 1660)

Be it enacted that in the case any English servant shall run away in company with any Negroes who are incapable of making satisfaction by addition of time . . . the English so running away in company with them shall serve for the time of the said Negroes absence as they are to do for their own by a former act.

II. On the Nativity Conditions of Slavery (December 1662)

Whereas some doubts have arisen whether children got by an Englishman upon a Negro woman should be slave or free, be it therefore enacted and declared by this present Grand Assembly, that all children born in this country shall be held bond or free only according to the condition of the mother; and that if any Christian shall commit fornication with a Negro man or woman, he or she so offending shall pay double the fines imposed by the former act.

III. On Baptism and Bondage (September 1667)

Whereas some doubts have risen whether children that are slaves by birth, and by the charity and piety of their owners made partakers of the blessed sacrament of baptism, should by virtue of their baptism be made free, it is enacted and declared by this Grand Assembly, and the authority thereof, that the conferring of baptism does not alter the condition of the person as to his bondage or freedom; that diverse masters, freed from this doubt may more carefully endeavor the propagation of Christianity by permitting children though slaves, or those of greater growth if capable, to be admitted to that sacrament.

IV. On Corporal Punishment (September 1668)

Whereas it has been questioned whether servants running away may be punished with corporal punishment by their master or magistrate, since the act already made gives the master satisfaction by prolonging their time by service, it is declared and enacted by this Assembly that moderate corporal punishment inflicted by master or magistrate upon a runaway servant shall not deprive the master of the satisfaction allowed by the law, the one being as necessary to reclaim them from persisting in that idle course as the other is just to repair the damages sustained by the master.

V. On the Killing of Slaves (October 1669)

Whereas the only law in force for the punishment of refractory servants resisting their master, mistress, or overseer cannot be inflicted upon Negroes, nor the obstinacy of many of them be suppressed by other than violent means, be it enacted and declared by this Grand Assembly if any slave resists his master (or other by his master's order correcting him) and by the extremity of the correction should chance to die, that his death shall not be accounted a felony, but the master (or that person appointed by the master to punish him) be acquitted from molestation, since it cannot be presumed that premeditated malice (which alone makes murder a felony) should induce any man to destroy his own estate.

Source: William W. Herning, ed. *The Statues at Large; Being a Collection of All Laws of Virginia, from 1619,* Vol. II, 1823.

The Emancipation Proclamation

The Emancipation Proclamation was first issued by President Abraham

Lincoln on September 22, 1862. The final proclamation was issued on January 1, 1863.

By the President of the United States of America: A Proclamation:

Whereas on the 22nd day of September, A.D. 1862, a proclamation was issued by the President of the United States, containing, among other things, the following, to wit:

"That on the 1st day of January, A.D. 1863, all persons held as slaves within any State or designated part of a State the people whereof shall then be in rebellion against the United States shall be then, and forever free; and the executive government of the United States, including the military and naval authority thereof, will recognize and maintain the freedom of such persons and will do no act or acts to repress such persons, or any of them, in any efforts they may make for their actual freedom.

"That the executive will on the 1st day of January aforesaid, by proclamation, designate the States and parts of States, if any, in which the people thereof, respectively, shall then be in rebellion against the United States; and the fact that any State or the people thereof shall on that day be in good faith represented in the Congress of the United States by members chosen thereto at elections wherein a majority of the qualified voters of such States shall have participated shall, in the absence of strong countervailing testimony, be deemed conclusive evidence that such State and the people thereof are not then in rebellion against the United States."

Now, therefore, I, Abraham Lincoln, President of the United States, by virtue of the power in me vested as Commander-in-Chief of the Army and Navy of the United States in time of actual armed rebellion against the authority and government of the United States, and as a fit and necessary war measure for suppressing said rebellion, do, on this 1st day of January, A.D. 1863, and in accordance with my purpose so to do, publicly proclaimed for the full period of one hundred days from the first day above mentioned, order and designate as the States and parts of States wherein the people thereof, respectively, are this day in rebellion against the United States the following, to wit:

Arkansas, Texas, Louisiana (except the parishes of St. Bernard, Plaquemines, Jefferson, St. John, St. Charles, St. James, Ascension, Assumption, Terrebonne, Lafourche, St. Mary, St. Martin, and Orleans, including the city of New Orleans), Mississippi, Alabama, Florida, Georgia, South Carolina, North Carolina, and Virginia (except the forty-eight counties designated as West Virginia, and also the counties of Berkeley, Accomac, Northamption, Elizabeth City, York, Princess Anne, and Norfolk, including the cities of Norfolk and Portsmouth), and which excepted parts are for the present left precisely as if this proclamation were not issued.

And by virtue of the power and for the purpose aforesaid, I do order and declare that all persons held as slaves within said designated States and parts of States are, and henceforward shall be, free; and that the Executive Government of the United States, including the military and naval authorities thereof, will recognize and maintain the freedom of said persons.

And I hereby enjoin upon the people so declared to be free to abstain from all violence, unless in necessary self-defense; and I recommend to them that, in all cases when allowed, they labor faithfully for reasonable wages.

And I further declare and make known that such persons of suitable condition will be received into the armed service of the United States to garrison forts, positions, stations, and other places, and to man vessels of all sorts in said service.

And upon this act, sincerely believe to be an act of justice, warranted by the Constitution upon military necessity, I invoke the considerable judgment of mankind and the gracious favor of Almighty God.

The Thirteenth, Fourteenth, and Fifteenth Amendments to the United States Constitution

Article XIII (Ratified in 1865)

Section 1. Neither slavery nor involuntary servitude, except as a punishment for crime whereof the party shall have been duly convicted, shall exist within the United States, or any place subject to their jurisdiction.

Section 2. Congress shall have power to enforce this article by appropriate legislation.

Article XIV (Ratified in 1868)

Section 1. All persons born or naturalized in the United States, and subject to the jurisdiction thereof, are citizens of the United States and of the State wherein they reside. No State shall make or enforce any law which shall abridge the privileges or immunities of citizens of the United States; nor shall any State deprive any person of life, liberty, or property, without due process of law; nor deny to any person within its jurisdiction the equal protection of the laws.

Section 2. Representatives shall be apportioned among the several States according to their respective numbers, counting the whole number of persons in each State, excluding Indians not taxed. But when the right to vote at any election for the choice of electors for President and Vice President of the United States, Representatives in Congress, the executive and judicial officers of a State, or the members of the legislature thereof, is denied to any of the male inhabitants of such State, being twenty-one years of age, and citizens of the United States, or in any way abridged, except for participation in rebellion, or other crime, the basis of representation therein shall be reduced in the proportion which the number of such male citizens shall bear to the whole number of male citizens twenty-one years of age in such State.

Section 3. No person shall be a Senator or Representative in Congress, or elector of President and Vice President, or hold any office, civil or military, under the United States, or under any State, who, having previously taken an oath, as a member of Congress, or as an officer of the United States, or as a member of any State legislature, or as an executive or judicial officer of any state, to support the Constitution of the United States, shall have engaged in insurrection or rebellion against the same, or given aid or comfort to the enemies thereof. But Congress may by a vote of two-thirds of each house, remove such disability.

Section 4. The validity of the public debt of the United States, authorized by law, including debts incurred for payment of pensions and bounties for services in suppressing insurrection or rebellion, shall not be questioned. But neither the United States nor any State shall assume or pay any debt or obligation incurred in aid of insurrection or rebellion against the United States, or any claim for the loss of emancipation of any slave; but all such debts, obligations and claims shall be held illegal and void.

Section 5. The Congress shall have power to enforce, by appropriate legislation, the provisions of this article.

Article XV (Ratified in 1870)

Section 1. The right of citizens of the United States to vote shall not be denied or abridged by the United States or by any State on account of race, color, or previous condition of servitude.

Section 2. The Congress shall have power to enforce this article by appropriate legislation.

An excerpt taken from the Decision of the United States Supreme Court in the Case of *Plessy v. Ferguson*, May 18, 1896. (Justice H. B. Brown for the Majority, Justice John M. Harlan for the Dissenting Opinion.)

This case turns upon the constitutionality of an act of the General Assembly of the state of Louisiana, passed in 1890, providing for separate railway carriages for the white and colored races. . . . .

The 1st Section of the statute enacts

That all railway companies carrying passengers in their coaches in this state shall provide equal but separate accommodations for the white and colored races, by providing two or more passenger coaches by a partition so as to secure separate accommodations: Provided, that this section shall not be construed to apply to street railroads. No person or persons shall be admitted to occupy seats in coaches, other than the ones assigned to them on account of the race they belong to. . . .

By the 2nd Section it was enacted

That the officers of such passenger trains shall have power and are hereby required to assign each passenger to the coach or compartment used for the race to which such passenger belongs; any passenger insisting on going into a coach or compartment to which by race he does not belong shall be liable to a fine of $25, or, in lieu thereof, to imprisonment for a period of not more than twenty days in the parish prison; and should any passenger refuse to occupy the coach or compartment to which he or she is assigned by the officer of such railway, said officer shall have power to refuse to carry such passenger on his train, and for such refusal neither he nor the railway company which he represents shall be liable for damages in any of the courts of this state. . . .

The constitutionality of this act is attacked upon the ground that it conflicts both with the Thirteenth Amendment of the Constitution, abolishing slavery, and the Fourteenth Amendment, which prohibits certain restrictive legislation on the part of the states.

1. That it does not conflict with the Thirteenth Amendment, which abolished slavery and involuntary servitude except as a punishment for crime, is too clear for argument. . . . A statute which implies merely a legal distinction between the white and colored races—a distinction which is founded in the color of two races, and which must always exist so long as white men are distinguished from the other race by color—has no tendency to destroy the legal equality of the two races or reestablish that the Thirteenth Amendment is strenuously relied upon by the plaintiff in error in this connection.

2. By the Fourteenth Amendment, all persons born or naturalized in the United States and subject to the jurisdiction thereof are made citizens of the United States and of the state wherein they reside; and the states are forbidden from making or enforcing any law which shall abridge the privileges or immunities of citizens of the United States, or shall deprive any person of life, liberty, or property without due process of law, or deny to any person within their jurisdiction the equal protection of the laws.

The proper construction of this amendment was first called to the attention of this court in the Slaughter-House Cases which involved, however, not a question of race but one of exclusive privileges. The case did not call for any expression of opinion as to the exact rights it was intended to secure to the colored race, but it was said generally that its main purpose was to establish the citizenship of the Negro; to give definitions of citizenship of the United States and of the states, and to protect from the hostile legislation of the states the privileges and immunities of citizens of the United States as distinguished from those of citizens of the states.

The object of the amendment was undoubtedly to enforce the absolute equality of the two races before the law, but in the nature of things it could not have been intended to abolish distinctions based upon color, or to enforce social as distinguished from political equality, or a commingling of the two races upon terms unsatisfactory to either. Laws permitting, and even requiring, their separation in places where they are liable to be brought into contact do not necessarily imply the inferiority of either race to the other, and have been generally, if not universally, recognized as within the competency of the state legislatures in the exercise of their police power. The most common instance of this is connected with the establishment of separate schools for white and colored children, which has been held to be a valid exercise of the legislative power even by courts of states where the political rights of the colored race have been longest and most earnestly enforced. . . .

While we think the enforced separation of the races, as applied to the internal commerce of the state, neither abridges the privileges or immunities of the colored man, deprives him of his property without due process of law, nor denies him the equal protection of the laws, within the meaning of the Fourteenth Amendment, we are not prepared to say that the conductor, in assigning passengers to the coaches according to their race, does not act at his peril, or that the provision of the 2nd Section of the act, that denies to the passenger compensation in damages for a refusal to receive him into the coach in which he properly belongs, is a valid exercise of the legislative power. Indeed, we understand it to be conceded by the state's attorney, that such part of the act as exempts from liability the railway company and its officers is unconstitutional.

The power to assign to a particular coach obviously implies the power to determine to which race the passenger belongs, as well as the power to determine who, under the laws of the particular state, is to be deemed white and who a colored person. This question, though indicated in the brief of the plaintiff in error, does not properly arise upon the record in this case, since the only issue made is as to the unconstitutionality of the act, so far as it requires the railway to provide separate accommodations and the conductor to assign passengers according to their race.

It is claimed by the plaintiff in error that, in any mixed community, the reputation of belonging to the dominant race, in this instance the white race, is property, in the same sense that a right of action, or of inheritance, is property. Conceding this to be so for the purposes of this case, we are unable to see how this statute deprives him of, or in any way affects, his right to such property. If he be a white man and assigned to a colored coach, he may have his action for damages against the company for being deprived of his so-called property. Upon the other hand, if he be a colored man and be so assigned, he had been deprived of no property since he is not lawfully entitled to the reputation of being a white man.

In this connection, it is also suggested by the learned counsel for the plaintiff in error that the same argument that will justify the state legislature in requiring railways to provide separate accommodations for the two races will also authorize them to require separate cars to be provided for people whose hair is of a certain color, or who are aliens, or who belong to certain nationalities, or to enact laws requiring colored people to walk upon one side of the street and white people upon the other, or requiring white men's houses to be painted white and colored men's black, or their vehicles or business signs to be of different colors, upon the theory that one side of the street is as good as the other, or that a house or vehicle of one color is as good as one of another color. The reply to all this is that every exercise of the police power must be reasonable and extend only to such laws as are enacted in good faith for the promotion for the public good and not for the annoyance or oppression of a particular class. . . .

So far, then, as a conflict with the Fourteenth Amendment is concerned, the case reduces itself to the question whether the statute of Louisiana is a reasonable regulation, and with respect to this there must necessarily be a large discretion on the part of the legislature. In determining the question of reasonableness, it is at liberty to act with reference to the established usages, customs, and traditions of the people, and with a view to the promotion of their comfort, and the preservation of the public and good order. Gauged by this standard, we cannot say that a law which authorizes or even requires the separation of the two races in public conveyances is unreasonable or more obnoxious to the Fourteenth Amendment than the acts of Congress requiring separate schools for colored children in the District of Columbia, the constitutionality of which does not seem to have been questioned, or the corresponding acts of state legislatures.

We consider the underlying fallacy of the plaintiff's argument to consist in the assumption that the enforced separation of the two races stamps the colored race with a badge of inferiority. If this be so, it is not by reason of anything found in the act, but solely because the colored race chooses to put that construction upon it. The argument necessarily assumes that if, as has been more than once the case, and is not unlikely to be so again, the colored race should become the dominant power in the state legislature and should enact a law in precisely similar terms, it would thereby relegate the white race to an inferior position. We imagine that the white race, at least, would not acquiesce in this assumption. . . .

Legislation is powerless to eradicate racial instincts or to abolish distinctions based upon physical differences, and the attempt to do so can only result in accentuating the difficulties of the present situation. If the civil and political rights of both races be equal, one cannot be inferior to the other civilly or politically. If one race be inferior to the other socially, the Constitution of the United States cannot put them upon the same plane.

It is true that the question of the proportion of colored blood necessary to constitute a colored person as distinguished from a white person is one upon which there is a difference of opinion in the different states, some holding that any visible admixture of black blood stamps the person as belonging to the colored race (*State v. Chavers* 5 Jones, [N.C.] 1, p. 11); others that it depends upon the preponderance of blood (*Gray v. State*, 4 Ohio, 354; *Monroe v. Collins*, 17 Ohio St. 665); and still others that the predominance of white blood must only be in the proportion of three-fourths (*People v. Dean*, 14 Michigan, 406; *Jones v. Commonwealth*, 80 Virginia, 538). But these are questions to be determined under the laws of each state and are not properly put in issue in this case. Under the allegations of his petition it may undoubtedly become a question of importance whether, under the laws of Louisiana, the petitioner belongs to the white or colored race.

The judgment of the Court below is, therefore, affirmed. Mr. Justice Harlan:

In respect of civil rights, common to all citizens, the Constitution of the United States does not, I think, permit any public authority to know the race of those entitled to be protected in the enjoyment of such rights. Every true man has pride of race, and, under appropriate circumstances, when the rights of others, his equals before the law, are not to be affected, it is his privilege to express such pride and to take such action based upon it as to him seems proper. But I deny that any legislative body or judicial tribunal may have regard to the race of citizens when the civil rights of those citizens are involved. Indeed, such legislation as that here in question is inconsistent, not only with the equality of rights which pertains to citizenship, national and state, but with the personal liberty enjoyed by everyone within the United States.

The Thirteenth Amendment does not permit the withholding or the deprivation of any right necessarily inhering in freedom. It not only struck down the institution of slavery as previously existing in the United States but it prevents the imposition of any burdens or disabilities that constitute badges of slavery or servitude. It decreed universal civil freedom in this country. This Court has so adjudged. But that amendment having been found inadequate to the protection of the rights of those who had been in slavery, it was followed by the Fourteenth Amendment, which added greatly to the dignity and glory of American citizenship and to the security of personal liberty by declaring that "all persons born or naturalized in the United States and subject to the jurisdiction thereof are citizens of the United States and of the state wherein they reside," and that "no state shall make or enforce any law which shall abridge the privileges or immunities of citizens of the United States; nor shall any state deprive any person of life, liberty, or property without due process of law, nor deny to any person within its jurisdiction the equal protection of the laws."

These two amendments, if enforced according to their true intent and meaning, will protect all the civil rights that pertain to freedom and citizenship. Finally, and to the end that no citizen should be denied on account of his race the privilege of participation in the political control of his country, it was declared by the Fifteenth Amendment that "the right of citizens of the United States to vote shall not be denied or abridged by the United States or by any state on account of race, color, or previous condition of servitude."

These notable additions to the fundamental law were welcomed by the friends of liberty throughout the world. They removed the race line from our governmental systems. They had, as this Court has said, a common purpose; namely, to secure "to a race recently emancipated, a race that through many generations have been held in slavery, all the civil rights that the superior race enjoy." They declared, in legal effect, this Court has further said, "that the law in the states shall be the same for the black as for the white; that all persons, whether colored or white, shall stand equal before the laws of the states, and, in regard to the colored race, for whose protection the amendment was primarily designed, that no discrimination shall be made against them by law because of their color."

We also said: "The words of the amendment, it is true, are prohibitory, but they contain a necessary implication of a positive immunity, or right, most valuable to the colored race—the right to exemption from unfriendly legislation against them distinctively as colored—exemption from legal discriminations, implying inferiority in civil society, lessening the security of their enjoyment of the rights which others enjoy, and discriminations which are steps toward reducing them to the condition of a subject race." It was, consequently, adjudged that a state law that excluded citizens of the colored race from juries because of their race and however well-qualified in other respects to discharge the duties of jurymen was repugnant to the Fourteenth Amendment. . . .

The decisions referred to show the scope of the recent amendments of the Constitution. They also show that it is not within the power of a state to prohibit colored citizens, because of their race, from participating as jurors in the administration of justice.

It was said in argument that the statue of Louisiana does not discriminate against either race, but prescribes a rule applicable alike to white and colored citizens. But this argument does not meet the difficulty. Everyone knows that the statute in question had its origin in the purpose, not so much to exclude white persons from railroad cars occupied by blacks as to exclude colored people from coaches occupied by or assigned to white persons. Railroad corporations of Louisiana did not make discrimination among whites in the matter of accommodation for travelers. The thing to accomplish was, under the guise of giving equal accommodation for whites and blacks, to compel the latter to keep to themselves while traveling in railroad passenger coaches. No one would be so wanting in candor as to assert the contrary.

The fundamental objection, therefore, to the statute is that it interferes with the personal freedom of citizens. "Personal liberty," it has been well said, "consists in the power of locomotion, of changing situation, or removing one's person to whatsoever places one's own inclination may direct, without imprisonment or restraint, unless by due course of law." . . . If a white man and a black man choose to occupy the same public conveyance on a public highway, it is their right to do so, and no government proceeding alone on grounds of race can prevent it without infringing the personal liberty of each.

It is one thing for railroad carriers to furnish, or to be required by law to furnish, equal accommodations for all whom they are under a legal duty to carry. It is quite another thing for government to forbid citizens of the white and black races from traveling in the same public conveyance, and to punish officers of railroad companies for permitting persons of the two races to occupy the same passenger coach. If a state can prescribe, as a rule of civil conduct, that whites and blacks shall not travel as passengers in the same railroad coach, why may it not so regulate the use of the streets of its cities and towns as to compel white citizens to keep on one side of a street and black citizens to keep on the other?

Why may it not, upon like grounds, punish whites and blacks who ride together in streetcars or in open vehicles on a public road or street? Why may it not require sheriffs to assign whites to one side of a courtroom and blacks to the other? And why may it not also prohibit the commingling of the two races in the galleries of legislative halls or in public assemblages convened for the consideration of the political questions of the day? Further, if this statute of Louisiana is consistent with the personal liberty of citizens, why may not the state require the separation in railroad coaches of native and naturalized citizens of the United States, or of Protestants and Roman Catholics?

The answer given at the argument to these questions was that regulations of the kind they suggest would be unreasonable and could not, therefore, stand before the law. Is it meant that the determination of questions of legislative power depends upon the inquiry whether the statute whose validity is questioned is, in the judgment of the courts, a reasonable one, taking all the circumstances into consideration? A statute may be unreasonable merely because a sound public policy forbade its enactment. But I do not understand that the courts have anything to do with the policy or expediency of legislation. A statute may be valid, and yet, upon grounds of public policy, may well be characterized as unreasonable. Mr. Sedgwick correctly states the rule when he says that the legislative intention being clearly ascertained, "the courts have no other duty to perform than to execute the legislative will, without any regard to their views as to the wisdom or justice of the particular enactment." . . .

There is a dangerous tendency in these latter days to enlarge the functions of the courts by means of judicial interference with the will of the people as expressed by the legislature. Our institutions have the distinguishing characteristic that the three departments of government are coordinate and separate. Each must keep within the limits defined by the Constitution, and the courts best discharge their duty by executing the will of the lawmaking power, constitutionally expressed, leaving the results of legislation to be dealt with by the people through their representatives.

Statues must always have a reasonable construction. Sometimes they are to be construed strictly; sometimes, liberally, in order to carry out the legislative will. But however construed, the intent of the legislature is to be respected if the particular state in question is valid, although the courts, looking at the public interests, may conceive the statute to be both unreasonable and impolitic. If the power exists to enact a statute, that ends the matter so far as the courts are concerned. The adjudged cases in which statutes have been held to be void because unreasonable are those in which the means employed by the legislature were not at all germane to the end to which the legislature was competent.

The white race deems itself to be the dominant race in this country. And so it is, in prestige, in achievements, in education, in wealth, and in power. So, I doubt not, it will continue to be for all time if it remains true to its great heritage and holds fast to the principles of constitutional liberty. But in view of the

Constitution, in the eye of the law, there is in this country no superior, dominant, ruling class of citizens. There is no caste here. Our Constitution is color-blind and neither knows nor tolerates classes among citizens.

In respect of civil rights, all citizens are equal before the law. The humblest is the peer of the most powerful. The law regards man as man and takes no account of his surroundings or of his color when his civil rights as guaranteed by the supreme law of the land are involved. It is therefore to be regretted that this land has reached the conclusion that it is competent for a state to regulate the enjoyment by citizens of their civil rights solely upon the basis of race.

In my opinion, the judgment this day rendered will, in time, prove to be quite as pernicious as the decision made by this tribunal in the Dred Scott Case. It was adjudged in that case that the descendants of Africans who were imported into this country and sold as slaves were not included nor intended to be included under the word "citizens" in the Constitution and could not claim any of the rights and privileges which that instrument provided for and secured to citizens of the United States; that at the time of the adoption of the Constitution they were "considered as a subordinate and inferior class of beings who had been subjugated by the dominant race, and, whether emancipated or not, yet remained subject to their authority, and had no rights or privileges but such as those who held the power and the government might choose to grant them.". . .

The recent amendments of the Constitution, it was supposed, had eradicated these principles from our institutions. But it seems that we have yet, in some of the states, a dominant race—a superior class of citizens, which assumes to regulate the enjoyment of civil rights, common to all citizens, upon the basis of race. The present decisions, it may well be apprehended, will not only stimulate aggressions, more or less brutal and irritating, upon the admitted rights of colored citizens, but will encourage the belief that it is possible, by means of state enactments, to defeat the beneficent purposes which the people of the United States had in view when they adopted the recent amendments of the Constitution, by one of which the blacks of this country were made citizens of the United States and of the states in which they respectively reside, and whose privileges and immunities as citizens the states are forbidden to abridge.

[Sixty million whites] are in no danger from the presence here of 8 million blacks. The destinies of the two races in this country are indissolubly linked together, and the interests of both require that the common government of all shall not permit the seeds of race hate to be planted under the sanction of law. What can more certainly arouse race hate, what more certainly create and perpetuate a feeling of distrust between these races than state enactments, which in fact, proceed on the ground that colored citizens are so inferior and degraded that they cannot be allowed to sit in public coaches occupied by white citizens? That, as all will admit, is the real meaning of such legislation as was enacted in Louisiana.

The sure guarantee of the peace and security of each race is the clear, distinct, unconditional recognition by our governments, national and state, of every right that inheres in civil freedom and of the equality before the law of all citizens of the United States without regard to race. State enactments regulating the enjoyment of civil rights upon the basis of race, and cunningly devised to defeat legitimate results of the war under the pretense of recognizing equality of rights, can have no other result than to render permanent peace impossible and to keep alive a conflict of races, the continuance of which must do harm to all concerned.

This question is not met by the suggestion that social equality cannot exist between the white and black races in this country. That argument, if it can be properly regarded as one, is scarcely worthy of consideration; for the social equality no more exists between two races when traveling in a passenger coach or a public highway than when members of the same races sit by each other in a streetcar or in the jury box, or stand or sit with each other in a political assembly, or when they use in common the streets of a city or town, or when they are in the same room for the purpose of having their names placed on the registry of voters, or when they approach the ballot box in order to exercise the high privilege of voting.

There is a race so different from our own that we do not permit those belonging to it to become citizens of the United States. Persons belonging to it are, with few exceptions, absolutely excluded from our country. I allude to the Chinese race. But by the statue in question, a Chinaman can ride in the same passenger coach with white citizens of the United States, while citizens of the black race in Louisiana, many of whom, perhaps, risked their lives for the preservation of the Union, who are entitled, by law, to participate in the political control of the state and nation, who are not excluded, by law or by reason of their race, from public stations of any kind, and who have all the legal rights that belong to white citizens, are yet declared to be criminals, liable to imprisonment, if they ride in a public coach occupied by citizens of the white race.

It is scarcely just to say that a colored citizen should not object to occupying a public coach assigned to his own race. He does not object, nor, perhaps, would he object to separate coaches for his race, if his rights under the law were recognized. But he objects, and ought never to cease objecting, to the proposition that citizens of the white and black races can be adjudged criminals because they sit, or claim the right to sit, in the same public coach on a public highway. The arbitrary separation of citizens, on the basis of race, while they are on a public highway, is a badge of servitude wholly inconsistent with the civil freedom and the equality before the law established by the Constitution. It cannot be justified upon any legal grounds.

If evils will result from the commingling of the two races upon public highways established for the benefit of all, they will be infinitely less than those that will surely come from state legislation regulating the enjoyment of civil rights upon the basis of race. We boast of the freedom enjoyed by our people above all other peoples. But it is difficult to reconcile that boast with a state of law which, practically, puts the brand of servitude and degradation upon a large class of our fellow citizens, our equals before the law. The thin disguise of "equal" accommodations for passengers in railroad coaches will not mislead anyone, nor atone for the wrong this day done.

The result of the whole matter is that while this Court has frequently adjudged, and at the present term has recognized the doctrine, that a state cannot, consistently with the Constitution of the United States, prevent white and black citizens, having the required qualifications for jury service, from sitting in the same jury box, it is now solemnly held that a state may prohibit white and black citizens form sitting in the same passenger coach on a public highway, or may require that they be separated by a "partition," when in the same passenger coach. . . .

I am of the opinion that the statute of Louisiana is inconsistent with the personal liberty of citizens, white and black, in that state, and hostile to both the spirit and letter of the Constitution of the United States. If laws of like character should be enacted in the several states of the Union, the effect would be in the highest degree mischievous. Slavery, as an institution tolerated by law, would, it is true, have disappeared from our country, but there would remain a power in the states, by sinister legislation, to interfere with the full enjoyment of the blessings of freedom; to regulate civil rights, common to all citizens, upon the basis of race; and to place in a condition of legal inferiority a large body of American citizens now constituting a part of the political community called the People of the United States, for whom, and by whom through representatives, our government is administered. Such a system is inconsistent with the guarantee given by the Constitution to each state of a republican form of government and may be stricken down by Congressional action or by the courts in the discharge of their solemn duty to maintain the supreme law of the land, anything in the constitution or law of any state to the contrary notwithstanding.

For the reasons stated, I am constrained to withhold my assent from the opinion and judgment of the majority.

Source: 163 U.S. 537

"Lift Every Voice and Sing" by James Weldon Johnson and J. Rosamond Johnson (1900)

Lift every voice and sing
Till earth and heaven ring,
Ring with the harmonies of Liberty;
Let our rejoicing rise
High as the listening skies,
Let it resound loud as the rolling sea.
Sing a song full of the faith that the dark past has
taught us,
Sing a song full of the hope that the present has
brought us,
Facing the rising sun of our new day begun
Let us march on till victory is won.

Stony the road we trod,
Bitter the chastening rod,
Felt in the days when hope unborn had died;
Yet with a steady beat,
Have not our weary feet
Come to the place for which our fathers sighed?
We have come over a way that with tears have been
watered,
We have come, treading our path through the blood
of the slaughtered,
Out from the gloomy past,
Till now we stand at last
Where the white gleam of our bright star is cast.

God of our weary years,
God of our silent tears,
Thou who has brought us thus far on the way;
Thou who has by Thy might
Led us into the light,
Keep us forever in the path, we pray.
Lest our feet stray from the places, Our God, where
we met Thee,
Lest, our hearts drunk with the wine of the world,
we forget Thee;
Shadowed beneath Thy hand,
May we forever stand.
True to our GOD,
True to our native land.

William Monroe Trotter's Protest against the
Segregation Policies of President Woodrow Wilson

One year ago we presented a national petition, signed by Afro-Americans in thirty-eight states, protesting against the segregation of employees of the national government whose ancestry could be traced in whole or in part to Africa, as instituted under your administration in the Treasury and Post Office departments. We then appealed to you to undo this race segregation in accord with your duty as president and with your pre-election pledges. We stated that there could be no freedom, no respect from others, and no equality of citizenship under segregation for races, especially when applied to but one of the many racial elements in the government employ. For such placement of employees means a charge by the government of physical indecency or infection, or of being a lower order of beings, or a subjection to the prejudices of other citizens, which constitutes inferiority of status. We protested such segregation as to working positions, eating tables, dressing rooms, rest rooms, lockers and especially public toilets in government buildings. We stated that such segregation was a public humiliation and degradation, entirely unmerited and far-reaching in its injurious effects, a gratuitous blow against ever-loyal citizens and against those many of whom aided and supported your elevation to the presidency of our common country.

At that time you stated you would investigate conditions for yourself. Now, after the lapse of a year, we have come back, having found that all forms of segregation of government employees of African extraction are still practiced in the Treasury and Post Office department buildings, and to a certain extent have spread into other government buildings.

Under the Treasury Department, in the Bureau of Engraving and Printing, there is segregation not only in dressing rooms, but in working positions. Afro-American employees being herded at separate tables, in eating, and in toilets. In the Navy Department there is herding at desks and separation in lavatories; in the Post Office Department there is separation in work for Afro-American women in the alcove on the eighth floor, of Afro-American men in rooms on the seventh floor, with forbidding even of entrance into an adjoining room occupied by white clerks on the seventh floor, and of Afro-American men in separate rooms just instituted on the sixth floor, with separate lavatories for Afro-American men on the eighth floor; in the main Treasury building in separate lavatories, which were specifically pointed out to you at our first hearing; in the state and other departments in separate lavatories; in marine hospital service building in separate lavatories; though there is but one Afro-American clerk to use it; in the War Department in separate lavatories; in the Post Office Department building separate lavatories; in the Sewing and Bindery Divisions of the Government Printing Office on the fifth floor there is herding at working positions of Afro-American women and separation in lavatories, and new segregation instituted by the division chief since our first audience with you. This lavatory segregation is the most degrading, most insulting of all. Afro-American employees who use the regular public lavatories on the floors where they work are cautioned and are then warned by superior officers against insubordination.

We have come by vote of this league to set before you this definite continuance of race segregation and to renew the protest and to ask you to abolish segregation of Afro-American employees in the Executive Department.

Because we cannot believe you capable of any disregard of your pledges we have been sent by the alarmed American citizens of color. They realize that if they can be segregated and thus humiliated by the national government at the national capital, the beginning is made for the spread of that persecution and prosecution which makes property and life itself insecure in the South, the foundation of the whole fabric of their citizenship is unsettled.

They have made plain enough to you their opposition to segregation last year by a national anti-segregation petition, this year by a protest registered at the polls, voting against every Democratic candidate save those outspoken against segregation. The only Democrat elected governor in the eastern states was Governor Walsh of Massachusetts, who appealed to you by letter to stop segregation. Thus have the Afro-Americans shown how they detest segregation.

In fact, so intense is their resentment that the movement to divide this solid race vote and make peace with the national Democracy, so suspiciously revived when you ran for the presidency, and which some of our families for two generations have been risking all to promote, bids fair to be undone.

Only two years ago you were heralded as perhaps the second Lincoln, and now the Afro-American leaders who supported you are hounded as false leaders and traitors to their race. What a change segregation has wrought!

You said that your "Colored fellow citizens could depend upon you for everything which would assist in advancing the interests of their race in the United States." Consider that pledge in the face of the continued color segregation! Fellow citizenship means congregation. Segregation destroys fellowship and citizenship. Consider that any passerby on the streets of the national capital, whether he be black or white, can enter and use the public lavatories in government buildings, while citizens of color who do the work of the government are excluded.

As equal citizens and by virtue of your public promises, we are entitled at your hands to freedom from discrimination, restriction, imputation and insult in

456

government employ. Have you a "new freedom" for white Americans and a new slavery for your "Afro-American fellow citizens"? God forbid!

We have been delegated to ask you to issue an Executive Order against any and all segregation of government employees because of race and color, and to ask whether you will do so. We await your reply, that we may give it to the waiting citizens of the United States of African extraction.

Source: *The Chicago Defender*, November 21, 1914.

Opinion of United States Supreme Court Justice Oliver Wendell Holmes in the Case of *Nixon v. Herndon*, March 7, 1927.

This is an action against the judges of elections for refusing to permit the plaintiff to vote at a primary election in Texas. It lays the damages at $5,000. The petition alleges that the plaintiff is a Negro, a citizen of the United States and of Texas, and a resident of El Paso, and in every way qualified to vote, as set forth in detail, except that the statue to be mentioned interferes with this right; that on July 26, 1924 a primary election was held at El Paso for the nomination of candidates for a senator and representatives in Congress and state and other offices, upon the Democratic ticket; that the plaintiff, being a member of the Democratic Party, sought to vote but was denied the right by defendants; that the denial Article 3039a, by the words of which "in no event shall a Negro be eligible to participate in a Democratic Party primary election held in the state of Texas," etc., and that this statute is contrary to the Fourteenth and Fifteenth Amendments to the Constitution of the United States.

The defendants moved to dismiss upon the ground that the subject matter of the suit was political and not within the jurisdiction of the court and that no violation of the amendments was shown. The suit was dismissed, and a writ of error was taken directly to this Court. Here no argument was made on behalf of the defendants, but a brief was allowed to be filed by the attorney general of the state.

The objection that the subject matter of the suit is political is little more than a play upon words. Of course, the petition concerns political action, but it alleges and seeks to recover for private damage. That private damage may be caused by such political action and may be recovered for in a suit at law hardly has been doubted for over 200 years.

If the defendants' conduct was a wrong to the plaintiff, the same reasons that allow a recovery for denying the plaintiff a vote at a final election allow it for denying a vote at the primary election that may determine the final result.

The important question is whether the statute can be sustained. But although we state it as a question, the answer does not seem to us open to a doubt. We find it unnecessary to consider the Fifteenth Amendment because it seems to us hard to imagine a more direct and obvious infringement of the Fourteenth. That amendment, while it applies to all, was passed, as we know, with a special intent to protect the blacks from discrimination against them (Slaughter House Cases). That amendment not only gave citizenship and the privileges of citizenship to persons of color, but it denied to any state the power to withhold from them the equal protection of the laws. . . . What is this but declaring that the law in the states shall be the same for the black as for the white; that all persons, whether colored or white, shall stand equal before the laws of the states, and, in regard to the colored race, for whose protection the amendment was primarily designed, that no discrimination shall be made against them by law because of their color? . . .

The statute of Texas in the teeth of the prohibitions referred to assumes to forbid Negroes to take part in a primary election, the importance of which we have indicated, discriminating against them by the distinction of color alone. States may do a good deal of classifying that it is difficult to believe rational, but there are limits, and it is too clear for extended argument that color cannot be made the basis of a statutory classification affecting the right set up in this case.

Source: 273 U.S. 536

The Origins of "Jim Crow"

Thomas "Daddy" Rice, a white minstrel performer, allegedly created "Jim Crow," a stereotypical Negro figure that became a famous minstrel show personality. Using the melody of a song entitled "Jump, Jim Crow," Rice performed a dance routine in blackface in which he "imitated the jerky movements and unintelligible utterance of a decrepit and malformed Negro he claimed he had once seen." In 1930, Rice published the song "Jump, Jim Crow," and since that time it has undergone numerous alterations. The version below is apparently from the early 1930s:

Come listen all you girls and boys
I'm just from Tuckahoe;
I'm going to sing a little song—
My name's Jim Crow.

CHORUS:

Wheel about, turn about,

Do just so;
Every time I wheel about
I jump Jim Crow.

I'm a roarer on the fiddle,
And down in old Virginny,
They say I play the scientific
Like Massa Pagganninny.
Then I go to Washington
With bank memorial;
But find they talk such nonsense
I spend my time with Sal.

Then I go to the President
He ask me what I do;
I put the veto on the boot
And nullify the shoe.

Then I go to New York,
To put them right all there;
But find so many tick heads
I give up in despair.

I walk down to the Battery
With Dina by my side;
And there we see Miss Watson,
the Paganini bride.

She sing so lovely that my heart
Go pit a pat just so;
I wish she'd fall in love with me,
I'd let Miss Dina go.

The term Jim Crow was later employed to denote racial segregation in public facilities throughout the nation.

An excerpt taken from the Decision of the United States Supreme Court in the Case of *Oliver Brown v. Board of Education of Topeka*, May 17, 1954.

Summary of Decision

In each of the four cases involved [*Brown v. Board of Education, Briggs v. Elliott, Davis v. County School Board of Prince Edward County*, and *Gebhart v. Belton*] the plaintiffs, Negro children, were denied admission to state public schools attended by white children under state laws requiring or permitting segregation according to race. There were findings below that the Negro and white schools involved had been equalized, or were being equalized, with respect to buildings, curricula, qualifications and salaries of teachers, and other tangible factors.

In an opinion by [Chief Justice Warren], the Supreme Court unanimously held that the plaintiffs, by reason of the segregation complained of, were deprived of the equal protection of the laws guaranteed by the Fourteenth Amendment. The "separate but equal" doctrine announced in *Plessy v. Ferguson*, involving equality in transportation facilities, under which equality of treatment is accorded by providing Negroes and whites substantially equal, though separate, facilities, was held to have no place in the field of public education.

In view of the complex problems presented by the formulation of the decrees, the cases were restored to the docket for argument by the parties.

Mr. Chief Justice Warren delivered the opinion of the Court:

These cases come to us from the States of Kansas, South Carolina, Virginia, and Delaware. They are premised on different facts and different local conditions, but a common legal question justifies their consideration together in this consolidated opinion.

In each of these cases, minors of the Negro race, through their legal representatives, seek the aid of the courts in obtaining admission to the public schools of their community on a nonsegregated basis. In each instance, they had been denied admission to schools attended by white children under laws requiring or permitting segregation according to race. This segregation was alleged to deprive the plaintiffs of the equal protection of the laws under the Fourteenth Amendment. In each of the cases other than the Delaware case, a three-judge federal district court denied relief to the plaintiffs on the so-called "separate but equal" doctrine announced by this Court in *Plessy v. Ferguson*. . . . Under that doctrine, equality of treatment is accorded when the races are provided substantially equal facilities, even though these facilities be separate. In the

Delaware case, the Supreme Court of Delaware adhered to that doctrine, but ordered that the plaintiffs be admitted to the white schools because of their superiority to the Negro schools.

The plaintiffs contend that segregated public schools are not "equal" and cannot be made "equal," and that hence they are deprived of the equal protection of the laws. Because of the obvious importance of the question presented, the Court took jurisdiction. Argument was heard in the 1952 Term, and reargument was heard this Term on certain questions propounded by the Court.

Reargument was largely devoted to the circumstances surrounding the adoption of the Fourteenth Amendment in 1868. It covered exhaustively consideration of the Amendment in Congress, ratification by the states, then existing practices in racial segregation, and the views of proponents and opponents of the Amendment. This discussion and our own investigation convince us that, although these sources cast some light, it is not enough to resolve the problem with which we are faced. At best, they are inconclusive. The most avid proponents of the post-War Amendments undoubtedly intended them to remove all legal distinctions among "all persons born or naturalized in the United States." Their opponents, just as certainly, were antagonistic to both the letter and the spirit of the Amendments and wished them to have the most limited effect. What others in Congress and the state legislatures had in mind cannot be determined with any degree of certainty.

An additional reason for the inconclusive nature of the Amendment's history, with respect to segregated schools, is the status of public education at that time. In the South, the movement toward free common schools, supported by general taxation, had not yet taken hold. Education of white children was largely in the hands of private groups. Education of Negroes was almost nonexistent, and practically all of the race were illiterate. In fact, any education of Negroes was forbidden by law in some states. Today, in contrast, many Negroes have achieved outstanding success in the arts and sciences as well as in the business and professional world. It is true that public school education at the time of the Amendment had advanced further in the North, but the effect of the Amendment on Northern States was generally ignored in the congressional debates. Even in the North, the conditions of public education did not approximate those existing today. The curriculum was usually rudimentary; ungraded schools were common in rural areas; the school term was but three months a year in many states; and compulsory school attendance was virtually unknown. As a consequence, it is not surprising that there should be so little in the history of the Fourteenth Amendment relating to its intended effect on public education.

In the first cases in this Court construing the Fourteenth Amendment, decided shortly after its adoption, the Court interpreted it as proscribing all state-imposed discriminations against the Negro race. The doctrine of "separate but equal" did not make its appearance in this Court until 1896 in the case of *Plessy v. Ferguson* . . . , involving not education but transportation. American courts have since labored with the doctrine for over half a century. In this Court, there have been six cases involving the "separate but equal" doctrine in the field of public education. In *Cumming v. County Board of Education* . . . and *Gong Lum v. Rice* . . . , the validity of the doctrine itself was not challenged. In more recent cases, all on the graduate school level, inequality was found in that specific benefits enjoyed by white students were denied to Negro students of the same educational qualifications. In none of these cases [*Missouri ex rel. Gaines v. Canada, Sipuel v. University of Oklahoma, Sweatt v. Painter,* and *McLaurin v. Oklahoma State Regents*] was it necessary to reexamine the doctrine to grant relief to the Negro plaintiff. And in *Sweatt v. Painter* . . . , the Court expressly reserved decision on the question whether *Plessy v. Ferguson* should be held inapplicable to public education.

In the instant cases, that question is directly presented. Here, unlike *Sweatt v. Painter,* there are findings below that the Negro and white schools involved have been equalized, or are being equalized, with respect to buildings, curricula, qualifications and salaries of teachers, and other "tangible" factors. Our decision, therefore, cannot turn on merely a comparison of these tangible factors in the Negro and white schools involved in each of the cases. We must look instead to the effect of segregation itself on public education.

In approaching this problem, we cannot turn the clock back to 1868 when the Amendment was adopted, or even to 1896 when *Plessy v. Ferguson* was written. We must consider public education in the light of its full development and its present place in American life throughout the Nation. Only in this way can it be determined if segregation in public schools deprives these plaintiffs of the equal protection of the laws.

Today, education is perhaps the most important function of state and local governments. Compulsory school attendance laws and the great expenditures for education both demonstrate our recognition of the importance of education to our democratic society. It is required in the performance of our most basic public responsibilities, even service in the armed forces. It is the very foundation of good citizenship. Today it is a principal instrument in awakening the child to cultural values, in preparing him for later professional training, and in helping him to adjust normally to his environment. In these days, it is doubtful that any child may reasonably be expected to succeed in life if he is denied the opportunity of an education. Such an opportunity, where the state has undertaken to provide it, is a right which must be made available to all on equal terms.

We come then to the question presented: Does segregation of children in public schools solely on the basis of race, even though the physical facilities and other "tangible" factors may be equal, deprive the children of the minority group of equal educational opportunities? We believe that it does.

In *Sweatt v. Painter* in finding that a segregated law school for Negroes could not provide them equal educational opportunities, this Court relied in large part on "those qualities which are incapable of objective measurement but which make for greatness in the law school." In *McLaurin v. Oklahoma State Regents* . . . the Court, in requiring that a Negro admitted to a white graduate school be treated like all other students, again resorted to intangible considerations: " . . . his ability to study, to engage in discussions and exchange views with other students, and, in general, to learn his profession." Such considerations apply with added force to children in grade and high schools. To separate them from others of similar age and qualifications solely because of their race generates a feeling of inferiority as to their status in the community that may affect their hearts and minds in a way unlikely ever to be undone. The effect of this separation on their educational opportunities was well stated by a finding in the Kansas case by a court which nevertheless felt compelled to rule against the Negro plaintiffs:

"Segregation of white and colored children in public schools has a detrimental effect upon the colored children. The impact is greater when it has the sanction of the law; for the policy of separating the races is usually interpreted as denoting the inferiority of the negro group. A sense of inferiority affects the motivation of a child to learn. Segregation with the sanction of law, therefore, has a tendency to [retard] the educational and mental development of Negro children and to deprive them of some of the benefits they would receive in a racial[ly] integrated school system."

Whatever may have been the extent of psychological knowledge at the time of *Plessy v. Ferguson,* this finding is amply supported by modern authority. Any language in *Plessy v. Ferguson* contrary to this finding is rejected.

We conclude that in the field of public education the doctrine of "separate but equal" has no place. Separate educational facilities are inherently unequal. Therefore, we hold that the plaintiffs and others similarly situated for whom the actions have been brought are, by reason of the segregation complained of, deprived of the equal protection of the laws guaranteed by the Fourteenth Amendment. This disposition makes unnecessary any discussion whether such segregation also violates the Due Process Clause of the Fourteenth Amendment.

Because these are class actions, because of the wide applicability of this decision, and because of the great variety of local conditions, the formulation of decrees in these cases presents problems of considerable complexity. On reargument, the consideration of appropriate relief was necessarily subordinated to the primary question—the constitutionality of segregation in public education. We have now announced that such segregation is a denial of the equal protection of the laws. In order that we may have the full assistance of the parties in formulating decrees, the cases will be restored to the docket, and the parties are requested to present further argument on Questions 4 and 5 previously propounded by the Court for the reargument this Term. The Attorney General of the United States is again invited to participate. The Attorneys General of the states requiring or permitting segregation in public education will also be permitted to appear as amici curiae upon request to do so by September 15, 1954, and submission of briefs by October 1, 1954.

It is so ordered.

Source: 347 US 483

An excerpt taken from the text of "I Have a Dream," a speech delivered by Dr. Martin Luther King, Jr. at the Lincoln Memorial in Washington, D.C., on August 28, 1963.

I am happy to join with you today in what will go down in history as the greatest demonstration for freedom in the history of our nation. Five score years ago a great American in whose symbolic shadow we stand today, signed the Emancipation Proclamation. This momentous decree came as a great beacon light of hope to millions of Negro slaves who had been seared in the flames of withering injustice. It came as a joyous daybreak to end the long night of their captivity.

In a sense we have come to our nation's capitol to cash a check. When the architects of our republic wrote the magnificent words of the Constitution and the Declaration of Independence, they were signing a promissory note to which every American was to fall heir. This note was a promise that all men, yes black men as well as white men, would be guaranteed the unalienable rights of life, liberty, and the pursuit of happiness. It is obvious today that America has defaulted on this promissory note insofar as her citizens of color are concerned. Instead of honoring this sacred obligation, America has given the Negro people a bad check: a check which has come back marked "insufficient funds." But we refuse to believe that the bank of justice is bankrupt. We refuse to believe that there are insufficient funds in the great vaults of opportunity of this nation. So we have come to cash this check—a check that will give us upon demand the riches of freedom and the security of justice.

We have also come to this hallowed spot to remind America of the fierce urgency of *now*. This is not the time to engage in the luxury of cooling off or to take the tranquilizing drug of gradualism. *Now* is the time. To make real the promises of democracy. *Now* is the time. To rise from the dark and desolate valley of segregation to the sunlit path of racial justice, *now* is the time. To lift our nation from the quicksands of racial injustice to the solid rock of brotherhood, *now* is the time. To make justice a reality for all of God's children.

It would be fatal for the nation to overlook the urgency of the moment and to underestimate the determination of the Negro. This sweltering summer of the Negro's legitimate discontent will not pass until there is an invigorating autumn of freedom and equality. Nineteen-hundred and sixty-three is not an end, but a beginning. Those who hope that the Negro needed to blow off steam, and will now be content will have a rude awakening if the Nation returns to business as usual. There will neither be rest nor tranquility in America until the Negro is granted his citizenship rights. The whirlwinds of revolt will continue to shake the foundations of our Nation until the bright day of justice emerges.

But there is something that I must say to my people who stand on the warm threshold which leads into the palace of justice. In the process of gaining our rightful place we must not be guilty of wrongful deeds. Let us not seek to satisfy our thirst for freedom by drinking from the cup of bitterness and hatred.

We must forever conduct our struggle on the high plane of dignity and discipline. We must not allow our creative protest to degenerate into physical violence. Again and again we must rise to the majestic heights of meeting physical force with soul force. The marvelous new militancy which has engulfed the Negro community must not lead us to a distrust of all white people, for many of our white brothers, as evidenced by their presence here today, have come to realize that their destiny is tied up with our destiny and their freedom is inextricably bound to our freedom. We cannot walk alone.

And as we walk, we must make the pledge that we shall always march ahead. We cannot turn back. There are those who are asking the devotees of civil rights, "when will you be satisfied?" We can never be satisfied as long as the Negro is the victim of the unspeakable horrors of police brutality. We can never be satisfied as long as our bodies, heavy with the fatigue of travel, cannot gain lodging in the motels of the highways and the hotels of the cities. We cannot be satisfied as long as the Negro's basic mobility is from a smaller ghetto to a larger one. We can never be satisfied as long as our children are stripped of their selfhood and robbed of their dignity by signs reading "For Whites Only." We can never be satisfied as long as a Negro in Mississippi cannot vote and a Negro in New York believes he has nothing for which to vote. No. No we are not satisfied, and we will not be satisfied until justice rolls down like waters and righteousness like a mighty stream.

I am not unmindful that some of you have come here out of great trials and tribulations. Some of you have come fresh from narrow jail cells. Some of you have come from areas where your quest for freedom left you battered by the storms of persecution and staggered by the winds of police brutality. You have been the victims of creative suffering. Continue to work with the faith that unearned suffering is redemptive.

Go back to Mississippi, go back to Alabama, go back to South Carolina, go back to Georgia, go back to Louisiana, go back to the slums and ghettos of our northern cities, knowing that somehow this situation can and will be changed. Let us not wallow in the valley of despair.

I say to you today, my friends, that in spite of the difficulties and frustrations of the moment, I still have a dream. It is a dream deeply rooted in the American dream. I have a dream that one day this nation will rise up and live out the true meaning of its creed: "We hold these truths to be self-evident—that all men are created equal."

I have a dream that one day on the red hills of Georgia the sons of former slaves and the sons of former slaveowners will be able to sit down together at the table of brotherhood. I have a dream that one day even the state of Mississippi, a desert state sweltering with the heat of injustice and oppression, will be transformed into an oasis of freedom and justice.

I have a dream that my four little children will one day live in a nation where they will not be judged by the color of their skin but by the content of their character.

I have a dream today.

I have a dream that one day the state of Alabama, whose governor's lips are presently dripping with the words of interposition and nullification, will be transformed into a situation where little black boys and black girls will be able to join hands with little white boys and white girls and walk together as sisters and brothers.

I have a dream today.

I have a dream that one day every valley shall be exalted, every hill and mountain shall be made low, the rough places will be made plain, and the crooked places will be made straight, and the glory of the Lord shall be revealed, and all flesh shall see it together.

This is our hope. This is the faith with which I return to the South. With this faith we will be able to hew out of the mountain of despair a stone of hope. With this faith we will be able to transform the jangling discords of our nation into a beautiful symphony of brotherhood. With this faith we will be able to work together, to pray together, to struggle together, to go to jail together, to stand up for freedom together, knowing that we will be free one day.

This will be the day when all of God's children will be able to sing with new meaning "My country 'tis of thee, sweet land of liberty, of thee I sing. Land where my fathers died, land of the pilgrim's pride, from every mountainside, let freedom ring."

And if America is to be a great nation this must become true. So let freedom ring from the prodigious hilltops of New Hampshire! Let freedom ring from the mighty mountains of New York! Let freedom ring from the heightening Alleghenies of Pennsylvania!

Let freedom ring from the snowcapped Rockies of Colorado!

Let freedom ring from the curvaceous peaks of California!

But not only that; let freedom ring from Stone Mountain of Georgia!

Let freedom ring from every hill and mole hill of Mississippi. From every mountainside, let freedom ring.

When we let freedom ring, when we let it ring from every village and every hamlet, from every state and every city, we will be able to speed up that day when all God's children, black men and white men, Jews and Gentiles, Protestants and Catholics, will be able to join hands and sing in the words of that old Negro spiritual, Free at last! Free at last! Thank God almighty, we are free at last!

Key Provisions of the Civil Rights Act of 1964

Title I - Voting Rights

Barred unequal application of registration procedures, and rejections for minor errors; made a sixth-grade education a rebuttable presumption of literacy;

required that literacy tests be administered in writing and that copies of the test and an individual's answers be furnished on request.

Title II - Public Accommodation

Barred discrimination in restaurants, hotels, motels, places of amusement and gasoline stations if the discrimination were "supported by state laws or action," or involved interstate commerce. It specifically exempted owner-occupied lodging houses with five or fewer rooms for rent (the "Mrs. Murphy" clause) and private clubs.

Title III - Desegregation of Public Facilities

Permitted the Justice Department to initiate suits to secure desegregation of state or locally owned, operated, or managed public facilities—parks, playgrounds, swimming pools, libraries, etc.

Title IV - Desegregation of Public Education

Authorized the attorney general to file school desegregation suits on written complaint, but did not cover busing of pupils or other such steps to end "racial imbalance." Required the United States Office of Education to make a survey and report to Congress within two years on the progress of desegregation of public schools at all levels.

Title V - Civil Rights Commission

Extended life of the Civil Rights Commission through January 31, 1968, and broadened the Commission's duties by authorizing it to serve as a national clearinghouse on civil rights information.

Title VI - Federally Assisted Programs

Barred discrimination under any federally assisted activity against any person because of race, color, or national origin; ordered federal agencies extending aid to issue rules (to be approved by the President) to carry out the title's provisions.

Title VII - Equal Employment Opportunity

Barred discrimination by employers or unions with 100 or more employees or members, but the number would be reduced over four years to 25 employees/ members or more.

Title VIII - Registration and Voting Statistics

Directed the Census Bureau to compile registration and voting statistics based on race, color, and national origin wherever recommended by the Civil Rights Commission.

Title IX - Intervention

Permitted the attorney general to intervene in private suits where persons alleged denial of equal protection of the laws under the Fourteenth Amendment and where he found the case to be of "general public importance."

Title X - Community Relations Service

Provided for a Community Relations Service in the Commerce Department to help communities resolve discrimination disputes.

Title XI - Miscellaneous

Guaranteed jury trials for criminal contempt cases under any part of the act but Title I, with a limit on the sentences of six months in prison and a $1,000 fine.

Title I or voting rights cases were covered by the 1957 jury-trial provision that a judge may try a case without a jury but that in such cases sentences were limited to a $300 fine and forty-five days in prison; in voting rights cases tried by jury, sentences were limited to six months and a fine of $1,000.

Public Law 88-352.

"Qualifications for Independence: We Must First Be Brothers," by the Honorable Elijah Muhammad, Spiritual Leader of the Nation of Islam.

The so-called American Negro needs self-education and the education of others in order to get the respect and recognition of others. He is not independent. He does not own any land that he can call his own. He does not have an organized government of his own; he needs even more than equal education. He needs superior education to that which is ruling the nations of the earth today.

It is essential for a nation—if they want recognition—to be united and to enjoy self-control and in a country of their own.

We call this independence. Now, we do not have self-education, self-control, or a country—not even some of this earth that we can call our own. We need a superior education or teaching in order to achieve the respect of others who are now enjoying such recognition.

The most essential qualification is the art of practicing that which we need in order to be accepted. Cleanliness, inwardly and outwardly, is number one on the list. Manners, along with general moral aspects, are second. The so-called American Negroes' warped minds and disrespect of self is one of the main objections of the self-respected societies.

There are no members of an educated and clean self-respecting society who want their society disgraced by a member who has ill and disrespecting morals. The so-called American Negroes (the majority of us) have been reared by southern white people who have the most profound hatred and dislike for us. And, this being true, they have made us (just as they did our foreparents) a degree below nothing for the last 400 years. At the same time, they frightened the so-called American Negro slaves to such a degree, they have no hope of ever being recognized as authorities among themselves.

They try to please the same white people as did our fathers under servitude and

470

slavery. Whether this "please" is for or against them, they will do it, because they fear the white man. We must remember that the Bible closes with announcing this fear in Revelation 21:8. Our people are afraid of the slave master and his children, afraid to displease them in their dislike of the salvation that has come to the slave, and God (Allah) has not offered the same to them (the slave master and his children).

The so-called Negro, who tries to please his master, displeases himself. He would love to see the Hereafter and live in a kingdom (a government) of peace and security, but he would not like to accept any such glory if this acceptance is not liked by the slave master. Therfore, he suffers the consequence of the slave master's children, which is referred to in Revelation 19:20 under the name beast (clearly symbolized as human beings in Revelation 19:19).

Destruction

Those who refuse (of the so-called Negroes) to accept God (Allah) as their King, and the people of God (Allah) as their brothers and nation, will suffer the destruction of hell-fire with the enemies.

You must wash and be clean as Isaiah 1:16 warns you. Proverbs 30:12 specifies us as a generation not washed. Hebrews 10:22 makes mention that it is necessary that our bodies be washed with pure water to enter into the recognition and respect of God (Allah). Revelation 1:5 reads in a parable of Jesus, who will wash us inwardly but from our sins. I want you to remember that this does not mean the Jesus who was here 2,000 years ago. It means a Jesus at the end of time. One whom Jesus prophesied God would sent under the title of a Comforter (in the Bible) and as Ahmad in the 61st Chapter of the Holy Qur'an.

Elijah Malachi had to first come and wash and clean up a people and make them self-respecting so that God would accept them in His presence. So, if we want white or Black to respect us, we must clean and wash ourselves of the filth in and out. No self-respecting nations will accept you as you are today, because of your ill-mannered behavior.

HURRY AND JOIN ONTO YOUR OWN KIND. THE TIME OF THIS WORLD IS NOW AT HAND!

Source: *Muhammad Speaks*, January 22, 1971, pp. 16-17.

The Muslim Program:

What the Muslims Want.

This is the question asked most frequently by both the whites and the blacks. The answers to this question I shall state as simply as possible.

1. We want freedom. We want a full and complete freedom.

2. We want justice. Equal justice under the law. We want justice applied equally to all, regardless of creed or class or color.

3. We want equality of opportunity. We want equal membership in society with the best in civilized society.

4. We want our people in America whose parents or grandparents were descendants from slaves, to be allowed to establish a separate state or territory of their own—either on this continent or elsewhere. We believe that our former slave masters are obligated to provide such land and that the area must be fertile and minerally rich. We believe that our former slave masters are obligated to maintain and supply our needs in this separate territory for the next 20 to 25 years—until we are able to produce and supply our own needs.

Since we cannot get along with them in peace and equality, after giving them 400 years of our sweat and blood and receiving in return some of the worst treatment human beings have ever experienced, we believe our contributions to this land and the suffering forced upon us by white America, justifies our demand for complete separation in a state or territory of our own.

5. We want freedom for all Believers of Islam now held in federal prisons. We want freedom for all black men and women now under death sentence in innumerable prisons in the North as well as the South.

We want every black man and woman to have the freedom to accept or reject being separated from the slave master's children and establish a land of their own.

We **know** that the above plan for the solution of the black and white conflict is the best and only answer to the problem between two people.

6. We want an immediate end to the police brutality and mob attacks against the so-called Negro throughout the United States.

We believe that the federal government should intercede to see that black men and women tried in white courts receive justice in accordance with the laws of the land—or allow us to build a new nation for ourselves, dedicated to justice, freedom, and liberty.

7. As long as we are not allowed to establish a state or territory of our own, we demand not only equal justice under the laws of the United States, but equal employment opportunities—**NOW!**

We do not believe that after 400 years of free or nearly free labor, sweat and blood, which has helped America become rich and powerful, that so many thousands of black people should have to subsist on relief, charity or live in poor houses.

8. We want the government of the United States to exempt our people from ALL taxation as long as we are deprived of equal justice under the laws of the land.

9. We want equal education—but separate schools up to 16 for boys and 18 for girls on the condition that the girls be sent to women's colleges and universities. We want all black children educated, taught and trained by their own teachers.

Under such schooling system we believe we will make a better nation of people. The United States government should provide, free, all necessary text books and equipment, schools and college buildings. The Muslim teachers shall be left free to teach and train their people in the way of righteousness, decency and self-respect.

10. We believe that intermarriage or race mixing should be prohibited. We want the religion of Islam taught without hindrance or suppression.

These are some of the things that we, the Muslims, want for our people in North America.

Source: *The Final Call*, Vol. 10, No. 8, April 8, 1991.

An excerpt taken from the Keynote Address delivered by Mayor Richard Hatcher of Gary, Indiana, at the National Black Political Convention held in Little Rock, Arkansas, on March 16, 1974.

After two years of wandering through the wilderness of Watergate, thank God we're together again.

After two years of reading the last rites over civil rights, thank God we're together again.

After two years of living in a land without a leader, thank God we're together again.

After two years of milk deals rather than fair deals, thank God we're together again.

After two years of cutting back on wheat and meat and heat, thank God we're together again.

After two years of grieving while West Africa filled with corpses, thank God we're together again.

After two years of watching white minorities oppress black majorities in Rhodesia and South Africa, thank God we're together again.

After two years of waiting in the wings while women's movements, Indian movements, ecology movements, and youth movements took center stage and precedence over black liberation, thank God we're together again.

We have come to Little Rock tonight to recommit ourselves to a common purpose.

We have come to Little Rock tonight to heal our wounds.

We have come to Little Rock to tell this country that our cries for justice will not be denied or turned aside.

We have come to Little Rock to demand a new era of black unity and leadership.

We have traveled more miles than any map will show from Gary, Indiana to Little Rock, Arkansas.

We were sure of ourselves, and of our newborn plans, in Gary. We must deal with deepening doubts and divisions today.

We challenged the heavens with visions in Gary. We hoped the sun would stand still until our cries for justice and equality were heard. We prayed that the red sea of racism would part and let us through to the promised land.

I am here tonight to tell you, to tell those incurable optimists among you that the age of miracles is over. The age of slogans is over. The age of progress without a plan is over. The age of striding without a strategy, of running without a flight plan is OVER! The waters of reaction are not going to turn into the wine of justice. Not today. Not tomorrow. Not ever. If we do not come together.

What we must understand here tonight, what our long struggle and suffering should have told us, is that if we are to survive as a people, we must save ourselves. Others can help, but we must assume the leadership in this struggle.

An excerpt taken from "The FBI and Dr. King's Assassination," by the Reverend Jesse Jackson.

What suggests that the FBI was involved?

1. The FBI had the greatest motive. Hoover's personal hatred of blacks, but especially Dr. King, is well-known and publicly documented. Others in authority at the FBI and many in the ranks shared his views, took his lead and carried out his wishes with great zeal.

The background of James Earl Ray, a professional subculture criminal, tends to lead one to believe that he would do anything for money, rather than engaging in criminal activity for a cause—racial or ideological. Hoover, on the other hand, wrote memos directing the FBI to "disrupt, discredit or otherwise destroy the black movement" and "to neutralize black leadership and prevent the rise of a black messiah."

2. The FBI is implicated in Dr. King's death because of actions taken by it. . . . The FBI used the same and similar surveillance and disruptive techniques against Dr. King that it used against Soviet agents. The FBI spent more of the taxpayer's money violating the constitutional rights of Dr. King then it did any other American citizen in the history of this country. Wiretaps were placed in his home and offices and in the homes and offices of associates and friends, as well as in hotel and motel rooms where he traveled. Attempts were made by the FBI to discredit him with churches, politicians, unions and financial supporters. The FBI attempted to manipulate the press by leaking alleged damaging information about Dr. King, cultivated reporters writing negative articles about him and attempted to prevent positive articles about him (and others by him) from appearing.

When Dr. King received the Nobel Peace Prize, the FBI tried to both sabotage receptions given by foreign heads of state and undermine a huge banquet and special "day" held in his honor. It attempted to use Cardinal Spellman to prevent King from having an audience with the Pope. The FBI sought to influence universities to withhold honorary degrees from Dr. King. It also attempted to use the IRS against him and his organization. They even sought to destroy King's marriage. Even two years after King's death, Hoover and the FBI continued to attempt to smear and discredit his accomplishments, honors, character and integrity, and to undermine Mrs. King's efforts to perpetuate his legacy.

The ACLU revealed FBI and right-wing political collusion which resulted in violence against the "Freedom Riders" of the 1960s, and the present Alabama attorney general alleges similar FBI and political actions during the civil rights movement in Alabama.

Pulitzer Prize-winning reporter Les Payne has revealed the strange actions by Memphis public safety director, Frank Holloman, in removing the black police officer in charge of security for Dr. King, Ed Redditt, just two hours before his assassination. Holloman spent 25 years working for the FBI (eight years as inspector-in-charge of J. Edgar Hoover's personal office) prior to his Memphis job. Dr. King had been under constant electronic and physical surveillance from the time he received the Nobel Peace Prize in 1964 until approximately an hour before his death by as many as 25 and never fewer than seven agents.

3. The FBI is implicated because of actions not taken by them. Their investigation lacked thoroughness. I was standing in the parking lot below the balcony talking with Dr. King when the shot was fired, yet the FBI has never interviewed me. Interviewing eyewitnesses is normally a routine matter. Rev. Ralph Abernathy, who was also present, has said that he has never been interviewed either. If the FBI overlooked routine investigative procedures, what else did it overlook?

If we knew as much about another organization (e.g. the Minutemen) as we knew about the FBI in relation to Dr. King, it would be difficult, even irresistible, for reasonable people not to conclude that the FBI was involved. We know it engaged in character assassination. It is the task of [the House Select Committee on Assassinations] to establish whether the FBI went further and engaged in physical assassination. . . .

Source: *The Atlanta Constitution*, September 11, 1978, p. 5A.

An excerpt taken from the editorial "The South Doesn't Want to Go Back."

The South owes its modern dynamism to the freedom its people won in the 1960s from the chains of racial segregation, chains which had weighed us down, black and white equally, and had marked the region off from the national mainstream. This freedom was hard-wrought in social, legal, and legislative struggles. It was paid for, sometimes, with lives. . . .

The new era has freed up the natural talent of the region, relieving it of the fatiguing preoccupation with race. It has opened the region to an enlivening, creative admixture of new residents and modern business. . . .

Few understand the importance of these changes better than the South's current governors. Governor-elect George Wallace, could return in Alabama only by convincing black voters he had put Jim Crow behind him.

This progress is now being challenged, not from within the South but from without, from Washington. Perhaps the danger is not yet great, but it is real. Where the federal government was once an active and needed partner in the birth of the modern South, a new and perverse federal activism toys with racial politics, even to the point of trying to roll back integration. Its efforts, increasingly visible, risk inciting residual constituencies which would demand that Southern politics play to them once again. . . .

By common account, nothing makes President Reagan bristle more than suspicions he is racist or even that he is racially insensitive. The President, then, must not know all that is being done in his name, or perhaps, he does not understand the potential burden of his administration's regressive activism. . . .

The administration had undercut the high purpose of the U.S. Civil Rights Commission, purposes sustained through six previous presidencies under both political parties, with appointees who oppose the Commission's fundamental charge. It has offered tax exemption to racially discriminatory schools. It has cut civil rights enforcement, especially in employment, where the administration has confused affirmative action with quotas. It has reinterpreted laws to release numerous federally financed programs from compliance with the Civil Rights Act. . . .

President Reagan may not realize that it is so, but his administration is playing with fire, and it is playing with it most dangerously in the South. Our governors dare not wait until they smell smoke before they answer the alarm bell.

Source: *The Atlanta Constitution*, December 15, 1982.

An excerpt taken from "Martin Luther King, Jr.: A Dream Deterred," by Hodding Carter III.

The 15th anniversary of Martin Luther King Jr.'s assassination was marked by memorial services across the country this week, and that was just about all there was to it for white America and much of black America as well. It has been less than two decades, but in many ways those tumultuous, riotous days of the late 1960s might as well have occurred 200 years ago, so far removed do we seem from the passion and commitment of those times.

But that is a surface impression, misleading and finally wrong in its implications. The events of the 1960s and early 1970s had profound effects on the nation, forcing some changes and eventually fueling the reaction which culminated with the election of Ronald Reagan in 1980. The question now is whether the Reagan counter-revolution is the wave of the future, and therefore, of a profoundly changed America, or whether the vast array of unfinished racial business from the late 1960s will set the agenda for tomorrow.

Mr. King's assassination came after he had moved his campaign away from a relatively easy task, that of forcing America to face up to the inherent contradiction of a South which lived by a code of white supremacy within a nation whose basic documents spoke to the equality of all men. It was not actually easy, of course, because never-never defiance went beyond lip service in the South and adherence to equal rights for all often went no further than lip service in the North. But as the late, great activist Al Lowenstein once remarked, the police dogs in Birmingham did have the salutary effect of selling civil rights in Des Moines, and the President and Congress responded to public outrage by pulling down the pillars of legalized segregation. . . .

Structural racism was deeply embedded and it would take a wrenching act of collective will to alter that reality. Towards that end, the civil-rights forces turned to fields in which there was no consensus: affirmative action and quotas, busing and guaranteed income. Mr. King was killed in the midst of a campaign on behalf of municipal workers in Memphis who were overwhelmingly black. His earlier march through Cicero, Illinois, had convinced many Northern whites that he had quit preaching and, as the old joke had it, gone to meddling.

There have been advances since 1968 that shouldn't be ignored. But the final dominant theme from Washington and the nation has been that enough is enough. "What do these people want?" is a common question. The failures of some of the new approaches, the anxiety of some groups as they saw their own cherished prerogatives and accomplishments threatened by demands for what seemed to be preferential treatment for blacks, the bone-deep racism of others whose actions could be altered by law but whose beliefs were unchanged: all created a politically fertile field the plowmen weren't long in coming.

Richard Nixon and the George Wallace of old spoke in different accents but to the same purpose. . . . The Carter presidency briefly reversed the trend, but with the election of President Reagan, Wallace and Nixon were merged and what had been subtle became overt. The new administration was determined to undo much of the work of the past and rescind the accomplishments of the Second Reconstruction. If that seems an unfair assessment to the President and his partisans, it understates the way blacks perceive his administration's words and deeds. . . .

Lincoln notwithstanding, it is possible for a nation to endure half-slave and half-free. They do exist around the globe. All it takes is force. . . . If what is going forward in Washington, with the implied consent of a majority of the people, isn't repudiated soon, we should alter the Great Seal. The old dream, the dream not just of a black Southern minister but of the white framers of the Declaration of Independence, was what set us apart from the Old World. We haven't lived up to the dream, but at least we preserved it, holding it out as the goal for all Americans. To watch this administration do its work is to watch the deliberate destruction of all that the dream proclaims. It can work, but it will take high walls and far more guards. It can work, but it won't be America.

Source: *The Wall Street Journal*, April 7, 1983.

An excerpt taken from "A Letter to My Delegates on the Road to Atlanta," by the Reverend Jesse Jackson.

Dr. Martin Luther King said in his last speech in Memphis. . . . "I've been to the mountaintop. . . . And I've seen the promised land. I may not get there. . . . But . . . we as a people will get to the promised land."

This was his way of saying that the campaign for jobs, peace and justice has no end. Even as we achieve our goals, we will still have to work to secure them. That is what is meant by "eternal vigilance"—the struggle for liberty and equality is never done.

At the base of our campaign is the tenacity of Fanny Lou Hamer, the lives of Viola Luizzo, of Jimmy Lee Jackson, of the Rev. James Reed, of the darling little children of Birmingham, Alabama, of Vincent Chin—those who gave their lives that we might be free. Their blood helped to purify our nation. They cry out from their graves for us to continue the struggle to keep America strong and to make America better.

Thus the campaign for a new and fair equation is both ancient and without end. It requires that we set a moral tone, seek new human priorities, offer a vision to the nation and have a will to serve.

These are the roots, the commitments from which our campaign grows. This is no ordinary campaign. We are not just running for votes and for delegates. We are seeking to save the soul of our nation. We are seeking to uplift those who have been locked out. We are working to fulfill the prayers and the dreams of our grandparents who did not have the right to vote. We are struggling to make life better for our children and for the generations yet unborn. . . .

Let no one mislead you. This is not the time for the campaign to wind down, but the time for it to build up and expand. The Democratic National Convention (DNC) will be the high point of the primary season. Intensity will increase. The tension produced will be a creative tension that makes change possible. Healthy deliberation and debate stirs the soul of democracy. . . .

In Atlanta, the key issues will concern direction and priorities for the party and the country. In Atlanta we will debate these fundamental questions. From debate and deliberation will come decision. That is how a consensus is formed and a mandate to lead is forged. . . .

Recently there have been attempts by those who do not understand the historic roots of our campaign to reduce it to a personal quest for power or position. What does Jesse want?—a contemptuous question, disrespectful and distorted. It is not a question of what Jesse wants, it is a question of what we have built. For we go to Atlanta representing millions who have found common ground on a basic agenda, an agenda of jobs, peace and justice.

It is not about a job or title or a position that I seek. It is about a mission, a tradition, a cause that we serve. . . .

Source: The *Atlanta Constitution*, July 13, 1988.

Estimates of Amounts of Money Raised for the African National Congress (ANC) by Nelson Mandela During His Ten Day Tour of the United States.

NEW YORK: Fund-raising income: $1.75 million, expected to rise to nearly $2 million. Local fund-raising expenses: About $150,000. Municipal expenses: $2.6 million, including $2 million in police overtime.

BOSTON: Fund-raising income: About $500,000. Local fund-raising expenses: About $150,000. Municipal expenses: About $130,000, including $110,000 in police overtime.

WASHINGTON: Fund-raising income: About $150,000. Local fund-raising expenses: Less than income. Municipal expenses: Undetermined.

ATLANTA: Fund-raising income: Projected at about $400,000. Local fund-raising expenses: Perhaps $100,000 in police overtime.

MIAMI: Fund-raising income: About $300,000 donated by members of the American Federation of State, County and Municipal Employees, which Mr. Mandela addressed. Municipal expenses: About $20,000 in police overtime.

DETROIT: Fund-raising income: About $1.4 million. Local fund-raising expenses: Less than $250,000. Municipal expenses: Undetermined.

LOS ANGELES: Fund-raising income: About $1.7 million. Municipal expenses: Undetermined.

OAKLAND, CALIF: Fund-raising income: About $900,000. Municipal expenses: Undetermined.

Source: The Associated Press, 1990.

TABLE A Percentage of Southern Blacks in Predominately-White Schools

Year	Percentage
1968	18.4
1970	39.1
1972	44.4

TABLE B Percentage of Southern Blacks in All-Black Schools

Year	Percentage
1968	68
1970	14.1
1972	9.2

Source: United States Department of Health, Education, and Welfare (Office of Civil Rights)

TABLE C Black Elected Officials, 1969, 1973, 1974

Year	Number
1969	1,185
1973	2,621
1974	2,991

Source: Joint Center for Political Studies

TABLE D Black Elected Officials in the South, 1969, 1974

Year	Number	Increase
1969	299	
1974	805	169%

Source: Voter Education Project, Atlanta, Georgia

TABLE E Black Owned Insurance Companies in the United States, 1974

State	Number of Firms
Alabama	6
California	1
Florida	2
Georgia	3
Illinois	3
Louisiana	12
New York	1
North Carolina	2
Pennsylvania	3
Virginia	2

Source: United States Department of Commerce

TABLE F Black Officials Elected in Eleven Southern States, 1974

Office	Number
U. S. Congress	3
State Senate	9
State Houses	74
Municipal Legislatures	226
County Legislatures	55
School Boards	101
Mayors	8
Judges	4
Magistrates	14
Coroners	4
Justices of the Peace	10
Vice Mayors	3
City Recorders	1
Tax Collectors	1
Constables	3
Law Enforcement Officers	9

Source: Voter Education Project

TABLE G Blacks in the Military: Where They Serve (1986)

Service	Number of Blacks	Percentage
Army	205,192	26.9
Marines	36,954	18.8
Air Force	90,975	15.0
Navy	71,385	12.6

Source: United States Department of Defense

TABLE H The Nation's Largest Black–Owned Banks

Bank	Location/Year Started	Assets 12/31/87	Assets 9/30/88
IndeCorp	Chicago, IL 1964	106 mil.	227 mil.*
Seaway National Bank	Chicago, IL 1965	145 mil.	148 mil.
Freedom National Bank	New York, NY 1964	124 mil.	123 mil.
Industrial Bank	Washington, D.C. 1934	107 mil.	109 mil.
Citizens Trust Bank	Atlanta, GA 1921	106 mil.	105 mil.
First Independence National Bank	Detroit, MI 1970	87 mil.	105 mil.
Mechanics and Farmers	Durham, NC 1908	84 mil.	87 mil.
First Texas Bank	Dallas, TX 1975	79 mil.	87 mil.
City National Bank	Newark, NJ 1973	68 mil.	62 mil.
Consolidated Bank & Trust	Richmond, VA 1903	62 mil.	60 mil.

*As of February, 1989.

Sources: *Black Enterprise* magazine, *Reuters*, the *Atlanta–Journal Consitution*

TABLE I The Top Ten Black-Owned Banks in Return On Average Assets (ROA)

Bank	Location	ROA* (Percent)
1. United National Bank	Fayetteville, NC	1.57
2. Highland Community Bank	Chicago, IL	1.39
3. Seaway National Bank	Chicago, IL	1.36
4. IndeCorp	Chicago, IL	1.21
5. Tri-State Bank	Memphis, TN	1.17
6. Mechanics and Farmers Bank	Durham, NC	1.03
7. Consolidated Bank and Trust	Richmond, VA	0.37
8. First Texas Bank	Dallas, TX	0.86
9. Industrial Bank	Washington, D.C.	0.86
10. Citizens Trust Bank	Atlanta, GA	0.70

All FDIC-Insured Banks Average
*Return on Average Assets as of September 30, 1988

Sources: Sheshunoff Information Services, Inc., the *Atlanta-Journal Constitution*

TABLE J Black Population

The states with the highest number of blacks in 1985 and the change from the 1980 Census

State	1985	Change from 1980
1. New York	2,733,100	218,500
2. California	2,074,300	242,800
3. Texas	1,909,500	201,300
4. Illinois	1,774,800	93,400
5. Georgia	1,600,400	134,600
6. Florida	1,565,100	215,100
7. North Carolina	1,392,300	72,000
8. Louisiana	1,348,400	108,700
9. Michigan	1,242,900	43,200
10. Ohio	1,136,400	55,100

Source: United States Department of Commerce, Bureau of the Census

Changes in Racial Attitudes, 1963 - 1987

In your opinion, how well do you think blacks are treated in your community- the same as whites, not very well, or badly?

	1967		1978		1980		1987	
	White	Black	White	Black	White	Black	White	Black
Same as whites	76%	44%	71%	44%	68%	45%	64%	44%
Not very well	15%	44%	13%	39%	68%	45%	21%	44%
Badly	1%	9%	3%	10%	3%	14%	3%	8%
No opinion	8%	3%	13%	7%	12%	10%	12%	4%

Source: Gallup Poll

In general, do you think blacks have as good a chance as white people in your community to get any kind of job for which they are qualified, or don't you think they have as good a chance?

Do you believe that where there has been job discrimination against blacks in the past, preference in hiring or promotion should be given to blacks today?

	1963	1978
As good	43%	67%
Not as good	48%	24%
No opinion	9%	9%

	1985	1987
Yes, preference	43%	37%
No	46%	57%
Don't know/NA	12%	6%

Source: Gallup Poll   Source: CBS/New York Times Poll

Percentages for bottom two questions are from black and white respondents.

1989 Salaries of Notable African-American Professional Athletes

Basketball

Athlete	Team	1989 Salary
Patrick Ewing	New York Knicks	3.25 million
Kareem Abdul-Jabbar	Los Angeles Lakers	3 million
Earvin Johnson	Los Angeles Lakers	2.5 million
Michael Jordan	Chicago Bulls	2.15 million
Isiah Thomas	Detroit Pistons	2 million
Ralph Sampson	Golden State Warriors	1.97 million
Akeem Olajuwon	Houston Rockets	1.67 million
Alex English	Denver Nuggets	1.65 million
Danny Manning	Los Angeles Clippers	1.65 million
Dominique Wilkins	Atlanta Hawks	1.54 million
Charles Barkley	Philadelphia 76ers	1.53 million
Moses Malone	Atlanta Hawks	1.5 million
Brad Daugherty	Cleveland Cavaliers	1.41 million
Joe Barry Carroll	New Jersey Nets	1.39 million
Terry Cummings	Milwaukee Bucks	1.38 million
Robert Parish	Boston Celtics	1.36 million
Karl Malone	Utah Jazz	1.35 million
Buck Williams	New Jersey Nets	1.35 million
James Worthy	Los Angeles Lakers	1.3 million
Adrian Dantley	Dallas Mavericks	1.25 million
Bill Cartwright	Chicago Bulls	1.22 million
Clyde Drexler	Portland Trailblazers	1.2 million
Dale Ellis	Seattle Supersonics	1.1 million
Bernard King	Washington Bullets	1.1 million
Byron Scott	Los Angeles Lakers	1.1 million
Sidney Moncrief	Milwaukee Bucks	1.1 million
Wayman Tisdale	Indiana Pacers	1 million
Benoit Benjamin	Los Angeles Clippers	1 million
Charles Oakley	New York Knicks	1 million
Maurice Cheeks	Philadelphia 76ers	1 million
Charles Smith	Los Angeles Clippers	1 million

Baseball

Athlete	Team	1989 Salary
Dwight Gooden	New York Mets	2.41 million
Jim Rice	Boston Red Sox	2.35 million
Ozzie Smith	St. Louis Cardinals	2.34 million
Eddie Murray	Los Angeles Dodgers	2.33 million

Rickey Henderson	NY Yankees/Oakland A's	2.12 million
Willie Wilson	Kansas City Royals	2.11 million
Tim Raines	Montreal Expos	2.1 million
Andre Dawson	Chicago Cubs	2.1 million
Kirby Puckett	Minnesota Twins	2 million
Dave Winfield	New York Yankees	1.98 million
George Bell	Toronto Blue Jays	1. 9 million
Pedro Guerrero	St. Louis Cardinals	1. 83 million
Joe Carter	Cleveland Indians	1.63 million
Juan Samuel	Philadelphia Phillies	1.45 million
Lee Smith	Boston Red Sox	1.42 million
Darryl Strawberry	New York Mets	1.42 million
Willie McGee	St. Louis Cardinals	1.4 million
Tony Fernandez	Toronto Blue Jays	1.4 million
Eric Davis	Cincinnati Reds	1.35 million
Jesse Barfield	Toronto Blue Jays	1.4 million
Lloyd Moseby	Toronto Blue Jays	1.3 million
Chill Davis	California Angels	1.27 million
Alvin Davis	Seattle Mariners	1.25 million
Tony Gwynn	San Diego Padres	1.21 million
Harold Baines	Chicago White Sox	1.2 million
Tony Pena	St. Louis Cardinals	1.1 million
Danny Tartabull	Kansas City Royals	1.03 million
Lou Whitaker	Detroit Tigers	1.02 million
Frank White	Kansas City Royals	1 million
Mookie Wilson	New York Mets	1 million
Alfredo Griffin	Los Angeles Dodgers	1 million

Football

Athlete	Team	1989 Salary
Warren Moon	Houston Oilers	1.5 million
Herschel Walker	Dallas Cowboys	1.4 million
Randall Cunningham	Philadelphia Eagles	1.35 million
Bo Jackson	Los Angeles Raiders	1.26 million
Eric Dickerson	Indianapolis Colts	1.21 million
Wilbur Marshall	Washington Redskins	1.15 million
Doug Wililams	Washington Redskins	1 million
Lawrence Taylor	New York Giants	1 million
Marcus Taylor	Los Angeles Raiders	1 million

A Selected Bibliography

Major Repositories

The major collections of materials in African-American History are the Amistad Collection at Tulane University, the Moorland Collection at Howard University, the Slaughter Collection at Atlanta University, The James Weldon Johnson Collection at Yale University, the Washington Collection and the Records and Research Center at Tuskegee University, the Schomburg Collection at the New York Public Library, and the Hampton University Library.

Bibliographical Aids

For a long time the best aid in the study of black Americans was Monroe N. Work, *A Bibliography of the Negro in Africa and America* (1928). It continues to have some value, especially for the pre-twentieth-century periods, but has been largely supplanted, particularly with respect to the United States, by James M. McPherson, et al., *Blacks in America: Bibliographical Essays* (1971).

The standard African-American history text is John Hope Franklin, *From Slavery to Freedom* (sixth edition, 1988). Other general surveys are Lerone Bennett, *Before the Mayflower* (revised edition, 1966), a well-illustrated journalistic text; August Meier and Elliott M. Rudwick, *From Plantation to Ghetto* (1966), a reasoned interpretive study despite some factual errors; Rayford Logan, *The Negro in the United States* (1957); Eli Ginzberg and Alfred S. Eichner, *The Troublesome Presence: Democracy and the Negro*. The pioneer general works include: George Washington Williams, *History of the Negro Race in America, 1619-1880* (2 vols., 1883); James W. Pennington, *Text Book of the Origin and History of the Colored People* (1841); William T. Alexander, *History of the Colored Race in*

America (1887); Harold M. Tarver, *The Negro in the History of the United States from the Beginning of the English Settlements in 1607 to the Present Time* (1905); E. A. Johnson, *School History of the Negro Race* (1893); Booker T. Washington, *The Story of the Negro* (1909); Willis D. Weatherford, *The Negro from Africa to America* (1924); Charles S. Johnson, *The Negro in American Civilization* (1930); Benjamin Brawley, *The Negro Genius* (1937); Benjamin G. Brawley, *A Short History of the American Negro* (1913); Carter G. Woodson and Charles H. Wesley, *The Negro in Our History* (tenth edition, 1962); and Edwin R. Embree, *Brown Americans* (1945). Thomas F, Gossett, *Race: The History of an Idea in America* (1963) and Winthrop Jordan, *White over Black* (1968) as well as Louis Ruchames, *Racial Thought in America: From the Puritans to Abraham Lincoln* (1969) are reputable surveys of American racial attitudes. The best of the older biographical compilations is Richard Bardolph, *The Negro Vanguard* (1961 edition). Other useful biographical compilations are Benjamin Brawley, *Negro Builders and Heroes* (1937); Russell L. Adams, *Great Negroes Past and Present* (1963); and Langston Hughes, *Famous Negro Heroes of America* (1965). The better general studies in the intellectual and social history of African-Americans include: Horace Mann Bond, *The Education of the Negro in the American Social Order* (1934); Alain Locke, *Negro Art* (1936); Carter G. Woodson, *History of the Negro Church* (1921); Benjamin E. Mays and Joseph Nicholson, *The Negro's Church* (1933); E. Franklin Frazier, *The Negro Church in America* (1963); Joseph R. Washington, *Black Religion* (1964); Benjamin Brawley, *The Negro in Literature and Art in the United States* (1921); Hugh M. Gloster, *The Negro in American Fiction* (1948); Robert Bone, *The Negro Novel in America* (1958); Frederick G. Detweiler, *The Negro Press in the United States* (1922).

There are a number of collections of essays and readings in African-American history. The better of the older ones include: Talcott Parsons and Kenneth Clark, eds., *The Negro American* (1966); Howard Brotz, *Negro Social and Political Thought 1850-1920: Representative Texts* (1966); Dwight Hoover, ed., *Understanding Negro History* (1968); Langston Hughes and Milton Meltzer, *Pictorial History of the Negro in America* (1968), especially valuable for young readers; Melvin Drimmer, ed., *Black History* (1969); August Meier and Elliott M. Rudwick, eds., *The Making of Black History* (2 vols., 1969); Allen Weinstein and Frank O. Catell, eds., *The Segregation Era, 1863-1954* (1970); William G. Shade and Roy Herrenkohl, eds., *Seven on Black* (1969); Eric Foner, ed., *America's Black Past* (1970).

Useful collections of sources include Encyclopedia Brittanica's *The Negro in American History* (3 vols., 1969); Herbert Aptheker, ed., *A Documentary History of the Negro People in the United States* (1951), an especially good treatment of the nineteenth century; Gilbert Osofsky, ed., *The Burden of Race* (1967); William Loren Katz, ed., *Eyewitness: The Negro in American History* (1967); Leslie H. Fishel and Benjamin Quarles, eds., *The Negro American: A Documentary History* (1967), replacing Aptheker as the standard documentary work.

The better of the more recent surveys and collections of sources include Mary Frances Berry and John Blassingame, *Long Memory: The Black Experience in America* (1982); Philip S. Foner, *History of Black Americans* (3 vols., 1975), Vincent Franklin, *Black Self-Determination: A Cultural History of the Faith of the Fathers* (1984); Darlene Clark Hine, ed., *The State of Afro-American History* (1986); Vincent Harding, *There Is a River: The Black Struggle for Freedom in America* (1981); August Meier and Elliott Rudwick, *Black History and the Historical Profession, 1915-1980* (1986); Rayford W. Logan and Michael Winston, eds., *Dictionary of American Negro Biography* (1982); and Edgar A. Toppin, *A Biographical History of Blacks in America Since 1528* (1971); Samella Lewis, *Art: African-American* (1978); LeRoi Jones, *Blues People: Negro Music in White America* (1963); Eileen Southern, *The Music of Black Americans: A History* (1971); Robert Hayden, et al., eds., *Afro-American Literature: An Introduction* (1971); Robert B. Stepto and Michael S. Harper, eds., *Chant of Saints: A Gathering of Afro-American Literature, Art, and Scholarship* (1979); Jack Lyle, ed., *The Black American and the Press* (1968); and Henry Lewis Suggs, ed., *The Black Press in the South* (1981).

Out of Africa

Some of the better histories delineating African history, the slave trade, and slavery in the West Indies are: Maurice Delafosse, *The Negroes of Africa: History and Culture* (1931); Basil Davidson, *The Lost Cities of Africa* (revised edition, 1970); Melville J. Herskovits, *Myth of the Negro Past* (reprint, 1958); Roland F. Oliver, *Africa in the Iron Age* (1975); Daniel R. Mannix, *Black Cargoes: A History of the Atlantic Slave Trade, 1518-1865* (1962); Philip D. Curtin, *The Atlantic Slave Trade: A Census* (1969); Eric Williams, *Capitalism and Slavery* (1944); Leo Wiener, *Africa and the Discovery of America* (3 vols., 1922); Ivan Van Sertima, *They Came before Columbus* (1976); Rayford W. Logan, "Estevanico, Negro Discoverer of the Southwest," *Phylon* (Fourth Quarter, 1940); Lowell J. Ragats, *The Fall of the Planter Class in the British Caribbean* (1928); Herbert S. Klein, *Slavery in the Americas* (1967); David Barry Gaspar, *Bondsmen and Rebels: A Study of Master-Slave Relations in Antigua* (1985); Franklin W. Knight, *The African Dimension in Latin American Societies* (1970); and Carl N. Degler, *Neither Black nor White: Slavery and Race Relations in Brazil and the United States* (1971).

Involuntary Servitude, 1619-1860

The slave period in African-American history is exhaustively treated. Some of the more useful of the older works include: Oscar and Mary Handlin, "Origins of the Southern Labor System," *William and Mary Quarterly* (1950); Carl Degler, "Slavery and the Genesis of American Race Prejudice," *Comparative Studies in Society and History* (1959); Winthrop D. Jordan, "The Influence of the West Indies on the Origins of New England Slavery," *William and Mary Quarterly* (1961); Eugene Sirmans, "The Legal Status of the Slave in South Carolina, 1670-1740," Winthrop D. Jordan, "Modern Tensions and the Origins of American Slavery," *Journal of Southern History* (1962); Eugene D. Genovese, "The Legacy of Slavery and the Roots of Black Nationalism," *Studies on the Left* (1966), a controversial essay which can best be read in conjunction with the criticisms of Herbert Aptheker and C. Vann Woodward in the same issue. See also Robert Twombly and Robert H. Moore, "Black Puritan: The Negro in Seventeenth-Century Massachusetts," *William and Mary Quarterly* (1967); Edward R. Turner, "Slavery in Colonial Pennsylvania," *Pennsylvania Magazine of History and Biography* (1911); Don B. Kates, "Abolition, Deportation, Integration: Attitudes Toward Slavery in the Early Republic," *Journal of Negro History* (1968); Ernest J. Clarke, "Aspects of the North Carolina Slave Code, 1715-1860," *North Carolina Historical Review* (1962); Harold D. Woodman, "The Profitability of Slavery: An Historical Perennial," *Journal of Southern History* (1963); John H. Moore, "Simon Gray, Riverman: A Slave Who Was Almost Free," *Mississippi Valley Historical Review* (1962); John B. Cade, ed., "Out of the Mouths of Ex-Slaves," *Journal of Negro History* (1935); E.O. Settle, "Social Attitudes During the Slave Regime: Household Servants Versus Field Hands," *Publications of the American Sociological Society* (1934); and J. Ralph Jones, ed., "Portraits of Georgia Slaves," *Georgia Review* (1967), all good collections of the reminiscences of former slaves. For an excellent analysis of slave songs and folk beliefs, see Sterling Brown, "Negro Folk Expression: Spirituals, Secular Ballads, and Songs," *Phylon* (1953). Other noteworthy works about American slavery are Kenneth Scott, "The Slave Insurrection in New York in 1712," *New York Historical Society Quarterly* (1961); T.W. Clark, "The Negro Plot of 1741," *New York History* (1944); Ferene M. Szasz, "The New York Slave Revolt of 1741: A Re-examination," *New York History* (1967); Raymond and Alice Bauer, "Day to Day Resistance to Slavery," *Journal of Negro History* (1943); Richard Wade, "The Vesey Plot Reconsidered," *Journal of Southern History* (1964), a controversial analysis of the famous South Carolina slave conspiracy; Marion D. Kilson, "Toward Freedom: An Analysis of Slave Revolts in the United States," *Phylon* (1964); George M. Fredrickson and Christopher Lasch, "Resistance to Slavery," *Civil War History* (1967).

The best of the older books about American Negro slavery include: Lorenzo Greene, *The Negro in Colonial New England* (1942); Ulrich B. Phillips, *American Negro Slavery* (1918), extensive scholarly research, though it reflects the racism of that epoch; Kenneth M. Stampp, *The Peculiar Institution* (1956), a major revisionist work; U.B. Phillips, *Life and Labor in the Old South* (1929); Stanley Elkins, *Slavery* (1959), a controversial historical-psychological study; Matthew T. Mellon, *Early American Views of Negro Slavery* (1934); Charles Sydnor, *Slavery in Mississippi* (1933); Edward J. McManus, *A History of Negro Slavery in New York* (1966); Joe Gray Taylor, *Negro Slavery in Louisiana* (1961); James C. Ballagh, *A History of Slavery in Virginia;* Guion G. Johnson, *Ante-Bellum North Carolina* (1937). Frank J. Klingberg, *An Appraisal of the Negro in Colonial South Carolina (1941);* Ralph B. Flanders, *Plantation Slavery in Georgia* (1933); Staughton Lynd, *Class Conflict, Slavery, and the United States Constitution* (1967); Frederic Bancroft, *Slave Trading in the Old South* (1931); Richard C. Wade, *Slavery in the Cities* (1964); Eugene D. Genovese, *The Political Economy of Slavery* (1965); Alfred H. Conrad and John R. Meyer, *The Economics of Slavery* (1964); Frederick Douglass, *My Bondage and My Freedom* (1955), an autobiographical reminiscence; Gilbert Osofsky, ed., *Puttin' On Ole Massa* (1969); Arna Bontemps, ed., *Great Slave Narratives* (1969); Benjamin Botkin, ed., *Lay My Burden Down* (1945), a comprehensive compilation of the reminiscences of former slaves; Frank Tannenbaum, *Slave and Citizen* (1946), a comparative work; and James Mellon, *Bullwhip Days: The Slaves Remember, An Oral History* (1988).

Abolitionists and abolitionism are well treated in Arthur Zilversmit, *The First Emancipation* (1967); Frederick Douglass, *The Life and Times of Frederick Douglass* (1881); Miles M. Fisher, *Negro Slave Songs in the United States* (1953); Herbert Aptheker, *American Negro Slave Revolts* (1943), one of the most controversial works on the subject; John Lofton, *Insurrection in South Carolina* (1964), a study of Denmark Vesey's plot; William Freehling, *Prelude to Civil War* (1966), another account of the Vesey conspiracy; Herbert Aptheker, *Nat Turner's Slave Rebellion* (1966), perhaps a bit exaggerated; Louis Filler, *The Crusade against Slavery* (1960), an excellent study; Dwight Dumond, *Anti-Slavery* (1961); Benjamin Quarles, *Black Abolitionists* (1969), a long overdue work; Philip S. Foner, *The Life and Writings of Frederick Douglass* (4 vols., 1950-1955); Philip Foner, *Frederick Douglass* (1964); Benjamin Quarles, *Frederick Douglass* (1948); Herbert Aptheker, ed., *One Continual Cry* (1965); Larry Gara, *The Liberty Line* (1961), a study of the Underground Railroad; Herbert Aptheker *To Be Free* (1948); Martin Duberman, ed., *The Anti-Slavery Vanguard* (1965); Aileen Kraditor, *Means and Ends in American Abolitionism* (1969), a work weakened by the author's tendency to avoid controversy; Eugene H. Berwanger, *The Frontier against Slavery* (1967); Eric Foner, *Free Soil, Free Labor, Free Men* (1970); Henrietta Buckmaster, *Let My People Go: The Story of the Underground Railroad and the Growth of the Abolition Movement* (1941); David B. Davis, *The Problem of Slavery in Western Culture* (1958); Nicholas Halasz, *The Rattling Chains: Slave Unrest and Revolt in the American South* (1959), a novelistic treatment; Joseph C. Carroll, *Slave Insurrections in the United States, 1800-1860* (1938); Lorenzo J. Greene, "Mutiny on the Slave Ships," *Phylon* (1944), a fascinating but little studied subject; Ann Petry, *Harriett*

Tubman (1955); Herbert Aptheker, *The Negro in the Abolitionist Movement* (1941); David Walker, *Appeal in Four Articles* (1830), a militant anti-slavery pamphlet.

The better older works about the Ante-Bellum free Negroes are Charles S. Sydnor, "The Free Negro in Mississippi Before the Civil War," *American Historical Review* (1927); Horace Fitchett, "Origin and Growth of the Free Negro Population of Charleston, South Carolina," *Journal of Negro History* (1941); Dorothy B. Porter, "The Organized Educational Activities of Negro Literary Societies, 1818-1846," *Journal of Negro Education* (1936); Robert Ernst, "The Economic Status of New York City Negroes, 1850-1863," (1949); Lee Calligaro, "The Negro's Legal Status in Pre-Civil War New Jersey", *New Jersey History* (1967); Richard C. Wade, "The Negro in Cincinnati, 1800-1830," *Journal of Negro History* (1954); Benjamin Quarles, *The Negro in the American Revolution* (1961); Shirley Graham, *The Story of Phyllis Wheatley* (1949); William Nell, *The Colored Patriots of the American Revolution* (1855); William Wells Brown, *The Negro in the American Revolution* (1867); Howard H. Bell, "The Negro Emigration Movement, 1849-1854: A Phase of Negro Nationalism," *Phylon* (1959); H.H. Bell, "Expressions of Negro Militancy in the North, 1840-1860," *Journal of Negro History* (1960); H.H. Bell, "Negro Nationalism: A Factor in Emigration Projects, 1858-1861," *Journal of Negro History* (1962); Hollis R. Lynch, "Pan-Negro Nationalism in the New World Before 1862," *Boston University Papers on Africa* (1966); L. Mehlinger, "The Attitude of the Free Negro Toward African Colonization," *Journal of Negro History* (1916); H.N. Sherwood, "Paul Cuffe," *Journal of Negro History* (1923), the story of New England's most noted free black man; Leon Litwack, *North of Slavery* (1961), the standard account on the subject; John Hope Franklin, *The Free Negro in North Carolina 1790-1860,* (1943); John H. Russell, *The Free Negro in Virginia* (1913); Carter G. Woodson, *Free Negro Heads of Families in the United States in 1830* (1925); Emma Lou Thornbrough, *The Negro in Indiana before 1900* (1957); Charles H. Wesley, *Richard Allen* (1935), still the best biography of the founder of the A.M.E. Church; Philip J. Staudenraus, *The African Colonization Movement, 1816-1865* (1961); Roger W. Shugg, "Negro Voting in the Ante-Bellum South," *Journal of Negro History,* (October 1936); John H. Russell, "Colored Freemen as Slave Owners in Virginia," *Journal of Negro History* (1916); Carter G. Woodson, *Free Negro Owners of Slaves in the United States in 1830* (1925).

The role of free blacks in abolitionist activities appears in William Breser, "John B. Russwurm," *Journal of Negro History* (1928); Monroe Work, "The Life of Charles B. Ray." *Journal of Negro History* (1919); Dorothy Porter, "David Ruggles, An Apostle of Human Rights," *Journal of Negro History* (1943); Ray A. Billington, "James Forten, Forgotten Abolitionist," *Negro History Bulletin* (1949), an excellent though perhaps exaggerated account of this wealthy and influential black abolitionist; Larry Gara, "The Professional Fugitive in the Abolitionist Movement," *Wisconsin Magazine of History* (1965); Charles H. Wesley, "The

Negro in the Organization of Abolition," *Phylon* (1941), "The Participation of Negroes in Anti-Slavery Political Parties, *Journal of Negro History* (1944), and "The Negro in New York in the Emancipation Movement, *Journal of Negro History* (1939); William and Jane H. Pease, "Anti-Slavery Ambivalence: Immediatism, Expediency, Race," *American Quarterly* (1965); Leon F. Litwack, "The Abolitionist Dilemma: The Anti-Slavery Movement and the Northern Negro," *New England Quarterly* (1961); Benjamin Quarles, "The Breach Between Garrison and Douglass," *Journal of Negro History* (1938); William and Jane H. Pease, "Boston Garrisonians and the Problem of Frederick Douglass," *Canada Journal of History* (1967); Eric Foner, "Politics and Prejudice: The Free Soil Party and the Negro, 1819-1852," *Journal of Negro History* (1965).

The outpouring of works examining the African-American slave community and the period of involuntary servitude in general has continued. Among the best of the more recent works are: Herbert S. Klein, *The Middle Passage: Comparative Studies in the Atlantic Slave Trade* (1978); Gerald W. Mullin, *Flight and Rebellion: Slave Resistance in Eighteenth-Century Virginia* (1972); T.H. Breen and Stephen Innes, *"Myne Owne Ground": Race and Freedom on Virginia's Eastern Shore, 1640-1676* (1980); Ira Berlin and Ronald Hoffman, *Slavery and Freedom in the Age of the American Revolution* (1983); Sidney Kaplan, *The Black Presence in the Era of the American Revolution, 1770-1800* (1973); David Brion Davis, *The Problem of Slavery in the Age of Revolution* (1975); Stavghton Lynd, *Class Conflict, Slavery and the United States Constitution* (1967); Lamont D. Thomas, *Rise to Be a People, A Biography of Paul Cuffe* (1986); Eugene Genovese, *Roll Jordan Roll: The World the Slaves Made* (1974); John Blassingame, *The Slave Community: Plantation Life in the Antebellum South* (1974); Leslic Howard Owens, *This Species of Property: Slave Life and Culture in the Old South* (1976); Charles J. Joyner, *Down By the Riverside: A South Carolina Slave Community* (1984); Ann J. Lane, ed., *The Debate Over Slavery: Stanley Elkins and His Critics* (1971); William L. Van Deburg, *The Slave Drivers: Black Agricultural Labor Supervisors in the Ante-Bellum South* (1979); Deborah Gray White, *Arn't I a Woman? Female Slaves in the Plantation South* (1985). Also, R.J.M. Blackett, *Building an Anti-Slavery Wall: Black Americans in the Atlantic Abolitionist Movement* (1983); Waldo E. Martin, Jr., *The Mind of Frederick Douglass* (1984); Peter Wood, *Black Majority: Negroes in Colonial South Carolina from 1670 Through the Stono Rebellion* (1974). On free Negroes, particularly, the best of the recent works is Ira Berlin, *Slaves without Masters: The Free Negro in the Antebellum South* (1975). Others of significant value are: Michael P. Johnson and James L. Roark, *No Chariot Let Down: Charleston's Free People of Color on the Eve of the Civil War* (1984); James Oliver Horton and Lois Horton, *Black Bostonians: Family Life and Community Struggle in the Ante-Bellum North* (1979); Robert Cottrol, *The Afro-Yankees: Providence's Black Community in the Antebellum Era* (1982); Suzanne Lebsock, *The Free Women of Petersburg: Status and Culture in a Southern Town* (1984); and Juliet E.K. Walker, *Free Frank: A Black Pioneer on the Ante-Bellum Frontier* (1984).

War and Freedom, 1861-1876

Significant older works about blacks during the Civil War and Reconstruction include: Herbert Aptheker, "Negro Casualties in the Civil War," *Journal of Negro History* (1947); Edgar A. Toppin, "Humbly They Served: The Black Brigade in the Defense of Cincinnati," *Journal of Negro History* (1963); Richard H. Abbott, "Massachusetts and the Recruitment of Southern Negroes, 1863-1865," *Civil War History* (1986); N.W. Stephenson, "The Question of Arming the Slaves," *American Hisitorical Review* (1913); Harvey Wish, "Slave Disloyalty Under the Confederacy," *Journal of Negro History* (1938); Charles H. Wesley, "The Employment of Negroes as Soldiers in the Confederate Army," *Journal of Negro History* (1919); Charles H. Wesley, "Lincoln's Plan for Colonizing the Emancipated Negro," *Journal of Negro History* (1919); Bernard Weisberger, "The Dark and Bloody Ground of Reconstruction Historiography," *Journal of Southern History* (1959); W.E.B. Du Bois, "Reconstruction and its Benefits," *American Historical Review* (1910); Joseph A. Barome, ed., "The Autobiography of Hiram Revels," *Midwest Journal* (1952-53); A.E. Perkins, "Oscar James Dunn," *Phylon* (1943); Robert H. Woody, "Jonathan Jasper Wright," *Journal of Negro History* (1933); Edward F. Sweat, "Francis L. Cardozo-Profile of Integrity in Reconstruction Politics," *Journal of Negro History* (1961); LaWanda Cox, "The Promise of Land for the Freedman," *Mississippi Valley Historical Review* (1958); Patrick W. Riddleberger, "The Radical's Abandonment of the Negro During Reconstruction, *Journal of Negro History* (1960); Leslie H. Fishel, "Northern Prejudice and Negro Suffrage, 1865-1900," *Journal of Negro History* (1954), "The Negro in Northern Politics, 1870-1900," *Mississippi Valley Historical Review* (1953), and "Repercussions of Reconstruction: The Northern Negro, 1870-1883," *Civil War History* (1968); Benjamin Quarles, *The Negro in the Civil War* (1953); Dudley Cornish, *The Sable Arm* (1956); James M. McPherson, *The Negro's Civil War* (1965); Thomas Wentworth Higginson, *Army Life in a Black Regiment* (1870), relating the experiences of a white officer with black troops; John Hope Franklin, *The Emancipation Proclamation* (1962) and *The Militant South* (1964); Benjamin Quarles, *Lincoln and the Negro* (1962); James M. McPherson, *The Struggle for Equality* (1964); Bell I. Wiley, *Southern Negroes, 1861-1865* (1953); V. Jacque Voegel, *Free but Not Equal* (1967); C.L. Wagandt, *The Mighty Revolution: Negro Emancipation in Maryland* (1965); Charlotte L. Forten, *The Journal of Charlotte L. Forten* (1961), the diary of a black teacher in the South during the Civil War; Irvin H. Lee, *Negro Medal of Honor Men* (1967); W.E.B. Du Bois, *Black Reconstruction* (1935), the pioneer revisionist work; Kenneth Stampp, *The Era of Reconstruction* (1965), a leading modern revisionist survey; John Hope Franklin, *Reconstruction After the Civil War* (1961); Lerone Bennett, *Black Power USA: The Human Side of Reconstruction, 1867-77* (1967), a slightly exaggerated account; LaWanda and John Cox, *Politics, Principle, and Prejudice* (1963), a revisionist study of national politics in the Reconstruction period;

Henry L. Swint, *The Northern Teacher in the South* (1965); Robert Cruden, *The Negro in Reconstruction* (1965); Robert Cruden, *The Negro in Reconstruction* (1969); Theodore Wilson, *The Black Codes of the South* (1965); Henderson Donald, *The Negro Freedman* (1952), not a wholly satisfactory work; Joel Williamson, *After Slavery* (1965), and Willie Lee Rose, *Rehearsal for Reconstruction: The Port Royal Experiment* (1964), both fine studies of South Carolina. Joe M. Richardson, *The Negro in the Reconstruction of Florida* (1966); Vernon Lane Wharton, *The Negro in Mississippi, 1865-1890* (1947); A.A. Taylor, *The Negro in the Reconstruction of Virginia* (1926); Otis A. Singletary, *Negro Militia and Reconstruction* (1957); Samuel Smith, *The Negro in Congress, 1870-1901* (1940); John M. Langston, *From the Virginia Plantation to the National Capitol* (1894), and John R. Lynch, *The Facts of Reconstruction* (1913), reminiscences of black reconstruction politicians. Walter C. Fleming, *Documentary History of Reconstruction* (3 vols., 1906-1907); Harry Hyman, ed., *New Frontiers of the American Reconstruction* (1966); James P. Shenton, ed., *The Reconstruction* (1963); E. Merton Coulter, *Negro Legislators in Georgia During the Reconstruction Period* (1968) and *The South During Reconstruction* (1948), both warrant caution for anti-Negro bias; George Bentley, *A History of the Freedmen's Bureau* (1955), the standard work, although not entirely satisfactory; William McFeeley, *Yankee Stepfather: General Oliver O. Howard and the Freedmen* (1968), a recent work that tells much about the workings of the Freedmen's Bureau as well as the life of its federal commissioner. A good supplement for Bentley's older work on the Bureau; Martin Abbott, *The Freedman's Bureau in South Carolina* (1967); Walter L. Fleming, *The Freedmen's Savings Bank* (1927).

Among the more highly recommended of the recent works about the Civil War and Emancipation are: Hans L. Trefonsse, *Lincoln's Decision for Emancipation* (1975); Clarence L. Mohr, *On the Threshold for Freedom: Masters and Slaves in Civil War Georgia* (1985); C. Peter Ripley, *Slaves and Freedmen in Civil War Louisiana* (1975); Roger L. Ransom and Richard Sutch, *One Kind of Freedom: The Economic Consequences of Emancipation* (1977); Eric Foner, *Nothing but Freedom* (1983); Ira Berlin, et al., *The Black Military Experience* (1982); Peter Kolchin, *First Freedom: The Responses of Alabama's Blacks to Emancipation and Reconstruction* (1972); Leon F. Litwack, *Been in the Storm So Long: The Aftermath of Slavery* (1979); Claude F. Oubre, *Forty Acres and a Mule: The Freedmen's Bureau and Black Land Ownership* (1978); Lawrence Levine, *Black Culture and Black Consciousness* (1977); Howard Rabinowitz, ed., *Southern Black Leaders of the Reconstruction Era* (1982); and Ronald E. Butchart, *Northern Schools, Southern Blacks and Reconstruction: Freedmen's Education, 1862-1875.*

The Nadir, 1877-1900

Studies of black life in the post-Reconstruction era include: Clarence A.

Bacote, "Negro Proscription and Proposed Solutions in Georgia, 1880-1908," *Journal of Southern History* (1959); John Hope Franklin, "The Negro Goes to School: The Genesis of Legal Segregation in Southern Schools," *South Atlantic Quarterly* (1959); Jack Abramowitz, "The Negro in the Populist Movement," *Journal of Negro History* (1953); Charles Crowe, "Tom Watson, Populists, and Blacks Reconsidered," *Journal of Negro History* (1970), perhaps the best summary on the subject; Edwin S. Redkey, "Bishop Turner's African Dream," *Journal of American History* (1967); C. Vann Woodward, *Origins of the New South* (1951); Thomas Clark and Albert Kirwan, *The South Since Appomattox* (1967); Charles Wynes, ed., *The Negro in the South Since 1865* (1965); George B. Tindall, *South Carolina Negroes, 1877-1900* (1952); Frenise Logan, *The Negro in North Carolina, 1876-1894* (1964); Albert D. Kirwan, *Revolt of the Rednecks* (1951), a good work on Mississippi politics; Stanley P. Hirshon, *Farewell to the Bloody Shirt* (1962); Vincent P. DeSantis, *Republicans Face the Southern Question* (1959); Rayford Logan, *The Negro in American Life and Thought: The Nadir* also titled *The Betrayal of the Negro*, (1954), an excellent study of the entire period; C. Vann Woodward, *The Strange Career of Jim Crow* (third edition, 1966), the standard account of the origins of segregation; Horace Mann Bond, *Negro Education in Alabama* (1939); Louis R. Harlan, *Separate and Unequal* (1958); Henry Bullock, *A History of Negro Education in the South* (1967); Edwin S. Redkey, *Black Exodus* (1969); Charles E. Wynes, *Race Relations in Virginia, 1870-1902;* (1961); Everett L. Jones, *The Negro Cowboys* (1965); Shirley Graham and George D. Liscomb, *Dr. George Washington Carver, Scientist* (1965); Arthur F. Raper, *The Tragedy of Lynching* (1933); David M. Chalmers, *Hooded Americanism: The First Century of the Ku Klux Klan* (1965).

The best recent scholarship on the Nadir includes: Charles L. Flynn, *White Land, Black Labor: Caste and Class in Late 19th Century Georgia* (1983); Arnold Taylor, *Travail and Triumph: Black Life and Culture in the South Since the Civil War* (1976); Paula Giddings, *When and Where I Enter . . . The Impact of Black Women on Race and Sex in America* (1984); Howard Rabonwitz, *Race Relations in the Urban South, 1865-1890* (1978); and H. Leon Prather, *"We Have Taken a City": The Wilmington Massacre and Coup of 1898* (1984).

The Age of Booker T. Washington, 1901-1917

Noteworthy among the earlier studies about the Washington era in African-American history are August Meier's works, "Booker T. Washington and the Negro Press," *Journal of Negro History* (1953), "Booker T. Washington and the Rise of the NAACP," *The Crisis* (1954) and "Toward a Reinterpretation of Booker T. Washington," *Journal of Southern History* (1957); Daniel Walden, "The Contemporary Opposition to the Political Ideas of Booker T. Washington," *Journal of Negro History* (1960); Donald J. Calesta, "Booker T. Washington: Another Look," *Journal of Negro History* (1964); Louis R. Harlan, "Booker T. Washington and the White Man's Burden," *American Historical Review* (1966); Vincent Harding, "W.E.B. Du Bois and the Black Messianic Tradition," *Freedomways* (1969); Mary L. Chaffee, "W.E.B. Du Bois' Concept of the Racial Problem in the United States," *Journal of Negro History* (1956); Elliott M. Rudwick, "The Niagara Movement," *Journal of Negro History* (1957); Thomas R. Cripps, "The Reaction of the Negro to the Motion Picture 'Birth of a Nation'," *Historian* (1963); Dewey W. Grantham, "The Progressive Movement and the Negro," *South Atlantic Quarterly* (1955); Kathleen Wohlgemuth, "Woodrow Wilson and Federal Segregation," *Journal of Negro History* (1959); Nancy J. Weiss, "The Negro and the New Freedom: Fighting Wilsonian Segregation," *Political Science Quarterly* (1969); Bernard Mandel, "Samuel Gompers and the Negro Workers, 1886-1914," *Journal of Negro History* (1955); Hugh Hawkins, ed., *Booker T. Washington and His Critics* (1962); August Meier, *Negro Thought in America, 1880-1915* (1963); Samuel R. Spencer, *Booker T. Washington and the Negro's Place in American Life* (1957); Booker T. Washington's book-length works, *The Future of the American Negro* (1899), *Up from Slavery* (1900), *The Negro in the South* (1907), and *Selected Speeches* (1932); Francis Broderick, *W.E.B. Du Bois, Propagandist of the Negro Protest* (1961); Du Bois's autobiographies, *Dusk of Dawn* (1940) and *Autobiography of W.E.B. Du Bois* (1968), as well as his penetrating *The Souls of Black Folk* (1903); Kelly Miller, *Race Adjustment* (1908); Charles Kellogg, *NAACP* (1967); Langston Hughes, *Fight For Freedom: Story of the NAACP* (1962); Robert L. Jack, *History of the NAACP* (1943); Ray Stanndard Baker, *Following the Color Line* (1908); I.A. Newby, *Jim Crow's Defense: Anti-Negro Thought in America, 1900-1930* (1965); Charles Wesley, *Negro Labor in the United States 1850-1925* (1927); Elliott M. Rudwick, *Race Riot at East St. Louis, July 2, 1917* (1964); Emmett J. Scott, *The American Negro in the World War* (1919); Ullin W. Leavell, *Philanthropy in Negro Education* (1930); W.E.B. Du Bois, *Atlanta University Studies* (1898-1901).

Any examination of Booker T. Washington and his era must begin with Louis R. Harlan's *Booker T. Washington: The Making of a Black Leader, 1856-1901* (1972) and *Booker T. Washington: The Wizard of Tuskegee, 1901-1915* (1983). Other useful recent publications include: Arnold Rampersad, *The Art and Imagination of W.E.B. Du Bois* (1976); Alfred Moss, *The American Negro Academy: Voice of the Talented Tenth* (1981); and Walter B. Weare, *Black Business in the New South: A History of the North Carolina Mutual Insurance Company* (1975); Ann J. Lane, *The Brownsville Affair: National Crisis and Black Reaction* (1971); Willard B. Gatewood, *Black Americans and the White Man's Burden, 1898-1903* (1975); David M. Katzman, *Before the Ghetto: Black Detroit in the Nineteenth Century* (1973); Robert L. Zangrando, *The NAACP's Crusade against Lynching, 1909-1950* (1980); Nancy Weiss, *The National Urban League, 1910-1940* (1974); Alfreda M. Duster, ed., *Crusade For Justice: The Autobiography of Ida B. Wells* (1970); Stephen R. Fox,

Guardian of Boston: William Monroe Trotter (1971), the story of one of Booker T. Washington's most militant antagonists; and Emma Lou Thornborough, *T. Thomas Fortune: Militant Journalist* (1972).

Between War and Depression, 1918-1932

The better of the older works for this period include: Emmett J. Scott, ed., "Letters of Negro Migrants", *Journal of Negro History* (1919); Charles S. Johnson, "How Much Is the Migration a Flight from Persecution?," *Opportunity* (1923); Gilbert Osofsky, *Harlem: The Making of a Ghetto* (1966); James Weldon Johnson, *Black Manhattan* (1930); Seth Scheiner, *Negro Mecca* (1965); Claude McKay, *Harlem: Negro Metropolis* (1940); Allan Spear, *Black Chicago* (1967); St. Clair Drake and Horace Cayton, *Black Metropolis* (1940), a classic study of black Chicagoans; Emmett J. Scott, *Negro Migration during the War* (1920); Thomas J. Woofter, *The Negro Problem in Cities* (1928); Louise V. Kennedy, *The Negro Peasant Turns Cityward* (1930); Claude V. Kiser, *Sea Island to City* (1932); Carter G. Woodson, *A Century of Negro Migration* (1918); Arna Bontemps and Jack Conroy, *Anyplace but Here* (1966); Robert Kerdin, ed., *Voice of the Negro* (1919) (1920); Edmund D. Cronon, *Black Moses* (1955), the standard biography of Marcus Garvey; Amy Garvey, *Garvey and Garveyism* (1968); Charles S. Johnson, *The Economic Status of Negroes* (1933); Arthur Fauset, *Black Gods of the Metropolis* (1944); John Hoshor, *God in a Rolls-Royce* (1936) and Sara Harris, *Father Divine: Holy Husband* (1953), both about Father Divine, leader of a pseudo-religious cult; Milton Meltzer and August Meier, *Time of Trial, Time of Hope: The Negro in America, 1919-1941* (1966); Roi Ottley, *The Lonely Warrior: The Life and Times of Robert S. Abbott* (1955), biography of the publisher of the militant newspaper, the *Chicago Defender;* Arthur I. Waskow, *From Race Riot to Sit-In* (1966), traces black protest from the riots of 1919 to the 1960s. Theodore Gross, eds., *Dark Symphony* (1968); John Henrik Clarke, ed., *American Negro Short Stories* (1966); Langston Hughes ed., *The Best Short Stories by Negro Writers* (1967); Abraham Chapman, ed., *Black Voices* (1968); Sterling Brown, *The Negro in American Fiction* (1937); Saunders Redding, *To Make a Poet Black* (1939); Stephen Bronz, *Roots of Negro Racial Consciousness* (1969); Mercer Cook and Stephen Henderson, *The Militant Black Writer in Africa and the United States* (1969); Alain Locke, ed., *The New Negro* (1925), an anthology of the works by the Harlem Renaissance writers; Blanche Ferguson, *Countee Cullen and the Negro Renaissance* (1966); James Weldon Johnson, *Along This Way* (1933), an autobiographical treatment, as is Langston Hughes's *The Big Sea* (1940); Benjamin Brawley, "The Negro Literary Renaissance," *The Southern Workman* (1927).

Among the most recommended newer studies about this era are: Robert V.

Haynes, *A Night of Violence: The Houston Riot of 1917* (1976); William Tuttle, *Race Riot: Chicago in the Red Summer of 1919* (1970); Mary F. Berry, *Black Resistance, White Law: A History of Constitutional Racism in America* (1971); Theodore Draper, *The Rediscovery of Black Nationalism* (1970); Nathan I. Huggins, *Harlem Ranaissance* (1971); James Richard Giles, *Claude McKay* (1976); Robert E. Hemenway, *Zora Neale Hurston: A Literary Biography* (1978); Russell J. Linnerman, ed., *Alain Locke: Reflections of a Modern Renaissance Man* (1983); Kenneth R. Manning, *Black Apollo of Science: The Life of Ernest Everett Just* (1983); Linda O. McMurry, *George Washington Carver: Scientist and Symbol* (1981); and Marcia M. Mathews, *Henry Ossawa Tanner: American Artist* (1969).

A New Deal—A New Life?, 1933-1940

The African-American in the New Deal era is still an inadequately treated subject. There are, however, some good studies. Among the older ones are James A. Harrell, "Negro Leadership in the Election Year 1936," *Journal of Southern History* (1968); John A. Salmond, "The CCC and the Negro," *Journal of American History* (1965); Leslie H. Fishel, "The Negro in the New Deal Era," *Wisconsin Magazine of History* (1964-65); Bernard Sternsher, ed., *The Negro in Depression and War* (1969); Arnold Hill, *The Negro and Economic Reconstruction* (1937); Abram Harris, *The Negro as Capitalist* (1936); Charles S. Johnson, et al., *The Collapse of Cotton Tenancy* (1938); Charles S. Johnson, *Shadow of the Plantation* (1934); John Dollar, *Caste and Class in a Southern Town,* (1937), an indepth study of black life and race relations in a Mississippi town, considered by many to be a classic; Harold Gosnell, *Negro Politicians* (1935), a standard account focusing on Chicago; Wilson Record, *The Negro and the Communist Party* (1951); E. Franklin Frazier, *Negro Youth at the Crossroads* (1949); St. Clair Drake and Horace Cayton, *Black Metropolis* (cited above); James W. Ford, *Hunger and Terror in Harlem* (1935); the story of that year's Harlem riot; Roi Ottley, *New World A-Coming* (1943), treats FDR's Black Cabinet; Robert C. Weaver, *Negro Labor* (1946); Marian Anderson, *My Lord What a Morning* (1956), an autobiography of the well known contralto; and Catherine O. Peare, *Mary McLeod Bethune* (1961).

More recent works which have added to a better understanding of blacks during the New Deal era include: Raymond Wolters, *Negroes and the Great Depression: The Problem of Economic Recovery;* Nancy Weiss, *Farewell to the Party of Lincoln: Black Politics in the Age of F.D.R.* (1983); Nell I. Painter, *The Narrative of Hosea Hudson: His Life as a Negro Communist in the South* (1979); Charles H. Martin, *The Angelo Herndon Case and Southern Justice* (1976); Mark Naison, *Communists in Harlem During the Depression* (1983); John H. Kirby, *Black Americans in the Roosevelt Era: Liberalism and Race* (1980); William H. Harris, *Keeping the Faith: A. Philip Randolph, Milton P. Webster, and the Brotherhood of Sleeping Car Porters, 1925-1937* (1977); and Harvard Sitkoff, *A New Deal for Blacks: The Emergence of Civil Rights as a National Issue.*

War Again, 1941-1945

The most noteworthy works about Africans-Americans during the war years are Richard M. Dalfiume, "The Forgotten Years of the Negro Revolution," *Journal of American History* (1968); Dan T. Carter, *Scottsboro* (1969), the story of the multifaceted Alabama rape case; Alfred M. Lee, *Detroit Race Riot* (1943); Ulysses Lee, *The Employment of Negro Troops* (1966); Herbert Garfinkel, *When Negroes March* (1959), the story of A. Philip Randolph's proposed March on Washington; Rayford Logan, ed., *What the Negro Wants* (1944); Loren Miller, *The Petitioners* (1968), treats the legal cases of the NAACP; Walter White, *A Rising Wind* (1945), a fine account of blacks on the fighting front; Louis Ruchames, *Race, Jobs and Politics: The Story of FEPC* (1953); Gunnar Myrdal, *An American Dilemma* (1944), a classic study of American race relations; Louis Kesselman, *The Social Politics of FEPC* (1953); B.R. Brazeal, *The Brotherhood of Sleeping Car Porters* (1946); Carl N. Degler, "The Negro in America—Where Myrdal Went Wrong," *New York Times Magazine* (1969); Poppy Cannon, *A Gentle Knight* (1956), a biography of the NAACP leader Walter F. White written by his wife. Richard Wright, *Black Boy* (1945), an autobiographical novel; John D. Silvera, *The Negro in World War II* (1946); Seymour J. Schorsfield, *The Negro in the Armed Forces* (1945); Earl Brown, "American Negroes and the War," *Harper's Magazine* (1942); John Temple Graves, "The Southern Negro and the War Crisis," *Virginia Quarterly Review* (1942); and Morris J. MacGregor, Jr., *Integration of the Armed Forces: 1940-1965* (1981).

The Attack against Segregation, 1945-1954

The most useful early studies about the post-war years include: Elliott M. Rudwick, "How CORE Began," *Social Science Quarterly* (1969); Thurgood Marshall, "An Evaluation of Recent Efforts to Achieve Racial Integration Through Resort to the Courts," *Journal of Negro Education* (1952); L.D. Reddick, "The Negro Policy of the United States Army, 1775-1945," *Journal of Negro History* (1949); Walter F. White, *A Man Called White* (1948), the autobiography of the second executive secretary of the NAACP; Henry L. Moon, *Balance of*

Power: The Negro Vote (1948), examining the role of the black vote in the election of 1948; Richard J. Stillman, *Integration of the Negro in the United States Armed Forces* (1968); Richard Dalfiume, *Desegregation of the U.S. Armed Forces* (1969); Harry S. Ashmore, *The Negro and the Schools* (1954); Abram Kardiner and Lionel Ovesey, *The Mark of Oppression* (1951); a classic study of the psychological effects of discrimination; J. Alvin Kugelmann, *Ralph J. Bunche, Fighter for Peace* (1952); Robert Penn Warren, *Who Speaks for the Negro?* (1954); Rayford W. Logan, *The Negro and the Post-War World* (1954); Robert C. Weaver, *The Negro Ghetto* (1948).

Recent works about the post-war years in African-American history include: Paul Burstein, *Discrimination, Jobs, and Politics: The Struggle for Equal Employment Opportunity in the United States Since the New Deal* (1985); Gerald Horne, *Black and Red: W.E.B. Du Bois and the Afro-American Response to the Cold War, 1944-1963* (1986); William C. Berman, *The Politics of Civil Rights in the Truman Administration* (1970); Donald R. McCoy and Richard T. Ruetten, *Quest and Response: Minority Rights and the Truman Administration* (1973); and Jules Tygiel, *Baseball's Great Experiment: Jackie Robinson and His Legacy* (1984).

"The Second Reconstruction," 1954-1964

A flood of articles and books has appeared about the Civil Rights era; the better studies include: August Meier, "On the Significance of Martin Luther King," *New Politics* (1965); Edward A. Leonard, "Nonviolence and Violence in American Racial Protests, 1945-1967," *Rocky Mountain Social Science Journal* (1969); Lerone Bennett, "The South and the Negro: Martin Luther King, Jr., *Ebony* (1957); Lerone Bennett, Jr., "Daisy Bates: First Lady of Little Rock," *Ebony* (1958), about the Little Rock NAACP leader who spearheaded school integration in her town; Benjamin Muse, *Ten Years of Prelude* (1964) and *The American Negro Revolution* (1968); Lerone Bennett, *What Manner of Man?* (1964), *Where Do We Go From Here?* (1967), *The Trumpet of Conscience* (1969); James Peck, *Freedom Ride* (1962); James Farmer, *Freedom-When?* (1965); Waskow, *From Race Riot to Sit-In* (cited above); Merill Proudfoot, *Diary of a Sit-In* (1962); Howard Zinn, *The New Abolitionists* (1964), mostly a story about SNCC, Elizabeth Sutherland, ed., *Letters from Mississippi* (1965), views of civil rights workers in Mississippi; Len Holt, *The Summer That Didn't End* (1965) and Sally Belfrage, *Freedom Summer* (1965), both detailing civil rights work in Mississippi during 1964; James Silver, *Mississippi, The Closed Society* (second edition, 1966); Louis Lomax, *The Negro Revolt* (1962); Charles Silberman, *Crisis in Black and White* (1964); Alan Westin, ed., *Freedom Now!* (1964); Lerone Bennett, *The Negro Mood* (1964); James Q. Wilson, *Negro Politics: The Search For Leadership* (1960); Jack Greenberg, *Race Relations and American Law* (1969), memoirs of an NAACP

503

lawyer; William Brink and Louis Harris, *The Negro Revolution in America* (1964); C. Eric Lincoln, *The Black Muslims in America* (1969); E.U. Essien-Udom, *Black Nationalism* (1962), also on the Muslims; E. Franklin Frazier, *Black Bourgeoisie* (1957), a classic work on the black middle class; Robert F. Williams, *Negroes with Guns* (1962); Carl Rowan, *Go South to Sorrow* (1957); United States Commission on Civil Rights, *Freedom to the Free* (1963); Doris E. Saunders, *The Day They Marched* (1963), an illustrated account of the 1963 March on Washington; Vivian W. Henderson, *The Economic Status of Negroes* (1963); Robert Brisbane, *Black Activism: Black Revolution in the U.S., 1954-1970* (1984); Clayborne Carson, *In Struggle, SNCC and the Black Awakening of the 1960s* (1981); William H. Chafe, *Civilities and Civil Rights: Greensboro, North Carolina and the Black Struggle for Freedom* (1980); Roy Wilkins, *Standing Fast: The Autobiography of Roy Wilkins* (1982); Tony Freyer, *The Little Rock Crisis: A Constitutional Interpretation* (1984); Aldon D. Morris, *The Origins of the Civil Rights Movement: Black Communities Organizing for Change* (1984); and Theodore Cross, *The Black Power Imperative: Racial Inequality and the Politics of Nonviolence* (1984).

"The Second Reconstruction" Wanes, 1964-1973 and "The Second Reconstruction" Betrayed, 1973-1990

The renewed interest in African-American history and the Black Revolution, as well as contemporary conditions, have produced a great outpouring of works. Some of the most useful studies are: Robert Fogelson, "From Resentment to Confrontation: The Police, the Negroes and the Outbreak of the 1960s Riots," *Political Science Quarterly* (1968); Nathan S. Caplan and Jeffrey M. Paige, "A Study of Ghetto Rioters," *Scientific American* (1968); Ulf Hannerz, "What Negroes Mean by Soul," *Trans-Action* (1968); Martin Kilson, "Black Power: Anatomy of a Paradox," *Harvard Journal of Negro Affairs* (1968); A.J. Gregor, *Science and Society* (1963); Stokely Carmichael, "What We Want," *The New York Review of Books* (1966); Kenneth Clark, *Dark Ghetto* (1965); Thomas F. Pettigrew, *A Portrait of the Negro American* (1964); Alphonso Pincney, *Black Americans* (1969), a compact, interdisciplinary study; Karl E. and Alma F. Taeuber, *Negroes in Cities* (1965); Paul Jacobs, *Prelude to Riot: A View of Urban America from the Bottom Up* (1967); Lee Rainwater and William Yancey, *The Moynihan Report and the Politics of Controversy* (1967); Robert Conot, *Rivers of Blood, Years of Darkness* (1967), about the Watts Riot; Fred Shapiro and James Sullivan, *Race Riot* (1969); Ben W. Gilbert, *Ten Blocks from the White House* (1969), about the Washington, D.C. riot; John Hersey, *The Algiers Motel Incident* (1968), a novelistic treatment of one aspect of the 1967 Detroit riot; Louis H. Masottli and Don R. Bowen eds., *Riots and Rebellion* (1969); William H. Grier and Price M. Cobbs, *Black Rage* (1968), a psychological study; Ulf Hannerz, *Soulside*

(1969); Claude Brown, *Manchild in the Promised Land* (1965), a critically acclaimed autobiography of ghetto life; Alex Haley, *The Autobiography of Malcolm X* (1965), has become somewhat of a classic; George Brietman, *Malcolm X: The Man and His Times* (1969); Floyd Barbour, ed., *The Black Power Revolt* (1968), a documentary collection; Stokeley Carmichael and Charles Hamilton, *Black Power* (1967), a political definition of the controversial slogan by one of the originators of the concept; H. Rap Brown, *Die, Nigger, Die* (1969), a loosely autobiographical account written while Brown was in exile; Whitney M. Young, Jr., *Beyond Racism: Building an Open Society* (1969), views of the moderate head of the National Urban League; Floyd McKissick, *Three-Fifths of a Man* (1969), views of the militant CORE leader; Nathan Wright, *Black Power and Urban Unrest* (1967); Lewis M. Killian, *Impossible Revolution? Black Power and the American Dream* (1968); Eldridge Cleaver, *Soul on Ice* (1968), *Eldridge Cleaver* (1969), *Post-Prison Writings and Speeches* (1969), writings of the exiled Black Panther leader; Harold Cruse, *The Crisis of the Negro Intellectual and Rebellion or Revolution* (1968); C. Eric Lincoln, ed., *Is Anybody Listening to Black America?* (1968), essays on the contemporary black mood; Gary T. Marx, *Protest and Prejudice* (revised edition, 1968); Robert Allen, *Black Awakening in Capitalist America* (1969); Elijah Muhammad, *Message to the Black Man in America* (1965), words from the head of the Muslim sect; Calvin Hernton, *Sex and Racism in America* (1967), an interesting, though slightly exaggerated work; Floyd B. Barbour, *The Black Power Revolt* (1968); Charles E. Fager, *White Reflections on Black Power* (1967); William Bradford Huie, *Three Lives for Mississippi* (1965), a well told story of the 1964 murders of civil rights workers Goodman, Cheney, and Schwerner; Fred Powledge, *Black Power, White Resistance: Notes on the New Civil War* (1967); *Report of the National Commission on Civil Disorders* (1968); Thomas F. Gossett, *Race: The History of An Idea in America* (1963); Vincent Harding, *Black Radicalism in America* (1970); Hanes Walton, *The Negro Pilgrimage in America* (1969); Hubert G. Locke, *The Detroit Riot of 1967* (1969); Robert H. Brisbane, *The Black Vanguard* (1970), traces the origins of the Negro "social revolution"; Lee Rainwater, *Behind Ghetto Walls* (1970); and Theodore Draper, *The Rediscovery of Black Nationalism* (1970), the book is not entirely satisfactory, but attempts to give a basic general treatment of the subject; Debbie Louis, *And We Are Not Saved: A History of the Movement as People* (1970), contains first-hand data from a young white CORE worker; C. Eric Lincoln, ed., *Martin Luther King, Jr.: A Profile* (1970) includes excerpts taken from King's own writings as well as the assessments of others; James Boggs, *Racism and the Class Struggle*, a radical essay on the conditions of black Americans; Peter Goldman, *Report from Black America* (1970); a study of contemporary black public opinion. New works on religion and racism include Joseph C. Hough, *Black Power and White Protestants* (1968), Charles F. Sleeper, *Black Power and Christian Responsibility* (1969), and Robert S. Lecky and H. Elliott Wright, eds., *Black Manifesto: Religion, Racism, and Reparations* (1969). Important critical studies of black capitalism include Robert L. Allen, *Black Awakening in Capitalist America* (1969) and Earl Ofari, *The Myth of Black Capitalism* (1970). Recent noteworthy writings on the era which began in 1964 include: Donald Freed, *Agony in New Haven: The Trial of Bobby Seale, Ericka Huggins and the Black Panther Party* (1973); John Henry Cutter, *Ed Brooke: Biography of a Senator* (1972); Edwin K. Norton, *Juror Number Four* (1973), the story of the trial of thirteen Black Panthers as seen by one of the jurors; Peter Goldman, *The Death and Life of Malcolm X* (1973); Stephen Henderson, *Understanding the New Black Poetry* (1972) and Huey P. Newton, *Revolutionary Suicide* (1973); Stephen B. Oates, *Let the Trumphet Sound: The Life of Martin Luther King, Jr.* (1982), is perhaps the best biography of the slain civil rights leader to date; David J. Garrow, *Protest At Selma: Martin Luther King, Jr. and the Voting Rights Act of 1965* and Garrow's *The FBI and Martin Luther King, Jr.* (1981); Richard Reeves, *The Reagan Detour* (1985); Adolph Reed, Jr., *The Jesse Jackson Phenomenon: The Crisis in Afro-American Politics* (1986); Barbara Reynolds, *Jesse Jackson, America's David* (1985); John A. Davis, ed., *Africa As Seen by American Negroes* (1958); and Wallace Terry, *Bloods: An Oral History of the Vietnam War by Black Veterans* (1984); John Hope Franklin, *Racial Equality in America* (1976); and William J. Wilson, *The Declining Significance of Race: Blacks and Changing American Institutions* (1978).

Index

Aaron, Henry, 218, 245
Abbott, Robert S., 61-2
Abernathy, Ralph David, 133, 141-42, 191, 208-09, 230, 408-10, 422, 427-28
Ablerman v. Booth, 30
Abolition movement, 7-9, 16-18, 21-4, 26, 29-31, 50-1
Adams, Cylinda, 405
Adams, John Hurst, 408
Adams, John Quincy, 19-20
Adderley, Julian "Cannonball," 264-65
Address to the Negroes of the State of New York (Hammon), 5
Affirmative Action, 335-38, 342, 362, 375, 381, 383-84, 392
Africa:
  aid to, 424
  emigration to, 13-15, 34, 57, 66-7, 72
  Empire of, 72
  liberation movements in, 217, 424
  See also Liberia; South Africa; Zaire
African Free School, 8-9
African Methodist Episcopal Church (A.M.E.), 9, 11-12, 14, 16, 18, 66-7
African National Congress (ANC), 422, 433, 480-81
African-American Patrolmen's League, 261

Afro-American Studies, 136, 219-20
Agriculture, 41, 53, 74, 79
  See also Cotton production; Plantations
Agyeman, Jaramazi Abebe, 258
AIDS, blacks and, 386-87
Ailey, Alvin, 416
Akron, Ohio, 135
Alabama, 78, 81, 106, 123-24, 125, 131, 142, 145, 187, 190, 193, 200, 229, 242, 265, 407, 415, 429
Alabama, University of, 103-04, 113-14
Albany, Georgia, 112
Alcorn College for Negroes, 43
Alexander, Clifford, Jr., 281
Alexander v. Holmes, 137
Ali, Muhammad, 159, 181, 239, 245, 258, 278-79, 287, 291, 293, 304, 309
Allen, Andy, 406
Allen, Marcus, 327
Allen, Richard, 9, 11-12, 14, 16
Allen, William Barclay, 409
Alliance Theater Company, 432
Amendments to the U.S. Constitution:
  the Thirteenth, 39, 442
  the Fourteenth, 40, 42, 126-27, 153, 196-97, 442-43
  the Fifteenth, 43, 443
  the Twenty-fourth, 117

American Civil Liberties Union (ACLC), 302
American Colonization Society, 14, 15, 57
American Federation of State, County, and Municipal Employees (AFSCME), 434
American Heritage Magazine, 287
American Revolution, 7-8
Amerson, Lucius D., 164, 172
Ames, Wilmer, 404
Amistad, 20
And the Walls Came Tumbling Down (Abernathy), 408-10, 422
Anderson, Marian, 85, 102, 116
Anderson, Reuben V., 336
Annenberg, Walter H., 423-24
Annie Allen (Brooks), 97
Antoine, C. C., 42
Apollo Theater, 337, 426
Appeal (Walker), 16-17
Arafat, Yassar, 436
Arkansas, 31, 102, 116
Armstrong, Louis, 118
Armstrong, Samuel C., 41, 62
Ashe, Arthur, 255
Ashely, Kimberly, 415
Ashford, Evelyn, 333
Ashum Institute, 27
Assad, Hafez, 326-27
Association of Social and Behavioral Scientists (ASBS), 224
Association for the Study of Negro Life and History (ASNLH), 66, 78, 97, 379-80, 407
Atlanta Child Murder Cases, 309-10
"Atlanta Compromise," 55, 63, 208
Atlanta, Georgia, 54-5, 63, 77, 82-4, 96, 99, 106, 112, 130, 140, 142, 209, 221, 225, 228-29, 235, 398
Atlanta Life Insurance Company, 61, 262
Atlanta University, 38, 40-1, 54-5, 63, 82-3, 99, 190, 394

Attenborough, Richard, 314-15
Attica prison, 189
Attucks, Crispus, 5
Atwater, Lee, 384-85
Atwood, Margaret, 368-69
Auburn, New York, 23-4, 65-6
Austin, Texas, 172, 183-84, 185, 199
Autobiography (Malcolm X), 124
Autobiography of an Ex-Colored Man, The (J. W. Johnson), 75-6

Baker, James E., 198
Baker, Josephine, 259
Baldwin, James, 354-55
Baltimore, Maryland, 101
Banneker, Benjamin, 11
Baraka, Imamu Amiri, 204, 217
Barnett, Ross, 113
Barrow, Joe Louis (*See* Joe Louis)
Barrow, Tom, 412
Barry, Marion, S., Jr., 345, 432
Barthelemy, Sidney, 341
Baseball, blacks in, 41, 94, 183, 210-11, 218, 236-37, 245, 277, 335, 373, 388, 391
Basie, William "Count," 331-32, 337
Bates, Eric, 407
Bearden, Harold Irwin, 424-25
Beckwith, Barbara, 401
Begle, Howell, 414
Beloved (Morrison), 368-69, 378
Bensonhurst (New York City), 399, 400, 402
Bentley, Mary Denise, 290
Bergman, Walter, 302, 328
Berry, Mary Francis, 325-26
Bethune, Mary McLeod, 78, 83, 92, 103
Bill Kenny Is Back, 296
Birmingham, Alabama, 105, 106, 113, 116, 265
Black, Hugo L., 113, 177, 187, 190

"Black Agenda," 194-95
Black and White (Fortune), 51
"Black Cabinet," 83, 84, 126
Black Caucus, 157-58, 167, 172-73, 198, 351-52
Black Christian Nationalist Church (BCN), 258
Black Codes, 39
Black Cultural Association (BCA), 217
"Black Laws," 12, 38
Black Leadership Forum, 415
Black militancy, 16, 59-60
Black Muslims, 81-2, 110, 111, 117, 124, 150, 181, 253-54, 283-84, 400, 409
Black National Network (BNN) (*See* National Black Network (NBN))
Black nationalism, 72, 110, 133, 217
Black P. Stone Nation, 146-47, 161
Black Panther Party, 128-29, 133, 136, 137, 140-41, 146-47, 148, 150, 151-52, 155, 159, 166, 171, 173-74, 176, 180, 181-82, 187, 196, 203, 239, 260, 266, 295-96
"Black Patti" (*See* Jones, Sissieretta)
"Black Power," 127, 128-29
Black Studies (*See* Afro-American Studies)
"Black Swan" (*See* Greenfield, Elizabeth Taylor)
Blackbirds, 317
Blackwell, Gordon C., 418
Blake, Elias, 287-88
Blake, Eubie, 73, 316-17
Bland, James A., 85
"Bleeding Kansas," 27
Bob Jones University, 320
Bolick, Clint, 387-88
Bolinger, Jimmy, 406
Bollander, William, 417
Bond, Alice, 349
Bond, Horace Mann, 205-06
Bond, Julian, 126, 129, 133, 199, 205, 231, 244, 254, 349, 410

Book of American Negro Poetry, The (J. W. Johnson), 74, 76
Borders, William Holmes, 199
Boston, Massachusetts, 2, 5, 7, 21, 24, 27, 114, 189, 215, 227, 233-34, 242-43, 247, 264, 433
Boston Guardian, 59
Bottoms, Lawrence W., 226
Bouchet, Edward A., 49
Bowers, Samuel H., Jr., 135
Bowler, Jack, 12
Bowman, Thea, 425-26
Boxing, blacks in, 82, 84, 93, 159, 181, 239, 245, 258
Boycotts, 99, 103, 105, 106, 116, 124, 175, 184, 233
Boyd, J. Mitchell, 406
Bradley, Gilbert H., Jr., 191
Bradley, Thomas, 207, 235, 262-63, 308
Brandeis University, 134-35
Brawley, Tawana, 376
Brennan, William, 342
Brewer, J. Mason, 248
Bridgeport, Connecticut, 207
Brimmer, Andrew, 134, 379-80
Brock, Lou, 335
Brooke, Edward W., 113, 129, 264
Brooklyn, New York, 400
Brooks, Gwendolyn, 97
Brooks, Jack, 414
Brooks, Preston S., 27
Brooks, Tyrone, 251, 254
Brotherhood of Sleeping Car Porters, 75, 89
Brown, Charles, 414
Brown, Ego, 387
Brown, H. Rap, 130, 196, 203
Brown, James, 204-05
Brown, Jim, 292
Brown, John, 27, 29-30
Brown, Lee, 311
Brown, Morris, 14, 16
Brown, Ruth, 414
Brown, Tony, 402

Brown, William H., 26, 134-35
Brown, William Wells, 26
*Brown v. Board of Education of Topeka,
    Kansas,* 101, 103, 154-55, 157,
    219, 223-24, 391-92, 395, 407,
    460-64
Brownsville, Texas, 61, 63
Bruce, Blanche K., 45-6, 50, 56
Bryan, Andrew, 5
Bryant, Hubert H., 291
Buchanan v. Warley, 68
Buckner, Linda Brown, 392
Buffalo, New York, 153
Bunche, Ralph, 92, 96, 98, 193
Bureau of the Census, 300-01, 322,
    338, 385, 389, 393-94, 423
Burger, Warren E., 137, 148, 189
Burgess, James R., Jr., 291
Burke, Yvonne Braithwaite, 201,
    211-12, 231, 240
Burleigh, Harry T., 68-9
Burns, Anthony, 27
Burse, Luther, 323-24
Bush, George, 380-81, 390, 396-97,
    409, 414, 415, 419, 423, 427, 434
Business, blacks in, 387
Busing, 148, 151, 154-55, 161-62,
    169-70, 172, 181, 185, 187, 188-
    89, 194, 195-96, 197, 199-200,
    406
    See also Integration, of schools
Butler, Andrew, 27
Butz, Earl L., 279
Bynoe, Peter, 395

Caesar, Shirley, 337
Cairo, Illinois, 156, 174, 214
Calhoun, John C., 14
Califano, Joseph A., 296
California, 22-3, 28-9, 113, 126-
    27, 140, 146, 149, 151, 435
Campbell, Joan Salmon, 392
Canada, 18, 23
Cardozo, Francis L., 42

Carmichael, Stokely, 127
"Carry Me Back to Old Virginny,"
    420
Carswell, G. Harrold, 141-42
Carter, Hodding, III, 415
Carter, Jimmy, 211, 226, 276, 280-
    81, 291, 305, 327, 409, 419
Carter, Ron, 260
Carter, Rubin "Hurricane," 274
Carver, George Washington, 74, 89,
    91, 212
    See also Tuskegee Institute
Cary, W. Sterling, 204
Case Western University, 289-90
Castro, Fidel, 436
Cater, Nathaniel, 309-10
Cato, 4
Central Intelligence Agency (CIA),
    295
Chambliss, Robert Edward, 291
Chapelle, Richard Allen, 275
Charles, Ezzard, 293
Charles, Ray, 414
Charleston, South Carolina, 10, 15,
    33, 41
Charlotte, North Carolina, 151, 154,
    169
Chattanooga, Tennessee, 173
Chenault, Marcus Wayne, 259
Cheney, James E., 121, 200, 410
Chesnutt, Charles W., 57
Chicago, Illinois, 6, 71, 91, 116,
    121, 124, 128, 130, 174, 188, 213
Chicago Defender (Abbott), 61-2
Chisholm, Shirley, 133, 158, 193,
    198-99, 240, 260
Cicero, Illinois, 98
Cinque, 20
Citizens League for Fair Play, 77
Citizenship, of blacks, 28, 29, 40, 42
City of Richmond v. J.A. Coson Co.,
    381
Civil Rights Act:
    of 1866, 40, 393
    of 1875, 45, 50

of 1957, 110
of 1964, 117-18, 121, 136, 139,
  143-44, 156, 157, 162, 170, 172,
  202, 205, 212, 329, 467-70
of 1968, 157
Civil Rights Restoration Act, 365-
  67
Civil War, 23, 33-5, 37-8
Clark, Mark, 137, 140-41
Clark, Septima Poinsetta, 355-56
Clark College, 394
Clay, Cassius (*See* Ali, Muhammad)
Clay, Henry, 14, 24
Cleaver, Eldridge, 151, 176, 266
Clement, Emma Clarissa, 93
Clement, Rufus E., 93, 99
Cleveland, Ohio, 128, 130, 131, 133
Clotel (Brown), 26
Clothilde, 30
Coalition of Friends and
  Beneficiaries of the Martin Luther
  King, Jr. Dream, 410
Cole, Olivia, 290
Cole, Thomas W., Jr. 404
Coleman, Frederick, 291
Coleman, J. Marshall, 412
College education, of blacks, 18, 27,
  38, 39-40, 41, 50, 63, 92, 150,
  153, 164, 178, 188, 190, 199, 219-
  20, 226-27, 229-30, 323, 401
  See also individual colleges and
    universities
Colonel's Dream, The (Chesnutt), 57
Colonizationists (*See* Africa,
  emigration to)
Color (Cullen), 74
Colored American, The (Cornish), 16
Colored Farmer's Alliance, 53
Colored Merchants Association, 77
Colored Methodist Episcopal
  Church, 84
Columbus, Georgia, 174-75, 180,
  212
Commission on Civil Disorders

(Kerner Commission), 130, 132,
  362-63
Commission on Civil Rights (CCR),
  154, 155, 171, 185, 192, 202, 246-
  47, 308-09, 325-26, 389, 409
Commission on Interracial
  Cooperation, 63
Committee on Civil Rights, 94, 95
Committee on Policy for Racial
  Justice, 390
Committee to Stop Children's
  Murder (STOP), 309-10
Compromise of 1850, 24-5, 27
*Condition, Elevation, Emigration and
  Destiny of the Colored People of the
  United States, The* (Delany), 13-14
Confederacy, 33-5, 37-8
Confiscation Act, 33
Congress, U.S.:
  civil rights legislation, 110, 117-
    18, 122, 136, 139
  Civil War and Reconstruction,
    33-5, 38-42
  pre-Civil War, 19, 22-3, 24-5,
    27
  voting rights legislation, 106, 110,
    124, 143
Congress of Racial Equality
  (CORE), 91, 94, 112, 124, 126,
  127, 194, 216
Conjure Woman, The (Chesnutt), 57
Connecticut, 8
Constitution, U.S., 10
  See also Amendments to the U.S.
    Constitution
Conyers, John, Jr., 143, 144
Cook, Howard E., 431
Cook, Samuel DuBois, 241, 275
Cook, Will Marion, 57
Cornish, Samuel, 16, 18
Cosby, Bill, 377
Cotton gin, 11
Cotton production, 55
Cotton States International
  Exposition, 55

Crim, Alonzo A., 207-08, 233
Crime, blacks and, 223, 294-95, 309-10
Crisis, The (NAACP), 65
Cuffee, Paul, 14-15
Cullen, Countee, 74
Cuomo, Mario M., 400

Dahmer, Vernon, 135
Daley, Richard, 124, 128
Dallas, Texas, 201
Daniels, John, 412-13
Davage, Matthew, 278
Davis, Abraham Lincoln, 301
Davis, Angela, 146, 155, 157, 158-59, 168, 194, 196, 201, 205, 230, 431
Davis, Benjamin O., Jr., 86
Davis, Benjamin O., Sr., 85-6
Davis, Jefferson, 38, 43
Davis, Miles, 335
Davis, Sammy, Jr., 431
Dawson, William L., 91
Days, Drew, 281
De Priest, Oscar, 76-7, 81, 102, 144
Deacons, The, 133
Decatur, Georgia, 246, 258
Declaration of Independence, 8
Dees, Morris, 294
DeKlerk, Frederick W., 422
Delany, Martin R., 13-14
Dellums, Ronald V., 217, 231, 390, 409
Demakos, Thomas A., 417
DeMascio, Robert, 265, 273
Dennard, Cleveland L., 289, 294
Denver, Colorado, 218
Department of Commerce, U.S., 433
Depression, Great, 77, 78-9
Desegregation, of schools (See Integration, of schools)
Detroit, Michigan, 91, 130, 156, 197, 211, 235, 265-66, 435

Dett, Robert Nathaniel, 72-3
Dickinson, Eric, 313
Diggs, Charles C., Jr., 104, 144, 304
Dinkins, David, 400, 411-12, 413, 415, 436
Disfranchisement (See Voting Rights)
District of Columbia (See Washington, D.C.)
District of Columbia v. John R. Thompson Co., 99
Dixiecrats, 96
Doctor, Bobby, 389
Donald, Michael, 328
Douglas, James "Buster," 422
Douglas, Stephen A., 27
Douglass, Frederick, 16, 21, 21-2, 30, 38, 40, 49, 50, 51, 54, 66, 416
Dred Scott v. Sandford, 28
Drew, Charles R., 97
Drug Enforcement Administration (DEA), 309
Du Bois, W.E.B., 54, 55, 60, 61, 65, 71, 92
Dukakis, Michael, 363, 366, 370-72, 419
Dunbar, Paul Laurence, 57, 62-3, 260-61
Dunmore Proclamation, 7-8
Dunn, Oscar J., 41-2
DuSable, Jean Baptiste Point, 6
Dykes, J. D., 404

East St. Louis, Illinois, 67, 168
Economic Opportunity Act, 122
Edgar, R. Allan, 343-44
Education, of blacks, 4, 10, 21, 24, 38, 39, 40-1, 50-1, 433
   See also Busing; College education, of blacks; Integration, of schools
Eisenhower, Dwight D., 101, 106, 109-10
Elbow Room (McPherson), 297
Elder, Lee, 303

Ellington, Duke, 224-25
Elliott, Robert B., 42
Ellis, Carl, 314
Ellison, Ralph, 355
Emancipation, of blacks, 34, 39
Emancipation Proclamation, 34, 440-42
Emory University, 298
Empire of Africa, 72
Employment, of blacks:
　as corporate executives, 152, 158
　during Depression, 77, 83
　as lawyers, 162, 182, 186, 201-02
　pre-Civil War, 31
　since 1945, 136, 143-44, 145, 149-50, 159, 165, 170, 171, 174, 182, 190, 207, 208, 212, 213-14, 215, 218, 219, 229, 232, 235-6, 243, 247, 252
　as teachers, 177, 194, 221, 263
　in unions, 75, 89, 103, 156-57
　in war-time industries, 79, 89-90
Enforcement Acts, 43
Enfranchisement (*See* Voting rights)
Enslen, Richard, 328
Equal Employment Opportunity Commission (EEOC), 172, 219, 253, 402
Estevanico, 1-2
Evers, Charles, 137, 176, 191, 202, 262
Evers, Medgar W., 137, 176, 410
"Exodus of 1879," 49

Fair Employment Practice Committee, 89-90, 92
Fair Housing Act, 133
Fair Housing Practice Ordinance, 106
Fard, W. D., 81-2, 253
Farentold, Frances, 257
Farino, Thomas, 417
Farmer, James, 124, 126, 133, 135, 166

Farrakhan, Louis, 400, 409
Faubus, Orval, 106
Fauntroy, Walter E., 166-67, 198, 258, 409
"The FBI and Dr. King's Assassination" (Jackson), 475-76
Federal Bureau of Investigation (FBI), 298-99, 304-05, 375
Feminists, black (*See* Women's rights)
Fetchit, Stepin (*See* Perry, Lincoln Theodore Andrew)
Fisk University, 38, 39-40, 95, 99, 190
Fitzgerald, Ella, 327
Flake, Floyd H., 409
Flemming, Arthur S., 308-09
Fletcher, Arthur A., 135, 174, 423
Florida, 140, 142, 384, 406
Florida A and M University, 291
Florida, University of, 169
Floyd, James A., 158
Fludd, Willie, 404
Fogg v. Hobbs, 20
Foraker, Joseph, 63
Forbes, George, 412
Ford, Claire, 290
Ford, Gerald R., 243, 246-47, 250, 251, 257, 266, 279
Ford, Harold, 428
Foreman, George, 239
Forsyth County, Georgia, 345-47
Fort Pillow, Tennessee, 35
Fort Stewart-Hunter, 303-04
Fort Valley State College, 251-52
Forten, James, 18
Fortune, T. Thomas, 51
Foster, Tabatha, 359
Franklin, Aretha, 332-33
Franklin, C. L., 332-33
Franklin, John Hope, 324
Free blacks, 8-9, 10, 12-13, 15-16, 31
Freedmen's Bank, 22, 38

Freedmen's Bureau, 14, 27-8, 38, 40, 41, 51, 67, 302, 328
Freedom Riders, 94, 112, 302, 328
Freedom's Journal (Russwurm and Cornish), 16
Fremond, John C., 33
Fugitive Slave Laws, 11, 24-5, 27, 30
See also Runaway slaves
Fuller, S.B., 377

"Gag rule," 19
Gaines, Lloyd, 84
Galanos, Chris, 328
Gantt, Harvey, 353-54, 431
Gardner, Newport, 10
Garfield, James A., 50
Garnet, Henry Highland, 20
Garrison, William Lloyd, 18, 22
Garvey, Marcus, 51, 72, 76, 85
Gaston, Cato, 391
Gates, Henry Louis, Jr., 355
Gay rights, 150
Gayles, Joseph N., Jr., 288-89
Georgia, 5, 8, 52, 66-7, 112, 113, 126, 129, 142, 162-63, 178-9, 200-1, 209, 211, 226, 239, 404, 405, 406, 418
Georgia, University of, 111, 240
Gerrymandering, 106, 175, 406
Giamatti, A. Bartlett, 391
Gibbs v. Board of Education, 83
Gibson, Kenneth, 145, 204, 221, 231
Gist, Carole, 424
Giuliani, Rudolph W., 400, 410
Gleaves, Richard, 42
Glickman, Loretta, 311
Gloster, Hugh M., 131
God's Trombones (J. W. Johnson), 76
Godwin, Mills E., 289
Gomillion v. Lightfoot, 106
Gone with the Wind, 85, 282
Goode, W. Wilson, 326, 358

Gooden, Dwight, 347
Goodman, Andrew, 121, 200, 410
Goodman, Carolyn, 410
Goodman, James A., 386
Goodman, Robert, 326-27
Gordy, Berry, Jr., 327
Gossett, Louis, Jr., 290, 320
"Grandfather clauses," 66
Grant, Ulysses S., 44, 46
Gray, William H., III, 409
Greenberg, Reuben M., 310
Greener, Richard T., 45
Greenfield, Elizabeth Taylor, 25
Gregory, Dick, 124, 410
Griffin, Michael, 344, 360
Griffith, Michael, 417
Growing Up in the Black Belt (C. S. Johnson), 95
Guardian Angels, The, 310
Guinn v. the United States, 66

Haiti, 20, 22, 34
Haley, Alex, 282, 284, 287, 290
Hall, Anthony, 417
Hall, Prince, 9-10
Hammon, Jupiter, 4-5
Hampton, Fred, 137, 140-41
Hampton Institute, 38, 41, 62, 73, 190, 192
Handy, W. C., 65, 211
Hankerson, Joseph "Big Lester," 373
Hansberry, Lorraine, 107
Harlan, John, 55, 444-47
Harlem, 75, 77, 91, 114, 121, 144
See also New York City
Harlem Renaissance, 74, 416
Harlem Shadows (McKay), 74
Harper's Ferry, Virginia, 30
Harris, Barbara, 282
Harris, Marcelite J., 419
Harris, Patricia Roberts, 280
Harris, William H., 324, 370
Harrison, Benjamin, 52-3

Harvard University, 136, 262, 361
Hastie, William, 84, 93, 97, 286
Hastings, Alcee, 387
Hatcher, Andrew, 111
Hatcher, Richard B., 131, 170, 191, 217-18, 231, 473-75
Hawkins, Augustus F., 113, 144, 194
Hawkins, Yusef, 399, 400, 342-32
Hayes, Roland, 75
Hayes, Rutherford B., 44, 49
Haynsworth, Clement, 144
Hays, Henry, 328
Head Start, 122
Health, Education, and Welfare (HEW), 282-83, 289, 308
Healy, James Augustine, 17-18, 45
Healy, Patrick Francis, 45
Heifetz, Alan W., 418
Height, Dorothy, 415
Henderson, F. L., 274
Henderson, Vivian W., 271-72
Henson, Matthew H., 64
Herndon, Alonzo F., 61
Hesburgh, Theodore M., 154, 202
Hill, Herbert, 182
Hill, Oliver W., 96
Hill, Richmond, 209
Hilliard, David, 150
Hine, Darlene Clark, 324
His Eye Is on the Sparrow (Waters), 288
Holley, Mary Anne, 404
Holman, M. Carl, 373-74
Holsey, Albon, 77
Homicide, of blacks, 289-90, 374, 386
Hooks, Benjamin L., 408, 410, 415
Hoover, Herbert, 77-8
Hoover, J. Edgar, 138, 159, 165
Hope, John, 63, 82-3, 131
Horton, Willie, 385
House behind the Cedars, The (Chesnutt), 57
Housing, of blacks, 68, 96, 107, 111, 113, 126, 127, 133, 135, 137, 167, 176, 177, 183, 215-16, 231-32, 375-76, 378, 389
Housing and Urban Development (HUD), 307, 418
Houston, Charles H., 85
Howard, Oliver O., 40
Howard Beach (New York City), 344, 359, 399, 400, 402, 417
Howard University, 38, 40, 99, 104-05, 124, 291, 297, 384-85, 388
Howells, William Dean, 62-3
Huggins, Ericka, 173
Huggins, Nathan I., 416
Hughes, Langston, 28, 74
Humphrey, Hubert H., 227, 292
Hunter, David, 34
Hunter, G. William, 291
Hurley, Ruby, 299-300
Hurston, Zora Neale, 74
Husni, Samir, 404

"I Have a Dream" (King), 464-67
Iftony, Rose, 294
Illinois, 64
Indentured servants, 3
Indians, 15, 49, 56
Ink Spots, The, 296
Inman, John, 225, 228
Innis, Roy, 216
Integration, of schools:
    in the North, 152, 153, 160, 188-89, 195-96, 197, 199-200, 215-16, 218, 219, 226-27, 232-33, 235, 240, 246-47, 263, 265-66, 379
    in the South, 101, 103, 106, 111, 112, 137, 138, 138-40, 142, 143, 145, 147, 148, 149, 162-63, 167, 169-70, 178-79, 180, 181, 183-84, 186, 187, 189, 193, 215, 219, 226-27, 232-33, 246-47, 251-52, 255-56, 318-19, 406
See also Busing

Intelligence, of blacks, 214-15, 216, 329
Internal Revenue Service (IRS), 320
Interracial marriage, 3, 96, 190

Jack, Hulan, 99
Jackson, Andrew, 15, 16
Jackson, Jesse, 161, 185, 253-54, 256-57, 265, 326-27, 363, 366, 370-73, 379, 409, 410, 411, 413
Jackson, Jimmie Lee, 410
Jackson, Lester Kendel, 283
Jackson, Lydia Monice, 302
Jackson, Mahalia, 193-94
Jackson, Maynard Holbrook, 142, 209, 225, 228, 229, 231, 235, 249, 258, 405
Jackson, Michael, 327, 337, 376-77, 402
Jackson, Mississippi, 114, 149, 157, 175, 177, 180, 186, 218, 356
Jackson, Prince, Jr., 286
Jackson, Reggie, 290-91
Jackson State University, 291
Jacksonville, Florida, 179
Jacob, John, 315, 336, 345
James, Daniel "Chappie", Jr., 266, 293
James, William, 408
Jamestown, Virginia, 1
Jefferson, Thomas, 8, 11
Jenkins, Chester, 412
Jewett, Doug, 413
Jim Crowism, 59, 81, 193, 458-59
"Jobs for Negroes" movement, 77
Johnson, Andrew, 22, 39-40
Johnson, Ben, 376
Johnson, Charles Spurgeon, 95
Johnson, Frank, 20
Johnson, Frank M., Jr., 224
Johnson, Jack, 98
Johnson, James Weldon, 71, 74, 75-76, 454

Johnson, Leroy R., 113, 249
Johnson, Lyndon B., 117, 118, 123, 124, 125, 126, 131, 133, 134, 242
Johnson, Mordecai, 92, 104-05, 277
Joint Center for Political Studies (JCPS), 337
Jones, Absalom, 9
Jones, John, 37
Jones, LeRoi (*See* Baraka, Imamu Amiri)
Jones, Sissieretta, 53-4
Jordan, Barbara, 201, 231, 240, 257, 291-92
Jordan, Howard, Jr., 162
Jordan, Vernon, 150, 177-78, 184-85, 209-10, 231, 271
Jubilee Singers, 40
Julian, Percy, 94-5
"Jump, Jim Crow" (Rice), 458-59

Kansas, 27, 49, 98
Kaunda, Kenneth D., 298
Kenny, Bill, 296
Kennedy, Arthur, 393
Kennedy, Ethel, 410
Kennedy, John F., 111, 112, 113-14, 116, 117, 126
Kennedy, Robert F., 111, 410
Kenyatta, Muhammad, 257
Kerner Commission (*See* Commission on Civil Disorders)
Kerr, Edward, 204
Khan, Chaka, 337
Killens, John Oliver, 352-53
King, Alberta, 228-29, 230, 233, 259
King, Bernice, 313
King, Chevene Bowers, 364
King, Clennon, 279-80, 302-03
King, Coretta Scott, 240, 243-244, 245, 257, 318, 325, 361, 380, 415
King, Dexter Scott, 380
King, Martin Luther, Jr., 77, 103, 106, 107, 108, 111, 112, 113, 114-

16, 118, 121, 122, 123-24, 127, 128, 129-30, 131, 132-33, 136, 139, 140, 166, 193, 209, 211, 226, 227, 228-29, 238-39, 241, 243-45, 248, 266, 298, 304-05, 313, 325, 339-40, 347, 356-58, 408, 410, 422, 427-28
King, Martin Luther, Sr., 314-15, 334
King, Martin Luther, III, 358
Kitt, Eartha, 241
Koch, Edward, 344, 356
Korean War, 98
Ku Klux Klan (KKK), 40, 43, 66, 109, 124, 135, 190, 230, 345, 347, 410, 429, 431

Labor unions (*See* Employment)
Lamar, South Carolina, 143, 164
Landrieu, Moon, 419
Lane, Isaac, 94
Langston, John Mercer, 27-8, 55
Larsen, Nella, 74
Laveau, Marie, 42-3
Lawson, Marjorie, 126
League for Non-Violent Civil Disobedience against Military Segregation, 95
Lee, Bernard, 410
Lee, Bertram, 395
Lee, Howard N., 137
Lee, Robert E., 38
Lee, Samuel, 42
Lee, Spike, 400
LeFlore, John, 200, 272
Leile, George, 5
Leland, George "Mickey," 396, 414, 417
Leon, Kenny, 432
Leonard, Sugar Ray, 403
Lester, Jon, 359
"Letter to My Delegates on the Road to Atlanta" (Jackson), 479-80

Lewis, Carl, 333
Lewis, Jesse W., 211, 248-29
Lewis, John, 239, 244, 245, 248, 324-25, 377, 390, 398, 409, 410
Liberator (Garrison), 18, 22, 26
Liberia, 15, 34, 67, 72, 74
   See also Africa
Liberty City (*See* Miami, Florida)
"Lift Every Voice and Sing" (Johnson), 454
Lightfoot, Sara Lawrence, 390
Lightner, Clarence, 230
Lin, Maya, 411
Lincoln, Abraham, 31, 33-5, 38-9, 67
Lincoln University, 27
Lipscombe, Andrew, 276
Liston, Sonny, 293
Literacy tests, 52, 124, 143
Little, Joann, 259-60, 261, 265
Little, Malcolm (*See* Malcolm X)
Little Rock, Arkansas, 106, 217
Liuzzo, Viola, 124, 125
Locke, Alain, 64
Lomax, Michael, 405
Long, Richard, 416
Looby, Z. Alexander, 98, 110, 194
Lorance v. A T and T Technologies, Inc., 393
Los Angeles, California, 140, 207, 235, 262-63, 435
   See also Watts
Louis, Joe, 82, 84, 245, 412
Louisiana, 35, 41-3, 45, 99, 111, 112, 187, 202, 207, 235, 262-63
Lowery, Joseph, 283, 298, 323, 373-75, 399-400, 409, 410, 415
Lowery, Peter, 24
Lucas, William, 382, 395-96
Lucas, William "Bill," 277-78
Lynchings, 71, 76, 77, 84, 99, 103, 107

Maddox, Alton H., Jr., 376

Maddox, Lester, 149, 191
Maine, 17-18
Malcolm X, 111, 117, 124
Mandela, Nelson R., 416, 422, 433-36
Mandela, Winnie, 416
Mansfield, Gordon H., 418
Mapp, James, 344
March on Washington (1963), 114-16, 374-75
Marino, Eugene Antonio, 364-65
Marrow of Tradition, The (Chesnutt), 57
Marsalis, Wynton, 337
Marshall, Thurgood, 101, 112, 125, 177, 181, 225, 350-51, 392, 401
"Martin Luther King, Jr.: A Dream Deferred" (Carter, H.), 319, 477-79
Martin Luther King, Jr. Center for Non-Violent Social Change, 298, 396
Maryland, 3, 18, 23, 213
Mason, C. Vernon, 376
Massachusetts, 3, 5, 6, 7, 14-15, 21, 24, 40, 113, 129
Massachusetts, University of, 360-61
Matzeliger, Jan E., 50
Mays, Benjamin E., 131, 142, 327, 329-31
McCree, Floyd, 131
McCree, Wade, 134
McDaniel, Hattie, 85
McDuffie, Arthur, 306
McGovern, George, 198, 199, 203
McKay, Claude, 74
McKinney, Calvin, 184
McKissick, Flloyd, 126, 199
McLauren v. Oklahoma, 97
McLucas, Lonnie, 148, 152
McNair, Denise, 291
McNair, Ronald E., 340
McPherson, James A., 297

Meharry Medical College, 46, 110, 297
Memphis, Tennessee, 40, 132-33, 190, 212-13
Memphis Blues (Handy), 65
Meredith, James H., 113, 127, 196, 225
Merrick, John, 61
Miami, Florida, 306-07, 314, 317-18
Miami Beach, Florida, 434
Michaux, Henry M., 291
Michigan, 152, 153, 384
Military, blacks in:
    Civil War, 23, 33-5, 37-8
    integration in, 95, 102, 184
    Korean War, 98, 101-2
    as officers, 73-4, 85-6, 101-02, 157-58, 167-68, 172, 266
    post-Vietnam War era, 342, 378
    racial tension on bases, 157-58, 177, 227-28, 303-04
    recruitment of, 167-68, 172, 378
    Revolutionary War, 7
    Spanish-American War, 56
    Vietnam War, 141, 145-46
    War of 1812, 9
    World War I, 51, 67
    World War II, 85-6, 90, 101-02
Miller, Doris "Dorie," 90
Milliken v. Michigan Road Builders, 384
Milton, Lorimer Douglas, 340-41
Mississippi, 35, 42, 43, 45-6, 52, 112, 121-22, 137, 138-39, 142, 151, 153, 174, 176, 186, 200, 220-21
Mississippi, University of, 113, 319-20, 403
Missouri Compromise, 15, 27
Missouri ex rel Gaines, 84
Mitchell, Arthur L., 81, 89
Mitchell, Charles L., 40
Mitchell, Nannie, 248
Mitchell, Parren, 409

Mitchell, Theo, 432
Mobile, Alabama, 91, 150-51, 154-55, 170, 181, 187
Mondale, Walter, 333
Monroe, George, 31
Monroe, James, 12, 15
Montgomery, Alabama, 103, 105, 108, 123-24, 215, 224, 410
Montgomery, Jackie, 405
Moody, Charles, Sr., 402
Moon, Mollie, 436
Moore, Harry T., 98
Morehouse College, 40, 63, 82, 99, 131, 297, 390
Morgan, Garrett A., 75
Morgan State College, 291
Morgan v. Virginia, 93
Morial, Ernest Nathan "Dutch," 311, 341, 418-19
Morial, Leonie, 418
Morial, Walter, 418
Moron, Alonzo G., 192
Morris Brown College, 388
Morrison, Toni, 368-69, 378
Morton, Franklin W., 231
Moses, Edwin, 333
Motley, Constance Baker, 126
Moton, Robert Russa, 66
Motown Records, 327
MOVE, 353
Moynihan, Daniel P., 143
Muhammad, Elijah, 81-2, 110, 117, 253-54, 470-71
Muhammad Speaks, 117
Mulzac, Hugh, 91
Murphy, Eddie, 402
Muslim Program, The, 472-73
Muslims (*See* Black Muslims)

NAACP v. Alabama, 106
Naantaanbuu, Abjua Abi, 410, 422
Nabrit, James M., Jr., 104-05
Nash, Beverly, 41

Nashville, Tennessee, 24, 40, 106, 108, 110, 181, 199-200, 316
Nation of Islam (*See* Black Muslims)
National Alliance of Black School Educators, 402
National Association for the Advancement of Colored People (NAACP):
after 1945, 98, 102-03, 106, 107, 112, 127, 131, 139-40, 141, 144, 154-55, 167, 179, 182, 192-93, 194, 195, 198, 263, 342-43, 399, 408, 410, 415, 417, 418
before 1945, 65, 66, 67, 75-6, 78, 81, 82, 86
founding of, 60, 63, 64
National Association of Colored Women, 55
National Black Alcoholism Council (NBAC), 351
National Black Feminist Organization, 208
National Black Network (NBN), 208, 232
National Black Political Convention, 194-95, 217-18
National Catholic Educational Association, 295
National Collegiate Black Caucus (NCBC), 432
National Committee Against Discrimination in Housing (NCADH), 232
National Committee to Combat Fascism (NCCF), 147, 151-52, 156
National Congress of Black Churches, 408
National Council of Colored People, 18, 25
National Council of Negro Women, 78, 415
National Liberty Congress of Colored People, 71

National Negro Business League, 58, 77

National Negro Convention, 18, 25

National Urban League (NUL), 65, 77, 110-11, 166, 177, 184, 185, 209, 292-93, 315, 336, 345, 396-97, 419

National Urban League Guild, 436

National Welfare Rights Organization (NWRO), 205

Native Son (Wright), 85

Naylor, Gloria, 414-15

Negro in the American Rebellions, The (Brown), 26

Negro College Graduate, The (C. S. Johnson), 95

Negro Convention Movement (*See* National Negro Convention)

Negro National Anthem, The (J. W. Johnson), 76
    See also "Lift Every Voice and Sing"

Negro World (Garvey), 72

Nesmith, Kevin, 343

New Bethel Baptist Church, 333

"New Deal," 78, 84

New England, 2, 12, 14

New Hampshire, 9

New Jersey, 9, 121, 145, 153-54, 158, 400

New Orleans, Louisiana, 111, 182, 313

New York (state), 4, 8, 23, 167, 189, 400, 401

New York Age (Fortune), 51

New York City, 4, 8, 16, 35, 64, 77, 99, 106, 121, 129, 167, 171, 400, 411, 413, 433
    See also Harlem

Newark, New Jersey, 130, 145, 204, 221

Newton, Huey P., 128-29, 133, 149, 150, 182, 192, 239, 398-99

Niagara Movement, 60, 61, 63

Nielson, A. C., 326

Night Creature (Balliett), 331

Nino, Pedro Alonso, 1

Nix, Robert N. C., Jr., 144, 327

Nix, Robert N. C., Sr., 327

Nixon, Edgar Daniel, 347-49

Nixon, Richard M., 135, 136, 137, 139, 142, 143, 144, 147, 154, 163, 166, 167, 171, 172, 173, 176, 179, 182, 183, 185, 189, 192, 194, 197, 199, 201, 202, 203, 209-10, 224, 225-26, 243-44, 247

Nixon v. Herndon, 76, 457-58

Norfolk State College, 291

Norris, Clarence "Willie," 279

North, the (*See* individual states and cities)

North Carolina, 12, 81, 154, 161-62, 189, 230, 296

North Carolina, University of, 81, 98

North Carolina A and T State University, 291

North Carolina Mutual Insurance Company, 58, 61, 262

North Star (Douglass), 16, 22

Northwest Territory, 9

Norton, Eleanor Holmes, 208, 231, 257, 402

Oakland, California, 435

Obadele, Imari A., 210

O'Connor, Sandra Day, 381

Officer and a Gentleman, An, 320

Ohio, 12

O'Kelley, William C., 406

Oklahoma, University of, 95

"One Third of a Nation," 367-68

Operation Breadbasket, 161, 185

Operation PUSH, 253, 256-57, 409

Operation Zebra, 220, 222

Opportunities Industrialization Centers (OIC), 250-51

Owens, Anthony, 295

Owens, Bob, 406

Owens, Jesse, 83, 333

Paige, Satchel, 183
Palestine Liberation Organization
   (PLO), 305-06, 436
Pan-Africanism, 66-7, 71
Parker, Charlie, 416
Parks, Rosa, 335, 347, 435
Parsons, James B., 112, 128
Passaic, New Jersey, 184
Patterson, Floyd, 293
Patterson, James O., Jr., 199
Payne, Jimmy Ray, 309-10
Payton, Benjamin F., 308
Payton, Walter, 292
Pease, Joachim, 37
Pendleton, Clarence, 308-09, 369
Pennsylvania Society for the
   Abolition of Slavery, 7
Pensacola, Florida, 205, 273-74
Periton, Paul L., 403
Perkins, Edward, 342
Perry, B. L., 284-85
Perry, Lincoln Theodore Andrew,
   338-39
Philadelphia, Pennsylvania, 7, 8, 9,
   18, 19, 71, 93, 121, 148, 249
Philadelphia Negro, The (Du Bois), 55
"Philadelphia Plan," 136, 143-44,
   147, 170
Picott, J. Rupert, 407
Pierce, Franklin, 27
Pierce, Samuel Riley, 307-08, 403
Pinchback, P.B.S., 42, 45, 46
Pinky, 288
Plantations, 3
   See also Agriculture
Plessy v. Ferguson, 55, 101, 444-53
*Poems on Various Subjects, Religious and
   Moral* (Wheatley), 5-6
Pointer Sisters, The, 337
Poitier, Sidney, 117
Police brutality, 113, 121, 123, 131-
   32, 184, 209, 243

Poll tax, 52, 117, 124
Pollard, Fritz, 405
Pontiac, Michigan, 153-54, 188-89
Pony Express, 31
Poor, Salem, 7
Poor Peoples Campaign, 428
Population, black, 3, 79, 138, 161,
   164-65, 169, 184, 208, 214, 236,
   300-01, 322-23, 338, 382, 385,
   393-94, 419, 423
Port Gibson, Mississippi, 312
Porter v. Metropolitan Dade County,
   384
Poussaint, Alvin, 223
Povinelli, James, 417
Powell, Adam Clayton, Jr., 92, 194,
   224
Powell, Colin L., 397, 403
Powell, Lewis F., 304
Prairie View A and M University,
   291
Prater, Oscar, 285-86
Pratt, John, 291
Princc, 336-37, 403
Prince Hall Masonic Lodge, 9-10
Principle of Ethnology (Delany), 13
Prisons, 156, 188, 198, 217, 218
Prosser, Gabriel, 12
Pulitzer Prize, 97, 297, 368-69
Punishment, of slaves, 3, 25

Qaddafi, Muammar al-, 436
Quakers, 4, 7, 11, 12
"Qualifications for Independence:
   We Must First Be Brothers"
   (Muhammad, E.), 470-71

Race Relations Information Center
   (RRIC), 178
Race riots and disturbances, 35, 40,
   42, 46, 58, 60-1, 63-4, 67, 71, 84,
   90, 91, 93, 99, 121, 123-24, 125,
   128, 130, 132-33, 143, 144, 145,

152, 163, 171, 173, 174-75, 179,
190, 260, 400, 401
See also individual cities; Slave
uprisings
Racial Classification, 321
Rainbow Coalition, 428
Rainey, Joseph H., 44
Raisin in the Sun, A (Hansberry), 107
Ramirez, Blandina C., 325-26
Randolph, A. Philip, 75, 89, 95, 103
Rangel, Charles, 92, 143, 231
Ransier, Alonzo J., 42
Rawls, Lou, 335
Ray, James Earl, 136, 139, 227,
228, 238-39, 254
Reagan, Ronald, 151, 307-09, 315-
16, 321, 325, 333-34, 342, 345,
350-51, 365-66, 375-76, 380,
403, 413, 419
Reconstruction, 39-46
"Red Summer," 71
Reeb, James, 123, 125
Reed, Thomas, 370
Rehnquist, William, 392
Republic of New Africa (RNA),
186, 210
Resurrection City, 133
Revels, Hiram R., 43, 59
Revolutionary War (*See* American
Revolution)
Rhode Island, 8
Rice, Thomas "Daddy," 458
Richardson, Elliott L., 147, 153,
189, 197
Richie, Lionel, 337
Richmond, Virginia, 96, 186, 193,
196
Rights of All (Cornish), 16
Rillieux, Norbert, 21
Rives, Richard T., 312
Roberts, Adelbert H., 75
Roberts, Benjamin, 24
Robeson, Paul, 268-70
Robinson, Aubrey E., 309
Robinson, Frank, 236-37, 405

Robinson, Jackie, 94
Robinson, Max, 378-79
Robinson, Randall, 422, 424, 433
Robinson, Robert E., 417-18
Rochester, New York, 18, 25
Rochon, Donald, 375
Rockefeller, Nelson, A., 110-11,
140, 171
Rooks, C. Shelby, 218-19
Roosevelt, Eleanor, 78, 85
Roosevelt, Franklin D., 78, 83, 84,
89-90, 126
Roosevelt, Theodore, 56, 60, 63
"Roots" (Haley), 282, 287, 290
Roussell, Noward, 421-22
Rowan, Carl T., 117, 201, 223-24,
413
Runaway slaves, 11, 23-4, 30
See also Fugitive Slave Laws
Russell, Bill, 405
Russwurm, John, 16
Rust College, 285, 403
Rustin, Bayard, 143, 349-50

Salem, Peter, 7
Salter, Bruce, 410
Salter, Rose, 408, 410
*Salvation by Christ with Penetential
Cries* (Hammon), 4
San Francisco, California, 186, 189,
200, 212, 220, 222
Savannah, Georgia, 5
Savannah State College, 286
Sawyer, Eugene, 383
Schaeffer, Bob, 401
Schmoke, Kurt, 353
Schwerner, Michael, 121, 200, 410
Scott, Dred, 21, 28
Scott, Emmett J., 68
Scott, Stanley, 267
Scottsboro, Alabama, 78
"Scottsboro Boys," 78
Seale, Bobby, 128-29, 136, 148,
155, 173, 203

Segregation:
  de facto, 112, 116, 157-58, 170, 240
  declared illegal, 93, 99, 103, 105, 328-29, 343-44
  legalized, 21, 50, 55, 81, 84, 89, 177
  See also Integration, of schools
Sellers, Cleveland L., Jr., 152
Selma, Alabama, 123-24, 402
Separate-but-equal doctrine, 24, 55, 81, 89
Sessions, William S., 375
Seward, William H., 23
Shadow of the Plantation (C.S. Johnson), 95
Shadur, Milton, 314, 321
Shah, Syed Riaz Hussain, 294
Sharpton, Al, 359, 376, 399, 400
Shavers, Ernie, 291
Shelley v. Kraemer, 96
Shockley, William B., 214-15, 216
Shuttlesworth, F. L, 105, 106
Simmons, Calvin, 312
Simpson, O. J., 292
Singleton, Benjamin, 49, 252-53
Singleton, Peter T., Jr., 252
Singleton v. Jackson, 178
Sipuel v. University of Oklahoma, 95
Sit-Ins, 108, 109-10, 110-11, 138-39, 201
Sixteenth Street Baptist Church, 116, 291
Slave codes, 3, 12-13, 18, 39, 439-40
Slave traders, 1-2, 5, 13, 24-5, 31
Slave uprisings, 3, 4, 12, 13, 15, 16-17, 18
  See also Race riots and disturbances
Slavery, as legal institution, 2, 3
Slavery period, 1-31
Sledge, Percy, 414
Sloan, Margaret, 208
Smalls, Robert, 34

Smith, Lillian, 414-15
Smith, Moreland Griffith, 394-95
Smith v. Allwright, 91
Smothers, Curtis R., 157-58
Snow, Percy, 416-17
Soledad Brothers, 194
Sollors, Werner, 388
Soul food, 242
Souls of Black Folks, The (Du Bois), 55-61
South, the (*See* individual states and cities)
South Africa, Republic of, 198, 422, 424, 429, 433, 480-81
  See also Africa
South Carolina, 4, 8, 10, 15-16, 31, 32, 34, 41, 42, 43, 44, 46, 98, 131-32, 408
South Carolina, University of, 45
"The South Doesn't Want to Go Back," 476-77
Southern Christian Leadership Conference (SCLC), 106, 125, 127, 133, 161, 191, 201, 208, 228, 303-04, 323, 399, 405, 408, 409, 415, 429
Southern Regional Council, 63, 99, 167, 178, 232, 236
Southern University, 112, 202, 207, 225, 291
Spaulding, C. C., 61
Speakes, Larry, 345
Spelman College, 50, 82, 421
Spingarn, Arthur B., 192-93
Spinks, Leon, 293, 304, 395
Sports, blacks in, 41, 53, 82, 83, 84, 93, 94, 159, 181, 183, 210-11, 218, 236-37, 239, 245, 255, 256-57, 259, 260
Spottswood, Stephen G., 141, 144, 182
Stanley, Frank, 237-38
Stargell, Willie, 373
Steele, Shirley Greenard, 280-81
Stevens, John Paul, 391, 392

Stewart, Donald, 401
Stokes, Carl B., 131, 137, 169
Stokes, Louis, 144
Stone, James, 33
STOP (*See* Committee to Stop Children's Murder)
Storey, Moorfield, 64
Stowe, Harriet Beecher, 25
Strawbridge, Nelson, 412
Stride toward Freedom (King), 107
Student Non-Violent Coordinating Committee (SNCC), 110, 126, 127, 130, 152, 196, 203, 245, 255, 258
Suburbs, blacks in, 161, 179, 236
Suicide among blacks, 301
Sullivan, Leon Howard, 158, 250-51
Sullivan, Louis Wade, 298, 385
Sumner, Charles, 27
Suppression of the African Slave Trade to America, The (Du Bois), 55
Supreme Court, U.S., 20, 28, 30, 50, 55, 66, 68, 76, 77-8, 84, 89, 91, 93, 95, 96, 97, 101, 103, 105, 106, 121, 126, 127, 129, 135, 137, 139-40, 141-42, 144, 154-55, 159, 165, 169-70, 172, 175, 177, 178, 180, 181, 189, 196, 197, 198, 205, 214, 215, 275-76, 280, 293-94, 302, 311-12, 316, 320, 328, 332, 342, 365-66, 381, 384, 391-93, 444-53, 457-58, 460-64
Sutton, Percy, 337
Swann v. Charlotte-Mecklenburg, 169-70, 172, 178, 180
Sweatt v. Painter, 97
Symbionese Liberation Army (SLA), 217

Tampa, Florida, 347
Taylor, Hobart, 134
Taylor, Walter S., 191
Taylor, Zachary, 23

Tennessee, 24, 35, 40, 50
Tennessee, University of, 99
Tennessee State University, 291, 423
Terrell, Mary Church, 55, 98
Texas, 61, 63, 67, 71, 76, 91
Texas Southern University, 291
Thompson, William H., 98
Threatt, Robert, 210
"Three-Fifths Compromise," 10
Thurman, Wallace, 74
Till, Emmett, 410
Tiller, Frank, 404
Topeka, Kansas, 101, 214, 223-24
Townsend, Willard, 103
TransAfrica, 422, 424, 433
Trenton, New Jersey, 153-54
Trotter, William Monroe, 60-1, 455-57
Trout, Nelson, 320-24, 455-57
Truman, Harry, 94, 96
Truth, Sojourner, 50-1
Tubbs, Tony, 366-67
Tubman, Harriet, 23-4
Tucker, Cynthia, 414
Tureard, A. P., 418
Turner, Debbye, 402
Turner, Gerald, 403
Turner, Henry McNeal, 66-7
Turner, Nat, 18
Turner, Tina, 336
Tuskegee Institute, 50, 66, 99, 108, 190, 212, 308
  See also Carver, George Washington; Washington, Booker T.
Tutu, Desmond, 340
TV Guide, 423
Tyson, Cicely, 240, 340
Tyson, Mike, 366-67, 383, 395, 402, 422

Uncle Tom's Cabin (Stowe), 25

Underground Railroad, 23-4, 26, 38
Union, the (*See* Civil War; Confederacy)
United Auto Workers (UAW), 435
United Nations, role of blacks in, 92, 96, 98, 193, 290, 342, 433
United Negro College Fund (UNCF), 92, 150, 177-78, 229-30, 335, 423-24
United Negro Improvement Association (UNIA), 72, 85
Up from Slavery (Washington), 59
Upward Bound, 122, 134
Urban Crisis Council, 184
Urban League (*See* National Urban League)
Urban migration of blacks, 65, 67, 74, 79, 138, 161, 164-65, 208, 236

Vance, Robert S., 417-18
Vaughan, Sarah, 426-27
Vermont, 8
Vesey, Denmark, 15-16
Vietnam War, 126, 129-30, 133, 141, 145-46
Virginia, 1-2, 7-8, 12, 18, 85, 163, 289, 401, 412-13
Vision of a Better Way: A Black Appraisal of Public Schooling, 390
Voodoo, 42-3
Voter Education Project (VEP), 178, 216, 222, 239, 245, 247-48, 324-25
Voting rights:
　after 1945, 106, 117, 123-24, 126, 134, 143, 160, 170, 175, 221-22, 244, 262-63, 322
　before 1945, 52-3, 66, 76, 91
　pre-Civil War, 13, 15-16, 20
　Reconstruction, 38-43
　women's suffrage, 50-1
Voting Rights Act:
　of 1957, 106, 110
　of 1960, 110
　of 1965, 134, 143-44, 160, 221-22, 244, 262-63

Walden, Austin T., 117
Walker, David, 16
Walker, Edward G., 40
Walker, Herschel, 313, 318
Walker, William, 37
Wallace, George C., 113-14, 124, 187, 190-91, 222, 229-30, 248-49, 251
Walters, Ron, 415
War of 1812, 9
"War on Poverty," 122
Ward, Horace T., 296-97
Washington, 311
Washington, Booker T., 50-1, 55, 58-9, 60-1, 63, 66, 68, 81, 208, 212
　See also Tuskegee Institute
Washington, Craig A., 417
Washington, D. C., 11, 25, 34, 40, 49-50, 71, 99, 101, 114-16, 130-31, 133, 166, 208, 212
Washington, George, 6-8
Washington, Harold, 318-19, 354, 383
Washington, Walter, 131, 135
Watergate, 242
Waters, Ethel, 288
Watts (Los Angeles), 125
Wayne State University, 388
Weaver, Robert C., 111, 126
Weekly Advocate (Cornish), 16
Weinberger, Caspar, 397
Weiss, John, 401
Weiss, Ted, 403
Wells, Curtis, 400
Wells, Mary, 414
WERD-AM, 96
"What We Have Seen and Heard," 307
Wheat, Alan D., 409

Wheatley, Phillis, 5-6
White, Bill, 388
White, Byron, 391
White, George H., 59
White, James C., 313-14
White, Michael, 412
White, Walter, 74, 84, 92, 102
Whitney, Eli, 11
Why Blacks Kill Blacks (Poussaint), 223
Widener, Warren, 168
Wife of His Youth, The (Chesnutt), 57
Wilder, Lawrence D., 412-13, 414-15, 420-21, 429
Wiley, George, 205
Wilkins, J. Ernest, Jr., 101
Wilkins, Roger, 362-63
Wilkins, Roy, 102, 167, 179, 193, 299
Williams, Carl "The Truth," 395
Williams, Daniel Hale, 78
Williams, Doug, 360
Williams, Hosea, 199, 225, 228, 240, 250, 345-47, 405
Williams, James E., 168
Williams, John Bell, 138, 139, 187
Williams, Poindexter E., 147-48
Williams, Samuel, 400
Williams, Vanessa, 324
Williams, Wayne, 309-10
Wilmington, North Carolina, 163
Wilmot Proviso, 23

Wilson, A. W., 396
Wilson, Kenneth, 289
Wilson, Woodrow, 61
Winfrey, Oprah, 389-90, 403
Winthrop, John, 2
Womble, Maxine, 351
Women's rights, 51, 55, 78, 92, 150, 193, 208, 253, 257
Wonder, Stevie, 325, 327
Wonder Woman Foundation, 334-35
Woodson, Carter G., 66, 97
World War I, 67-8, 71
World War II, 90, 92
Wright, Jonathan Jasper, 43
Wright, Richard, 85

Yes I Can (Davis), 430
Young, Andrew J., 199, 201, 231, 280-82, 290, 305-06, 349, 409-10, 428
Young, Charles R., 68, 73-4
Young, Coleman, 311, 412
Young, Whitney M., Jr., 166, 177-78, 185

Zaire, 239
See also Africa
"Zebra" killings, 220, 222